SUMMER OF

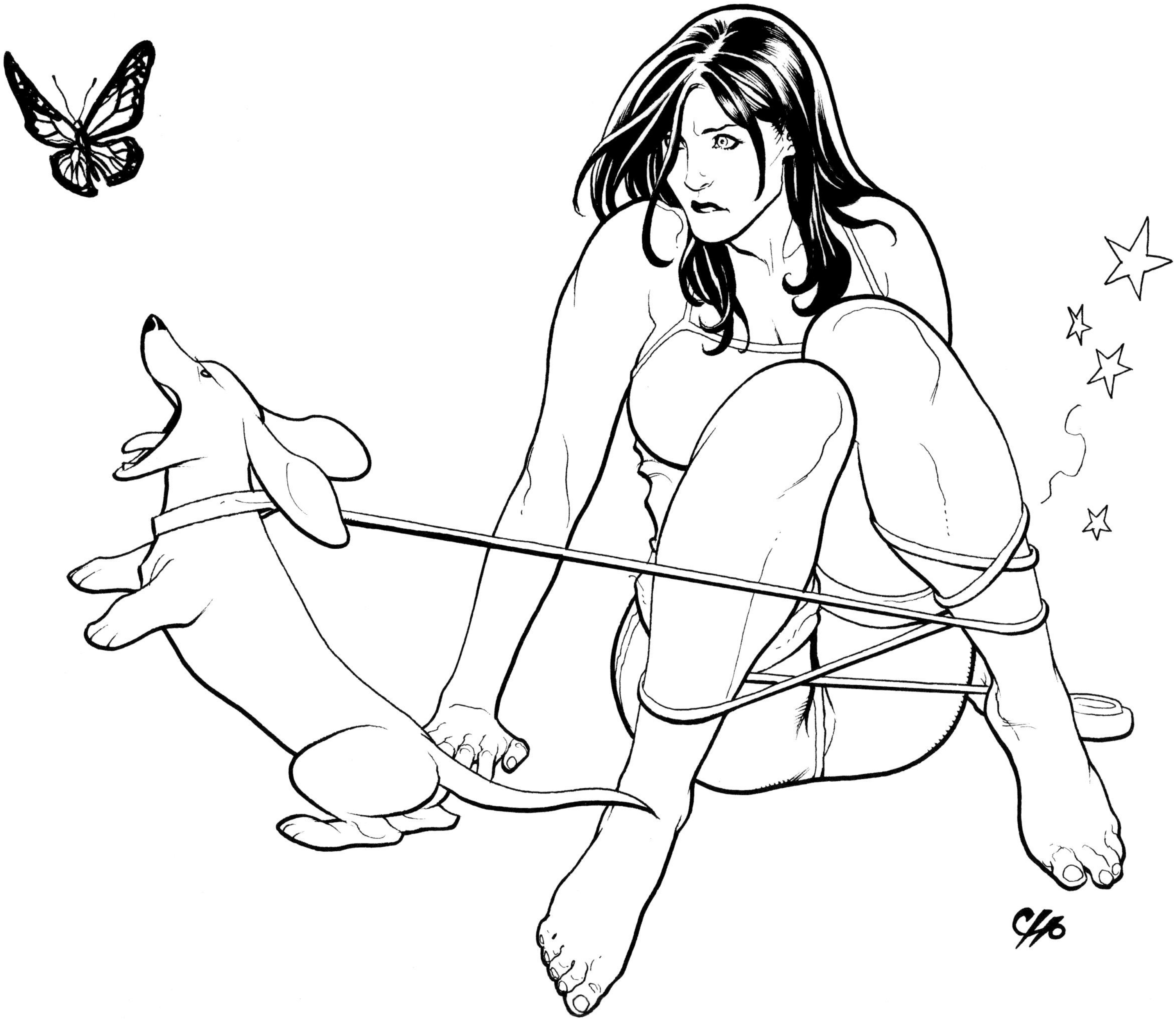
CHO

LOVE

LIBERTY MEADOWS™

by FRANK CHO

SUMMER OF LOVE

BOOK THREE

INTRODUCTION BY
DAVID MANDEL

Image®
BERKELEY, CALIFORNIA

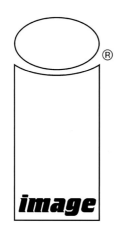

Image Comics, Inc.

Erik Larsen - Publisher
Todd McFarlane - President
Marc Silvestri - CEO
Jim Valentino - Vice-President
Eric Stephenson - Executive Director
Jim Demonakos - PR & Marketing Coordinator
Mia MacHatton - Accounts Manager
Traci Hui - Administrative Assistant
Joe Keatinge - Traffic Manager
Allen Hui - Production Artist
Jonathan Chan - Production Artist
Drew Gill - Production Artist

www.imagecomics.com

LIBERTY MEADOWS, BOOK THREE: SUMMER OF LOVE. 2006. Second Printing. Published by Image Comics, Inc., Office of publication: 1942 University Avenue, Suite 305, Berkeley, California 94704.

Dedicated to my newest daughter,
═══ Samantha ═══

With all my love and joy.

INTRODUCTION

Hello, and welcome to the third collection of Frank Cho's Liberty Meadows. If you have never heard of Liberty Meadows, have no idea who Frank Cho is, and have accidentally opened this book-- while your wife is in Loehmann's doing some shopping-- because of the cute girl on the cover, then you my friend are a pervert. How dare you check out the "bazangas" on a cartoon character! Put this book down and get the hell out of the store! You disgust me! I'll have you know that Liberty Meadows—first seen as a syndicated newspaper strip, and now as an ongoing comic series—is gloriously hilarious, evoking the funny-animal humor of classic strips mixed with a sly, modern take on male-female relationships. So stop gawking at the hot babe, sewer-brain, and go!

Is he is gone? I think he's gone. Now we real fans of Liberty Meadows can finally discuss the essential truth of Frank Cho's strip. And that is: holy crap, Brandy is hot!!! Look at those bazangas! She is crazy hot, and Frank Cho always draws her in tight t-shirts, bending over and stuff. I always think she looks a little like Claire Forlani who was in Mallrats, but maybe that's me. And better than Brandy is Jen. Oh man, Jen. She's hot too, but she knows it, and that makes her hotter. And she's blonde. And the whole idea of Brandy and Jen living together is really hot. There should be more strips about living together and how they tickle each other.

Crap, somebody else is coming to read this introduction. Damn it, it's my mother. She loves seeing my name in print. Everybody play along. Just act natural... Ahem, blah, blah, blah art and society. And what of Cho himself? It is easy to think of him as the classic unwashed comic book nerd drawing gravity-defying women—a classic Bloom County daily (Berkeley Breathed no doubt influenced Liberty Meadows, especially early on) famously showed a large-bosomed Super-heroine standing next to her artist's table, offering to "Sharpen your pencil, Stan". But there is more than that to Cho. It feels silly just to call him a cartoonist. Look at that line work. He is more than a cartoonist, he is an illustrator—a fact we are reminded of every time Cho throws the on-going strip aside and decides, just for the hell of it, to give us a powerful King Kong or a heroic Tarzan. It is in those moments that comparisons to the greats like Foster and Krenkel don't seem out of line, and—OK, she is gone.

Where was I? Right, hot girls. This collection includes one of my all-time favorite stories "Evil Brady", which features not one, but two Brandys. And then they wrestle, and pull each other's hair, and tear their clothes. And I like to think that if it wasn't for the close-mindedness of America's prudish newspaper editors and the post-Janet Jackson new morality, Brandy and evil Brandy could have made out. In fact, I drew my own ending to the story where they made out a lot, and then Frank got to sleep with them both. Only it wasn't Frank, it was me. And then—Oh no!!

It's my girlfriend, and all her friends. I lied to her and told her I was doing an introduction for a book on German pre-war cinema. She will kill me if she sees what Brandy looks like. She thinks all comic fans are emotionally retarded freaks who get off on pictures of wonder woman. God, wouldn't Brandy look great as Wonder Woman? Here she comes. Hide!

And so in conclusion, Fritz Lang turned down Hitler's offer to run the Nazi film office and made his way to America where he continued to deliver on the promise of Metropolis. America would soon declare war on Germany, thus ending the golden Age of German pre-war cinema. But in this book, you can relive that age thanks to Frank Cho, a professor of film at the University of Berlin. Unless you are my girlfriend, in which case please close the book.

David Mandel
Los Angeles, California
September 6, 2004

David Mandel is a former writer for *Saturday Night Live* and *Seinfeld*. He recently wrote and co-directed *Eurotrip*, a movie with a lot of hot naked girls. Please buy it, as he gets a nickel for every DVD sale. If anyone asks, you can tell them it is a documentary on the history of German pre-war cinema.

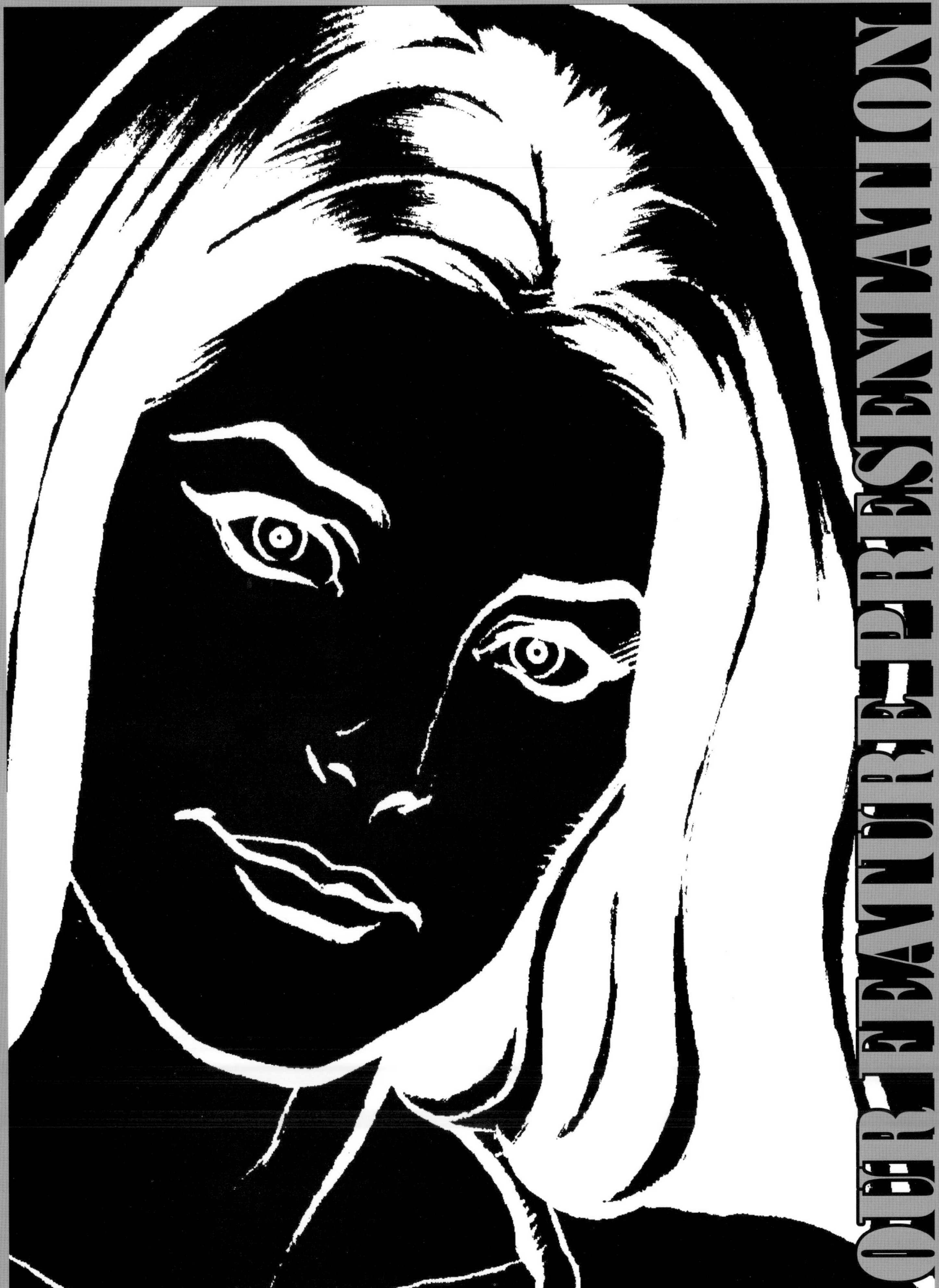
OUR FEATURE PRESENTATION

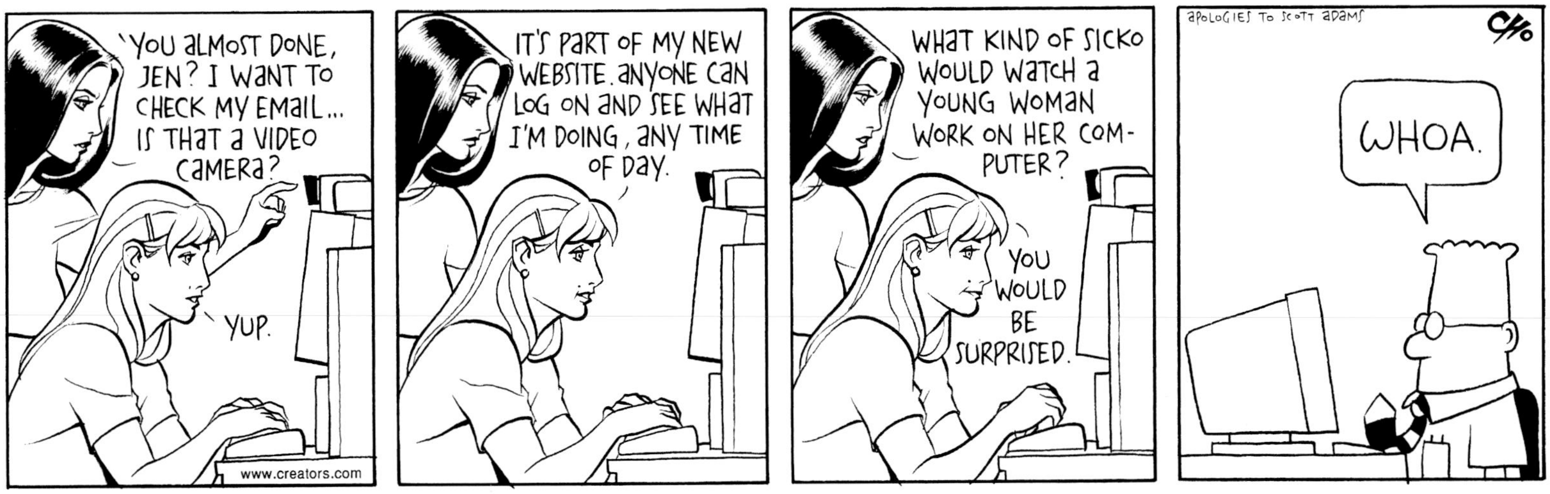
YOU ALMOST DONE, JEN? I WANT TO CHECK MY EMAIL... IS THAT A VIDEO CAMERA?
YUP.
www.creators.com
IT'S PART OF MY NEW WEBSITE. ANYONE CAN LOG ON AND SEE WHAT I'M DOING, ANY TIME OF DAY.
WHAT KIND OF SICKO WOULD WATCH A YOUNG WOMAN WORK ON HER COMPUTER?
YOU WOULD BE SURPRISED.
APOLOGIES TO SCOTT ADAMS
CHO
WHOA.

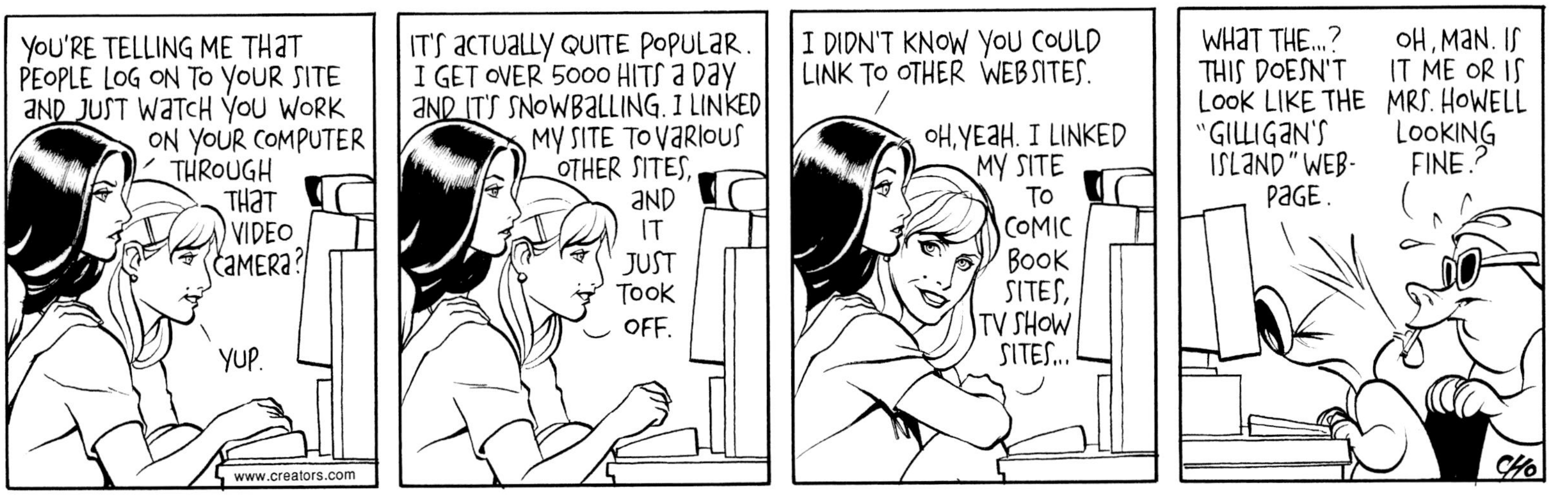
YOU'RE TELLING ME THAT PEOPLE LOG ON TO YOUR SITE AND JUST WATCH YOU WORK ON YOUR COMPUTER THROUGH THAT VIDEO CAMERA?
YUP.
www.creators.com
IT'S ACTUALLY QUITE POPULAR. I GET OVER 5000 HITS A DAY AND IT'S SNOWBALLING. I LINKED MY SITE TO VARIOUS OTHER SITES, AND IT JUST TOOK OFF.
I DIDN'T KNOW YOU COULD LINK TO OTHER WEBSITES.
OH, YEAH. I LINKED MY SITE TO COMIC BOOK SITES, TV SHOW SITES...
WHAT THE...? THIS DOESN'T LOOK LIKE THE "GILLIGAN'S ISLAND" WEB-PAGE.
OH, MAN. IS IT ME OR IS MRS. HOWELL LOOKING FINE?
CHO

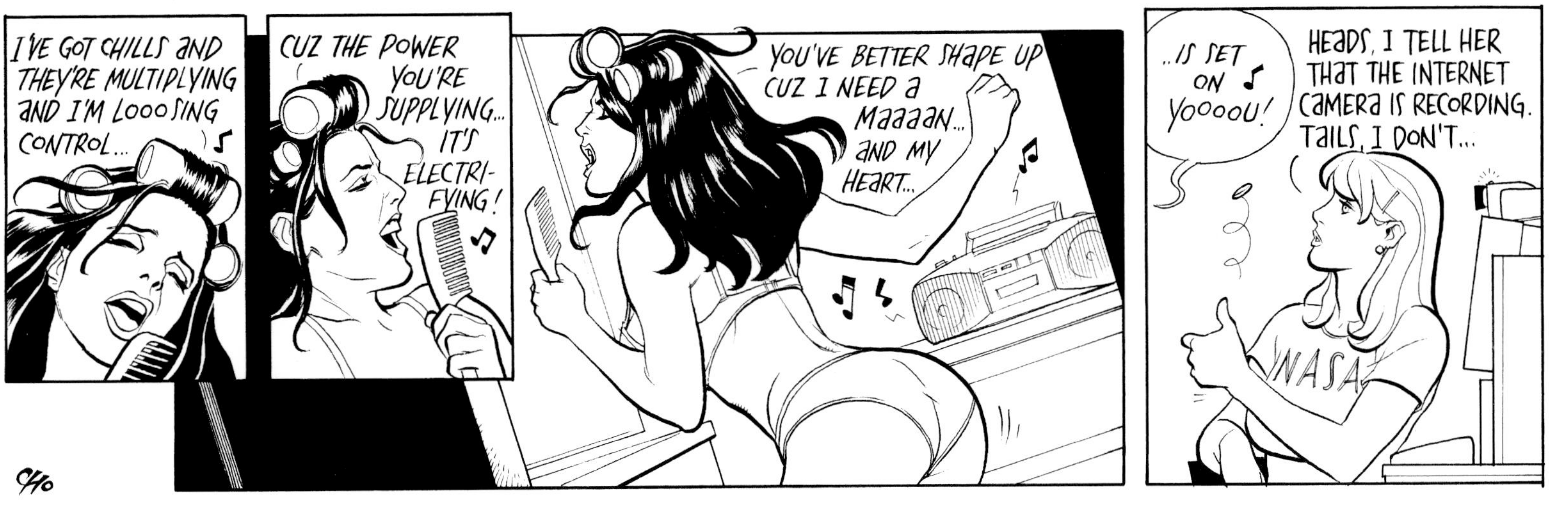
I'VE GOT CHILLS AND THEY'RE MULTIPLYING AND I'M LOOOSING CONTROL...
CUZ THE POWER YOU'RE SUPPLYING... IT'S ELECTRIFYING!
YOU'VE BETTER SHAPE UP CUZ I NEED A MAAAAN... AND MY HEART...
CHO
..IS SET ON YOOOOU!
HEADS, I TELL HER THAT THE INTERNET CAMERA IS RECORDING. TAILS, I DON'T...
NASA

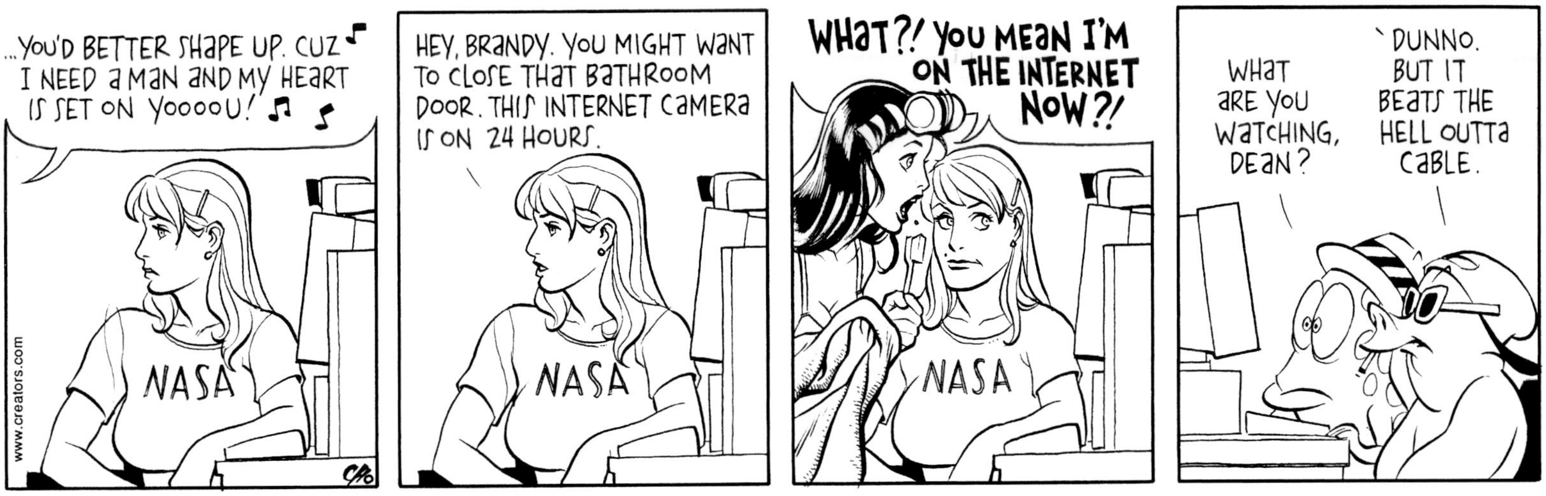
...YOU'D BETTER SHAPE UP. CUZ I NEED A MAN AND MY HEART IS SET ON YOOOOU!
NASA
www.creators.com
CHO
HEY, BRANDY. YOU MIGHT WANT TO CLOSE THAT BATHROOM DOOR. THIS INTERNET CAMERA IS ON 24 HOURS.
NASA
WHAT?! YOU MEAN I'M ON THE INTERNET NOW?!
NASA
WHAT ARE YOU WATCHING, DEAN?
DUNNO. BUT IT BEATS THE HELL OUTTA CABLE.

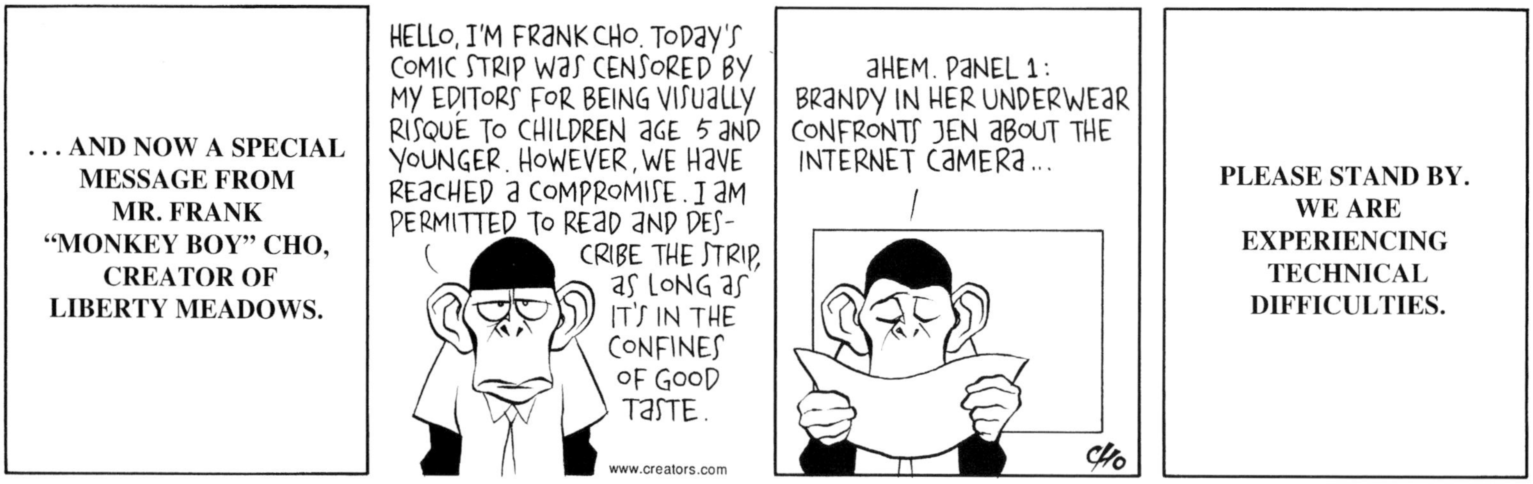

. . . AND NOW A SPECIAL MESSAGE FROM MR. FRANK "MONKEY BOY" CHO, CREATOR OF LIBERTY MEADOWS.
HELLO, I'M FRANK CHO. TODAY'S COMIC STRIP WAS CENSORED BY MY EDITORS FOR BEING VISUALLY RISQUÉ TO CHILDREN AGE 5 AND YOUNGER. HOWEVER, WE HAVE REACHED A COMPROMISE. I AM PERMITTED TO READ AND DESCRIBE THE STRIP, AS LONG AS IT'S IN THE CONFINES OF GOOD TASTE.
www.creators.com
AHEM. PANEL 1: BRANDY IN HER UNDERWEAR CONFRONTS JEN ABOUT THE INTERNET CAMERA...
CHO
PLEASE STAND BY. WE ARE EXPERIENCING TECHNICAL DIFFICULTIES.

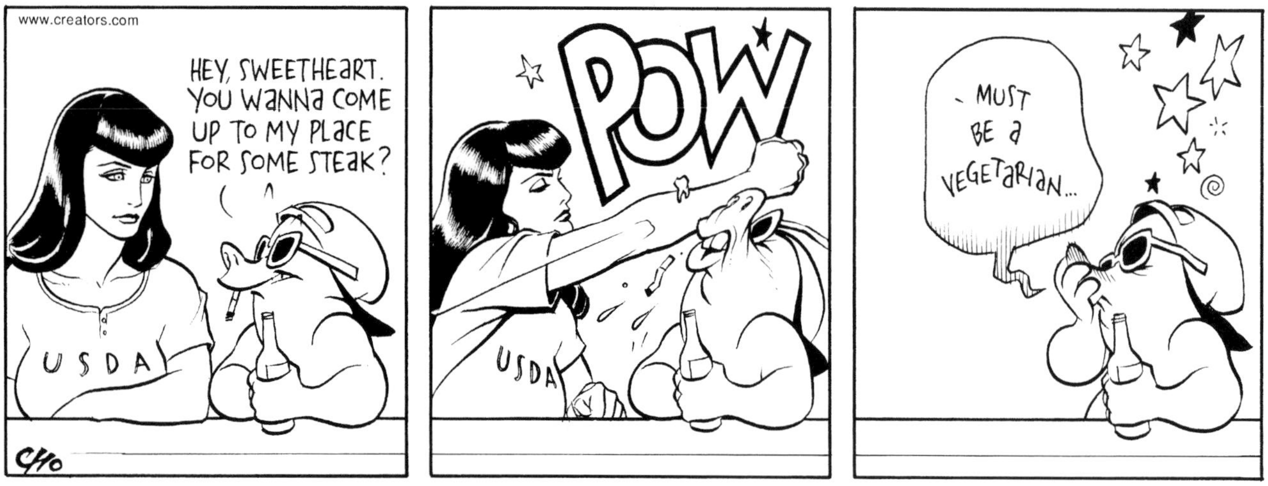

www.creators.com
HEY, SWEETHEART. YOU WANNA COME UP TO MY PLACE FOR SOME STEAK?
USDA
CHO
POW
USDA
- MUST BE A VEGETARIAN...

PORK

THE OTHER WHITE MEAT

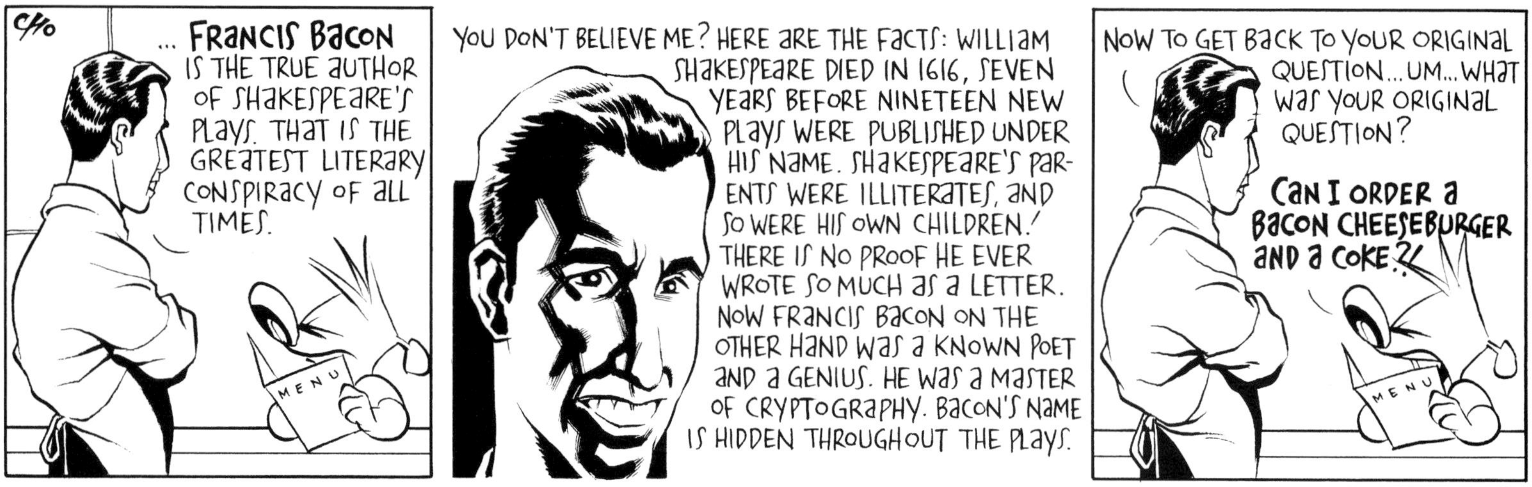

CHO
... FRANCIS BACON IS THE TRUE AUTHOR OF SHAKESPEARE'S PLAYS. THAT IS THE GREATEST LITERARY CONSPIRACY OF ALL TIMES.
MENU
YOU DON'T BELIEVE ME? HERE ARE THE FACTS: WILLIAM SHAKESPEARE DIED IN 1616, SEVEN YEARS BEFORE NINETEEN NEW PLAYS WERE PUBLISHED UNDER HIS NAME. SHAKESPEARE'S PARENTS WERE ILLITERATES, AND SO WERE HIS OWN CHILDREN! THERE IS NO PROOF HE EVER WROTE SO MUCH AS A LETTER. NOW FRANCIS BACON ON THE OTHER HAND WAS A KNOWN POET AND A GENIUS. HE WAS A MASTER OF CRYPTOGRAPHY. BACON'S NAME IS HIDDEN THROUGHOUT THE PLAYS.
NOW TO GET BACK TO YOUR ORIGINAL QUESTION...UM...WHAT WAS YOUR ORIGINAL QUESTION?
CAN I ORDER A BACON CHEESEBURGER AND A COKE?!
MENU

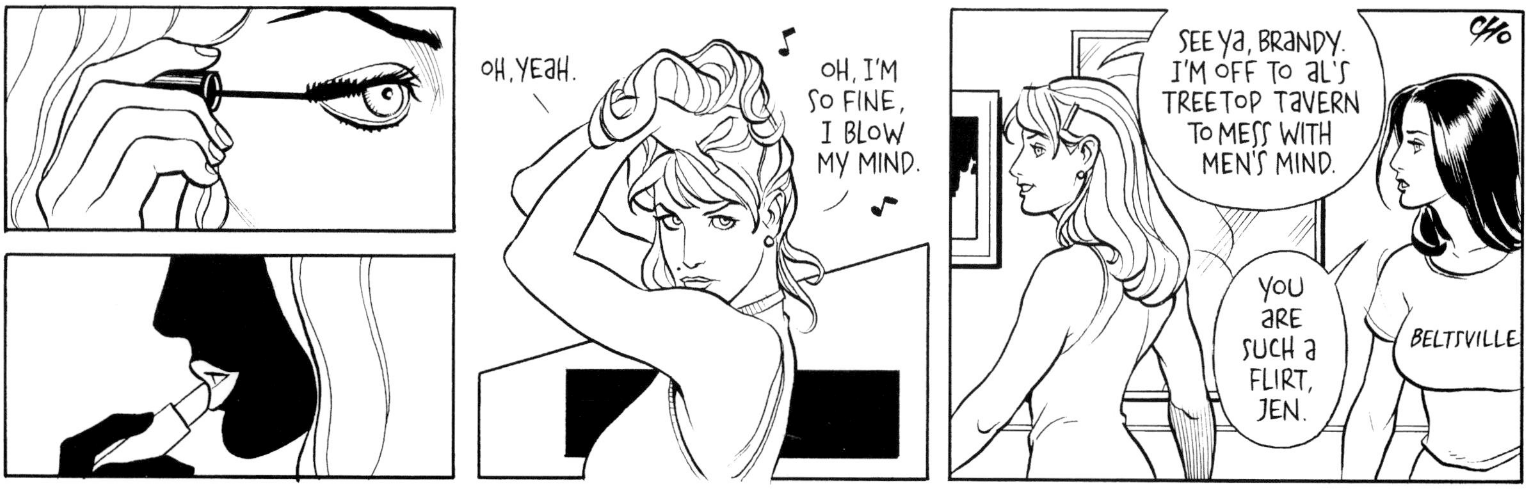

OH, YEAH.
OH, I'M SO FINE, I BLOW MY MIND.
CHO
SEE YA, BRANDY. I'M OFF TO AL'S TREETOP TAVERN TO MESS WITH MEN'S MIND.
YOU ARE SUCH A FLIRT, JEN.
BELTSVILLE

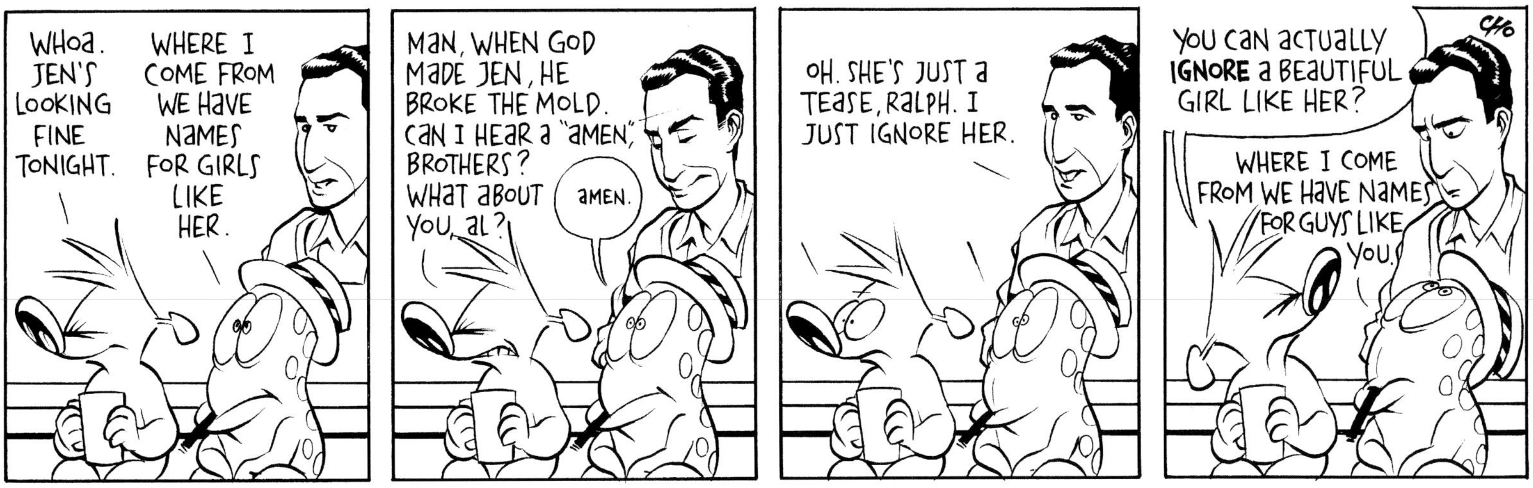
WHOA. JEN'S LOOKING FINE TONIGHT.
WHERE I COME FROM WE HAVE NAMES FOR GIRLS LIKE HER.
MAN, WHEN GOD MADE JEN, HE BROKE THE MOLD. CAN I HEAR A "AMEN," BROTHERS? WHAT ABOUT YOU, AL?
AMEN.
OH. SHE'S JUST A TEASE, RALPH. I JUST IGNORE HER.
YOU CAN ACTUALLY IGNORE A BEAUTIFUL GIRL LIKE HER?
WHERE I COME FROM WE HAVE NAMES FOR GUYS LIKE YOU.
CHO

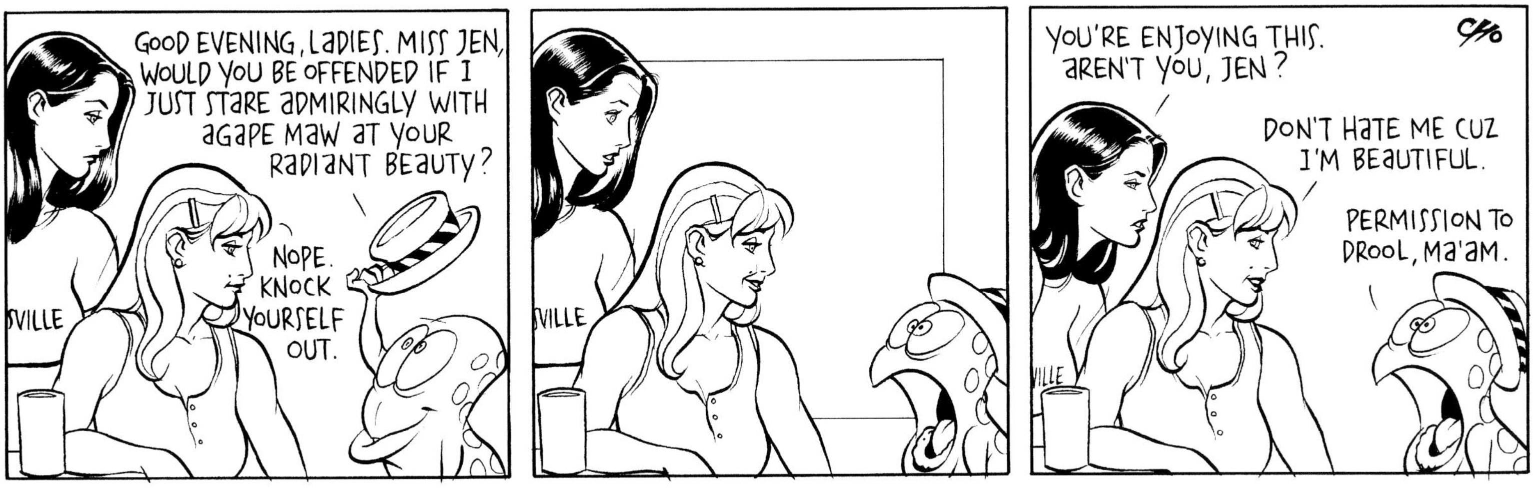
GOOD EVENING, LADIES. MISS JEN, WOULD YOU BE OFFENDED IF I JUST STARE ADMIRINGLY WITH AGAPE MAW AT YOUR RADIANT BEAUTY?
NOPE. KNOCK YOURSELF OUT.
YOU'RE ENJOYING THIS. AREN'T YOU, JEN?
DON'T HATE ME CUZ I'M BEAUTIFUL.
PERMISSION TO DROOL, MA'AM.
CHO

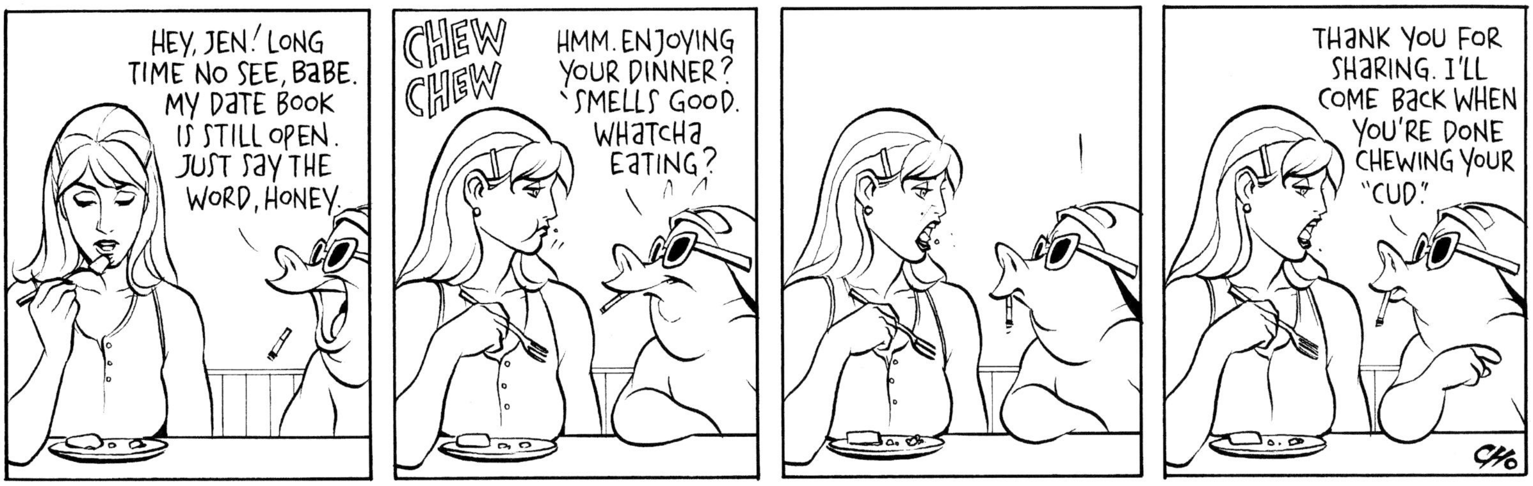
HEY, JEN! LONG TIME NO SEE, BABE. MY DATE BOOK IS STILL OPEN. JUST SAY THE WORD, HONEY.
CHEW CHEW
HMM. ENJOYING YOUR DINNER? SMELLS GOOD. WHATCHA EATING?
THANK YOU FOR SHARING. I'LL COME BACK WHEN YOU'RE DONE CHEWING YOUR "CUD."
CHO

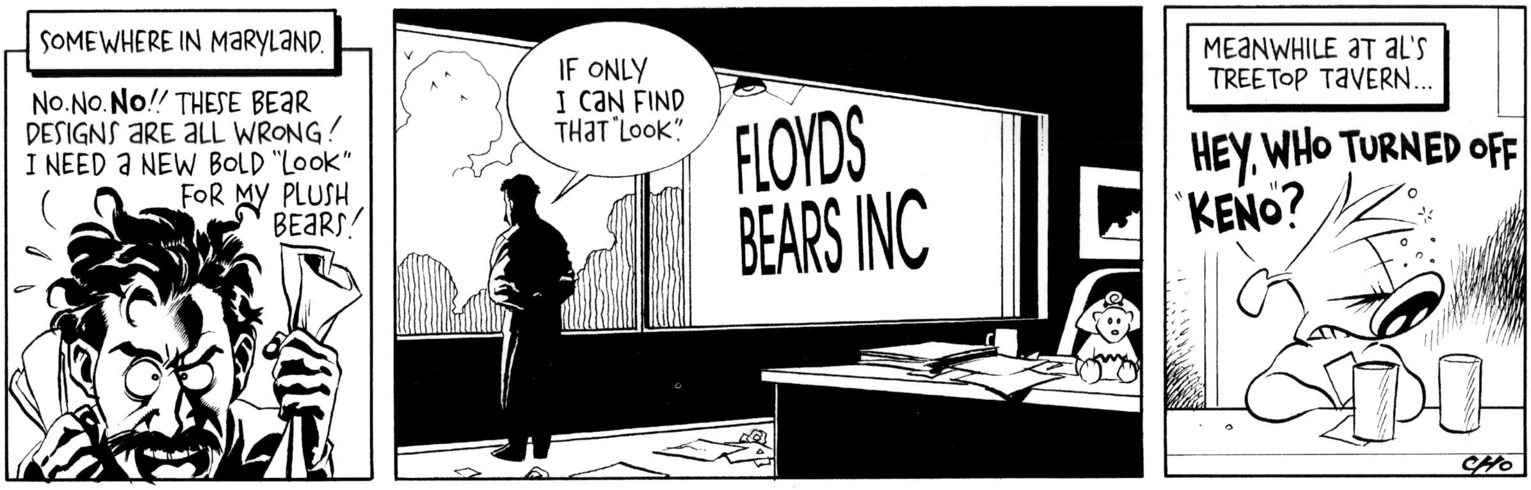
SOMEWHERE IN MARYLAND.
NO. NO. NO!! THESE BEAR DESIGNS ARE ALL WRONG! I NEED A NEW BOLD "LOOK" FOR MY PLUSH BEARS!
IF ONLY I CAN FIND THAT "LOOK."
FLOYDS BEARS INC
MEANWHILE AT AL'S TREETOP TAVERN...
HEY, WHO TURNED OFF "KENO"?
CHO

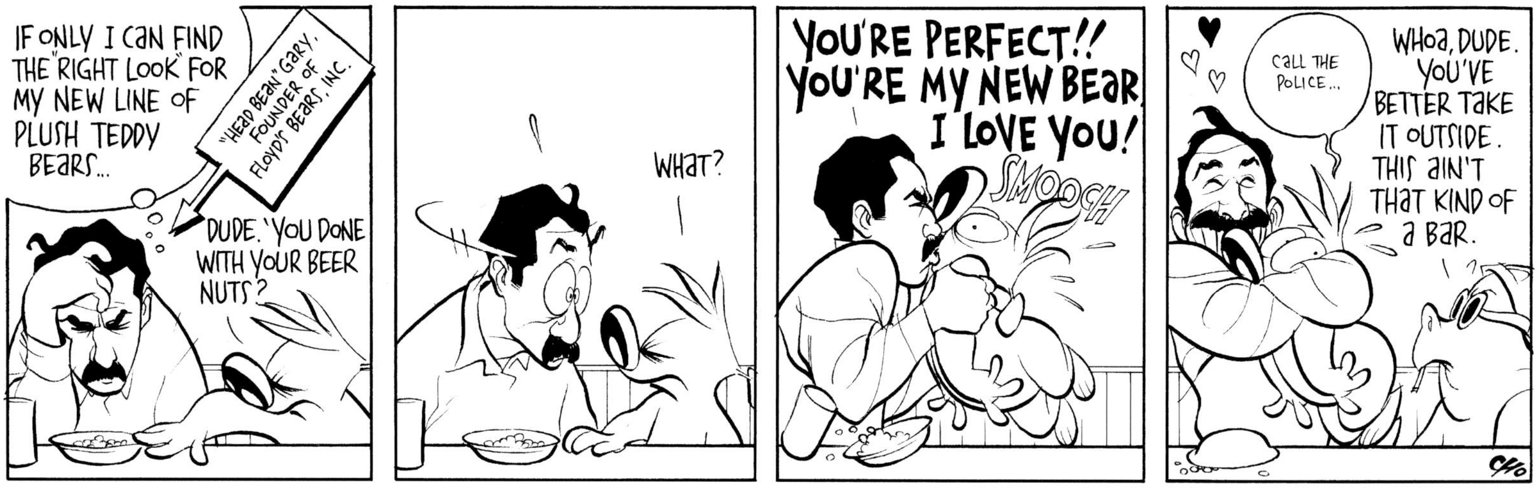
IF ONLY I CAN FIND THE "RIGHT LOOK" FOR MY NEW LINE OF PLUSH TEDDY BEARS...
"HEAD BEAN" GARY, FOUNDER OF FLOYDS BEARS, INC.
DUDE. YOU DONE WITH YOUR BEER NUTS?
WHAT?
YOU'RE PERFECT!! YOU'RE MY NEW BEAR. I LOVE YOU!
SMOOCH
CALL THE POLICE...
WHOA, DUDE. YOU'VE BETTER TAKE IT OUTSIDE. THIS AIN'T THAT KIND OF A BAR.
CHO

MAKING OF A STAR

Part 1
"CHANCE DISCOVERY"

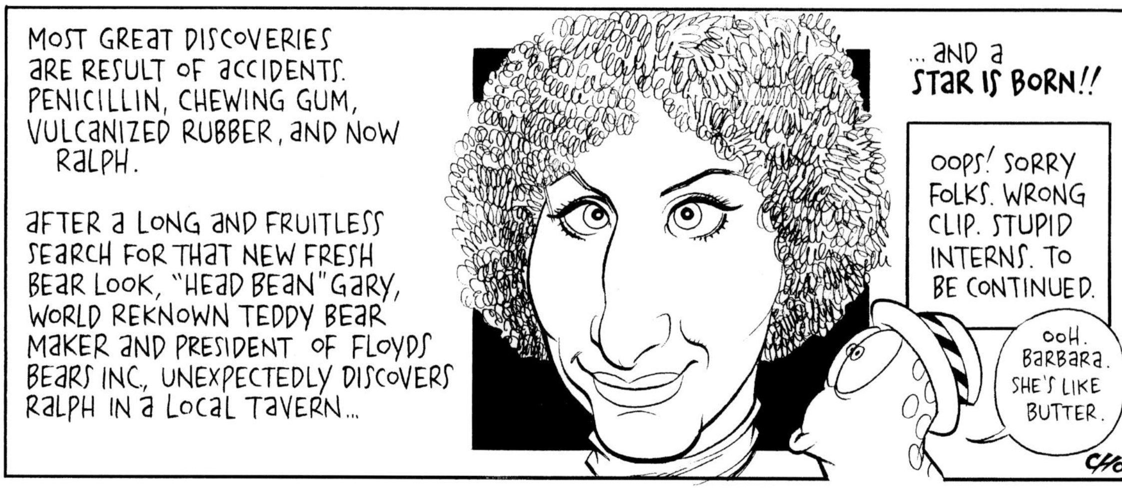
MOST GREAT DISCOVERIES ARE RESULT OF ACCIDENTS. PENICILLIN, CHEWING GUM, VULCANIZED RUBBER, AND NOW RALPH.
AFTER A LONG AND FRUITLESS SEARCH FOR THAT NEW FRESH BEAR LOOK, "HEAD BEAN" GARY, WORLD REKNOWN TEDDY BEAR MAKER AND PRESIDENT OF FLOYDS BEARS INC., UNEXPECTEDLY DISCOVERS RALPH IN A LOCAL TAVERN...
...AND A STAR IS BORN!!
OOPS! SORRY FOLKS. WRONG CLIP. STUPID INTERNS. TO BE CONTINUED.
OOH. BARBARA. SHE'S LIKE BUTTER.
CHO

MAKING OF A STAR

Part 2
"THE RIGHT CLOTHES. THE RIGHT LOOK"

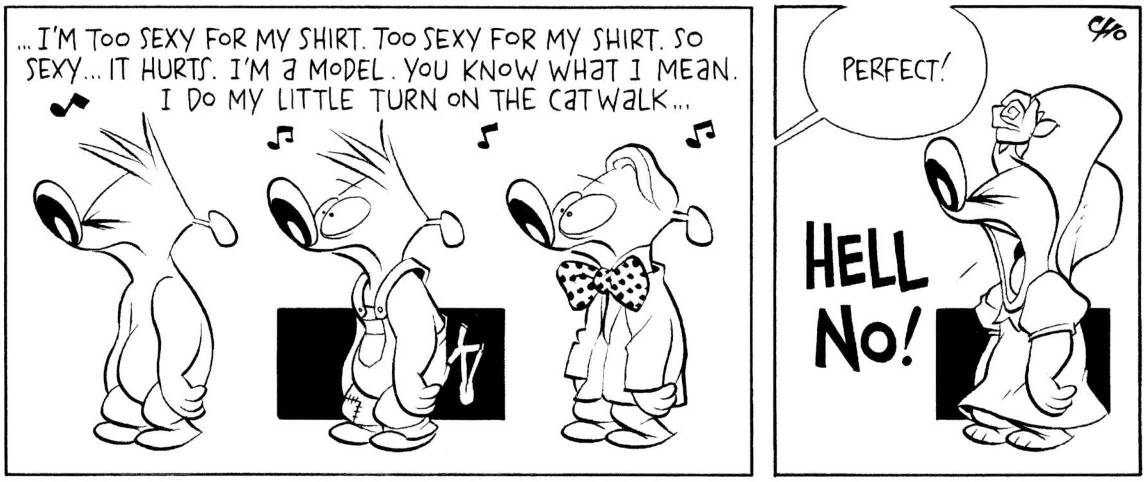
...I'M TOO SEXY FOR MY SHIRT. TOO SEXY FOR MY SHIRT. SO SEXY... IT HURTS. I'M A MODEL. YOU KNOW WHAT I MEAN. I DO MY LITTLE TURN ON THE CATWALK...
CHO
PERFECT!
HELL NO!

MAKING OF A STAR

Part 3
"MARKET TESTING"

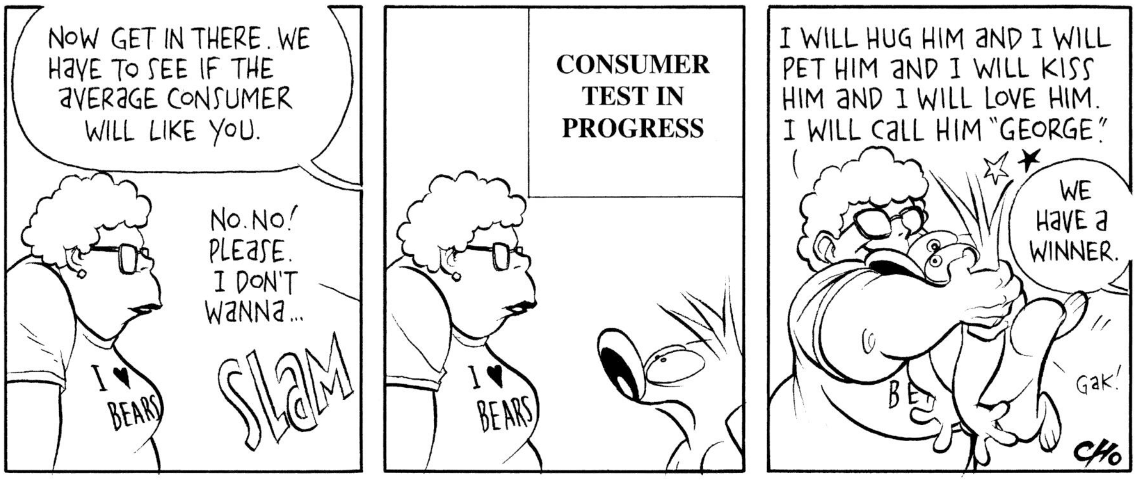
NOW GET IN THERE. WE HAVE TO SEE IF THE AVERAGE CONSUMER WILL LIKE YOU.
NO. NO! PLEASE. I DON'T WANNA...
I ♥ BEARS
SLAM
CONSUMER TEST IN PROGRESS
I ♥ BEARS
I WILL HUG HIM AND I WILL PET HIM AND I WILL KISS HIM AND I WILL LOVE HIM. I WILL CALL HIM "GEORGE".
WE HAVE A WINNER.
GAK!
CHO

MAKING OF A STAR

Part 4
"THE IMAGE MAKER"

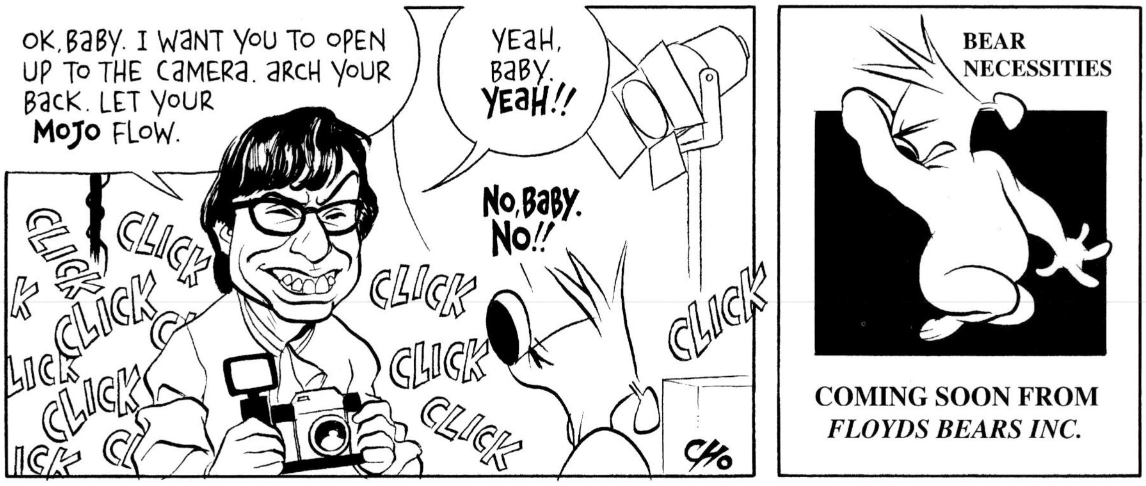
OK, BABY. I WANT YOU TO OPEN UP TO THE CAMERA. ARCH YOUR BACK. LET YOUR MOJO FLOW.
YEAH, BABY. YEAH!!
CLICK CLICK CLICK CLICK CLICK CLICK CLICK
NO, BABY. NO!!
CHO
BEAR NECESSITIES
COMING SOON FROM
FLOYDS BEARS INC.

MAKING OF A STAR

Part 5
"THE MEDIA BLITZ"

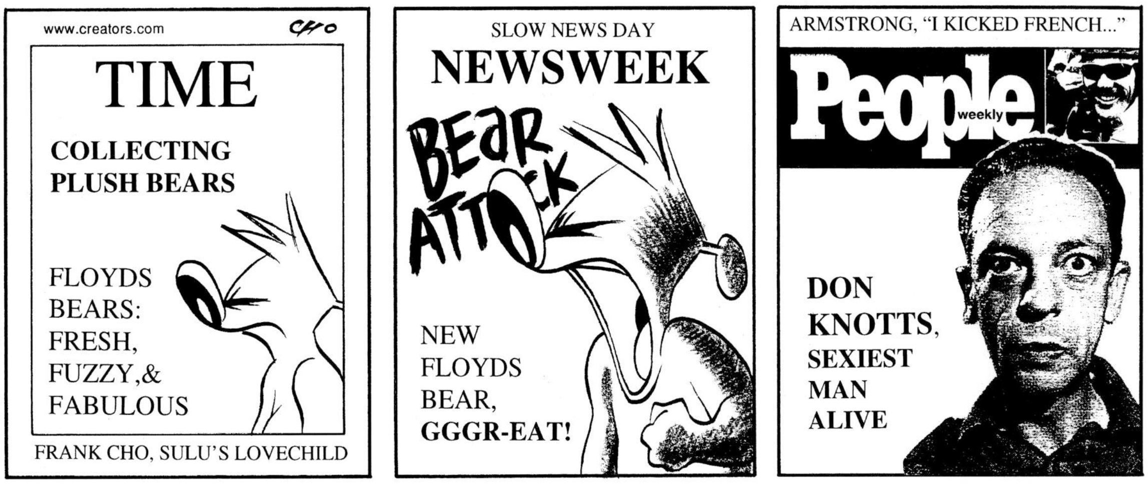
www.creators.com
CHO
TIME
COLLECTING PLUSH BEARS
FLOYDS BEARS: FRESH, FUZZY,& FABULOUS
FRANK CHO, SULU'S LOVECHILD
SLOW NEWS DAY
NEWSWEEK
BEAR ATTACK
NEW FLOYDS BEAR, GGGR-EAT!
ARMSTRONG, "I KICKED FRENCH..."
People weekly
DON KNOTTS, SEXIEST MAN ALIVE

MAKING OF A STAR

Part 6
"THE LAUNCH"

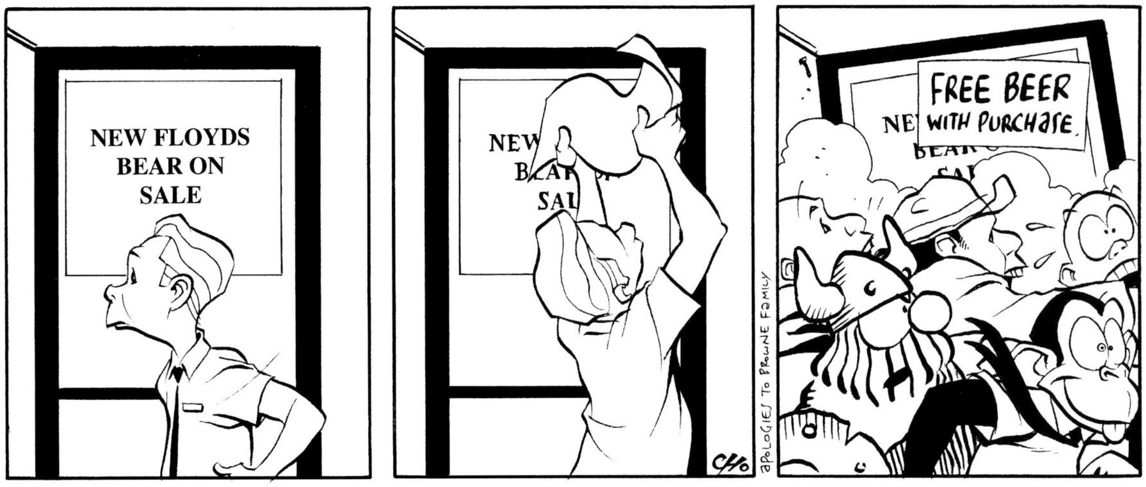
NEW FLOYDS BEAR ON SALE
CHO
APOLOGIES TO BROWNE FAMILY
FREE BEER WITH PURCHASE

MAKING OF A STAR

Part 7
"SUCCESS"

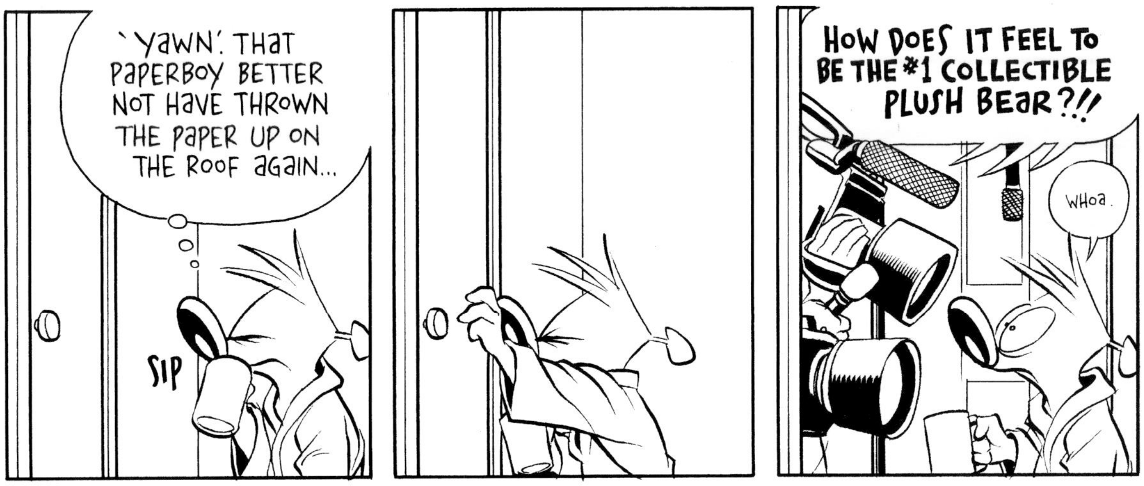
`YAWN'. THAT PAPERBOY BETTER NOT HAVE THROWN THE PAPER UP ON THE ROOF AGAIN...
SIP
HOW DOES IT FEEL TO BE THE #1 COLLECTIBLE PLUSH BEAR?!!
WHOA.

MAKING OF A STAR

Part 8
"THE TALK SHOWS"

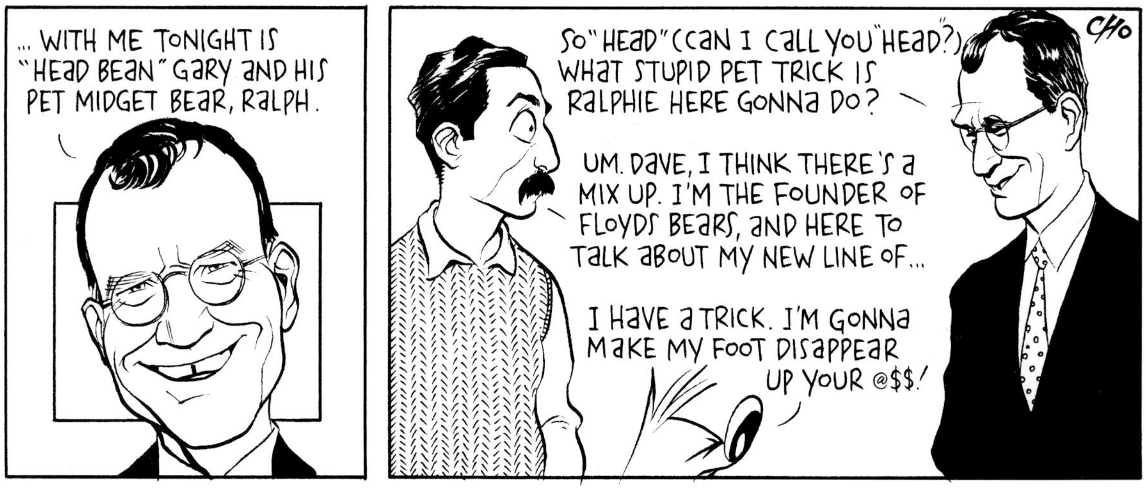

... WITH ME TONIGHT IS "HEAD BEAN" GARY AND HIS PET MIDGET BEAR, RALPH.
CHO
SO "HEAD" (CAN I CALL YOU "HEAD"?) WHAT STUPID PET TRICK IS RALPHIE HERE GONNA DO?
UM. DAVE, I THINK THERE'S A MIX UP. I'M THE FOUNDER OF FLOYDS BEARS, AND HERE TO TALK ABOUT MY NEW LINE OF...
I HAVE A TRICK. I'M GONNA MAKE MY FOOT DISAPPEAR UP YOUR @$$!

MAKING OF A STAR

Part 9
"MERCHANDISE, MERCHANDISE, MERCHANDISE"

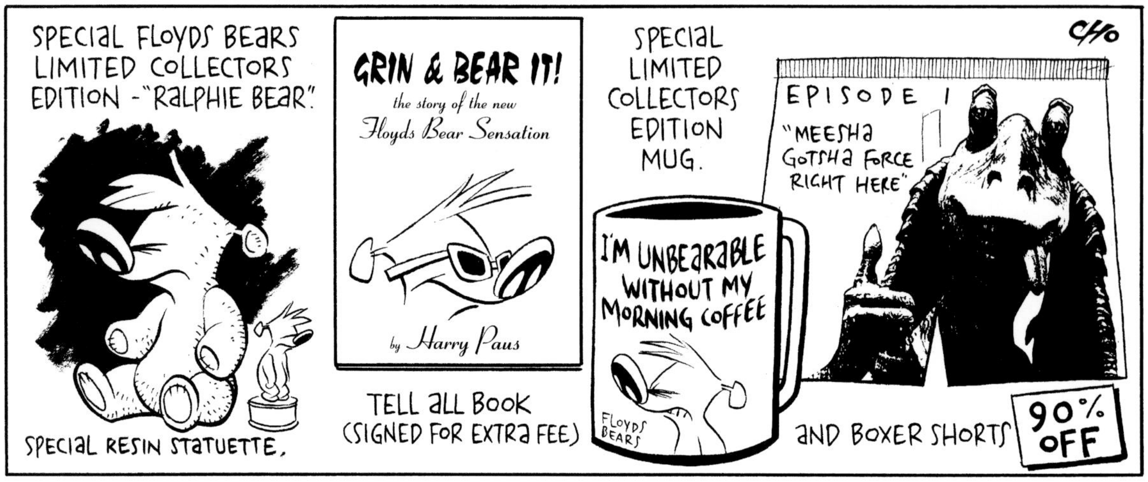

SPECIAL FLOYDS BEARS LIMITED COLLECTORS EDITION - "RALPHIE BEAR".
SPECIAL RESIN STATUETTE,
GRIN & BEAR IT!
the story of the new Floyds Bear Sensation
by Harry Paus
TELL ALL BOOK (SIGNED FOR EXTRA FEE)
SPECIAL LIMITED COLLECTORS EDITION MUG.
I'M UNBEARABLE WITHOUT MY MORNING COFFEE
FLOYDS BEARS
CHO
EPISODE I
"MEESHA GOTSHA FORCE RIGHT HERE"
AND BOXER SHORTS
90% OFF

MAKING OF A STAR

Part 10
"FAME"

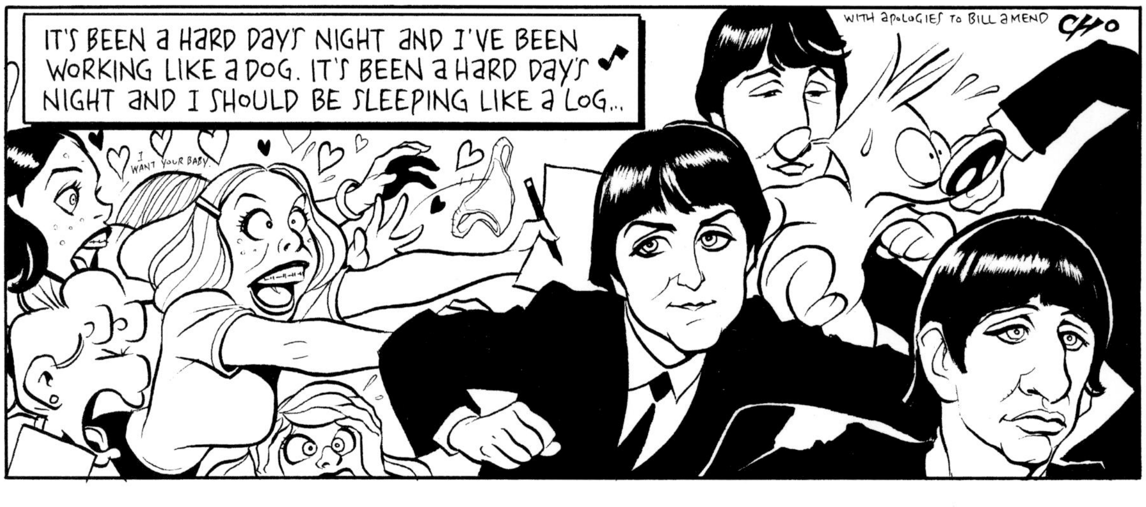

IT'S BEEN A HARD DAYS NIGHT AND I'VE BEEN WORKING LIKE A DOG. IT'S BEEN A HARD DAY'S NIGHT AND I SHOULD BE SLEEPING LIKE A LOG...
WITH APOLOGIES TO BILL AMEND
CHO
I WANT YOUR BABY

MAKING OF A STAR

Part 11
"BOOZE, DRUGS & WOMEN"

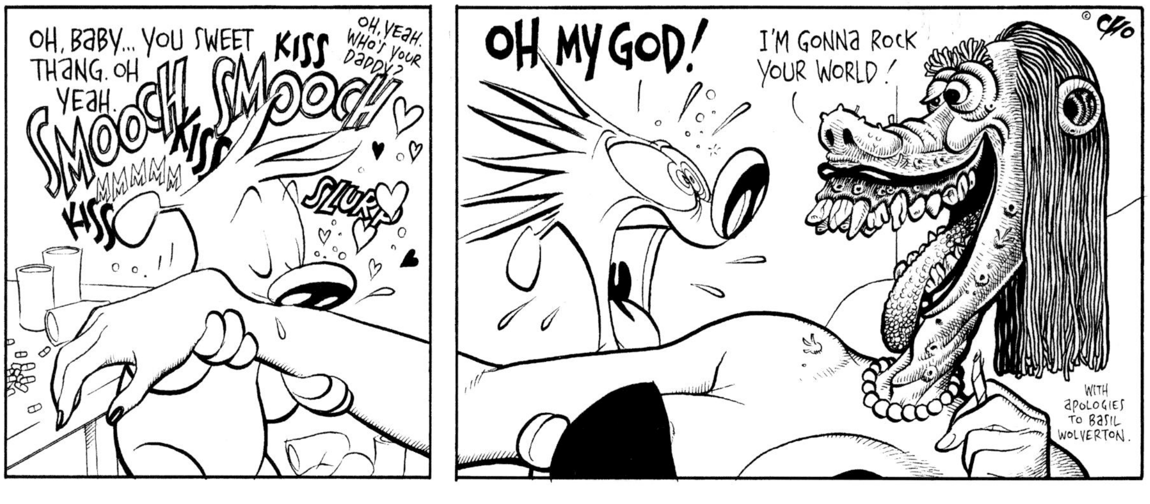

OH, BABY... YOU SWEET THANG. OH YEAH.
OH, YEAH. WHO'S YOUR DADDY?
KISS
SMOOCH
SMOOCH
KISS
MMMMM
KISS
SLURP
OH MY GOD!
I'M GONNA ROCK YOUR WORLD!
© CHO
WITH APOLOGIES TO BASIL WOLVERTON.

MAKING OF A STAR

Part 12
"SCANDAL"

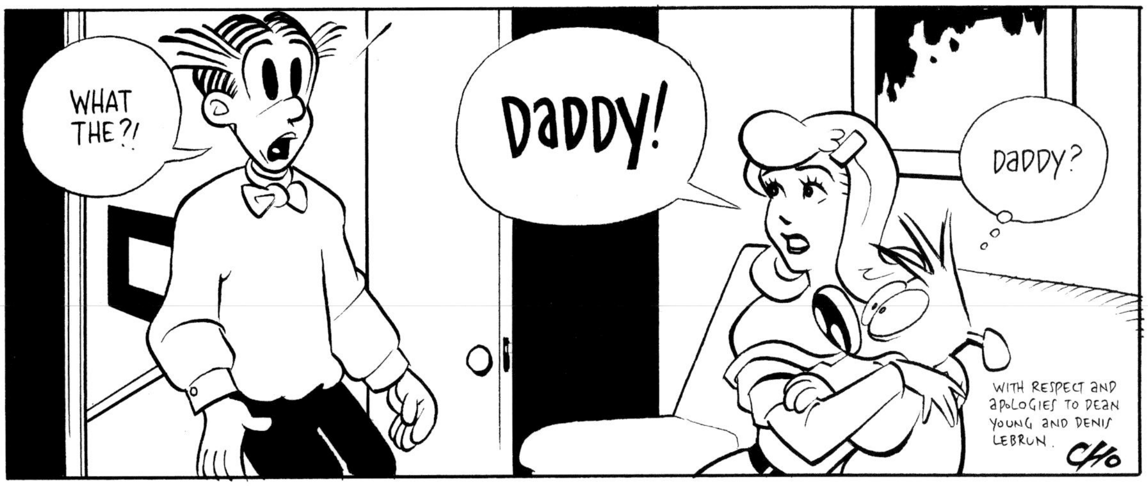
WHAT THE?!
DADDY!
DADDY?
WITH RESPECT AND APOLOGIES TO DEAN YOUNG AND DENIS LEBRUN.
CHO

MAKING OF A STAR

Part 13
"MEDIA FRENZY"

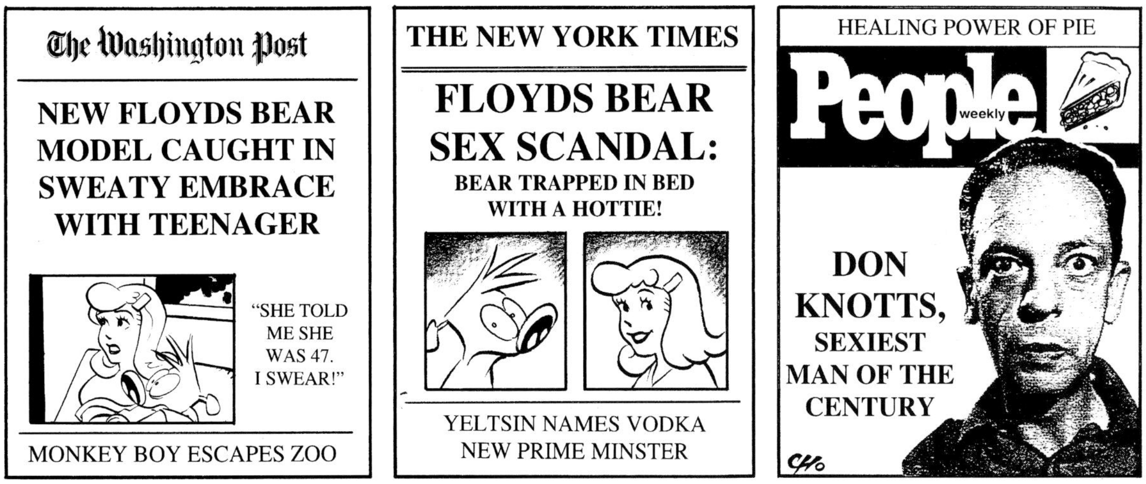
The Washington Post
NEW FLOYDS BEAR MODEL CAUGHT IN SWEATY EMBRACE WITH TEENAGER
"SHE TOLD ME SHE WAS 47. I SWEAR!"
MONKEY BOY ESCAPES ZOO
THE NEW YORK TIMES
FLOYDS BEAR SEX SCANDAL:
BEAR TRAPPED IN BED WITH A HOTTIE!
YELTSIN NAMES VODKA NEW PRIME MINSTER
HEALING POWER OF PIE
People weekly
DON KNOTTS,
SEXIEST MAN OF THE CENTURY
CHO

MAKING OF A STAR

Part 14
"REGROUP AND BUY TIME"

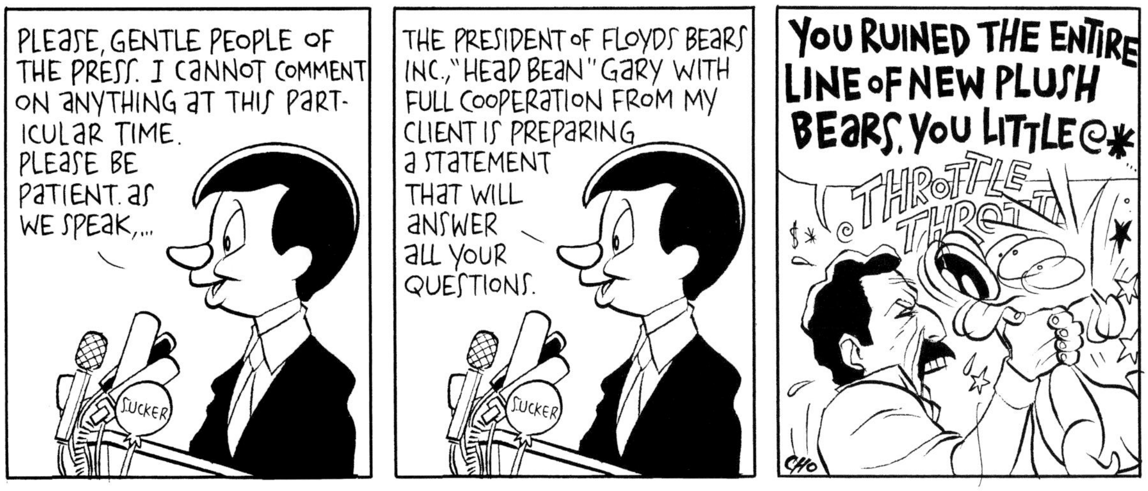
PLEASE, GENTLE PEOPLE OF THE PRESS. I CANNOT COMMENT ON ANYTHING AT THIS PARTICULAR TIME. PLEASE BE PATIENT. AS WE SPEAK,...
SUCKER
THE PRESIDENT OF FLOYDS BEARS INC., "HEAD BEAN" GARY WITH FULL COOPERATION FROM MY CLIENT IS PREPARING A STATEMENT THAT WILL ANSWER ALL YOUR QUESTIONS.
SUCKER
YOU RUINED THE ENTIRE LINE OF NEW PLUSH BEARS, YOU LITTLE @*...
THROTTLE
THROTTLE
CHO

MAKING OF A STAR

Part 15
"MEDIA DIGS FOR RATINGS"

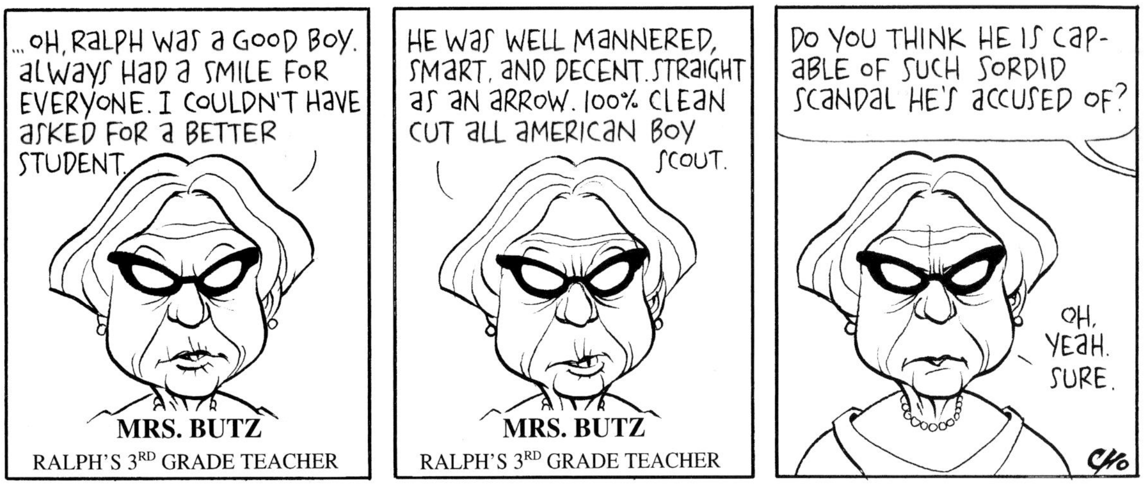
...OH, RALPH WAS A GOOD BOY. ALWAYS HAD A SMILE FOR EVERYONE. I COULDN'T HAVE ASKED FOR A BETTER STUDENT.
MRS. BUTZ
RALPH'S 3RD GRADE TEACHER
HE WAS WELL MANNERED, SMART, AND DECENT. STRAIGHT AS AN ARROW. 100% CLEAN CUT ALL AMERICAN BOY SCOUT.
MRS. BUTZ
RALPH'S 3RD GRADE TEACHER
DO YOU THINK HE IS CAPABLE OF SUCH SORDID SCANDAL HE'S ACCUSED OF?
OH, YEAH. SURE.
CHO

MAKING OF A STAR

Part 16
"DENIAL"

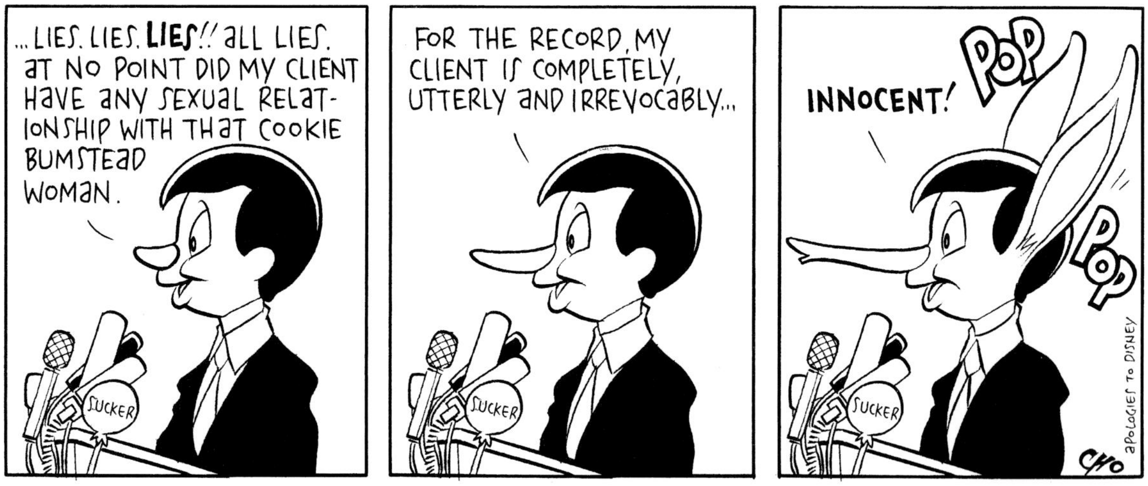
...LIES. LIES. LIES!! ALL LIES. AT NO POINT DID MY CLIENT HAVE ANY SEXUAL RELATIONSHIP WITH THAT COOKIE BUMSTEAD WOMAN.
SUCKER
FOR THE RECORD, MY CLIENT IS COMPLETELY, UTTERLY AND IRREVOCABLY...
SUCKER
INNOCENT!
POP
POP
SUCKER
APOLOGIES TO DISNEY
CHO

MAKING OF A STAR

Part 17
"THE FALL"

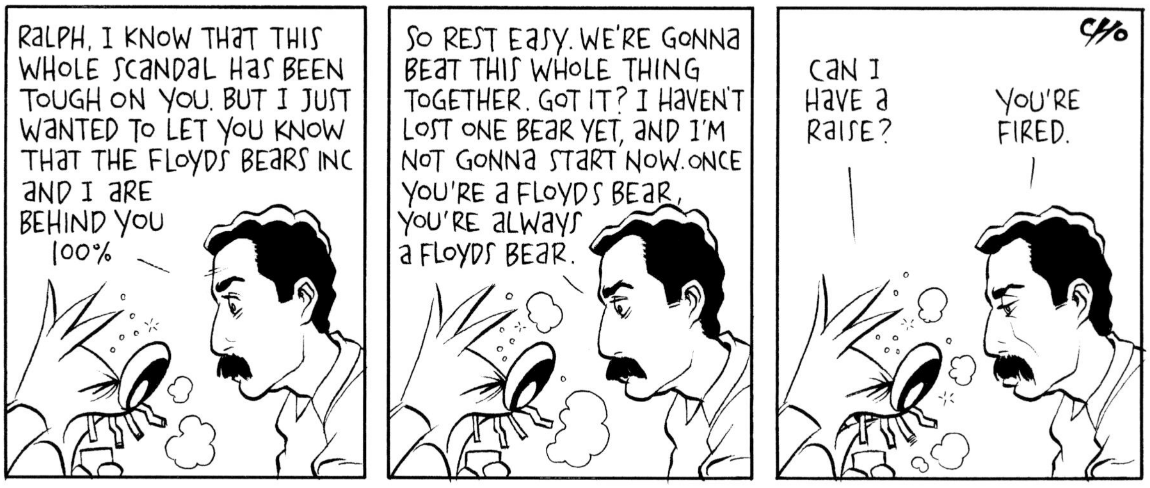
RALPH, I KNOW THAT THIS WHOLE SCANDAL HAS BEEN TOUGH ON YOU. BUT I JUST WANTED TO LET YOU KNOW THAT THE FLOYDS BEARS INC AND I ARE BEHIND YOU 100%
SO REST EASY. WE'RE GONNA BEAT THIS WHOLE THING TOGETHER. GOT IT? I HAVEN'T LOST ONE BEAR YET, AND I'M NOT GONNA START NOW. ONCE YOU'RE A FLOYDS BEAR, YOU'RE ALWAYS A FLOYDS BEAR.
CHO
CAN I HAVE A RAISE?
YOU'RE FIRED.

MAKING OF A STAR

Part 18
"ROCK BOTTOM"

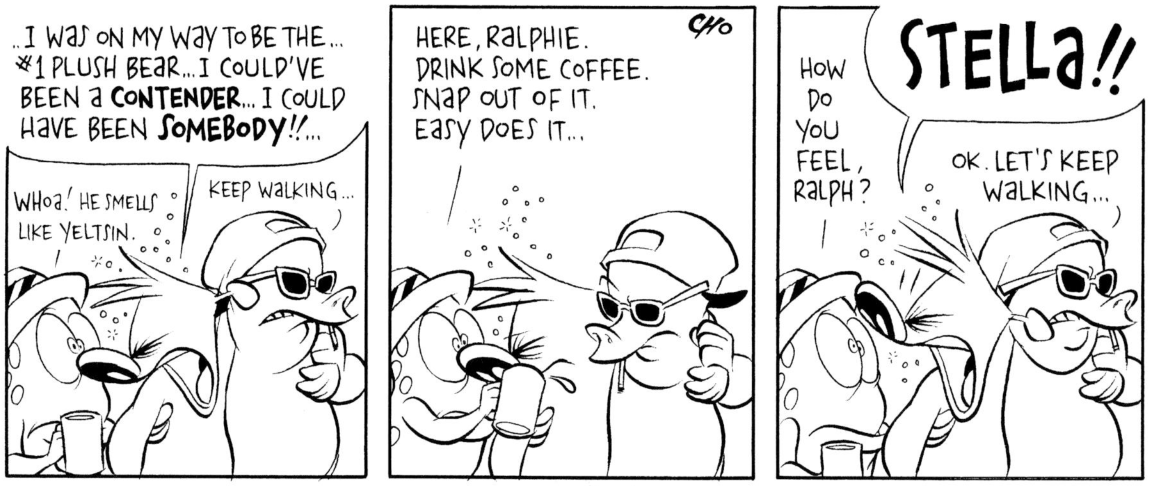
..I WAS ON MY WAY TO BE THE... #1 PLUSH BEAR... I COULD'VE BEEN A CONTENDER... I COULD HAVE BEEN SOMEBODY!!...
WHOA! HE SMELLS LIKE YELTSIN.
KEEP WALKING...
CHO
HERE, RALPHIE. DRINK SOME COFFEE. SNAP OUT OF IT. EASY DOES IT...
HOW DO YOU FEEL, RALPH?
STELLA!!
OK. LET'S KEEP WALKING...

MAKING OF A STAR

Part 19
"BORN AGAIN"

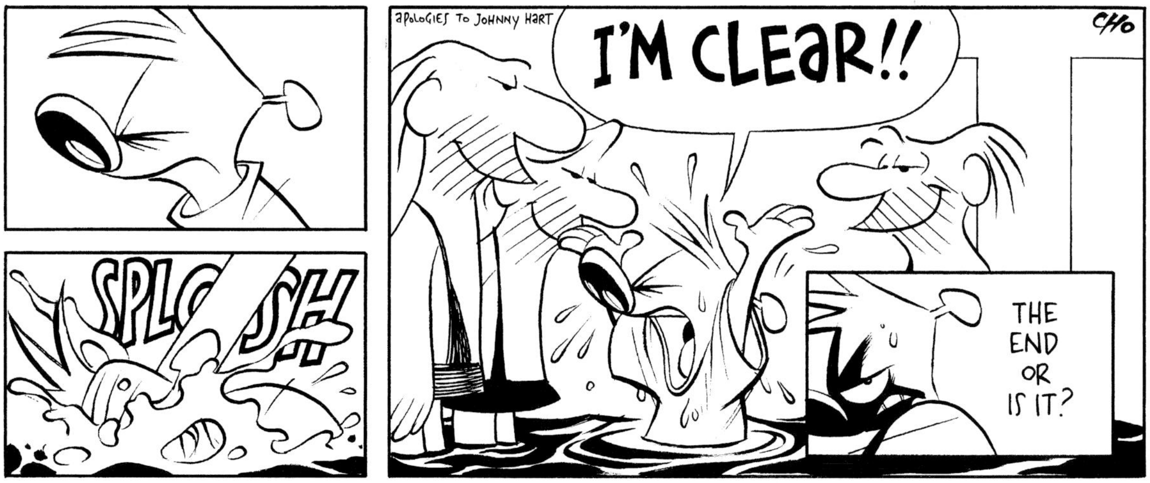
SPLOOSH
APOLOGIES TO JOHNNY HART
CHO
I'M CLEAR!!
THE END OR IS IT?

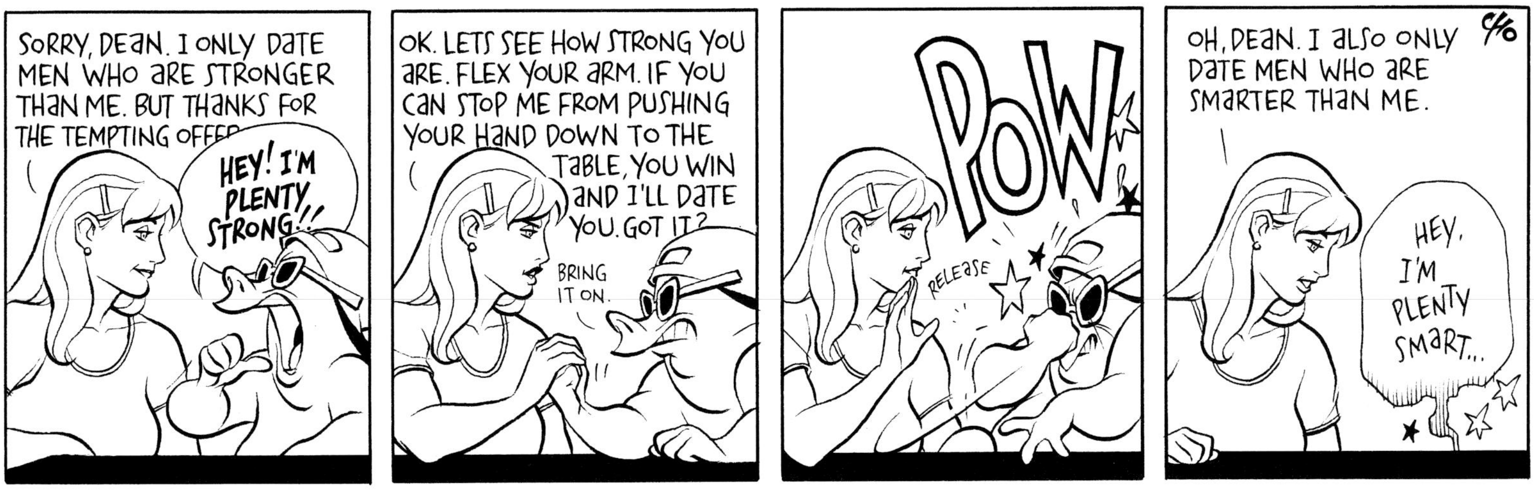
SORRY, DEAN. I ONLY DATE MEN WHO ARE STRONGER THAN ME. BUT THANKS FOR THE TEMPTING OFFER
HEY! I'M PLENTY STRONG!!!
OK. LETS SEE HOW STRONG YOU ARE. FLEX YOUR ARM. IF YOU CAN STOP ME FROM PUSHING YOUR HAND DOWN TO THE TABLE, YOU WIN AND I'LL DATE YOU. GOT IT?
BRING IT ON.
POW
RELEASE
OH, DEAN. I ALSO ONLY DATE MEN WHO ARE SMARTER THAN ME.
HEY, I'M PLENTY SMART...

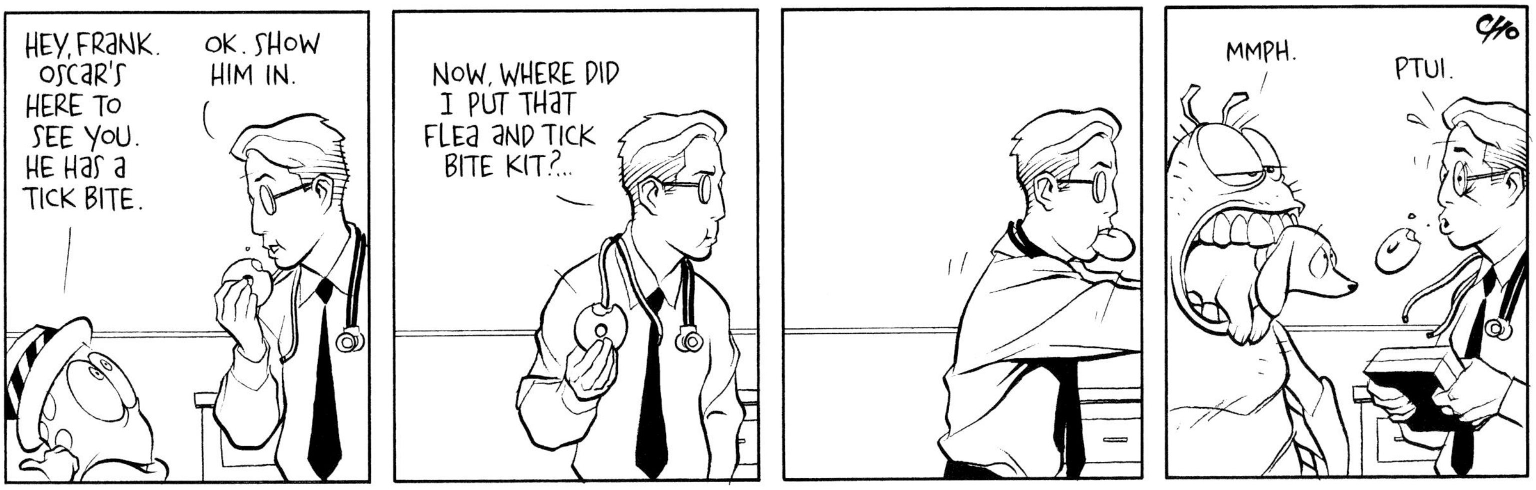
HEY, FRANK. OSCAR'S HERE TO SEE YOU. HE HAS A TICK BITE.
OK. SHOW HIM IN.
NOW, WHERE DID I PUT THAT FLEA AND TICK BITE KIT?...
MMPH.
PTUI.

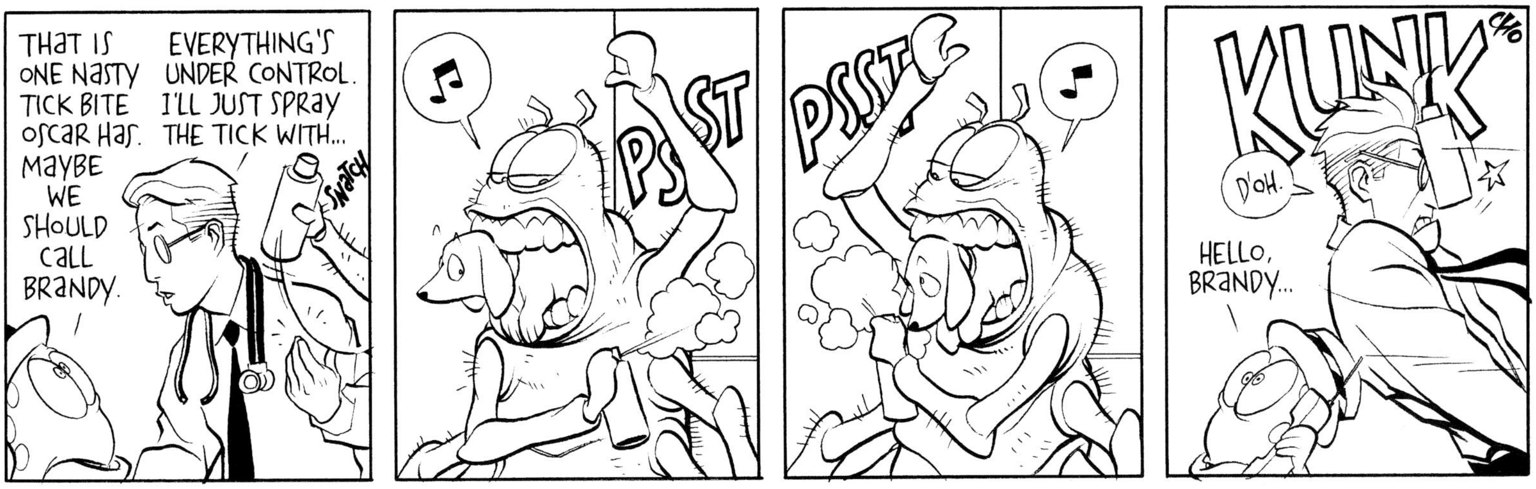
THAT IS ONE NASTY TICK BITE OSCAR HAS. MAYBE WE SHOULD CALL BRANDY.
EVERYTHING'S UNDER CONTROL. I'LL JUST SPRAY THE TICK WITH...
SNATCH
PSST
PSST
KUNK
D'OH.
HELLO, BRANDY...

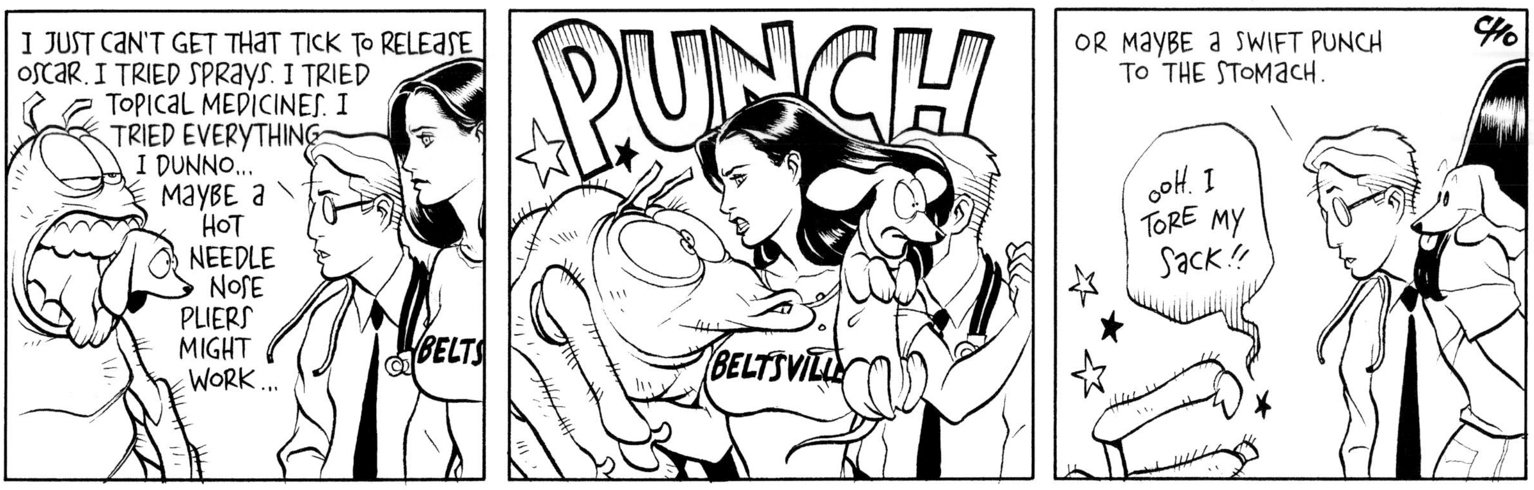
I JUST CAN'T GET THAT TICK TO RELEASE OSCAR. I TRIED SPRAYS. I TRIED TOPICAL MEDICINES. I TRIED EVERYTHING. I DUNNO... MAYBE A HOT NEEDLE NOSE PLIERS MIGHT WORK...
BELTS
PUNCH
BELTSVILLE
OR MAYBE A SWIFT PUNCH TO THE STOMACH.
OOH. I TORE MY SACK!!

MR. FRANK CHO
IS ATTENDING THE
SMALL PRESS EXPO
IN BETHESDA, MARYLAND
AND IS UNABLE TO
PRODUCE TODAY'S
COMIC STRIP.

REPLACING MR. CHO
TODAY IS A BELOVED
AMERICAN ARTIST WHO
NEEDS NO INTRODUCTION.

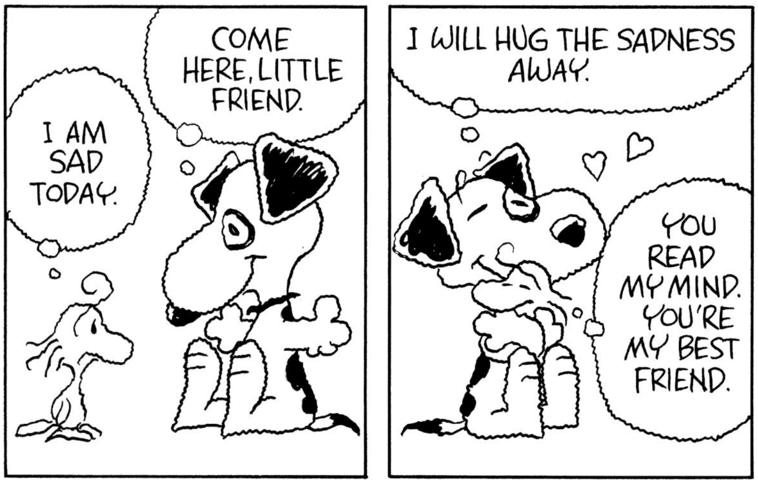

I AM SAD TODAY.
COME HERE, LITTLE FRIEND.
I WILL HUG THE SADNESS AWAY.
YOU READ MY MIND. YOU'RE MY BEST FRIEND.

NO. IT'S NOT
THOMAS KINKADE,
PAINTER OF LIGHT.

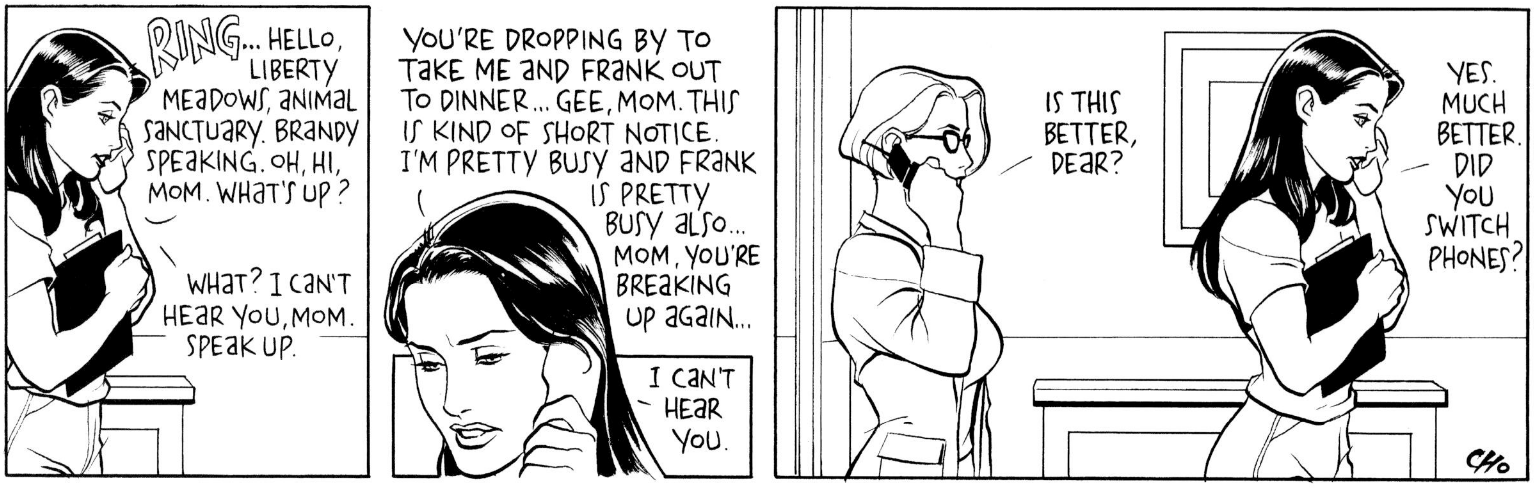

RING... HELLO, LIBERTY MEADOWS, ANIMAL SANCTUARY. BRANDY SPEAKING. OH, HI, MOM. WHAT'S UP?
WHAT? I CAN'T HEAR YOU, MOM. SPEAK UP.
YOU'RE DROPPING BY TO TAKE ME AND FRANK OUT TO DINNER... GEE, MOM. THIS IS KIND OF SHORT NOTICE. I'M PRETTY BUSY AND FRANK IS PRETTY BUSY ALSO... MOM, YOU'RE BREAKING UP AGAIN...
I CAN'T HEAR YOU.
IS THIS BETTER, DEAR?
YES. MUCH BETTER. DID YOU SWITCH PHONES?
CHO

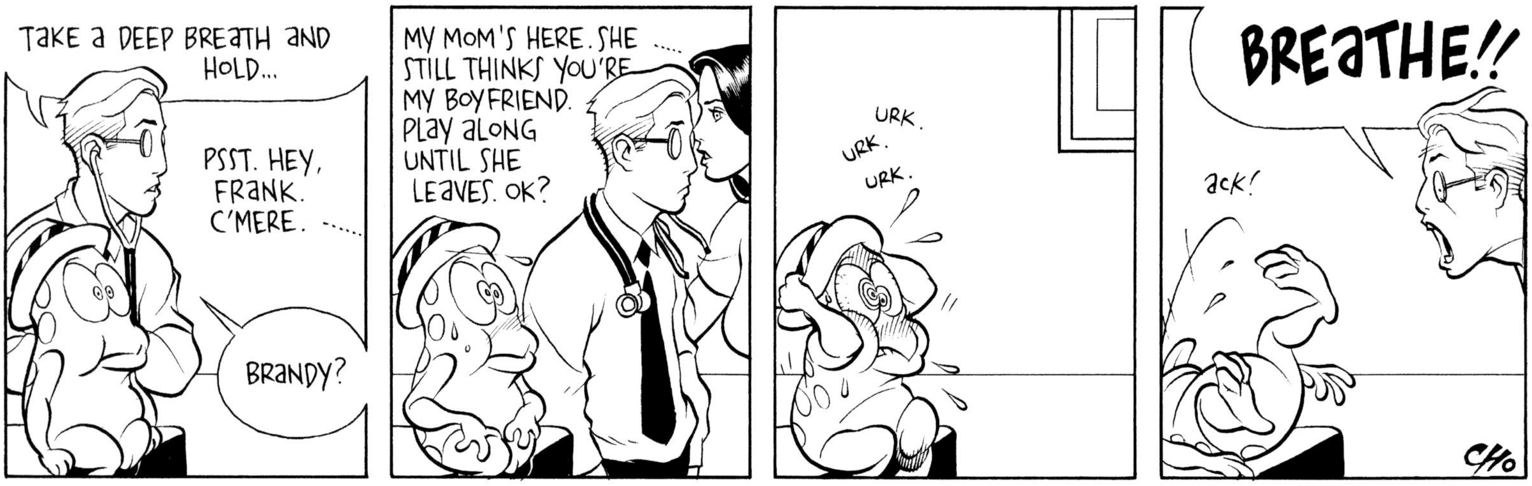

TAKE A DEEP BREATH AND HOLD...
PSST. HEY, FRANK. C'MERE.
BRANDY?
MY MOM'S HERE. SHE STILL THINKS YOU'RE MY BOYFRIEND. PLAY ALONG UNTIL SHE LEAVES. OK?
URK. URK. URK.
BREATHE!!
ACK!
CHO

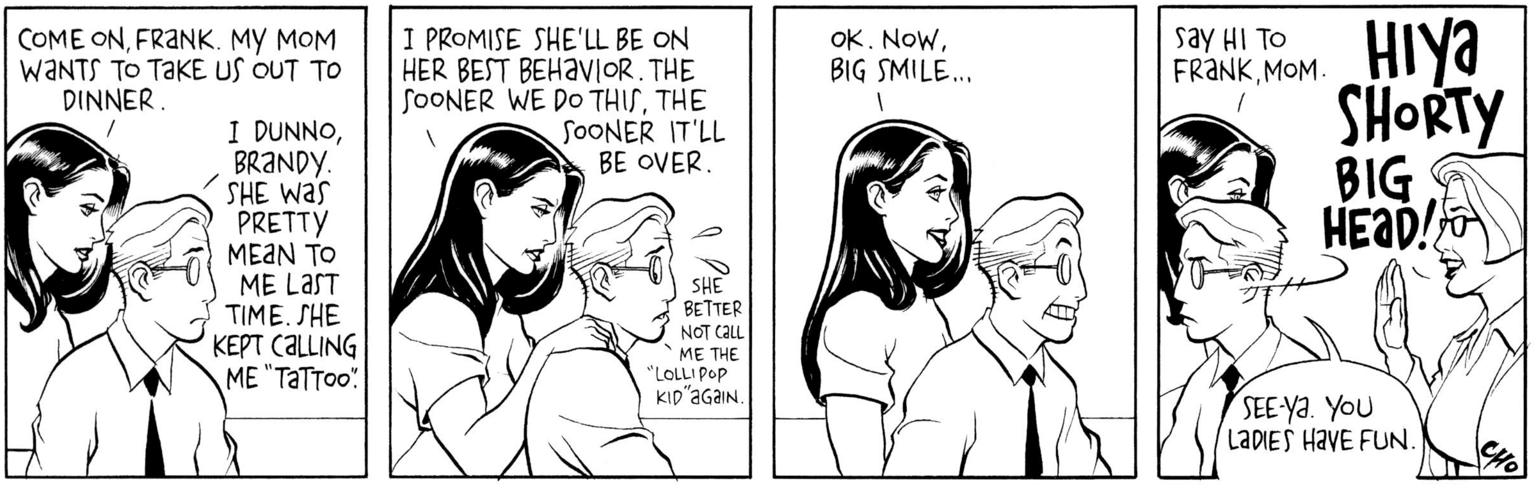

COME ON, FRANK. MY MOM WANTS TO TAKE US OUT TO DINNER.
I DUNNO, BRANDY. SHE WAS PRETTY MEAN TO ME LAST TIME. SHE KEPT CALLING ME "TATTOO".
I PROMISE SHE'LL BE ON HER BEST BEHAVIOR. THE SOONER WE DO THIS, THE SOONER IT'LL BE OVER.
SHE BETTER NOT CALL ME THE "LOLLIPOP KID" AGAIN.
OK. NOW, BIG SMILE...
SAY HI TO FRANK, MOM.
HIYA SHORTY BIG HEAD!
SEE-YA. YOU LADIES HAVE FUN.
CHO

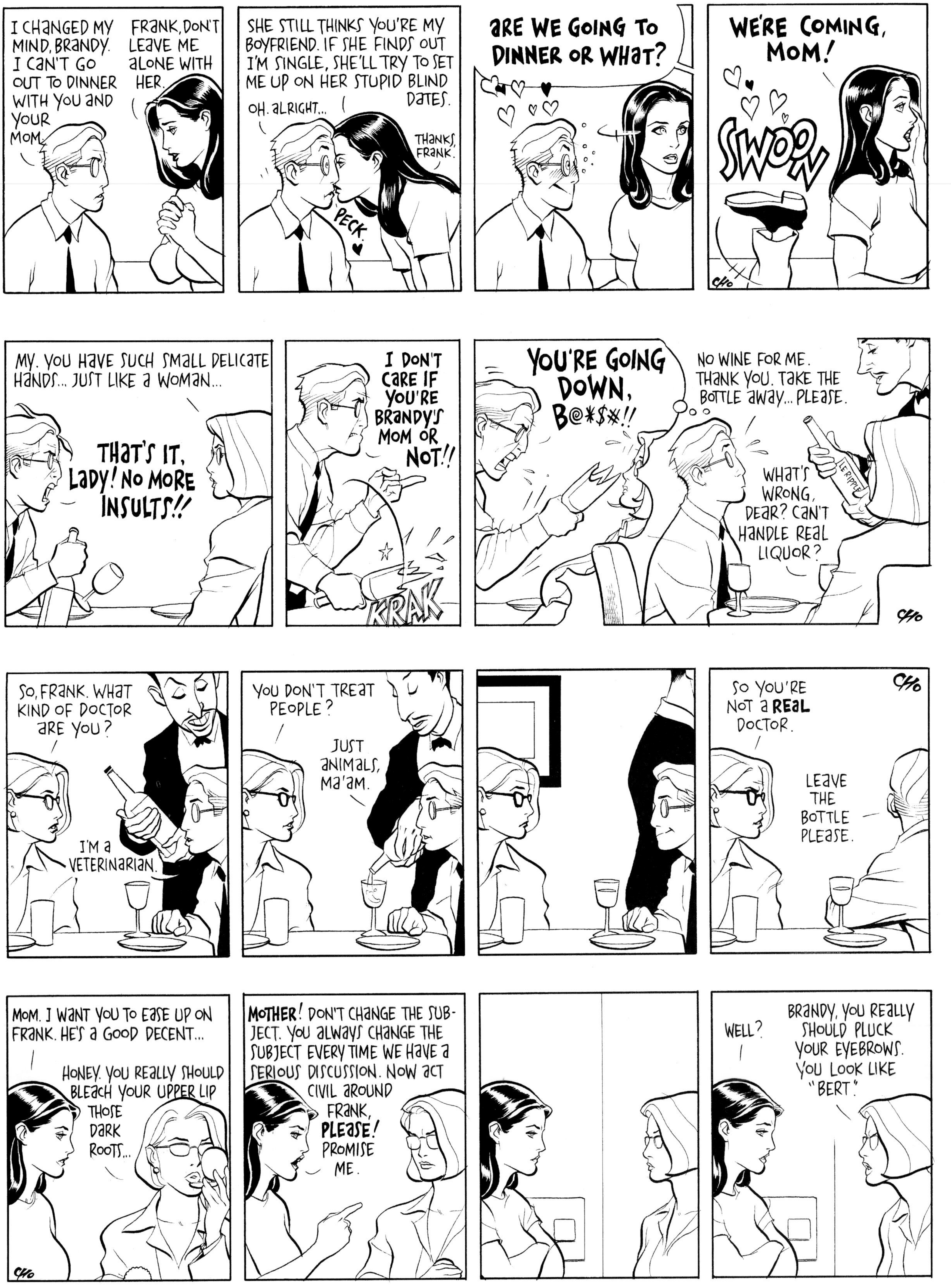

I CHANGED MY MIND, BRANDY. I CAN'T GO OUT TO DINNER WITH YOU AND YOUR MOM.
FRANK, DON'T LEAVE ME ALONE WITH HER.
SHE STILL THINKS YOU'RE MY BOYFRIEND. IF SHE FINDS OUT I'M SINGLE, SHE'LL TRY TO SET ME UP ON HER STUPID BLIND DATES.
OH. ALRIGHT...
THANKS, FRANK.
PECK
ARE WE GOING TO DINNER OR WHAT?
WE'RE COMING, MOM!
SWOON
CHO
MY. YOU HAVE SUCH SMALL DELICATE HANDS... JUST LIKE A WOMAN...
THAT'S IT, LADY! NO MORE INSULTS!!
I DON'T CARE IF YOU'RE BRANDY'S MOM OR NOT!!
KRAK
YOU'RE GOING DOWN, B@*$*!!
NO WINE FOR ME. THANK YOU. TAKE THE BOTTLE AWAY... PLEASE.
WHAT'S WRONG, DEAR? CAN'T HANDLE REAL LIQUOR?
LE RIPPLE
CHO
SO, FRANK. WHAT KIND OF DOCTOR ARE YOU?
I'M A VETERINARIAN.
YOU DON'T TREAT PEOPLE?
JUST ANIMALS, MA'AM.
CHO
SO YOU'RE NOT A REAL DOCTOR.
LEAVE THE BOTTLE PLEASE.
MOM. I WANT YOU TO EASE UP ON FRANK. HE'S A GOOD DECENT...
HONEY. YOU REALLY SHOULD BLEACH YOUR UPPER LIP THOSE DARK ROOTS...
CHO
MOTHER! DON'T CHANGE THE SUBJECT. YOU ALWAYS CHANGE THE SUBJECT EVERY TIME WE HAVE A SERIOUS DISCUSSION. NOW ACT CIVIL AROUND FRANK, PLEASE! PROMISE ME.
WELL?
BRANDY, YOU REALLY SHOULD PLUCK YOUR EYEBROWS. YOU LOOK LIKE "BERT."

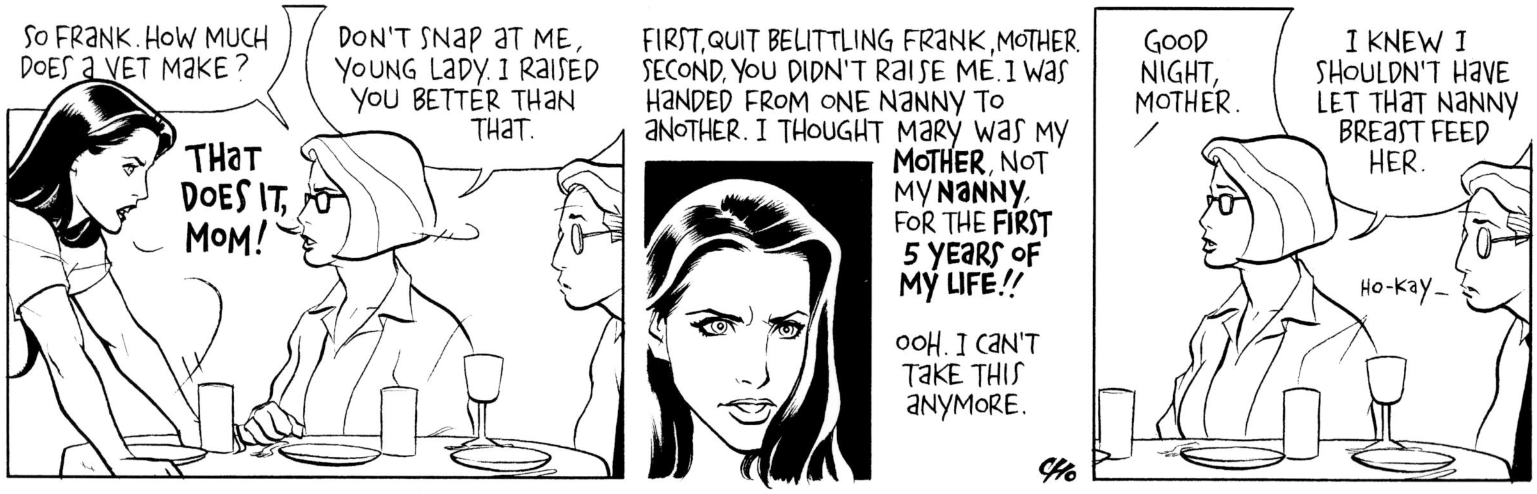
SO FRANK. HOW MUCH DOES A VET MAKE?
THAT DOES IT, MOM!
DON'T SNAP AT ME, YOUNG LADY. I RAISED YOU BETTER THAN THAT.
FIRST, QUIT BELITTLING FRANK, MOTHER. SECOND, YOU DIDN'T RAISE ME. I WAS HANDED FROM ONE NANNY TO ANOTHER. I THOUGHT MARY WAS MY **MOTHER**, NOT MY **NANNY**, FOR THE **FIRST 5 YEARS OF MY LIFE!!**
OOH. I CAN'T TAKE THIS ANYMORE.
GOOD NIGHT, MOTHER.
I KNEW I SHOULDN'T HAVE LET THAT NANNY BREAST FEED HER.
HO-KAY_

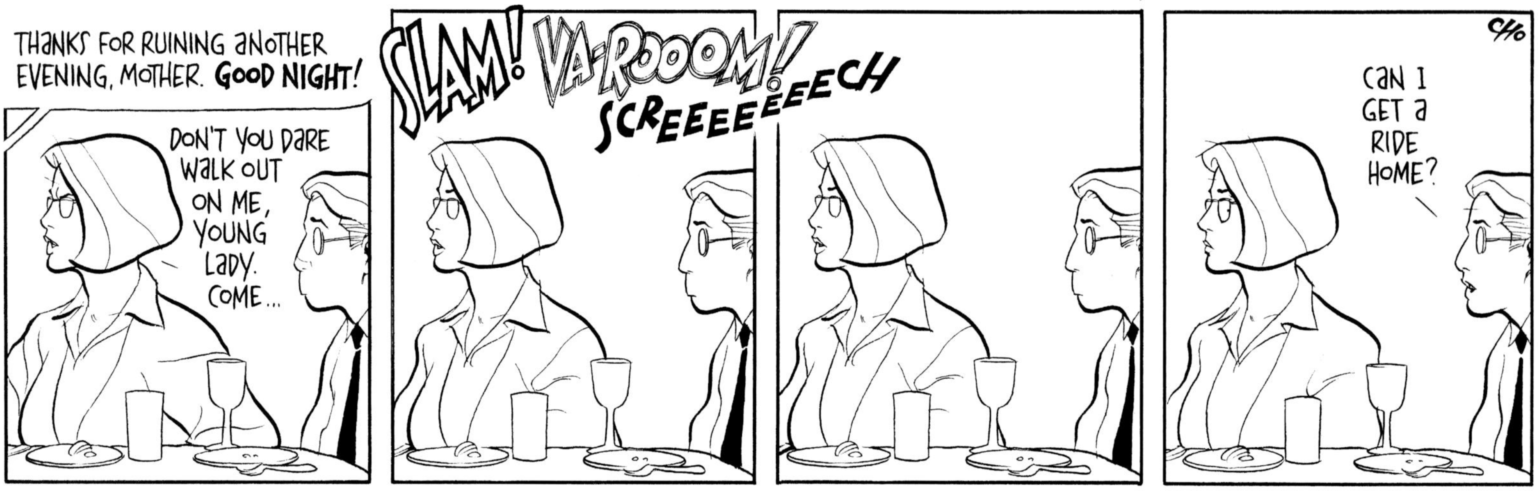
THANKS FOR RUINING ANOTHER EVENING, MOTHER. **GOOD NIGHT!**
DON'T YOU DARE WALK OUT ON ME, YOUNG LADY. COME...
SLAM!
VA-ROOOM!
SCREEEEEEECH
CAN I GET A RIDE HOME?

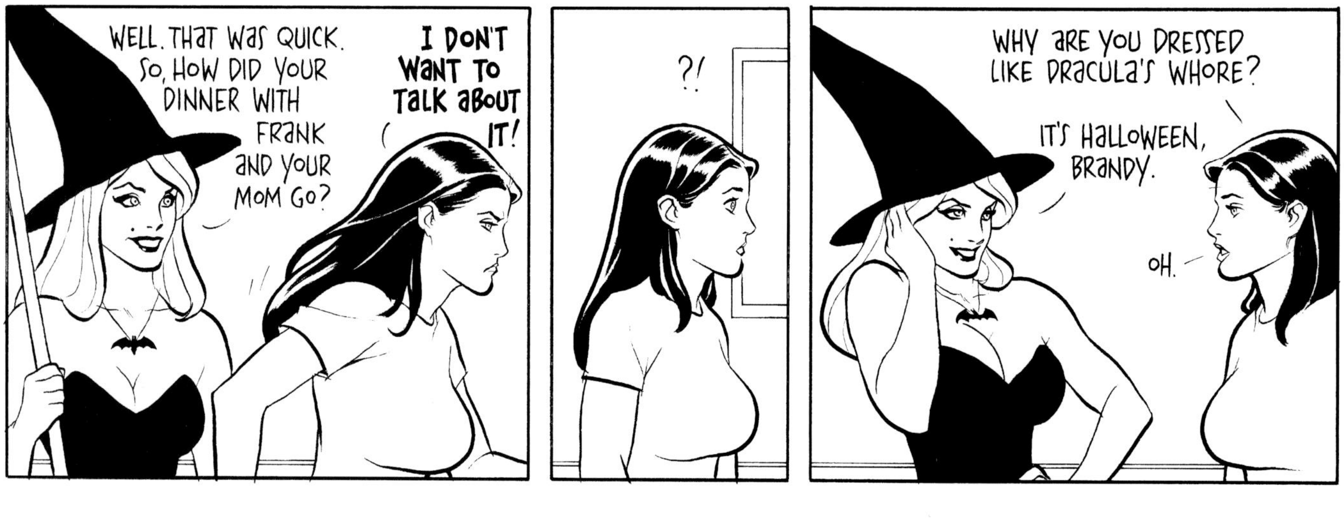
WELL. THAT WAS QUICK. SO, HOW DID YOUR DINNER WITH FRANK AND YOUR MOM GO?
I DON'T WANT TO TALK ABOUT IT!
?!
WHY ARE YOU DRESSED LIKE DRACULA'S WHORE?
IT'S HALLOWEEN, BRANDY.
OH.

THIS HAS BEEN FRANK CHO'S ***GRATUITOUS*** SHOT OF THE WEEK.

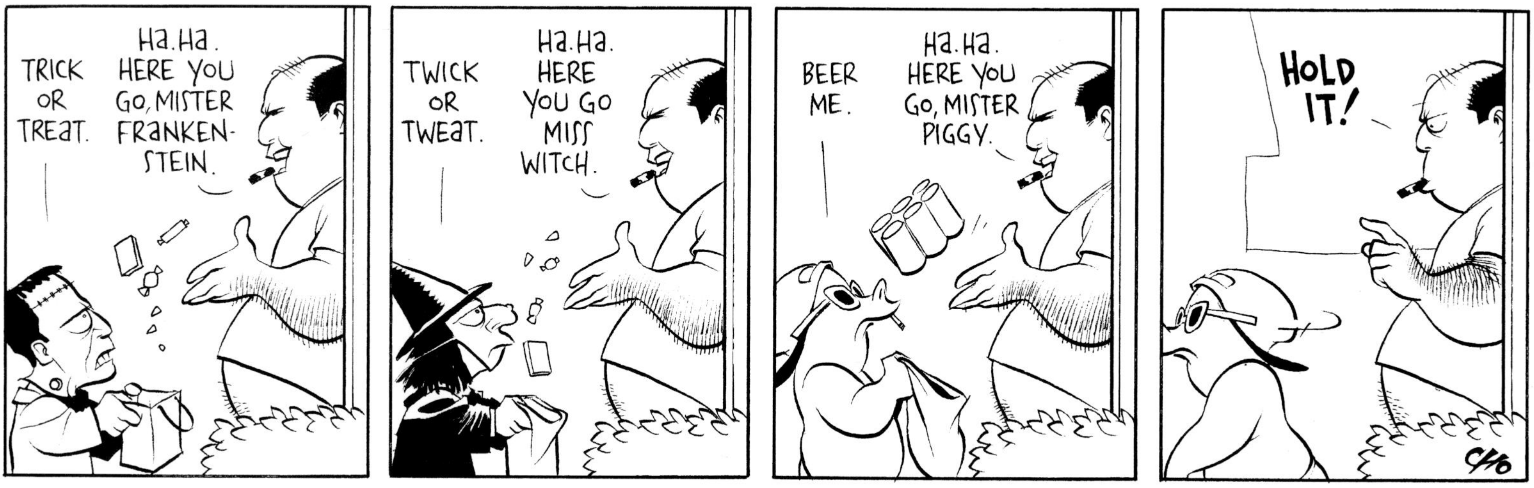
TRICK OR TREAT.
HA.HA. HERE YOU GO, MISTER FRANKENSTEIN.
TWICK OR TWEAT.
HA.HA. HERE YOU GO MISS WITCH.
BEER ME.
HA.HA. HERE YOU GO, MISTER PIGGY.
HOLD IT!

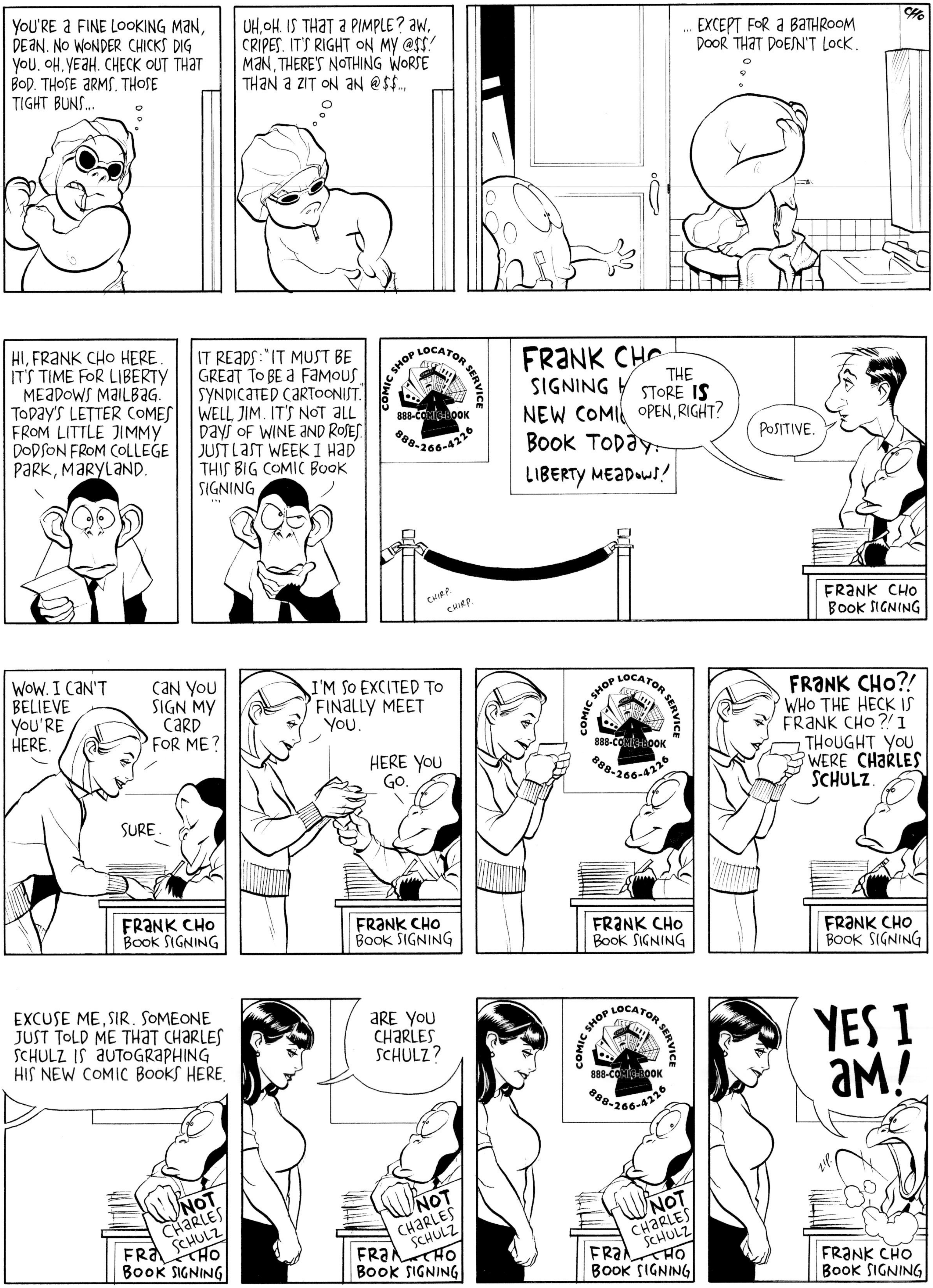
YOU'RE A FINE LOOKING MAN, DEAN. NO WONDER CHICKS DIG YOU. OH, YEAH. CHECK OUT THAT BOD. THOSE ARMS. THOSE TIGHT BUNS...
UH, OH. IS THAT A PIMPLE? AW, CRIPES. IT'S RIGHT ON MY @$$! MAN, THERE'S NOTHING WORSE THAN A ZIT ON AN @$$...
CHO
... EXCEPT FOR A BATHROOM DOOR THAT DOESN'T LOCK.
HI, FRANK CHO HERE. IT'S TIME FOR LIBERTY MEADOWS MAILBAG. TODAY'S LETTER COMES FROM LITTLE JIMMY DODSON FROM COLLEGE PARK, MARYLAND.
IT READS: "IT MUST BE GREAT TO BE A FAMOUS SYNDICATED CARTOONIST." WELL, JIM. IT'S NOT ALL DAYS OF WINE AND ROSES. JUST LAST WEEK I HAD THIS BIG COMIC BOOK SIGNING ...
COMIC SHOP LOCATOR SERVICE
888-COMIC-BOOK
888-266-4226
LIBERTY MEADOWS!
THE STORE IS OPEN, RIGHT?
POSITIVE.
CHIRP. CHIRP.
FRANK CHO BOOK SIGNING
WOW. I CAN'T BELIEVE YOU'RE HERE.
CAN YOU SIGN MY CARD FOR ME?
SURE.
FRANK CHO BOOK SIGNING
I'M SO EXCITED TO FINALLY MEET YOU.
HERE YOU GO.
FRANK CHO BOOK SIGNING
COMIC SHOP LOCATOR SERVICE
888-COMIC-BOOK
888-266-4226
FRANK CHO BOOK SIGNING
FRANK CHO?! WHO THE HECK IS FRANK CHO?! I THOUGHT YOU WERE CHARLES SCHULZ.
FRANK CHO BOOK SIGNING
EXCUSE ME, SIR. SOMEONE JUST TOLD ME THAT CHARLES SCHULZ IS AUTOGRAPHING HIS NEW COMIC BOOKS HERE.
NOT CHARLES SCHULZ
BOOK SIGNING
ARE YOU CHARLES SCHULZ?
NOT CHARLES SCHULZ
BOOK SIGNING
COMIC SHOP LOCATOR SERVICE
888-COMIC-BOOK
888-266-4226
NOT CHARLES SCHULZ
BOOK SIGNING
YES I AM!
ZIP.
FRANK CHO BOOK SIGNING

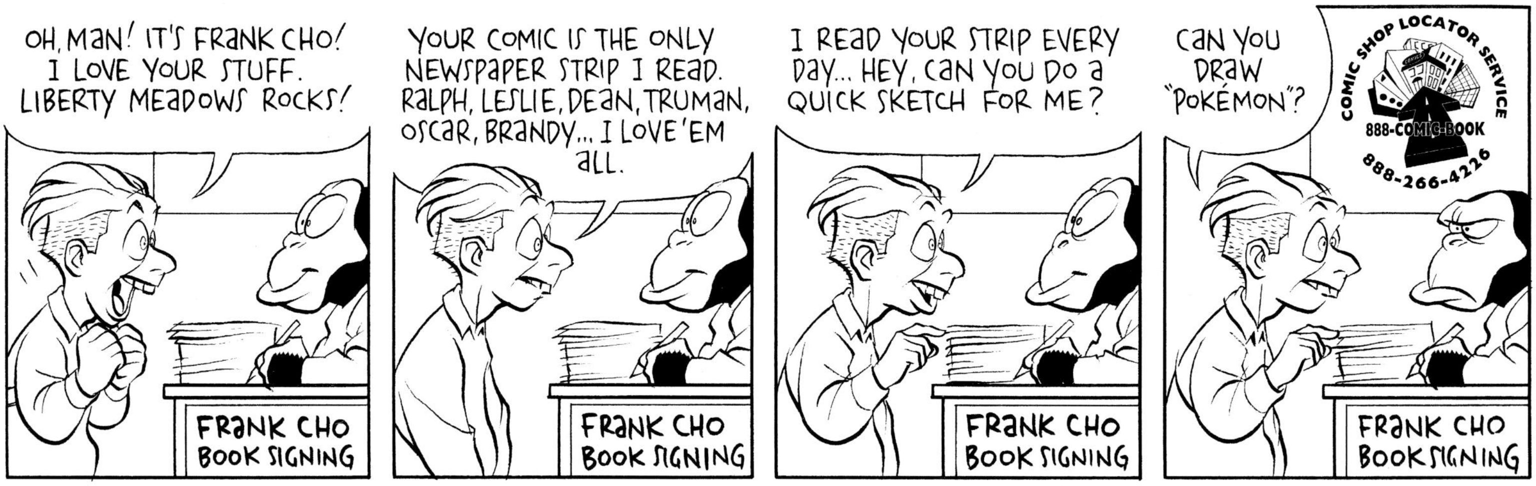
OH, MAN! IT'S FRANK CHO! I LOVE YOUR STUFF. LIBERTY MEADOWS ROCKS!
FRANK CHO BOOK SIGNING
YOUR COMIC IS THE ONLY NEWSPAPER STRIP I READ. RALPH, LESLIE, DEAN, TRUMAN, OSCAR, BRANDY... I LOVE 'EM ALL.
FRANK CHO BOOK SIGNING
I READ YOUR STRIP EVERY DAY... HEY, CAN YOU DO A QUICK SKETCH FOR ME?
FRANK CHO BOOK SIGNING
CAN YOU DRAW "POKÉMON"?
COMIC SHOP LOCATOR SERVICE
888-COMIC-BOOK
888-266-4226
FRANK CHO BOOK SIGNING
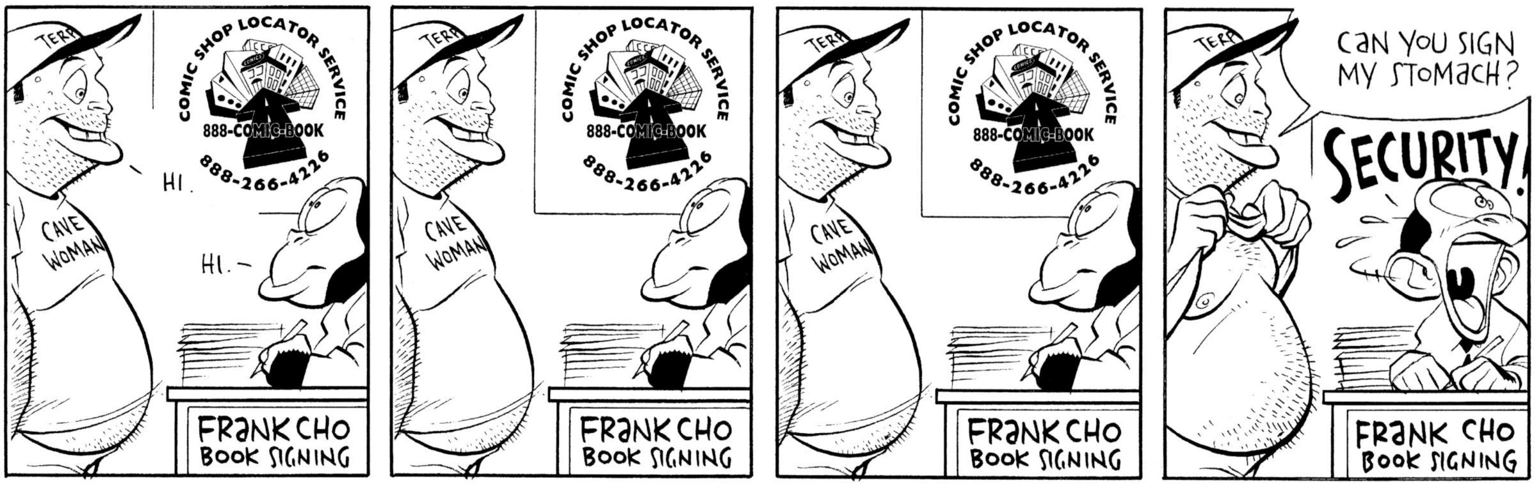
COMIC SHOP LOCATOR SERVICE
888-COMIC-BOOK
888-266-4226
CAVE WOMAN
HI.
HI.
FRANK CHO BOOK SIGNING
COMIC SHOP LOCATOR SERVICE
888-COMIC-BOOK
888-266-4226
CAVE WOMAN
FRANK CHO BOOK SIGNING
COMIC SHOP LOCATOR SERVICE
888-COMIC-BOOK
888-266-4226
CAVE WOMAN
FRANK CHO BOOK SIGNING
CAN YOU SIGN MY STOMACH?
SECURITY!
FRANK CHO BOOK SIGNING
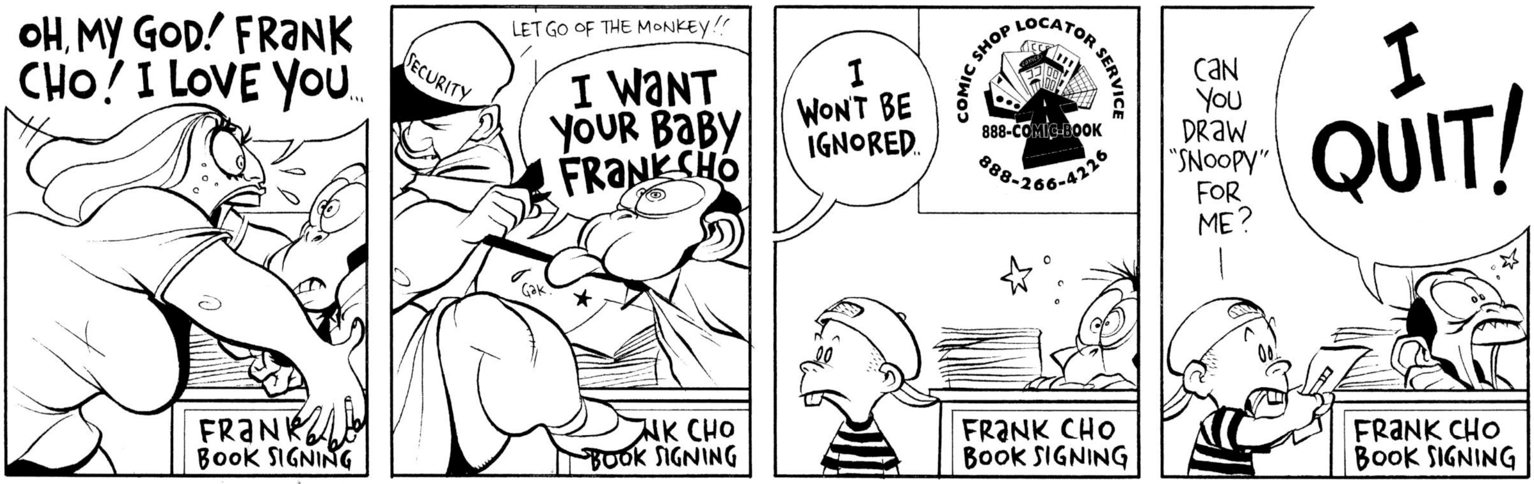
OH, MY GOD! FRANK CHO! I LOVE YOU...
BOOK SIGNING
LET GO OF THE MONKEY!!
SECURITY
I WANT YOUR BABY FRANK CHO
GAK
BOOK SIGNING
I WON'T BE IGNORED.
COMIC SHOP LOCATOR SERVICE
888-COMIC-BOOK
888-266-4226
FRANK CHO BOOK SIGNING
CAN YOU DRAW "SNOOPY" FOR ME?
I QUIT!
FRANK CHO BOOK SIGNING
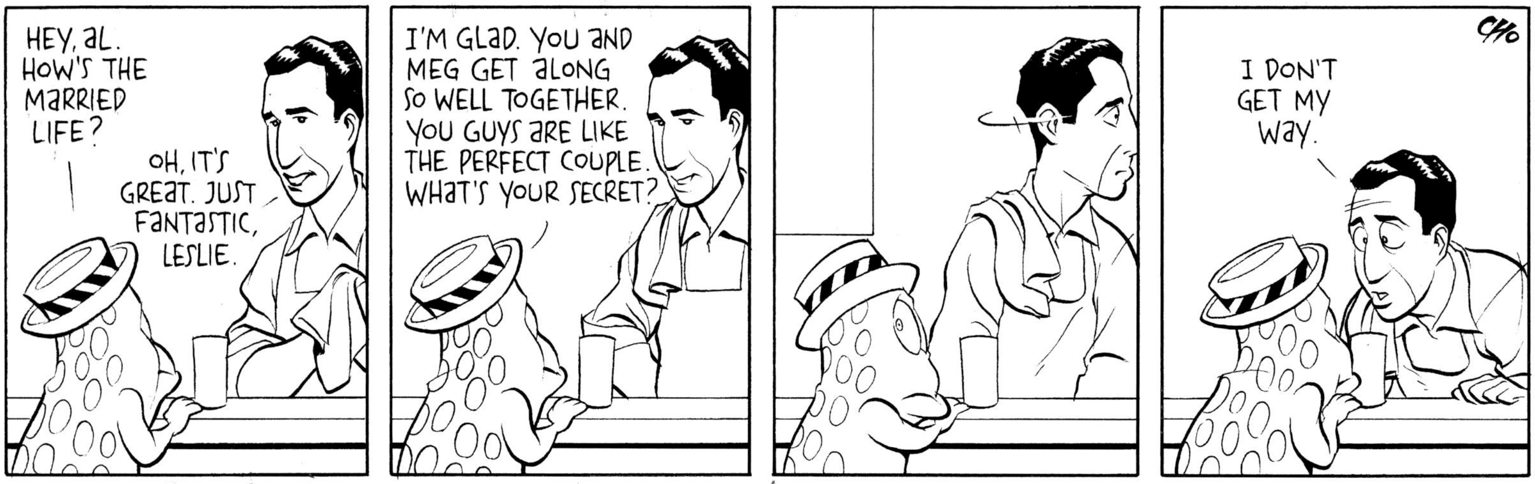
HEY, AL. HOW'S THE MARRIED LIFE?
OH, IT'S GREAT. JUST FANTASTIC, LESLIE.
I'M GLAD. YOU AND MEG GET ALONG SO WELL TOGETHER. YOU GUYS ARE LIKE THE PERFECT COUPLE. WHAT'S YOUR SECRET?
CHO
I DON'T GET MY WAY.

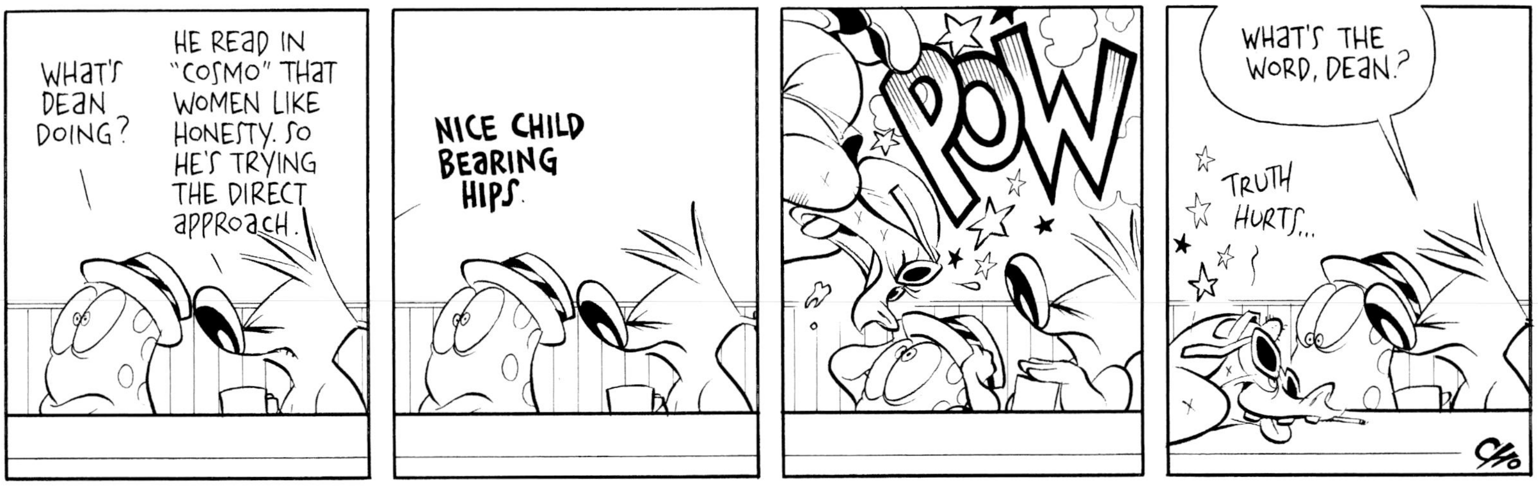
WHAT'S DEAN DOING?
HE READ IN "COSMO" THAT WOMEN LIKE HONESTY. SO HE'S TRYING THE DIRECT APPROACH.
NICE CHILD BEARING HIPS.
POW
WHAT'S THE WORD, DEAN?
TRUTH HURTS...
CHO

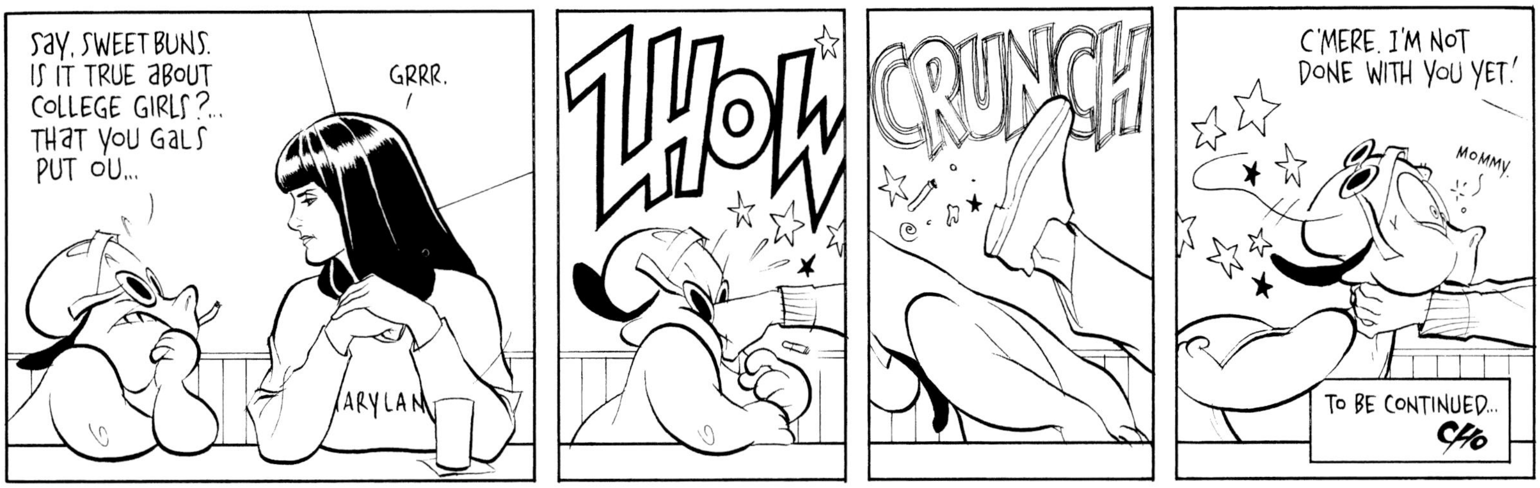
SAY, SWEET BUNS. IS IT TRUE ABOUT COLLEGE GIRLS?... THAT YOU GALS PUT OU...
GRRR.
MARYLAN
ZHOW
CRUNCH
C'MERE. I'M NOT DONE WITH YOU YET!
MOMMY.
TO BE CONTINUED...
CHO

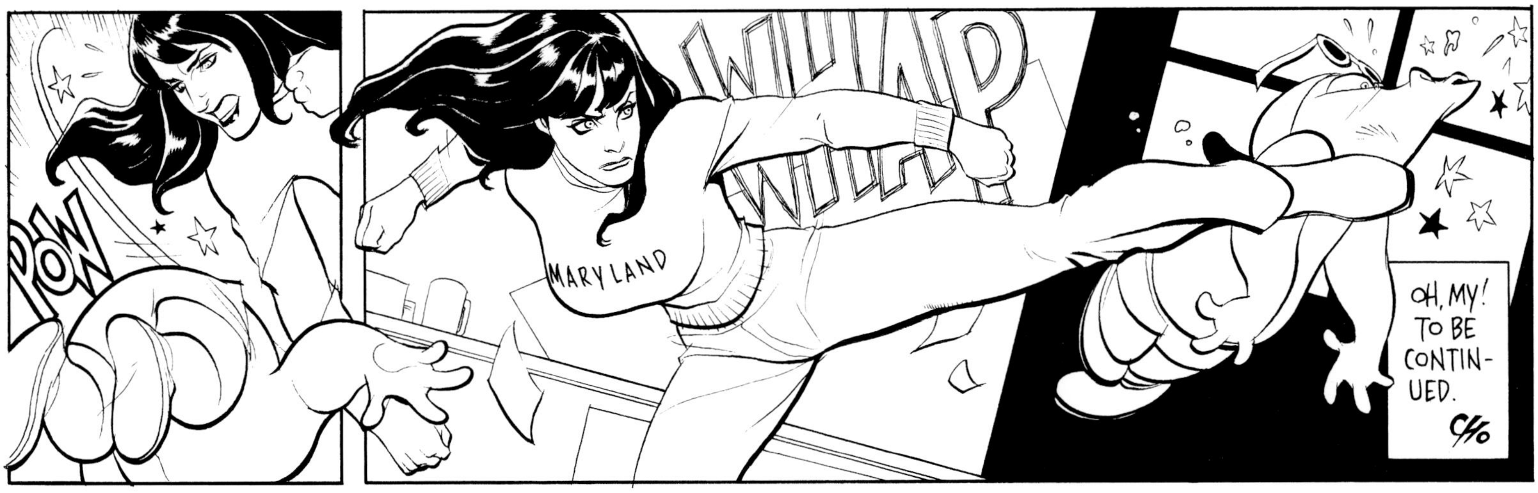
POW
WHAP
WHAP
MARYLAND
OH, MY! TO BE CONTIN-UED.
CHO

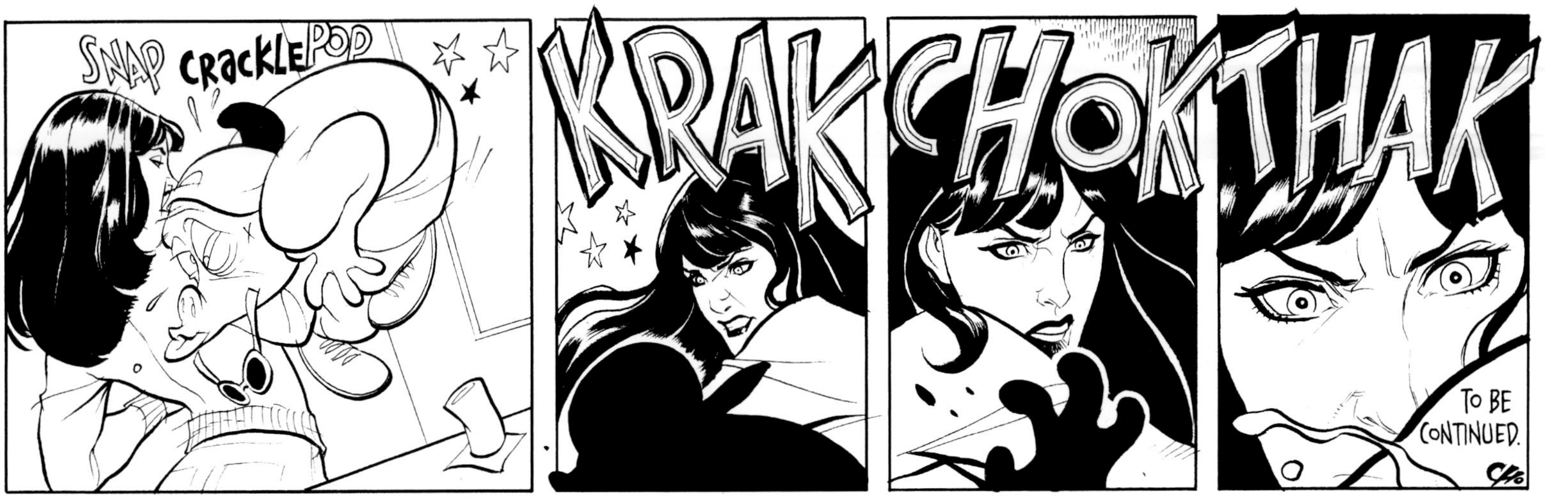
SNAP CRACKLE POP
KRAK
CHOK
THAK
TO BE CONTINUED.
CHO

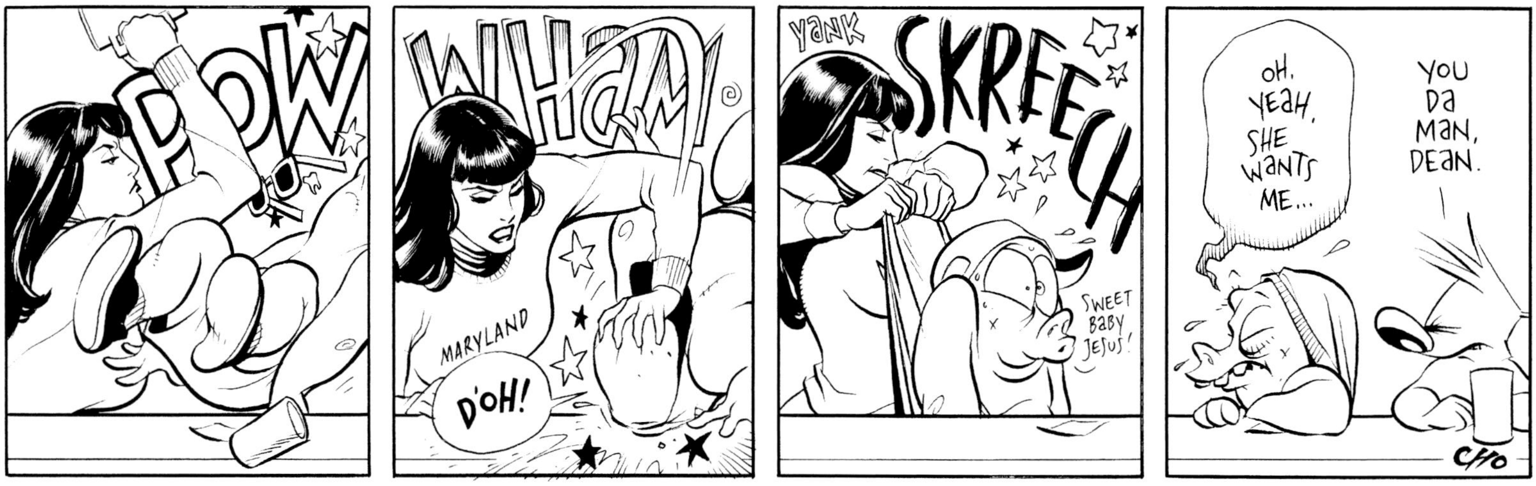
POW
WHAM
MARYLAND
D'OH!
YANK
SKREECH
SWEET BABY JESUS!
OH, YEAH, SHE WANTS ME...
YOU DA MAN, DEAN.
CHO

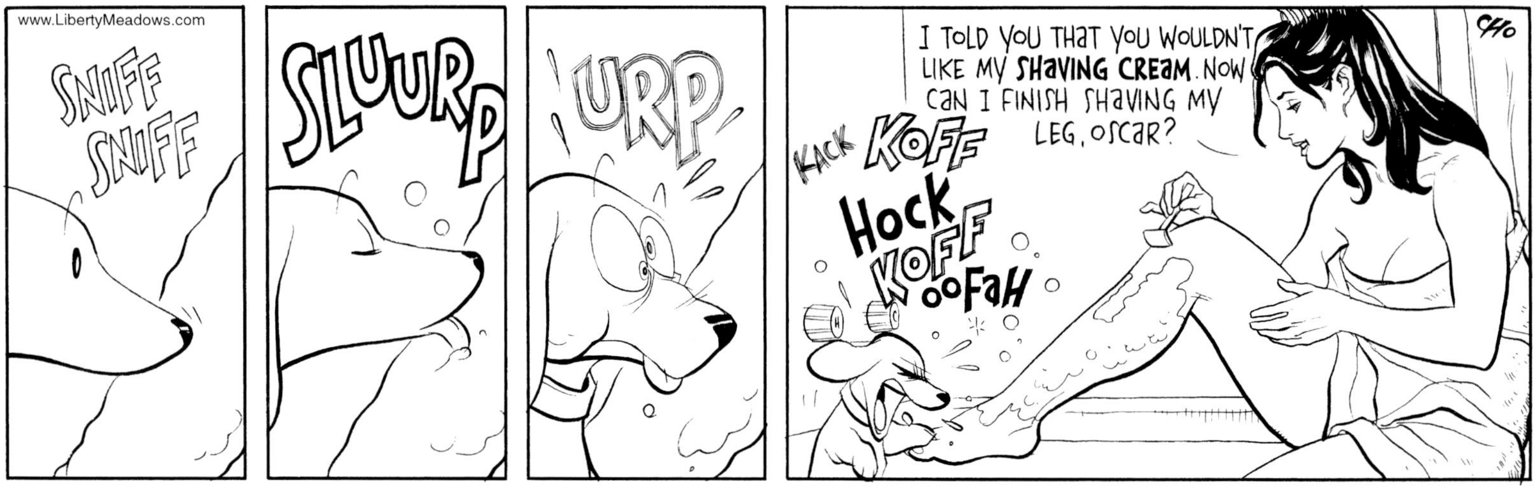
www.LibertyMeadows.com
SNIFF SNIFF
SLUURP
URP
CHO
I TOLD YOU THAT YOU WOULDN'T LIKE MY SHAVING CREAM. NOW CAN I FINISH SHAVING MY LEG, OSCAR?
KACK KOFF
HOCK
KOFF
OOFAH

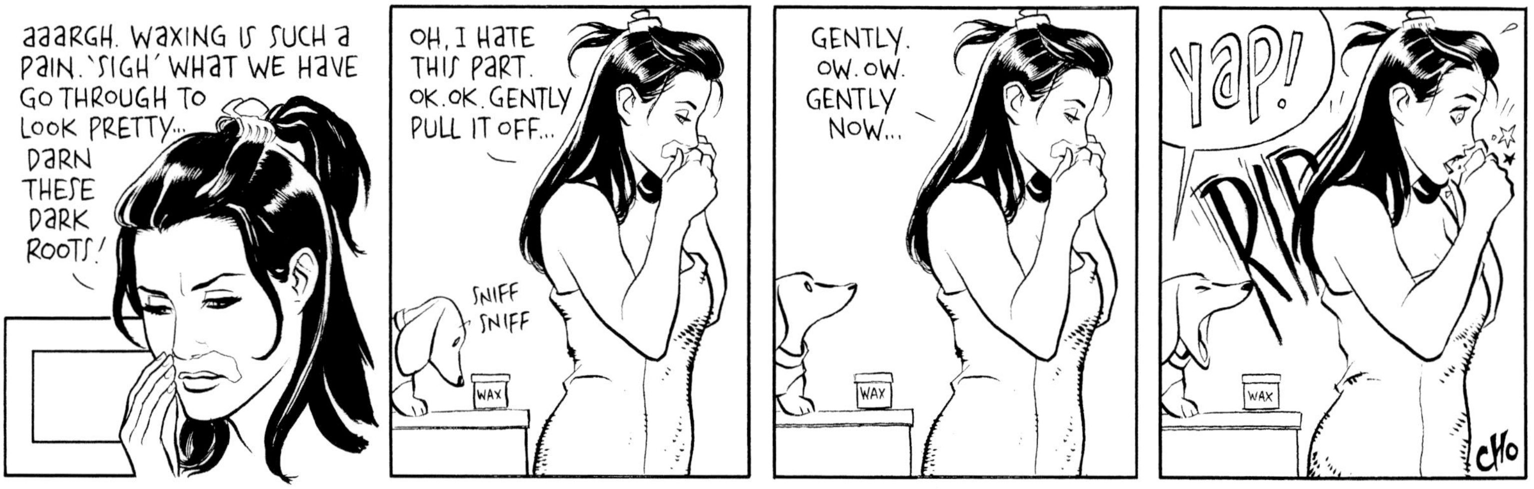
AAARGH. WAXING IS SUCH A PAIN. `SIGH´ WHAT WE HAVE GO THROUGH TO LOOK PRETTY... DARN THESE DARK ROOTS!
OH, I HATE THIS PART. OK. OK. GENTLY PULL IT OFF...
SNIFF SNIFF
WAX
GENTLY. OW. OW. GENTLY NOW...
WAX
YAP!
RIP
WAX
CHO

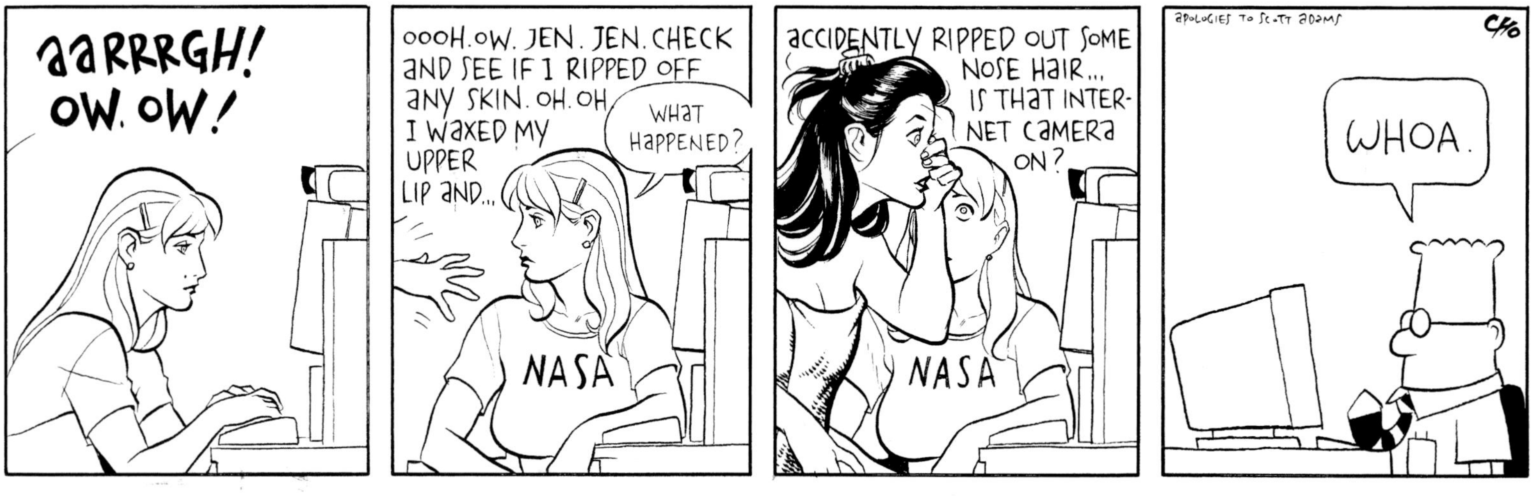
AARRRGH! OW. OW!
OOOH. OW. JEN. JEN. CHECK AND SEE IF I RIPPED OFF ANY SKIN. OH. OH. I WAXED MY UPPER LIP AND...
WHAT HAPPENED?
NASA
ACCIDENTLY RIPPED OUT SOME NOSE HAIR... IS THAT INTERNET CAMERA ON?
NASA
APOLOGIES TO SCOTT ADAMS
CHO
WHOA.

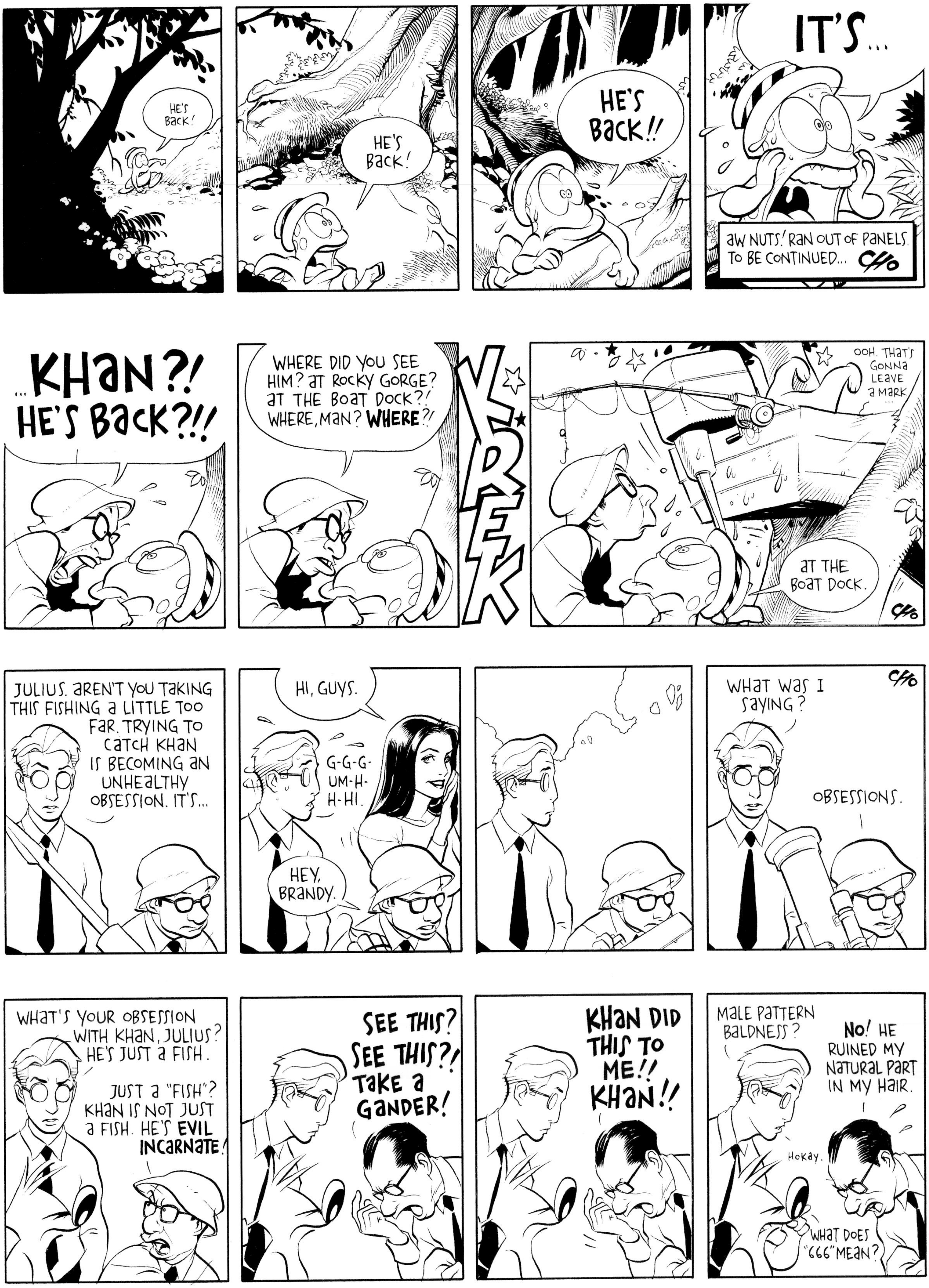
HE'S BACK!
HE'S BACK!
HE'S BACK!!
IT'S...
AW NUTS! RAN OUT OF PANELS. TO BE CONTINUED... CHO
...KHAN?! HE'S BACK?!!
WHERE DID YOU SEE HIM? AT ROCKY GORGE? AT THE BOAT DOCK?! WHERE, MAN? WHERE?!
KREK
OOH. THAT'S GONNA LEAVE A MARK...
AT THE BOAT DOCK.
CHO
JULIUS. AREN'T YOU TAKING THIS FISHING A LITTLE TOO FAR. TRYING TO CATCH KHAN IS BECOMING AN UNHEALTHY OBSESSION. IT'S...
HI, GUYS.
G-G-G-UM-H-H-HI.
HEY, BRANDY.
CHO
WHAT WAS I SAYING?
OBSESSIONS.
WHAT'S YOUR OBSESSION WITH KHAN, JULIUS? HE'S JUST A FISH.
JUST A "FISH"? KHAN IS NOT JUST A FISH. HE'S EVIL INCARNATE!
SEE THIS? SEE THIS?! TAKE A GANDER!
KHAN DID THIS TO ME!! KHAN!!
MALE PATTERN BALDNESS?
NO! HE RUINED MY NATURAL PART IN MY HAIR.
HOKAY.
WHAT DOES "666" MEAN?

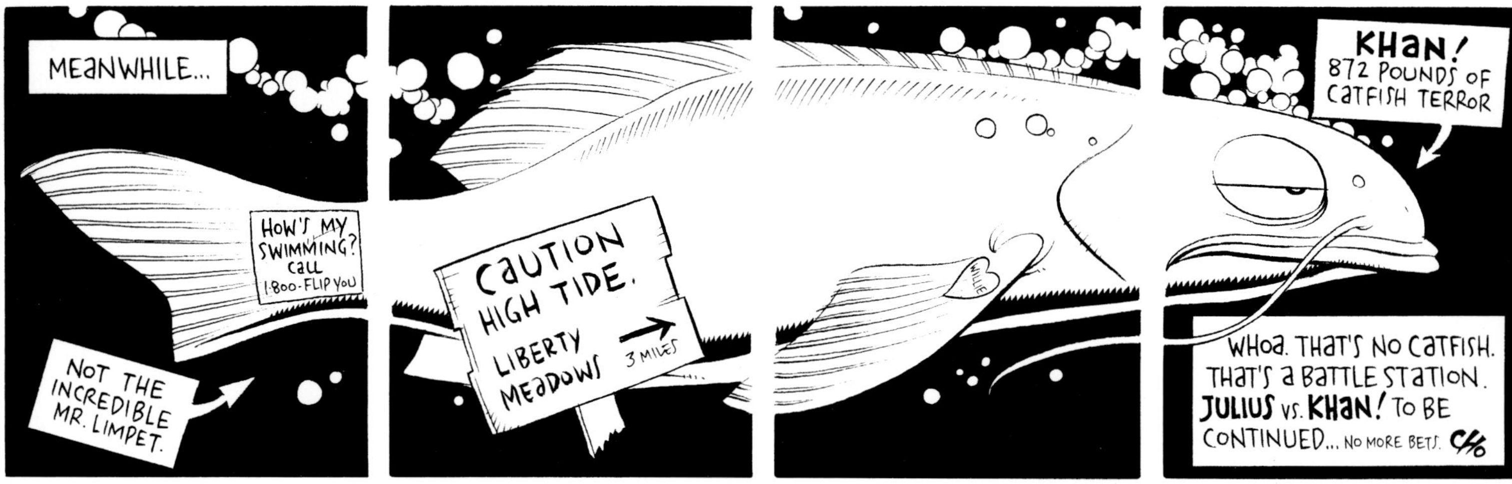
MEANWHILE...
HOW'S MY SWIMMING? CALL 1-800-FLIP YOU
NOT THE INCREDIBLE MR. LIMPET.
CAUTION HIGH TIDE.
LIBERTY MEADOWS 3 MILES
WILLIE
KHAN! 872 POUNDS OF CATFISH TERROR
WHOA. THAT'S NO CATFISH. THAT'S A BATTLE STATION. JULIUS VS. KHAN! TO BE CONTINUED... NO MORE BETS.
CHO

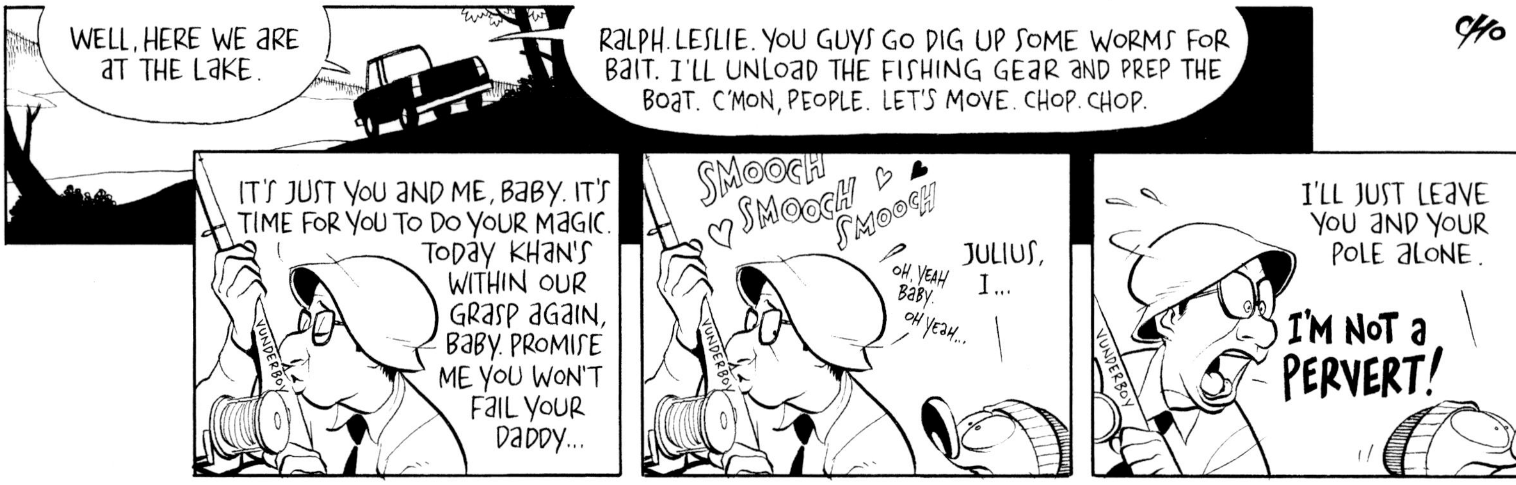
WELL, HERE WE ARE AT THE LAKE.
RALPH. LESLIE. YOU GUYS GO DIG UP SOME WORMS FOR BAIT. I'LL UNLOAD THE FISHING GEAR AND PREP THE BOAT. C'MON, PEOPLE. LET'S MOVE. CHOP. CHOP.
CHO
IT'S JUST YOU AND ME, BABY. IT'S TIME FOR YOU TO DO YOUR MAGIC. TODAY KHAN'S WITHIN OUR GRASP AGAIN, BABY. PROMISE ME YOU WON'T FAIL YOUR DADDY...
VUNDERBOY
SMOOCH SMOOCH SMOOCH
OH, YEAH BABY. OH YEAH...
JULIUS, I...
I'LL JUST LEAVE YOU AND YOUR POLE ALONE.
I'M NOT A PERVERT!

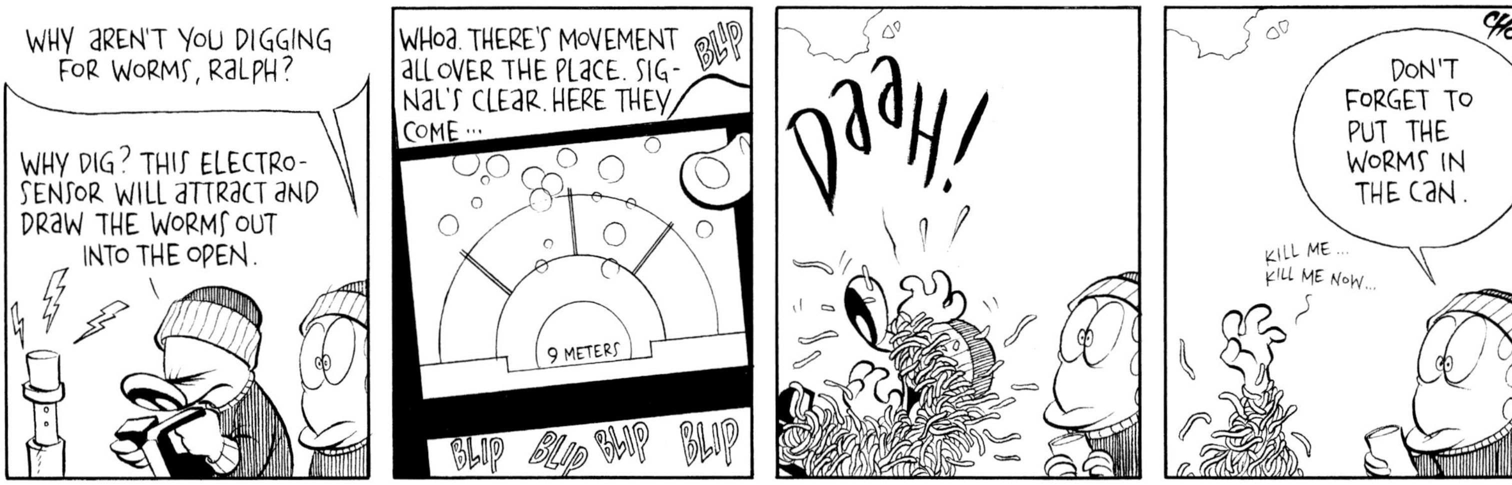
WHY AREN'T YOU DIGGING FOR WORMS, RALPH?
WHY DIG? THIS ELECTRO-SENSOR WILL ATTRACT AND DRAW THE WORMS OUT INTO THE OPEN.
WHOA. THERE'S MOVEMENT ALL OVER THE PLACE. SIG-NAL'S CLEAR. HERE THEY COME...
BLIP
9 METERS
BLIP BLIP BLIP BLIP
DAAH!
CHO
DON'T FORGET TO PUT THE WORMS IN THE CAN.
KILL ME... KILL ME NOW...

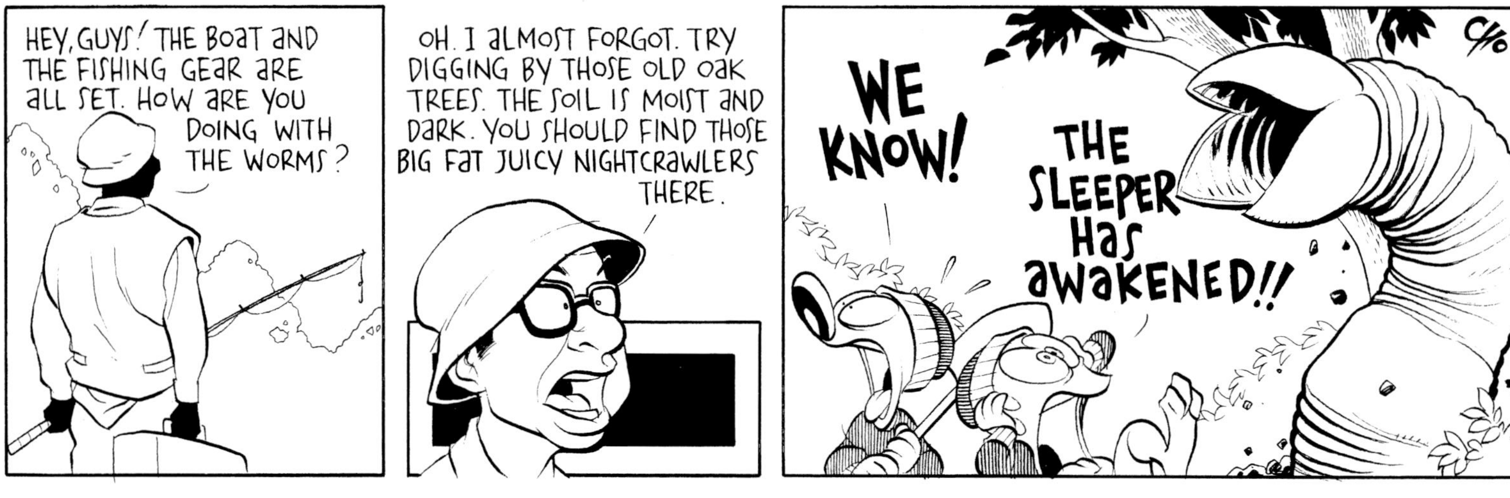
HEY, GUYS! THE BOAT AND THE FISHING GEAR ARE ALL SET. HOW ARE YOU DOING WITH THE WORMS?
OH. I ALMOST FORGOT. TRY DIGGING BY THOSE OLD OAK TREES. THE SOIL IS MOIST AND DARK. YOU SHOULD FIND THOSE BIG FAT JUICY NIGHTCRAWLERS THERE.
CHO
WE KNOW!
THE SLEEPER HAS AWAKENED!!

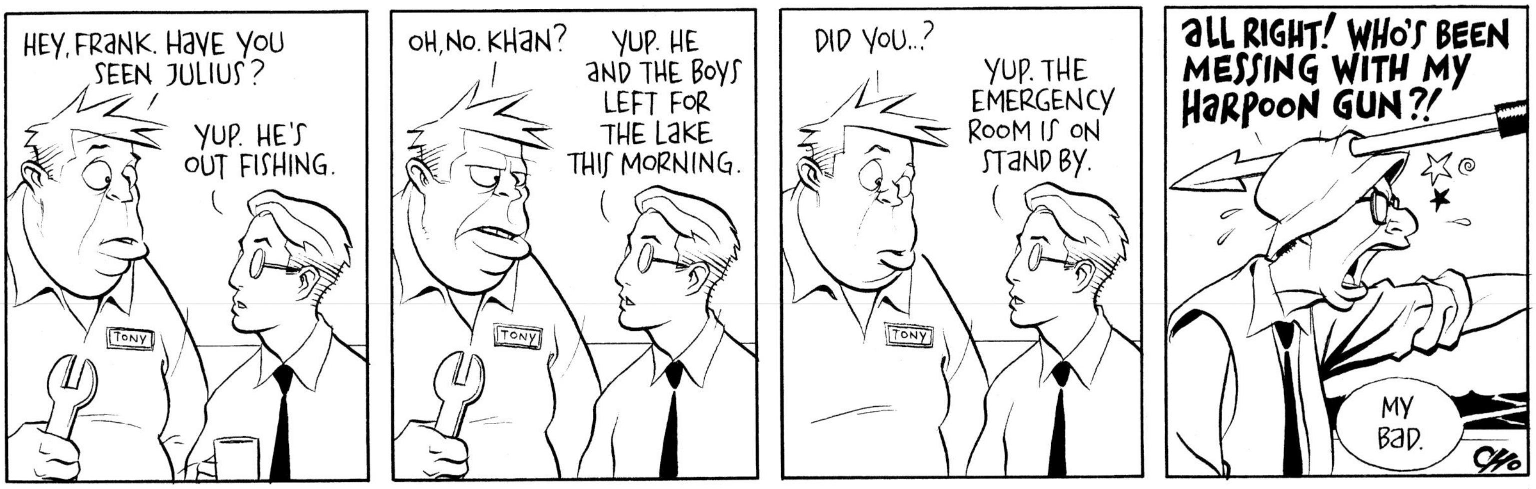
HEY, FRANK. HAVE YOU SEEN JULIUS?
YUP. HE'S OUT FISHING.
TONY
OH, NO. KHAN?
YUP. HE AND THE BOYS LEFT FOR THE LAKE THIS MORNING.
TONY
DID YOU..?
YUP. THE EMERGENCY ROOM IS ON STAND BY.
TONY
ALL RIGHT! WHO'S BEEN MESSING WITH MY HARPOON GUN?!
MY BAD.
CHO

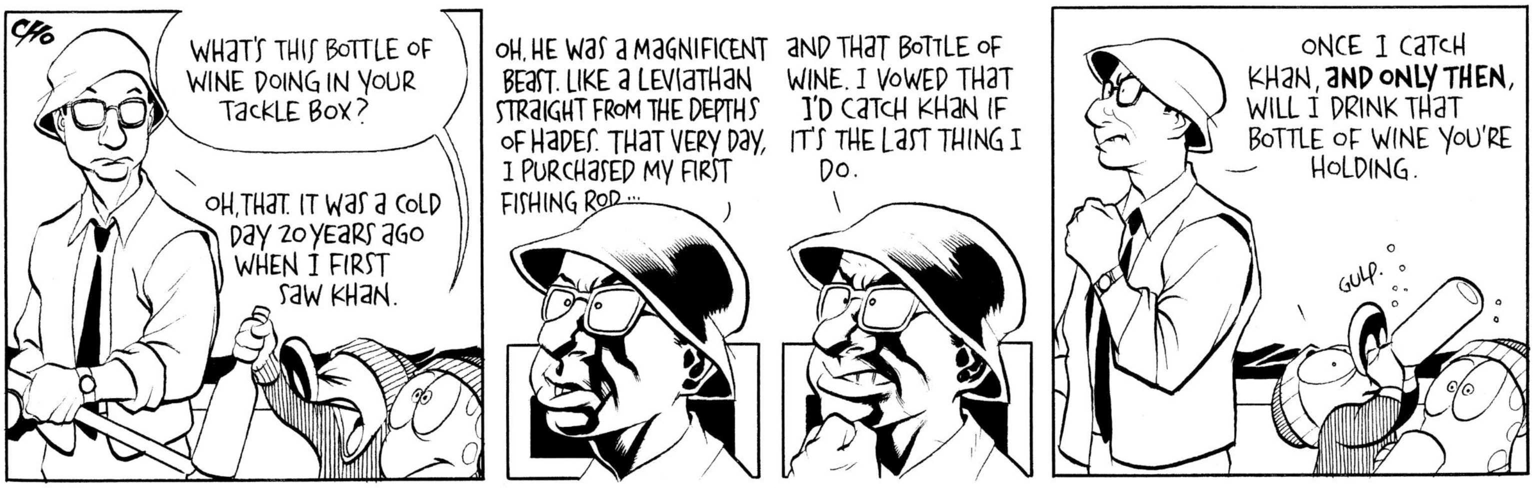
CHO
WHAT'S THIS BOTTLE OF WINE DOING IN YOUR TACKLE BOX?
OH, THAT. IT WAS A COLD DAY 20 YEARS AGO WHEN I FIRST SAW KHAN.
OH, HE WAS A MAGNIFICENT BEAST. LIKE A LEVIATHAN STRAIGHT FROM THE DEPTHS OF HADES. THAT VERY DAY, I PURCHASED MY FIRST FISHING ROD...
AND THAT BOTTLE OF WINE. I VOWED THAT I'D CATCH KHAN IF IT'S THE LAST THING I DO.
ONCE I CATCH KHAN, **AND ONLY THEN**, WILL I DRINK THAT BOTTLE OF WINE YOU'RE HOLDING.
GULP.

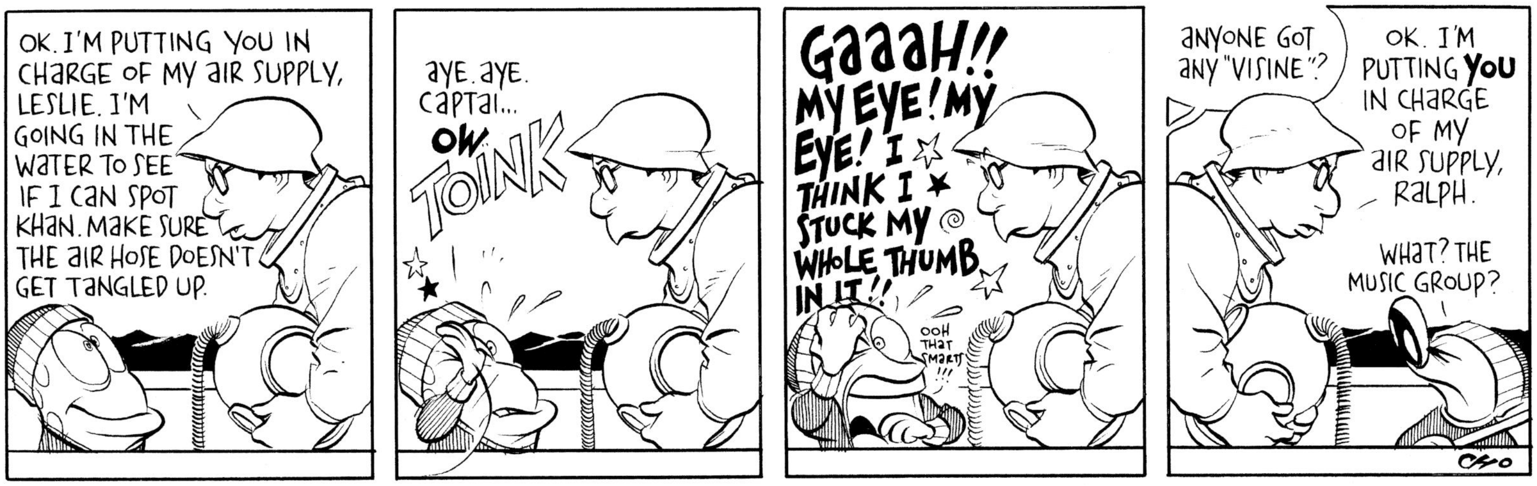
OK. I'M PUTTING YOU IN CHARGE OF MY AIR SUPPLY, LESLIE. I'M GOING IN THE WATER TO SEE IF I CAN SPOT KHAN. MAKE SURE THE AIR HOSE DOESN'T GET TANGLED UP.
AYE. AYE. CAPTAI...
OW
TOINK
GAAAH!! MY EYE! MY EYE! I THINK I STUCK MY WHOLE THUMB IN IT!!
OOH THAT SMARTS!!!
ANYONE GOT ANY "VISINE"?
OK. I'M PUTTING **YOU** IN CHARGE OF MY AIR SUPPLY, RALPH.
WHAT? THE MUSIC GROUP?
CHO

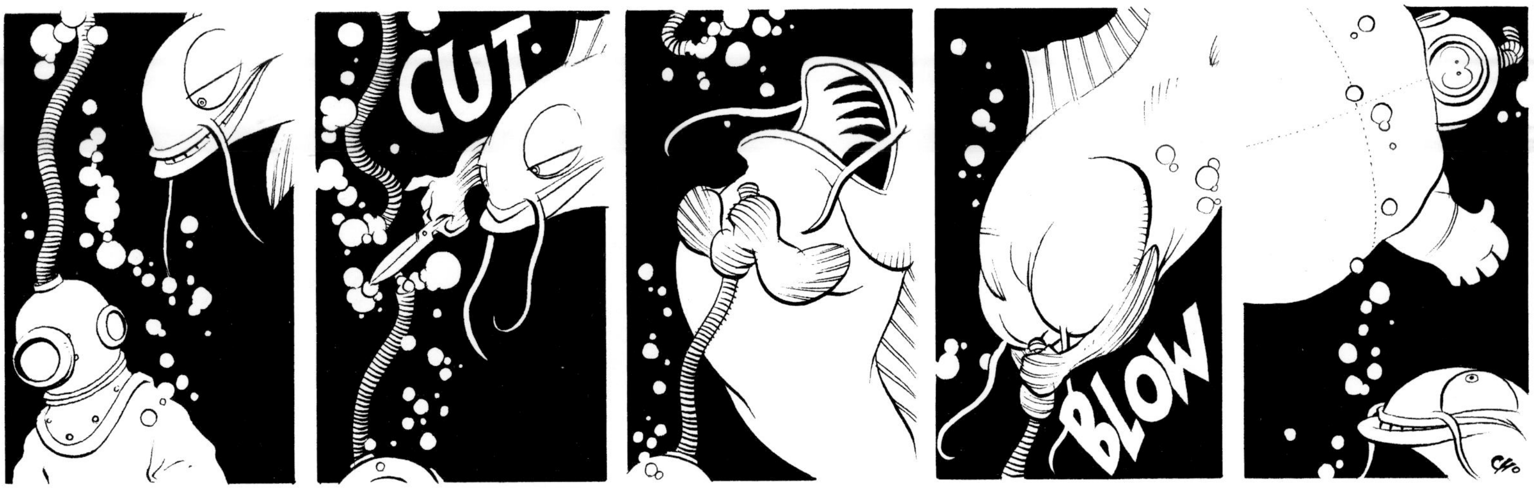
CUT
BLOW
CHO

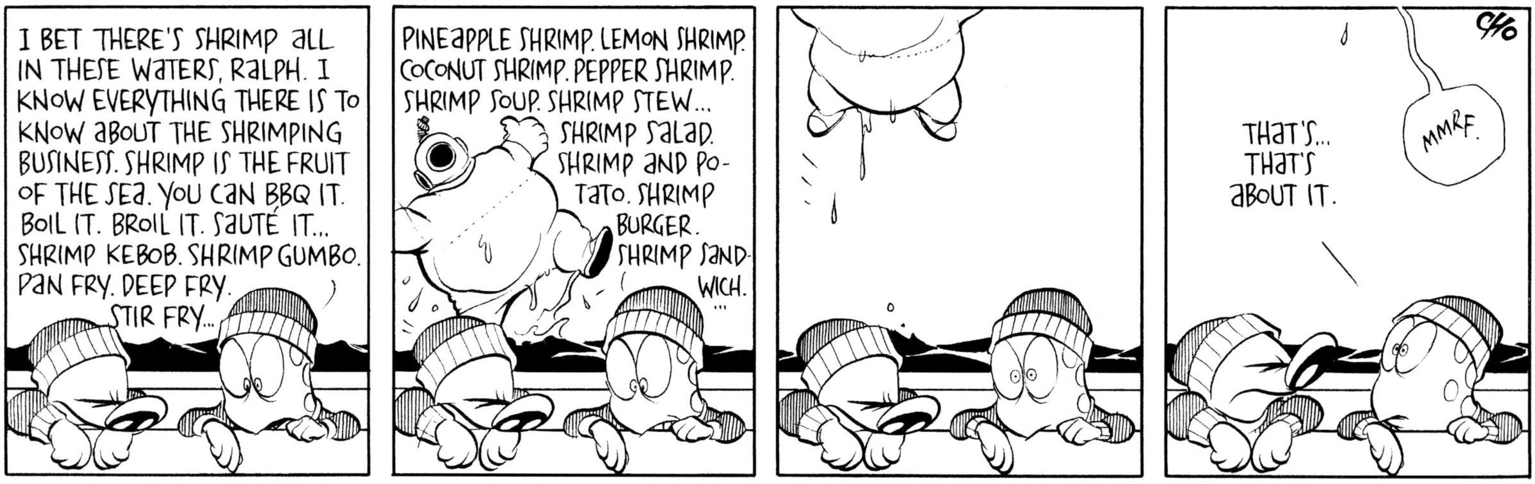
I BET THERE'S SHRIMP ALL IN THESE WATERS, RALPH. I KNOW EVERYTHING THERE IS TO KNOW ABOUT THE SHRIMPING BUSINESS. SHRIMP IS THE FRUIT OF THE SEA. YOU CAN BBQ IT. BOIL IT. BROIL IT. SAUTÉ IT... SHRIMP KEBOB. SHRIMP GUMBO. PAN FRY. DEEP FRY. STIR FRY...
PINEAPPLE SHRIMP. LEMON SHRIMP. COCONUT SHRIMP. PEPPER SHRIMP. SHRIMP SOUP. SHRIMP STEW... SHRIMP SALAD. SHRIMP AND PO-TATO. SHRIMP BURGER. SHRIMP SAND-WICH. ...
THAT'S... THAT'S ABOUT IT.
MMRF.
C/10

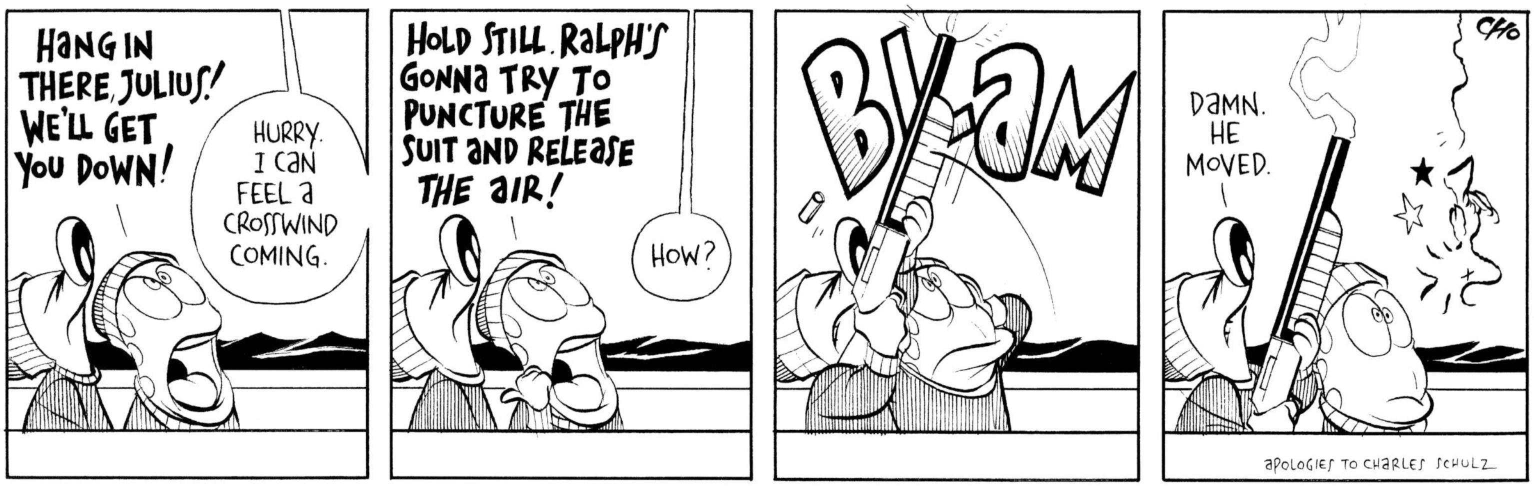
HANG IN THERE, JULIUS! WE'LL GET YOU DOWN!
HURRY. I CAN FEEL A CROSSWIND COMING.
HOLD STILL. RALPH'S GONNA TRY TO PUNCTURE THE SUIT AND RELEASE THE AIR!
HOW?
BLAM
DAMN. HE MOVED.
C/10
APOLOGIES TO CHARLES SCHULZ

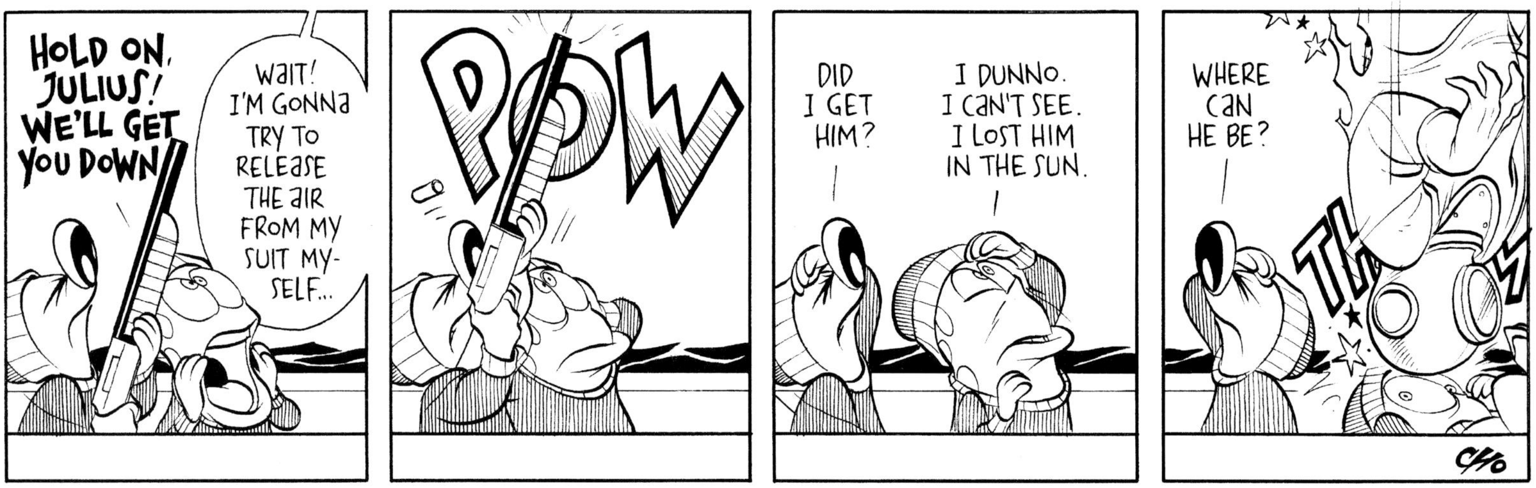
HOLD ON, JULIUS! WE'LL GET YOU DOWN!
WAIT! I'M GONNA TRY TO RELEASE THE AIR FROM MY SUIT MY-SELF...
POW
DID I GET HIM?
I DUNNO. I CAN'T SEE. I LOST HIM IN THE SUN.
WHERE CAN HE BE?
C/10

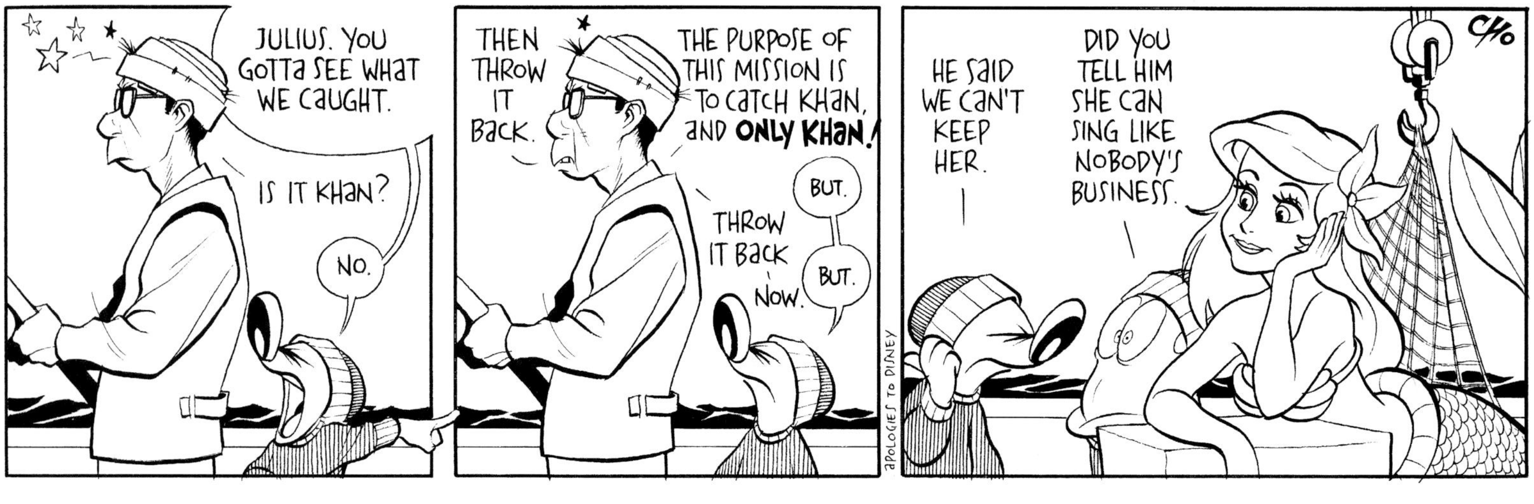
JULIUS. YOU GOTTA SEE WHAT WE CAUGHT.
IS IT KHAN?
NO.
THEN THROW IT BACK.
THE PURPOSE OF THIS MISSION IS TO CATCH KHAN, AND ONLY KHAN!
BUT.
BUT.
THROW IT BACK NOW.
APOLOGIES TO DISNEY
HE SAID WE CAN'T KEEP HER.
DID YOU TELL HIM SHE CAN SING LIKE NOBODY'S BUSINESS.
C/10

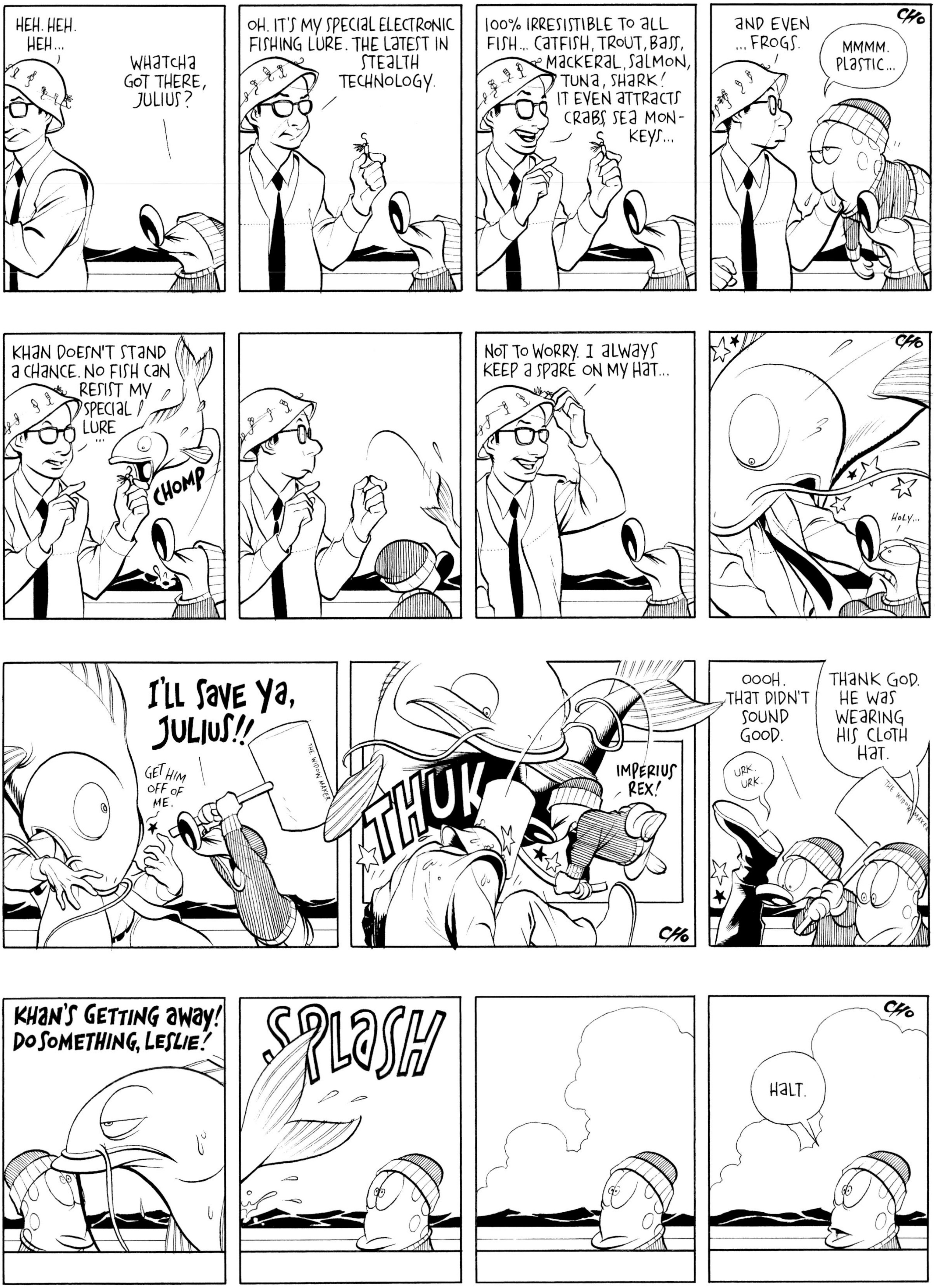
HEH. HEH. HEH...
WHATCHA GOT THERE, JULIUS?
OH. IT'S MY SPECIAL ELECTRONIC FISHING LURE. THE LATEST IN STEALTH TECHNOLOGY.
100% IRRESISTIBLE TO ALL FISH... CATFISH, TROUT, BASS, MACKERAL, SALMON, TUNA, SHARK! IT EVEN ATTRACTS CRABS, SEA MON-KEYS...
CHO
AND EVEN ...FROGS.
MMMM. PLASTIC...
KHAN DOESN'T STAND A CHANCE. NO FISH CAN RESIST MY SPECIAL LURE...
CHOMP
NOT TO WORRY. I ALWAYS KEEP A SPARE ON MY HAT...
CHO
HOLY...
I'LL SAVE YA, JULIUS!!
GET HIM OFF OF ME.
THE WIDOW MAKER
THUK
IMPERIUS REX!
CHO
OOOH. THAT DIDN'T SOUND GOOD.
THANK GOD. HE WAS WEARING HIS CLOTH HAT.
URK. URK.
THE WIDOW MAKER
KHAN'S GETTING AWAY! DO SOMETHING, LESLIE!
SPLASH
CHO
HALT.

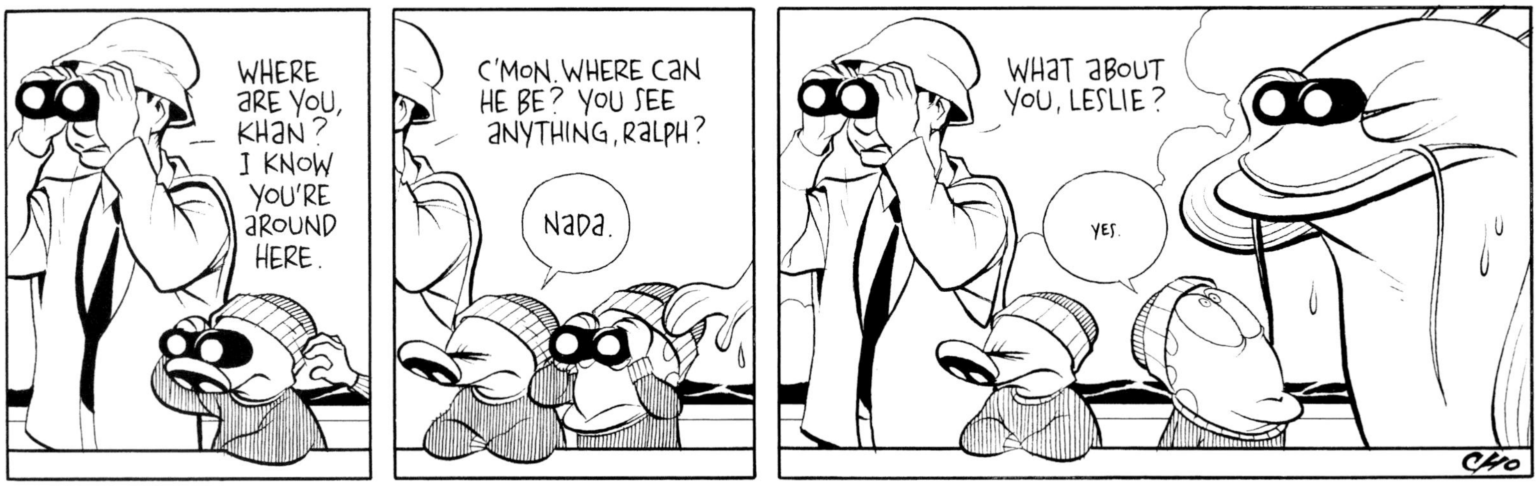
WHERE ARE YOU, KHAN? I KNOW YOU'RE AROUND HERE.
C'MON. WHERE CAN HE BE? YOU SEE ANYTHING, RALPH?
NADA.
WHAT ABOUT YOU, LESLIE?
YES.
CHO

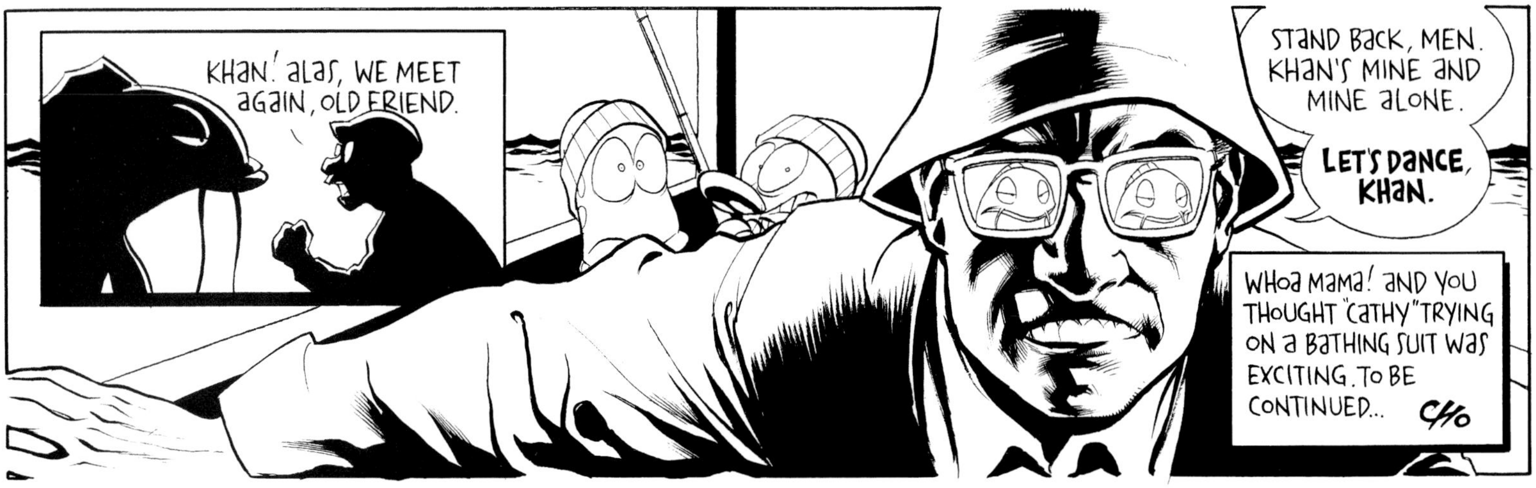
KHAN! ALAS, WE MEET AGAIN, OLD FRIEND.
STAND BACK, MEN. KHAN'S MINE AND MINE ALONE.
LET'S DANCE, KHAN.
WHOA MAMA! AND YOU THOUGHT "CATHY" TRYING ON A BATHING SUIT WAS EXCITING. TO BE CONTINUED...
CHO

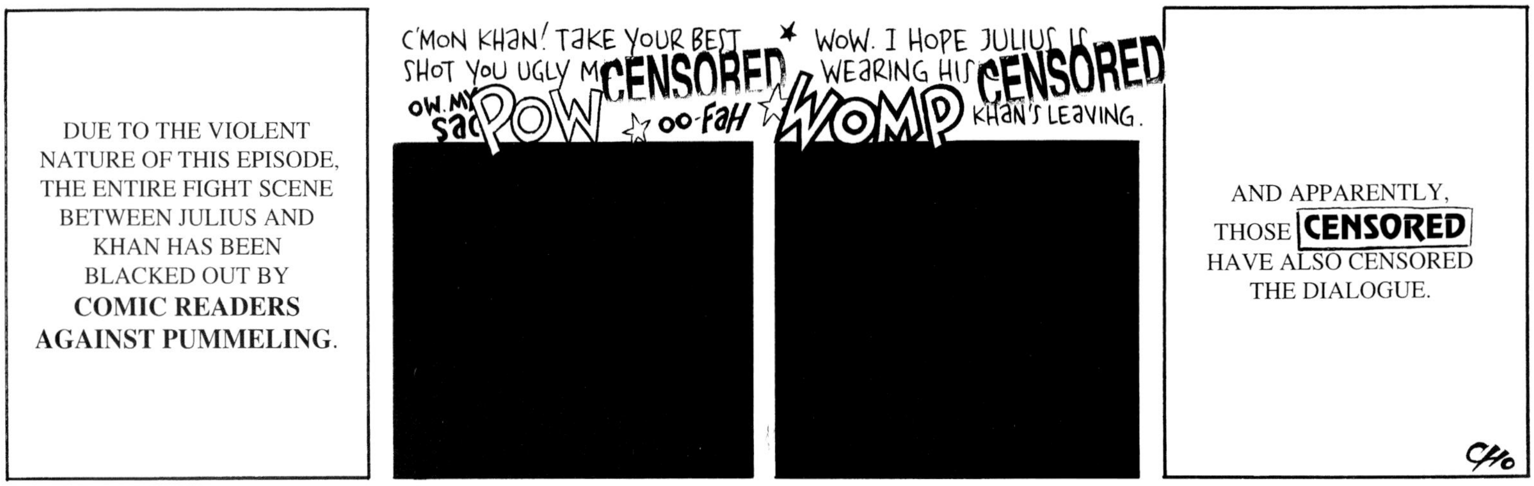
DUE TO THE VIOLENT NATURE OF THIS EPISODE, THE ENTIRE FIGHT SCENE BETWEEN JULIUS AND KHAN HAS BEEN BLACKED OUT BY **COMIC READERS AGAINST PUMMELING**.
C'MON KHAN! TAKE YOUR BEST SHOT YOU UGLY M
CENSORED
OW. MY SAC
POW
OO-FAH
WOW. I HOPE JULIUS IS WEARING HIS
CENSORED
WOMP
KHAN'S LEAVING.
AND APPARENTLY, THOSE CENSORED HAVE ALSO CENSORED THE DIALOGUE.
CHO

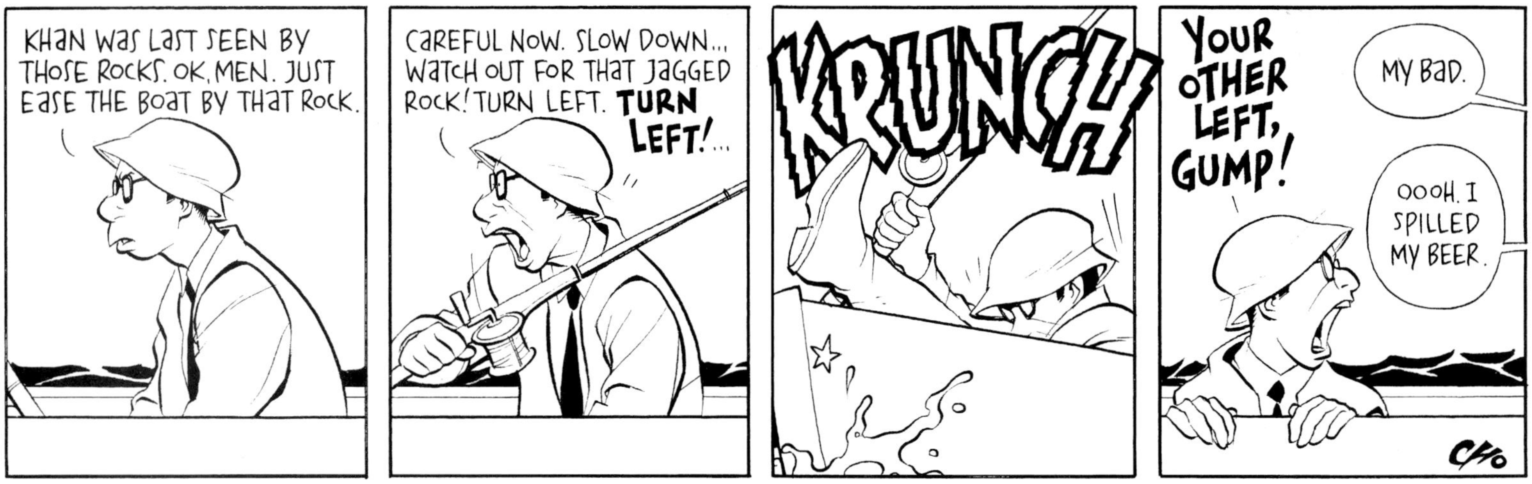
KHAN WAS LAST SEEN BY THOSE ROCKS. OK, MEN. JUST EASE THE BOAT BY THAT ROCK.
CAREFUL NOW. SLOW DOWN... WATCH OUT FOR THAT JAGGED ROCK! TURN LEFT. TURN LEFT!...
KRUNCH
YOUR OTHER LEFT, GUMP!
MY BAD.
OOOH. I SPILLED MY BEER.
CHO

HOW BAD'S THE DAMAGE?

I'VE SEEN WORSE.

THIS STRIP OF DUCT TAPE SHOULD KEEP THE WATER OUT. HERE, LESLIE. PUT YOUR HAND OVER THE TAPE, WHILE I START THE WATER PUMP.

RALPH!

HANG ON. I'LL CUT ANOTHER STRIP.

RALPH!

HANG ON, THIS TAPE SHOULD DO THE TRICK.

NOW. SIT TIGHT. DON'T MOVE YOUR HANDS. I'LL GET THE PUMP STARTED, THEN I'LL PATCH THAT HOLE UP.

ARE THE GUYS BACK FROM THEIR FISHING TRIP YET?

NO. NOT YET.

I HOPE THEY COME HOME SOON. IT'S GETTING PRETTY DARK OUT THERE.

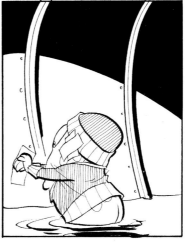

DON'T WORRY, BRANDY. JULIUS HAS BEEN FISHING IN THAT LAKE FOR YEARS. I'M SURE THEY'RE FINE.

WOW. THE BOAT SURE SANK FAST, HUH?

SHUT UP.

I'M SORRY THAT I SANK THE BOAT, JULIUS. LISTEN.. I WANNA MAKE IT UP TO YOU.

IF IT LOOKS LIKE WE'LL NEVER REACH THE SHORE AND FACE STARVATION, I WANT YOU TO EAT ME.

SHUT UP.

DUDE, IF I WERE YOU I'D TAKE THE OFFER. FROG LEGS ARE CONSIDERED DELICACY IN THE SOUTH.

SHUT UP!

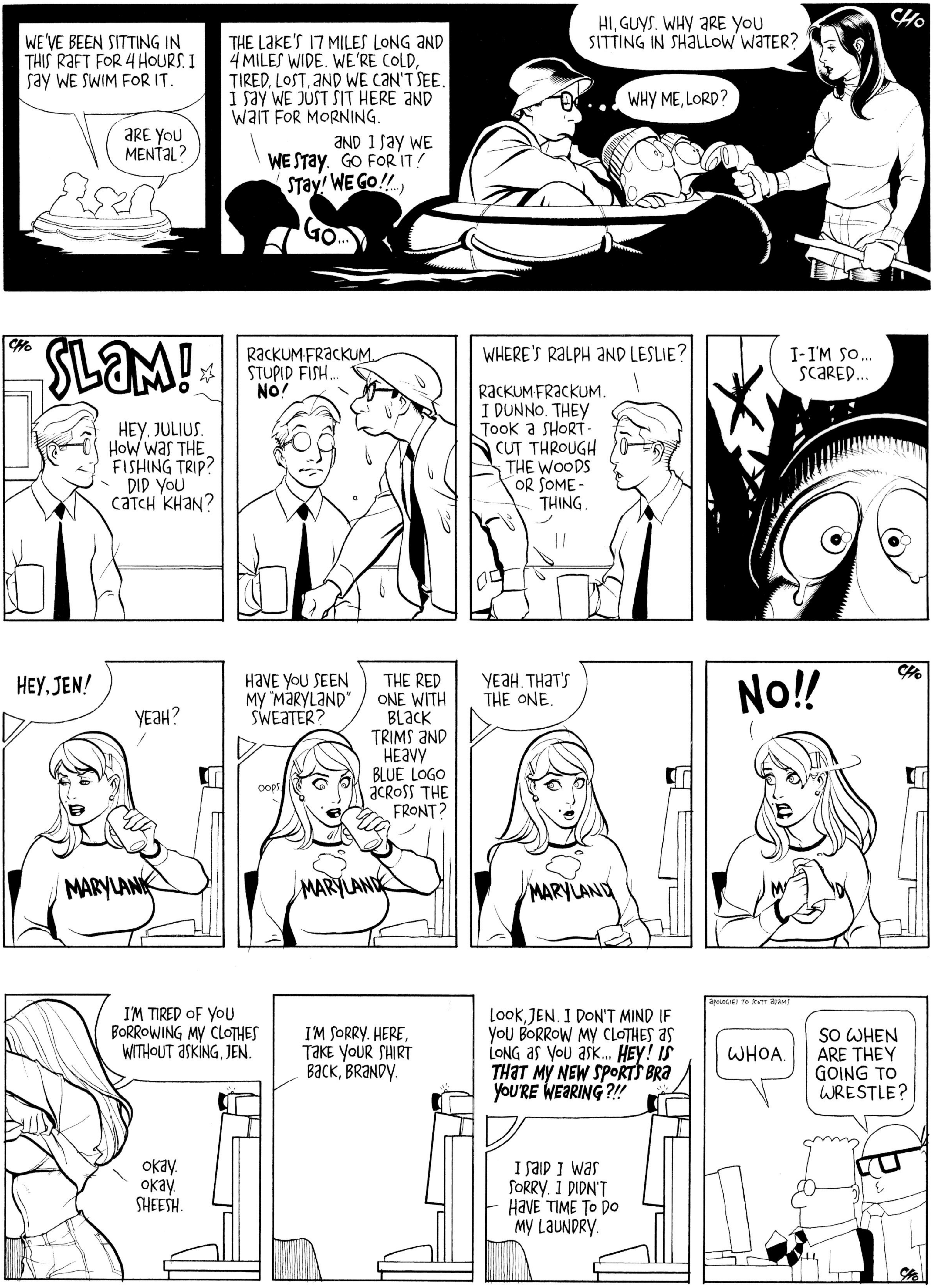
CHO
WE'VE BEEN SITTING IN THIS RAFT FOR 4 HOURS. I SAY WE SWIM FOR IT.
ARE YOU MENTAL?
THE LAKE'S 17 MILES LONG AND 4 MILES WIDE. WE'RE COLD, TIRED, LOST, AND WE CAN'T SEE. I SAY WE JUST SIT HERE AND WAIT FOR MORNING.
AND I SAY WE GO FOR IT!
WE STAY.
STAY!
WE GO!!
GO...
HI, GUYS. WHY ARE YOU SITTING IN SHALLOW WATER?
WHY ME, LORD?
CHO
SLAM!
HEY, JULIUS. HOW WAS THE FISHING TRIP? DID YOU CATCH KHAN?
RACKUM-FRACKUM. STUPID FISH...
NO!
WHERE'S RALPH AND LESLIE?
RACKUM-FRACKUM. I DUNNO. THEY TOOK A SHORT-CUT THROUGH THE WOODS OR SOME-THING.
I-I'M SO... SCARED...
HEY, JEN!
YEAH?
MARYLAND
HAVE YOU SEEN MY "MARYLAND" SWEATER?
THE RED ONE WITH BLACK TRIMS AND HEAVY BLUE LOGO ACROSS THE FRONT?
OOPS
MARYLAND
YEAH. THAT'S THE ONE.
MARYLAND
CHO
NO!!
I'M TIRED OF YOU BORROWING MY CLOTHES WITHOUT ASKING, JEN.
OKAY. OKAY. SHEESH.
I'M SORRY. HERE, TAKE YOUR SHIRT BACK, BRANDY.
LOOK, JEN. I DON'T MIND IF YOU BORROW MY CLOTHES AS LONG AS YOU ASK... HEY! IS THAT MY NEW SPORTS BRA YOU'RE WEARING?!!
I SAID I WAS SORRY. I DIDN'T HAVE TIME TO DO MY LAUNDRY.
APOLOGIES TO SCOTT ADAMS
WHOA.
SO WHEN ARE THEY GOING TO WRESTLE?
CHO

WHAT'S THAT, RALPHIE?

IT'S MY TRANSDIMENSIONAL PORTAL UNIT. IT FOLDS SPACE AND REALITY ALLOWING ME TO TRAVEL GREAT DISTANCES BY OPENING PORTALS TO ANY DESTINATION.

DID YOU KNOW IT TAKES ME FULL 32 SECONDS TO WALK FROM MY ROOM TO THE BATHROOM DOWN THE HALL? WITH THIS UNIT, I CAN OPEN A PORTAL AND TRAVEL DIRECTLY TO THE BATHROOM FROM MY ROOM WITHOUT WASTING PRECIOUS TIME WALKING UP AND DOWN THE HALL. I CAN SAVE 64 SECONDS OF MY LIFE PER TRIP. **THAT'S 4 MINUTES AND 16 SECONDS A DAY!**

YOU'RE TELLING ME YOU'VE CREATED THIS SCIENTIFIC MARVEL SO YOU CAN GO TO THE BATHROOM **FASTER**?

RIGHT.

CO/o

COOL BEANS!

IT ALSO DOUBLES AS A GIANT HARMONICA IF YOU BLOW ON IT.

TWEET!

OH, ANXIETY CLOSET. WHAT HORRERS HAVE YOU WROUGHT TONIGHT?

WITH APOLOGIES TO BERKE BREATHED

FIZZZ

THE PORTAL'S OPEN. GO IN AND SEE IF IT'S THE BATHROOM.

AAIGHH!

YOU'RE THE HORROR?

NOT THE FACE. NOT THE FACE. I'M A PRETTY MAN!!

CHO

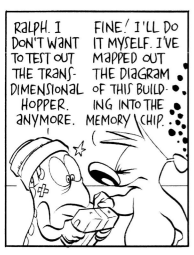

RALPH. I DON'T WANT TO TEST OUT THE TRANSDIMENSIONAL HOPPER. ANYMORE.

FINE! I'LL DO IT MYSELF. I'VE MAPPED OUT THE DIAGRAM OF THIS BUILDING INTO THE MEMORY CHIP.

THIS PORTAL SHOULD DIRECTLY TRANSPORT ME TO OUR BATHROOM DOWN THE HALL IN A MERE SECOND. HA. HA. HERE'S TO NO MORE WASTED TIME WALKING TO THE BATHROOM.

DAMN!

CHO

OK. OK. I MADE THE MINOR COORDINATE ADJUSTMENTS. THE TRANSDIMENSIONAL PORTAL SHOULD OPEN AWAY FROM THE TOILET BOWL.

ONCE AGAIN, HERE'S TO NO MORE WASTED TIME WALKING TO THE BATHROOM. "NOBEL", HERE I COME.

GODSPEED, ME BRAVE LAD.

DOUBLE DAMN!

CHO

37

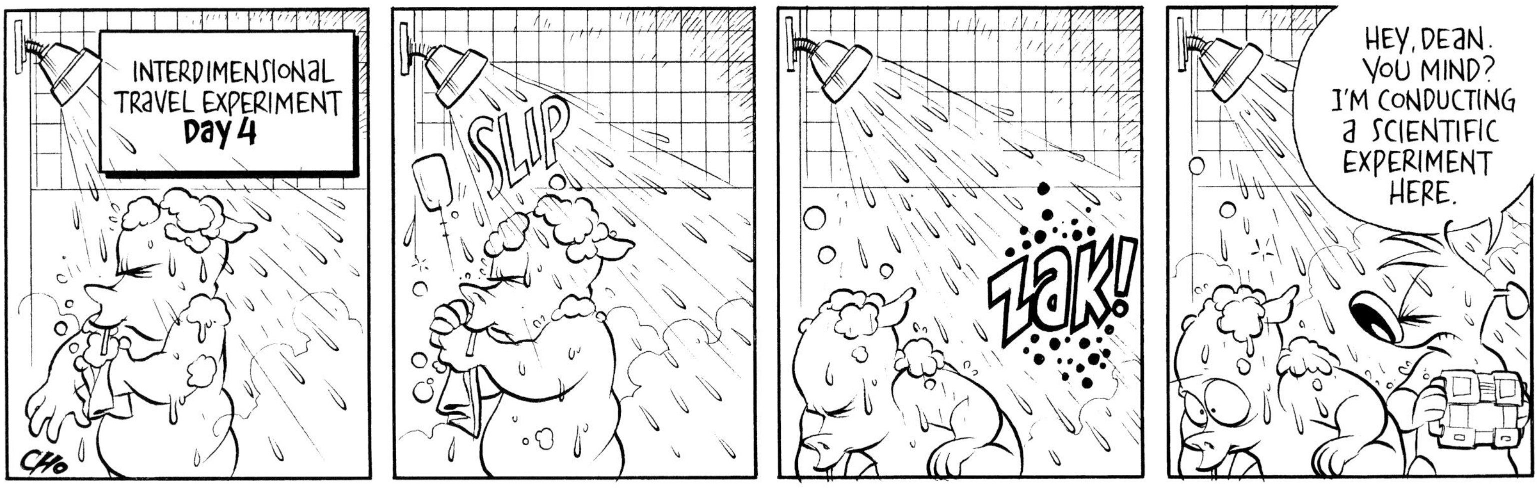
INTERDIMENSIONAL TRAVEL EXPERIMENT Day 4
SLIP
ZAK!
HEY, DEAN. YOU MIND? I'M CONDUCTING A SCIENTIFIC EXPERIMENT HERE.

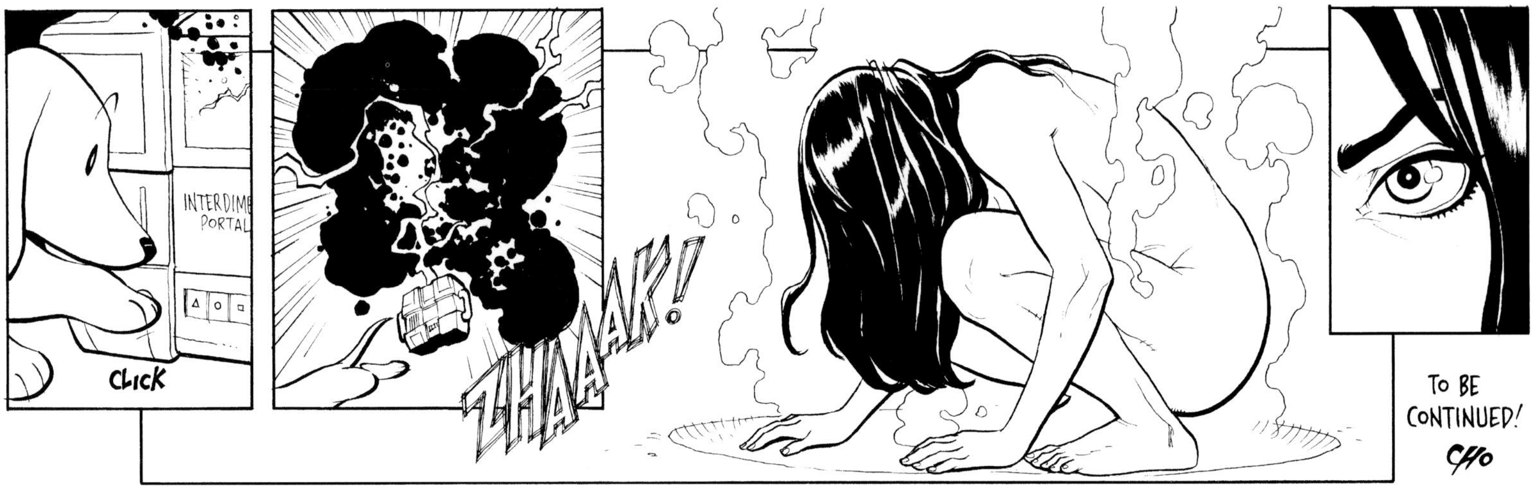
INTERDIME
PORTAL
CLICK
ZHAAAK!
TO BE CONTINUED!

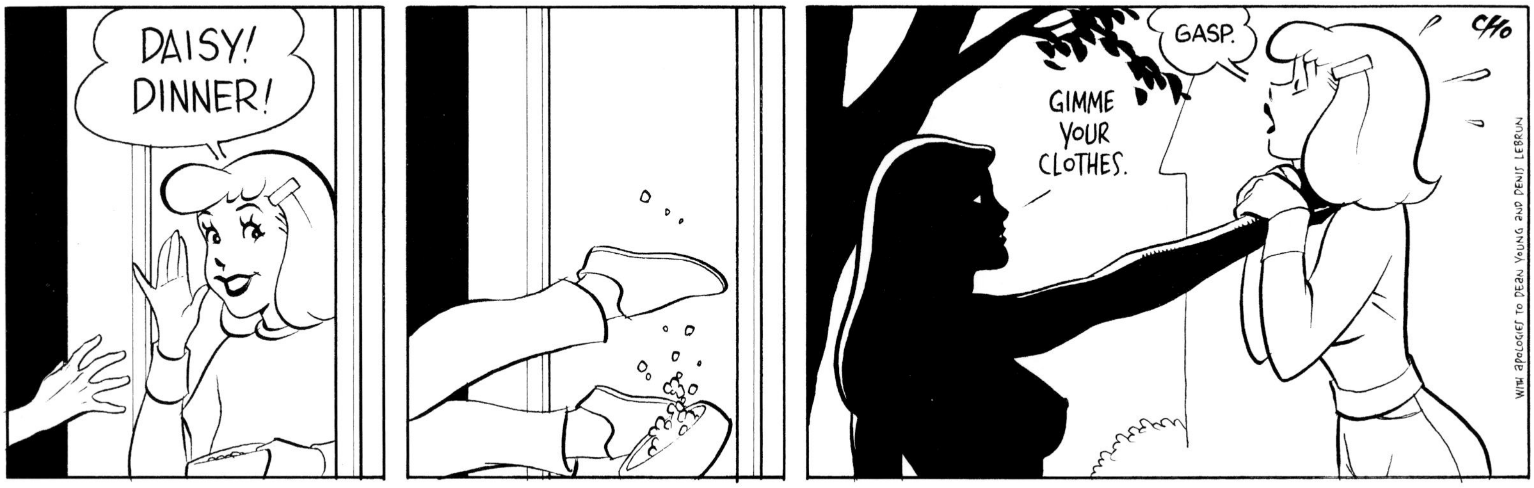
DAISY! DINNER!
GASP.
GIMME YOUR CLOTHES.
WITH APOLOGIES TO DEAN YOUNG AND DENIS LEBRUN

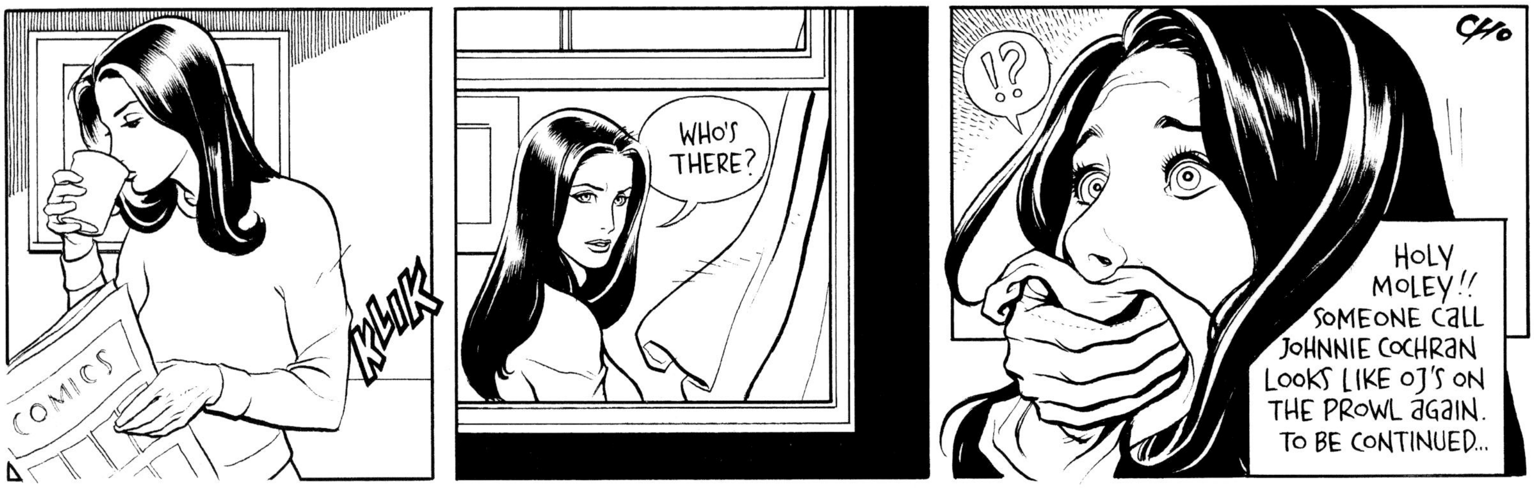
COMICS
KLIK
WHO'S THERE?
!?
HOLY MOLEY!! SOMEONE CALL JOHNNIE COCHRAN LOOKS LIKE OJ'S ON THE PROWL AGAIN.
TO BE CONTINUED...

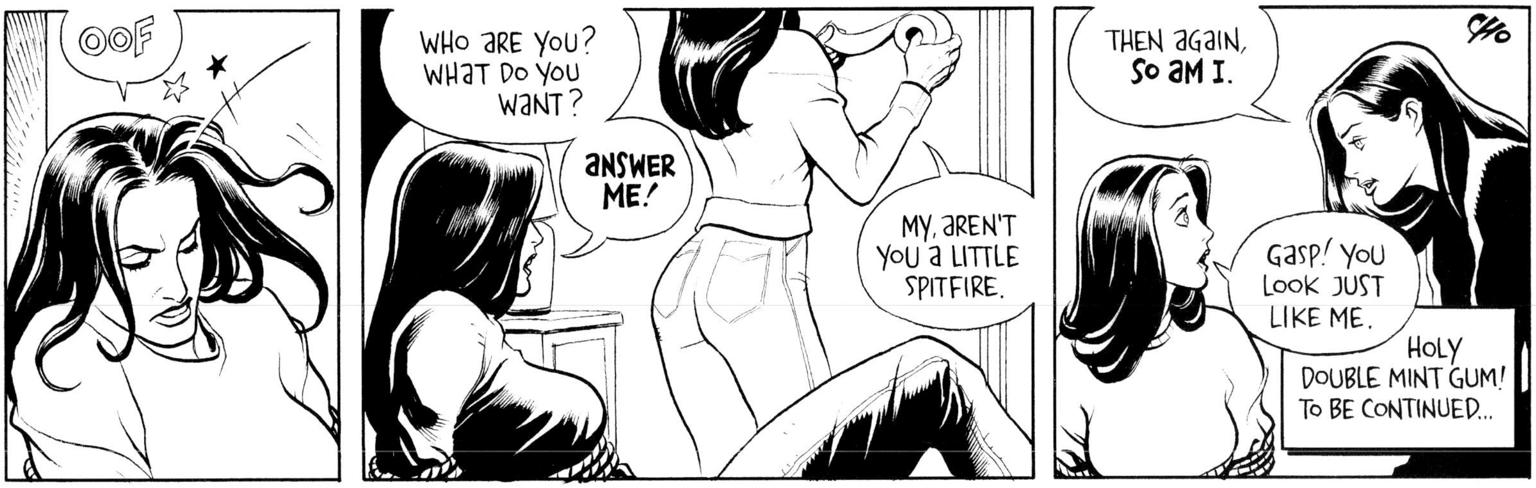
OOF
WHO ARE YOU? WHAT DO YOU WANT?
ANSWER ME!
MY, AREN'T YOU A LITTLE SPITFIRE.
CHO
THEN AGAIN, SO AM I.
GASP! YOU LOOK JUST LIKE ME.
HOLY DOUBLE MINT GUM! TO BE CONTINUED...

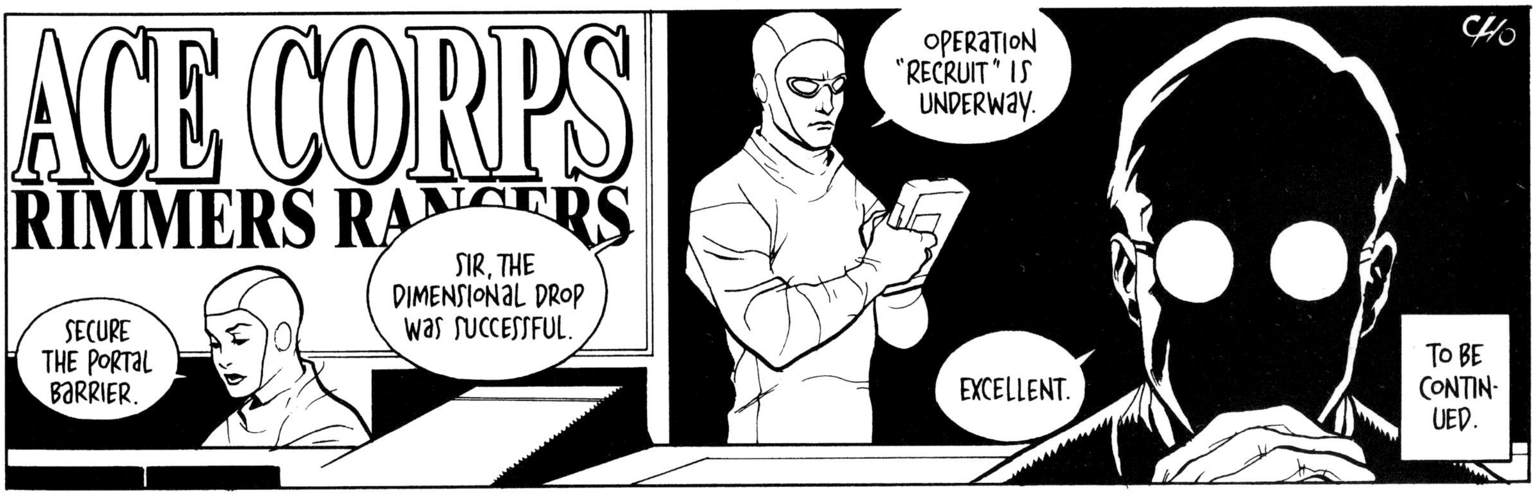
ACE CORPS
RIMMERS RANGERS
SECURE THE PORTAL BARRIER.
SIR, THE DIMENSIONAL DROP WAS SUCCESSFUL.
OPERATION "RECRUIT" IS UNDERWAY.
CHO
EXCELLENT.
TO BE CONTIN-UED.

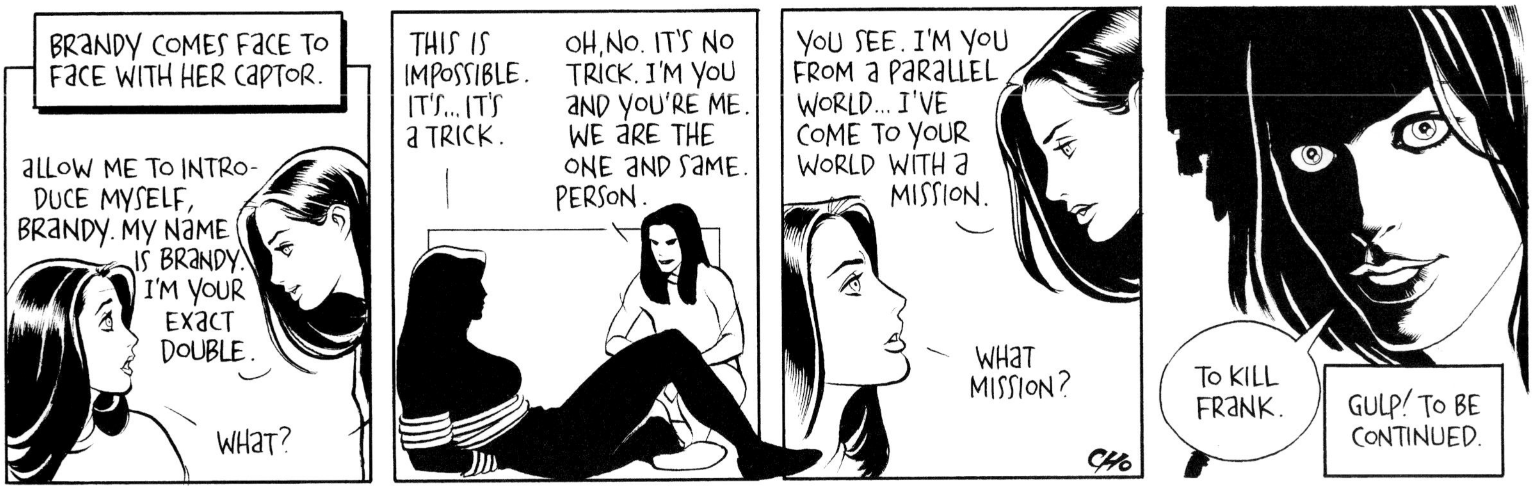
BRANDY COMES FACE TO FACE WITH HER CAPTOR.
ALLOW ME TO INTRO-DUCE MYSELF, BRANDY. MY NAME IS BRANDY. I'M YOUR EXACT DOUBLE.
WHAT?
THIS IS IMPOSSIBLE. IT'S... IT'S A TRICK.
OH, NO. IT'S NO TRICK. I'M YOU AND YOU'RE ME. WE ARE THE ONE AND SAME. PERSON.
YOU SEE. I'M YOU FROM A PARALLEL WORLD... I'VE COME TO YOUR WORLD WITH A MISSION.
WHAT MISSION?
CHO
TO KILL FRANK.
GULP! TO BE CONTINUED.

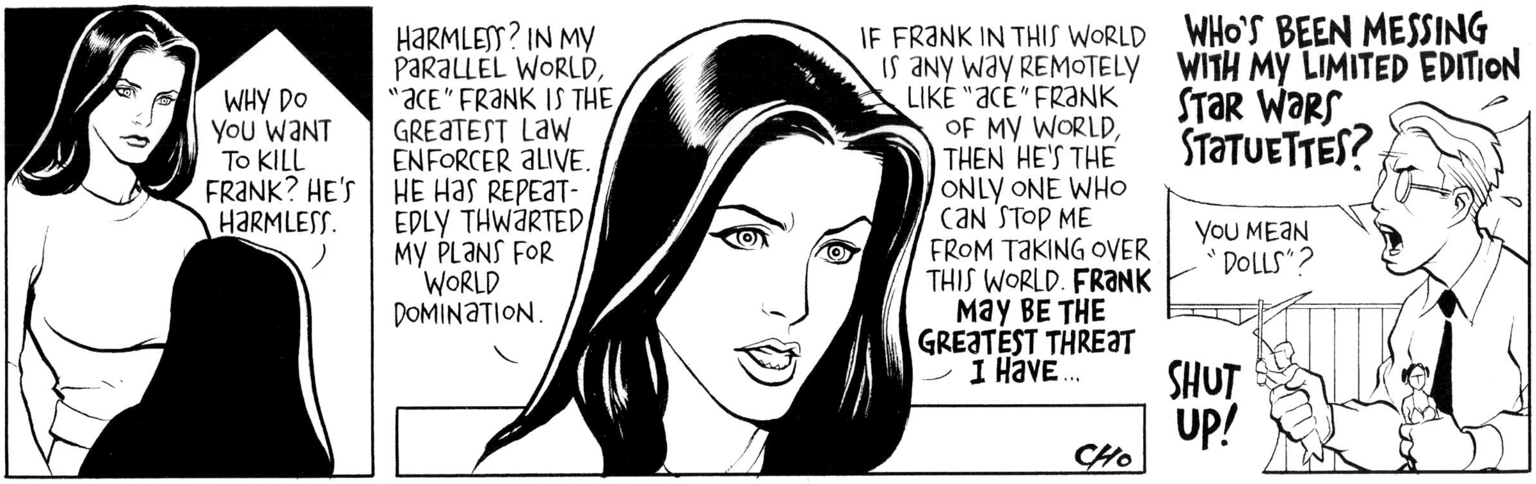
WHY DO YOU WANT TO KILL FRANK? HE'S HARMLESS.
HARMLESS? IN MY PARALLEL WORLD, "ACE" FRANK IS THE GREATEST LAW ENFORCER ALIVE. HE HAS REPEAT-EDLY THWARTED MY PLANS FOR WORLD DOMINATION.
IF FRANK IN THIS WORLD IS ANY WAY REMOTELY LIKE "ACE" FRANK OF MY WORLD, THEN HE'S THE ONLY ONE WHO CAN STOP ME FROM TAKING OVER THIS WORLD. FRANK MAY BE THE GREATEST THREAT I HAVE...
CHO
WHO'S BEEN MESSING WITH MY LIMITED EDITION STAR WARS STATUETTES?
YOU MEAN "DOLLS"?
SHUT UP!

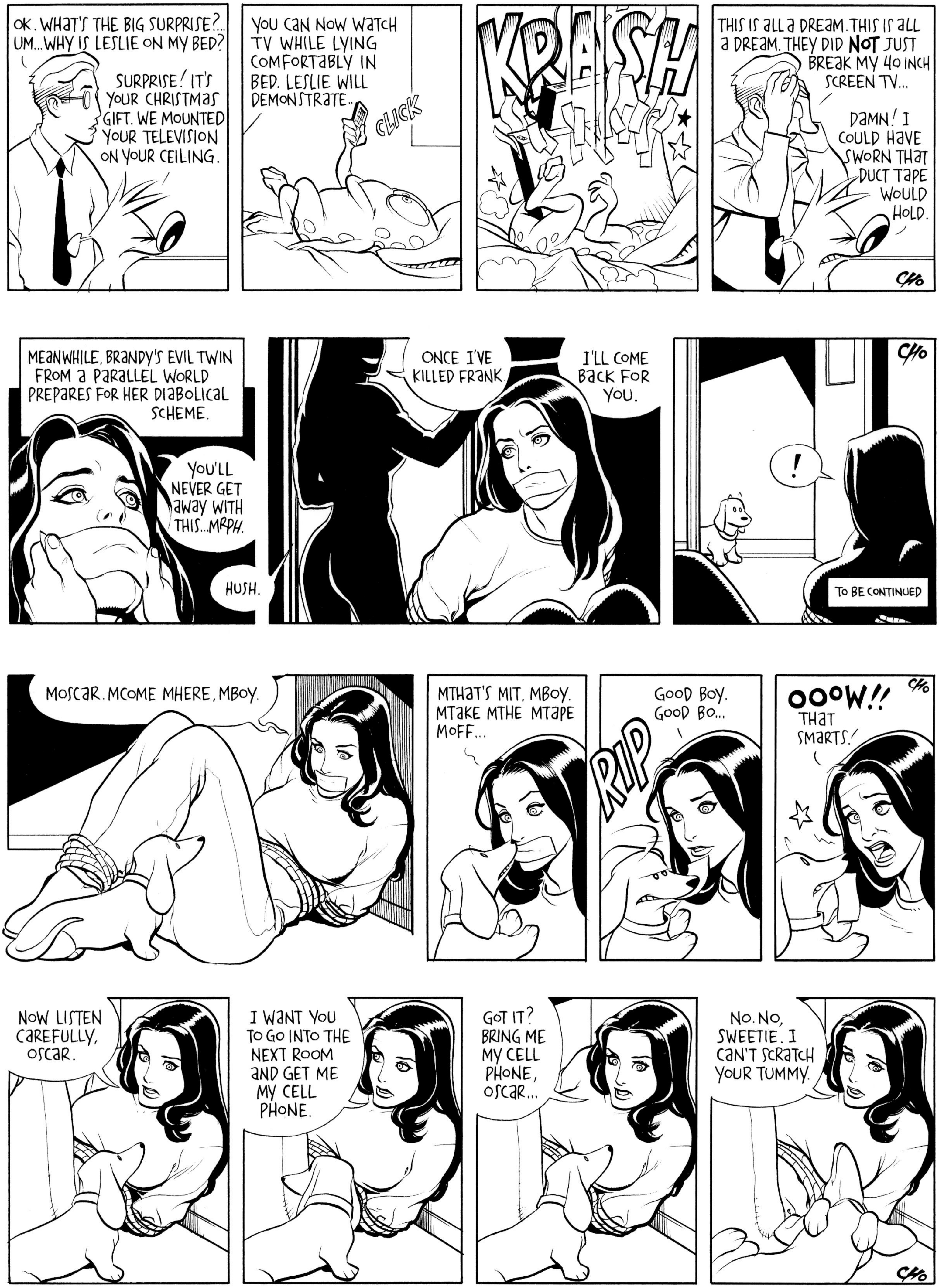
OK. WHAT'S THE BIG SURPRISE?... UM...WHY IS LESLIE ON MY BED?
SURPRISE! IT'S YOUR CHRISTMAS GIFT. WE MOUNTED YOUR TELEVISION ON YOUR CEILING.
YOU CAN NOW WATCH TV WHILE LYING COMFORTABLY IN BED. LESLIE WILL DEMONSTRATE...
CLICK
KRASH
THIS IS ALL A DREAM. THIS IS ALL A DREAM. THEY DID NOT JUST BREAK MY 40 INCH SCREEN TV...
DAMN! I COULD HAVE SWORN THAT DUCT TAPE WOULD HOLD.
MEANWHILE, BRANDY'S EVIL TWIN FROM A PARALLEL WORLD PREPARES FOR HER DIABOLICAL SCHEME.
YOU'LL NEVER GET AWAY WITH THIS...MRPH.
HUSH.
ONCE I'VE KILLED FRANK,
I'LL COME BACK FOR YOU.
!
TO BE CONTINUED
MOSCAR. MCOME MHERE, MBOY.
MTHAT'S MIT, MBOY. MTAKE MTHE MTAPE MOFF...
RIP
GOOD BOY. GOOD BO...
OOOW!! THAT SMARTS!
NOW LISTEN CAREFULLY, OSCAR.
I WANT YOU TO GO INTO THE NEXT ROOM AND GET ME MY CELL PHONE.
GOT IT? BRING ME MY CELL PHONE, OSCAR...
NO. NO, SWEETIE. I CAN'T SCRATCH YOUR TUMMY.

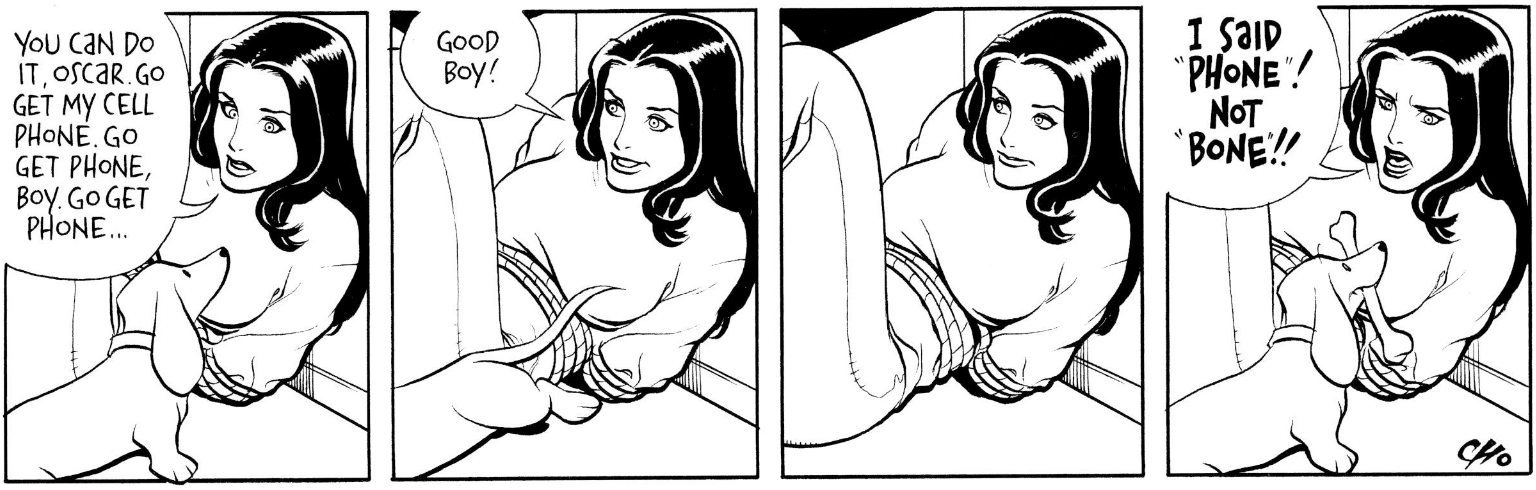
YOU CAN DO IT, OSCAR. GO GET MY CELL PHONE. GO GET PHONE, BOY. GO GET PHONE...
GOOD BOY!
I SAID "PHONE"! NOT "BONE"!!
CHO

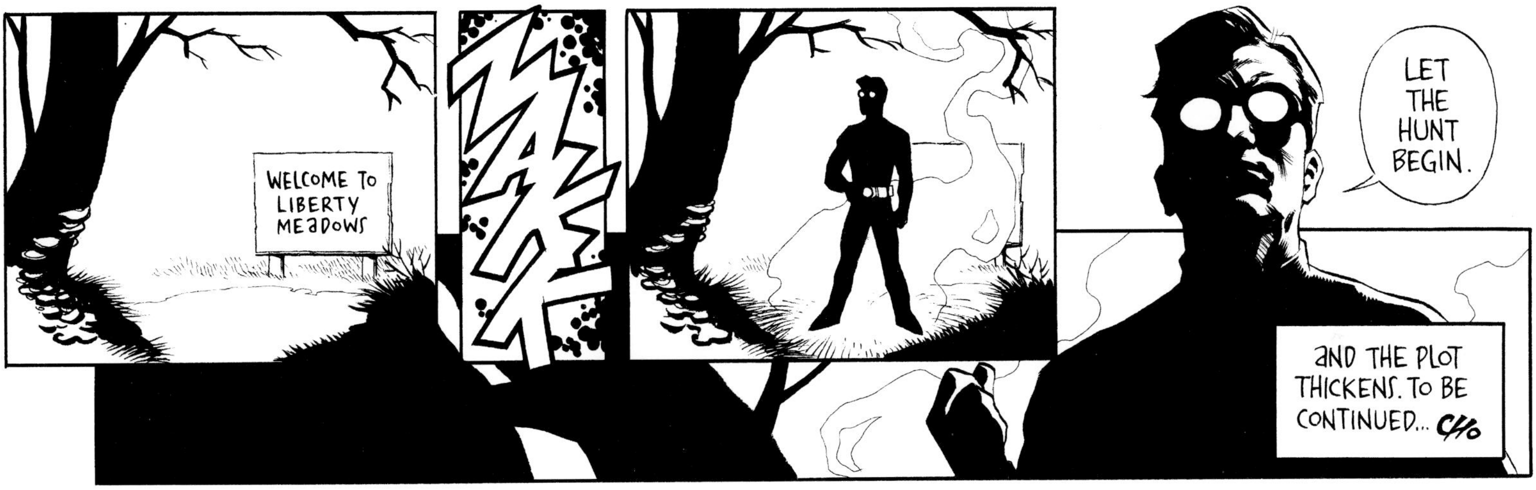
WELCOME TO LIBERTY MEADOWS
LET THE HUNT BEGIN.
AND THE PLOT THICKENS. TO BE CONTINUED... CHO

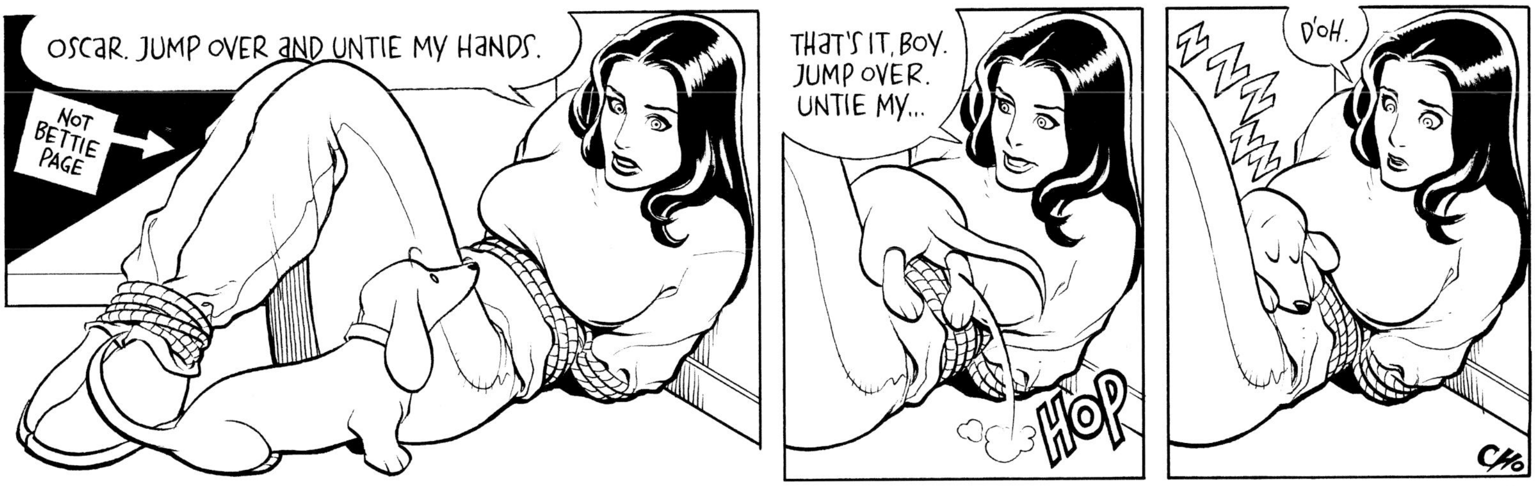
OSCAR. JUMP OVER AND UNTIE MY HANDS.
NOT BETTIE PAGE
THAT'S IT, BOY. JUMP OVER. UNTIE MY...
HOP
Z Z Z Z Z
D'OH.
CHO

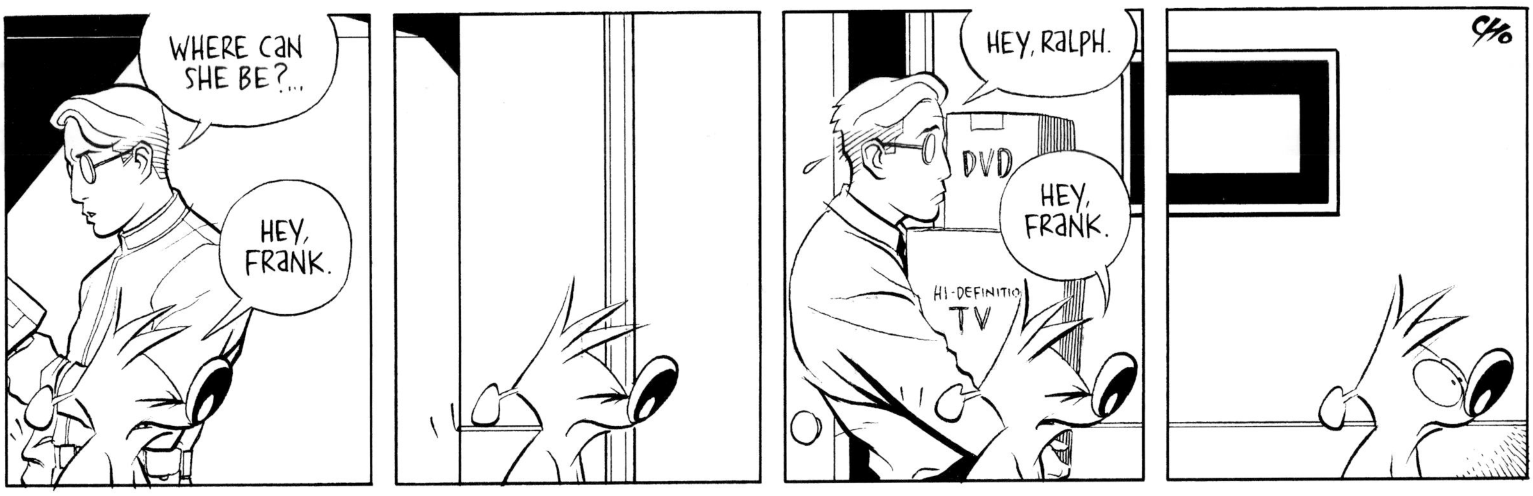
WHERE CAN SHE BE?...
HEY, FRANK.
HEY, RALPH.
DVD
HEY, FRANK.
HI-DEFINITIO TV
CHO

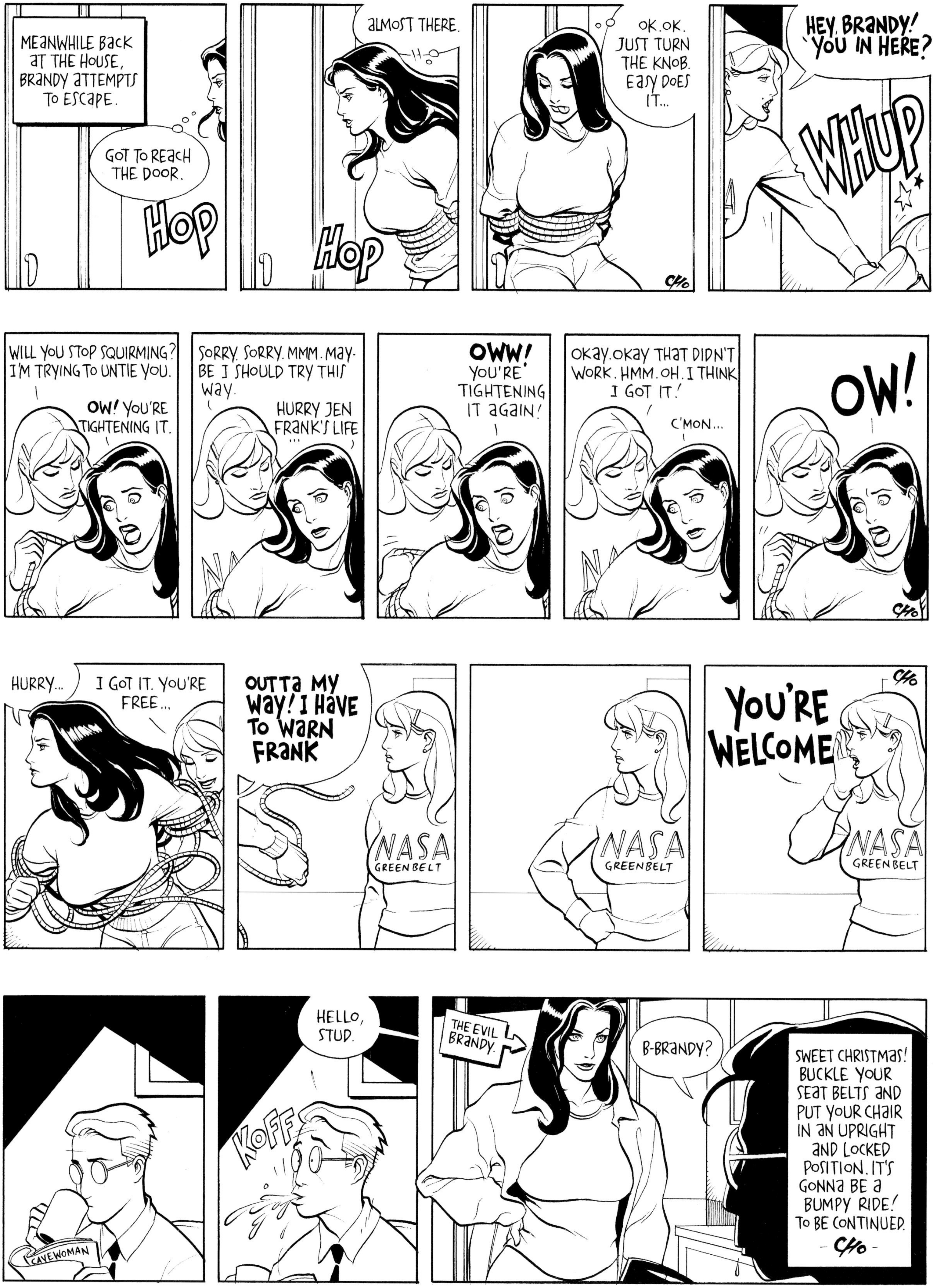
MEANWHILE BACK AT THE HOUSE, BRANDY ATTEMPTS TO ESCAPE.
GOT TO REACH THE DOOR.
HOP
ALMOST THERE.
HOP
OK.OK. JUST TURN THE KNOB. EASY DOES IT...
CHO
HEY, BRANDY! YOU IN HERE?
WHUP
WILL YOU STOP SQUIRMING? I'M TRYING TO UNTIE YOU.
OW! YOU'RE TIGHTENING IT.
SORRY. SORRY. MMM. MAY-BE I SHOULD TRY THIS WAY.
HURRY JEN FRANK'S LIFE ...
OWW! YOU'RE TIGHTENING IT AGAIN!
OKAY. OKAY THAT DIDN'T WORK. HMM. OH. I THINK I GOT IT!
C'MON...
OW!
CHO
HURRY...
I GOT IT. YOU'RE FREE...
OUTTA MY WAY! I HAVE TO WARN FRANK
NASA GREENBELT
NASA GREENBELT
CHO
YOU'RE WELCOME
NASA GREENBELT
CAVEWOMAN
HELLO, STUD.
KOFF
THE EVIL BRANDY.
B-BRANDY?
SWEET CHRISTMAS! BUCKLE YOUR SEAT BELTS AND PUT YOUR CHAIR IN AN UPRIGHT AND LOCKED POSITION. IT'S GONNA BE A BUMPY RIDE! TO BE CONTINUED.
- CHO -

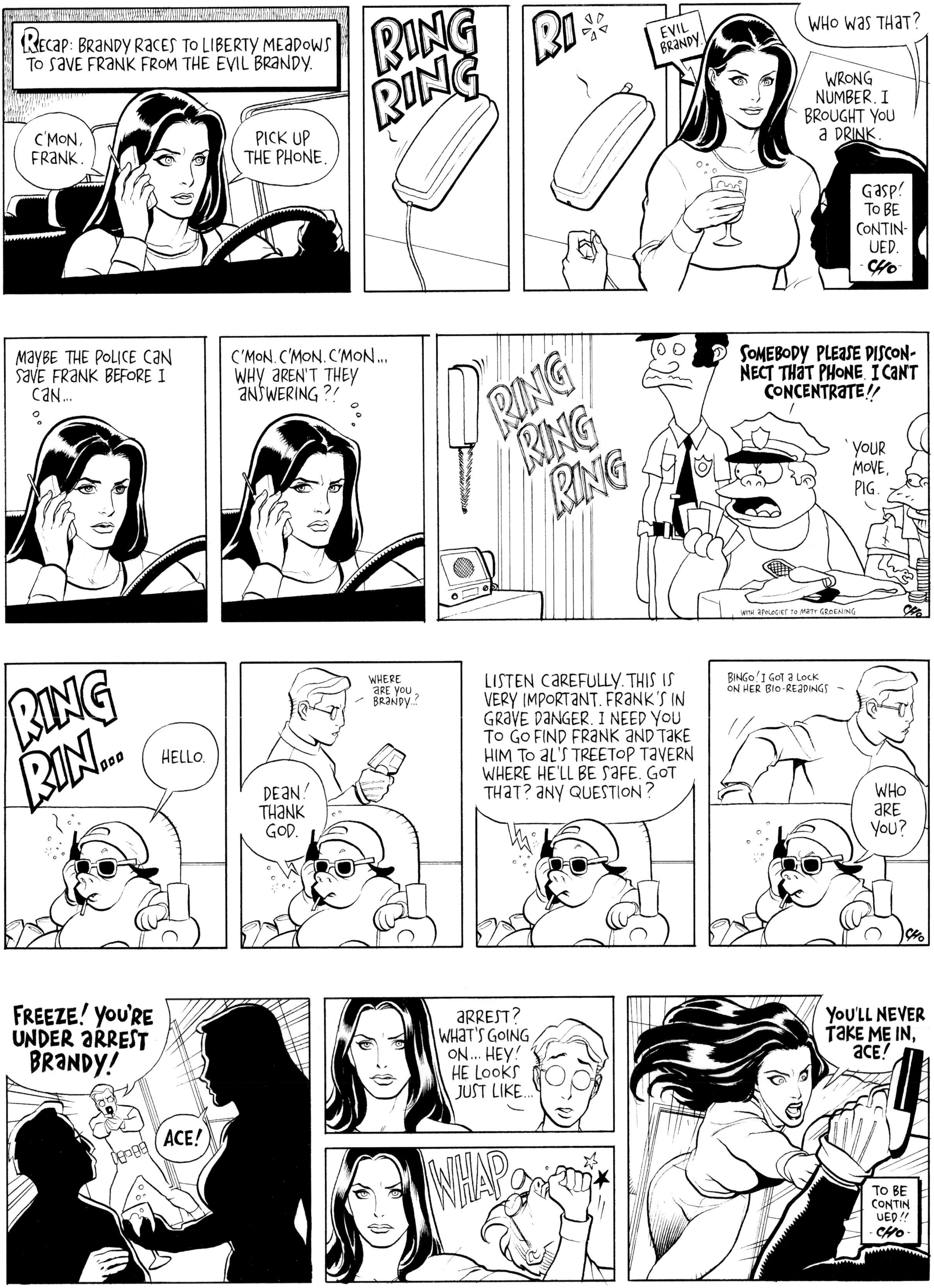
RECAP: BRANDY RACES TO LIBERTY MEADOWS TO SAVE FRANK FROM THE EVIL BRANDY.
C'MON, FRANK.
PICK UP THE PHONE.
RING RING
RI
EVIL BRANDY.
WHO WAS THAT?
WRONG NUMBER. I BROUGHT YOU A DRINK.
GASP! TO BE CONTIN-UED.
-CHO-
MAYBE THE POLICE CAN SAVE FRANK BEFORE I CAN...
C'MON. C'MON. C'MON... WHY AREN'T THEY ANSWERING?!
RING RING RING
SOMEBODY PLEASE DISCON-NECT THAT PHONE. I CAN'T CONCENTRATE!!
YOUR MOVE, PIG.
WITH APOLOGIES TO MATT GROENING
CHO
RING RIN...
HELLO.
WHERE ARE YOU BRANDY..?
DEAN! THANK GOD.
LISTEN CAREFULLY. THIS IS VERY IMPORTANT. FRANK'S IN GRAVE DANGER. I NEED YOU TO GO FIND FRANK AND TAKE HIM TO AL'S TREETOP TAVERN WHERE HE'LL BE SAFE. GOT THAT? ANY QUESTION?
BINGO! I GOT A LOCK ON HER BIO-READINGS
WHO ARE YOU?
CHO
FREEZE! YOU'RE UNDER ARREST BRANDY!
ACE!
ARREST? WHAT'S GOING ON... HEY! HE LOOKS JUST LIKE...
WHAP
YOU'LL NEVER TAKE ME IN, ACE!
TO BE CONTIN UED!!
-CHO-

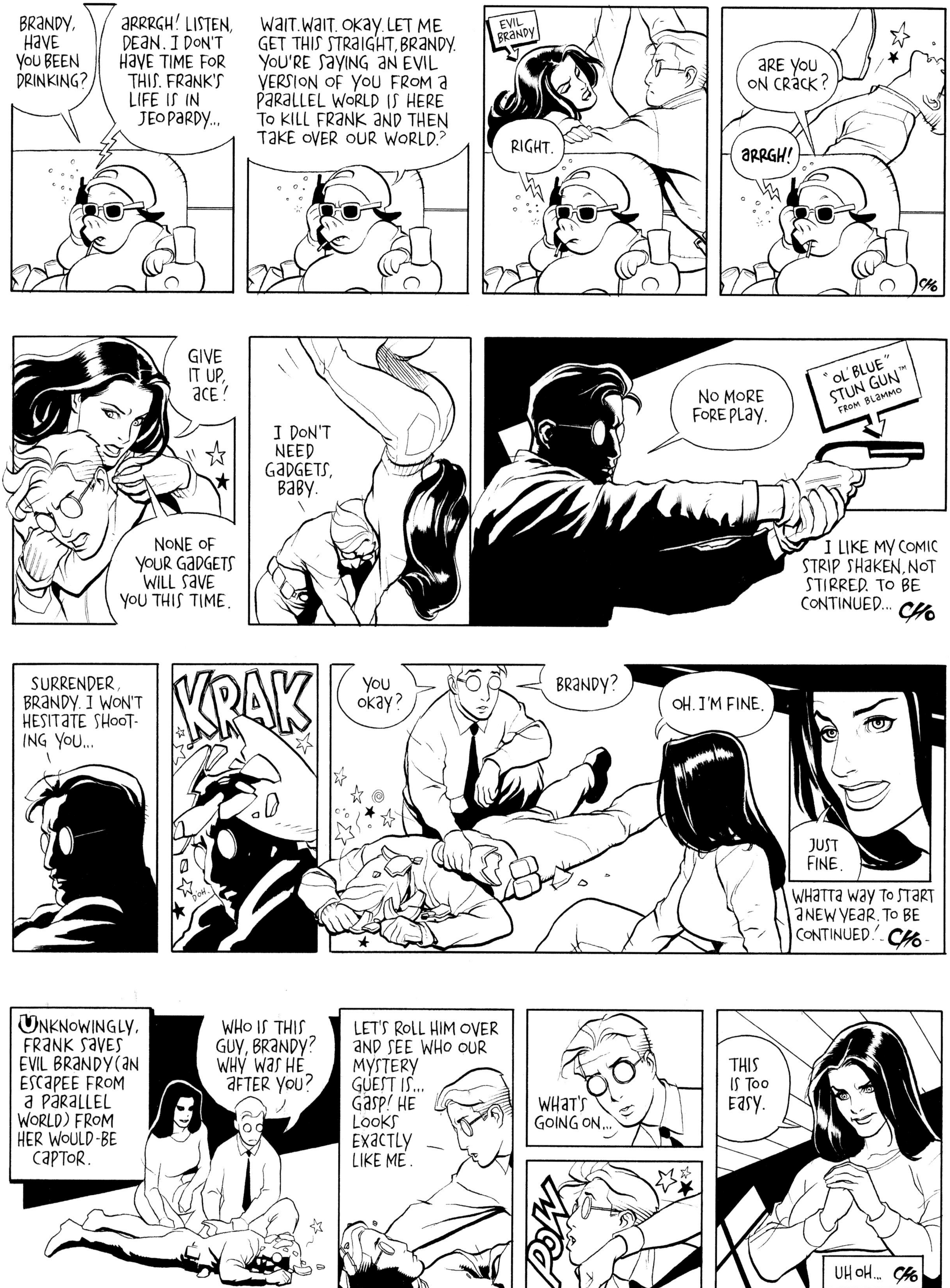
BRANDY, HAVE YOU BEEN DRINKING?
ARRRGH! LISTEN, DEAN. I DON'T HAVE TIME FOR THIS. FRANK'S LIFE IS IN JEOPARDY...
WAIT. WAIT. OKAY. LET ME GET THIS STRAIGHT, BRANDY. YOU'RE SAYING AN EVIL VERSION OF YOU FROM A PARALLEL WORLD IS HERE TO KILL FRANK AND THEN TAKE OVER OUR WORLD?
EVIL BRANDY
RIGHT.
ARE YOU ON CRACK?
ARRGH!
C/O
GIVE IT UP, ACE!
NONE OF YOUR GADGETS WILL SAVE YOU THIS TIME.
I DON'T NEED GADGETS, BABY.
NO MORE FOREPLAY.
"OL' BLUE" STUN GUN™ FROM BLAMMO
I LIKE MY COMIC STRIP SHAKEN, NOT STIRRED. TO BE CONTINUED...
C/O
SURRENDER, BRANDY. I WON'T HESITATE SHOOT-ING YOU...
KRAK
DOH.
YOU OKAY?
BRANDY?
OH. I'M FINE.
JUST FINE.
WHATTA WAY TO START A NEW YEAR. TO BE CONTINUED!
C/O
UNKNOWINGLY, FRANK SAVES EVIL BRANDY (AN ESCAPEE FROM A PARALLEL WORLD) FROM HER WOULD-BE CAPTOR.
WHO IS THIS GUY, BRANDY? WHY WAS HE AFTER YOU?
LET'S ROLL HIM OVER AND SEE WHO OUR MYSTERY GUEST IS... GASP! HE LOOKS EXACTLY LIKE ME.
WHAT'S GOING ON...
POW
THIS IS TOO EASY.
UH OH...
C/O

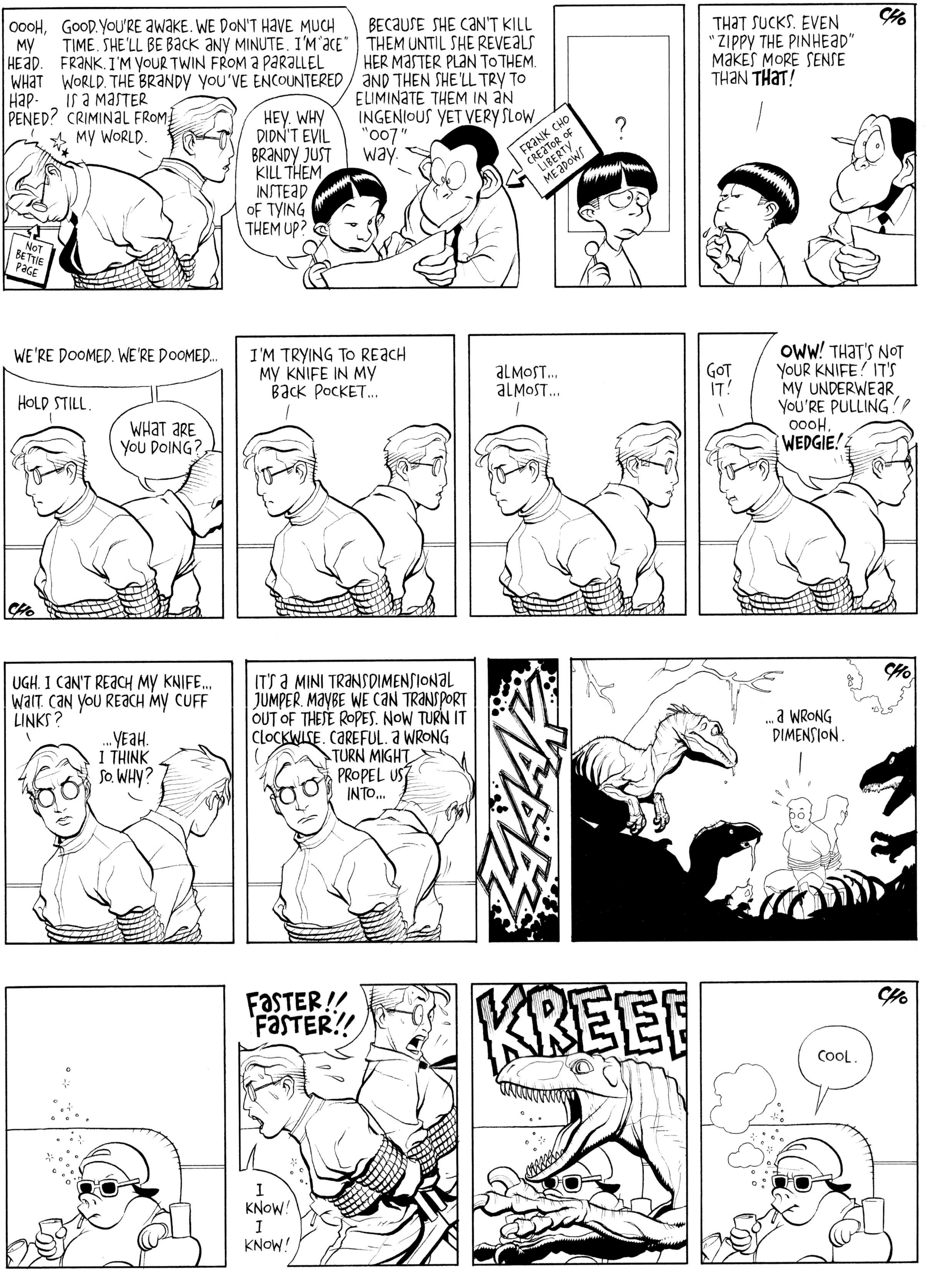

OOOH, MY HEAD. WHAT HAP-PENED?
GOOD. YOU'RE AWAKE. WE DON'T HAVE MUCH TIME. SHE'LL BE BACK ANY MINUTE. I'M "ACE" FRANK. I'M YOUR TWIN FROM A PARALLEL WORLD. THE BRANDY YOU'VE ENCOUNTERED IS A MASTER CRIMINAL FROM MY WORLD.
NOT BETTIE PAGE
HEY. WHY DIDN'T EVIL BRANDY JUST KILL THEM INSTEAD OF TYING THEM UP?
BECAUSE SHE CAN'T KILL THEM UNTIL SHE REVEALS HER MASTER PLAN TO THEM. AND THEN SHE'LL TRY TO ELIMINATE THEM IN AN INGENIOUS YET VERY SLOW "007" WAY.
FRANK CHO CREATOR OF LIBERTY MEADOWS
?
THAT SUCKS. EVEN "ZIPPY THE PINHEAD" MAKES MORE SENSE THAN THAT!
CHO
WE'RE DOOMED. WE'RE DOOMED...
HOLD STILL.
WHAT ARE YOU DOING?
CHO
I'M TRYING TO REACH MY KNIFE IN MY BACK POCKET...
ALMOST... ALMOST...
GOT IT!
OWW! THAT'S NOT YOUR KNIFE! IT'S MY UNDERWEAR YOU'RE PULLING!! OOOH, WEDGIE!
UGH. I CAN'T REACH MY KNIFE... WAIT. CAN YOU REACH MY CUFF LINKS?
...YEAH. I THINK SO. WHY?
IT'S A MINI TRANSDIMENSIONAL JUMPER. MAYBE WE CAN TRANSPORT OUT OF THESE ROPES. NOW TURN IT CLOCKWISE. CAREFUL. A WRONG TURN MIGHT PROPEL US INTO...
ZAAAK
CHO
...A WRONG DIMENSION.
FASTER!! FASTER!!!
I KNOW! I KNOW!
KREEE
CHO
COOL.

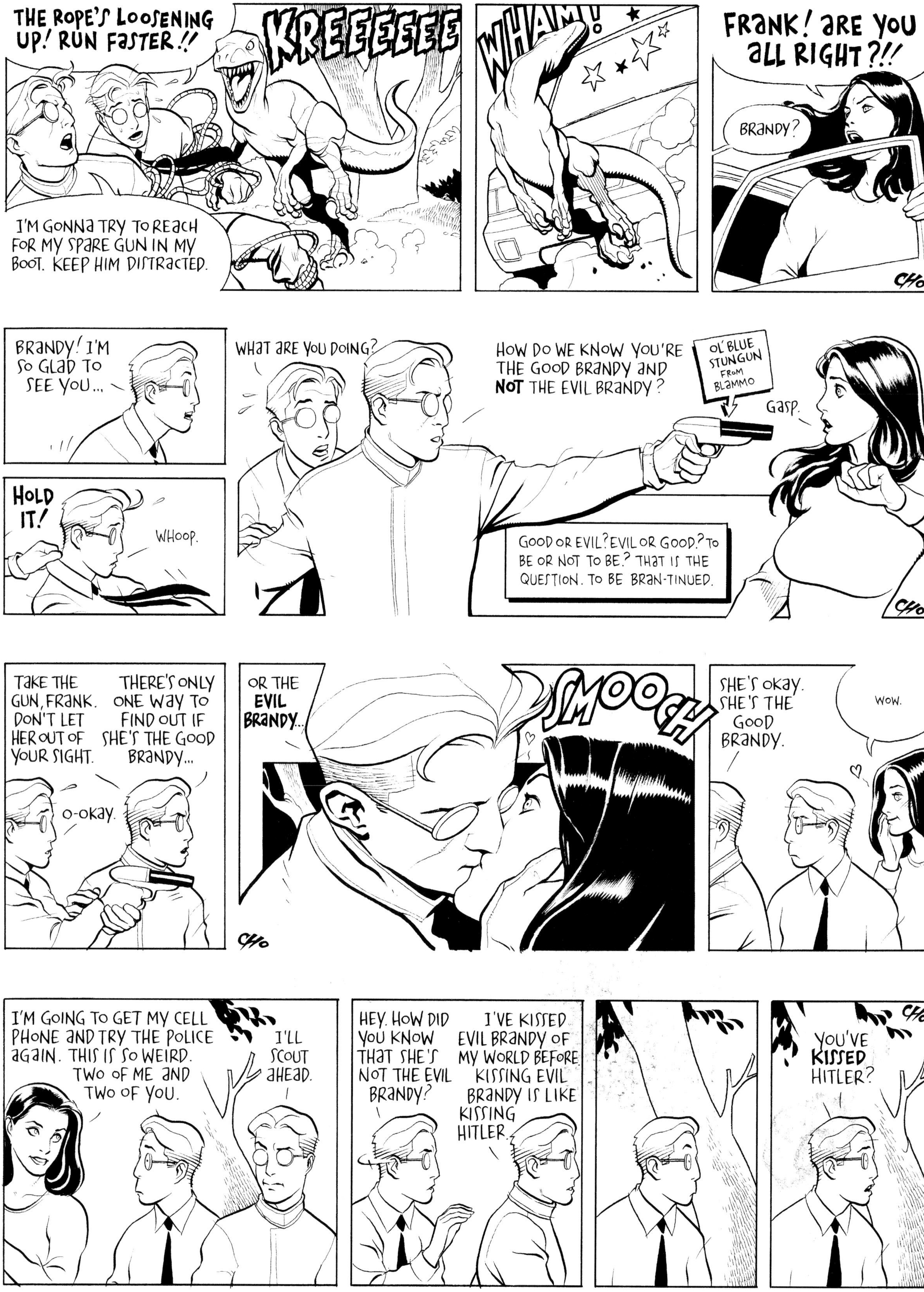
THE ROPE'S LOOSENING UP! RUN FASTER!!
KREEEEEE
I'M GONNA TRY TO REACH FOR MY SPARE GUN IN MY BOOT. KEEP HIM DISTRACTED.
WHAM!
FRANK! ARE YOU ALL RIGHT?!!
BRANDY?
CHO
BRANDY! I'M SO GLAD TO SEE YOU...
HOLD IT!
WHOOP.
WHAT ARE YOU DOING?
HOW DO WE KNOW YOU'RE THE GOOD BRANDY AND **NOT** THE EVIL BRANDY?
OL' BLUE STUNGUN FROM BLAMMO
GASP.
GOOD OR EVIL? EVIL OR GOOD? TO BE OR NOT TO BE? THAT IS THE QUESTION. TO BE BRAN-TINUED.
CHO
TAKE THE GUN, FRANK. DON'T LET HER OUT OF YOUR SIGHT.
THERE'S ONLY ONE WAY TO FIND OUT IF SHE'S THE GOOD BRANDY...
O-OKAY.
CHO
OR THE **EVIL BRANDY**...
SMOOCH
SHE'S OKAY. SHE'S THE GOOD BRANDY.
WOW.
I'M GOING TO GET MY CELL PHONE AND TRY THE POLICE AGAIN. THIS IS SO WEIRD. TWO OF ME AND TWO OF YOU.
I'LL SCOUT AHEAD.
HEY. HOW DID YOU KNOW THAT SHE'S NOT THE EVIL BRANDY?
I'VE KISSED EVIL BRANDY OF MY WORLD BEFORE. KISSING EVIL BRANDY IS LIKE KISSING HITLER.
CHO
YOU'VE **KISSED** HITLER?

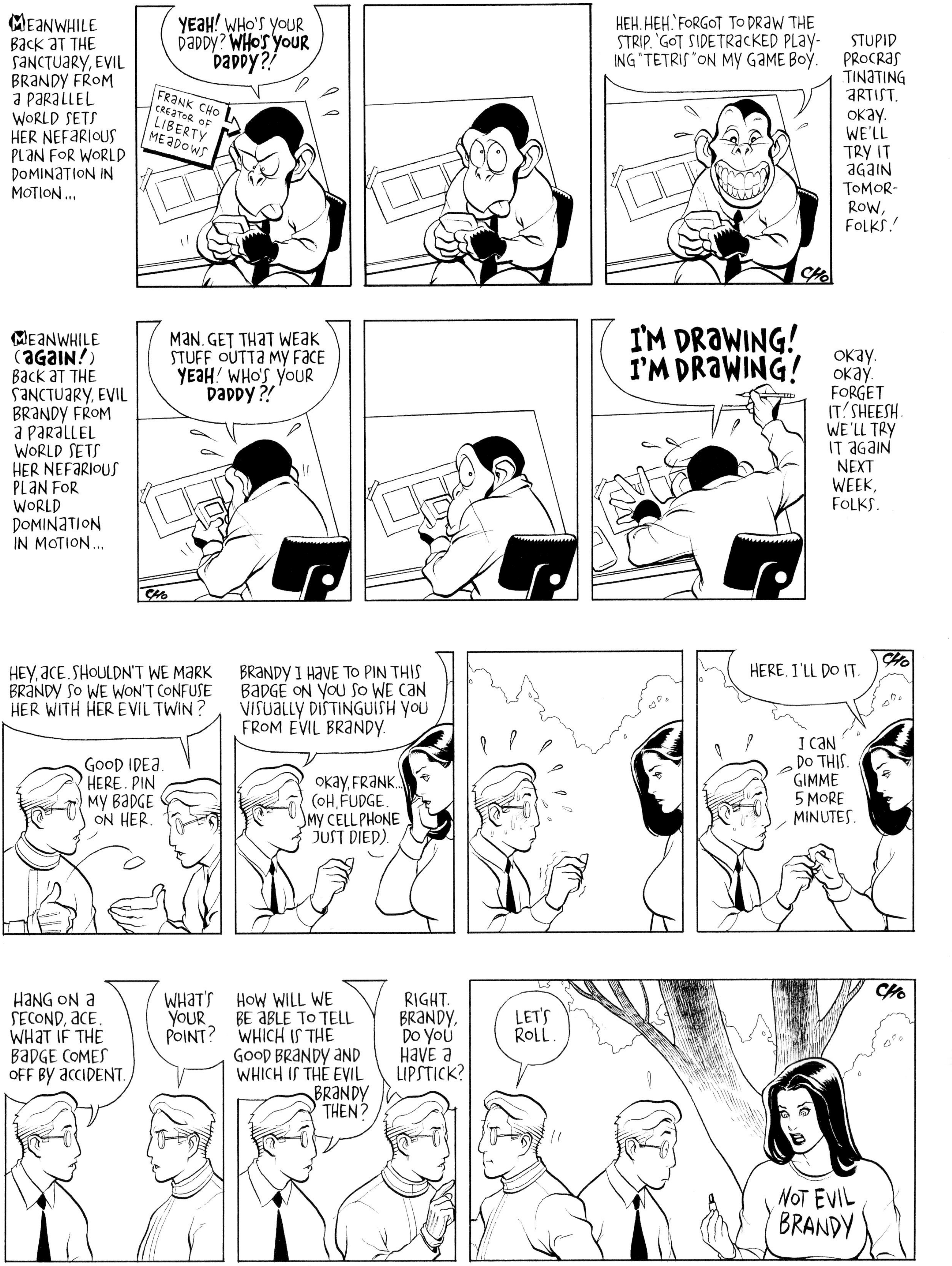
MEANWHILE BACK AT THE SANCTUARY, EVIL BRANDY FROM A PARALLEL WORLD SETS HER NEFARIOUS PLAN FOR WORLD DOMINATION IN MOTION...
YEAH! WHO'S YOUR DADDY? WHO'S YOUR DADDY?!
FRANK CHO CREATOR OF LIBERTY MEADOWS
HEH. HEH. 'FORGOT TO DRAW THE STRIP. 'GOT SIDETRACKED PLAYING "TETRIS" ON MY GAME BOY.
STUPID PROCRASTINATING ARTIST. OKAY. WE'LL TRY IT AGAIN TOMORROW, FOLKS!
CHO
MEANWHILE (AGAIN!) BACK AT THE SANCTUARY, EVIL BRANDY FROM A PARALLEL WORLD SETS HER NEFARIOUS PLAN FOR WORLD DOMINATION IN MOTION...
MAN. GET THAT WEAK STUFF OUTTA MY FACE YEAH! WHO'S YOUR DADDY?!
CHO
I'M DRAWING! I'M DRAWING!
OKAY. OKAY. FORGET IT! SHEESH. WE'LL TRY IT AGAIN NEXT WEEK, FOLKS.
HEY, ACE. SHOULDN'T WE MARK BRANDY SO WE WON'T CONFUSE HER WITH HER EVIL TWIN?
GOOD IDEA. HERE. PIN MY BADGE ON HER.
BRANDY I HAVE TO PIN THIS BADGE ON YOU SO WE CAN VISUALLY DISTINGUISH YOU FROM EVIL BRANDY.
OKAY, FRANK... (OH, FUDGE. MY CELLPHONE JUST DIED).
CHO
HERE. I'LL DO IT.
I CAN DO THIS. GIMME 5 MORE MINUTES.
HANG ON A SECOND, ACE. WHAT IF THE BADGE COMES OFF BY ACCIDENT.
WHAT'S YOUR POINT?
HOW WILL WE BE ABLE TO TELL WHICH IS THE GOOD BRANDY AND WHICH IS THE EVIL BRANDY THEN?
RIGHT. BRANDY, DO YOU HAVE A LIPSTICK?
CHO
LET'S ROLL.
NOT EVIL BRANDY

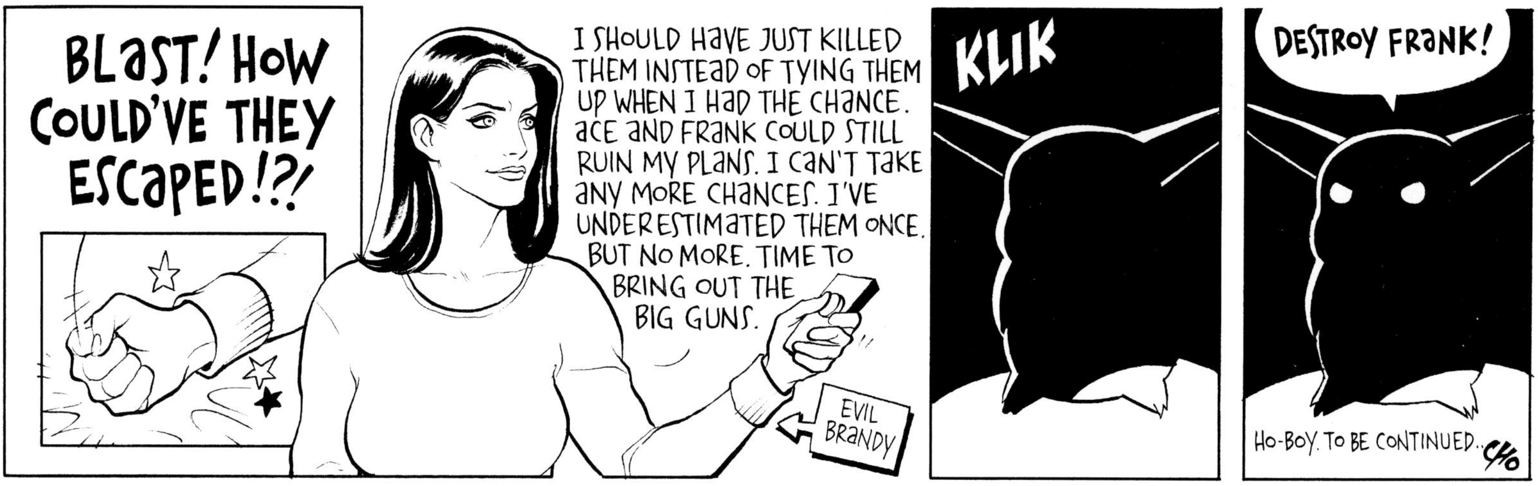
BLAST! HOW COULD'VE THEY ESCAPED!?!
I SHOULD HAVE JUST KILLED THEM INSTEAD OF TYING THEM UP WHEN I HAD THE CHANCE. ACE AND FRANK COULD STILL RUIN MY PLANS. I CAN'T TAKE ANY MORE CHANCES. I'VE UNDERESTIMATED THEM ONCE. BUT NO MORE. TIME TO BRING OUT THE BIG GUNS.
EVIL BRANDY
KLIK
DESTROY FRANK!
HO-BOY. TO BE CONTINUED...
CHO

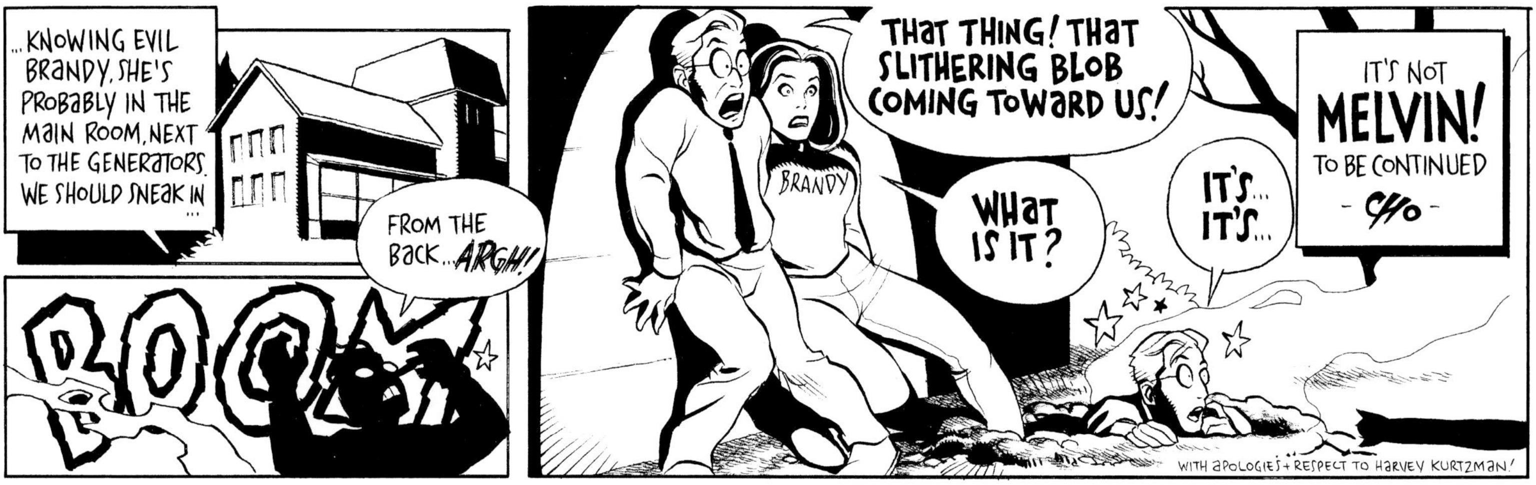
...KNOWING EVIL BRANDY, SHE'S PROBABLY IN THE MAIN ROOM, NEXT TO THE GENERATORS. WE SHOULD SNEAK IN...
FROM THE BACK...ARGH!
BOOM
THAT THING! THAT SLITHERING BLOB COMING TOWARD US!
BRANDY
WHAT IS IT?
IT'S... IT'S...
IT'S NOT MELVIN! TO BE CONTINUED
- CHO -
WITH APOLOGIES + RESPECT TO HARVEY KURTZMAN!

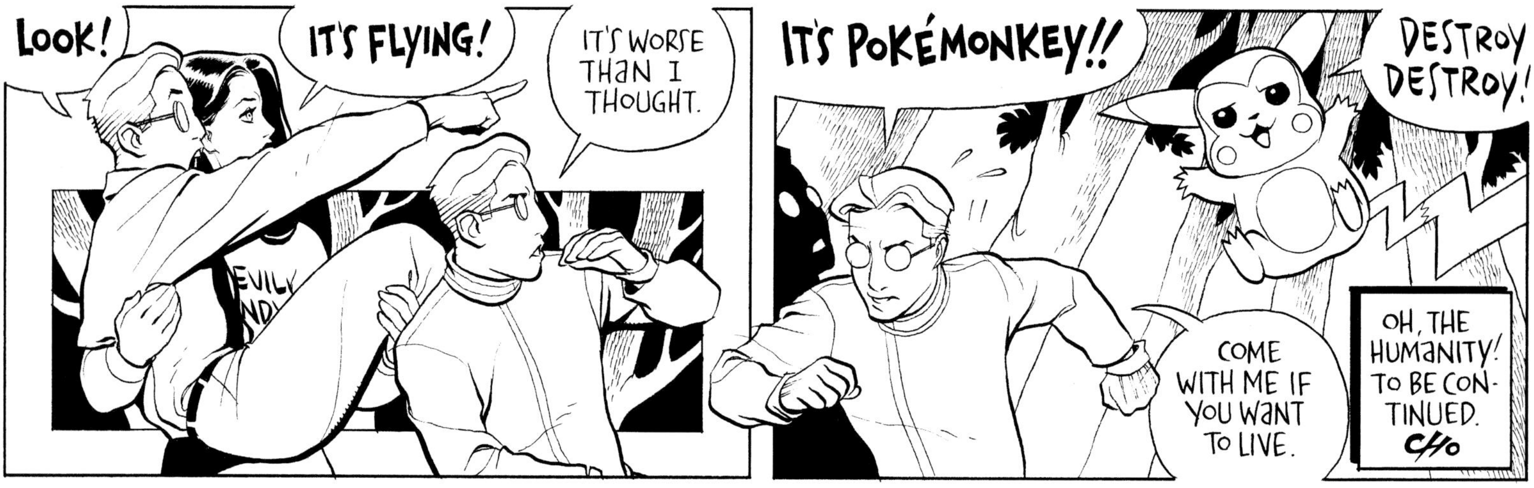
LOOK!
IT'S FLYING!
IT'S WORSE THAN I THOUGHT.
IT'S POKÉMONKEY!!
DESTROY DESTROY!
COME WITH ME IF YOU WANT TO LIVE.
OH, THE HUMANITY! TO BE CONTINUED.
CHO

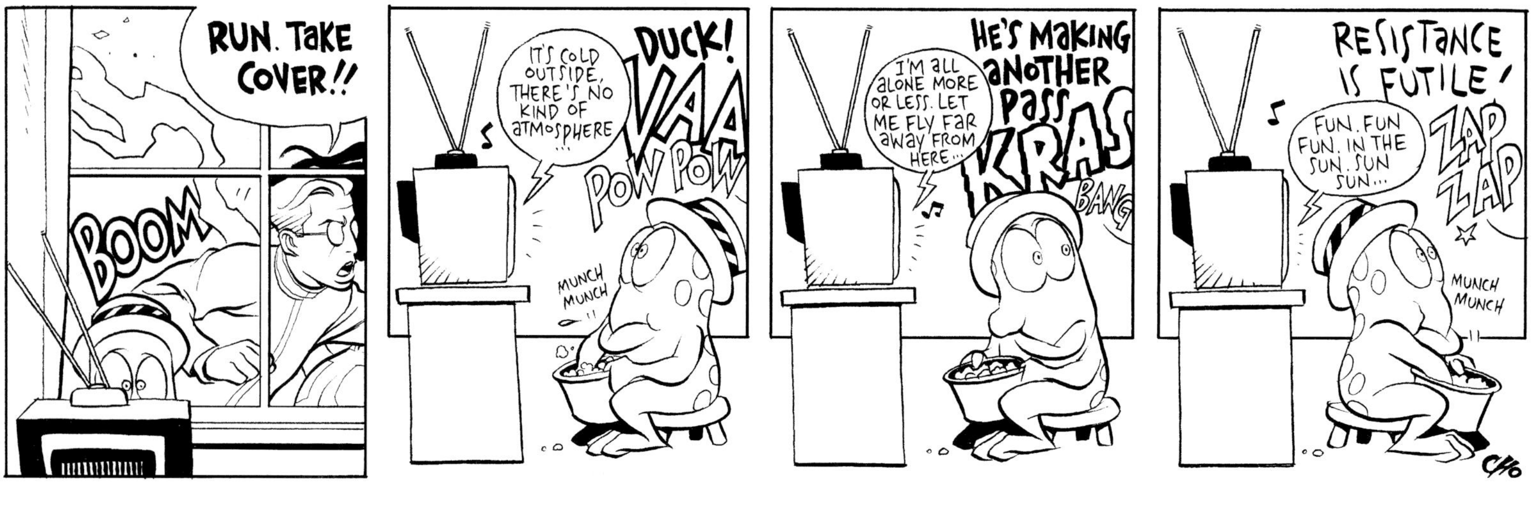
RUN. TAKE COVER!!
BOOM
IT'S COLD OUTSIDE, THERE'S NO KIND OF ATMOSPHERE...
DUCK!
VAA
POW POW
MUNCH MUNCH
HE'S MAKING ANOTHER PASS
I'M ALL ALONE MORE OR LESS. LET ME FLY FAR AWAY FROM HERE...
KRAS
BANG
RESISTANCE IS FUTILE!
FUN. FUN FUN. IN THE SUN. SUN SUN...
ZAP ZAP
MUNCH MUNCH
CHO

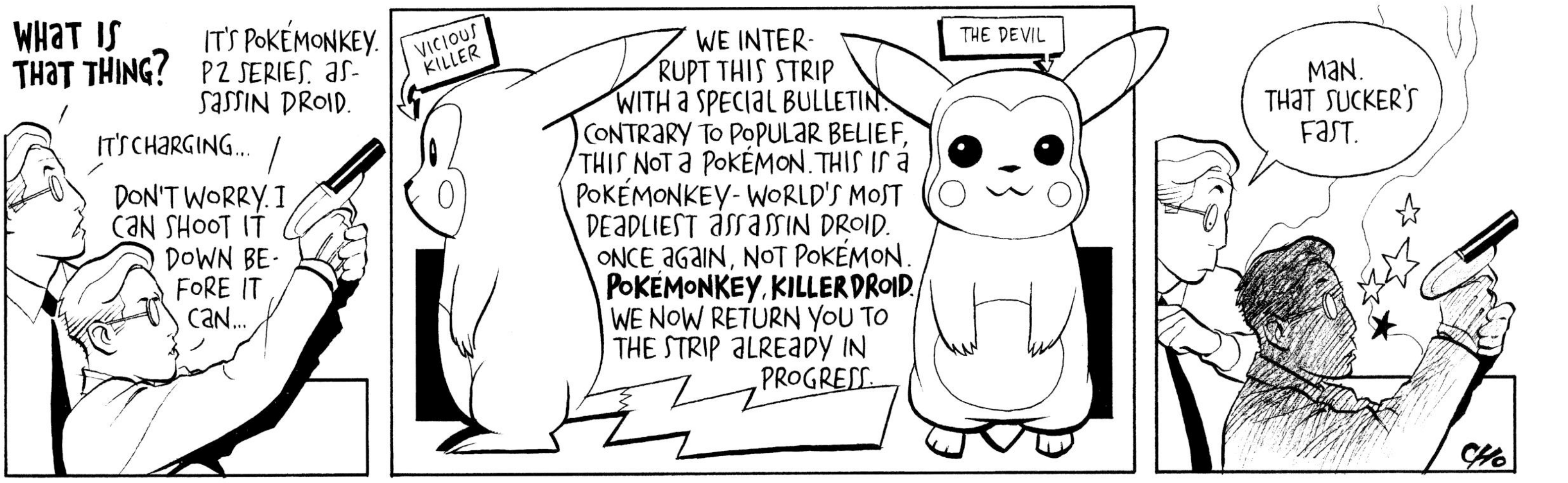
WHAT IS THAT THING?
IT'S POKÉMONKEY. P2 SERIES. AS-SASSIN DROID.
IT'S CHARGING...
DON'T WORRY. I CAN SHOOT IT DOWN BE-FORE IT CAN...
VICIOUS KILLER
WE INTER-RUPT THIS STRIP WITH A SPECIAL BULLETIN. CONTRARY TO POPULAR BELIEF, THIS NOT A POKÉMON. THIS IS A POKÉMONKEY- WORLD'S MOST DEADLIEST ASSASSIN DROID. ONCE AGAIN, NOT POKÉMON. POKÉMONKEY, KILLER DROID. WE NOW RETURN YOU TO THE STRIP ALREADY IN PROGRESS.
THE DEVIL
MAN. THAT SUCKER'S FAST.
CHO

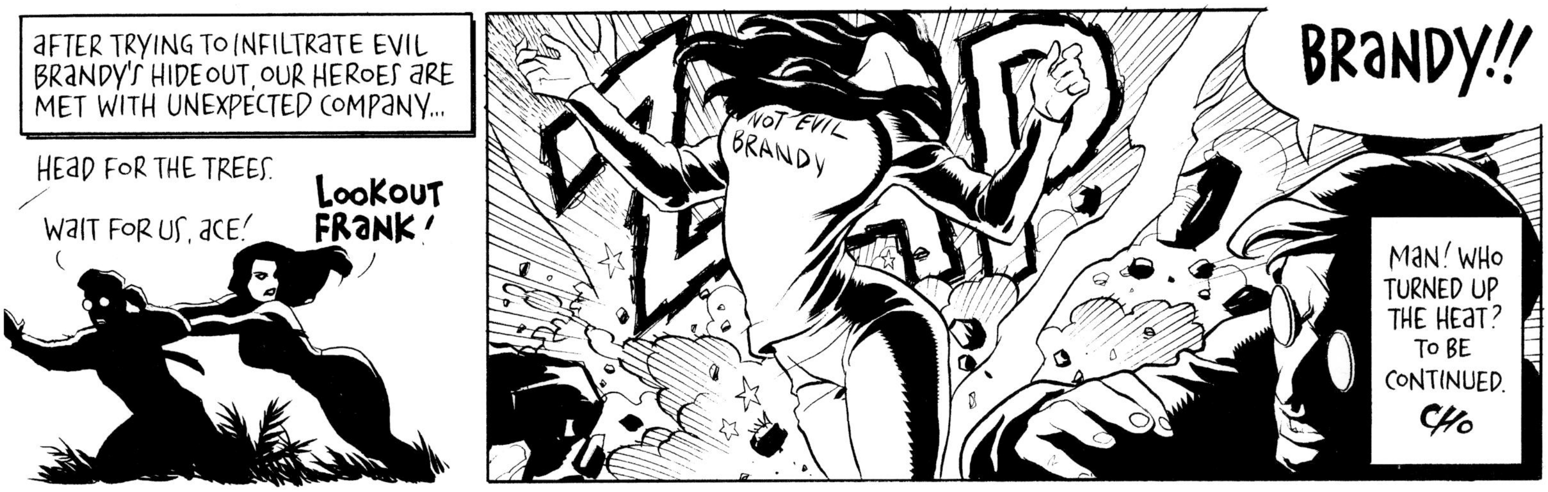
AFTER TRYING TO INFILTRATE EVIL BRANDY'S HIDEOUT, OUR HEROES ARE MET WITH UNEXPECTED COMPANY...
HEAD FOR THE TREES.
WAIT FOR US, ACE!
LOOKOUT FRANK!
NOT EVIL BRANDY
BRANDY!!
MAN! WHO TURNED UP THE HEAT? TO BE CONTINUED.
CHO

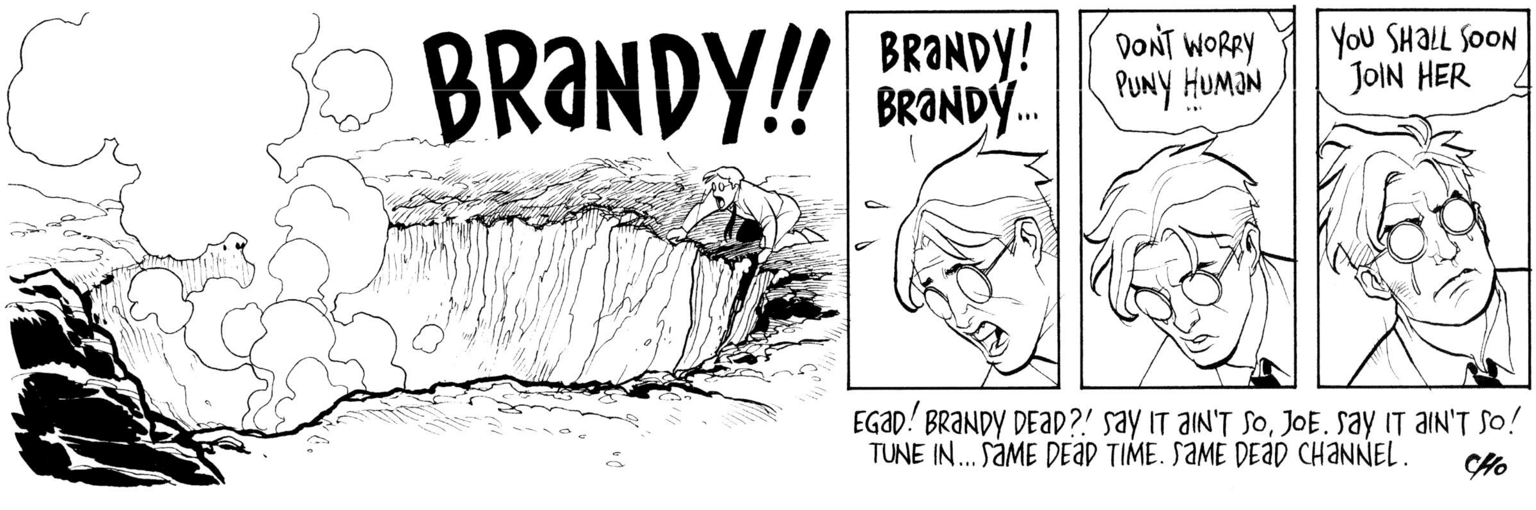
BRANDY!!
BRANDY! BRANDY...
DON'T WORRY PUNY HUMAN
YOU SHALL SOON JOIN HER
EGAD! BRANDY DEAD?! SAY IT AIN'T SO, JOE. SAY IT AIN'T SO!
TUNE IN... SAME DEAD TIME. SAME DEAD CHANNEL.
CHO

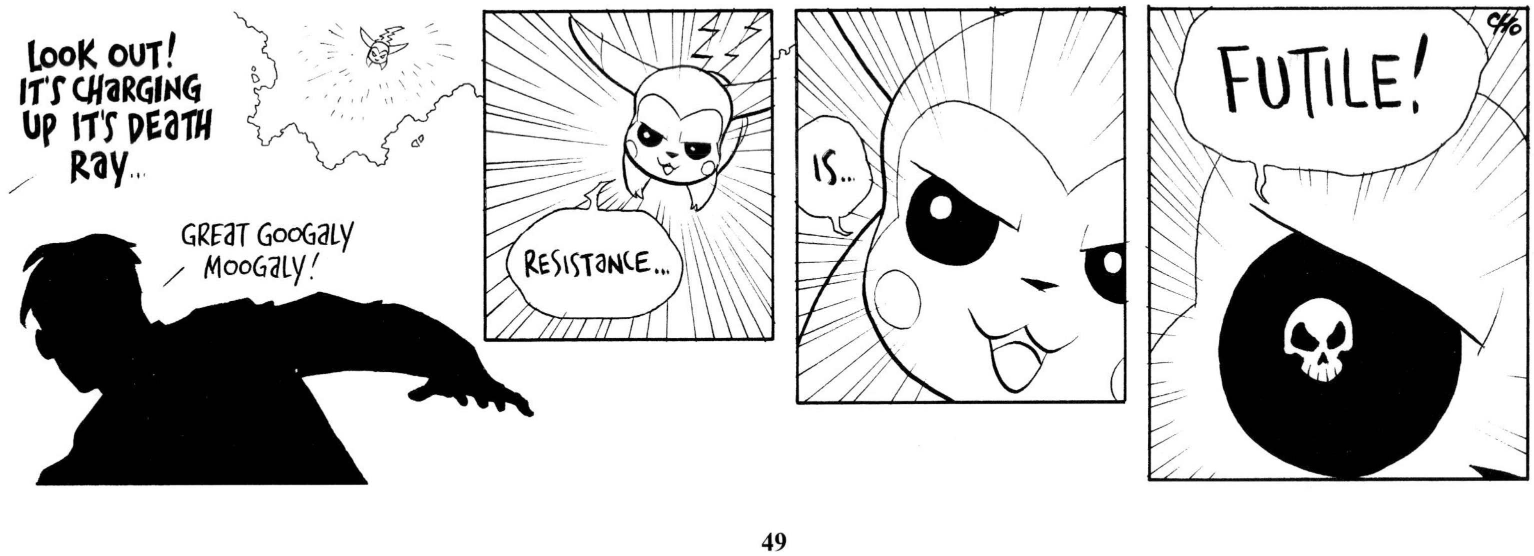
LOOK OUT! IT'S CHARGING UP IT'S DEATH RAY...
GREAT GOOGALY MOOGALY!
RESISTANCE...
IS...
FUTILE!
CHO

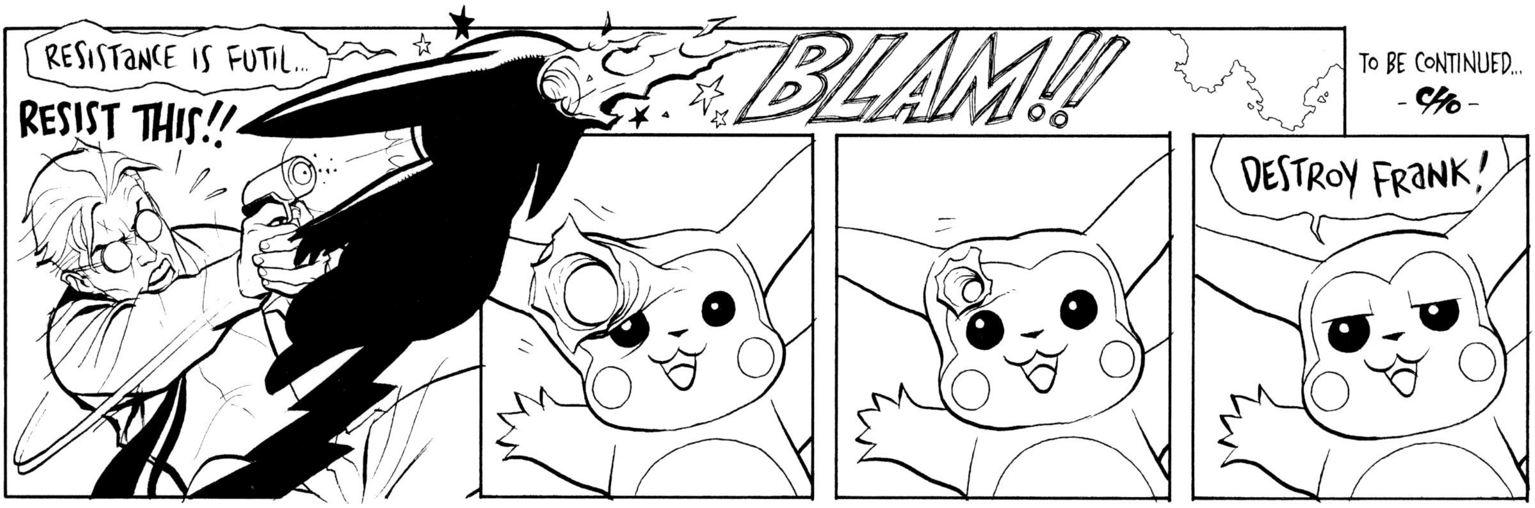
RESISTANCE IS FUTIL...
RESIST THIS!!
BLAM!!!
DESTROY FRANK!
TO BE CONTINUED...
- CHO -

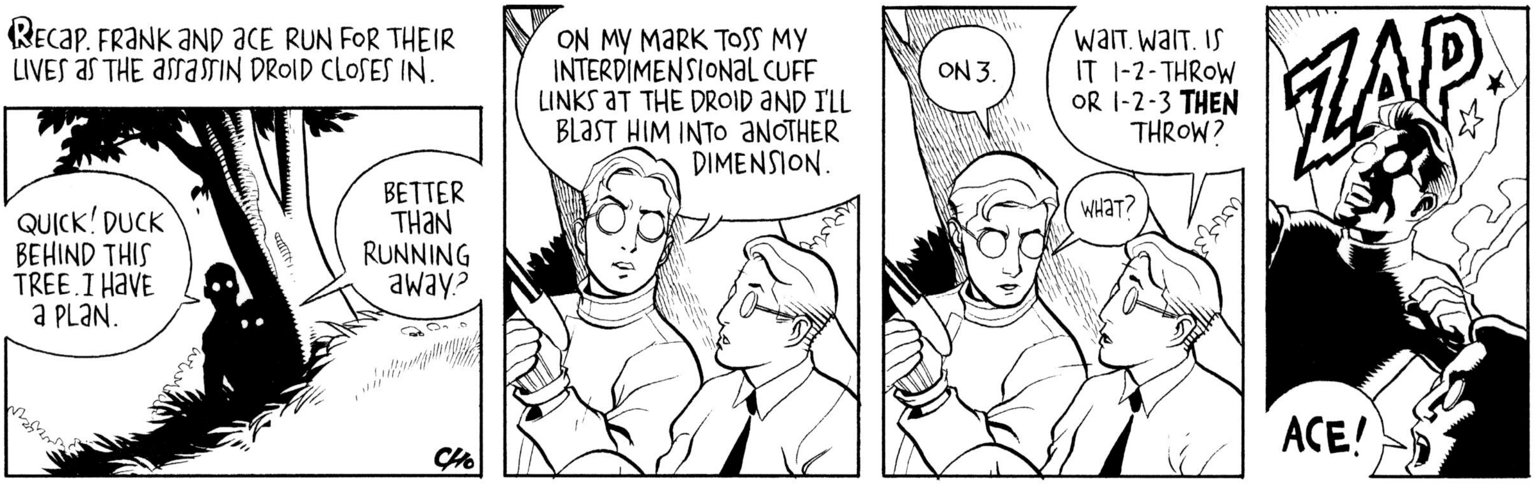
RECAP. FRANK AND ACE RUN FOR THEIR LIVES AS THE ASSASSIN DROID CLOSES IN.
QUICK! DUCK BEHIND THIS TREE. I HAVE A PLAN.
BETTER THAN RUNNING AWAY?
CHO
ON MY MARK TOSS MY INTERDIMENSIONAL CUFF LINKS AT THE DROID AND I'LL BLAST HIM INTO ANOTHER DIMENSION.
ON 3.
WAIT. WAIT. IS IT 1-2-THROW OR 1-2-3 THEN THROW?
WHAT?
ZAP
ACE!

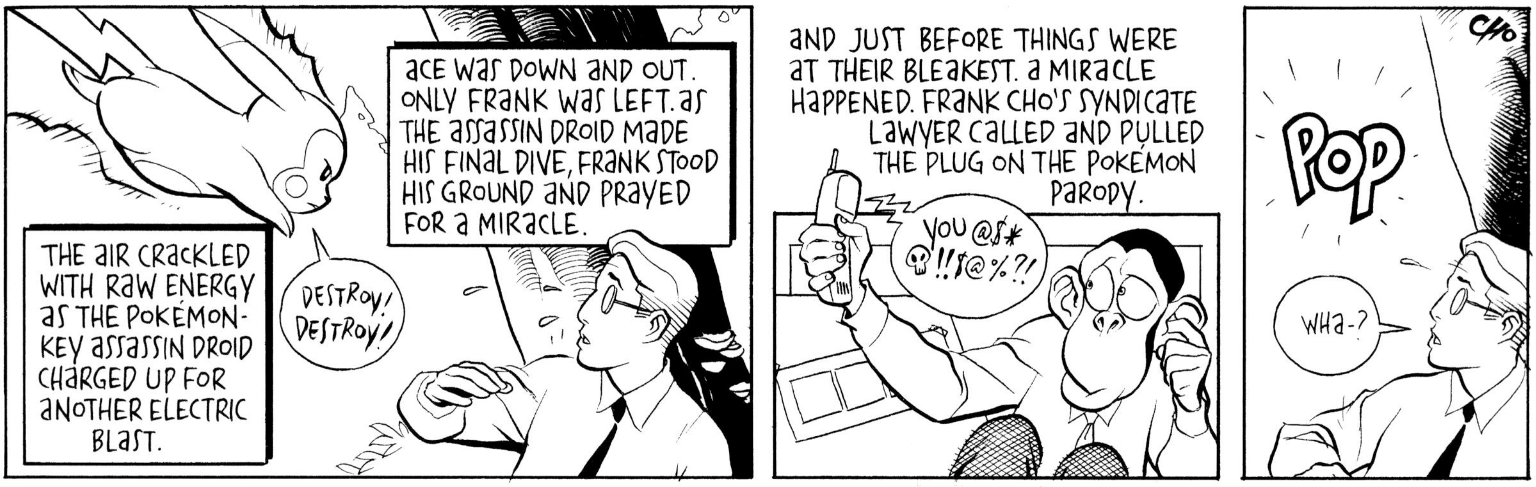
THE AIR CRACKLED WITH RAW ENERGY AS THE POKÉMONKEY ASSASSIN DROID CHARGED UP FOR ANOTHER ELECTRIC BLAST.
ACE WAS DOWN AND OUT. ONLY FRANK WAS LEFT. AS THE ASSASSIN DROID MADE HIS FINAL DIVE, FRANK STOOD HIS GROUND AND PRAYED FOR A MIRACLE.
DESTROY! DESTROY!
AND JUST BEFORE THINGS WERE AT THEIR BLEAKEST. A MIRACLE HAPPENED. FRANK CHO'S SYNDICATE LAWYER CALLED AND PULLED THE PLUG ON THE POKÉMON PARODY.
YOU @$* !!$@%?!
CHO
POP
WHA-?

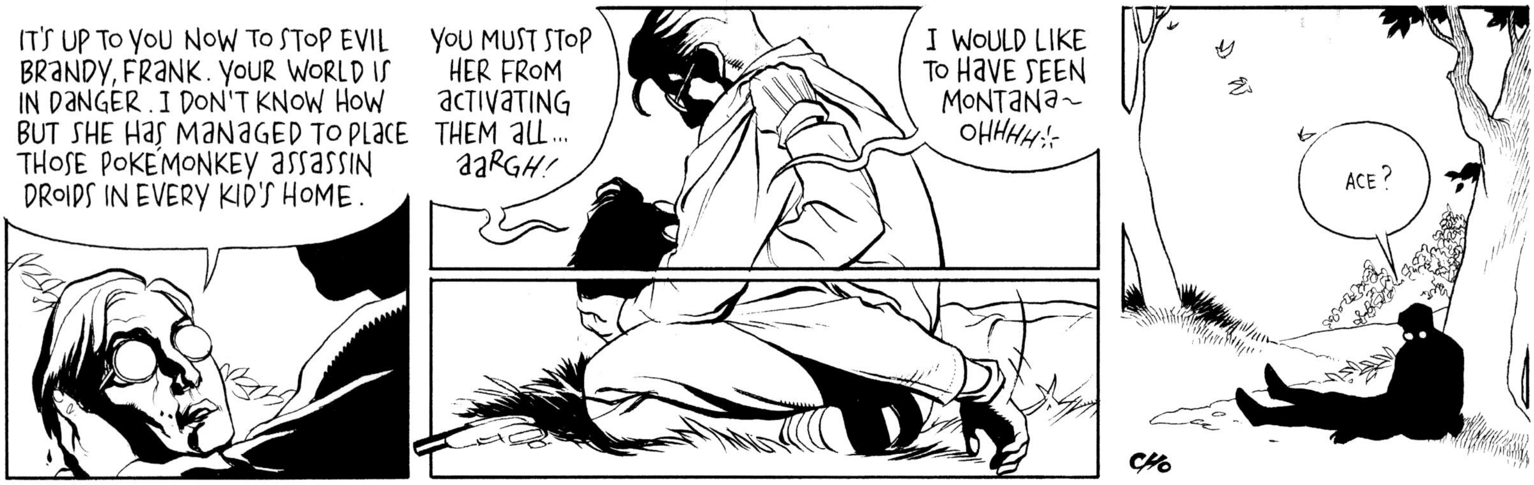
IT'S UP TO YOU NOW TO STOP EVIL BRANDY, FRANK. YOUR WORLD IS IN DANGER. I DON'T KNOW HOW BUT SHE HAS MANAGED TO PLACE THOSE POKÉMONKEY ASSASSIN DROIDS IN EVERY KID'S HOME.
YOU MUST STOP HER FROM ACTIVATING THEM ALL... AARGH!
I WOULD LIKE TO HAVE SEEN MONTANA~ OHHHH!
ACE?
CHO

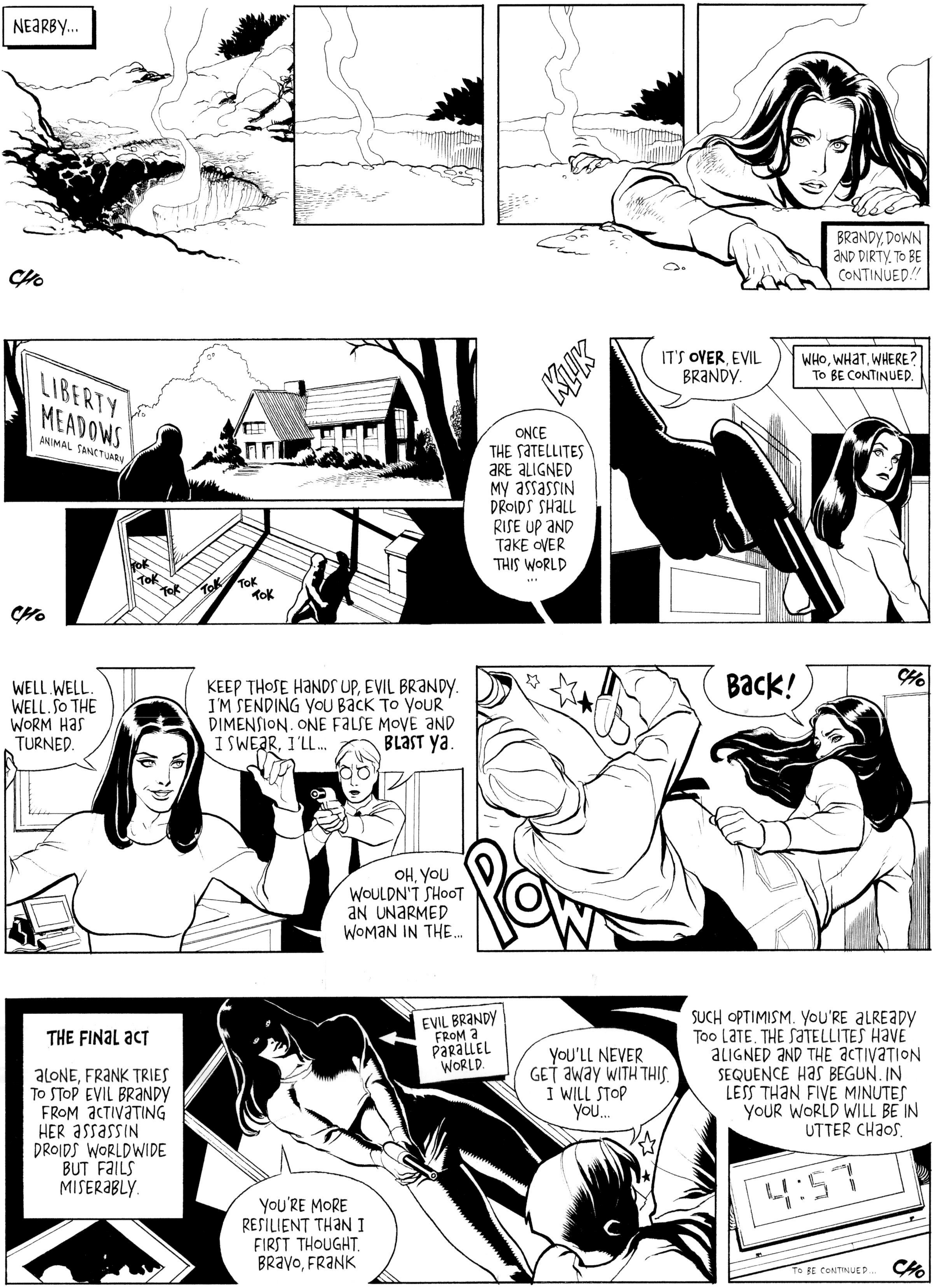
NEARBY...
BRANDY, DOWN AND DIRTY. TO BE CONTINUED!!
LIBERTY MEADOWS ANIMAL SANCTUARY
TOK TOK TOK TOK TOK TOK
KLIK
ONCE THE SATELLITES ARE ALIGNED MY ASSASSIN DROIDS SHALL RISE UP AND TAKE OVER THIS WORLD ...
IT'S OVER, EVIL BRANDY.
WHO, WHAT, WHERE? TO BE CONTINUED.
WELL. WELL. WELL. SO THE WORM HAS TURNED.
KEEP THOSE HANDS UP, EVIL BRANDY. I'M SENDING YOU BACK TO YOUR DIMENSION. ONE FALSE MOVE AND I SWEAR, I'LL... BLAST YA.
OH, YOU WOULDN'T SHOOT AN UNARMED WOMAN IN THE...
BACK!
POW
THE FINAL ACT
ALONE, FRANK TRIES TO STOP EVIL BRANDY FROM ACTIVATING HER ASSASSIN DROIDS WORLDWIDE BUT FAILS MISERABLY.
EVIL BRANDY FROM A PARALLEL WORLD.
YOU'RE MORE RESILIENT THAN I FIRST THOUGHT. BRAVO, FRANK
YOU'LL NEVER GET AWAY WITH THIS. I WILL STOP YOU...
SUCH OPTIMISM. YOU'RE ALREADY TOO LATE. THE SATELLITES HAVE ALIGNED AND THE ACTIVATION SEQUENCE HAS BEGUN. IN LESS THAN FIVE MINUTES YOUR WORLD WILL BE IN UTTER CHAOS.
4:57
TO BE CONTINUED...

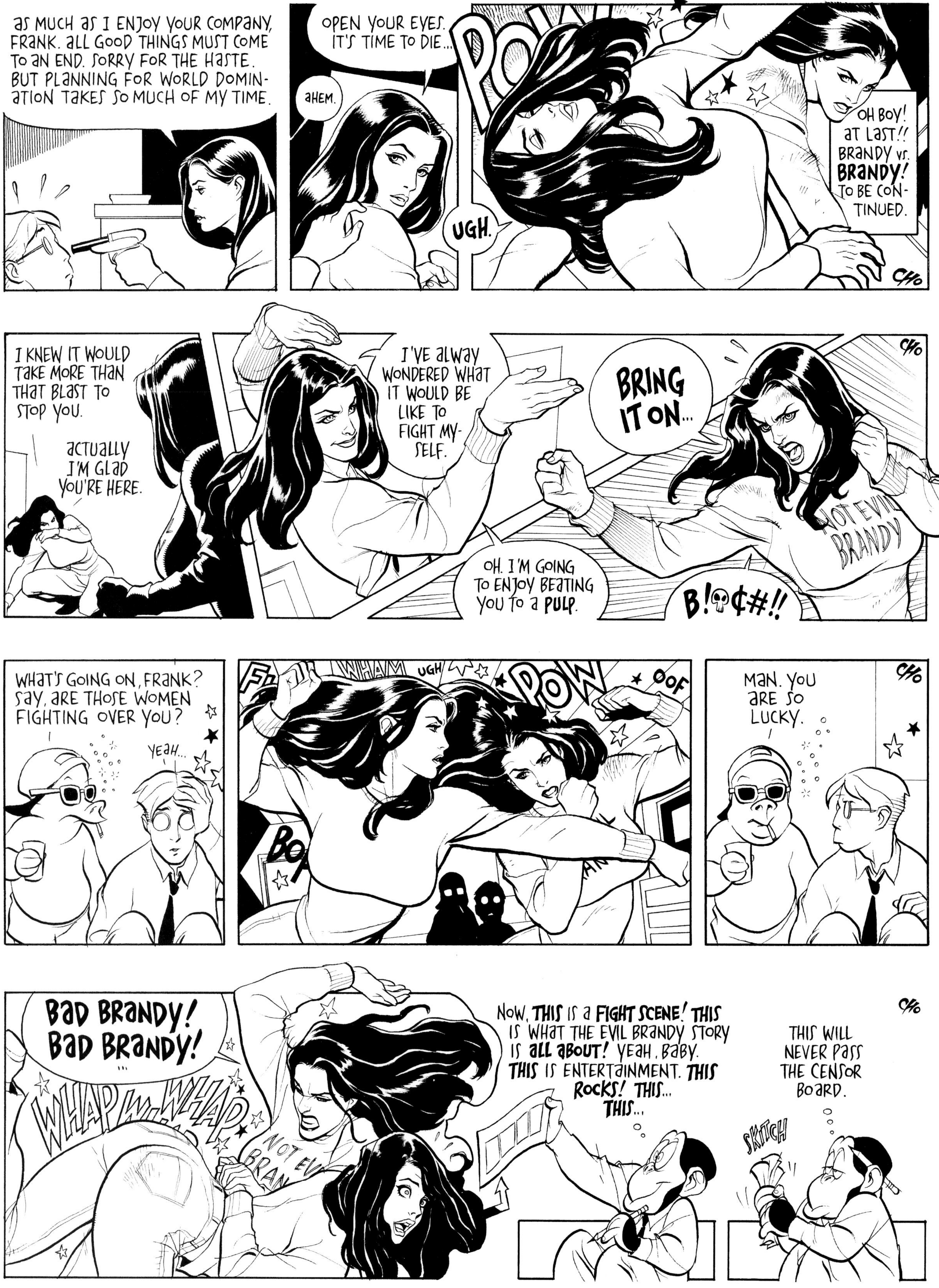
as MUCH as I ENJOY YOUR COMPANY, FRANK. aLL GOOD THINGS MUST COME TO AN END. SORRY FOR THE HASTE. BUT PLANNING FOR WORLD DOMINATION TAKES SO MUCH OF MY TIME.
OPEN YOUR EYES. IT'S TIME TO DIE...
aHEM.
POW
UGH.
OH BOY! aT LAST!! BRANDY vs. BRANDY! TO BE CONTINUED.
CHO
I KNEW IT WOULD TAKE MORE THAN THAT BLAST TO STOP YOU.
actually I'M GLAD YOU'RE HERE.
I'VE alway WONDERED WHAT IT WOULD BE LIKE TO FIGHT MYSELF.
OH. I'M GOING TO ENJOY BEATING YOU TO a PULP.
BRING IT ON...
NOT EVIL BRANDY
B!☠¢#!!
CHO
WHAT'S GOING ON, FRANK? SAY, ARE THOSE WOMEN FIGHTING OVER YOU?
YEAH...
WHAM
UGH
POW
OOF
MAN. YOU ARE SO LUCKY.
CHO
Bad Brandy! Bad Brandy!
...
WHAP W-WHAP
NOT EVIL BRAN
NOW, THIS IS a FIGHT SCENE! THIS IS WHAT THE EVIL BRANDY STORY IS all about! YEAH, BABY. THIS IS ENTERTAINMENT. THIS ROCKS! THIS... THIS...
THIS WILL NEVER Pass THE CENSOR BOARD.
SKRITCH
CHO

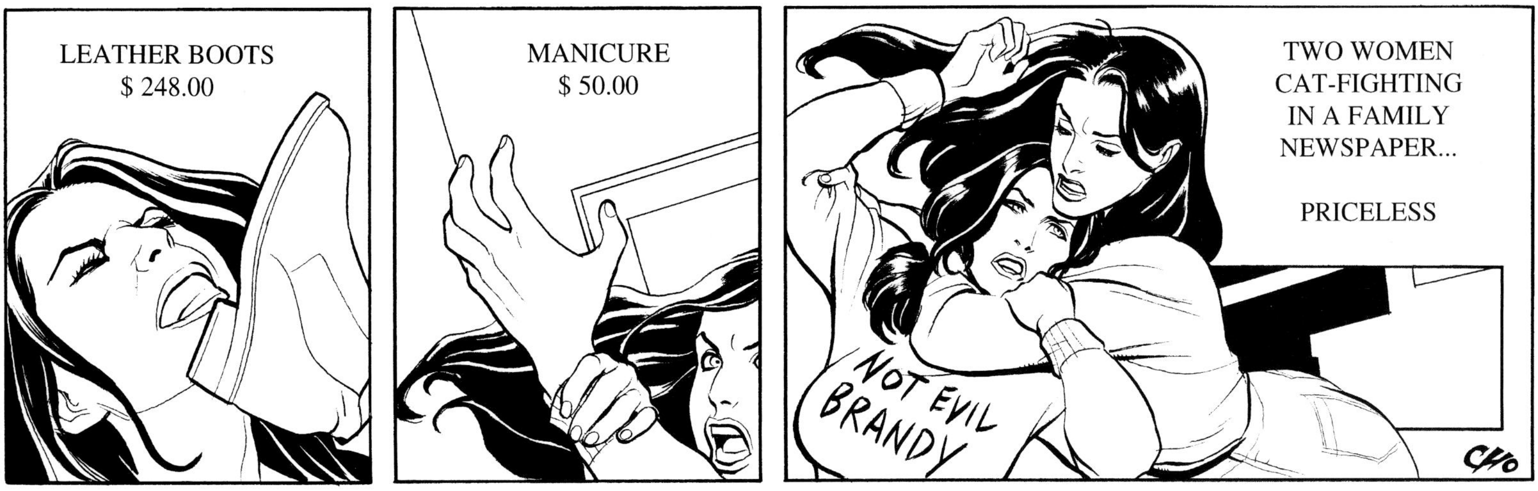
LEATHER BOOTS
$ 248.00
MANICURE
$ 50.00
TWO WOMEN CAT-FIGHTING IN A FAMILY NEWSPAPER...
PRICELESS
NOT EVIL BRANDY
CHO

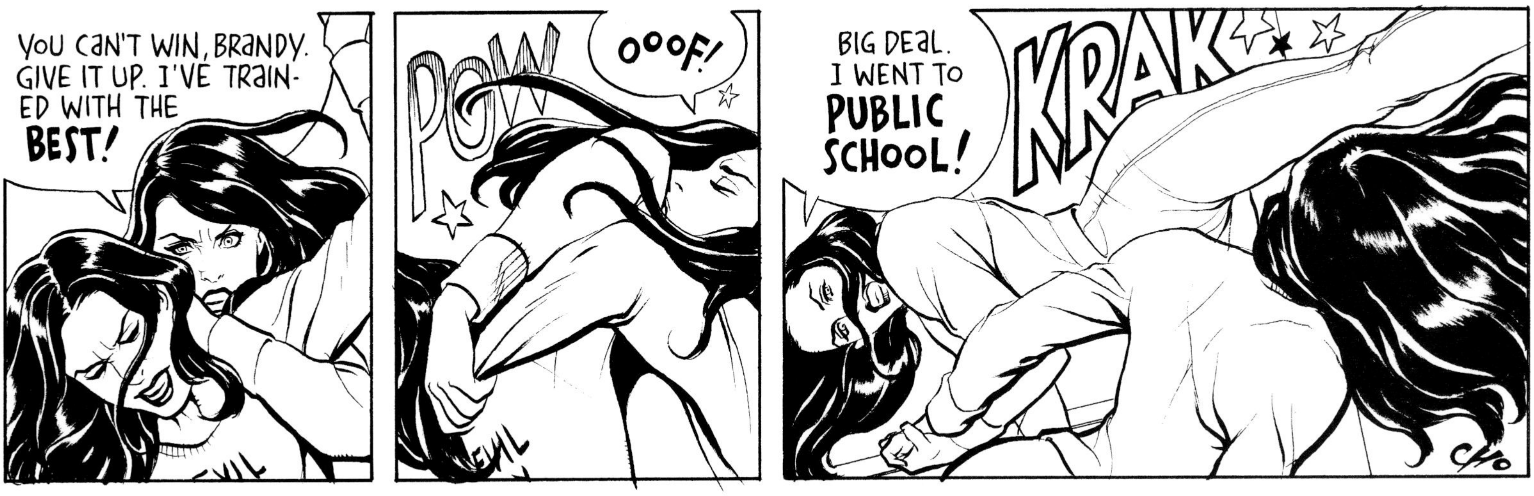
YOU CAN'T WIN, BRANDY. GIVE IT UP. I'VE TRAINED WITH THE BEST!
EVIL
POW
OOOF!
EVIL
BIG DEAL. I WENT TO PUBLIC SCHOOL!
KRAK
CHO

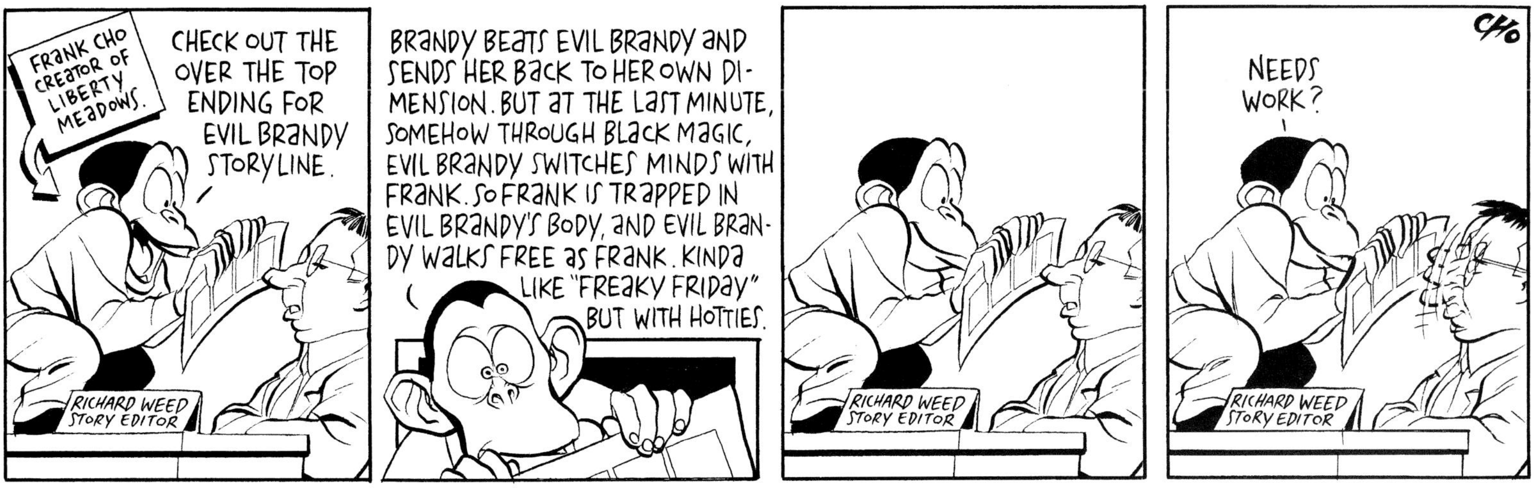
FRANK CHO CREATOR OF LIBERTY MEADOWS.
CHECK OUT THE OVER THE TOP ENDING FOR EVIL BRANDY STORYLINE.
RICHARD WEED STORY EDITOR
BRANDY BEATS EVIL BRANDY AND SENDS HER BACK TO HER OWN DIMENSION. BUT AT THE LAST MINUTE, SOMEHOW THROUGH BLACK MAGIC, EVIL BRANDY SWITCHES MINDS WITH FRANK. SO FRANK IS TRAPPED IN EVIL BRANDY'S BODY, AND EVIL BRANDY WALKS FREE AS FRANK. KINDA LIKE "FREAKY FRIDAY" BUT WITH HOTTIES.
RICHARD WEED STORY EDITOR
CHO
NEEDS WORK?
RICHARD WEED STORY EDITOR

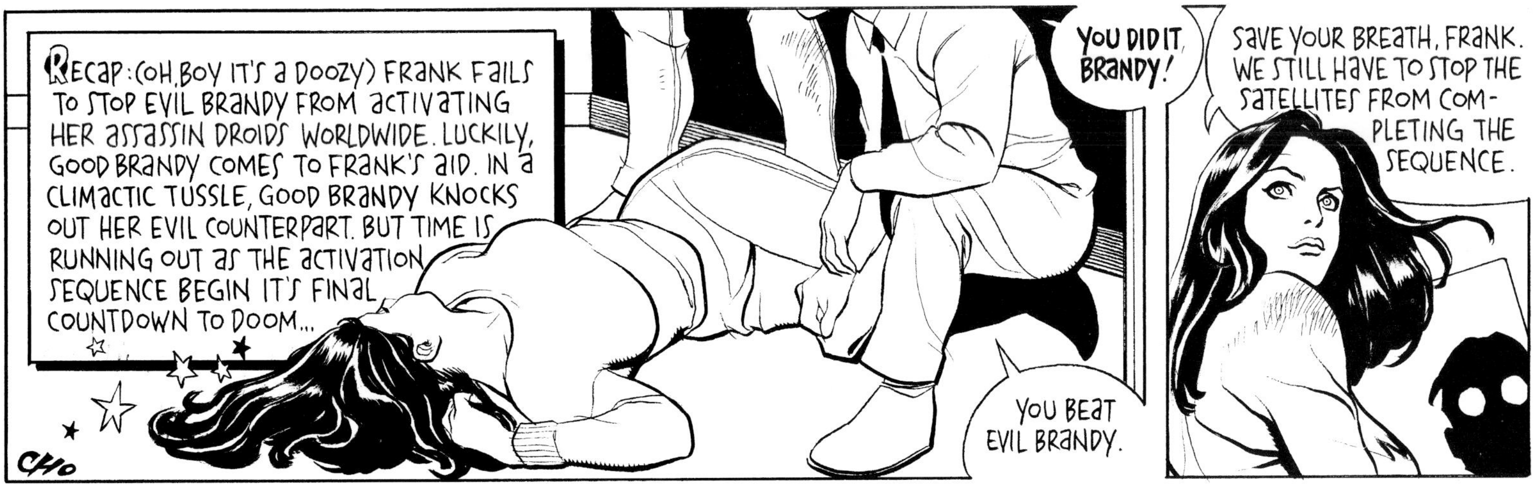
RECAP: (OH, BOY IT'S A DOOZY) FRANK FAILS TO STOP EVIL BRANDY FROM ACTIVATING HER ASSASSIN DROIDS WORLDWIDE. LUCKILY, GOOD BRANDY COMES TO FRANK'S AID. IN A CLIMACTIC TUSSLE, GOOD BRANDY KNOCKS OUT HER EVIL COUNTERPART. BUT TIME IS RUNNING OUT AS THE ACTIVATION SEQUENCE BEGIN IT'S FINAL COUNTDOWN TO DOOM...
YOU DID IT, BRANDY!
YOU BEAT EVIL BRANDY.
CHO
SAVE YOUR BREATH, FRANK. WE STILL HAVE TO STOP THE SATELLITES FROM COMPLETING THE SEQUENCE.

LOOK! WE HAVE LESS THAN 1 MINUTE TO DEFUSE THE TIMER BEFORE UTTER CHAOS IS UNLEASHED!

LOOK FOR THE FUSEBOX AND TRY TO CUT THE JUICE, FRANK.

I'LL TRY TO SMASH IT OPEN AND DISCONNECT THE WIRES.

FRANK! BRANDY! WAIT!

KLIK
0:08

IT STOPPED! BUT WHO...
0:07
0:07

WHO INDEED? TO BE CONTINUED. CHO

ACE! YOU'RE ALIVE! BUT I SAW YOU DIE!

?!

I MADE YOU BELIEVE THAT I DIED. THIS WAS ALL A TEST FOR YOU, FRANK.—

WHAT?

THIS IS ALL MY DOING. MY AGENCY AND I HAD EVERYTHING UNDER CONTROL FROM THE START. I LET EVIL BRANDY ESCAPE OUR DIMENSION AND WRECK HAVOC IN YOUR WORLD. I WANTED TO SEE IF YOU COULD RISE UP TO THE CHALLENGE AND DEFEAT HER. I WANTED TO SEE IF YOU'RE WORTHY ENOUGH TO TAKE MY PLACE AND CONTINUE THE LEGACY IF ANYTHING HAPPENED TO ME.

BACK TO PRISON FOR YOU, EVIL BRANDY

...IF IT WEREN'T FOR THOSE MEDDLING KIDS...

UH...DID I PASS?

NO.

CHO

YOU MEAN TO TELL ME THAT YOU RISKED OUR LIVES AND THE LIVES OF INNOCENT PEOPLE... ALMOST CAUSED A WORLD-WIDE DESTRUCTION **JUST** TO SEE IF FRANK IS MAN ENOUGH TO REPLACE YOU AND JOIN THE RIMMER'S RANGERS?!!

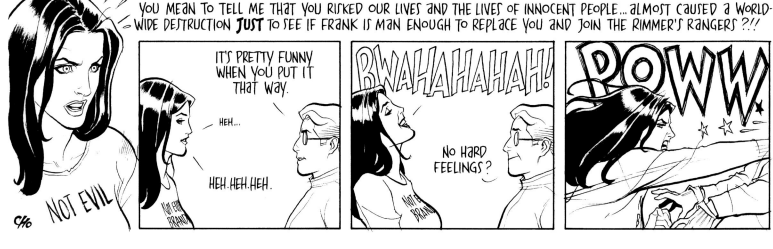
NOT EVIL

CHO

IT'S PRETTY FUNNY WHEN YOU PUT IT THAT WAY.

HEH...

HEH. HEH. HEH.

BWAHAHAHAH!

NO HARD FEELINGS?

POWW

...THUS CONCLUDES THE EVIL BRANDY SAGA. HI, I'M LANCE LOCKJAW. THE EVIL BRANDY STORYLINE WAS BY FAR THE MOST INTRIGUING STORY FRANK CHO HAS PRODUCED THIS YEAR. THE MORE FASCINATING ASPECT OF IT WAS THE GROUND BREAKING ROLES.

BUCKING THE TREND, CHO PUT THE FEMALE CHARACTERS IN THE TRADITIONAL MALE ROLES. IS THIS THE START OF THE END FOR WEAK WOMEN? IS THIS THE DAWNING OF STRONG & SMART FEMALE CHARACTERS IN COMIC STRIPS? HERE WITH A SPECIAL COMMENTARY IS "CATHY."

DO I LOOK FAT? DO I LOOK FAT? I'M FAT, RIGHT? BLEAH!

APOLOGIES TO CATHY GUISEWITE

APPARENTLY NOT.

WHY WON'T YOU RETURN MY CALLS, LANCE? ACK!!

CHO

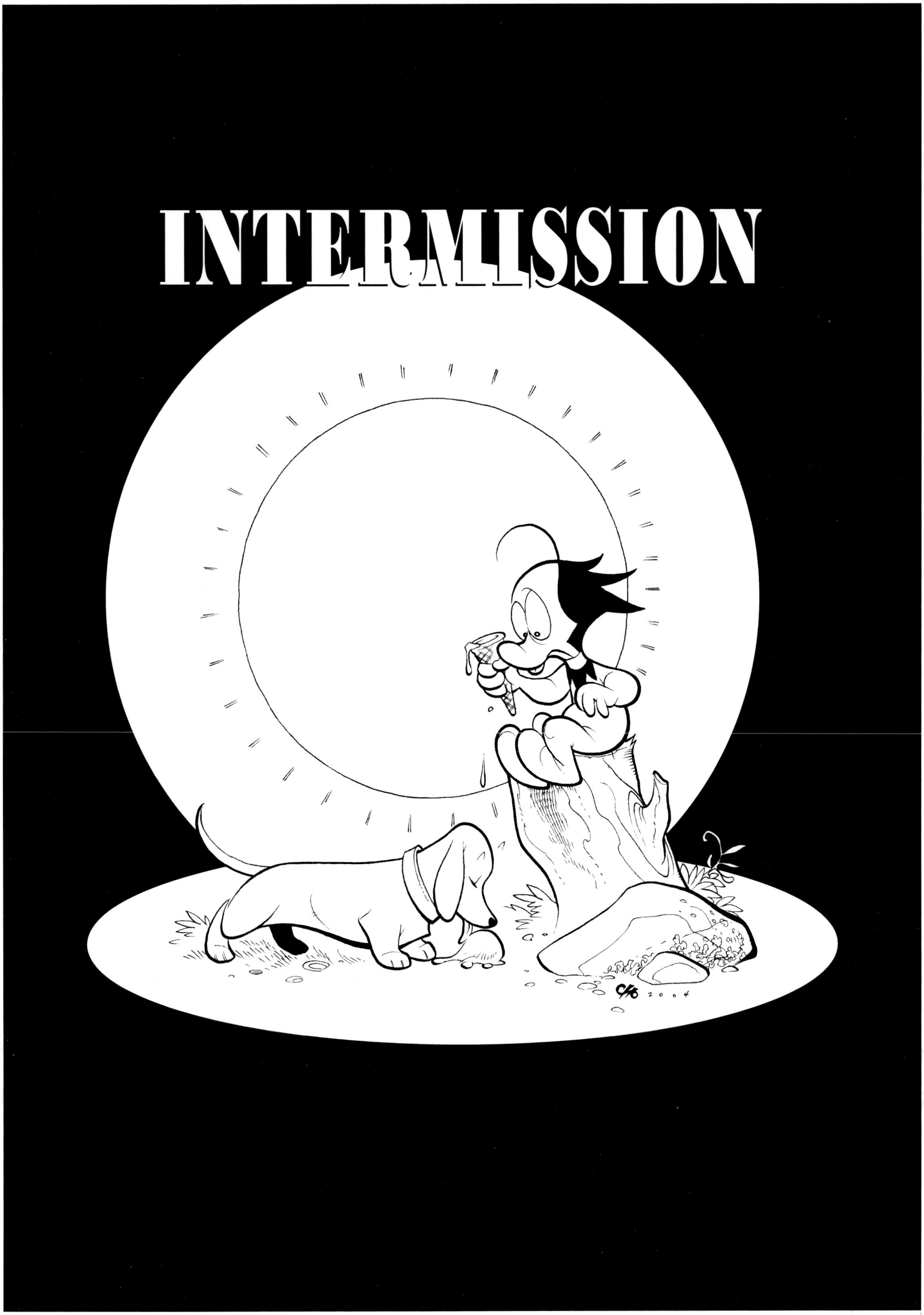
INTERMISSION

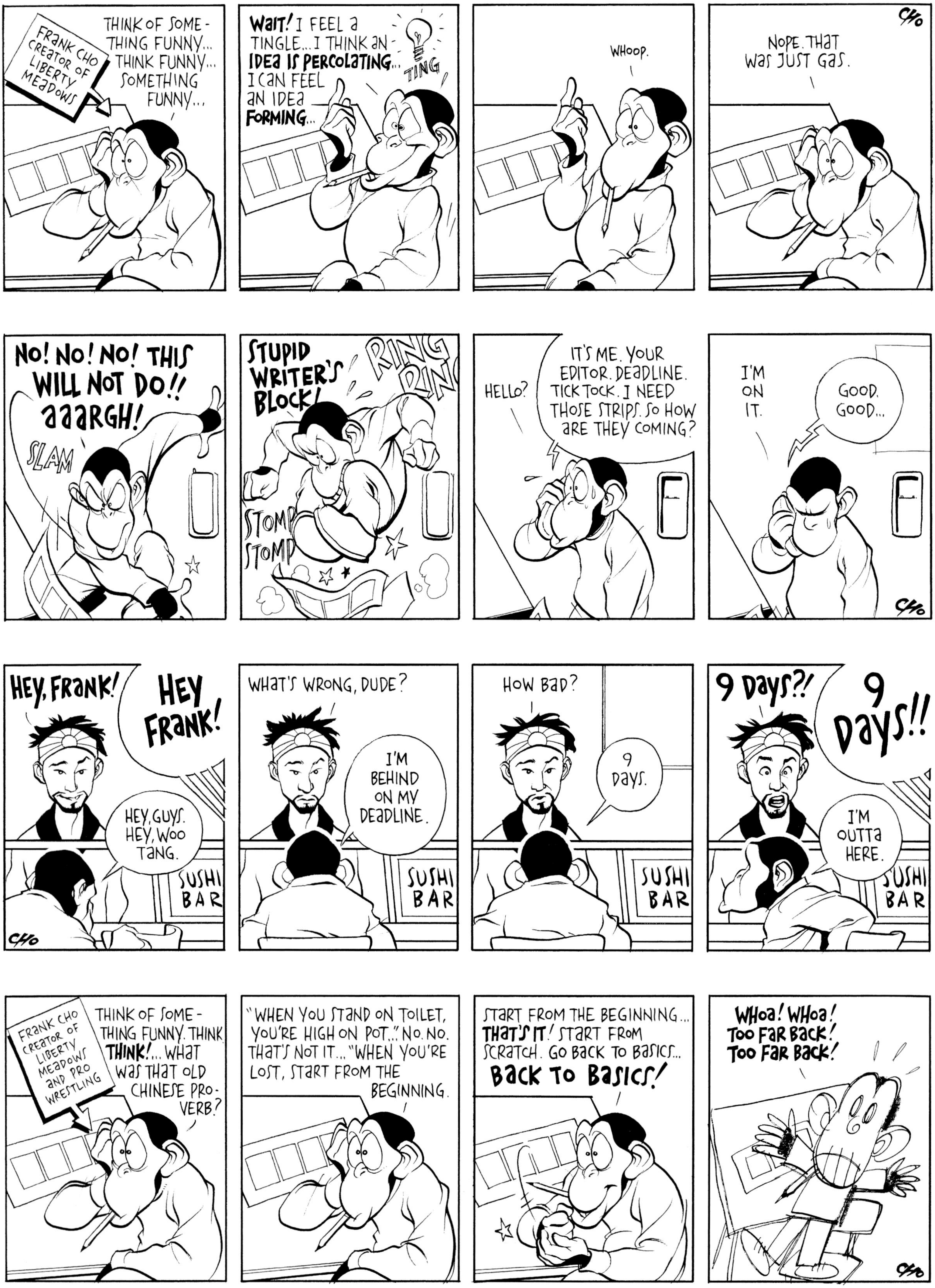
FRANK CHO CREATOR OF LIBERTY MEADOWS
THINK OF SOME-THING FUNNY... THINK FUNNY... SOMETHING FUNNY...
WAIT! I FEEL A TINGLE...I THINK AN IDEA IS PERCOLATING... I CAN FEEL AN IDEA FORMING...
TING
WHOOP.
CHO
NOPE. THAT WAS JUST GAS.
NO! NO! NO! THIS WILL NOT DO!! AAARGH!
SLAM
STUPID WRITER'S BLOCK!
RING RING
STOMP STOMP
HELLO?
IT'S ME. YOUR EDITOR. DEADLINE. TICK TOCK. I NEED THOSE STRIPS. SO HOW ARE THEY COMING?
I'M ON IT.
GOOD. GOOD...
CHO
HEY, FRANK!
HEY FRANK!
HEY, GUYS. HEY, WOO TANG.
SUSHI BAR
CHO
WHAT'S WRONG, DUDE?
I'M BEHIND ON MY DEADLINE.
SUSHI BAR
HOW BAD?
9 DAYS.
SUSHI BAR
9 DAYS?!
9 DAYS!!
I'M OUTTA HERE.
SUSHI BAR
FRANK CHO CREATOR OF LIBERTY MEADOWS AND PRO WRESTLING
THINK OF SOME-THING FUNNY. THINK. THINK!... WHAT WAS THAT OLD CHINESE PRO-VERB?
"WHEN YOU STAND ON TOILET, YOU'RE HIGH ON POT." NO. NO. THAT'S NOT IT... "WHEN YOU'RE LOST, START FROM THE BEGINNING.
START FROM THE BEGINNING... THAT'S IT! START FROM SCRATCH. GO BACK TO BASICS... BACK TO BASICS!
WHOA! WHOA! TOO FAR BACK! TOO FAR BACK!
CHO

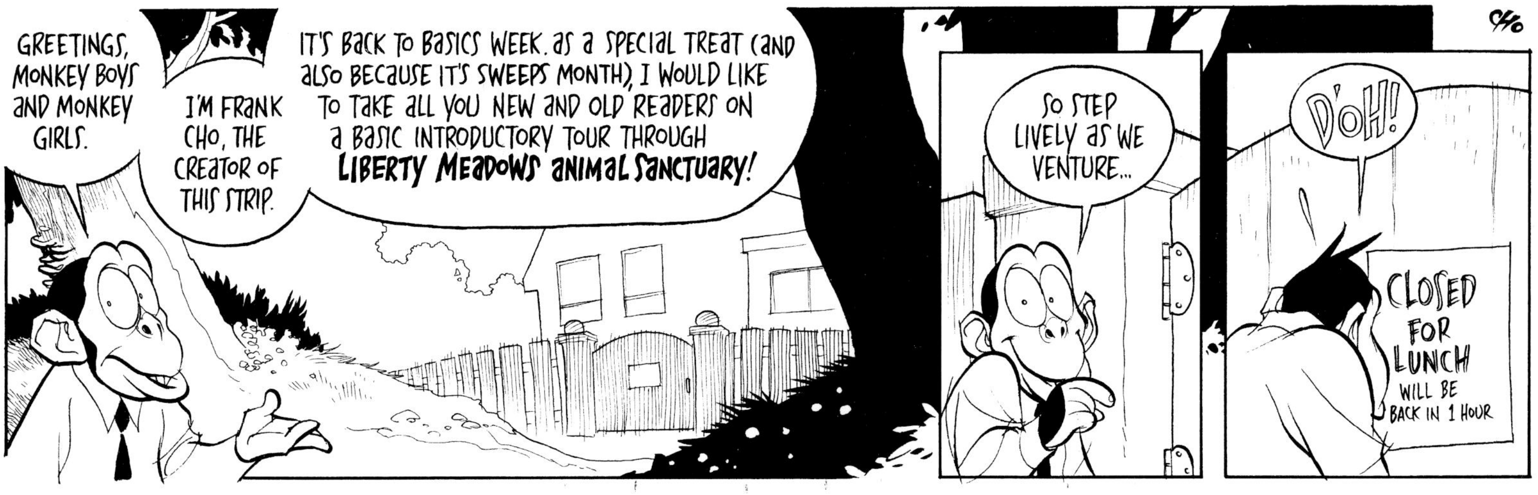
GREETINGS, MONKEY BOYS AND MONKEY GIRLS.
I'M FRANK CHO, THE CREATOR OF THIS STRIP.
IT'S BACK TO BASICS WEEK. AS A SPECIAL TREAT (AND ALSO BECAUSE IT'S SWEEPS MONTH), I WOULD LIKE TO TAKE ALL YOU NEW AND OLD READERS ON A BASIC INTRODUCTORY TOUR THROUGH **LIBERTY MEADOWS ANIMAL SANCTUARY!**
SO STEP LIVELY AS WE VENTURE...
D'OH!
CLOSED FOR LUNCH
WILL BE BACK IN 1 HOUR

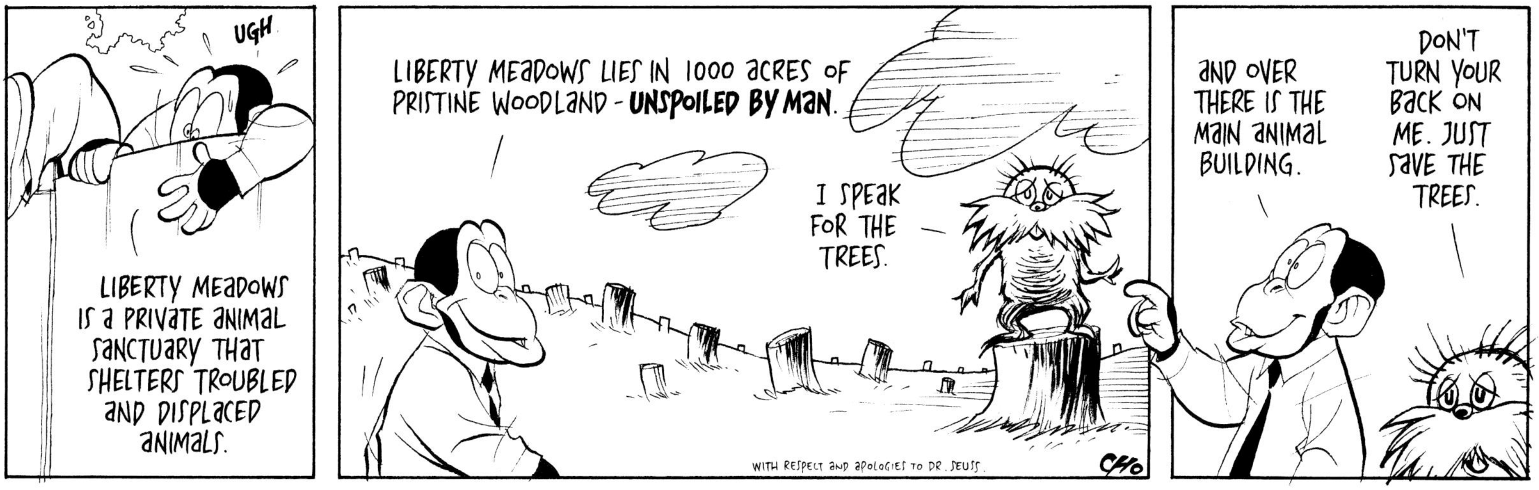
UGH
LIBERTY MEADOWS IS A PRIVATE ANIMAL SANCTUARY THAT SHELTERS TROUBLED AND DISPLACED ANIMALS.
LIBERTY MEADOWS LIES IN 1000 ACRES OF PRISTINE WOODLAND - **UNSPOILED BY MAN.**
I SPEAK FOR THE TREES.
WITH RESPECT AND APOLOGIES TO DR. SEUSS.
AND OVER THERE IS THE MAIN ANIMAL BUILDING.
DON'T TURN YOUR BACK ON ME. JUST SAVE THE TREES.

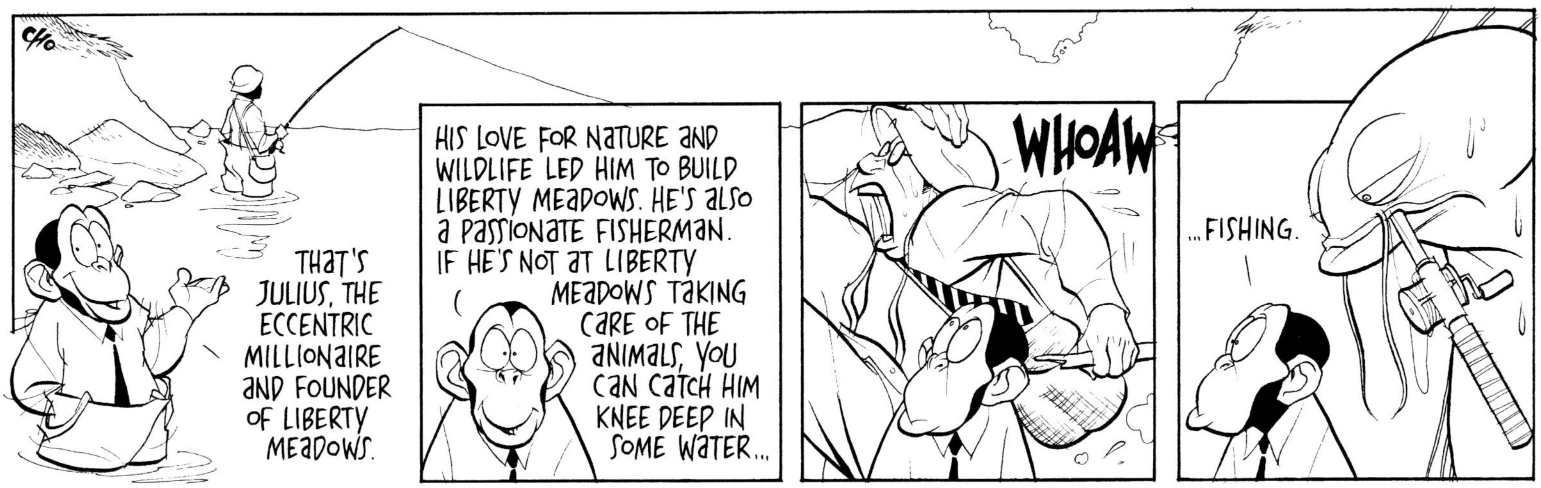
THAT'S JULIUS, THE ECCENTRIC MILLIONAIRE AND FOUNDER OF LIBERTY MEADOWS.
HIS LOVE FOR NATURE AND WILDLIFE LED HIM TO BUILD LIBERTY MEADOWS. HE'S ALSO A PASSIONATE FISHERMAN. IF HE'S NOT AT LIBERTY MEADOWS TAKING CARE OF THE ANIMALS, YOU CAN CATCH HIM KNEE DEEP IN SOME WATER...
WHOAW
...FISHING.

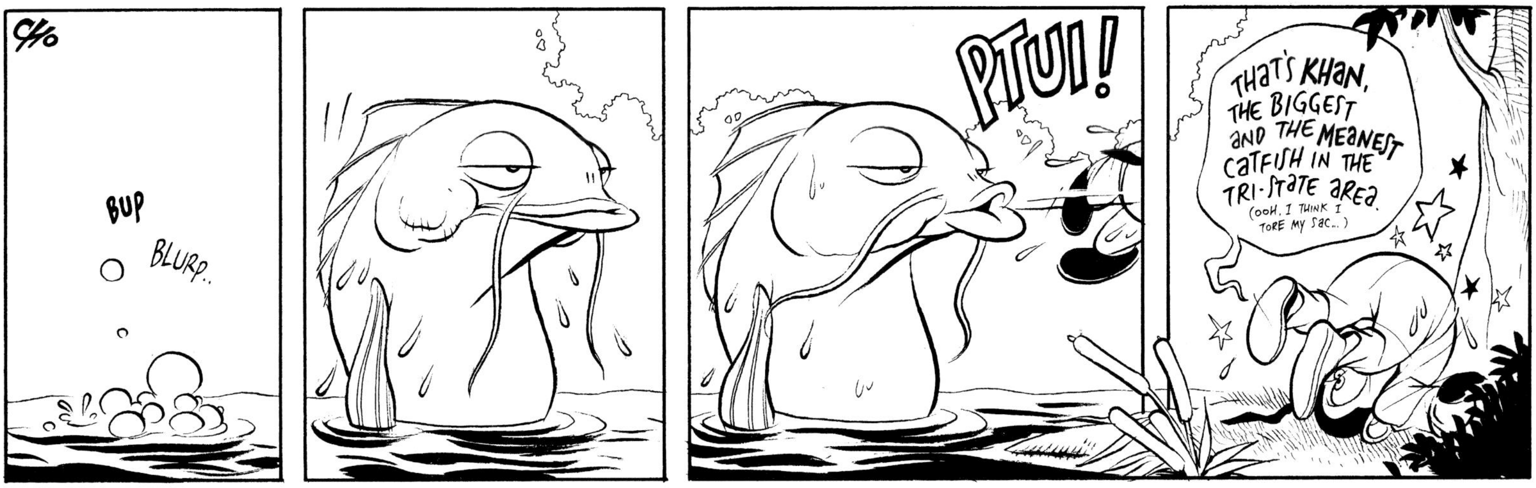
BUP
BLURP..
PTUI!
THAT'S **KHAN,** THE BIGGEST AND THE **MEANEST** CATFISH IN THE TRI-STATE AREA.
(OOH, I THINK I TORE MY SAC...)

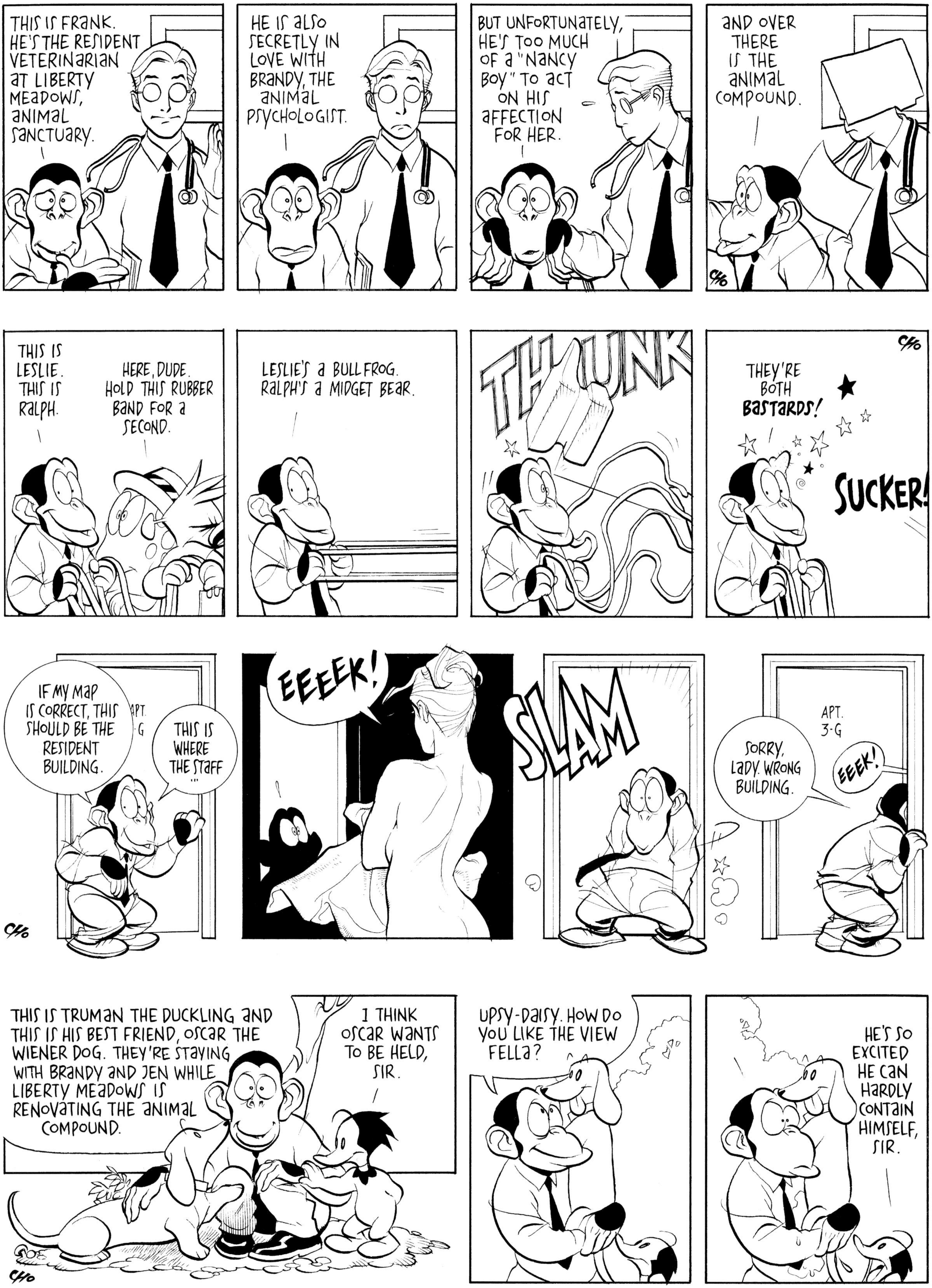
THIS IS FRANK. HE'S THE RESIDENT VETERINARIAN AT LIBERTY MEADOWS, ANIMAL SANCTUARY.
HE IS ALSO SECRETLY IN LOVE WITH BRANDY, THE ANIMAL PSYCHOLOGIST.
BUT UNFORTUNATELY, HE'S TOO MUCH OF A "NANCY BOY" TO ACT ON HIS AFFECTION FOR HER.
AND OVER THERE IS THE ANIMAL COMPOUND.
CHO
THIS IS LESLIE. THIS IS RALPH.
HERE, DUDE. HOLD THIS RUBBER BAND FOR A SECOND.
LESLIE'S A BULLFROG. RALPH'S A MIDGET BEAR.
THUNK
CHO
THEY'RE BOTH **BASTARDS!**
SUCKER!
IF MY MAP IS CORRECT, THIS SHOULD BE THE RESIDENT BUILDING.
THIS IS WHERE THE STAFF ...
CHO
EEEEK!
SLAM
APT. 3-G
SORRY, LADY. WRONG BUILDING.
EEEK!
THIS IS TRUMAN THE DUCKLING AND THIS IS HIS BEST FRIEND, OSCAR THE WIENER DOG. THEY'RE STAYING WITH BRANDY AND JEN WHILE LIBERTY MEADOWS IS RENOVATING THE ANIMAL COMPOUND.
I THINK OSCAR WANTS TO BE HELD, SIR.
CHO
UPSY-DAISY. HOW DO YOU LIKE THE VIEW FELLA?
HE'S SO EXCITED HE CAN HARDLY CONTAIN HIMSELF, SIR.

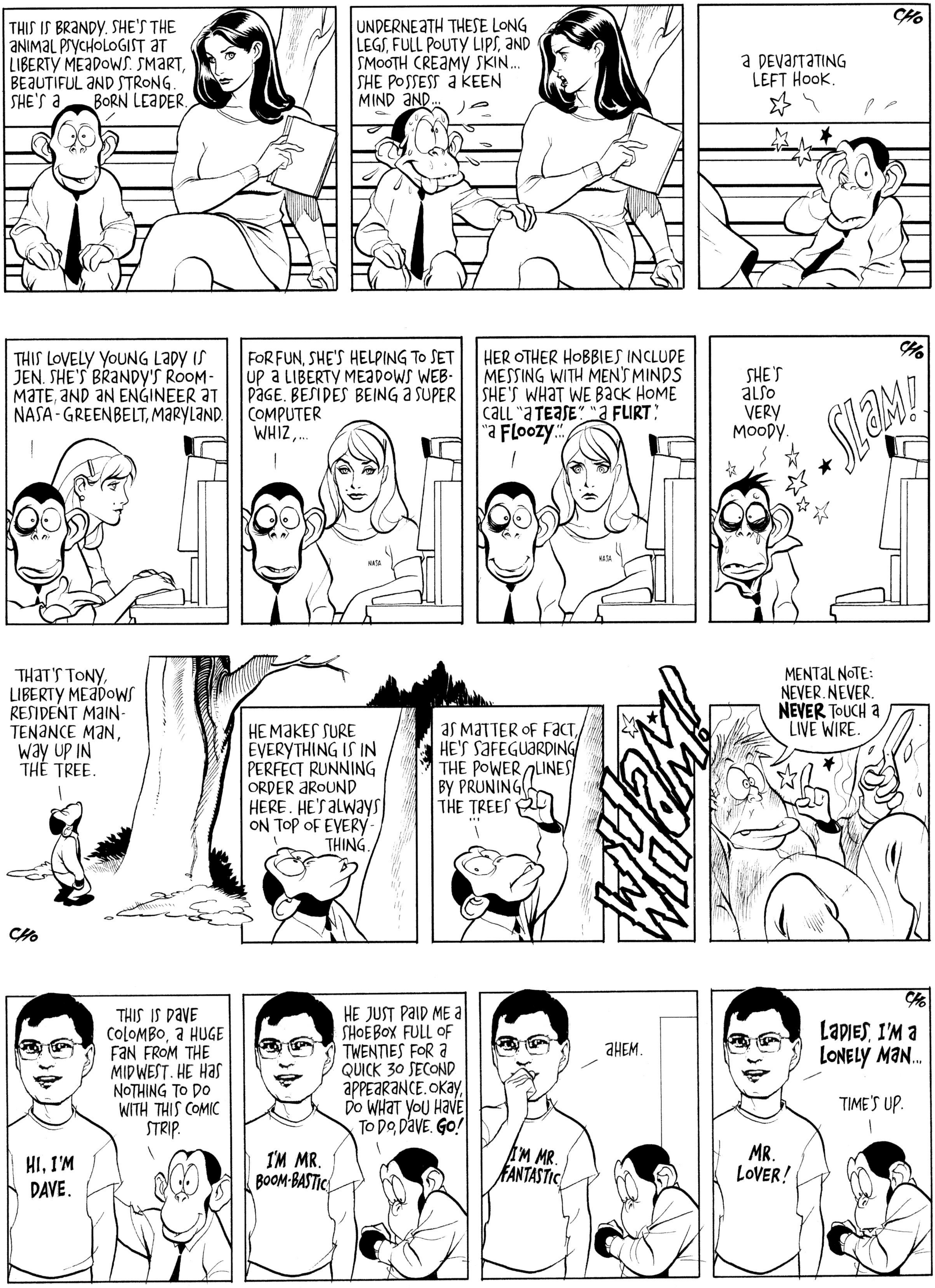

CHO
THIS IS BRANDY. SHE'S THE ANIMAL PSYCHOLOGIST AT LIBERTY MEADOWS. SMART, BEAUTIFUL AND STRONG. SHE'S A BORN LEADER.
UNDERNEATH THESE LONG LEGS, FULL POUTY LIPS, AND SMOOTH CREAMY SKIN... SHE POSSESS A KEEN MIND AND...
A DEVASTATING LEFT HOOK.
CHO
THIS LOVELY YOUNG LADY IS JEN. SHE'S BRANDY'S ROOM-MATE, AND AN ENGINEER AT NASA - GREENBELT, MARYLAND.
FOR FUN, SHE'S HELPING TO SET UP A LIBERTY MEADOWS WEB-PAGE. BESIDES BEING A SUPER COMPUTER WHIZ,...
NASA
HER OTHER HOBBIES INCLUDE MESSING WITH MEN'S MINDS SHE'S WHAT WE BACK HOME CALL "A **TEASE**," "A **FLIRT**," "A **FLOOZY**."...
NASA
SHE'S ALSO VERY MOODY.
SLAM!
THAT'S TONY, LIBERTY MEADOWS RESIDENT MAIN-TENANCE MAN, WAY UP IN THE TREE.
HE MAKES SURE EVERYTHING IS IN PERFECT RUNNING ORDER AROUND HERE. HE'S ALWAYS ON TOP OF EVERY-THING.
AS MATTER OF FACT, HE'S SAFEGUARDING THE POWER LINES BY PRUNING THE TREES ...
WHUMP!
MENTAL NOTE: NEVER. NEVER. **NEVER** TOUCH A LIVE WIRE.
CHO
THIS IS DAVE COLOMBO, A HUGE FAN FROM THE MIDWEST. HE HAS NOTHING TO DO WITH THIS COMIC STRIP.
HI, I'M DAVE.
HE JUST PAID ME A SHOEBOX FULL OF TWENTIES FOR A QUICK 30 SECOND APPEARANCE. OKAY, DO WHAT YOU HAVE TO DO, DAVE. **GO!**
I'M MR. BOOM-BASTIC
AHEM.
I'M MR. FANTASTIC
LADIES, I'M A LONELY MAN...
MR. LOVER!
TIME'S UP.

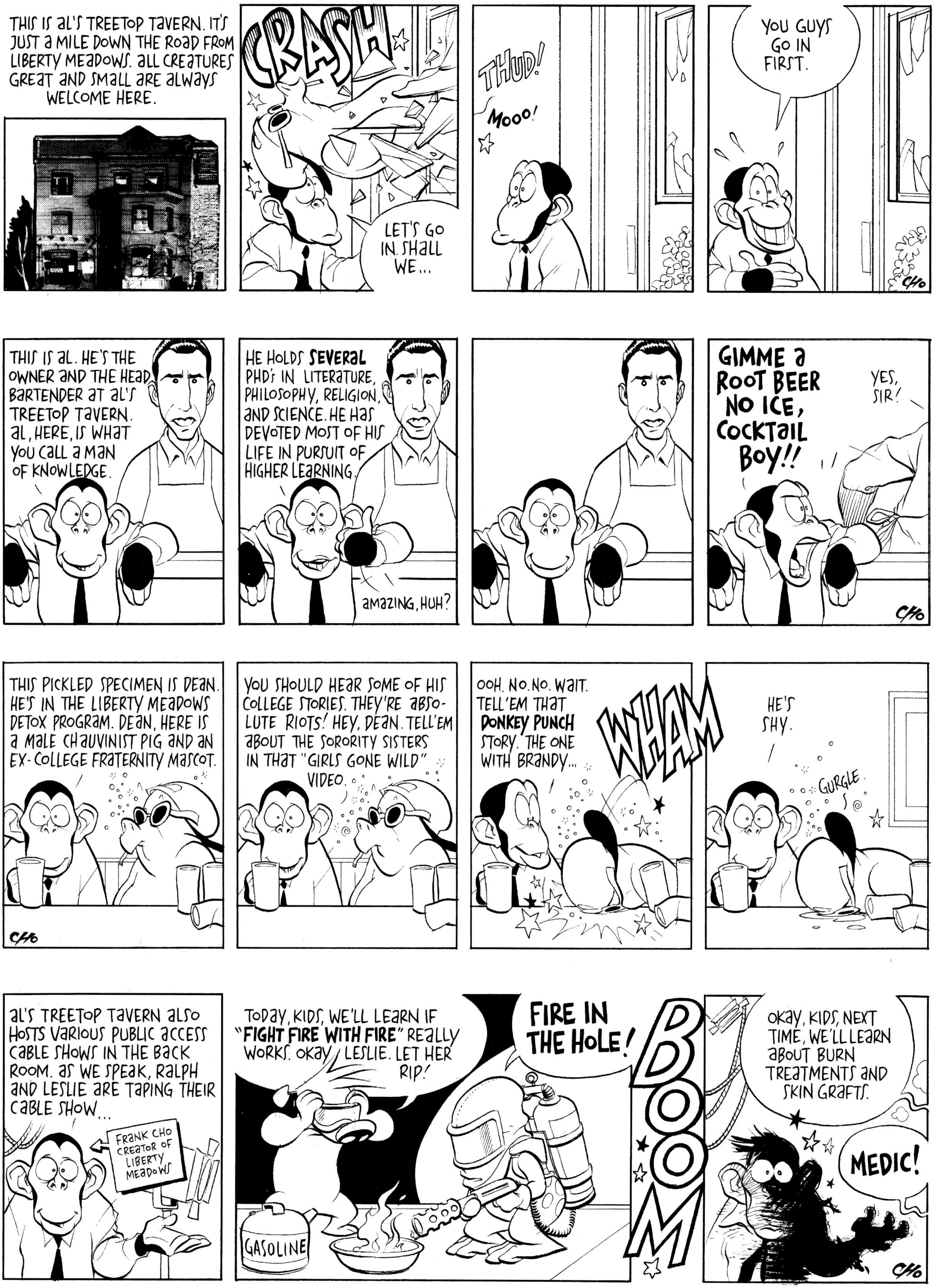

THIS IS AL'S TREETOP TAVERN. IT'S JUST A MILE DOWN THE ROAD FROM LIBERTY MEADOWS. ALL CREATURES GREAT AND SMALL ARE ALWAYS WELCOME HERE.
CRASH
LET'S GO IN. SHALL WE...
THUD!
MOOO!
YOU GUYS GO IN FIRST.
CHO
THIS IS AL. HE'S THE OWNER AND THE HEAD BARTENDER AT AL'S TREETOP TAVERN. AL, HERE, IS WHAT YOU CALL A MAN OF KNOWLEDGE.
HE HOLDS SEVERAL PHD'S IN LITERATURE, PHILOSOPHY, RELIGION, AND SCIENCE. HE HAS DEVOTED MOST OF HIS LIFE IN PURSUIT OF HIGHER LEARNING.
AMAZING, HUH?
GIMME A ROOT BEER NO ICE, COCKTAIL BOY!!
YES, SIR!
CHO
THIS PICKLED SPECIMEN IS DEAN. HE'S IN THE LIBERTY MEADOWS DETOX PROGRAM. DEAN, HERE IS A MALE CHAUVINIST PIG AND AN EX-COLLEGE FRATERNITY MASCOT.
CHO
YOU SHOULD HEAR SOME OF HIS COLLEGE STORIES. THEY'RE ABSOLUTE RIOTS! HEY, DEAN. TELL'EM ABOUT THE SORORITY SISTERS IN THAT "GIRLS GONE WILD" VIDEO.
OOH. NO. NO. WAIT. TELL'EM THAT DONKEY PUNCH STORY. THE ONE WITH BRANDY...
WHAM
HE'S SHY.
GURGLE
AL'S TREETOP TAVERN ALSO HOSTS VARIOUS PUBLIC ACCESS CABLE SHOWS IN THE BACK ROOM. AS WE SPEAK, RALPH AND LESLIE ARE TAPING THEIR CABLE SHOW...
FRANK CHO CREATOR OF LIBERTY MEADOWS
TODAY, KIDS, WE'LL LEARN IF "FIGHT FIRE WITH FIRE" REALLY WORKS. OKAY, LESLIE. LET HER RIP!
FIRE IN THE HOLE!
GASOLINE
BOOM
OKAY, KIDS, NEXT TIME, WE'LL LEARN ABOUT BURN TREATMENTS AND SKIN GRAFTS.
MEDIC!
CHO

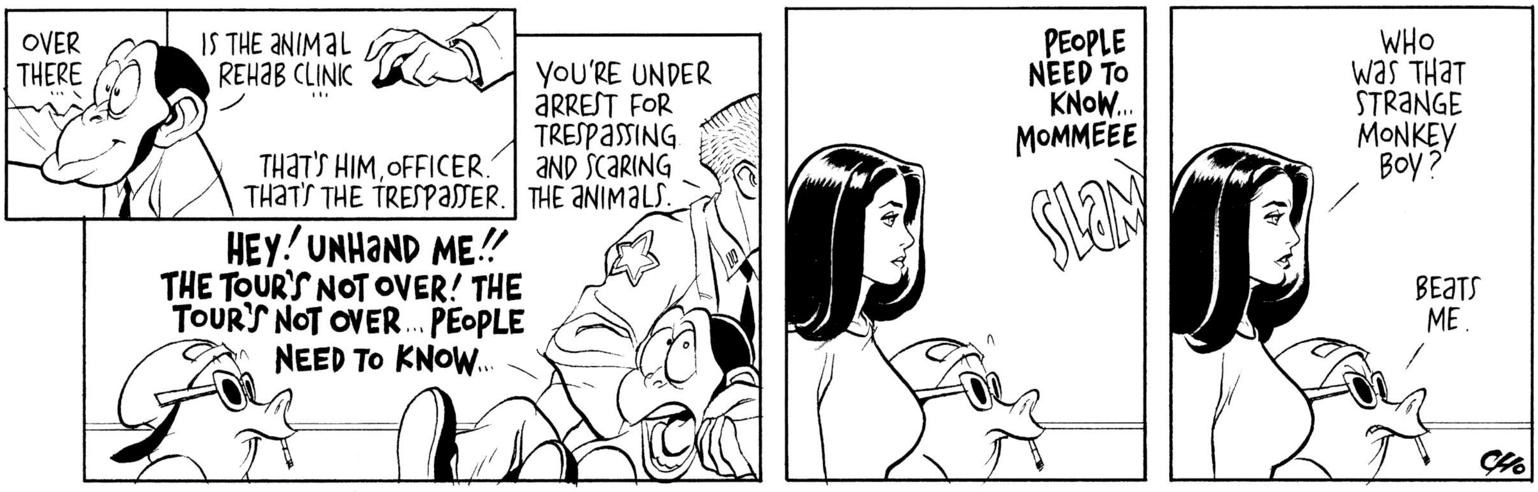
OVER THERE ...
IS THE ANIMAL REHAB CLINIC ...
THAT'S HIM, OFFICER. THAT'S THE TRESPASSER.
YOU'RE UNDER ARREST FOR TRESPASSING AND SCARING THE ANIMALS.
HEY! UNHAND ME!! THE TOUR'S NOT OVER! THE TOUR'S NOT OVER... PEOPLE NEED TO KNOW...
PEOPLE NEED TO KNOW... MOMMEEE
SLAM
WHO WAS THAT STRANGE MONKEY BOY?
BEATS ME.
CHO

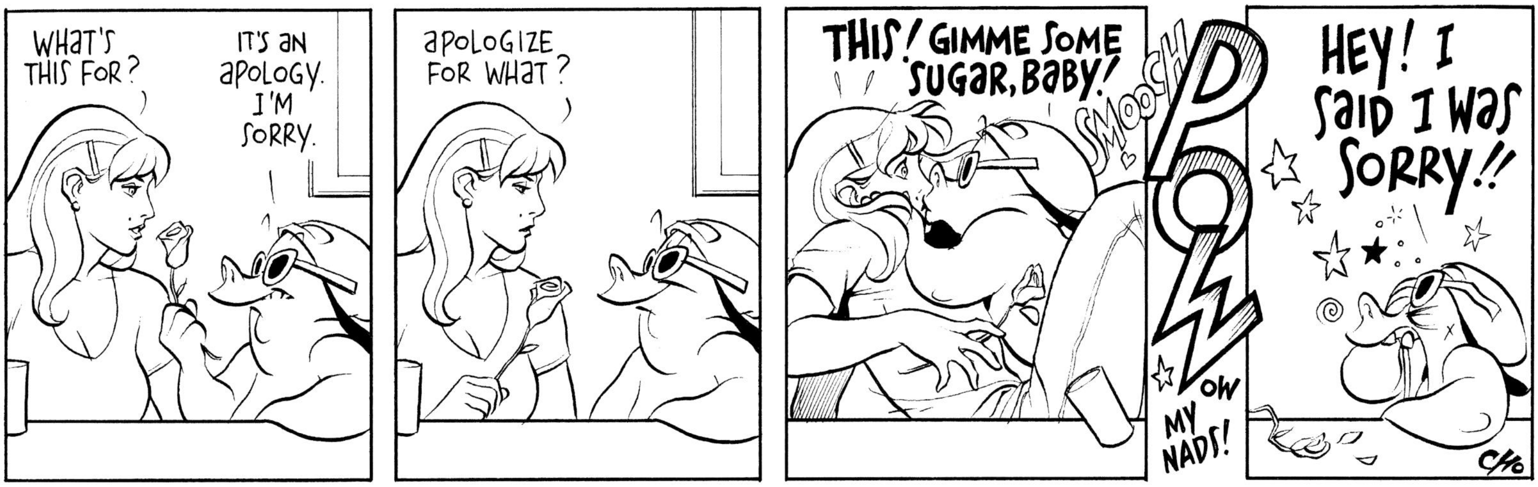
WHAT'S THIS FOR?
IT'S AN APOLOGY. I'M SORRY.
APOLOGIZE FOR WHAT?
THIS! GIMME SOME SUGAR, BABY!
SMOOCH
POW
OW MY NADS!
HEY! I SAID I WAS SORRY!!
CHO

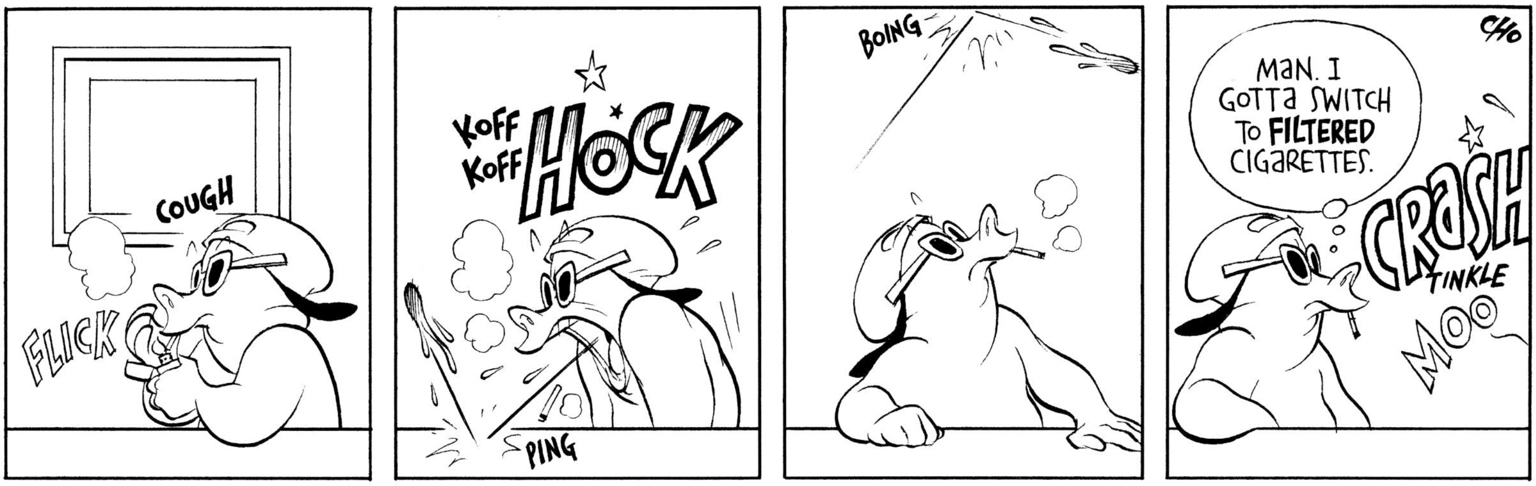
COUGH
FLICK
KOFF KOFF HOCK
PING
BOING
MAN. I GOTTA SWITCH TO FILTERED CIGARETTES.
CRASH
TINKLE
MOO
CHO

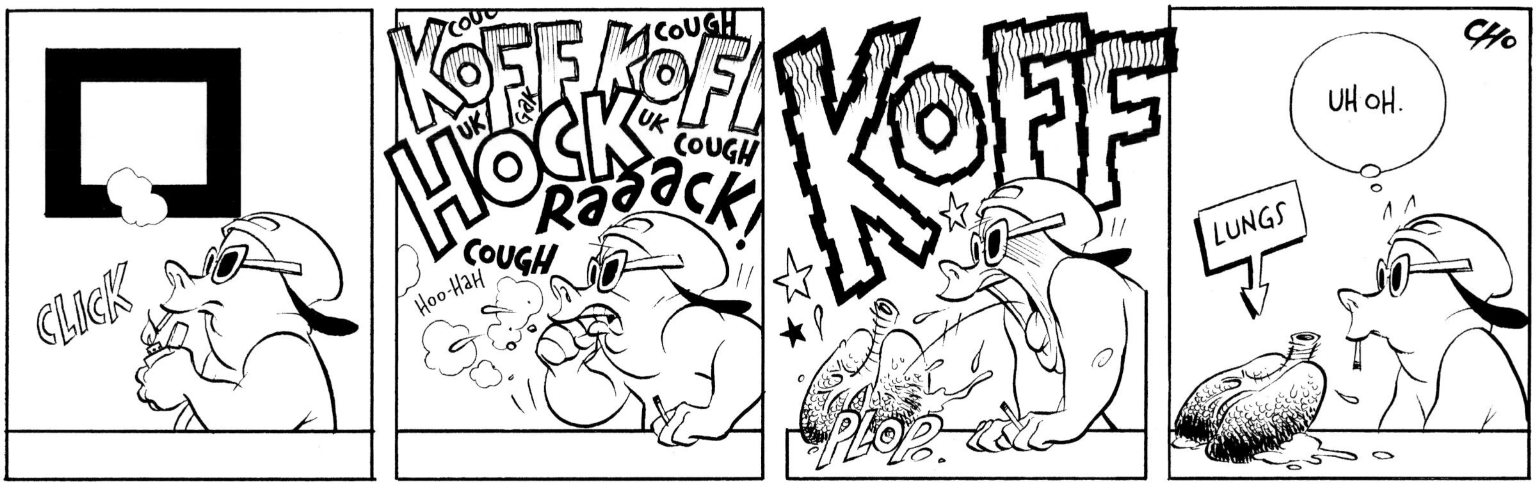
CLICK
KOFF KOFF
COUGH
UK
GAK
HOCK
UK
COUGH
RAAACK!
COUGH
HOO-HAH
KOFF
PLOP
CHO
UH OH.
LUNGS

OKAY CALM DOWN DEAN. SO YOU COUGHED UP YOUR LUNGS. SMOKING DOES THAT TO YOU SOMETIMES. THERE'S NO NEED TO PANIC...

DEAN'S LUNGS

CHOMP

TROT TROT TROT

OKAY... NOW PANIC.

CHO

WHAT HAPPENED? WHAT'S WRONG, DEAN?

HOCK ack
TOO MANY CIGARETTES...
GASP... ack
COUGHED UP LUNGS...

KOFF WHEEEEZZ gak
GASP CAN'T BREATHE
ack I'M KOFF
DONE FOR!
NEED AIR...
GASP

HI. I'M DEAN.

CHO

DEAN'S IN TROUBLE! HE COUGHED UP HIS LUNGS!!

HOW LONG HAS DEAN GONE WITHOUT OXYGEN?

DUNNO. BUT RALPH GOT HIM HOOKED UP TO HIS ARTIFICAL LUNG MACHINE.

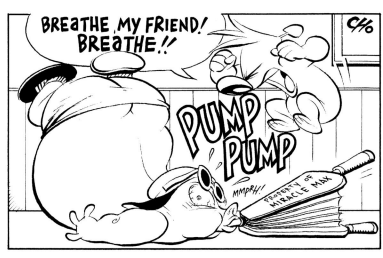

BREATHE, MY FRIEND! BREATHE!!

PUMP PUMP

MMPRH!

PROPERTY OF MIRACLE MAX

CHO

MAN. THOSE CIGARETTES DID A NUMBER ON YOU, DEAN. OKAY. BEFORE I PUT YOU UNDER, I WANT TO BRIEF YOU ON YOUR CONDITION.

YOU'VE COUGHED UP YOUR LUNGS DUE TO EXCESSIVE SMOKING. I'M GOING TO CLEAN AND REATTACH YOUR LUNGS. IT'S A DELICATE AND VERY INVASIVE OPERATION.

YOU'LL NEED A LONG AND INTENSIVE PHYSICAL THERAPY AFTERWARDS. BUT I THINK, YOU'LL MAKE A FULL RECOVERY. ANY QUESTIONS?

CAN I HAVE A CIGARETTE?

CHO

DEAN, CAN YOU HEAR ME? I SUCCESSFULLY REATTACHED YOUR LUNGS.
YOUR LUNGS ARE FINE AND WORKING PROPERLY. THERE ARE SOME POST OPERATIVE SYMPTOMS YOU SHOULD KNOW.
SOME SWELLING IS COMMON IN THIS TYPE OF THORACIC SURGERY.
...ESPECIALLY AROUND THE CHEST AREA.
MIRROR... NOW!
CENSORED
HEY, DEAN. GLAD TO SEE YOU UP AND ABOUT, MAN.
BELTSVILLE NEWS
GOATMAN ESCAPES USDA
PIG LOSES LUNGS
HOW DID YOUR LUNG SURGERY GO.... WHAT THE?!
ZOUNDS! WHAT MOUNDS!!
HEY, HEY! EYES UP FRONT! EYES UP FRONT, BUDDY!!
EXACTLY WHAT KIND OF SURGERY DID YOU HAVE, DEAN?
HOLY...
POST OPERATIVE SWELLING DUE TO MAJOR LUNG SURGERY.
WHOA.
WHAT?!
CAN I GET A HUG?
DEAN'S ROAD TO RECOVERY: DAY 5.
THERE! YOU'RE ALL STRAPPED IN. THIS "ICE VEST" I DESIGNED SHOULD EASE YOUR CHEST SWELLING DOWN.
HOW DO YOU FEEL, DEAN?
THUD...
FOOM
LIKE KICKING YOUR BUTT.
OH. IT ALSO COMES WITH AIRBAGS.

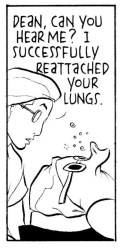

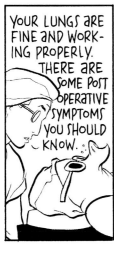

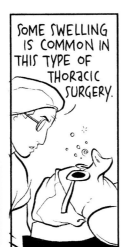

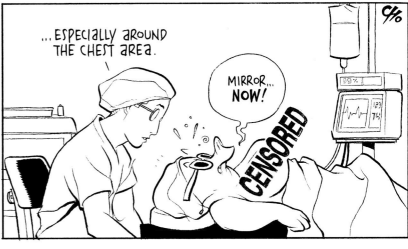

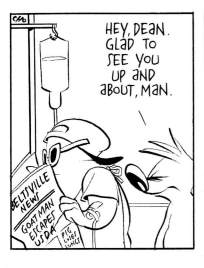

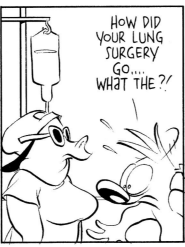

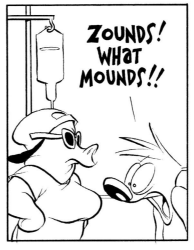

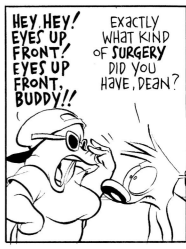

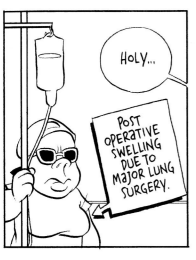

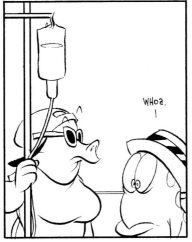

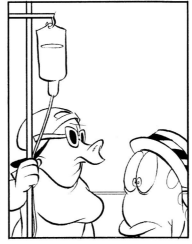

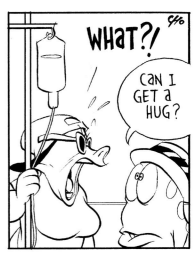

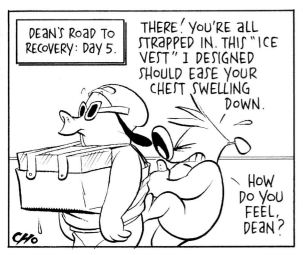

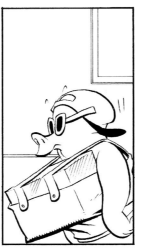

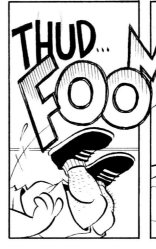

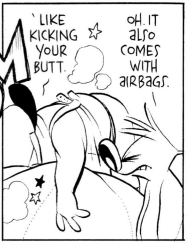

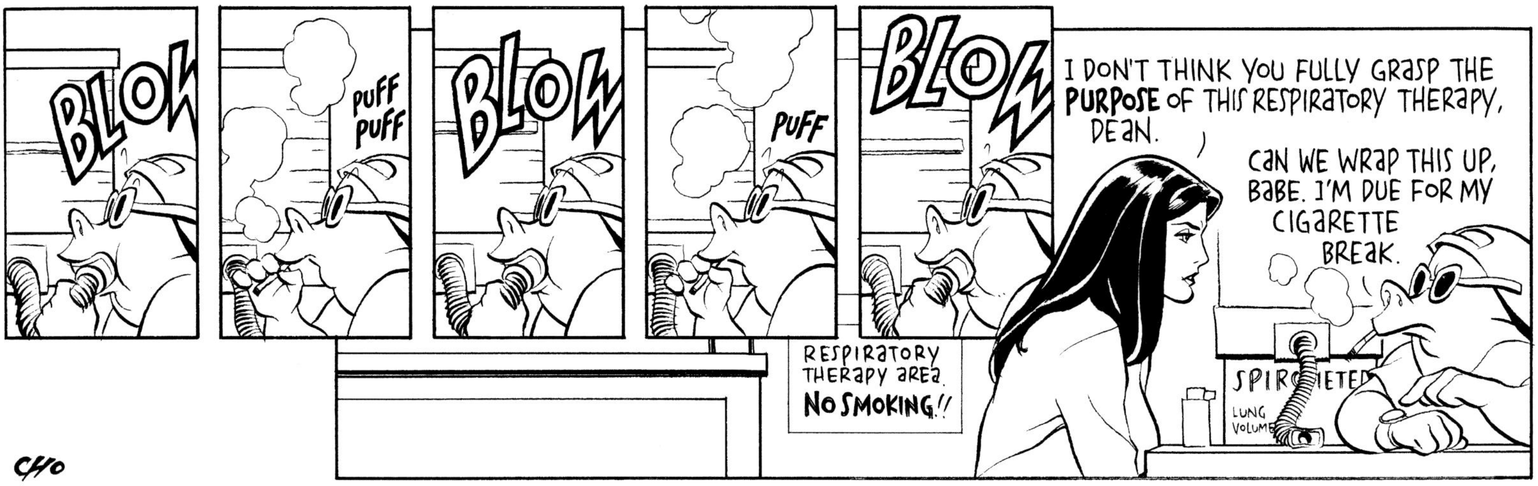
BLOW
PUFF PUFF
BLOW
PUFF
BLOW
I DON'T THINK YOU FULLY GRASP THE PURPOSE OF THIS RESPIRATORY THERAPY, DEAN.
CAN WE WRAP THIS UP, BABE. I'M DUE FOR MY CIGARETTE BREAK.
RESPIRATORY THERAPY AREA. NO SMOKING!!
LUNG VOLUME
CHO

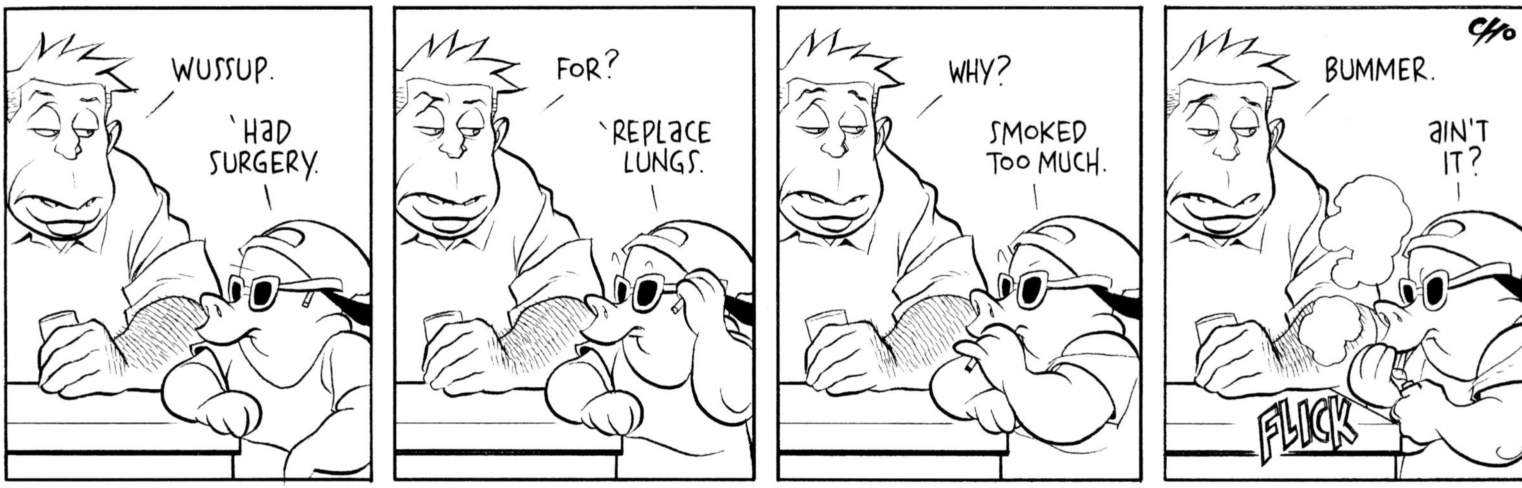
WUSSUP.
`HAD SURGERY.
FOR?
`REPLACE LUNGS.
WHY?
SMOKED TOO MUCH.
BUMMER.
AIN'T IT?
FLICK
CHO

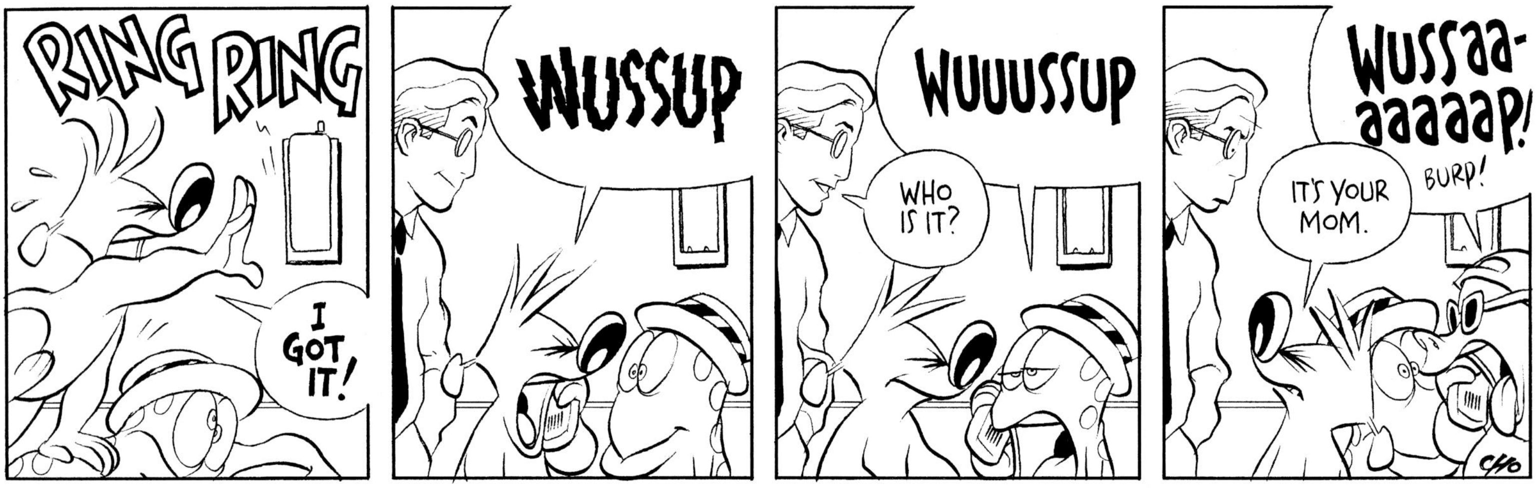
RING RING
I GOT IT!
WUSSUP
WHO IS IT?
WUUUSSUP
WUSSAA-AAAAAP!
IT'S YOUR MOM.
BURP!
CHO

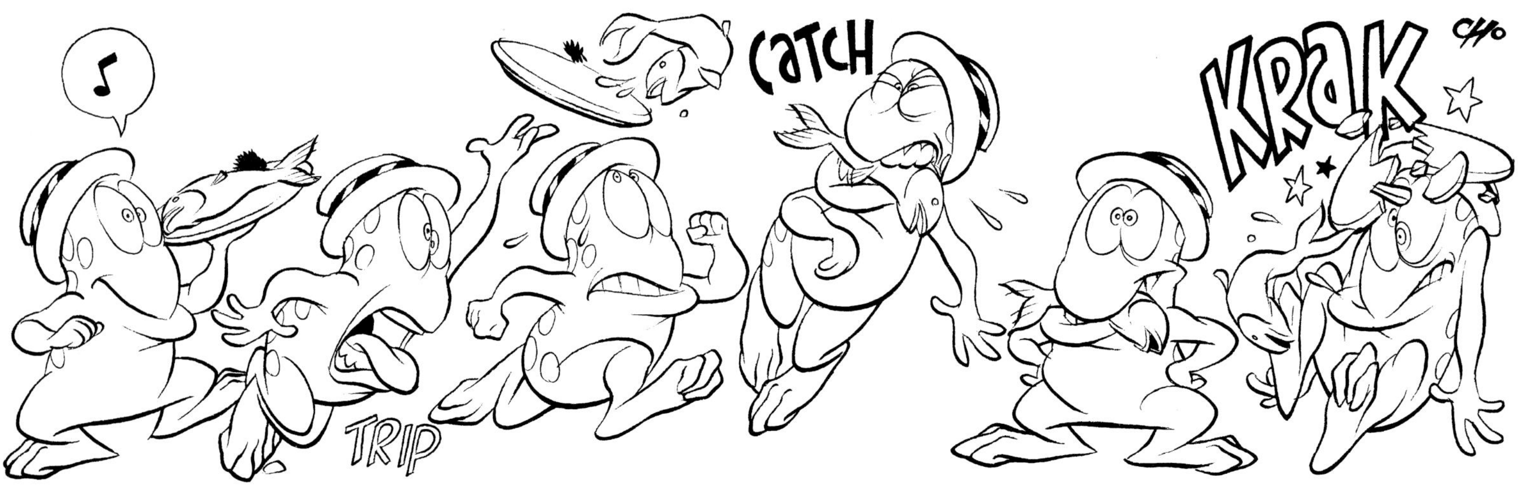
♪
TRIP
CATCH
KRAK
CHO

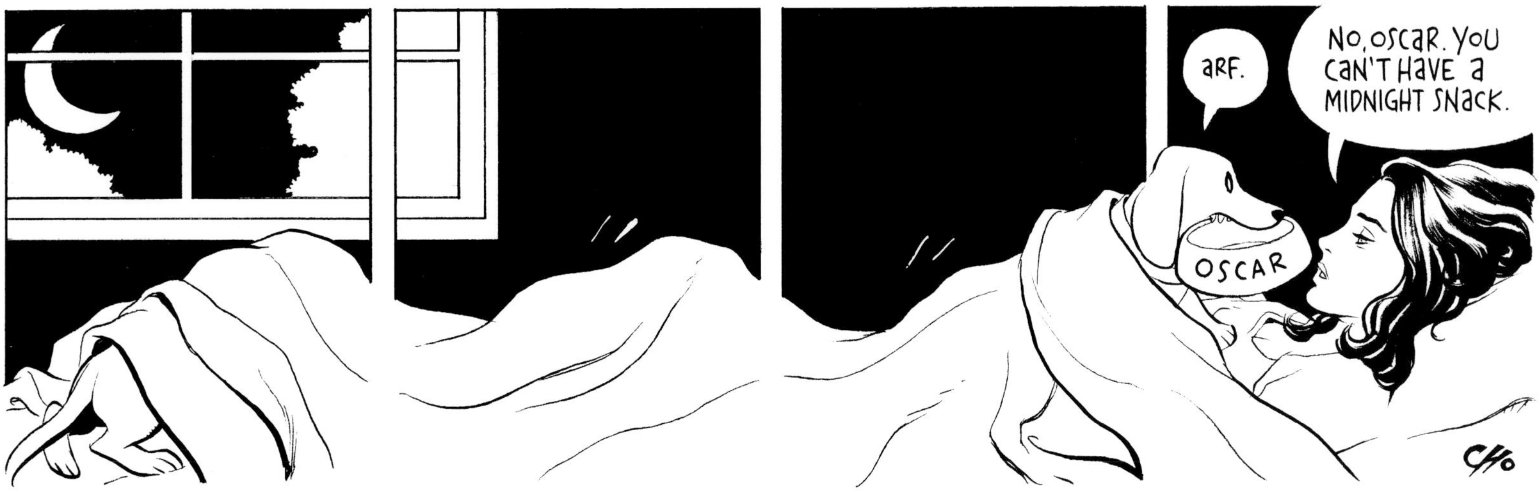
ARF.
OSCAR
NO, OSCAR. YOU CAN'T HAVE A MIDNIGHT SNACK.
CHO

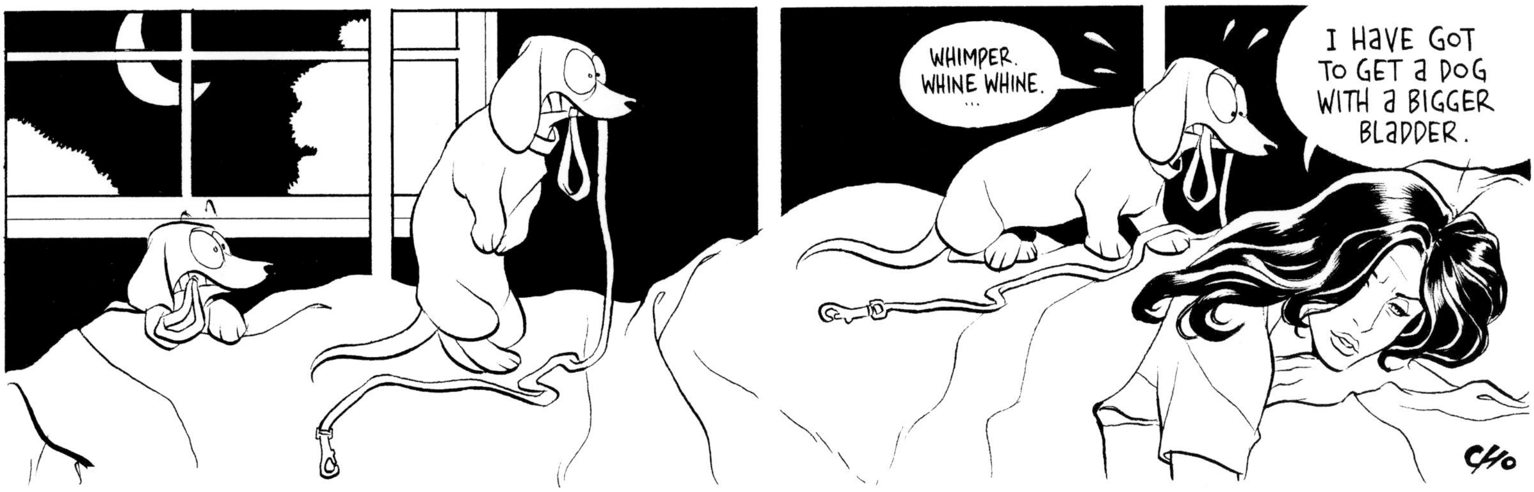
WHIMPER. WHINE WHINE. ...
I HAVE GOT TO GET A DOG WITH A BIGGER BLADDER.
CHO

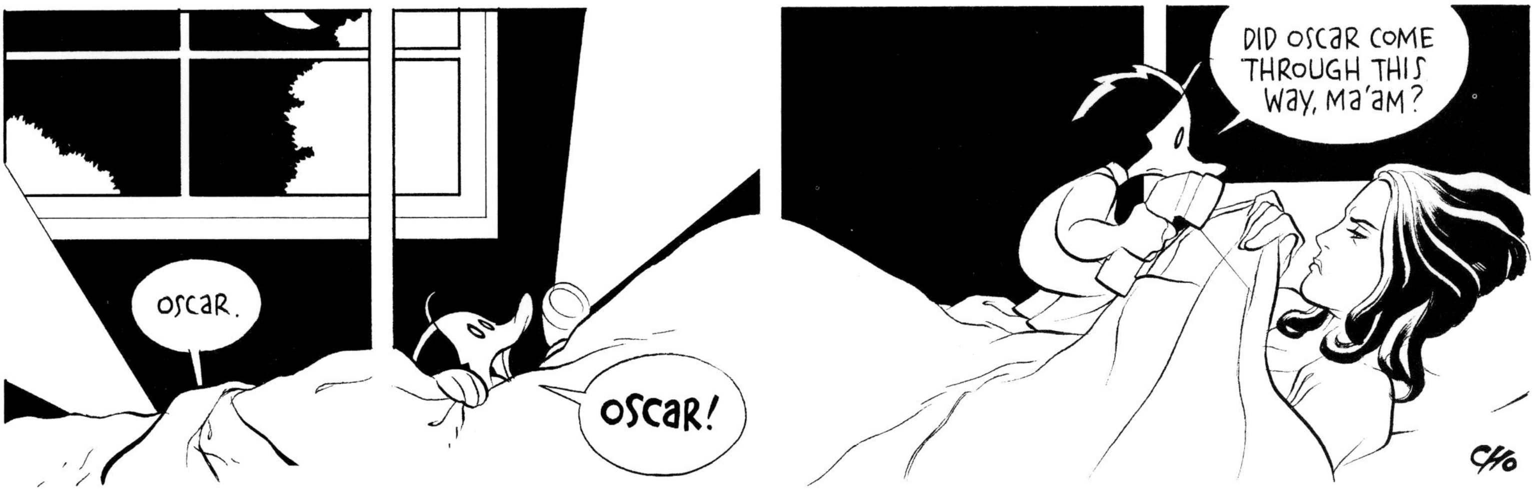
OSCAR.
OSCAR!
DID OSCAR COME THROUGH THIS WAY, MA'AM?
CHO

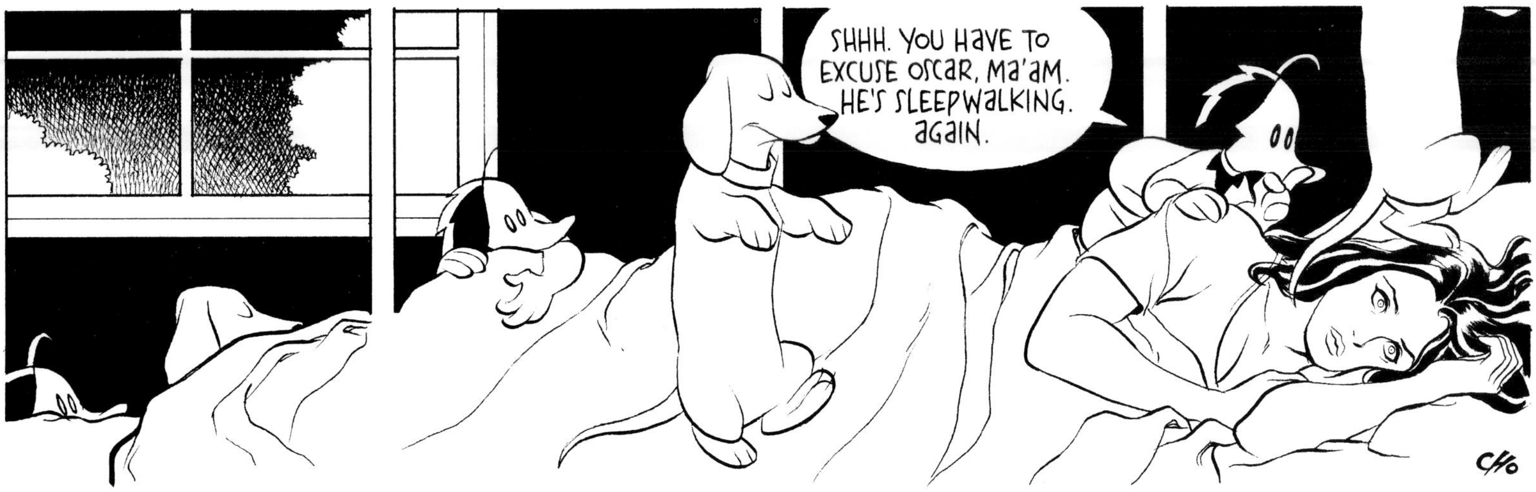
SHHH. YOU HAVE TO EXCUSE OSCAR, MA'AM. HE'S SLEEPWALKING. AGAIN.
CHO

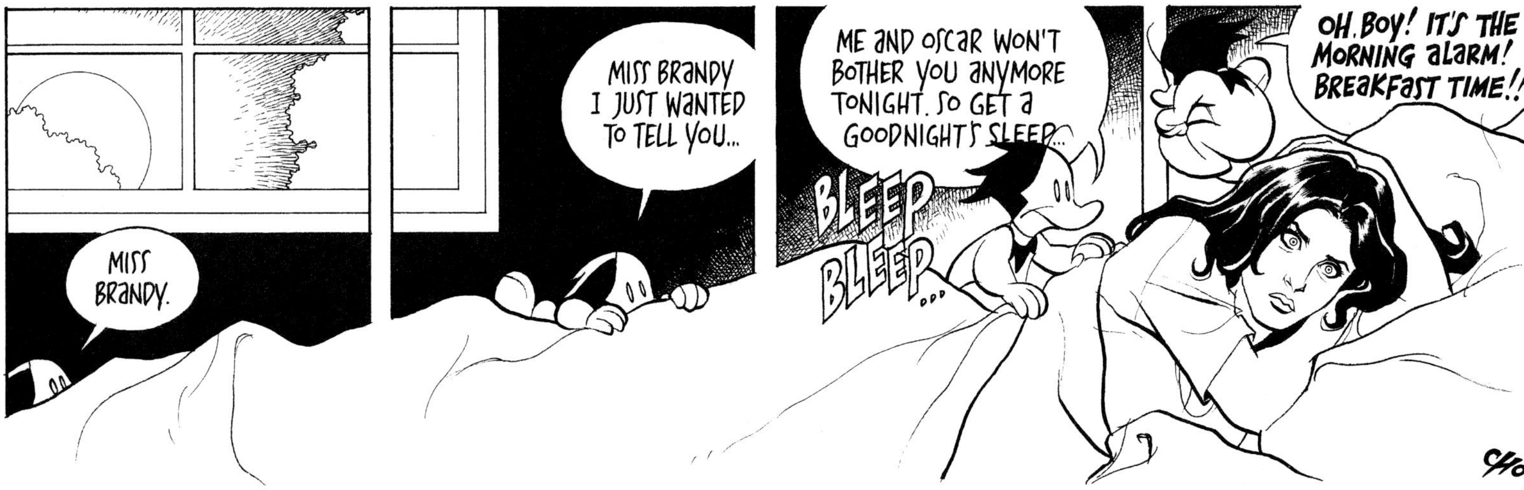

MISS BRANDY.
MISS BRANDY I JUST WANTED TO TELL YOU...
ME AND OSCAR WON'T BOTHER YOU ANYMORE TONIGHT. SO GET A GOODNIGHT'S SLEEP...
BLEEP BLEEP...
OH, BOY! IT'S THE MORNING ALARM! BREAKFAST TIME!!
CHO

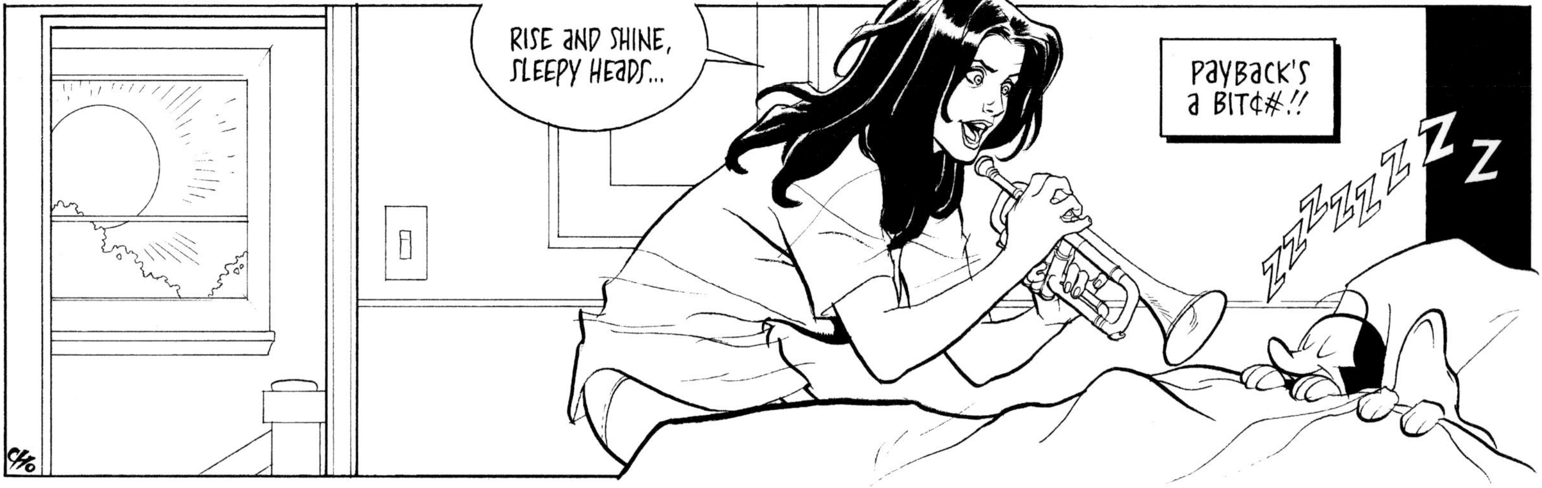

RISE AND SHINE, SLEEPY HEADS...
PAYBACK'S A BIT¢#!!
ZZZZZZZZ Z Z
CHO

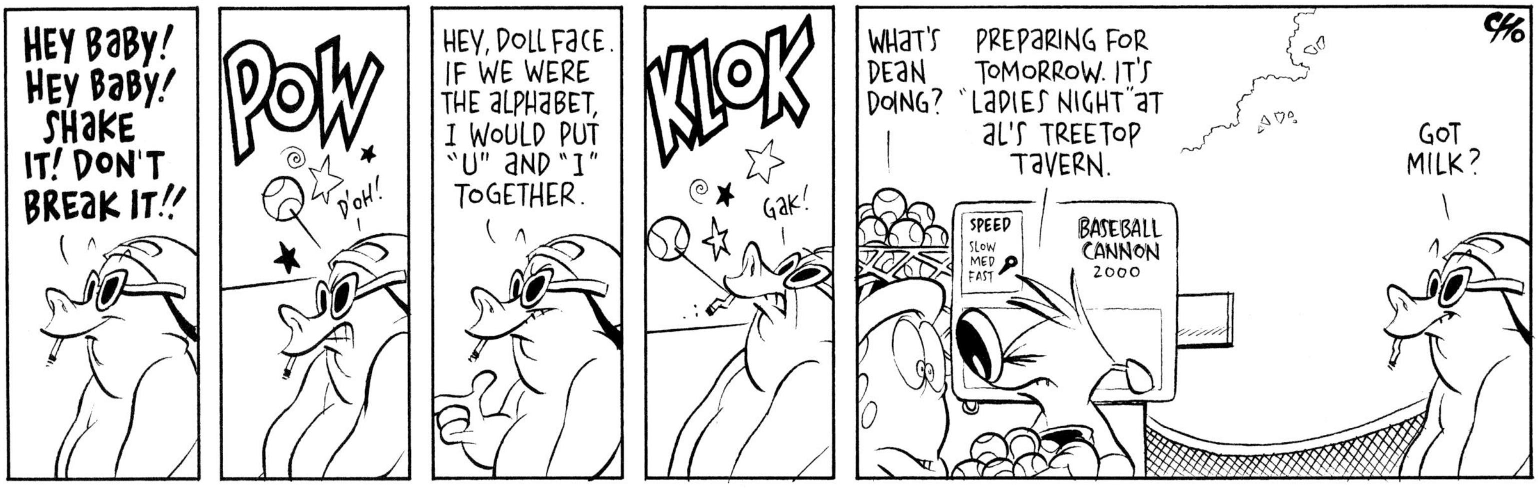

HEY BABY! HEY BABY! SHAKE IT! DON'T BREAK IT!!
POW
D'OH!
HEY, DOLL FACE. IF WE WERE THE ALPHABET, I WOULD PUT "U" AND "I" TOGETHER.
KLOK
GAK!
CHO
WHAT'S DEAN DOING?
PREPARING FOR TOMORROW. IT'S "LADIES NIGHT" AT AL'S TREETOP TAVERN.
SPEED SLOW MED FAST
BASEBALL CANNON 2000
GOT MILK?

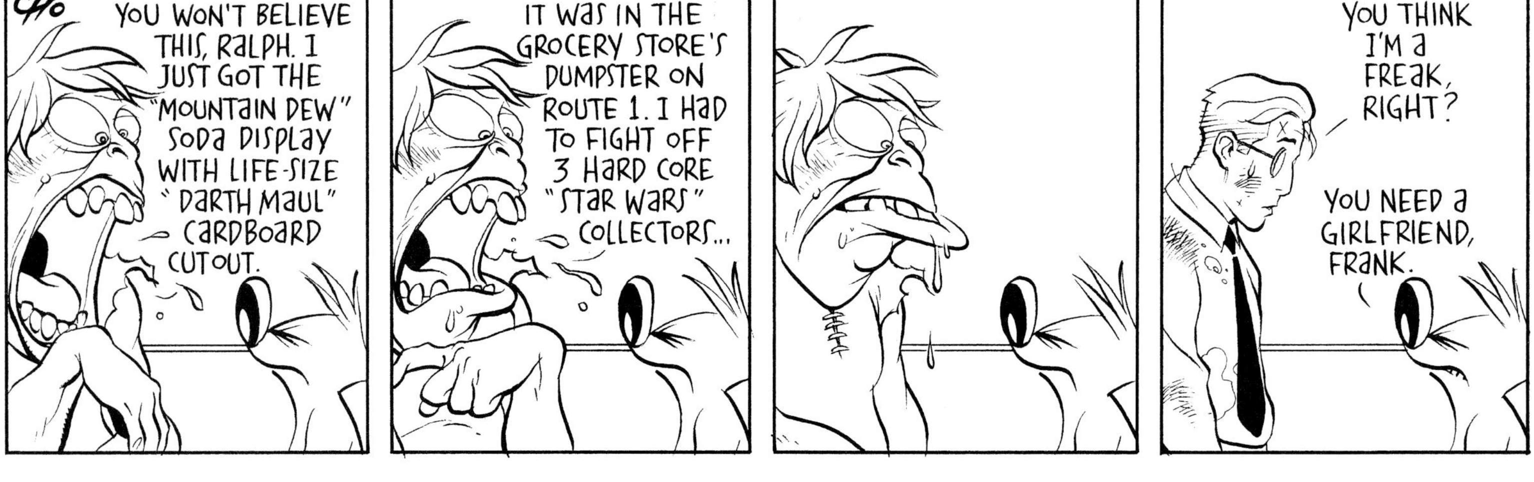

CHO
YOU WON'T BELIEVE THIS, RALPH. I JUST GOT THE "MOUNTAIN DEW" SODA DISPLAY WITH LIFE-SIZE "DARTH MAUL" CARDBOARD CUTOUT.
IT WAS IN THE GROCERY STORE'S DUMPSTER ON ROUTE 1. I HAD TO FIGHT OFF 3 HARD CORE "STAR WARS" COLLECTORS...
YOU THINK I'M A FREAK, RIGHT?
YOU NEED A GIRLFRIEND, FRANK.

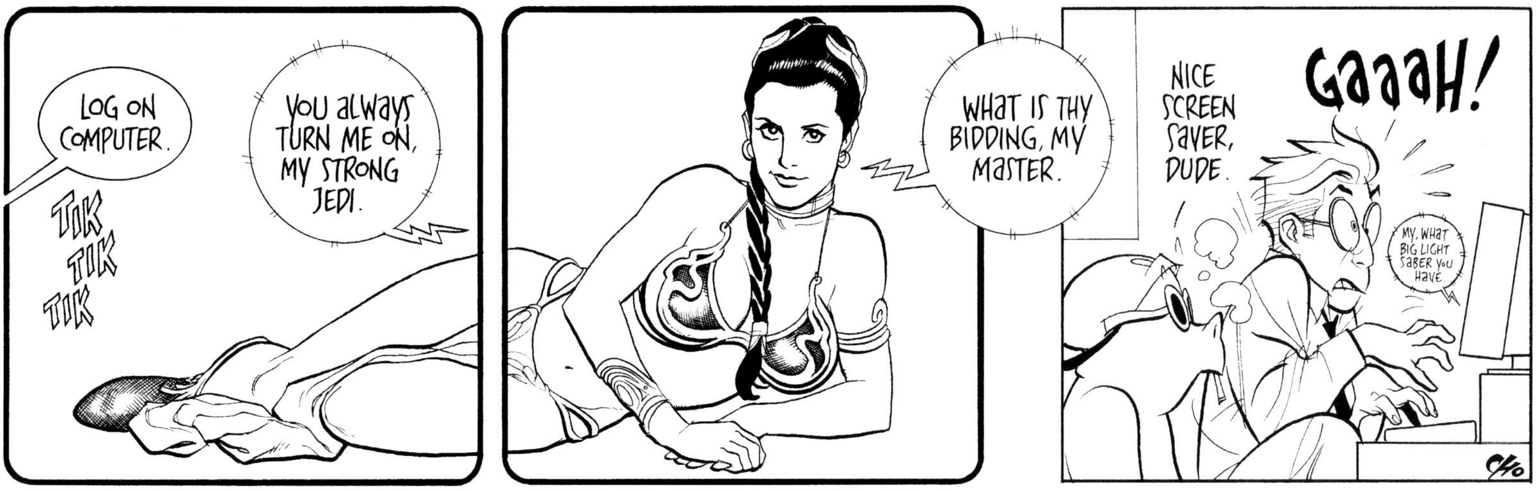
LOG ON COMPUTER.
TIK TIK TIK
YOU ALWAYS TURN ME ON, MY STRONG JEDI.
WHAT IS THY BIDDING, MY MASTER.
NICE SCREEN SAVER, DUDE.
GAAAH!
MY, WHAT BIG LIGHT SABER YOU HAVE.
CHO

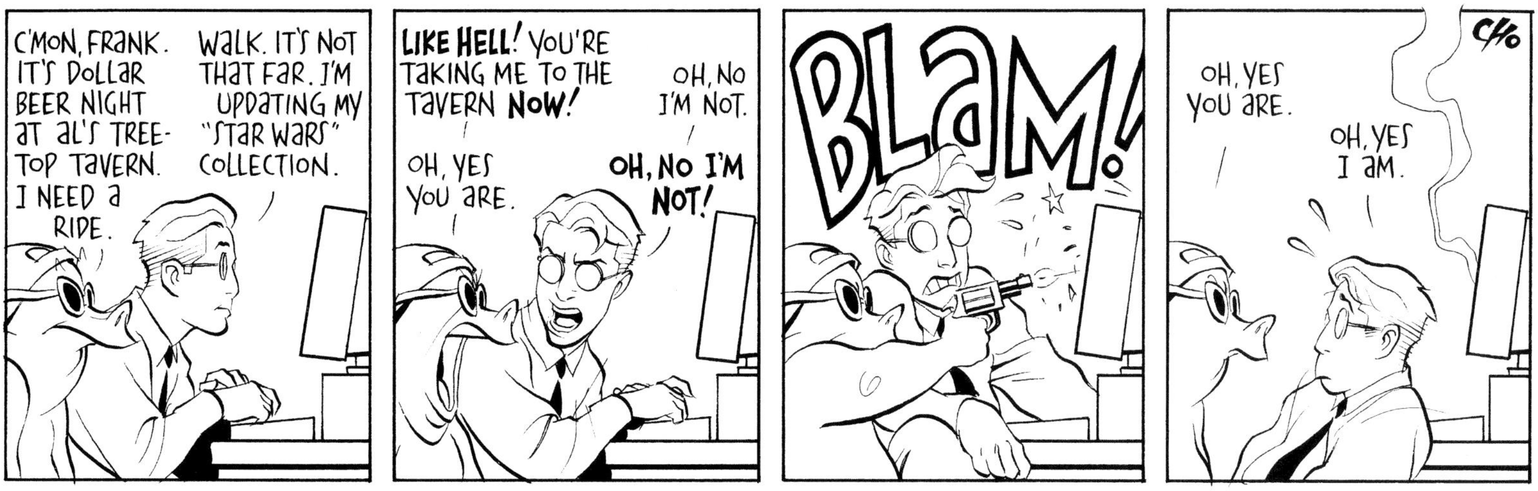
C'MON, FRANK. IT'S DOLLAR BEER NIGHT AT AL'S TREE-TOP TAVERN. I NEED A RIDE.
WALK. IT'S NOT THAT FAR. I'M UPDATING MY "STAR WARS" COLLECTION.
LIKE HELL! YOU'RE TAKING ME TO THE TAVERN NOW!
OH, NO I'M NOT.
OH, YES YOU ARE.
OH, NO I'M NOT!
BLAM!
OH, YES YOU ARE.
OH, YES I AM.
CHO

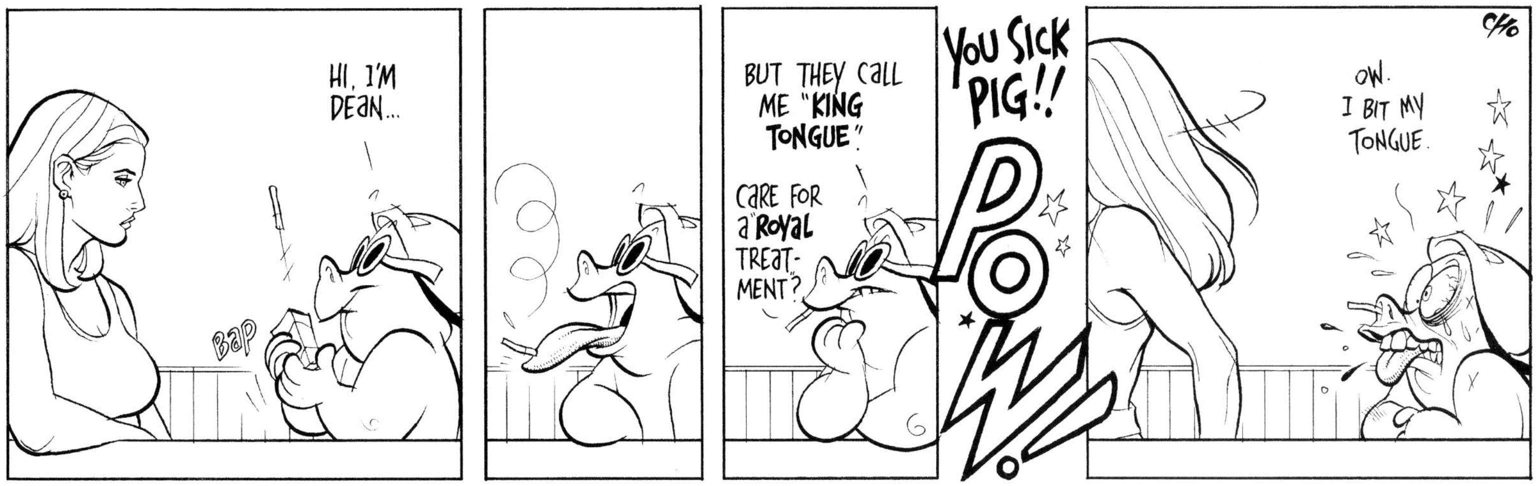
HI, I'M DEAN...
BAP
BUT THEY CALL ME "KING TONGUE".
CARE FOR A "ROYAL TREAT-MENT"?
YOU SICK PIG!!
POW!
OW. I BIT MY TONGUE.
CHO

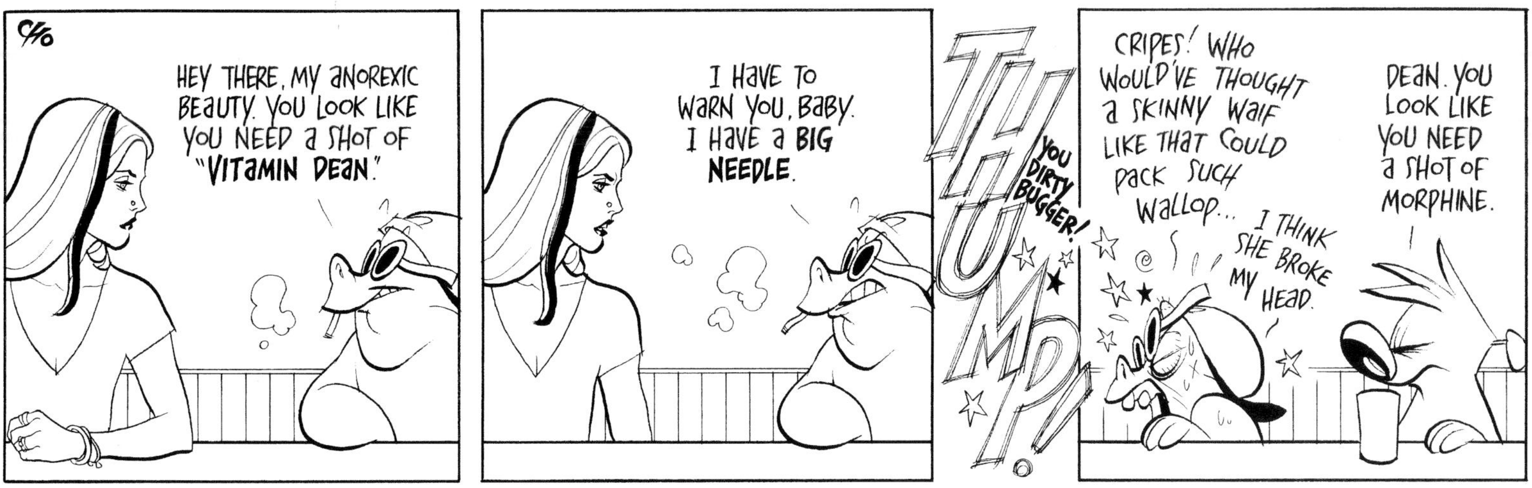
CHO
HEY THERE, MY ANOREXIC BEAUTY. YOU LOOK LIKE YOU NEED A SHOT OF "VITAMIN DEAN".
I HAVE TO WARN YOU, BABY. I HAVE A BIG NEEDLE.
THUMP!
YOU DIRTY BUGGER!
CRIPES! WHO WOULD'VE THOUGHT A SKINNY WAIF LIKE THAT COULD PACK SUCH WALLOP... I THINK SHE BROKE MY HEAD.
DEAN. YOU LOOK LIKE YOU NEED A SHOT OF MORPHINE.

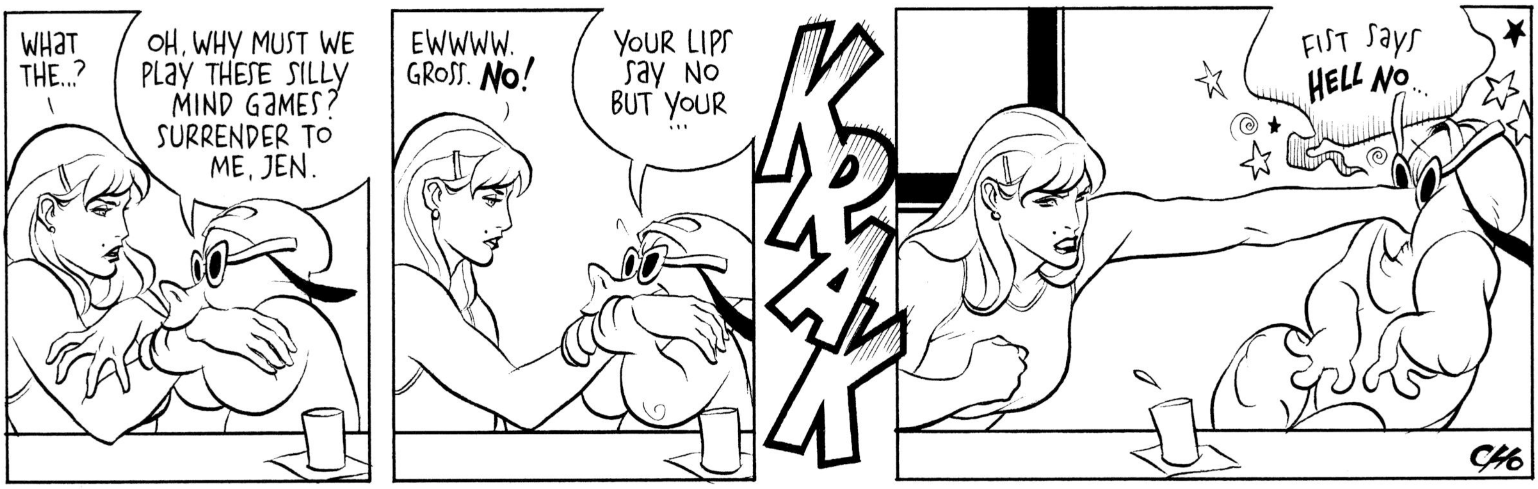

WHAT THE...?
OH, WHY MUST WE PLAY THESE SILLY MIND GAMES? SURRENDER TO ME, JEN.
EWWWW. GROSS. NO!
YOUR LIPS SAY NO BUT YOUR ...
KRAK
FIST SAYS HELL NO...
CHO

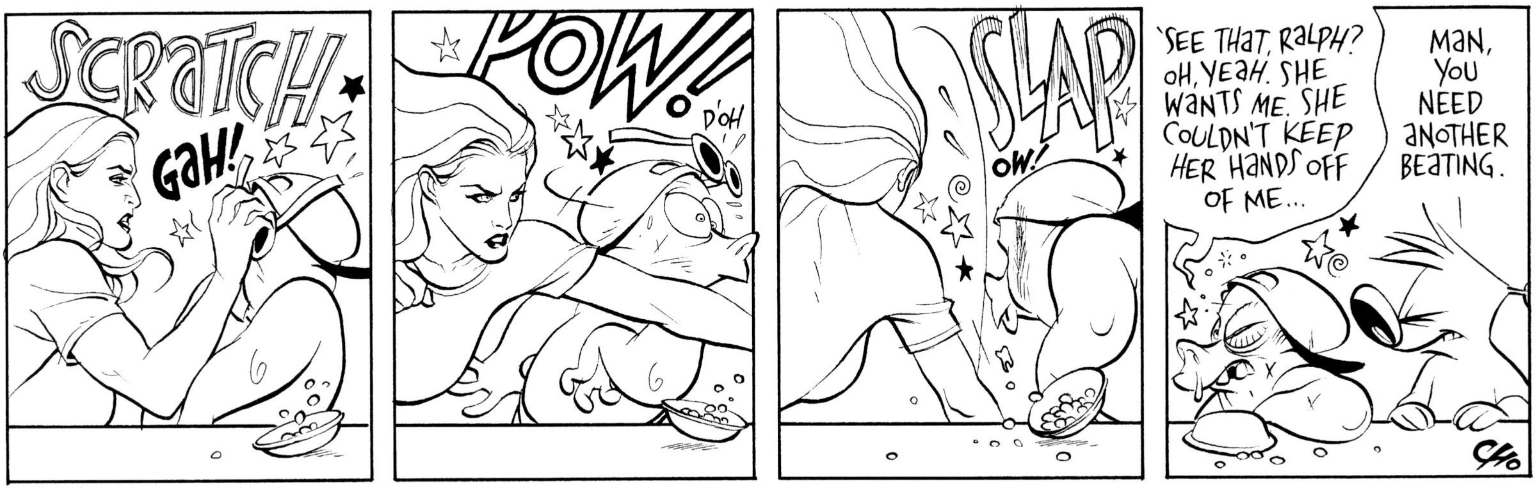

SCRATCH
GAH!
POW!
D'OH
SLAP
OW!
'SEE THAT, RALPH? OH, YEAH. SHE WANTS ME. SHE COULDN'T KEEP HER HANDS OFF OF ME...
MAN, YOU NEED ANOTHER BEATING.
CHO

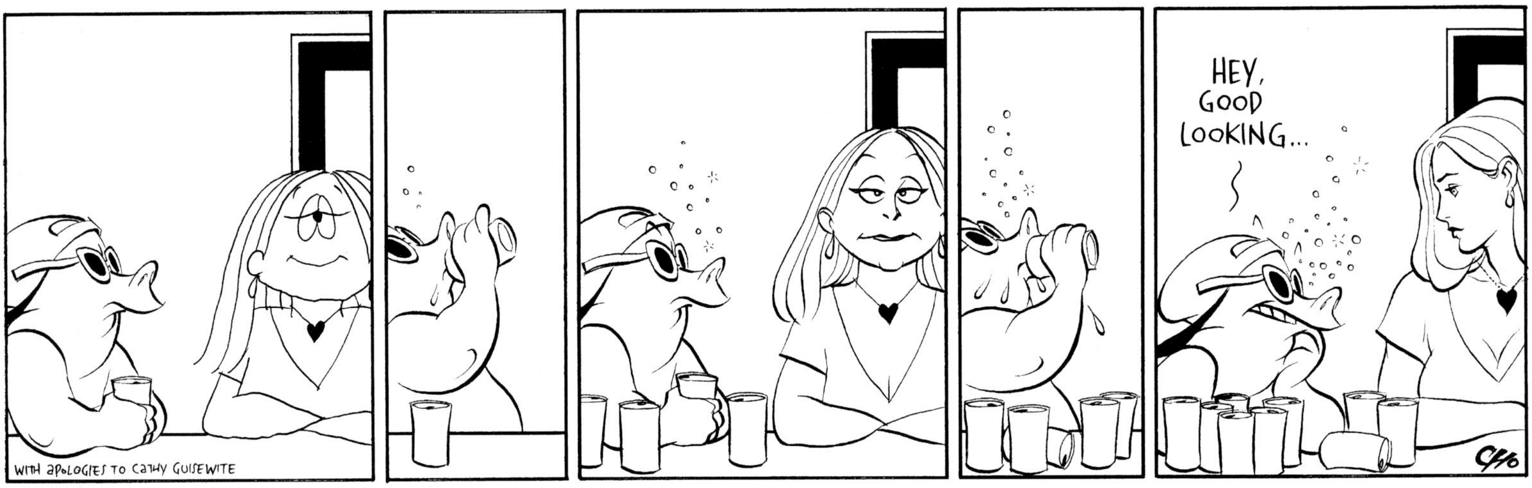

WITH APOLOGIES TO CATHY GUISEWITE
HEY, GOOD LOOKING...
CHO

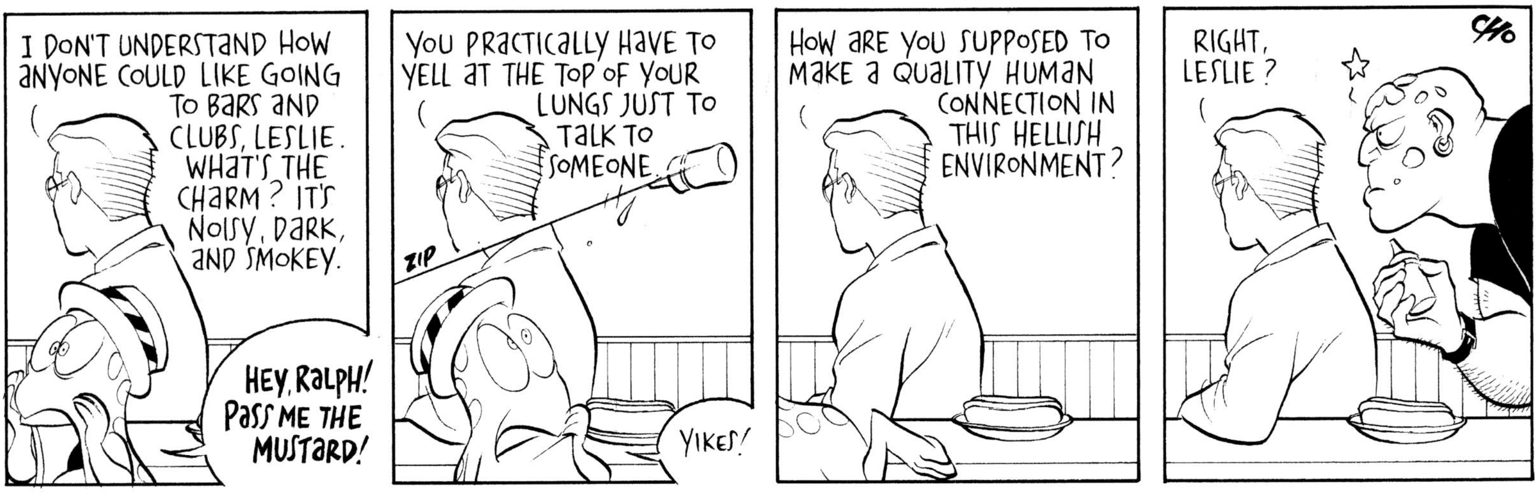

I DON'T UNDERSTAND HOW ANYONE COULD LIKE GOING TO BARS AND CLUBS, LESLIE. WHAT'S THE CHARM? IT'S NOISY, DARK, AND SMOKEY.
HEY, RALPH! PASS ME THE MUSTARD!
YOU PRACTICALLY HAVE TO YELL AT THE TOP OF YOUR LUNGS JUST TO TALK TO SOMEONE.
ZIP
YIKES!
HOW ARE YOU SUPPOSED TO MAKE A QUALITY HUMAN CONNECTION IN THIS HELLISH ENVIRONMENT?
CHO
RIGHT, LESLIE?

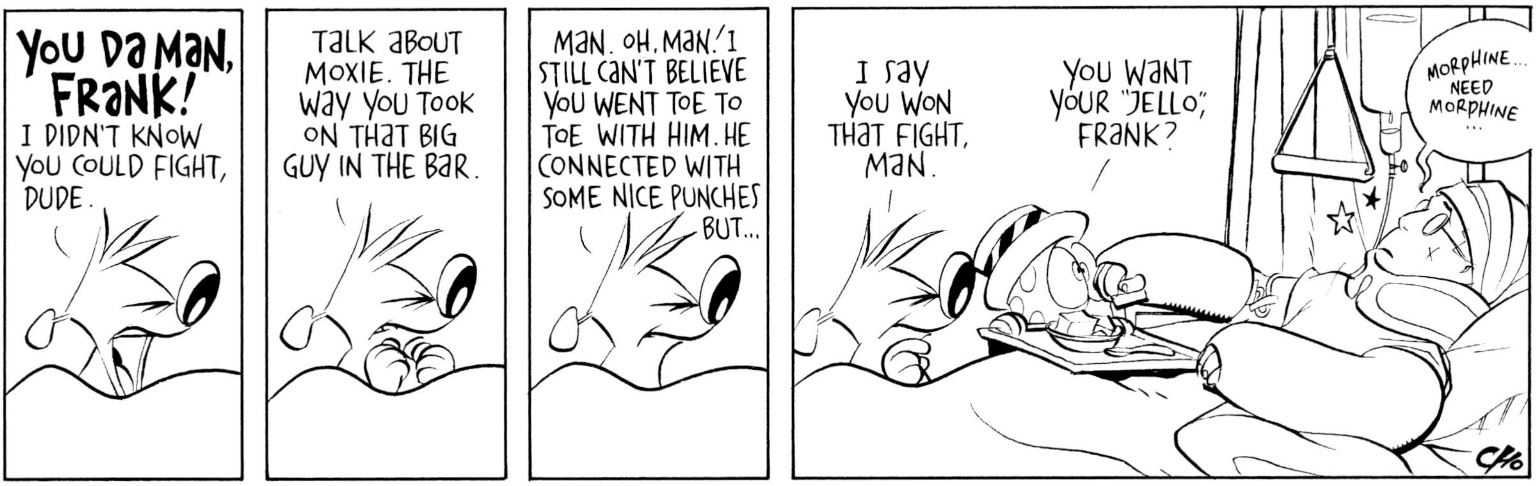

YOU Da MaN, FRANK! I DIDN'T KNOW YOU COULD FIGHT, DUDE.
TaLK aBOUT MOXIE. THE WaY YOU TOOK ON THaT BIG GUY IN THE BaR.
MaN. OH, MaN! I STILL CaN'T BELIEVE YOU WENT TOE TO TOE WITH HIM. HE CONNECTED WITH SOME NICE PUNCHES BUT...
I SaY YOU WON THaT FIGHT, MaN.
YOU WaNT YOUR "JELLO", FRANK?
MORPHINE... NEED MORPHINE...
CHO

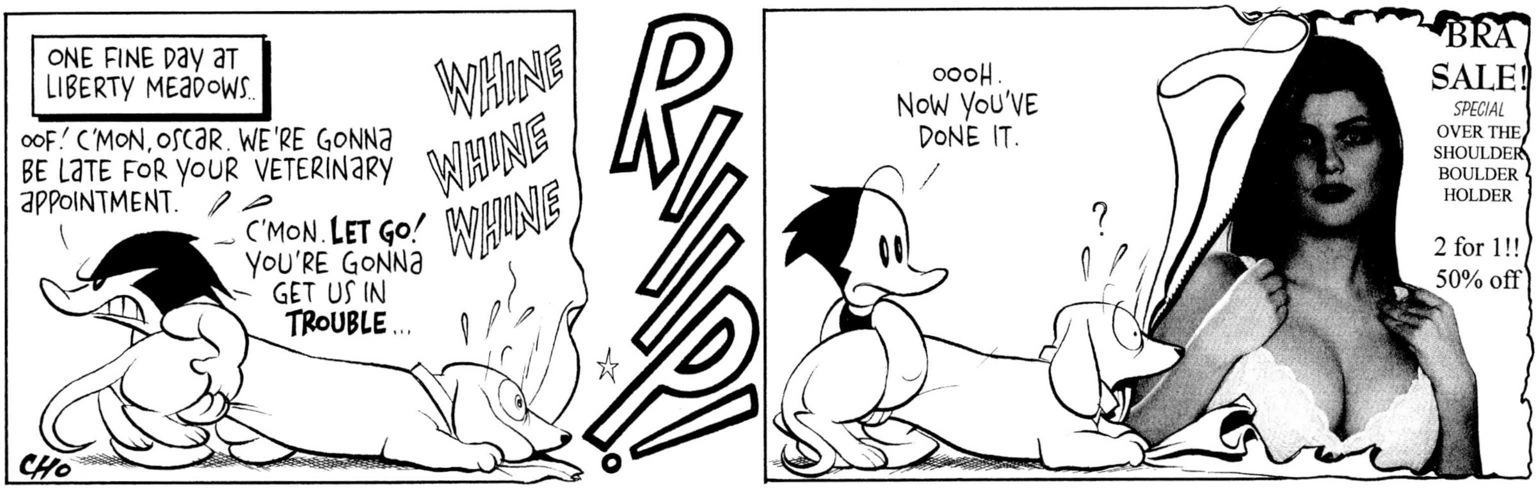

ONE FINE DaY aT LIBERTY MEaDOWS..
OOF! C'MON, OSCaR. WE'RE GONNa BE LaTE FOR YOUR VETERINaRY aPPOINTMENT.
C'MON. LET GO! YOU'RE GONNa GET US IN TROUBLE...
WHINE WHINE WHINE
RIIIP!
CHO
OOOH. NOW YOU'VE DONE IT.
?
BRA SALE!
SPECIAL
OVER THE SHOULDER BOULDER HOLDER
2 for 1!!
50% off

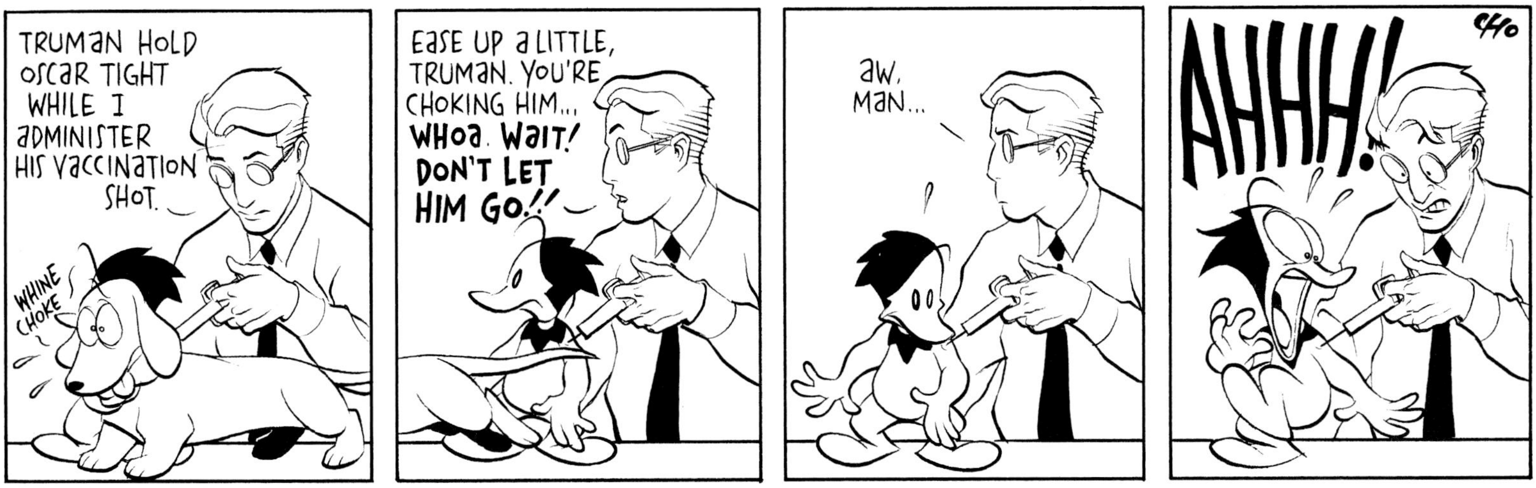

TRUMaN HOLD OSCaR TIGHT WHILE I aDMINISTER HIS VaCCINaTION SHOT.
WHINE CHOKE
EaSE UP a LITTLE, TRUMaN. YOU'RE CHOKING HIM... WHOa. WaIT! DON'T LET HIM GO!!
aW, MaN...
aHHH!
CHO

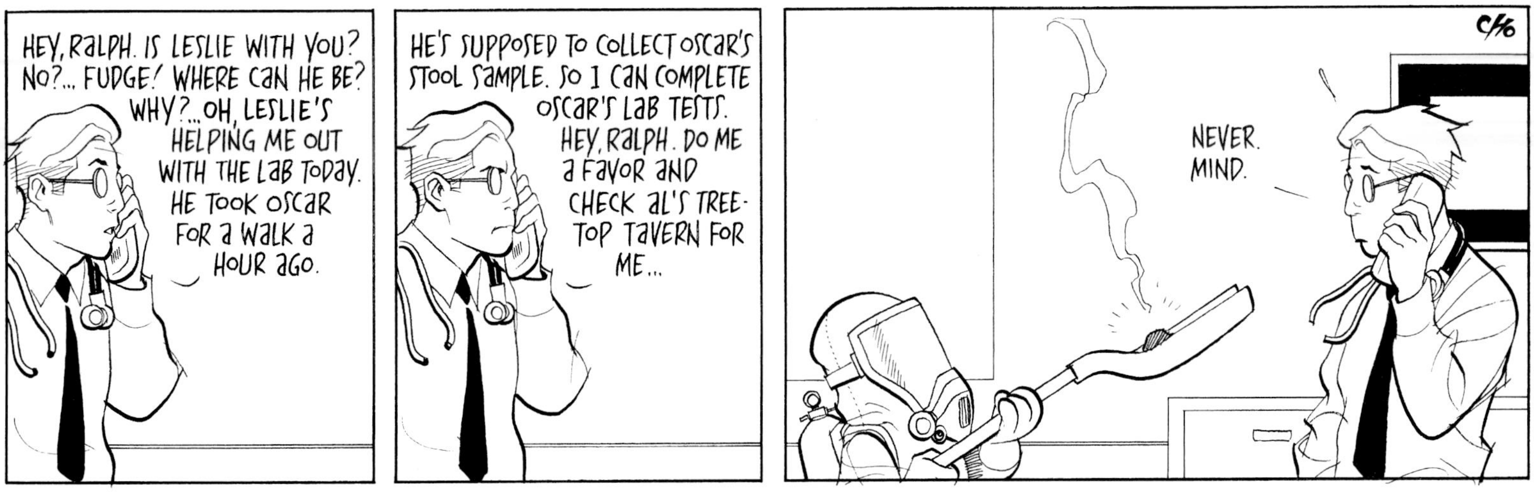

HEY, RaLPH. IS LESLIE WITH YOU? NO?... FUDGE! WHERE CaN HE BE? WHY?... OH, LESLIE'S HELPING ME OUT WITH THE LaB TODaY. HE TOOK OSCaR FOR a WaLK a HOUR aGO.
HE'S SUPPOSED TO COLLECT OSCaR'S STOOL SaMPLE. SO I CaN COMPLETE OSCaR'S LaB TESTS. HEY, RaLPH. DO ME a FaVOR aND CHECK aL'S TREE-TOP TaVERN FOR ME...
NEVER. MIND.
CHO

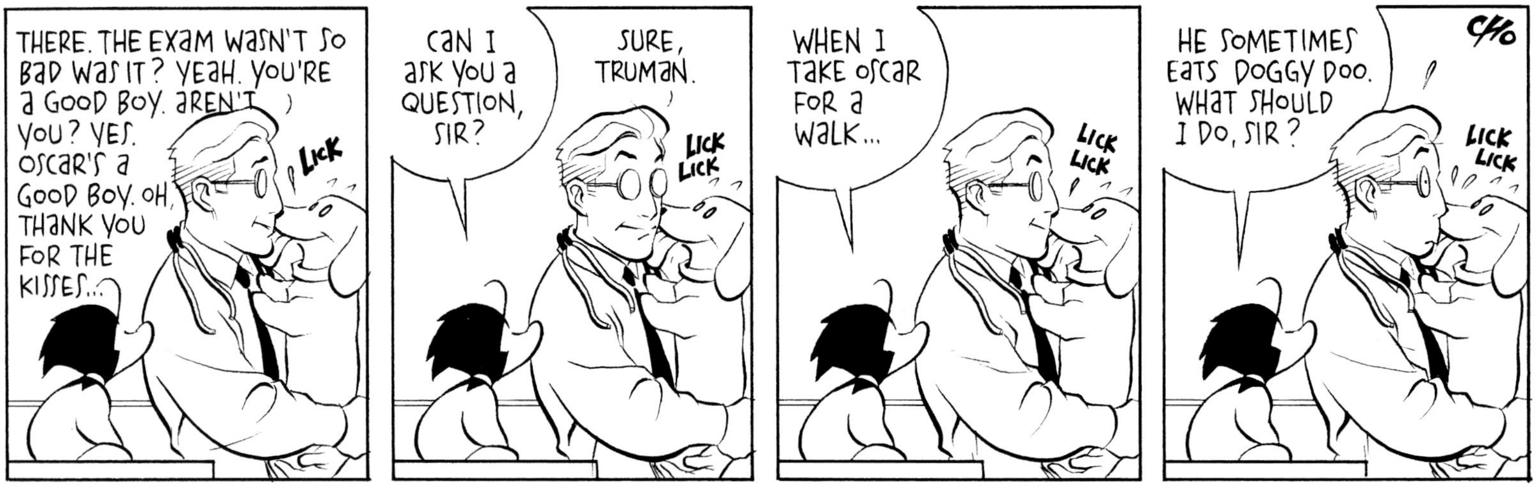
THERE. THE EXAM WASN'T SO BAD WAS IT? YEAH. YOU'RE A GOOD BOY. AREN'T YOU? YES. OSCAR'S A GOOD BOY. OH, THANK YOU FOR THE KISSES...
LICK
CAN I ASK YOU A QUESTION, SIR?
SURE, TRUMAN.
LICK LICK
WHEN I TAKE OSCAR FOR A WALK...
LICK LICK
HE SOMETIMES EATS DOGGY DOO. WHAT SHOULD I DO, SIR?
LICK LICK

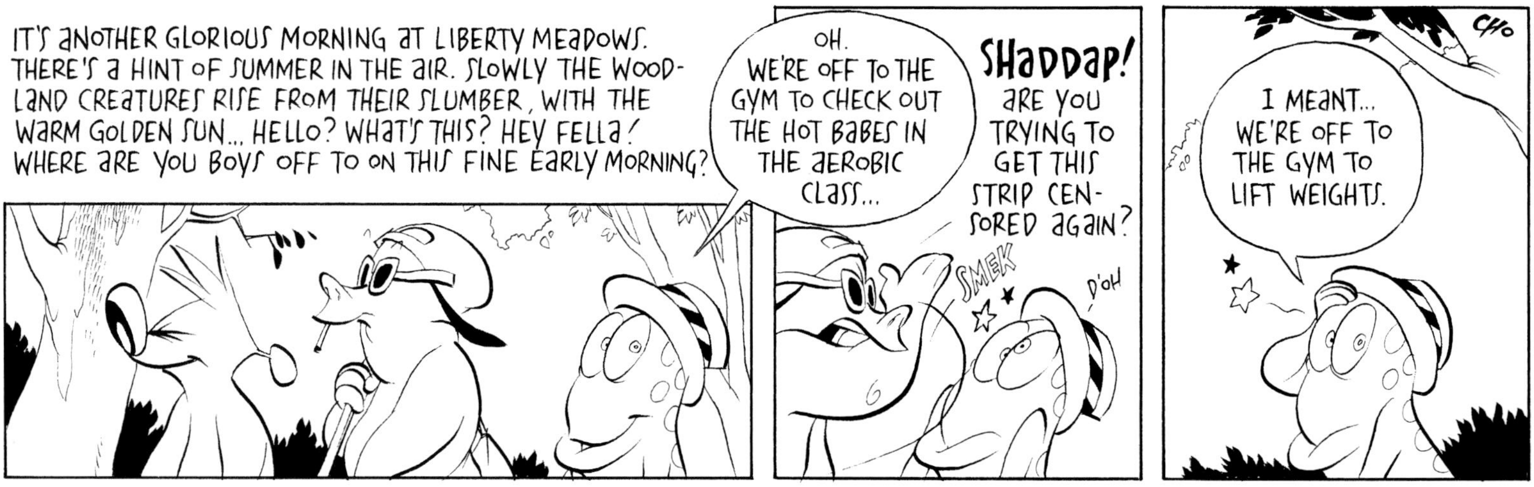
IT'S ANOTHER GLORIOUS MORNING AT LIBERTY MEADOWS. THERE'S A HINT OF SUMMER IN THE AIR. SLOWLY THE WOODLAND CREATURES RISE FROM THEIR SLUMBER, WITH THE WARM GOLDEN SUN... HELLO? WHAT'S THIS? HEY FELLA! WHERE ARE YOU BOYS OFF TO ON THIS FINE EARLY MORNING?
OH. WE'RE OFF TO THE GYM TO CHECK OUT THE HOT BABES IN THE AEROBIC CLASS...
SHADDAP! ARE YOU TRYING TO GET THIS STRIP CENSORED AGAIN?
SMEK
D'OH
I MEANT... WE'RE OFF TO THE GYM TO LIFT WEIGHTS.

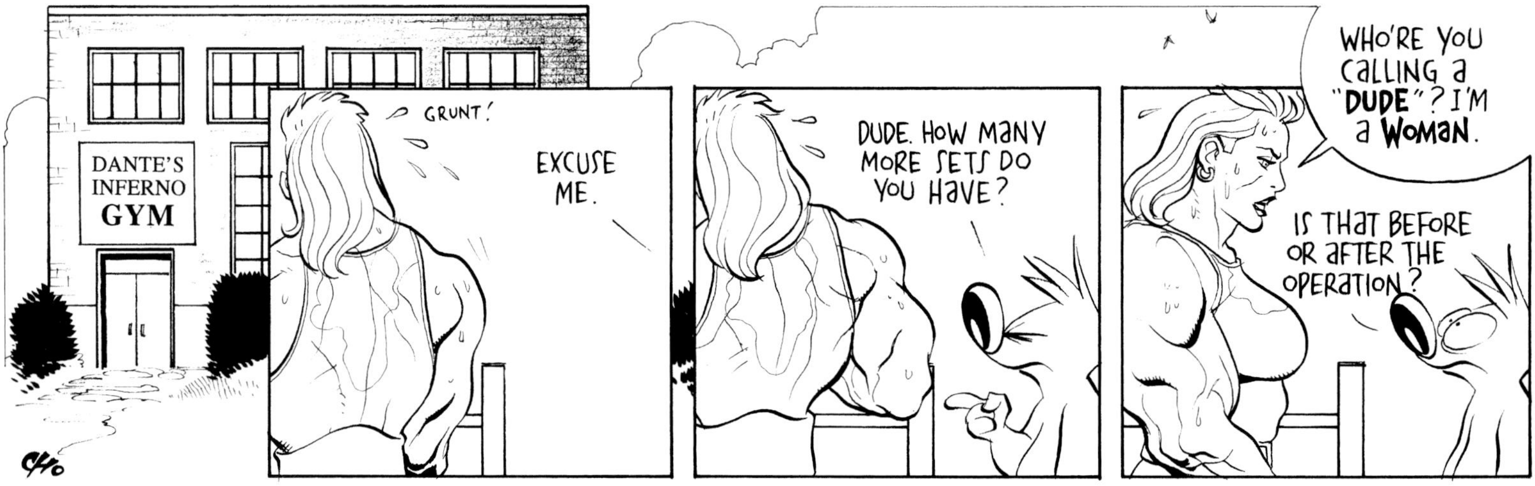
DANTE'S INFERNO GYM
GRUNT!
EXCUSE ME.
DUDE. HOW MANY MORE SETS DO YOU HAVE?
WHO'RE YOU CALLING A "DUDE"? I'M A WOMAN.
IS THAT BEFORE OR AFTER THE OPERATION?

FREE

FOR ALL

WHERE READERS RANT

TODAY:

MISS CINDY HAIRYBACK

FROM

ROID'S GYM

VENICE BEACH, CALIFORNIA

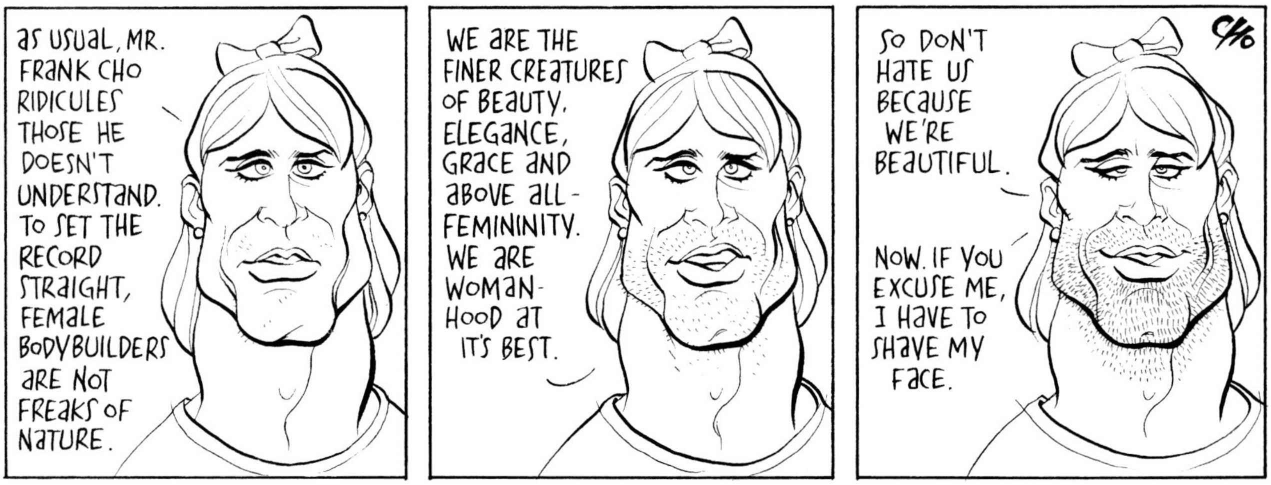
AS USUAL, MR. FRANK CHO RIDICULES THOSE HE DOESN'T UNDERSTAND. TO SET THE RECORD STRAIGHT, FEMALE BODYBUILDERS ARE NOT FREAKS OF NATURE.
WE ARE THE FINER CREATURES OF BEAUTY, ELEGANCE, GRACE AND ABOVE ALL - FEMININITY. WE ARE WOMANHOOD AT IT'S BEST.
SO DON'T HATE US BECAUSE WE'RE BEAUTIFUL.
NOW. IF YOU EXCUSE ME, I HAVE TO SHAVE MY FACE.

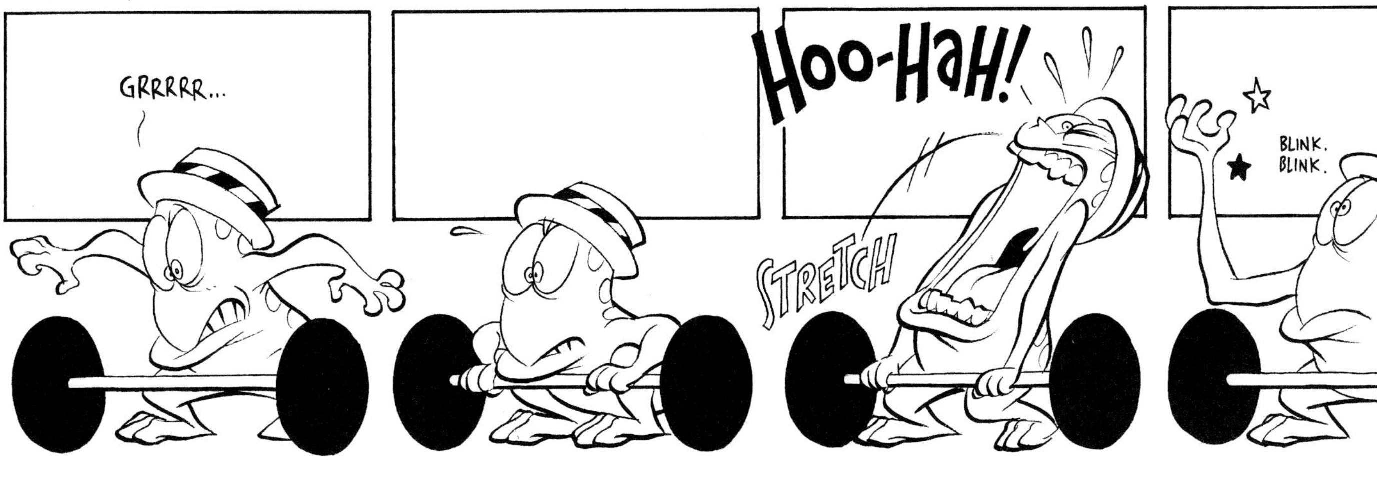

GRRRRR...
HOO-HAH!
STRETCH
CHO
BLINK. BLINK.

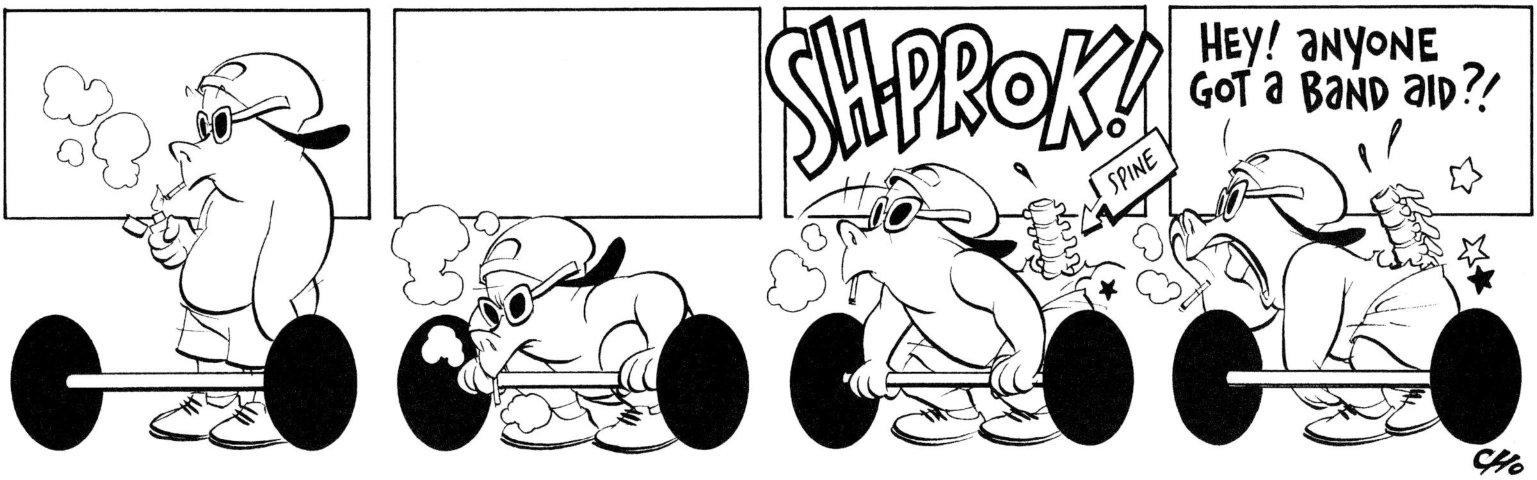

SH-PROK!
SPINE
HEY! ANYONE GOT A BAND AID?!
CHO

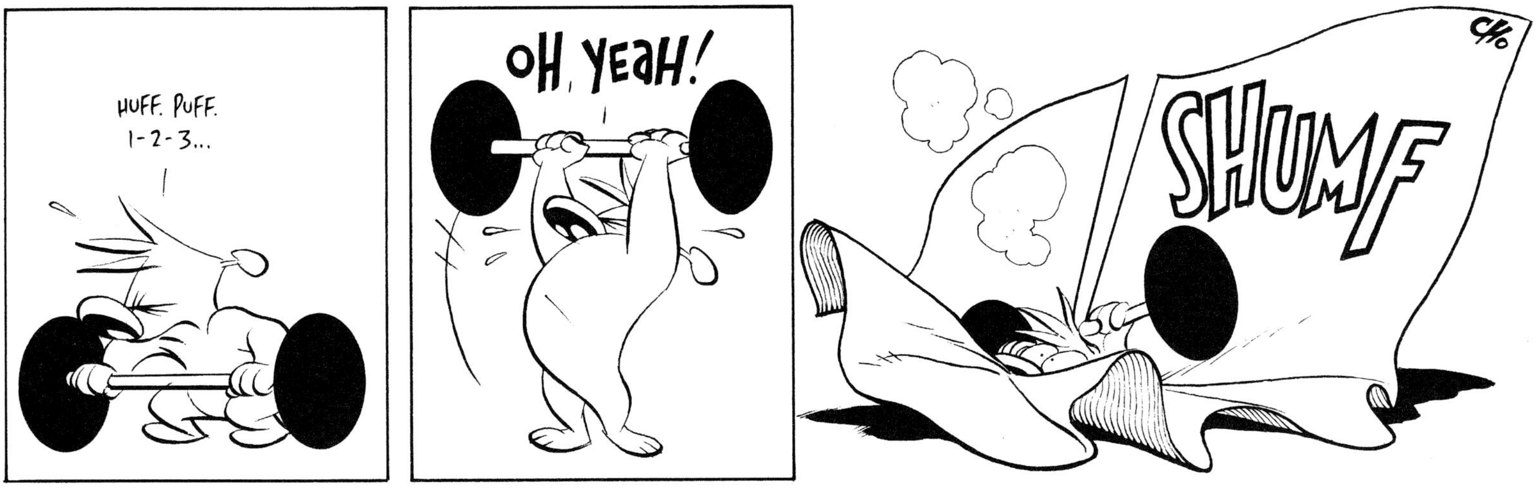

HUFF. PUFF. 1-2-3...
OH, YEAH!
CHO
SHUMF

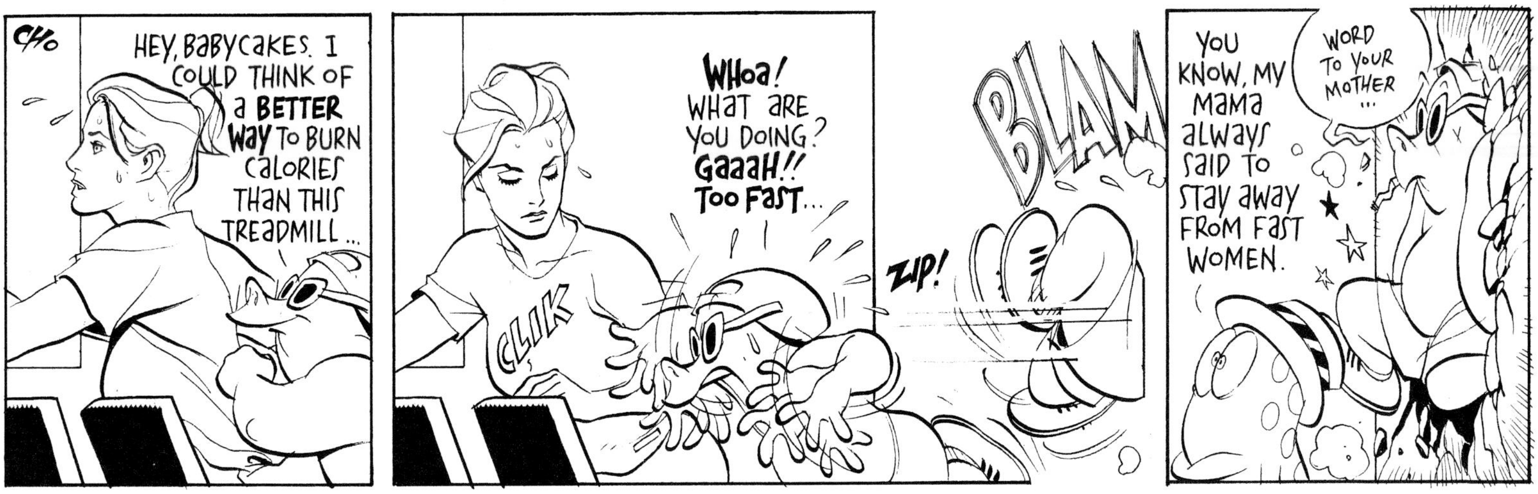

CHO
HEY, BABYCAKES. I COULD THINK OF A **BETTER WAY** TO BURN CALORIES THAN THIS TREADMILL...
CLIK
WHOA! WHAT ARE YOU DOING? **GAAAH!! TOO FAST**...
BLAM
ZIP!
YOU KNOW, MY MAMA ALWAYS SAID TO STAY AWAY FROM FAST WOMEN.
WORD TO YOUR MOTHER...

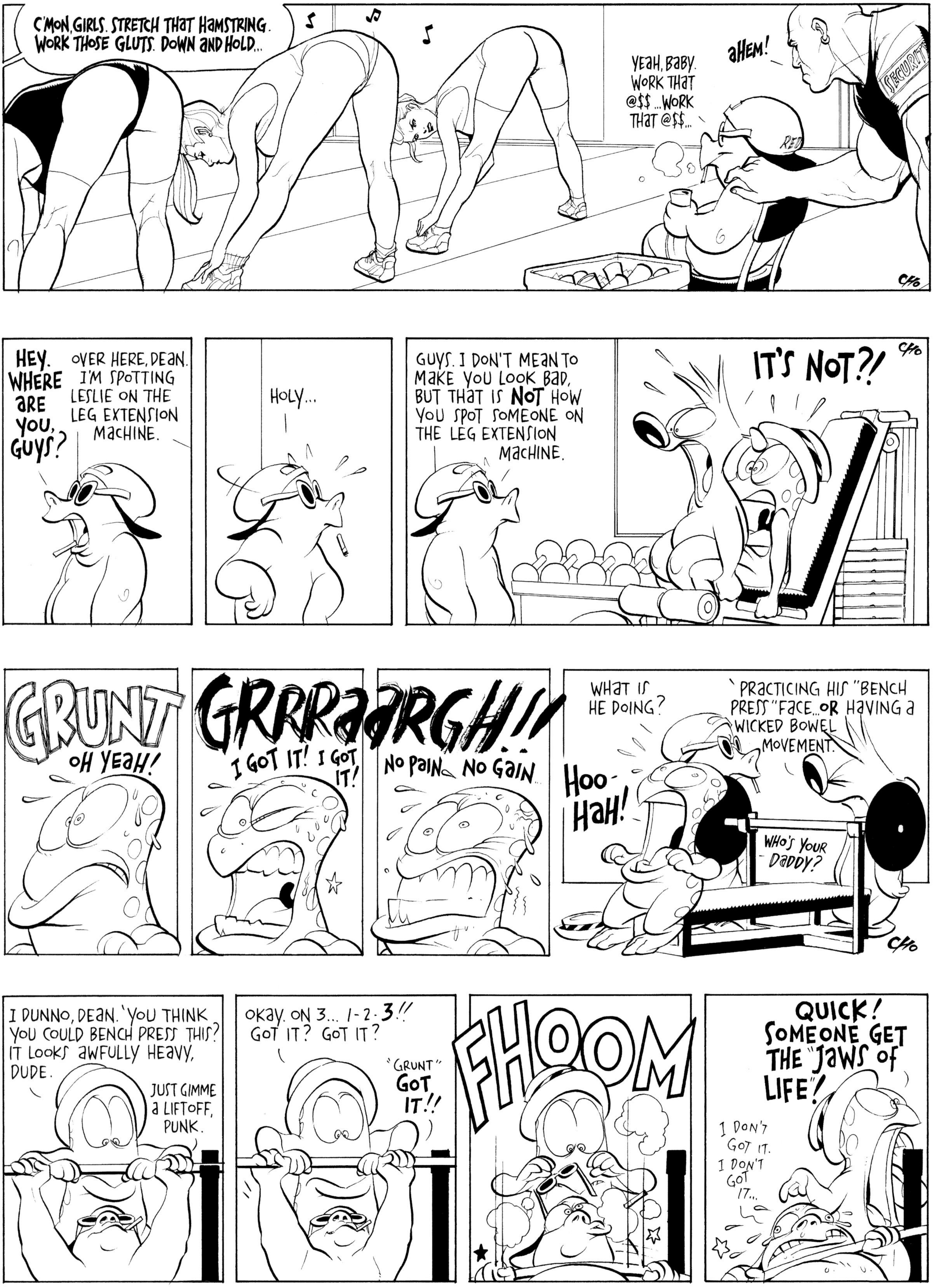
C'MON, GIRLS. STRETCH THAT HAMSTRING. WORK THOSE GLUTS. DOWN AND HOLD...
YEAH, BABY. WORK THAT @$$ ...WORK THAT @$$...
AHEM!
HEY. WHERE ARE YOU, GUYS?
OVER HERE, DEAN. I'M SPOTTING LESLIE ON THE LEG EXTENSION MACHINE.
HOLY...
GUYS. I DON'T MEAN TO MAKE YOU LOOK BAD, BUT THAT IS NOT HOW YOU SPOT SOMEONE ON THE LEG EXTENSION MACHINE.
IT'S NOT?!
GRUNT
OH YEAH!
GRRRAARGH!!
I GOT IT! I GOT IT!
NO PAIN... NO GAIN...
WHAT IS HE DOING?
PRACTICING HIS "BENCH PRESS" FACE...OR HAVING A WICKED BOWEL MOVEMENT.
HOO-HAH!
WHO'S YOUR DADDY?
I DUNNO, DEAN. YOU THINK YOU COULD BENCH PRESS THIS? IT LOOKS AWFULLY HEAVY, DUDE.
JUST GIMME A LIFTOFF, PUNK.
OKAY. ON 3... 1-2-3!! GOT IT? GOT IT?
"GRUNT" GOT IT!!
FHOOM
QUICK! SOMEONE GET THE "JAWS OF LIFE"!
I DON'T GOT IT. I DON'T GOT IT...

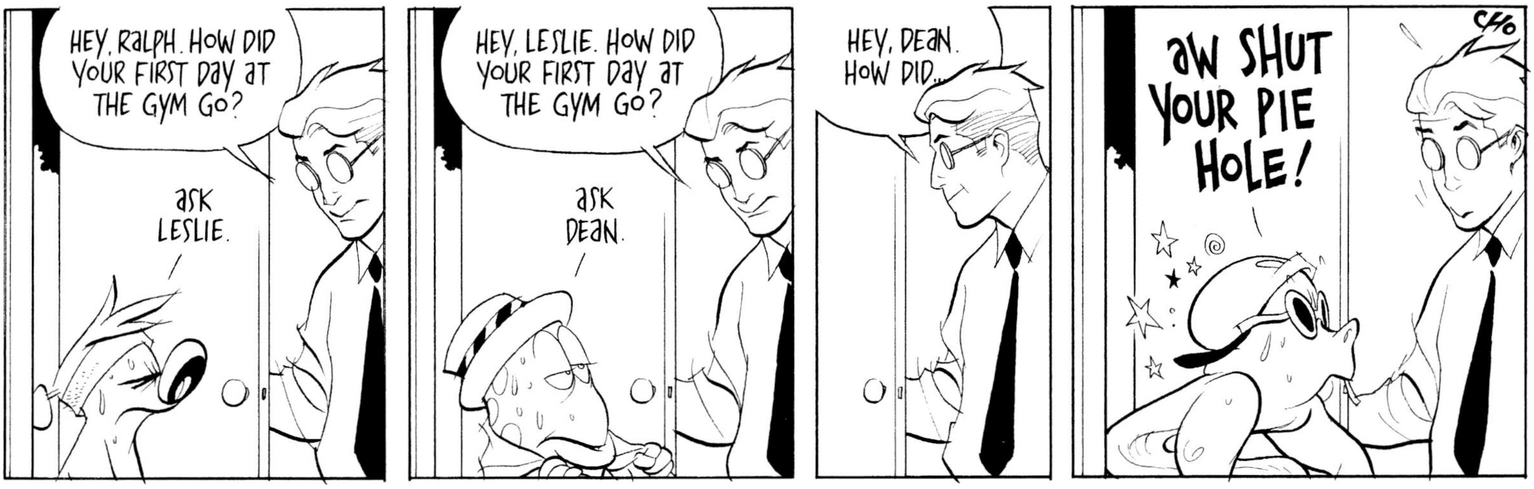
HEY, RaLPH. HOW DID YOUR FIRST DaY aT THE GYM GO?
aSK LESLIE.
HEY, LESLIE. HOW DID YOUR FIRST DaY aT THE GYM GO?
aSK DEaN.
HEY, DEaN. HOW DID...
aW SHUT YOUR PIE HOLE!
CHO

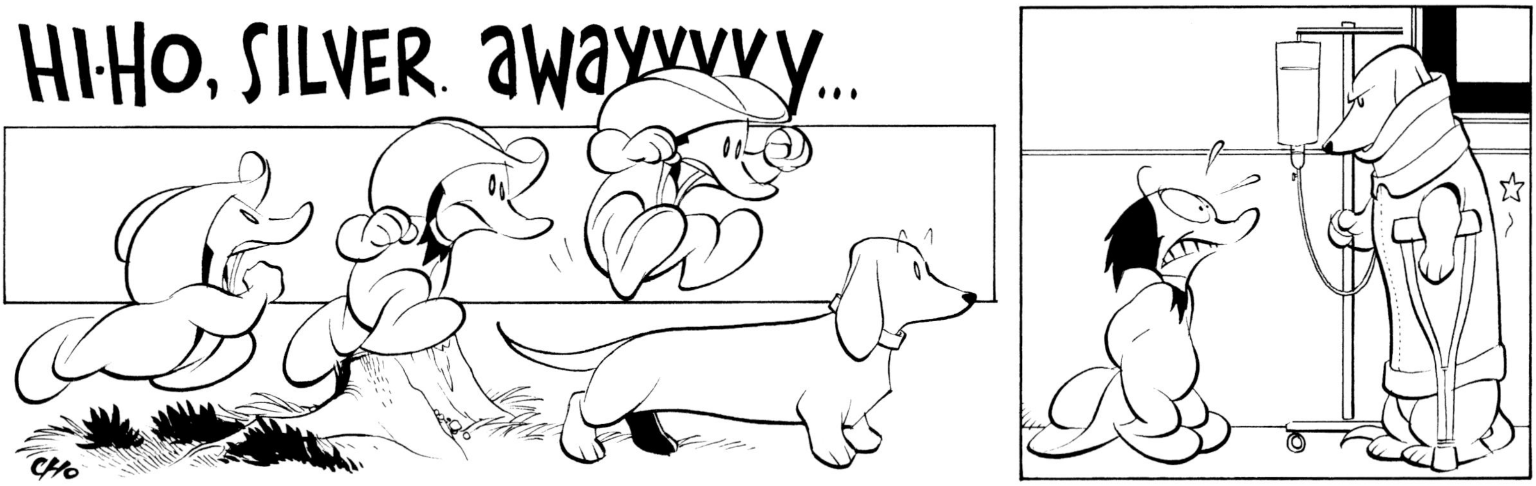
HI-HO, SILVER. awayyyyy...
CHO

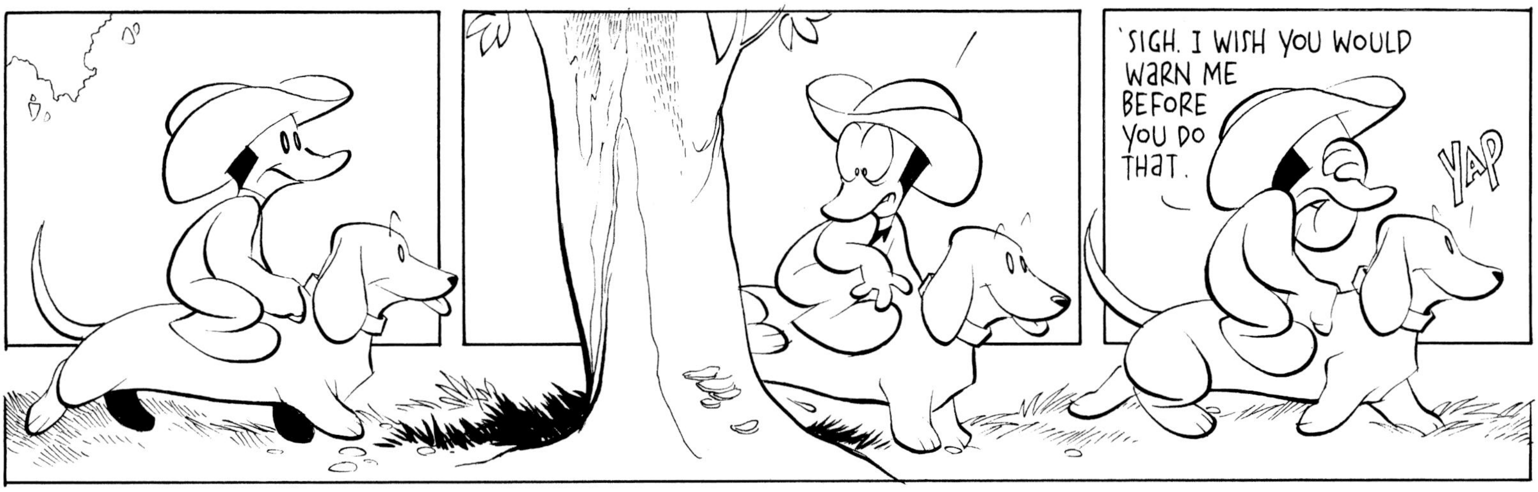
*SIGH. I WISH YOU WOULD WaRN ME BEFORE YOU DO THaT.
YaP

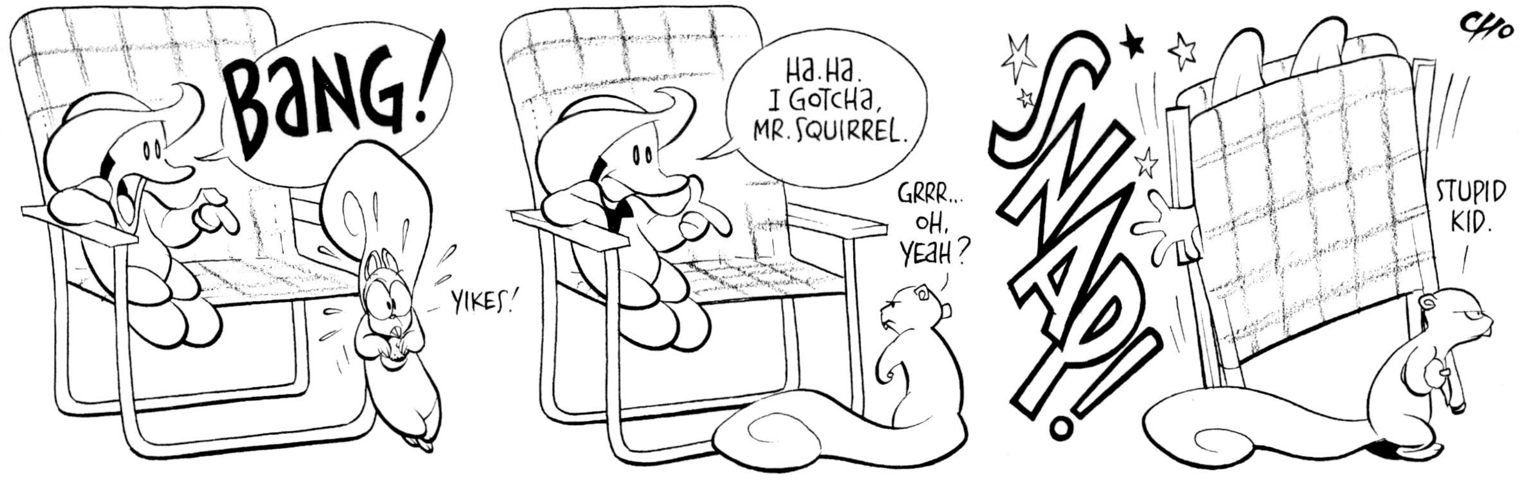
BaNG!
YIKES!
Ha. Ha. I GOTCHa, MR. SQUIRREL.
GRRR... OH, YEaH?
SNAP!
STUPID KID.
CHO

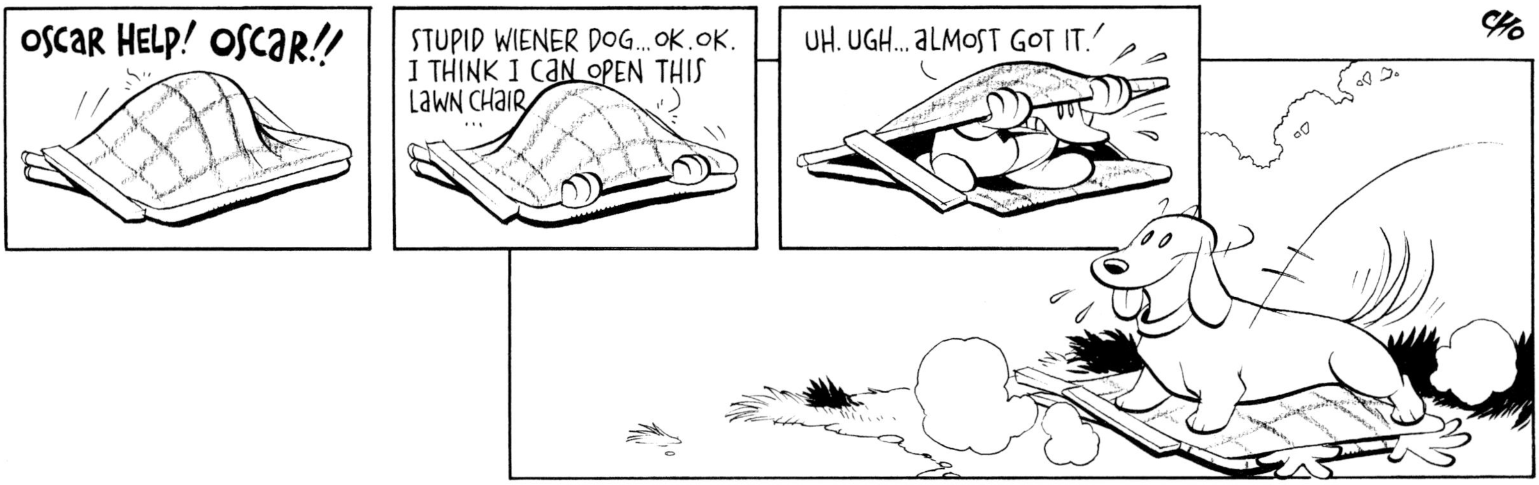
OSCAR HELP! OSCAR!!
STUPID WIENER DOG... OK. OK. I THINK I CAN OPEN THIS LAWN CHAIR ...
UH. UGH... ALMOST GOT IT!

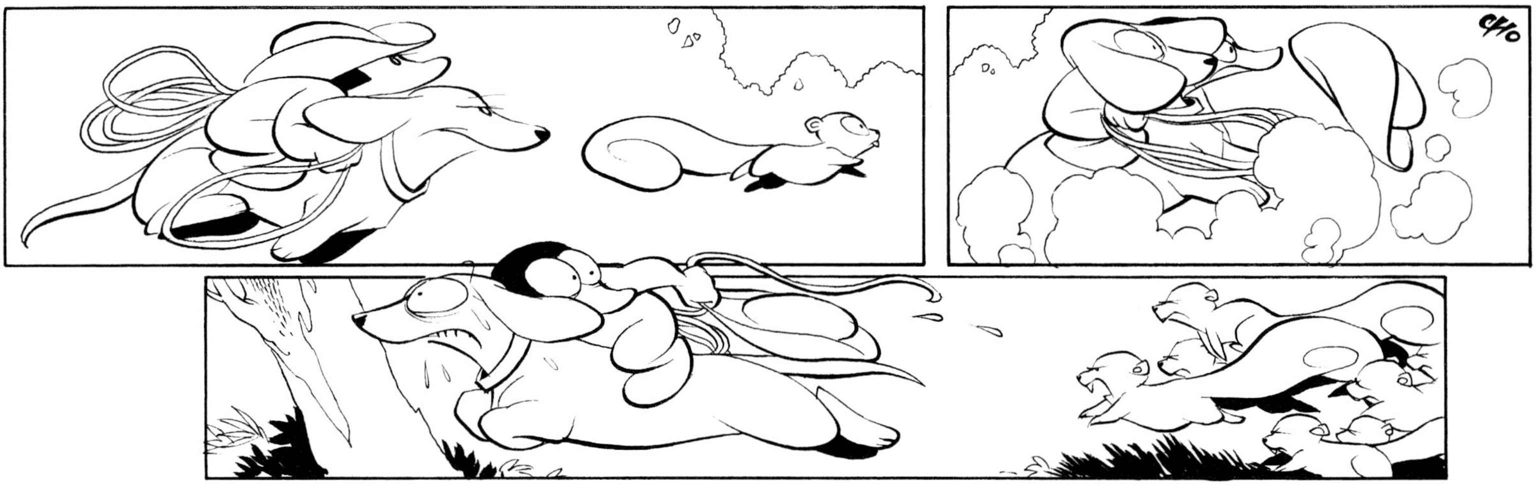

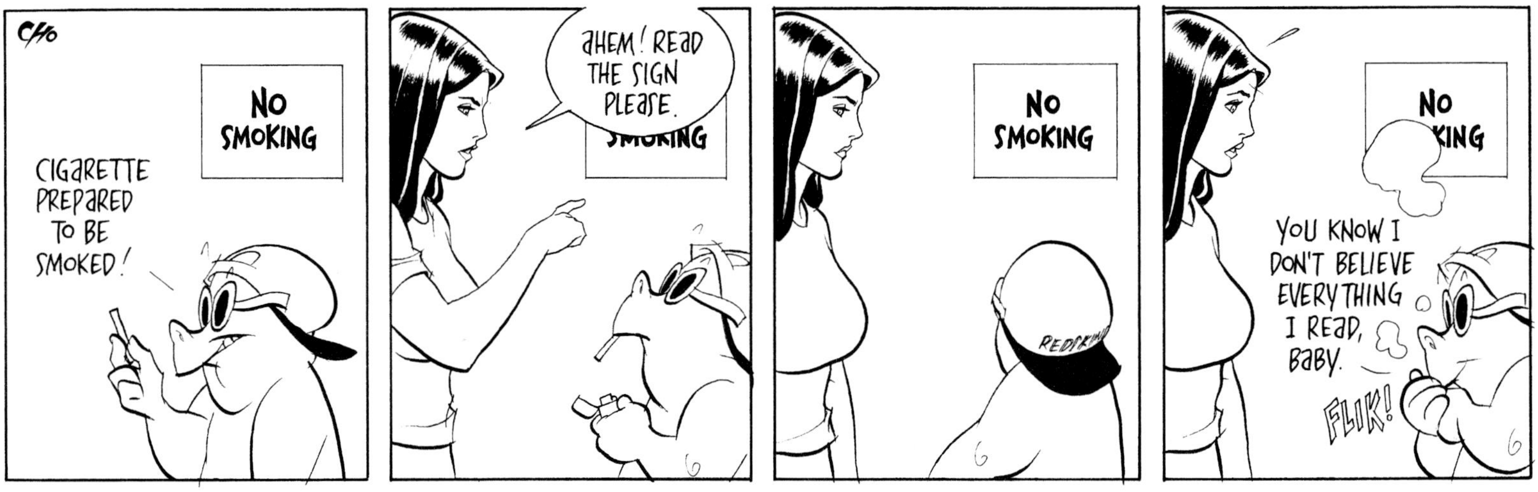
NO SMOKING
CIGARETTE PREPARED TO BE SMOKED!
AHEM! READ THE SIGN PLEASE.
SMOKING
NO SMOKING
NO KING
YOU KNOW I DON'T BELIEVE EVERYTHING I READ, BABY.
FLIK!

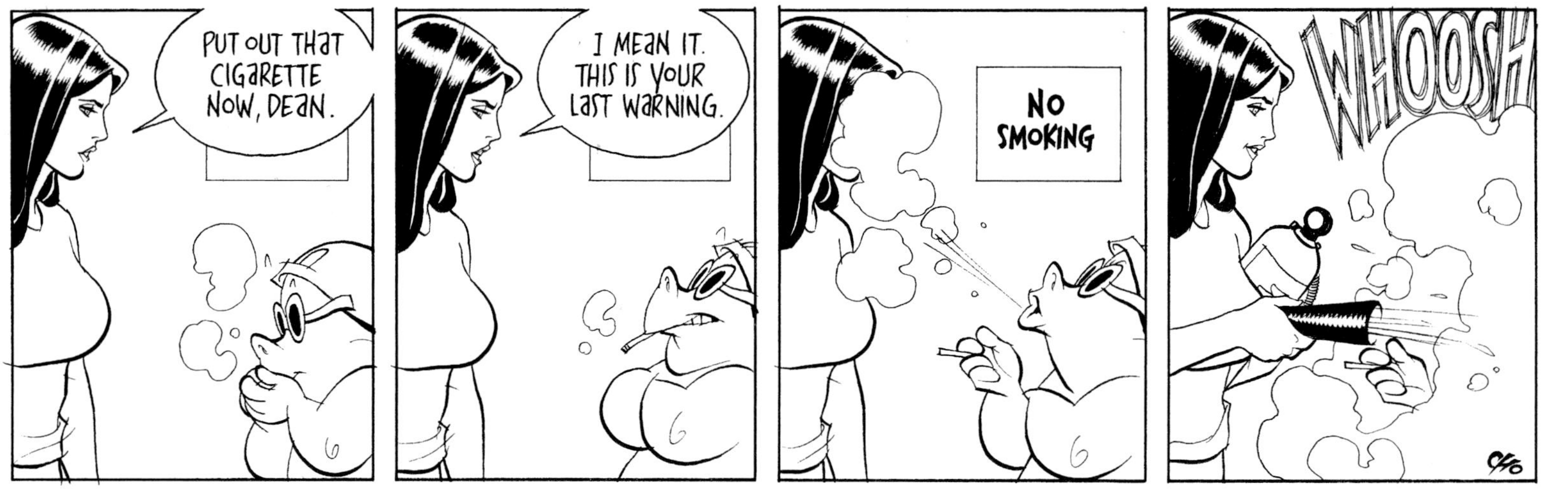
PUT OUT THAT CIGARETTE NOW, DEAN.
I MEAN IT. THIS IS YOUR LAST WARNING.
NO SMOKING
WHOOSH

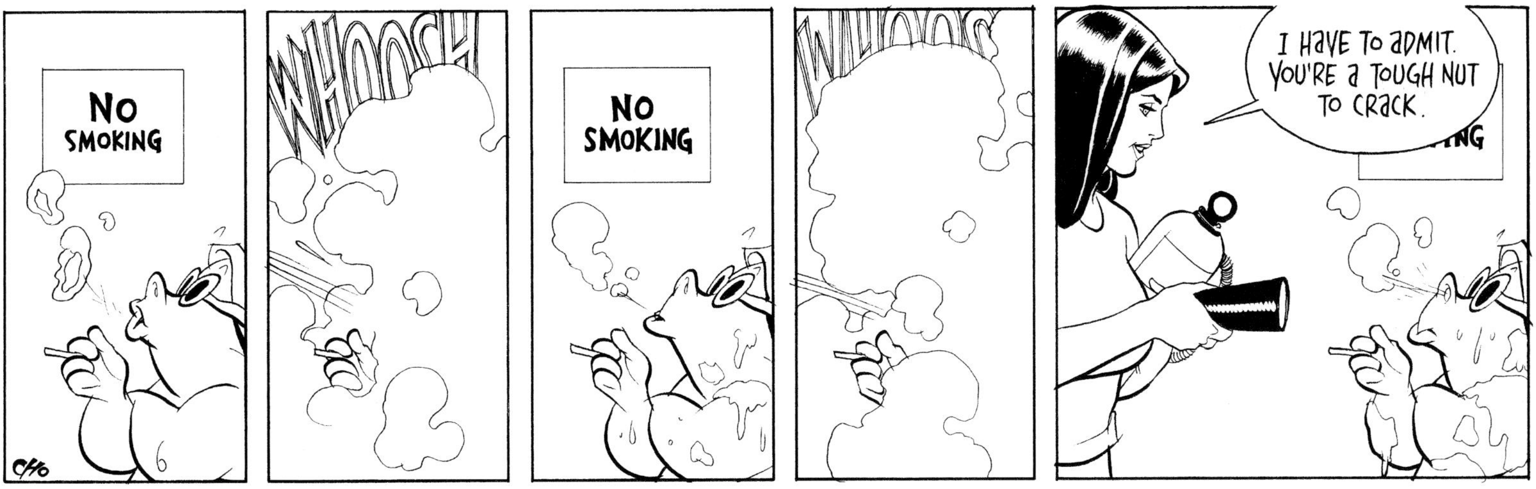
NO SMOKING
WHOOSH
NO SMOKING
WHOOSH
I HAVE TO ADMIT. YOU'RE A TOUGH NUT TO CRACK.

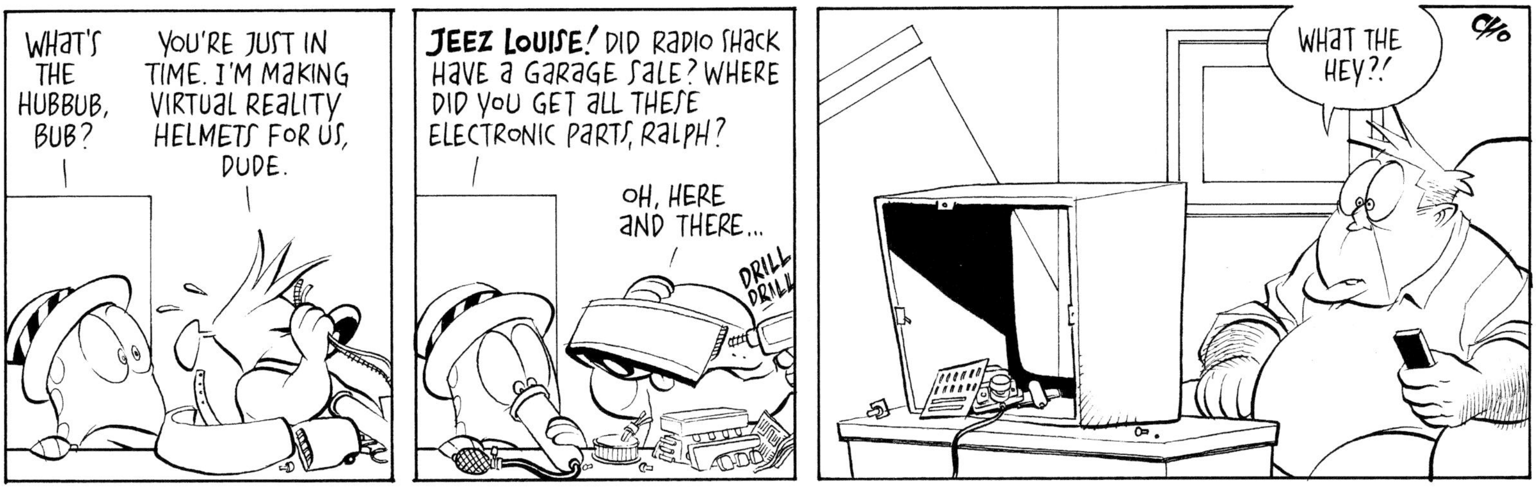
WHAT'S THE HUBBUB, BUB?
YOU'RE JUST IN TIME. I'M MAKING VIRTUAL REALITY HELMETS FOR US, DUDE.
JEEZ LOUISE! DID RADIO SHACK HAVE A GARAGE SALE? WHERE DID YOU GET ALL THESE ELECTRONIC PARTS, RALPH?
OH, HERE AND THERE...
DRILL DRILL
WHAT THE HEY?!

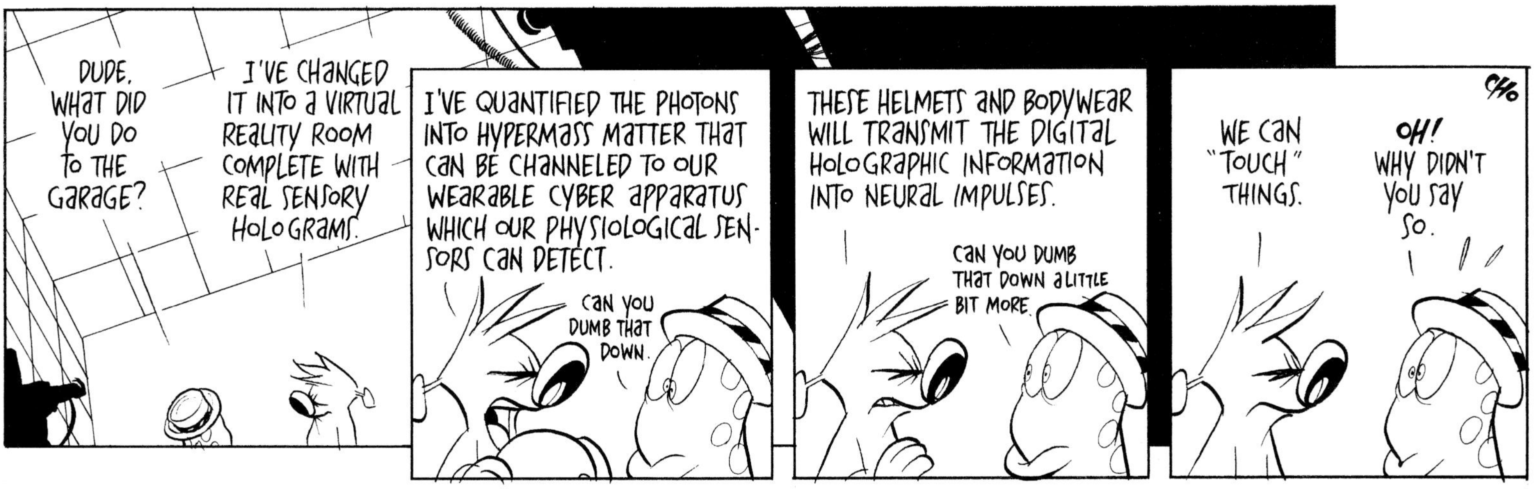
DUDE. WHAT DID YOU DO TO THE GARAGE?
I'VE CHANGED IT INTO A VIRTUAL REALITY ROOM COMPLETE WITH REAL SENSORY HOLOGRAMS.
I'VE QUANTIFIED THE PHOTONS INTO HYPERMASS MATTER THAT CAN BE CHANNELED TO OUR WEARABLE CYBER APPARATUS WHICH OUR PHYSIOLOGICAL SENSORS CAN DETECT.
CAN YOU DUMB THAT DOWN.
THESE HELMETS AND BODYWEAR WILL TRANSMIT THE DIGITAL HOLOGRAPHIC INFORMATION INTO NEURAL IMPULSES.
CAN YOU DUMB THAT DOWN A LITTLE BIT MORE.
WE CAN "TOUCH" THINGS.
OH! WHY DIDN'T YOU SAY SO.

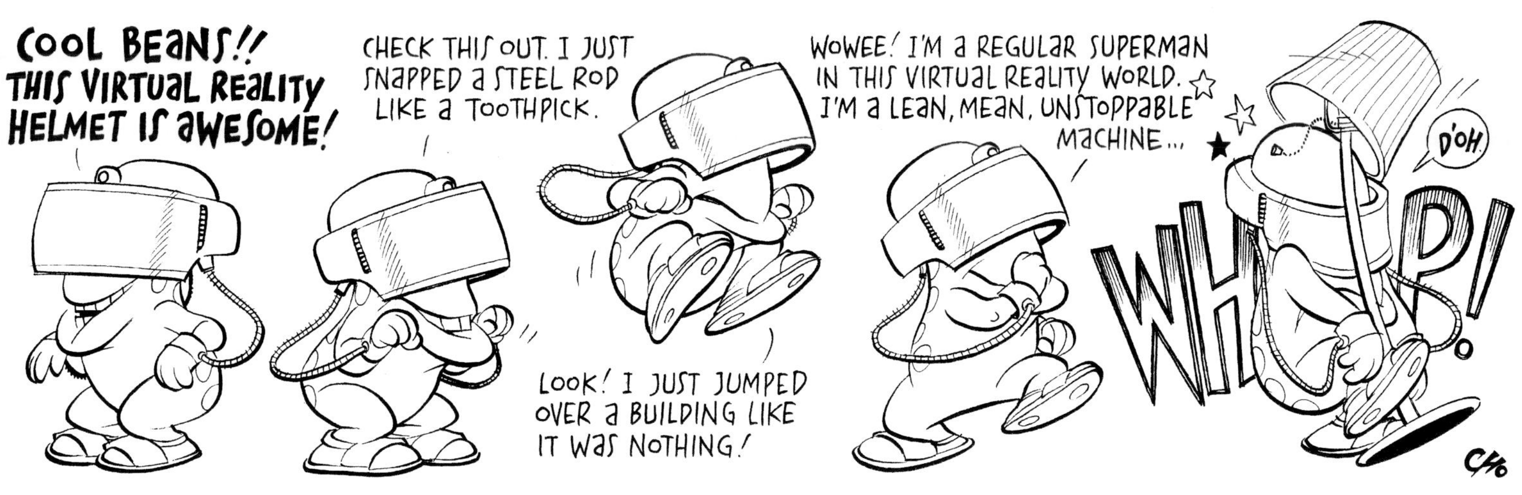
COOL BEANS!! THIS VIRTUAL REALITY HELMET IS AWESOME!
CHECK THIS OUT. I JUST SNAPPED A STEEL ROD LIKE A TOOTHPICK.
LOOK! I JUST JUMPED OVER A BUILDING LIKE IT WAS NOTHING!
WOWEE! I'M A REGULAR SUPERMAN IN THIS VIRTUAL REALITY WORLD. I'M A LEAN, MEAN, UNSTOPPABLE MACHINE...
D'OH
WHAP!

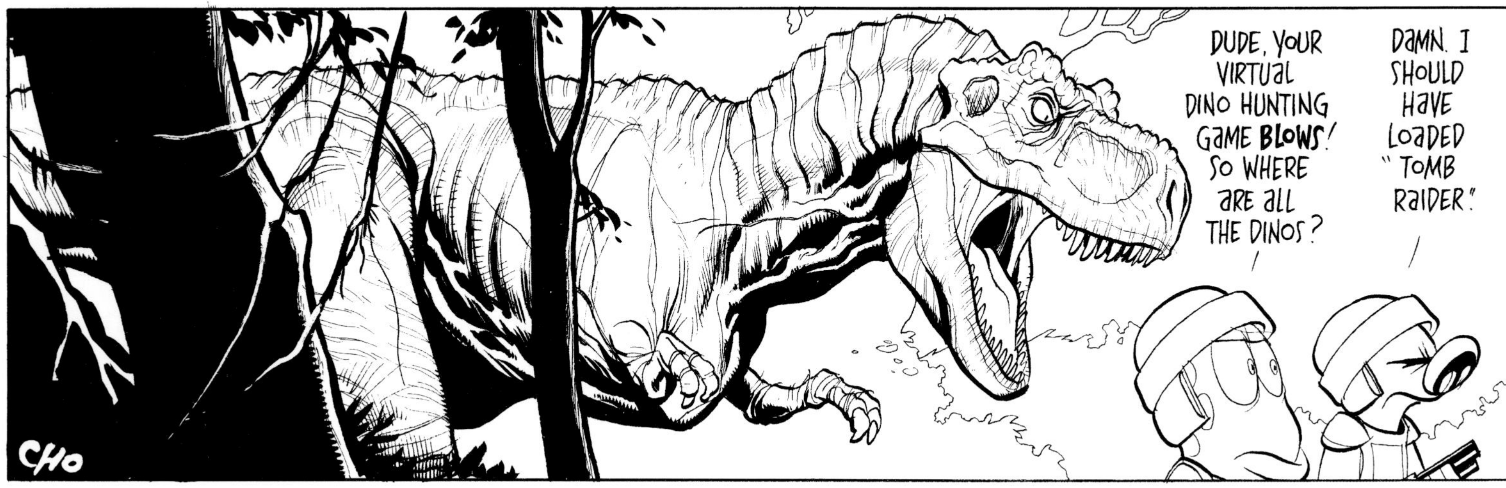
DUDE, YOUR VIRTUAL DINO HUNTING GAME **BLOWS**! SO WHERE ARE ALL THE DINOS?
DAMN. I SHOULD HAVE LOADED "TOMB RAIDER".

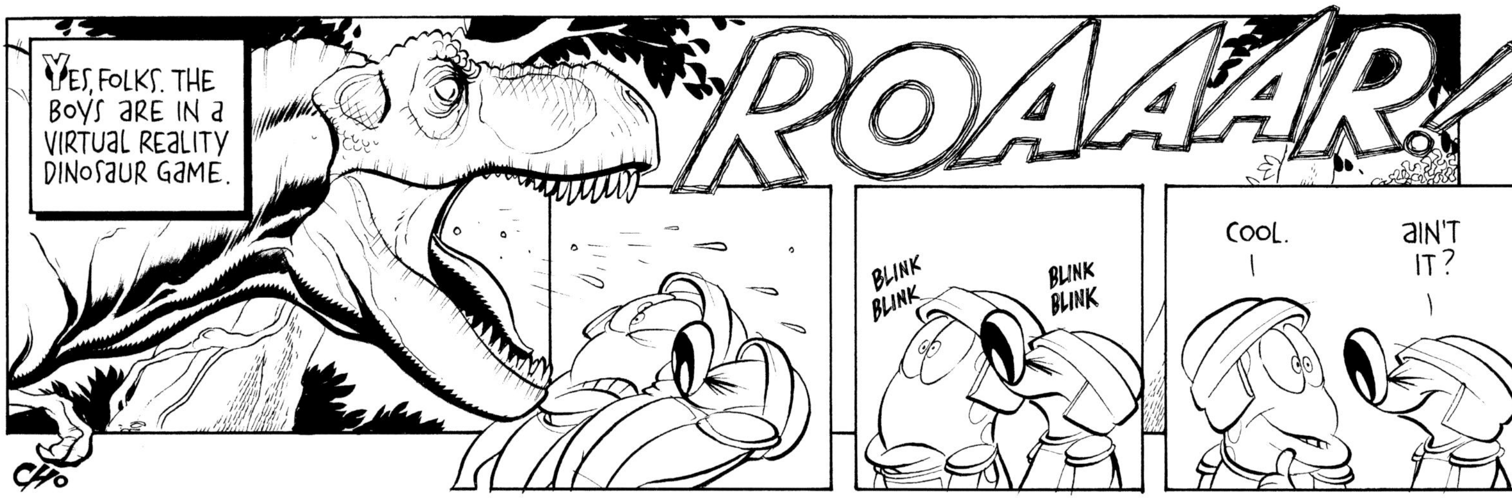
YES, FOLKS. THE BOYS ARE IN A VIRTUAL REALITY DINOSAUR GAME.
ROAAAR!
BLINK BLINK
BLINK BLINK
COOL.
AIN'T IT?

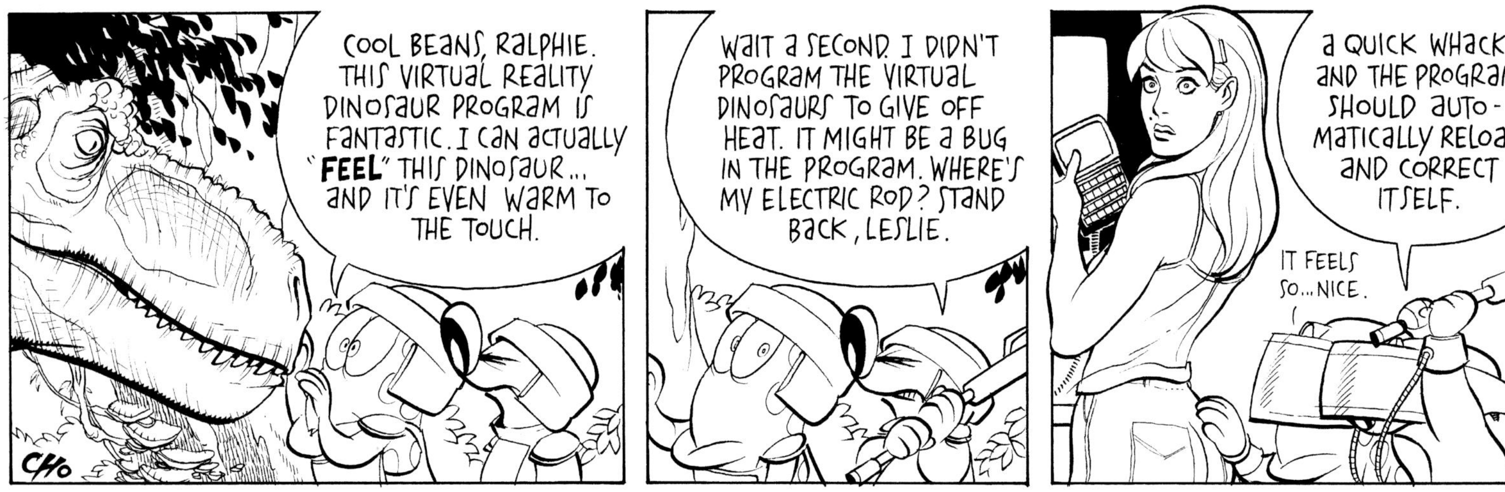
COOL BEANS, RALPHIE. THIS VIRTUAL REALITY DINOSAUR PROGRAM IS FANTASTIC. I CAN ACTUALLY "**FEEL**" THIS DINOSAUR... AND IT'S EVEN WARM TO THE TOUCH.
WAIT A SECOND. I DIDN'T PROGRAM THE VIRTUAL DINOSAURS TO GIVE OFF HEAT. IT MIGHT BE A BUG IN THE PROGRAM. WHERE'S MY ELECTRIC ROD? STAND BACK, LESLIE.
A QUICK WHACK AND THE PROGRAM SHOULD AUTO-MATICALLY RELOAD AND CORRECT ITSELF.
IT FEELS SO... NICE.

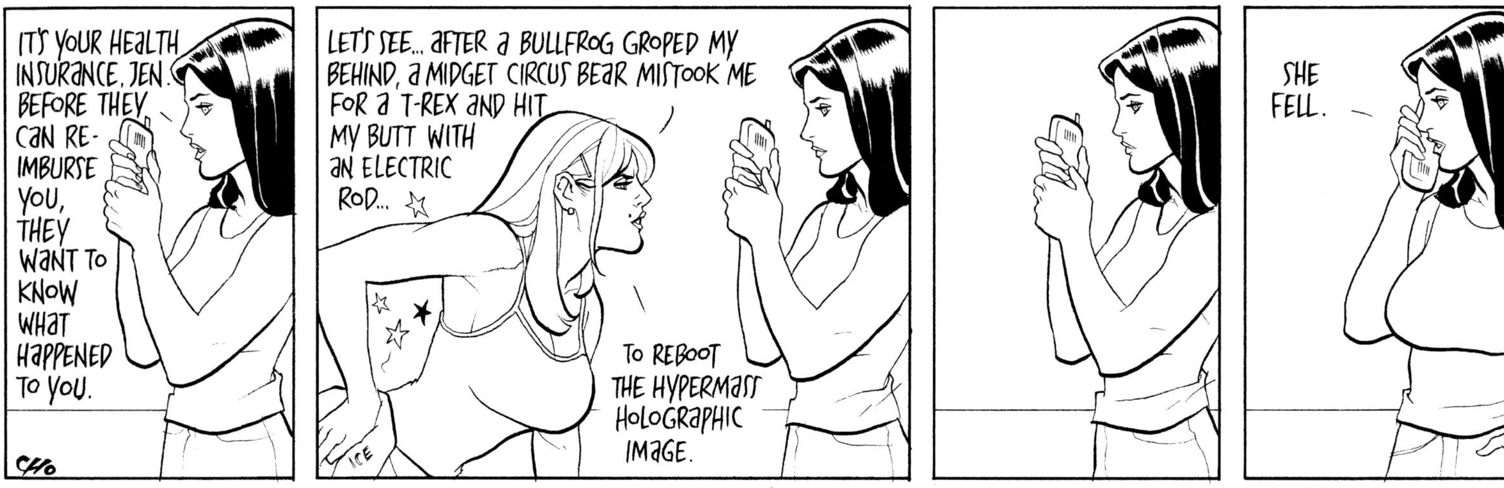
IT'S YOUR HEALTH INSURANCE, JEN. BEFORE THEY CAN RE-IMBURSE YOU, THEY WANT TO KNOW WHAT HAPPENED TO YOU.
LET'S SEE... AFTER A BULLFROG GROPED MY BEHIND, A MIDGET CIRCUS BEAR MISTOOK ME FOR A T-REX AND HIT MY BUTT WITH AN ELECTRIC ROD...
TO REBOOT THE HYPERMASS HOLOGRAPHIC IMAGE.
SHE FELL.

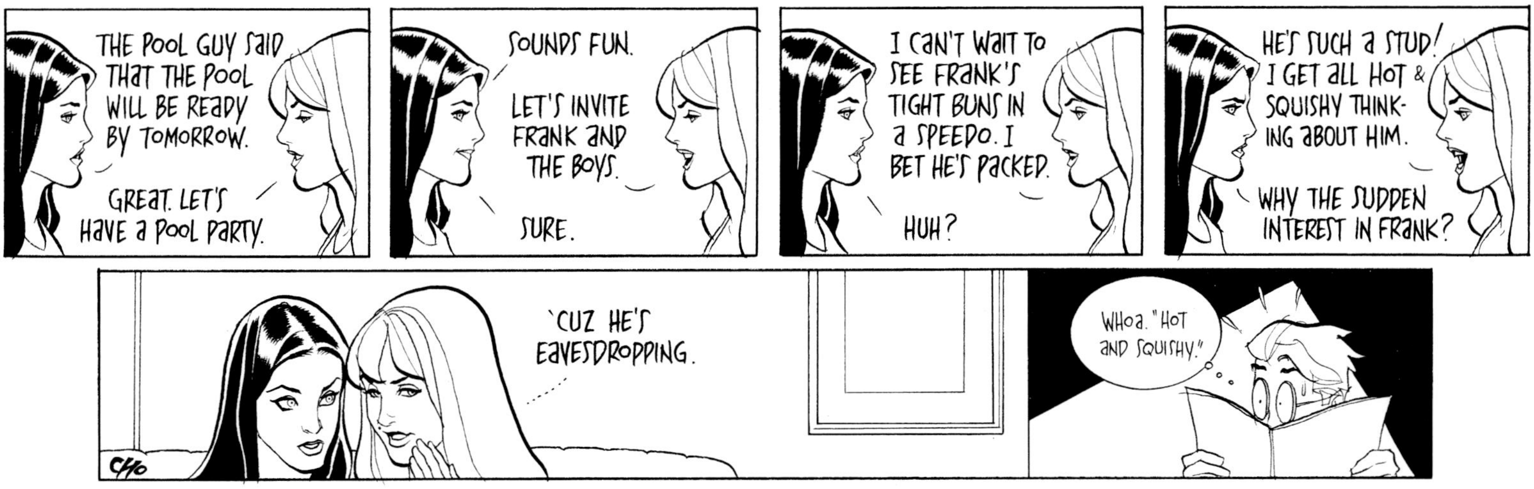
THE POOL GUY SAID THAT THE POOL WILL BE READY BY TOMORROW.
GREAT. LET'S HAVE A POOL PARTY.
SOUNDS FUN.
LET'S INVITE FRANK AND THE BOYS.
SURE.
I CAN'T WAIT TO SEE FRANK'S TIGHT BUNS IN A SPEEDO. I BET HE'S PACKED.
HUH?
HE'S SUCH A STUD! I GET ALL HOT & SQUISHY THINKING ABOUT HIM.
WHY THE SUDDEN INTEREST IN FRANK?
`CUZ HE'S EAVESDROPPING.
WHOA. "HOT AND SQUISHY."

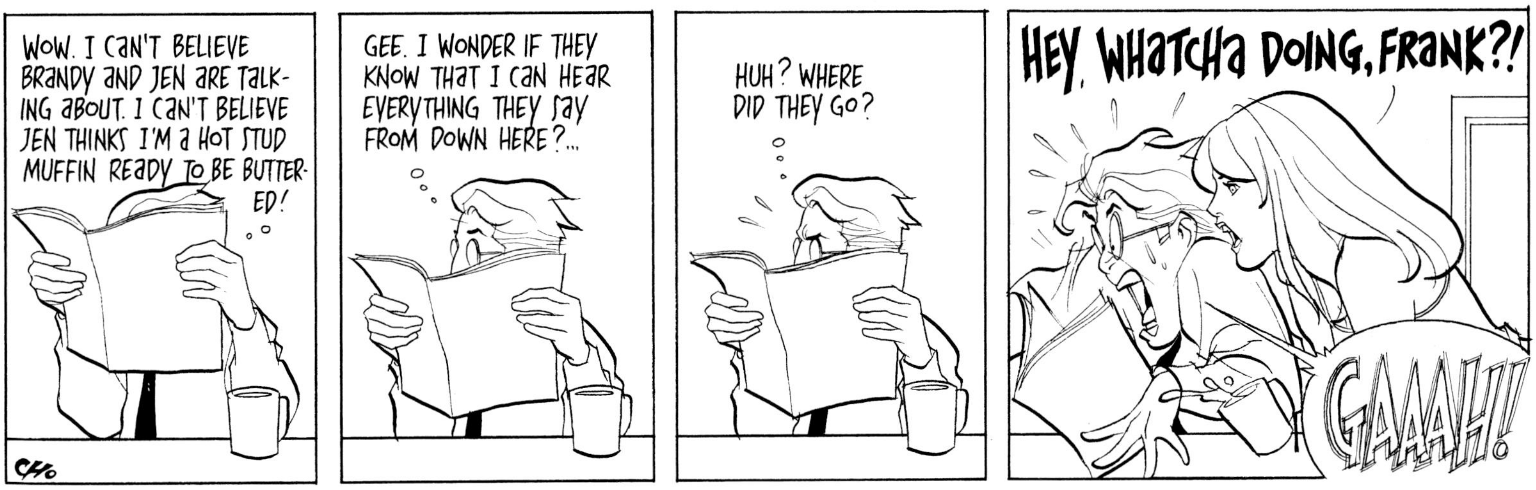
WOW. I CAN'T BELIEVE BRANDY AND JEN ARE TALKING ABOUT. I CAN'T BELIEVE JEN THINKS I'M A HOT STUD MUFFIN READY TO BE BUTTERED!
GEE. I WONDER IF THEY KNOW THAT I CAN HEAR EVERYTHING THEY SAY FROM DOWN HERE?...
HUH? WHERE DID THEY GO?
HEY, WHATCHA DOING, FRANK?!
GAAAH!

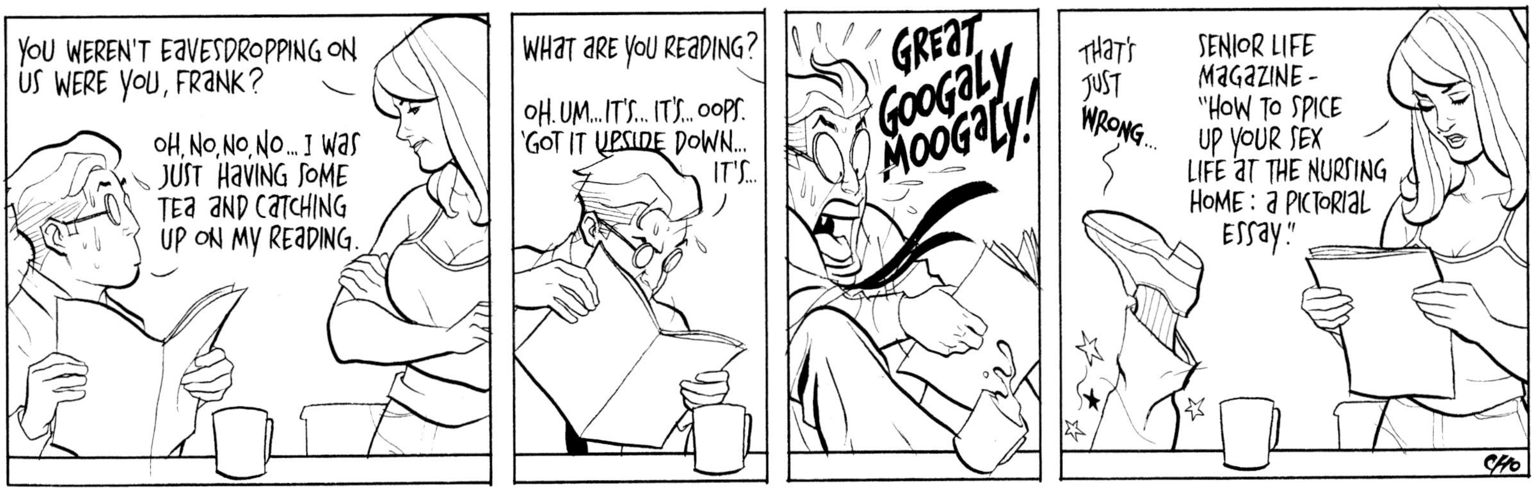
YOU WEREN'T EAVESDROPPING ON US WERE YOU, FRANK?
OH, NO, NO, NO... I WAS JUST HAVING SOME TEA AND CATCHING UP ON MY READING.
WHAT ARE YOU READING?
OH. UM... IT'S... IT'S... OOPS. 'GOT IT UPSIDE DOWN... IT'S...
GREAT GOOGALY MOOGALY!
THAT'S JUST WRONG...
SENIOR LIFE MAGAZINE - "HOW TO SPICE UP YOUR SEX LIFE AT THE NURSING HOME: A PICTORIAL ESSAY."

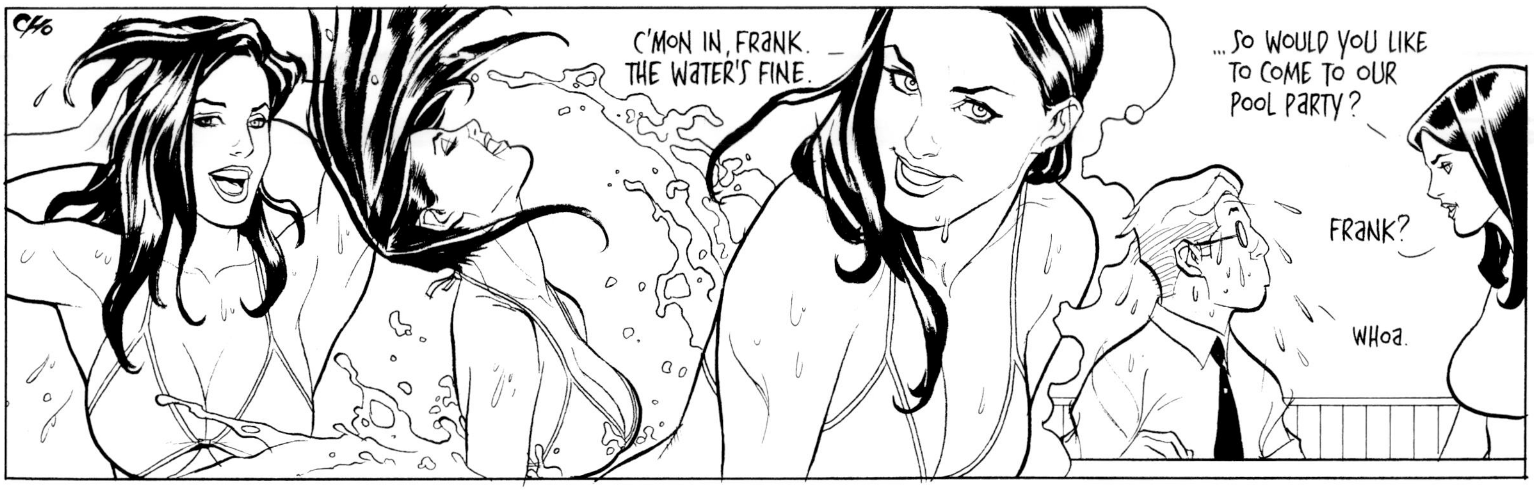
C'MON IN, FRANK. THE WATER'S FINE.
...SO WOULD YOU LIKE TO COME TO OUR POOL PARTY?
FRANK?
WHOA.

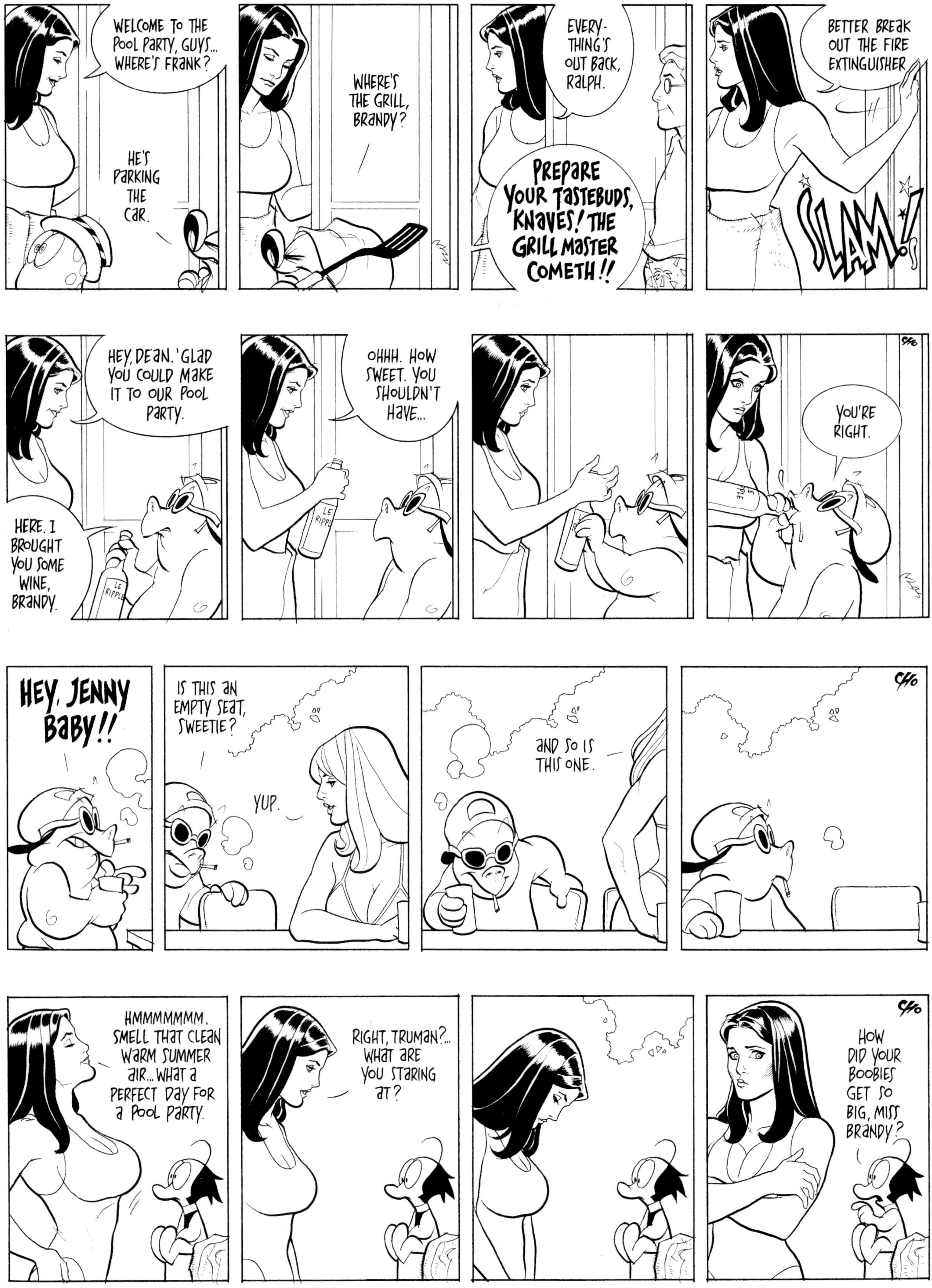
WELCOME TO THE POOL PARTY, GUYS... WHERE'S FRANK?
HE'S PARKING THE CAR.
WHERE'S THE GRILL, BRANDY?
EVERY-THING'S OUT BACK, RALPH.
PREPARE YOUR TASTEBUDS, KNAVES! THE GRILL MASTER COMETH!!
BETTER BREAK OUT THE FIRE EXTINGUISHER
SLAM!
HEY, DEAN. 'GLAD YOU COULD MAKE IT TO OUR POOL PARTY.
HERE. I BROUGHT YOU SOME WINE, BRANDY.
LE RIPPLE
OHHH. HOW SWEET. YOU SHOULDN'T HAVE...
LE RIPPLE
YOU'RE RIGHT.
CHO
HEY, JENNY BABY!!
IS THIS AN EMPTY SEAT, SWEETIE?
YUP.
AND SO IS THIS ONE.
CHO
HMMMMMMM. SMELL THAT CLEAN WARM SUMMER AIR... WHAT A PERFECT DAY FOR A POOL PARTY.
RIGHT, TRUMAN?... WHAT ARE YOU STARING AT?
HOW DID YOUR BOOBIES GET SO BIG, MISS BRANDY?
CHO

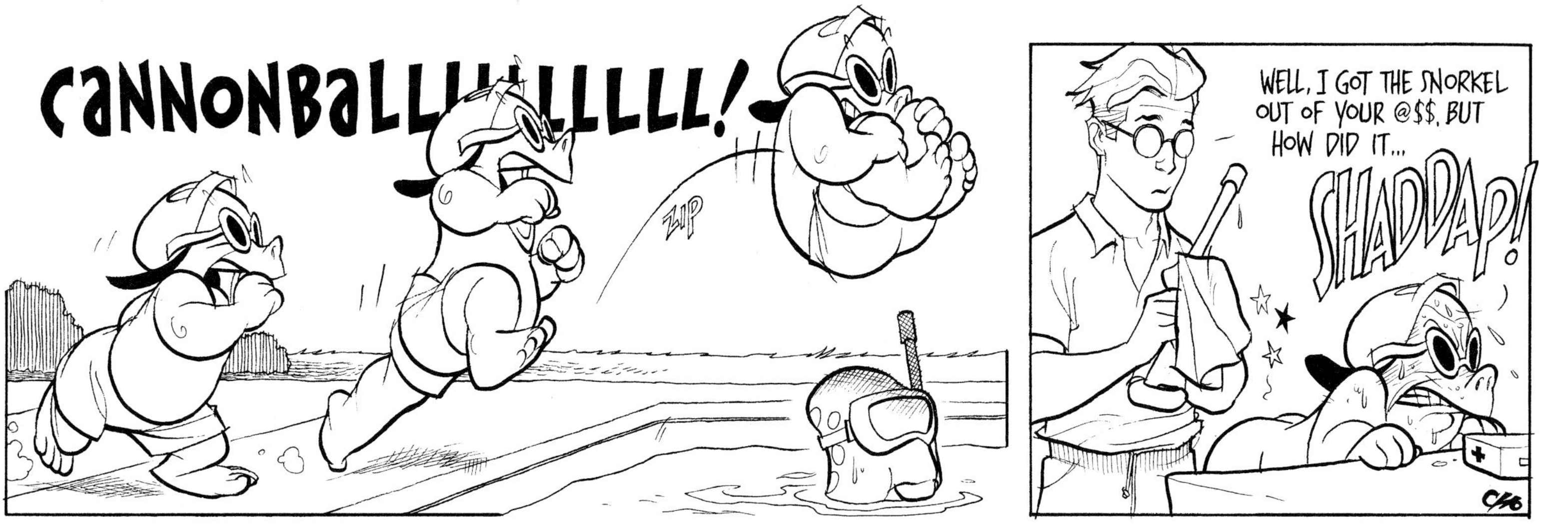
CANNONBALLLLLLLLL!
ZIP
WELL, I GOT THE SNORKEL OUT OF YOUR @$$, BUT HOW DID IT...
SHADDAP!

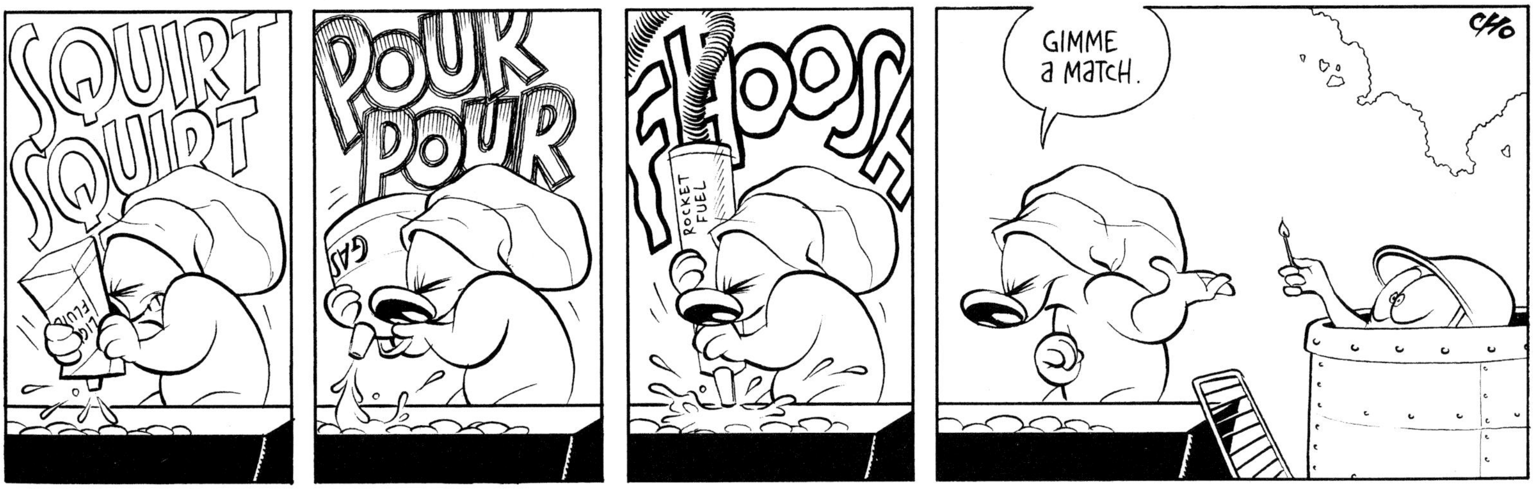
SQUIRT SQUIRT
POUR POUR
FWOOSH
ROCKET FUEL
GIMME A MATCH.

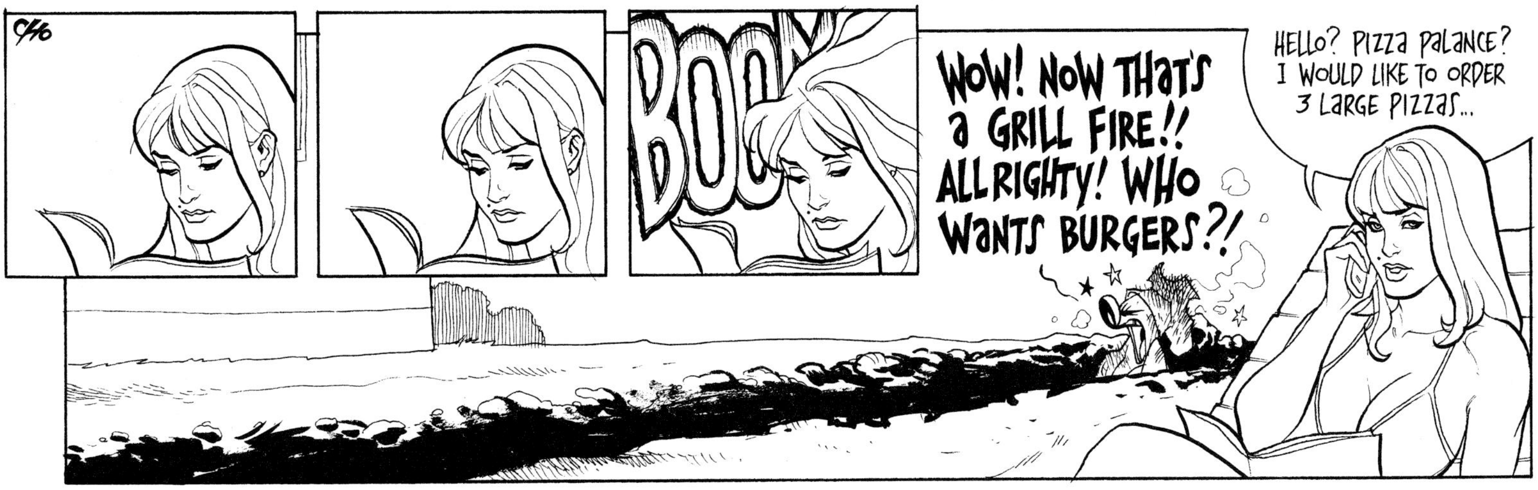
BOOM
WOW! NOW THAT'S A GRILL FIRE!! ALLRIGHTY! WHO WANTS BURGERS?!
HELLO? PIZZA PALANCE? I WOULD LIKE TO ORDER 3 LARGE PIZZAS...

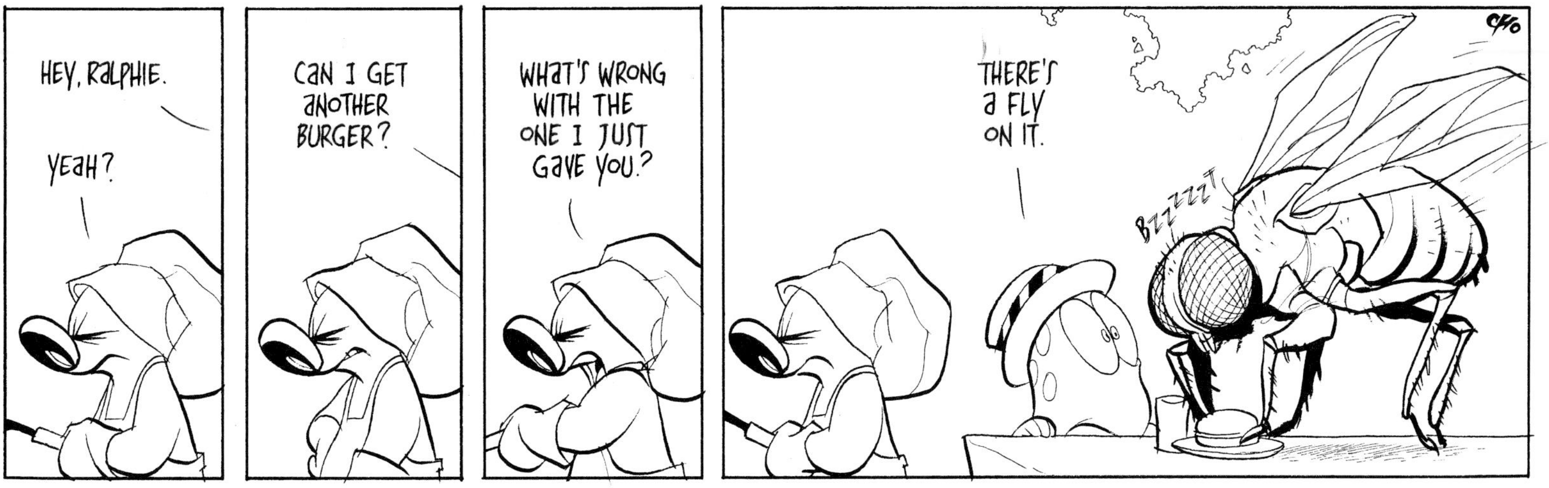
HEY, RALPHIE.
YEAH?
CAN I GET ANOTHER BURGER?
WHAT'S WRONG WITH THE ONE I JUST GAVE YOU?
THERE'S A FLY ON IT.
BZZZZZT

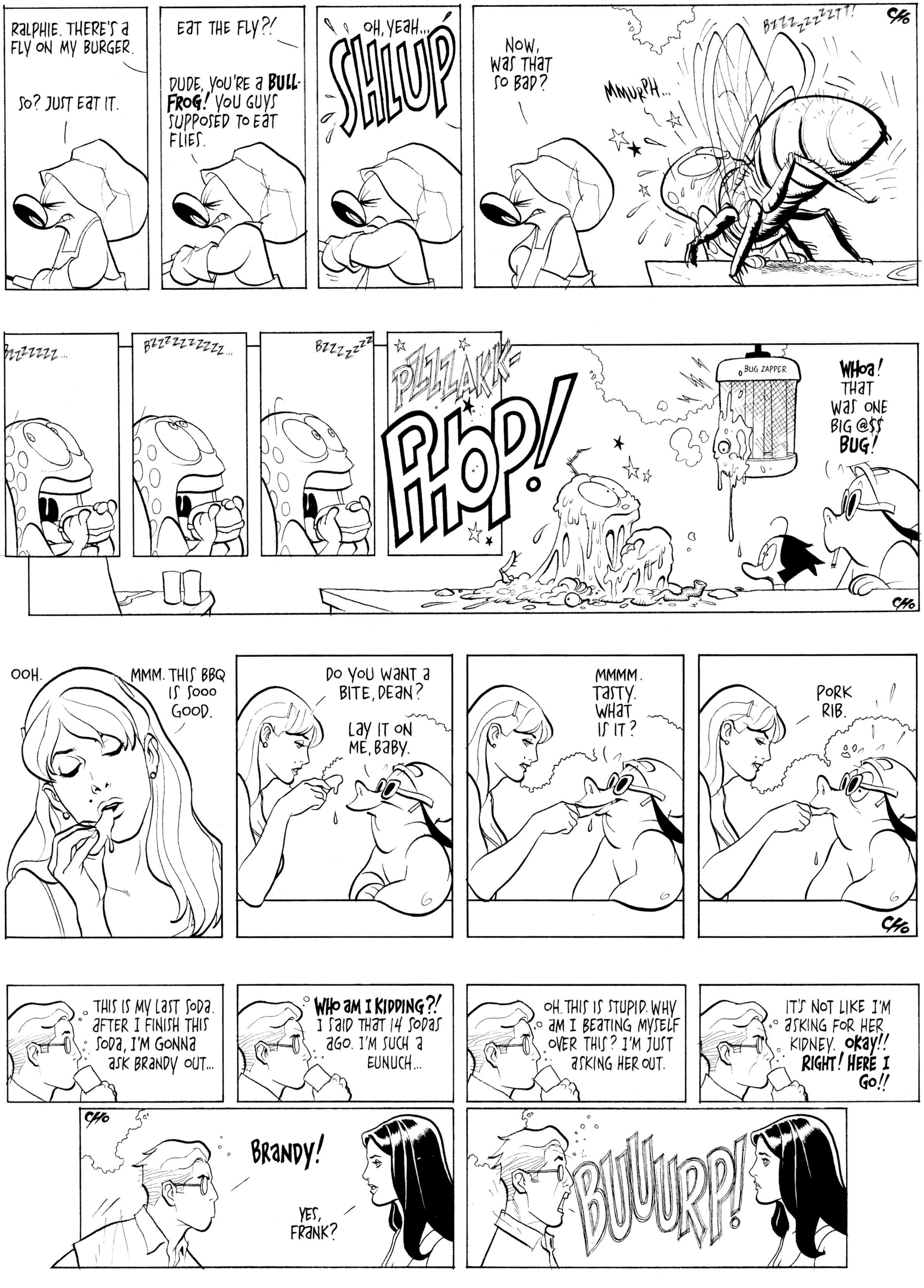
RALPHIE. THERE'S A FLY ON MY BURGER.
SO? JUST EAT IT.
EAT THE FLY?!
DUDE, YOU'RE A BULL-FROG! YOU GUYS SUPPOSED TO EAT FLIES.
OH, YEAH...
SHLUP
NOW, WAS THAT SO BAD?
MMMURPH...
BZZZZZZZZZT!
CHO
BZZZZZZZ...
BZZZZZZZZZZZ...
BZZZZZZZ
PZZZAKK-
PHOP!
BUG ZAPPER
WHOA! THAT WAS ONE BIG @$$ BUG!
CHO
OOH.
MMM. THIS BBQ IS SOOO GOOD.
DO YOU WANT A BITE, DEAN?
LAY IT ON ME, BABY.
MMMM. TASTY. WHAT IS IT?
PORK RIB.
CHO
THIS IS MY LAST SODA. AFTER I FINISH THIS SODA, I'M GONNA ASK BRANDY OUT...
WHO AM I KIDDING?! I SAID THAT 14 SODAS AGO. I'M SUCH A EUNUCH...
OH. THIS IS STUPID. WHY AM I BEATING MYSELF OVER THIS? I'M JUST ASKING HER OUT.
IT'S NOT LIKE I'M ASKING FOR HER KIDNEY. OKAY!! RIGHT! HERE I GO!!
CHO
BRANDY!
YES, FRANK?
BUUURP!

GREAT GOOGALY MOOGALY. I CAN'T BELIEVE I BURPED RIGHT IN BRANDY'S FACE. THIS IS SO HUMILIATING.

SHE'LL PROBABLY NEVER SPEAK TO ME AGAIN. THIS GOT TO BE ONE OF THE LOWEST POINT OF MY LIFE. IT CAN'T GET ANY WORSE...

D'OH!

THUNK

SURPRISE, BRANDY!

MOM?

GOODNESS. I DIDN'T KNOW YOU WERE HAVING A POOL PARTY.

YOU'RE MORE THAN WELCOME TO STAY AWHILE, MOM.

UH OH. SHE HAS THAT LOOK, AGAIN.

'WONDER WHAT SHE'S GOING TO CRITICIZE ME ABOUT THIS TIME: MY JOB? MY SOCIAL LIFE? MY APPEARANCE?...

ARE YOU PUTTING ON WEIGHT, DEAR?

BINGO!

HERE, MOM. HAVE SOME BURGERS.

THAT SOUNDS GOOD. WHO'S COOKING?

GRILL MASTER RALPH AT YOUR SERVICE, MA'AM.

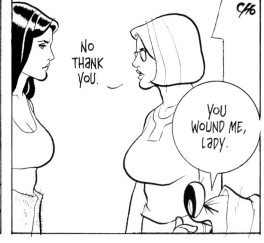

NO THANK YOU.

YOU WOUND ME, LADY.

DEAR, YOU HAVE TO WATCH WHAT YOU EAT. YOU HAVE YOUR GRANDMOTHER'S HIP AND ...

MOM. I AM NOT FAT. I'M NOT GOING TO TALK TO YOU.

UNLESS YOU CHANGE THE SUBJECT.

DO YOU HAVE A VIDEO PLAYER?

YEAH. WHY?

I HAVE SOME "TAE-BO" TAPES IF YOU WANT...

MOTHER!

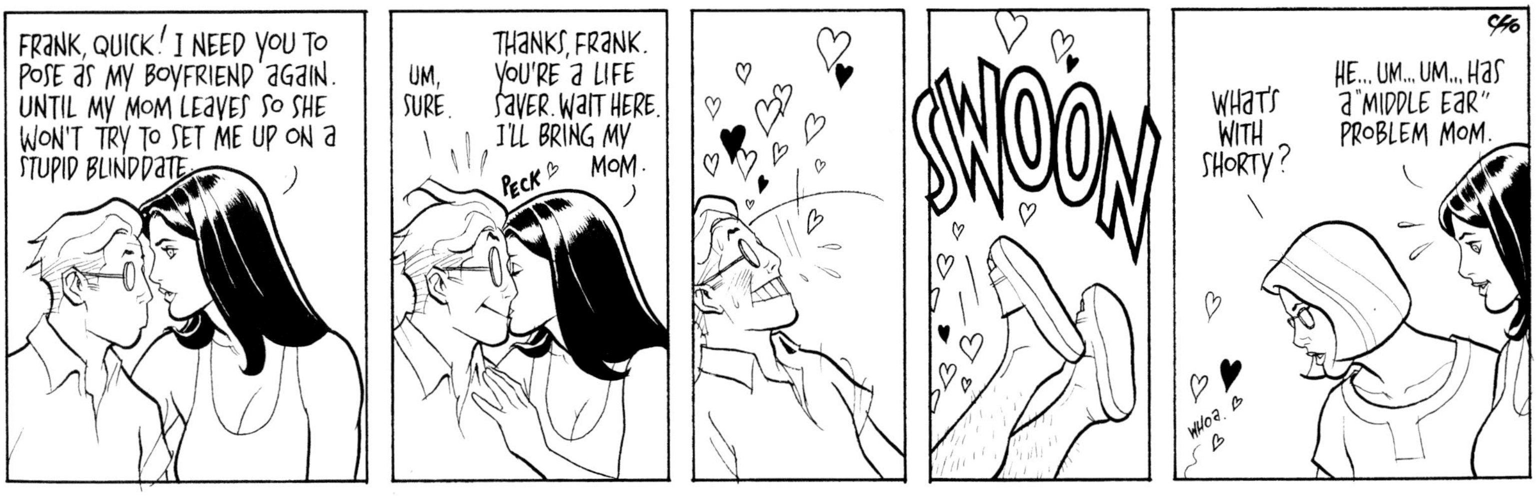

FRANK, QUICK! I NEED YOU TO POSE AS MY BOYFRIEND AGAIN. UNTIL MY MOM LEAVES SO SHE WON'T TRY TO SET ME UP ON A STUPID BLIND DATE.
UM, SURE.
THANKS, FRANK. YOU'RE A LIFE SAVER. WAIT HERE. I'LL BRING MY MOM.
PECK
SWOON
WHAT'S WITH SHORTY?
HE... UM... UM... HAS A "MIDDLE EAR" PROBLEM MOM.
WHOA.

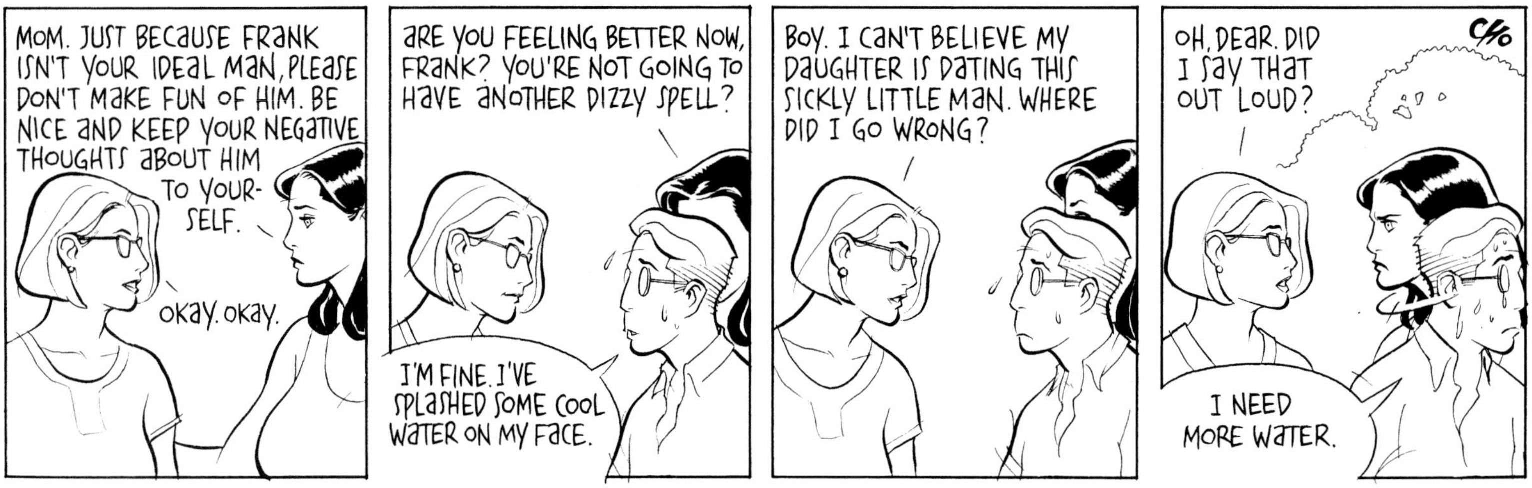

MOM. JUST BECAUSE FRANK ISN'T YOUR IDEAL MAN, PLEASE DON'T MAKE FUN OF HIM. BE NICE AND KEEP YOUR NEGATIVE THOUGHTS ABOUT HIM TO YOURSELF.
OKAY. OKAY.
ARE YOU FEELING BETTER NOW, FRANK? YOU'RE NOT GOING TO HAVE ANOTHER DIZZY SPELL?
I'M FINE. I'VE SPLASHED SOME COOL WATER ON MY FACE.
BOY. I CAN'T BELIEVE MY DAUGHTER IS DATING THIS SICKLY LITTLE MAN. WHERE DID I GO WRONG?
OH, DEAR. DID I SAY THAT OUT LOUD?
I NEED MORE WATER.

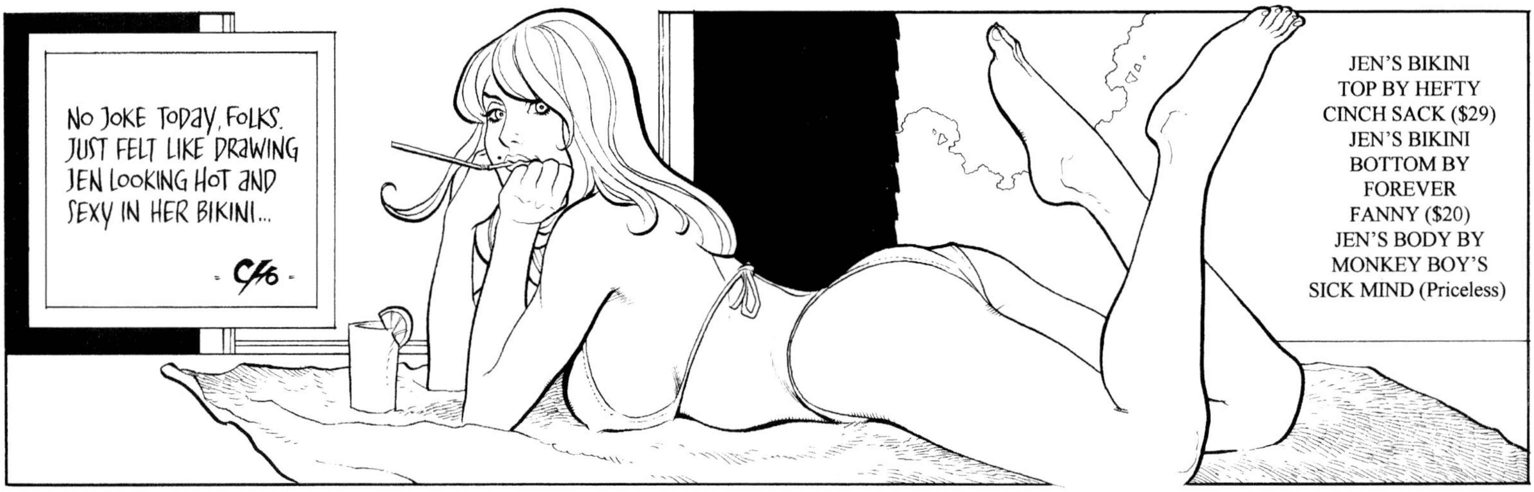

NO JOKE TODAY, FOLKS. JUST FELT LIKE DRAWING JEN LOOKING HOT AND SEXY IN HER BIKINI...
JEN'S BIKINI TOP BY HEFTY CINCH SACK ($29)
JEN'S BIKINI BOTTOM BY FOREVER FANNY ($20)
JEN'S BODY BY MONKEY BOY'S SICK MIND (Priceless)

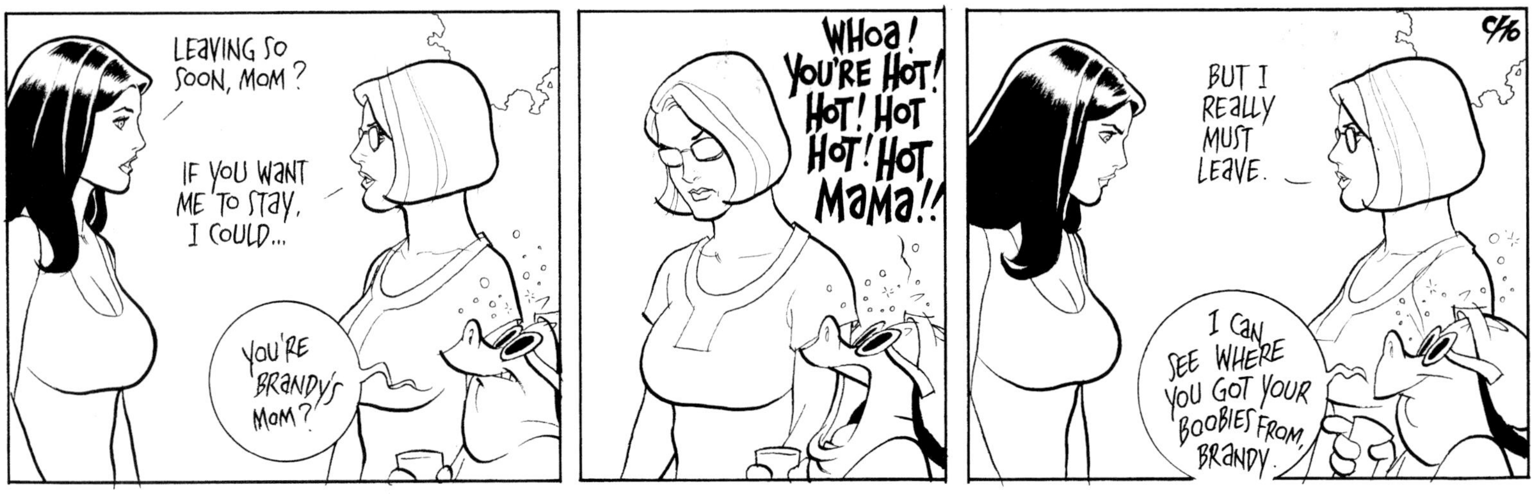

LEAVING SO SOON, MOM?
IF YOU WANT ME TO STAY, I COULD...
YOU'RE BRANDY'S MOM?
WHOA! YOU'RE HOT! HOT! HOT HOT! HOT MAMA!!
BUT I REALLY MUST LEAVE.
I CAN SEE WHERE YOU GOT YOUR BOOBIES FROM, BRANDY.

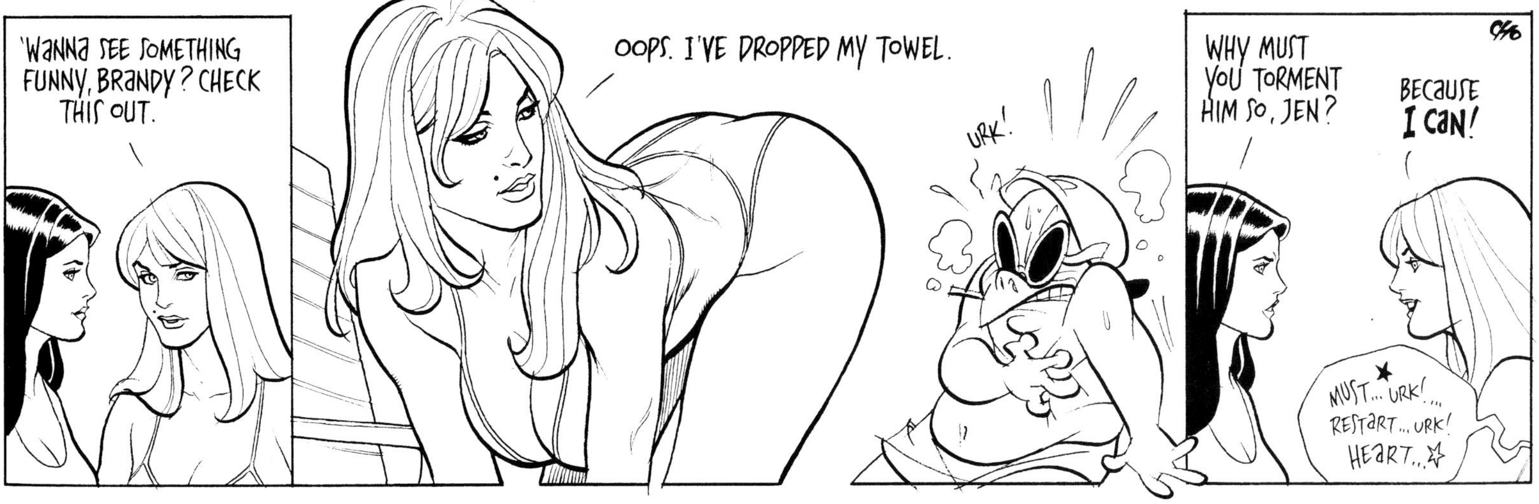
'WANNA SEE SOMETHING FUNNY, BRANDY? CHECK THIS OUT.
OOPS. I'VE DROPPED MY TOWEL.
URK!
WHY MUST YOU TORMENT HIM SO, JEN?
BECAUSE I CAN!
MUST... URK!... RESTART... URK! HEART...
CHO

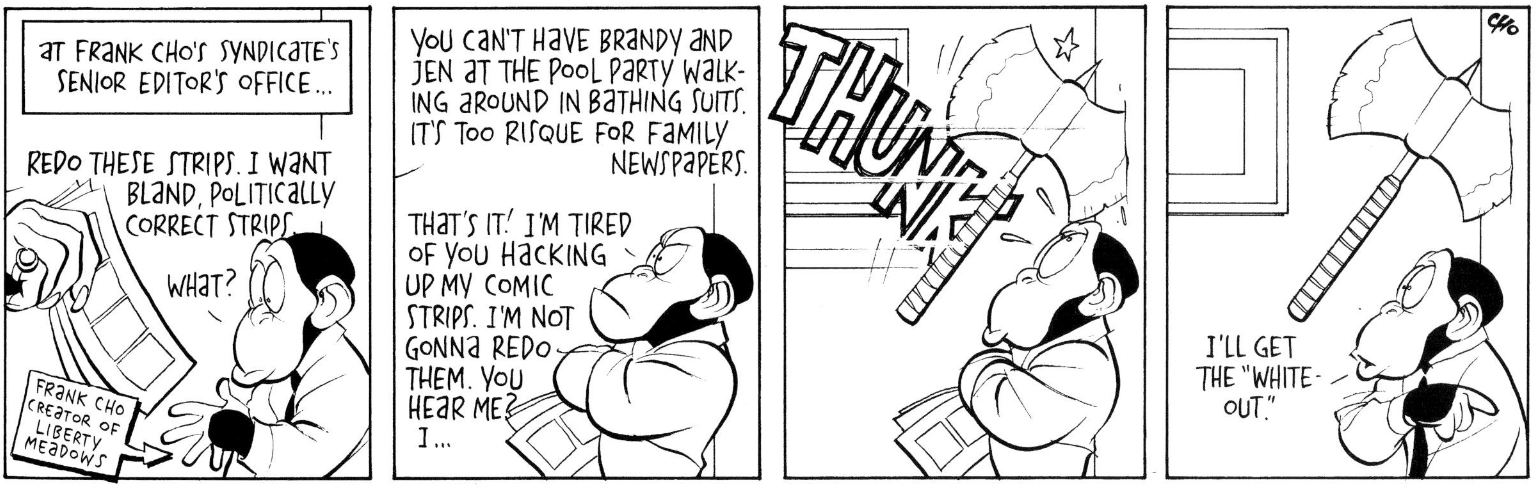
AT FRANK CHO'S SYNDICATE'S SENIOR EDITOR'S OFFICE...
REDO THESE STRIPS. I WANT BLAND, POLITICALLY CORRECT STRIPS.
WHAT?
FRANK CHO CREATOR OF LIBERTY MEADOWS
YOU CAN'T HAVE BRANDY AND JEN AT THE POOL PARTY WALKING AROUND IN BATHING SUITS. IT'S TOO RISQUE FOR FAMILY NEWSPAPERS.
THAT'S IT! I'M TIRED OF YOU HACKING UP MY COMIC STRIPS. I'M NOT GONNA REDO THEM. YOU HEAR ME? I...
THUNK!
I'LL GET THE "WHITE OUT."
CHO

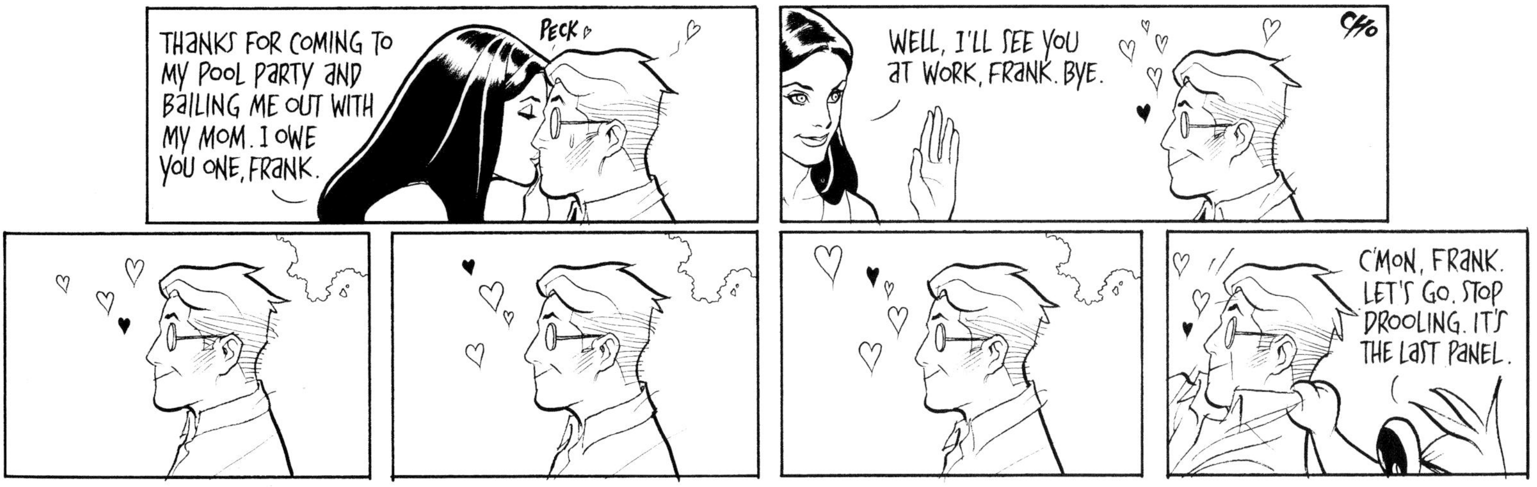
THANKS FOR COMING TO MY POOL PARTY AND BAILING ME OUT WITH MY MOM. I OWE YOU ONE, FRANK.
PECK
WELL, I'LL SEE YOU AT WORK, FRANK. BYE.
CHO
C'MON, FRANK. LET'S GO. STOP DROOLING. IT'S THE LAST PANEL.

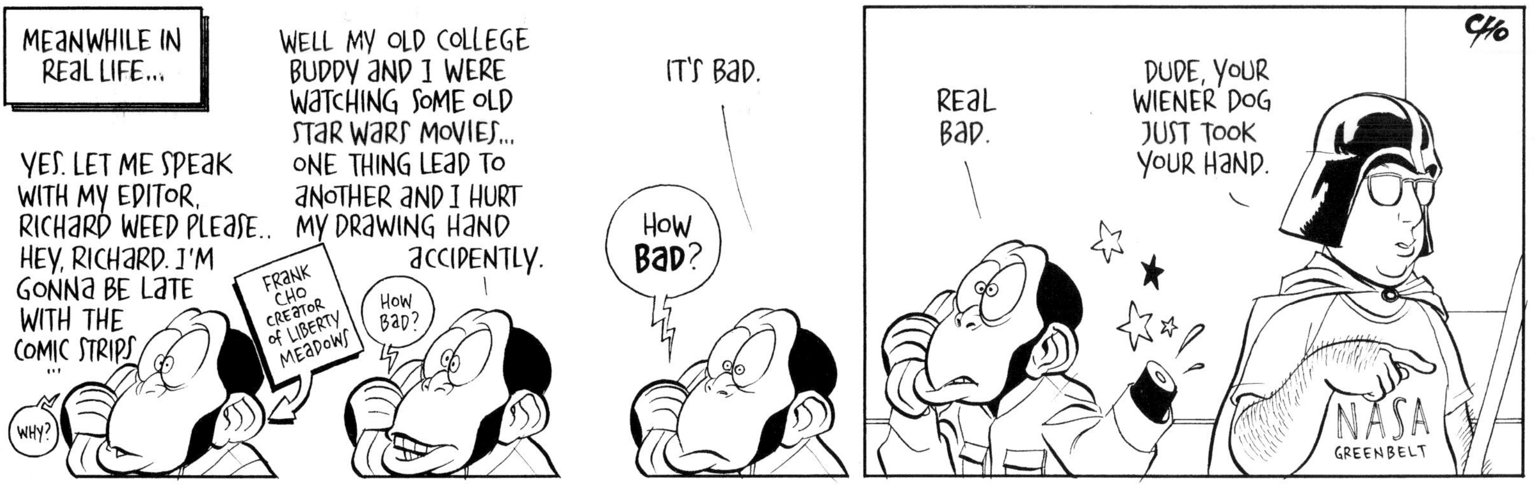
MEANWHILE IN REAL LIFE...
YES. LET ME SPEAK WITH MY EDITOR, RICHARD WEED PLEASE.. HEY, RICHARD. I'M GONNA BE LATE WITH THE COMIC STRIPS ...
WHY?
FRANK CHO CREATOR OF LIBERTY MEADOWS
WELL MY OLD COLLEGE BUDDY AND I WERE WATCHING SOME OLD STAR WARS MOVIES... ONE THING LEAD TO ANOTHER AND I HURT MY DRAWING HAND ACCIDENTLY.
HOW BAD?
IT'S BAD.
HOW BAD?
REAL BAD.
DUDE, YOUR WIENER DOG JUST TOOK YOUR HAND.
NASA GREENBELT
CHO

MR. FRANK CHO HAS INJURED HIS DRAWING HAND AND IS UNABLE TO PRODUCE TODAY'S COMIC STRIP.

FILLING IN FOR MR. CHO IS MR. BALDO SMUDGE, RENOWN AND BELOVED NEWSPAPER CARTOONIST FOR MANY GENERATIONS.

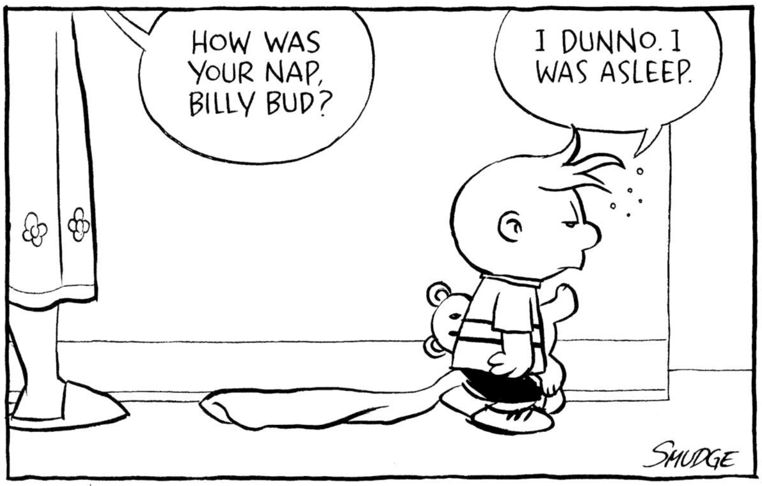
HOW WAS YOUR NAP, BILLY BUD?
I DUNNO. I WAS ASLEEP.
SMUDGE

LET'S PRAY FOR MR. FRANK CHO'S SPEEDY RECOVERY.

MR. FRANK CHO HAS INJURED HIS DRAWING HAND AND IS UNABLE TO PRODUCE TODAY'S COMIC STRIP.

FILLING IN FOR MR. CHO IS MR. BALDO SMUDGE, RENOWN AND BELOVED NEWSPAPER CARTOONIST FOR MANY GENERATIONS.

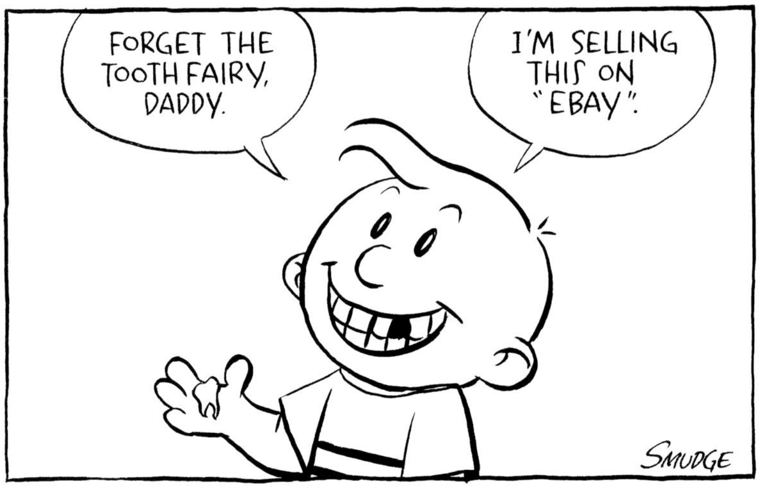
FORGET THE TOOTH FAIRY, DADDY.
I'M SELLING THIS ON "EBAY".
SMUDGE

LET'S PRAY REALLY HARD FOR MR. FRANK CHO'S SPEEDY RECOVERY.

MR. FRANK CHO HAS INJURED HIS DRAWING HAND AND IS UNABLE TO PRODUCE TODAY'S COMIC STRIP.

FILLING IN FOR MR. CHO IS MR. BALDO SMUDGE, RENOWN AND BELOVED NEWSPAPER CARTOONIST FOR MANY GENERATIONS.

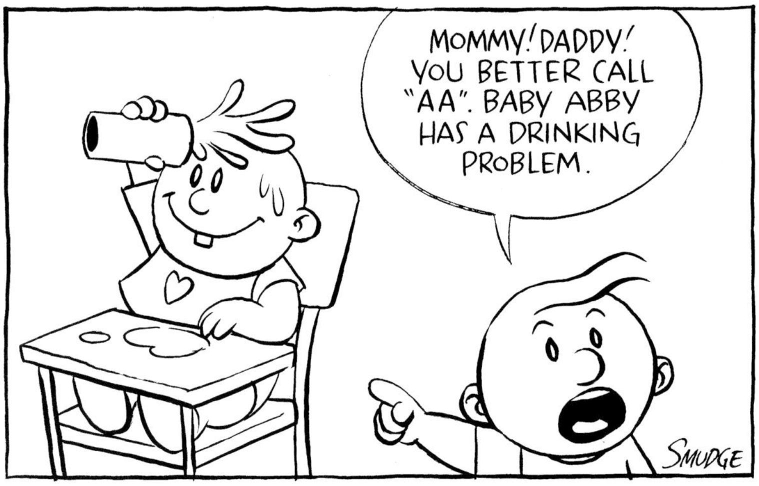
MOMMY! DADDY! YOU BETTER CALL "AA". BABY ABBY HAS A DRINKING PROBLEM.
SMUDGE

PRAY LIKE YOU'VE NEVER PRAYED BEFORE FOR MR. FRANK CHO'S SPEEDY RECOVERY.

MR. FRANK CHO HAS INJURED HIS DRAWING HAND AND IS UNABLE TO PRODUCE TODAY'S COMIC STRIP.

FILLING IN FOR MR. CHO IS MR. BALDO SMUDGE, RENOWN AND BELOVED NEWSPAPER CARTOONIST FOR MANY GENERATIONS.

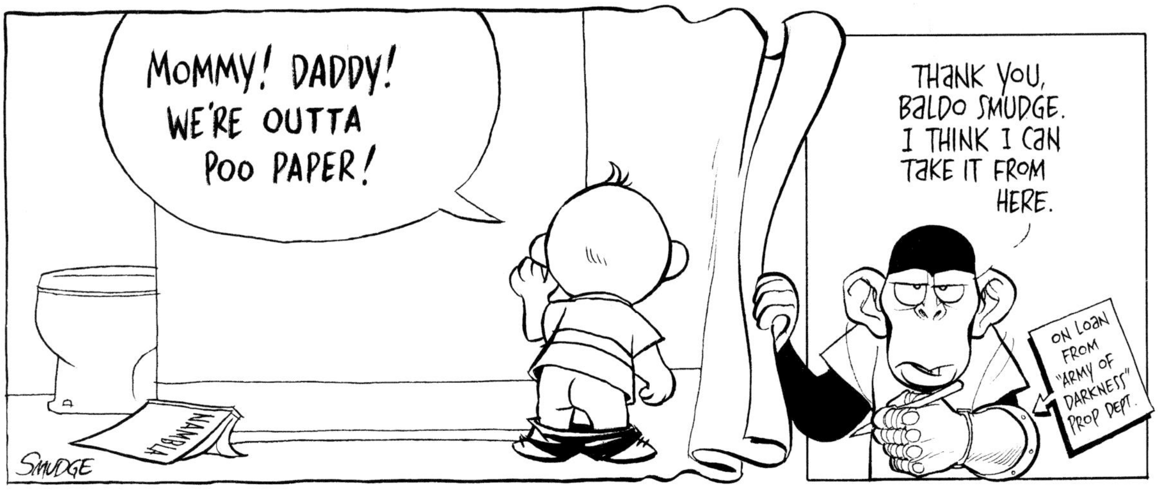
MOMMY! DADDY! WE'RE OUTTA POO PAPER!
SMUDGE
THANK YOU, BALDO SMUDGE. I THINK I CAN TAKE IT FROM HERE.
ON LOAN FROM "ARMY OF DARKNESS" PROP DEPT.

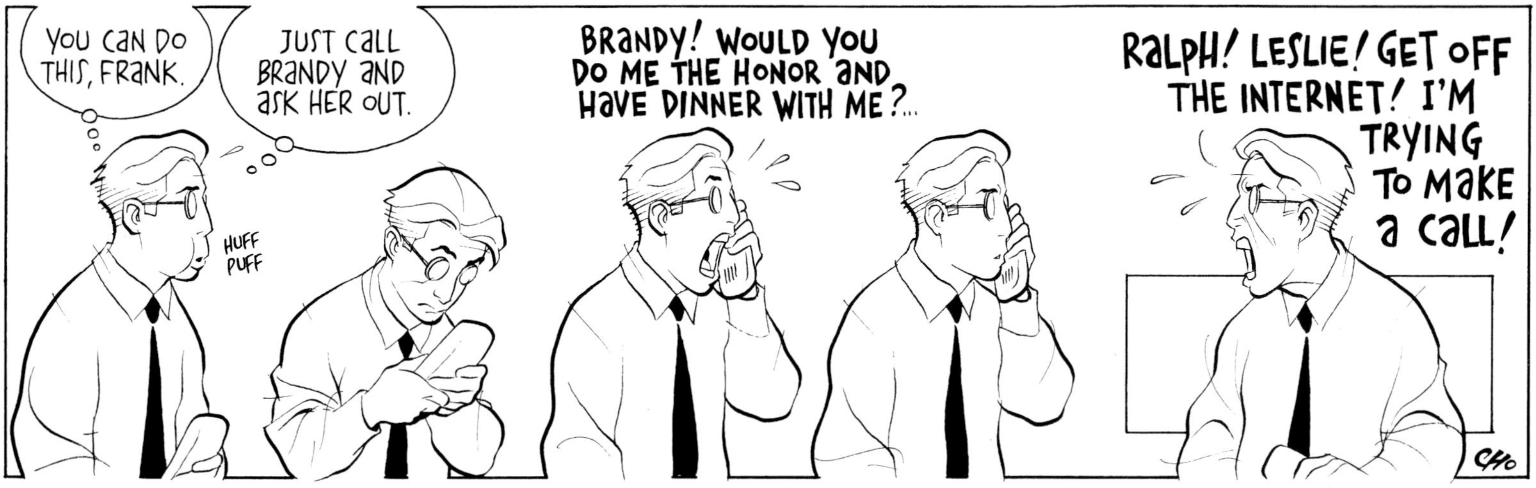
YOU CAN DO THIS, FRANK.
JUST CALL BRANDY AND ASK HER OUT.
HUFF PUFF
BRANDY! WOULD YOU DO ME THE HONOR AND HAVE DINNER WITH ME?...
RALPH! LESLIE! GET OFF THE INTERNET! I'M TRYING TO MAKE A CALL!
CHO

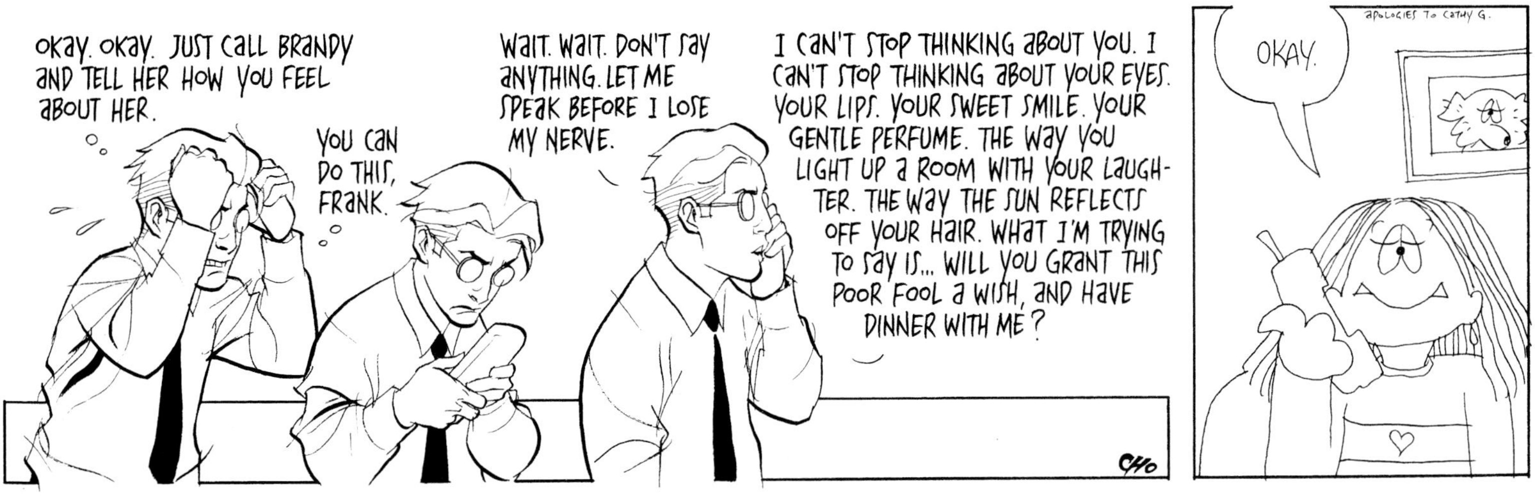
OKAY. OKAY. JUST CALL BRANDY AND TELL HER HOW YOU FEEL ABOUT HER.
YOU CAN DO THIS, FRANK.
WAIT. WAIT. DON'T SAY ANYTHING. LET ME SPEAK BEFORE I LOSE MY NERVE.
I CAN'T STOP THINKING ABOUT YOU. I CAN'T STOP THINKING ABOUT YOUR EYES. YOUR LIPS. YOUR SWEET SMILE. YOUR GENTLE PERFUME. THE WAY YOU LIGHT UP A ROOM WITH YOUR LAUGHTER. THE WAY THE SUN REFLECTS OFF YOUR HAIR. WHAT I'M TRYING TO SAY IS... WILL YOU GRANT THIS POOR FOOL A WISH, AND HAVE DINNER WITH ME?
CHO
APOLOGIES TO CATHY G.
OKAY.

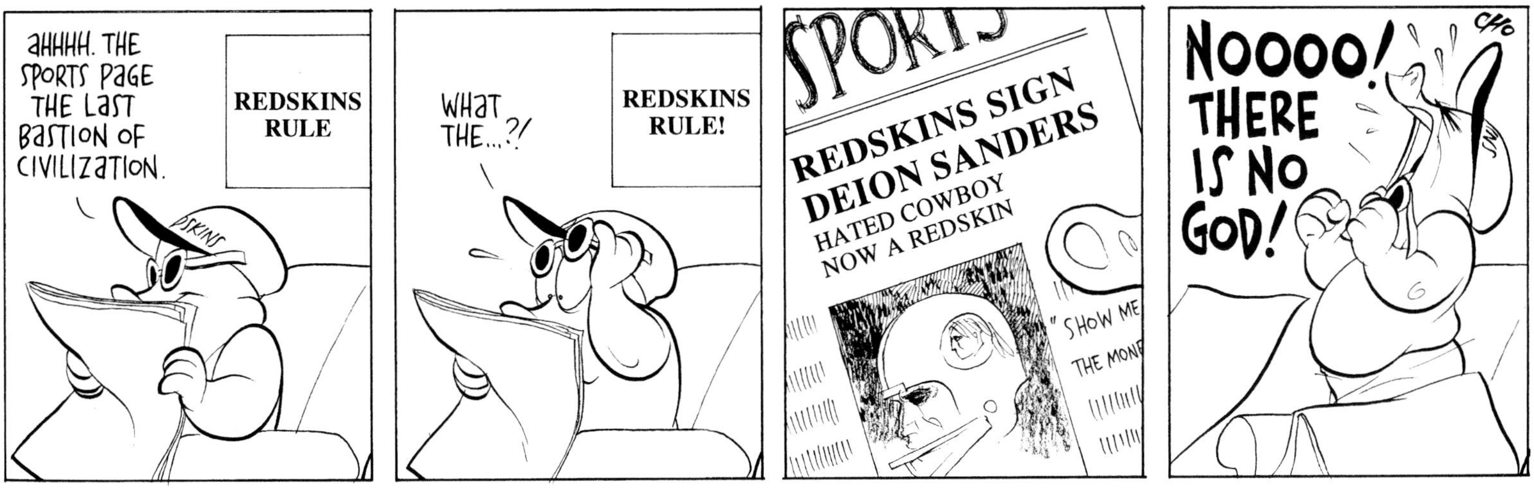
AHHHH. THE SPORTS PAGE THE LAST BASTION OF CIVILIZATION.
REDSKINS RULE
WHAT THE...?!
REDSKINS RULE!
SPORTS
REDSKINS SIGN DEION SANDERS
REDSKINS SIGN DEION SANDERS
HATED COWBOY NOW A REDSKIN
"SHOW ME THE MONE
NOOOO! THERE IS NO GOD!
CHO

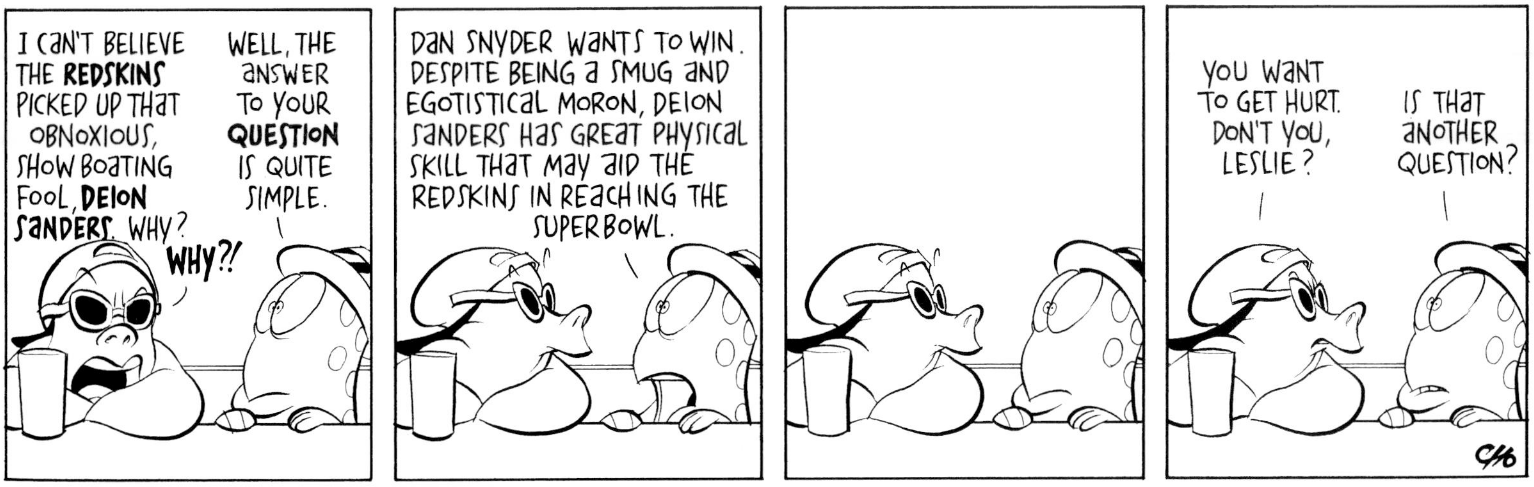
I CAN'T BELIEVE THE **REDSKINS** PICKED UP THAT OBNOXIOUS, SHOWBOATING FOOL, **DEION SANDERS**. WHY?
WHY?!
WELL, THE ANSWER TO YOUR **QUESTION** IS QUITE SIMPLE.
DAN SNYDER WANTS TO WIN. DESPITE BEING A SMUG AND EGOTISTICAL MORON, DEION SANDERS HAS GREAT PHYSICAL SKILL THAT MAY AID THE REDSKINS IN REACHING THE SUPERBOWL.
YOU WANT TO GET HURT. DON'T YOU, LESLIE?
IS THAT ANOTHER QUESTION?
CHO

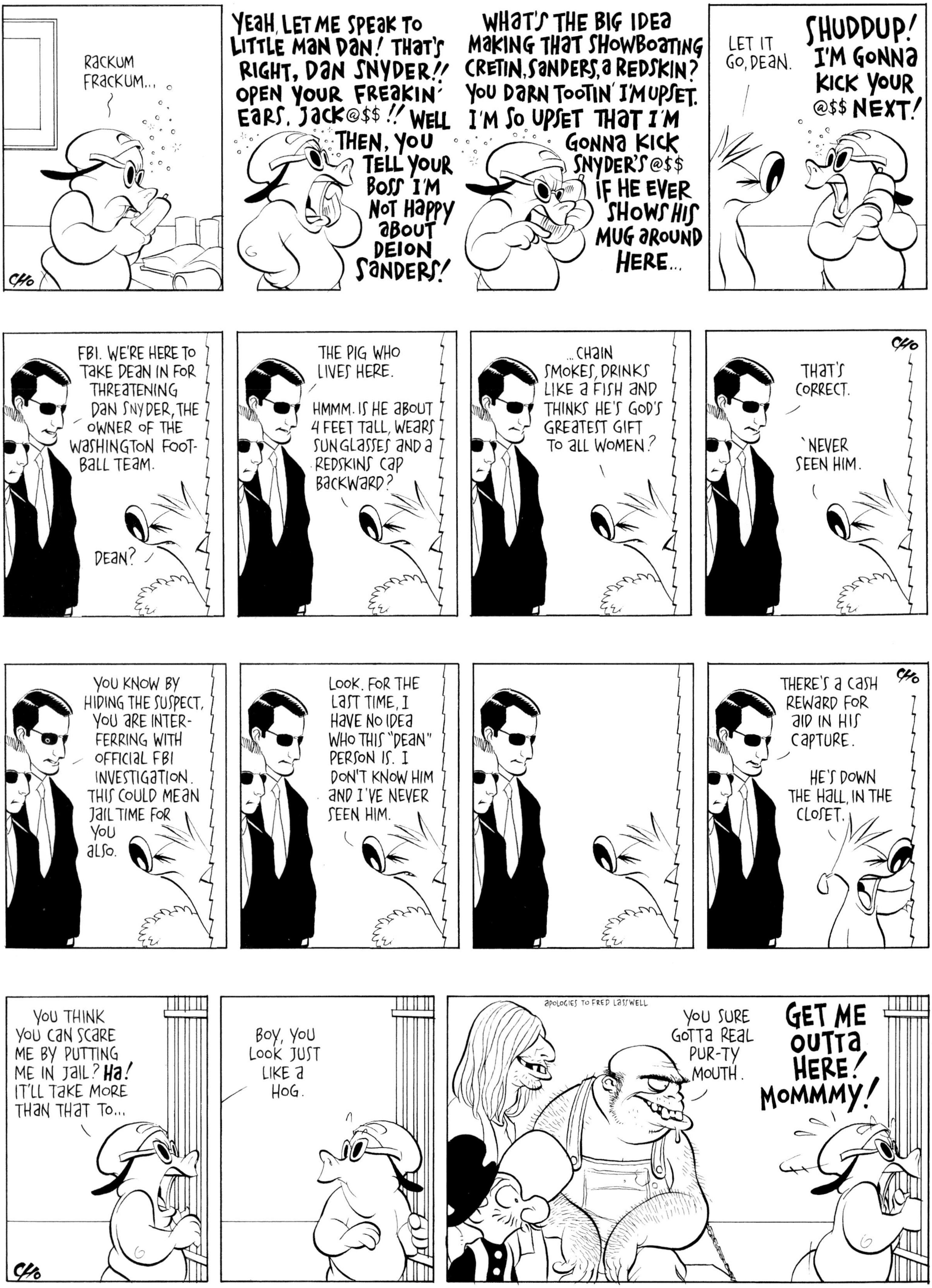

RACKUM FRACKUM...
CHO
YEAH, LET ME SPEAK TO LITTLE MAN DAN! THAT'S RIGHT, DAN SNYDER!! OPEN YOUR FREAKIN' EARS, JACK@$$!! WELL THEN, YOU TELL YOUR BOSS I'M NOT HAPPY ABOUT DEION SANDERS!
WHAT'S THE BIG IDEA MAKING THAT SHOWBOATING CRETIN, SANDERS, A REDSKIN? YOU DARN TOOTIN' I'M UPSET. I'M SO UPSET THAT I'M GONNA KICK SNYDER'S @$$ IF HE EVER SHOWS HIS MUG AROUND HERE...
LET IT GO, DEAN.
SHUDDUP! I'M GONNA KICK YOUR @$$ NEXT!
FBI. WE'RE HERE TO TAKE DEAN IN FOR THREATENING DAN SNYDER, THE OWNER OF THE WASHINGTON FOOT-BALL TEAM.
DEAN?
THE PIG WHO LIVES HERE.
HMMM. IS HE ABOUT 4 FEET TALL, WEARS SUNGLASSES AND A REDSKINS CAP BACKWARD?
...CHAIN SMOKES, DRINKS LIKE A FISH AND THINKS HE'S GOD'S GREATEST GIFT TO ALL WOMEN?
CHO
THAT'S CORRECT.
`NEVER SEEN HIM.
YOU KNOW BY HIDING THE SUSPECT, YOU ARE INTER-FERRING WITH OFFICIAL FBI INVESTIGATION. THIS COULD MEAN JAIL TIME FOR YOU ALSO.
LOOK. FOR THE LAST TIME, I HAVE NO IDEA WHO THIS "DEAN" PERSON IS. I DON'T KNOW HIM AND I'VE NEVER SEEN HIM.
CHO
THERE'S A CASH REWARD FOR AID IN HIS CAPTURE.
HE'S DOWN THE HALL, IN THE CLOSET.
YOU THINK YOU CAN SCARE ME BY PUTTING ME IN JAIL? HA! IT'LL TAKE MORE THAN THAT TO...
CHO
BOY, YOU LOOK JUST LIKE A HOG.
APOLOGIES TO FRED LASSWELL
YOU SURE GOTTA REAL PUR-TY MOUTH.
GET ME OUTTA HERE! MOMMMY!

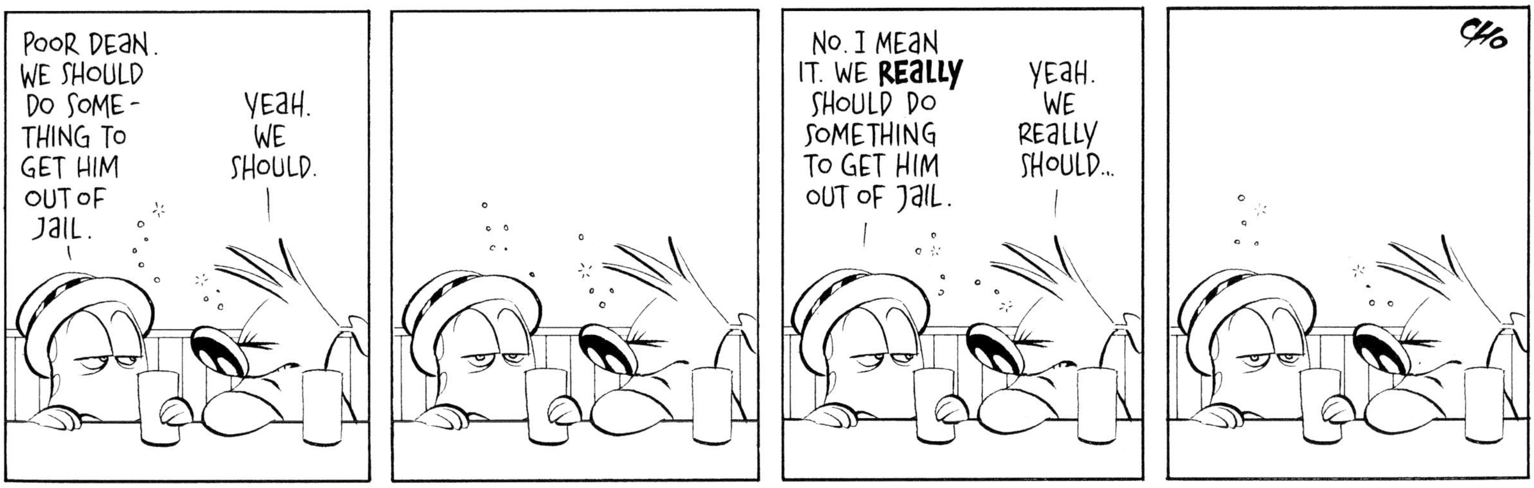
POOR DEAN. WE SHOULD DO SOME-THING TO GET HIM OUT OF JAIL.
YEAH. WE SHOULD.
NO. I MEAN IT. WE **REALLY** SHOULD DO SOMETHING TO GET HIM OUT OF JAIL.
YEAH. WE REALLY SHOULD...
CHO

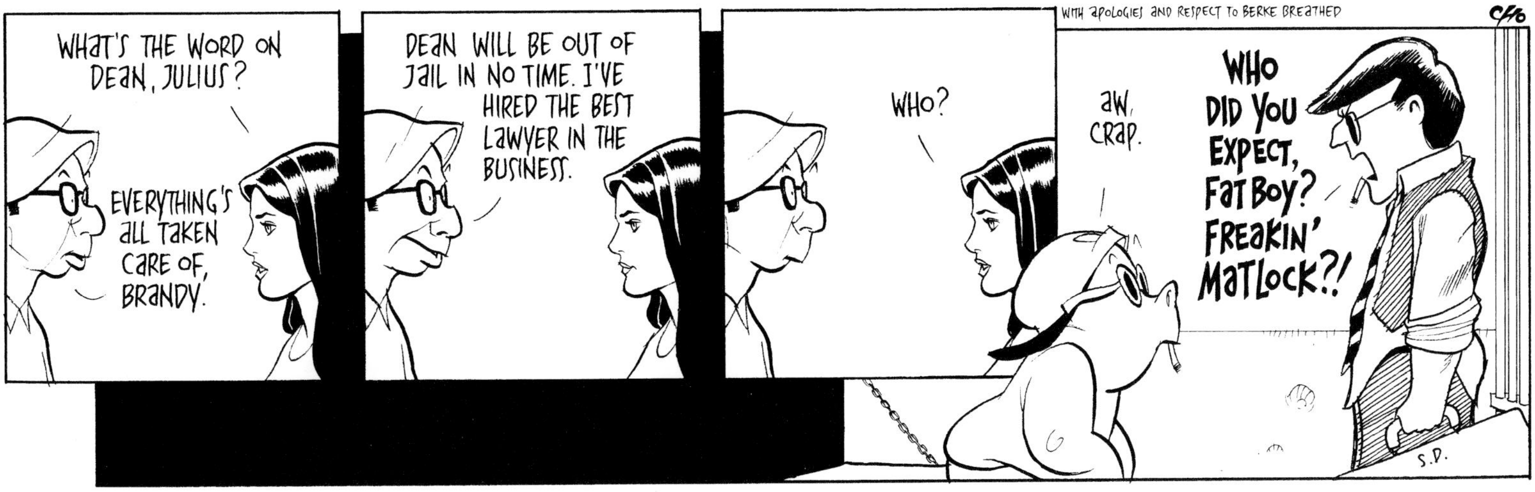
WHAT'S THE WORD ON DEAN, JULIUS?
EVERYTHING'S ALL TAKEN CARE OF, BRANDY.
DEAN WILL BE OUT OF JAIL IN NO TIME. I'VE HIRED THE BEST LAWYER IN THE BUSINESS.
WHO?
WITH APOLOGIES AND RESPECT TO BERKE BREATHED
CHO
AW, CRAP.
WHO DID YOU EXPECT, FAT BOY? FREAKIN' MATLOCK?!
S.D.

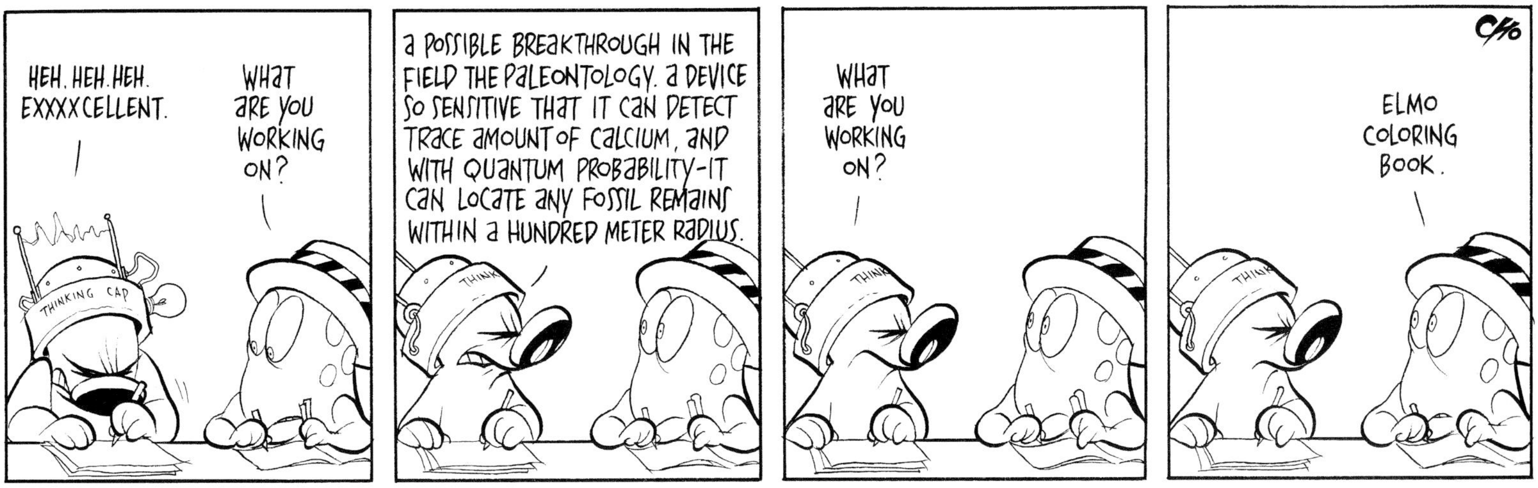
HEH. HEH. HEH. EXXXXCELLENT.
WHAT ARE YOU WORKING ON?
THINKING CAP
A POSSIBLE BREAKTHROUGH IN THE FIELD THE PALEONTOLOGY. A DEVICE SO SENSITIVE THAT IT CAN DETECT TRACE AMOUNT OF CALCIUM, AND WITH QUANTUM PROBABILITY-IT CAN LOCATE ANY FOSSIL REMAINS WITHIN A HUNDRED METER RADIUS.
WHAT ARE YOU WORKING ON?
CHO
ELMO COLORING BOOK.

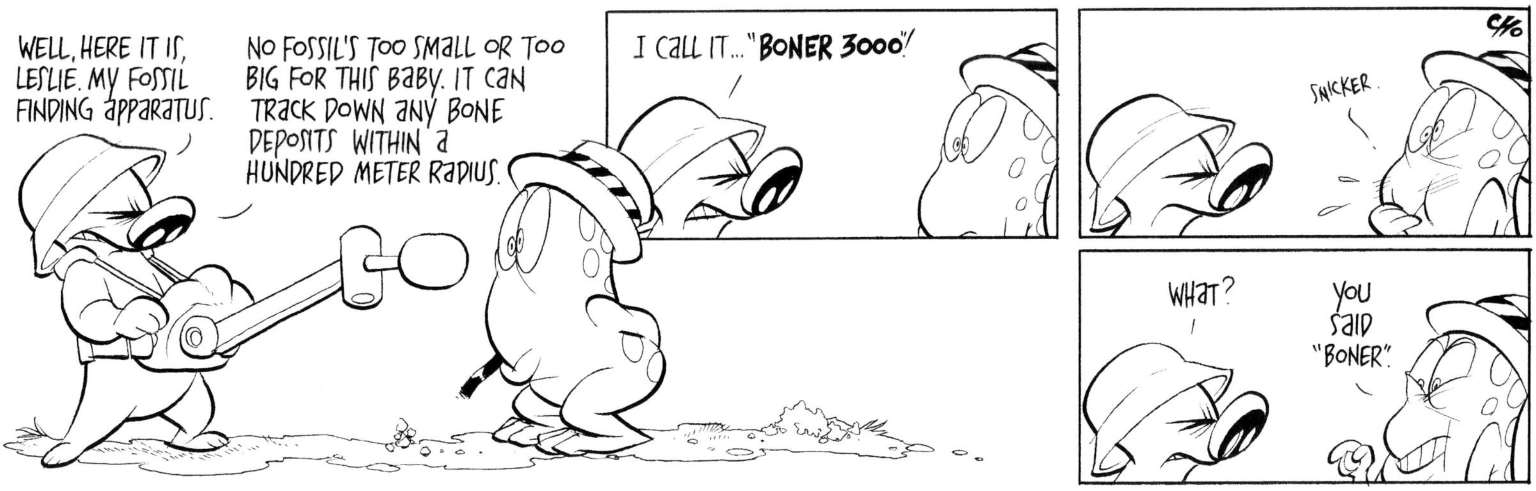
WELL, HERE IT IS, LESLIE. MY FOSSIL FINDING APPARATUS.
NO FOSSIL'S TOO SMALL OR TOO BIG FOR THIS BABY. IT CAN TRACK DOWN ANY BONE DEPOSITS WITHIN A HUNDRED METER RADIUS.
I CALL IT... "**BONER 3000**"!
CHO
SNICKER.
WHAT?
YOU SAID "BONER".

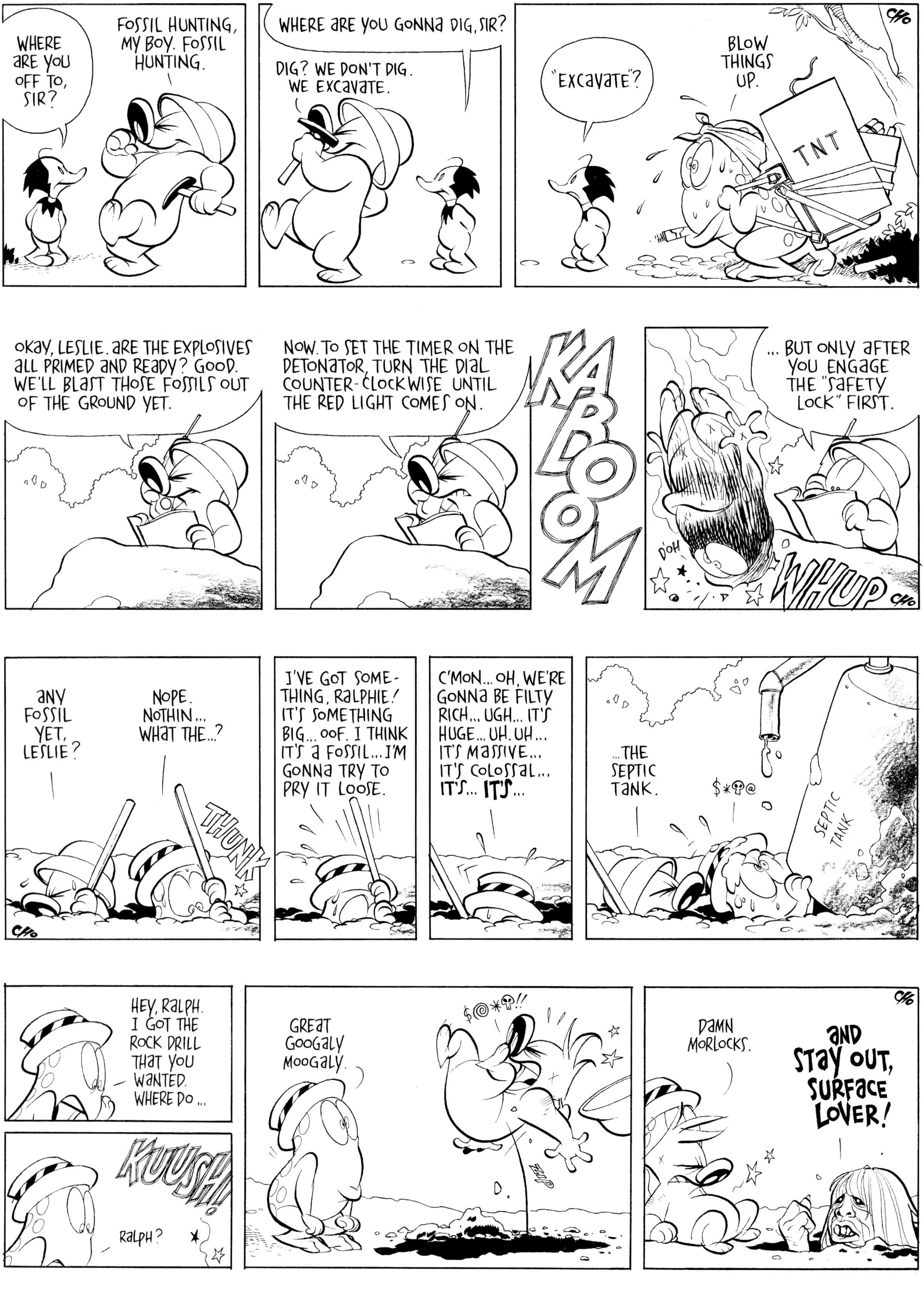
WHERE ARE YOU OFF TO, SIR?
FOSSIL HUNTING, MY BOY. FOSSIL HUNTING.
WHERE ARE YOU GONNA DIG, SIR?
DIG? WE DON'T DIG. WE EXCAVATE.
CHO
"EXCAVATE"?
BLOW THINGS UP.
TNT
OKAY, LESLIE. ARE THE EXPLOSIVES ALL PRIMED AND READY? GOOD. WE'LL BLAST THOSE FOSSILS OUT OF THE GROUND YET.
NOW. TO SET THE TIMER ON THE DETONATOR, TURN THE DIAL COUNTER-CLOCKWISE UNTIL THE RED LIGHT COMES ON.
KABOOM
... BUT ONLY AFTER YOU ENGAGE THE "SAFETY LOCK" FIRST.
D'OH
WHUP
CHO
ANY FOSSIL YET, LESLIE?
NOPE. NOTHIN... WHAT THE...?
THUNK
CHO
I'VE GOT SOMETHING, RALPHIE! IT'S SOMETHING BIG... OOF. I THINK IT'S A FOSSIL... I'M GONNA TRY TO PRY IT LOOSE.
C'MON... OH, WE'RE GONNA BE FILTY RICH... UGH... IT'S HUGE... UH. UH... IT'S MASSIVE... IT'S COLOSSAL... IT'S... IT'S...
...THE SEPTIC TANK.
SEPTIC TANK
HEY, RALPH. I GOT THE ROCK DRILL THAT YOU WANTED. WHERE DO ...
KUUSH!
RALPH?
GREAT GOOGALY MOOGALY.
CHO
DAMN MORLOCKS.
AND STAY OUT, SURFACE LOVER!

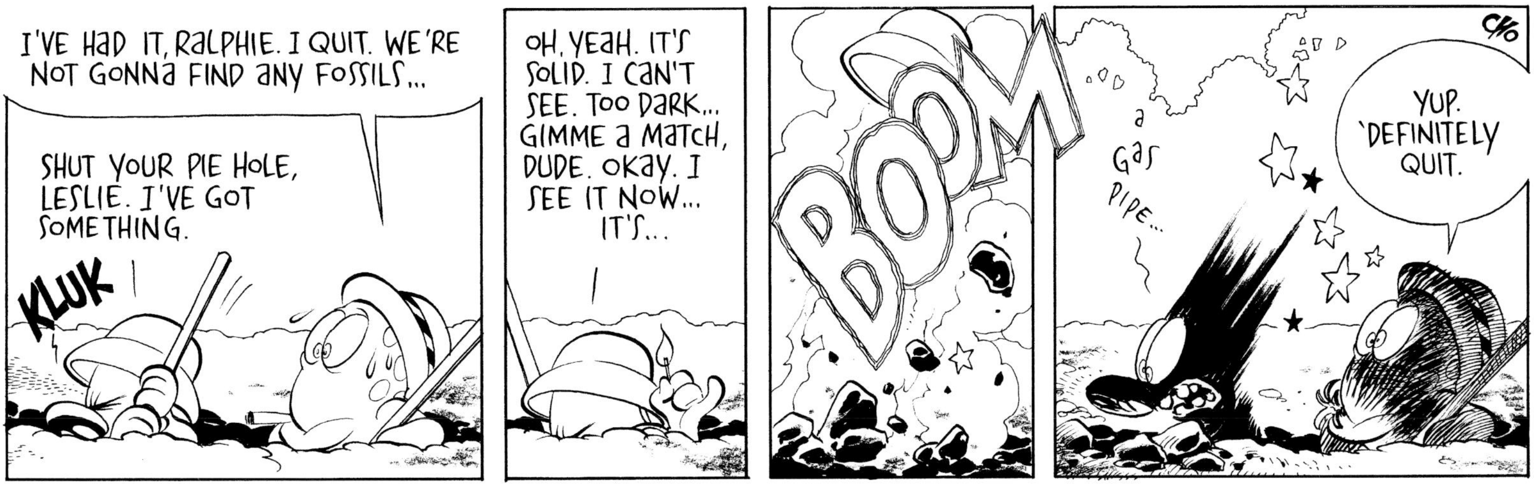
I'VE HAD IT, RALPHIE. I QUIT. WE'RE NOT GONNA FIND ANY FOSSILS...
SHUT YOUR PIE HOLE, LESLIE. I'VE GOT SOMETHING.
KLUK
OH, YEAH. IT'S SOLID. I CAN'T SEE. TOO DARK... GIMME A MATCH, DUDE. OKAY. I SEE IT NOW... IT'S...
BOOM
A GAS PIPE...
YUP. 'DEFINITELY QUIT.
CHO

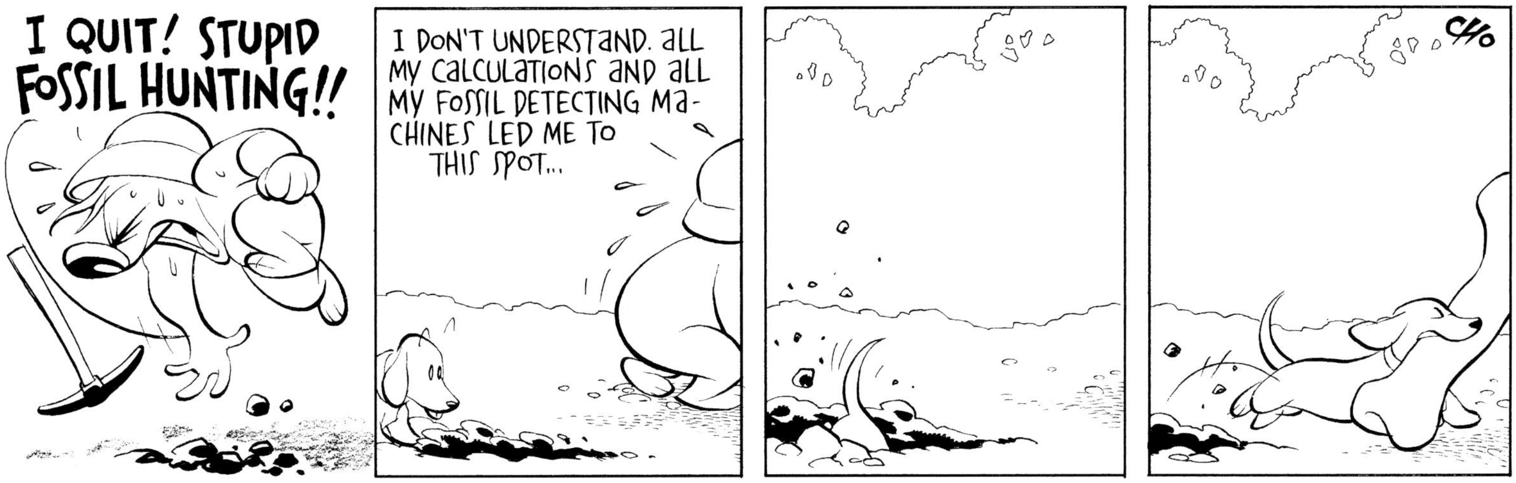
I QUIT! STUPID FOSSIL HUNTING!!
I DON'T UNDERSTAND. ALL MY CALCULATIONS AND ALL MY FOSSIL DETECTING MACHINES LED ME TO THIS SPOT...
CHO

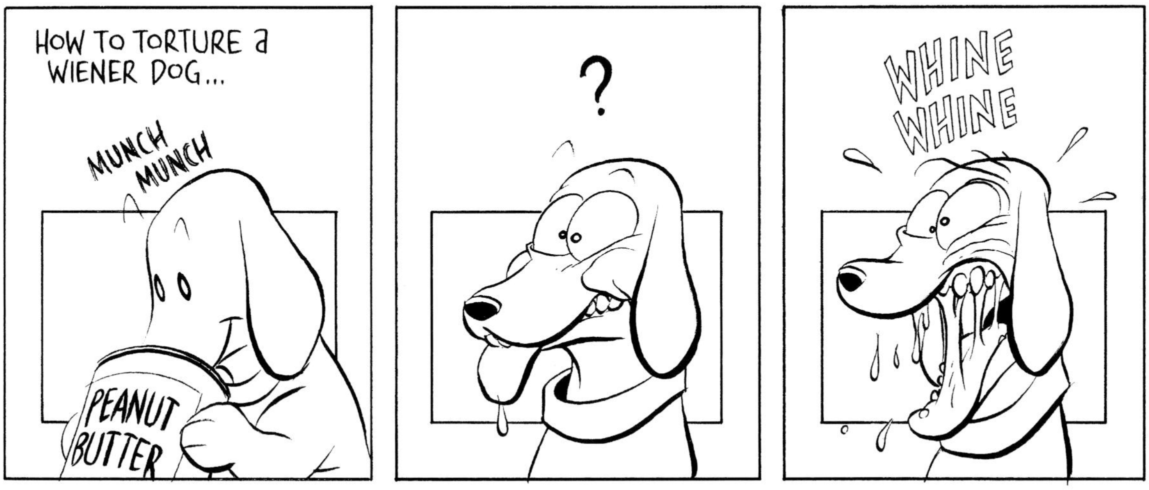
HOW TO TORTURE A WIENER DOG...
MUNCH MUNCH
PEANUT BUTTER
?
WHINE WHINE

SORRY FOR THE LAME GAG, FOLKS. IT'S 4:23 IN THE MORNING AND IT'S THE ONLY JOKE MY CAFFEINE AND GIN SATURATED BRAIN COULD MUSTER.

OH. AND NO WIENER DOGS OR PEANUT BUTTER WERE HARMED DURING THE MAKING OF THIS STRIP.

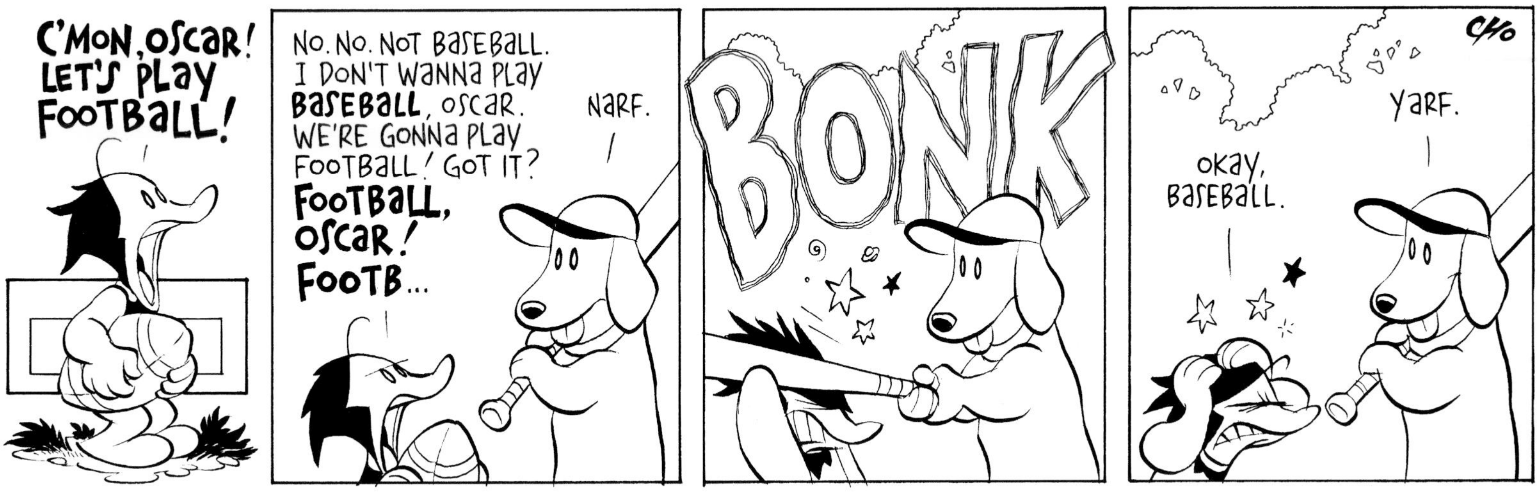
C'MON, OSCAR! LET'S PLAY FOOTBALL!
NO. NO. NOT BASEBALL. I DON'T WANNA PLAY BASEBALL, OSCAR. WE'RE GONNA PLAY FOOTBALL! GOT IT? FOOTBALL, OSCAR! FOOTB...
NARF.
BONK
OKAY, BASEBALL.
YARF.
CHO

SWOOSH GRUNT!

THOK

I HATE YOUR SLOW BALLS...

C'MON, OSCAR. THROW THE BALL. RIGHT HERE. C'MON. C'MON. GIMME A FAST BALL. ATTABOY. RIGHT HERE. PUT SOME HEAT ON IT. MAKE IT SIZZLE, BABY. C'MON.

THAT'S RIGHT. PUT SOME PEPPER ON IT, BOY. PUT SOME PEPPER ON IT. C'MON. C'MON. ATTABOY. HURT ME...

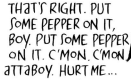

WOOH

HEY, LESLIE! HOW'S MY FAVORITE HYPOCHONDRIAC? SO, WHAT'S THE ILLNESS OF THE WEEK?

IT'S THE WORST MALADY YET. IT'S **FREAKIN'** ME OUT.

WHAT IS IT?

BRACE YOURSELF. I THINK, I HAVE "**OVARIAN CYST**."

LESLIE, YOU'RE A **GUY**.

I KNOW. THAT'S WHY IT'S FREAKIN' ME OUT.

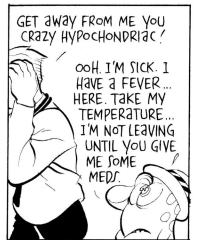

GET AWAY FROM ME YOU CRAZY HYPOCHONDRIAC!

OOH. I'M SICK. I HAVE A FEVER... HERE. TAKE MY TEMPERATURE... I'M NOT LEAVING UNTIL YOU GIVE ME SOME MEDS.

OKAY. OKAY. SINCE YOU PUT IT THAT WAY. HERE. TAKE THIS TWICE A DAY FOR A WEEK. IT SHOULD HELP YOU WITH THE FEVER.

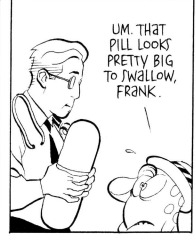

UM. THAT PILL LOOKS PRETTY BIG TO SWALLOW, FRANK.

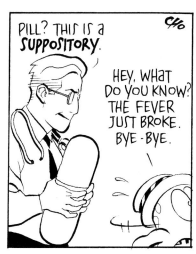

PILL? THIS IS A **SUPPOSITORY**.

HEY, WHAT DO YOU KNOW? THE FEVER JUST BROKE. BYE-BYE.

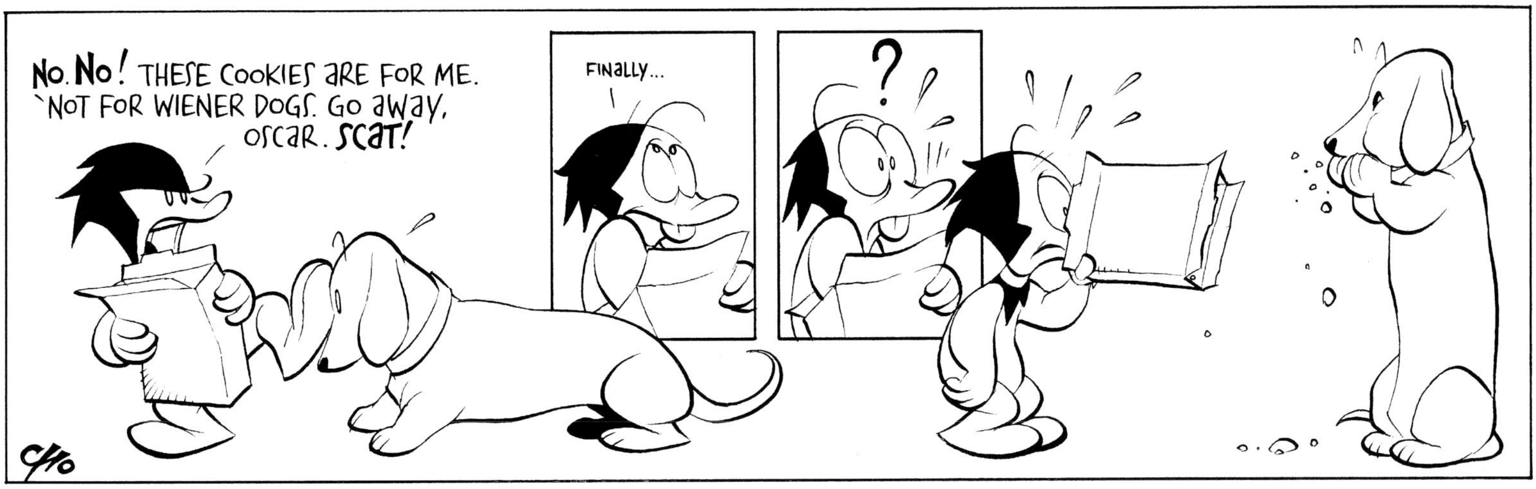
No. No! THESE COOKIES ARE FOR ME. `NOT FOR WIENER DOGS. GO AWAY, OSCAR. SCAT!
CHO
FINALLY...
?

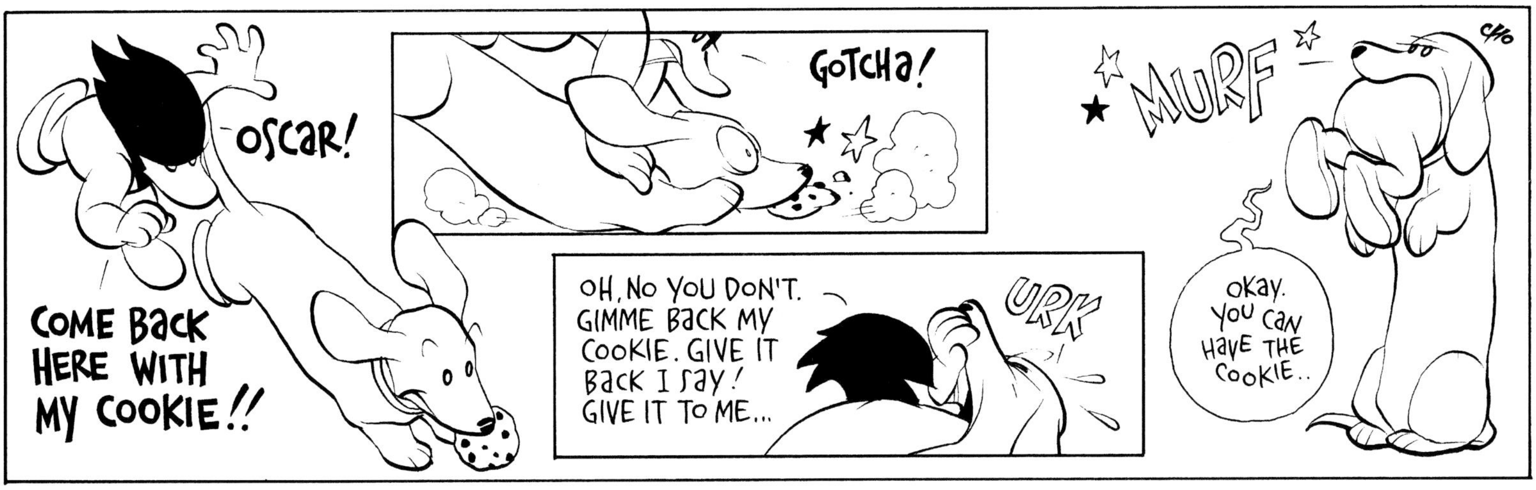
OSCAR!
COME BACK HERE WITH MY COOKIE!!
GOTCHA!
OH, NO YOU DON'T. GIMME BACK MY COOKIE. GIVE IT BACK I SAY! GIVE IT TO ME...
URK
MURF
CHO
OKAY. YOU CAN HAVE THE COOKIE..

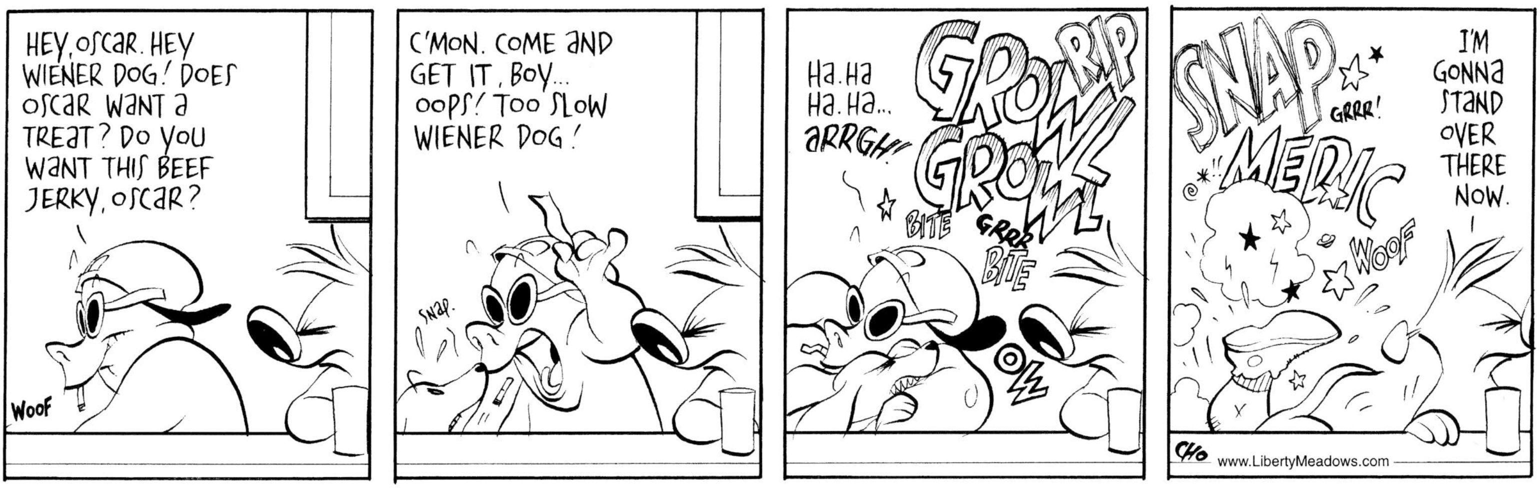
HEY, OSCAR. HEY WIENER DOG! DOES OSCAR WANT A TREAT? DO YOU WANT THIS BEEF JERKY, OSCAR?
WOOF
C'MON. COME AND GET IT, BOY... OOPS! TOO SLOW WIENER DOG!
SNAP.
HA. HA HA. HA... ARRGH!!
GROWL
RIP
GROWL
BITE
GRRR
BITE
OW
SNAP
GRRR!
MEDIC
WOOF
I'M GONNA STAND OVER THERE NOW.
CHO
www.LibertyMeadows.com

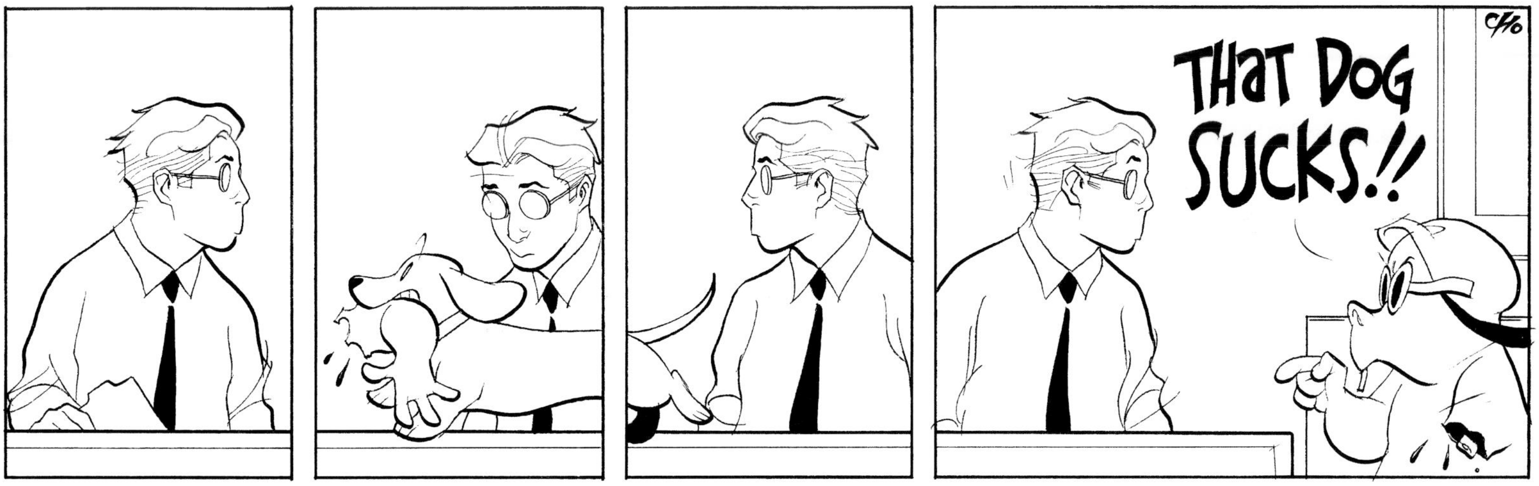
CHO
THAT DOG SUCKS!!

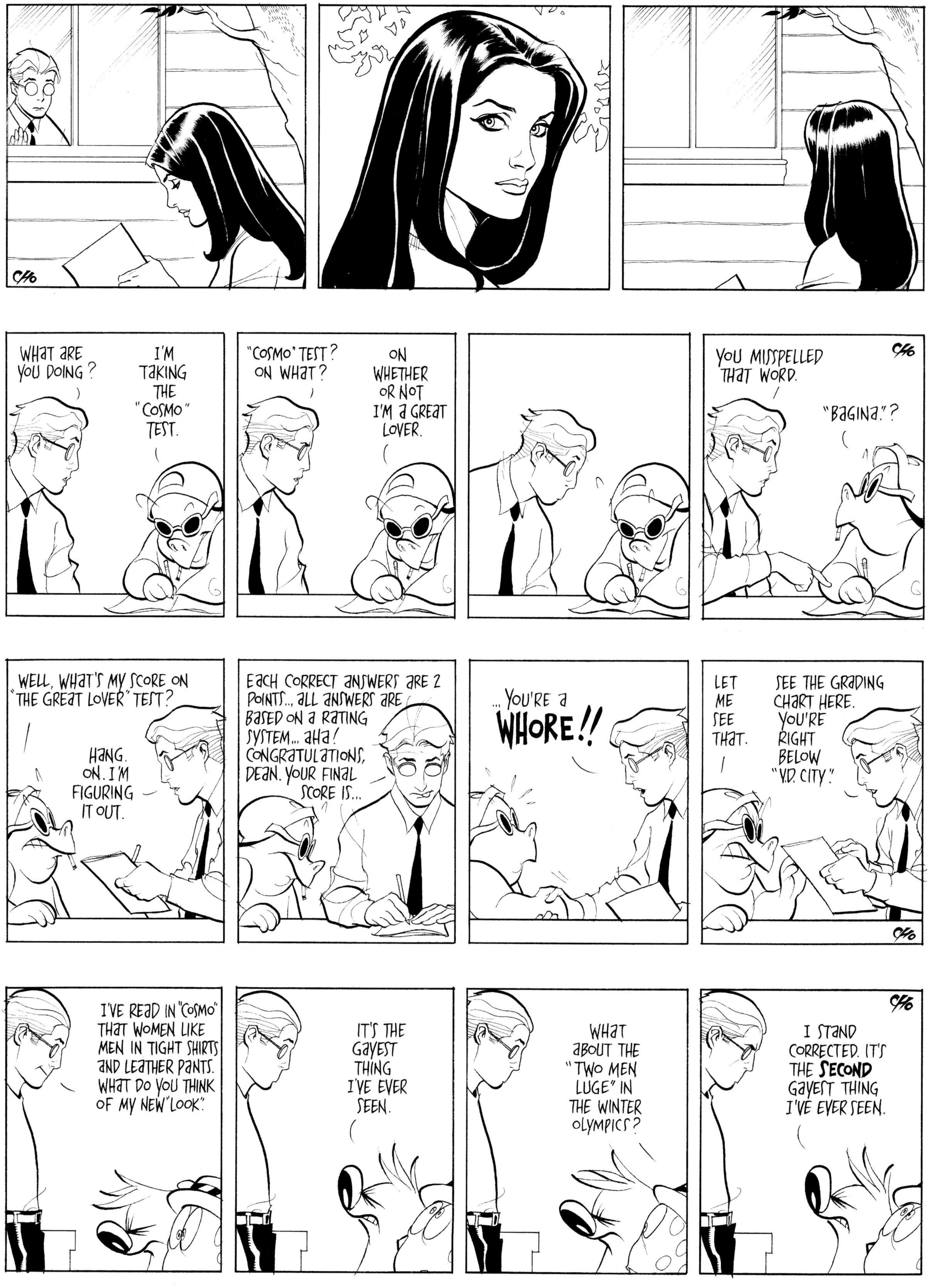
WHAT ARE YOU DOING?
I'M TAKING THE "COSMO" TEST.
"COSMO" TEST? ON WHAT?
ON WHETHER OR NOT I'M A GREAT LOVER.
YOU MISSPELLED THAT WORD.
"BAGINA."?
WELL, WHAT'S MY SCORE ON "THE GREAT LOVER" TEST?
HANG. ON. I'M FIGURING IT OUT.
EACH CORRECT ANSWERS ARE 2 POINTS... ALL ANSWERS ARE BASED ON A RATING SYSTEM... AHA! CONGRATULATIONS, DEAN. YOUR FINAL SCORE IS...
...YOU'RE A WHORE!!
LET ME SEE THAT.
SEE THE GRADING CHART HERE. YOU'RE RIGHT BELOW "V.D. CITY."
I'VE READ IN "COSMO" THAT WOMEN LIKE MEN IN TIGHT SHIRTS AND LEATHER PANTS. WHAT DO YOU THINK OF MY NEW "LOOK".
IT'S THE GAYEST THING I'VE EVER SEEN.
WHAT ABOUT THE "TWO MEN LUGE" IN THE WINTER OLYMPICS?
I STAND CORRECTED. IT'S THE **SECOND** GAYEST THING I'VE EVER SEEN.

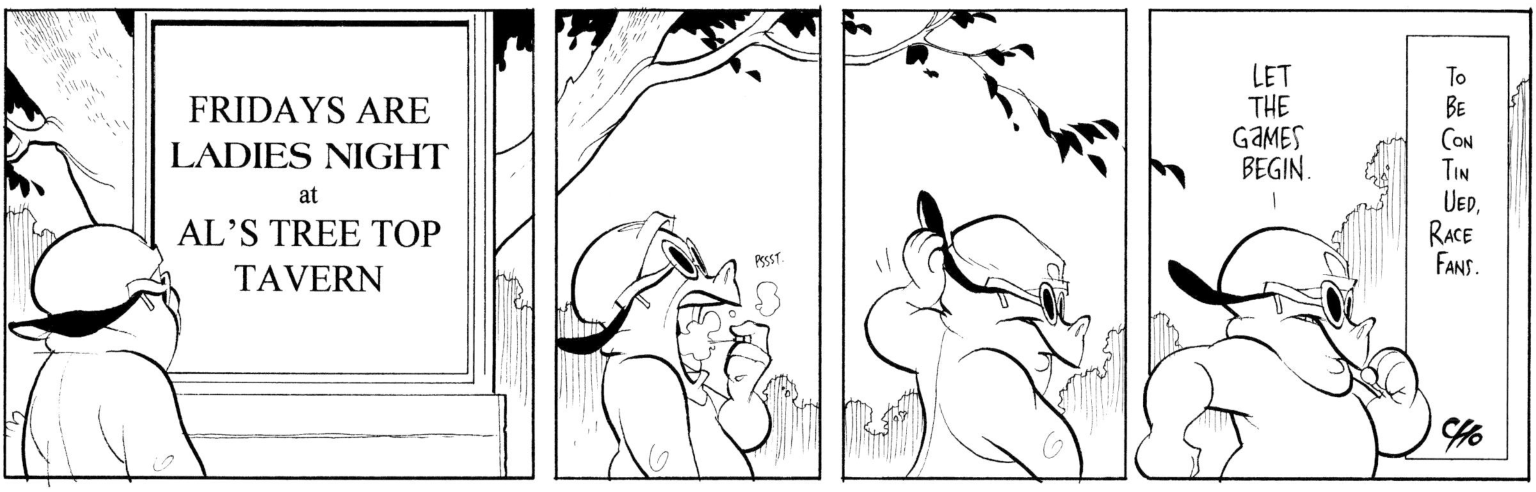
FRIDAYS ARE LADIES NIGHT at AL'S TREE TOP TAVERN
PSSST.
LET THE GAMES BEGIN.
To Be Con Tin Ued, Race Fans.

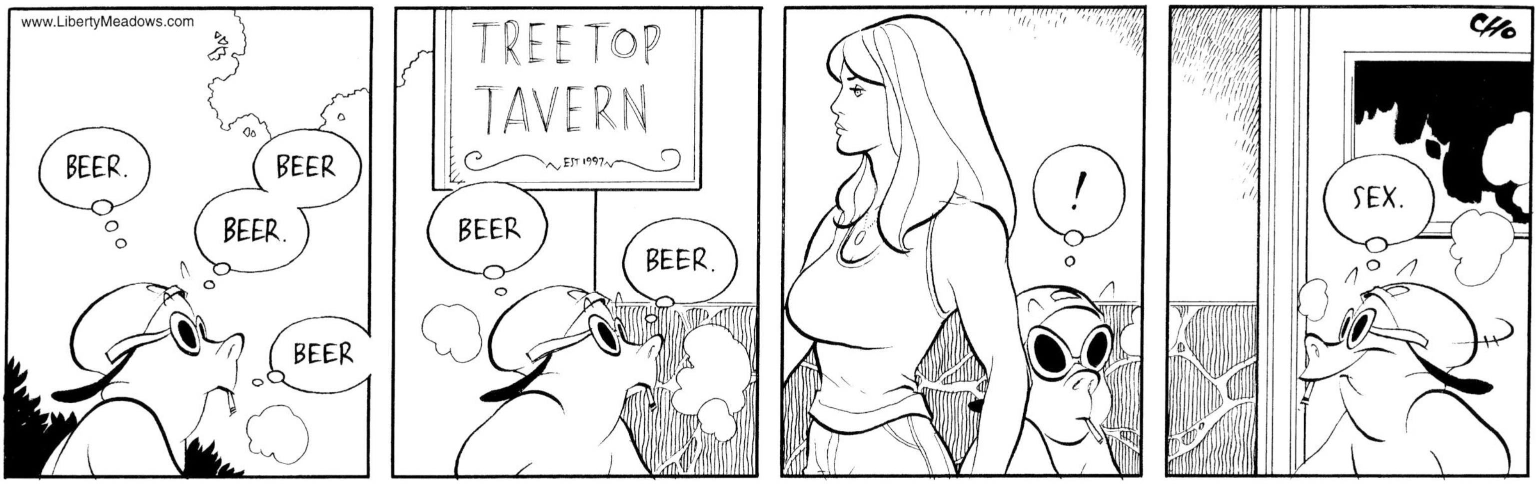
www.LibertyMeadows.com
BEER.
BEER
BEER.
BEER
TREE TOP TAVERN
EST 1997
BEER
BEER.
!
SEX.

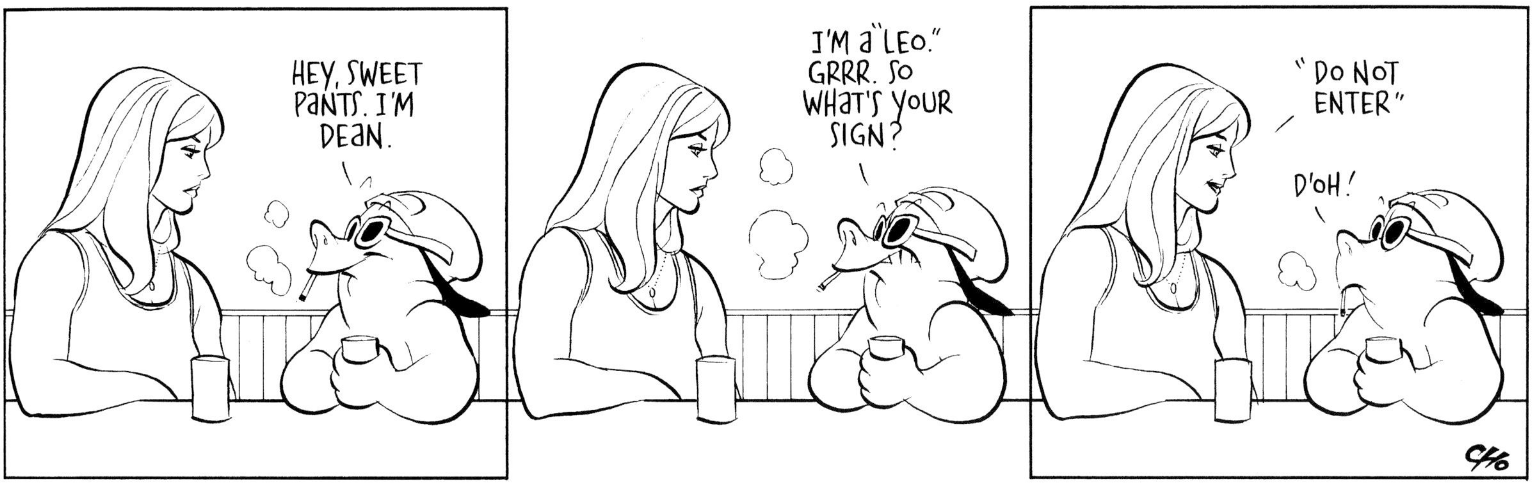
HEY, SWEET PANTS. I'M DEAN.
I'M a "LEO." GRRR. SO WHAT'S YOUR SIGN?
"DO NOT ENTER"
D'OH!

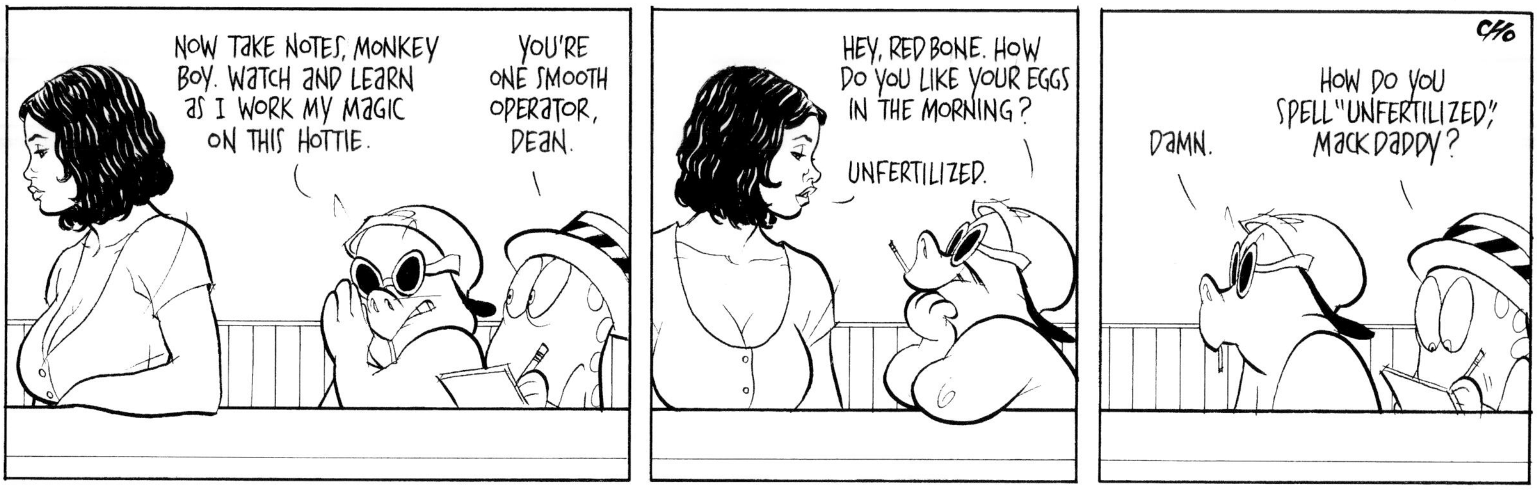
NOW TAKE NOTES, MONKEY BOY. WATCH AND LEARN AS I WORK MY MAGIC ON THIS HOTTIE.
YOU'RE ONE SMOOTH OPERATOR, DEAN.
HEY, RED BONE. HOW DO YOU LIKE YOUR EGGS IN THE MORNING?
UNFERTILIZED.
DAMN.
HOW DO YOU SPELL "UNFERTILIZED," MACK DADDY?

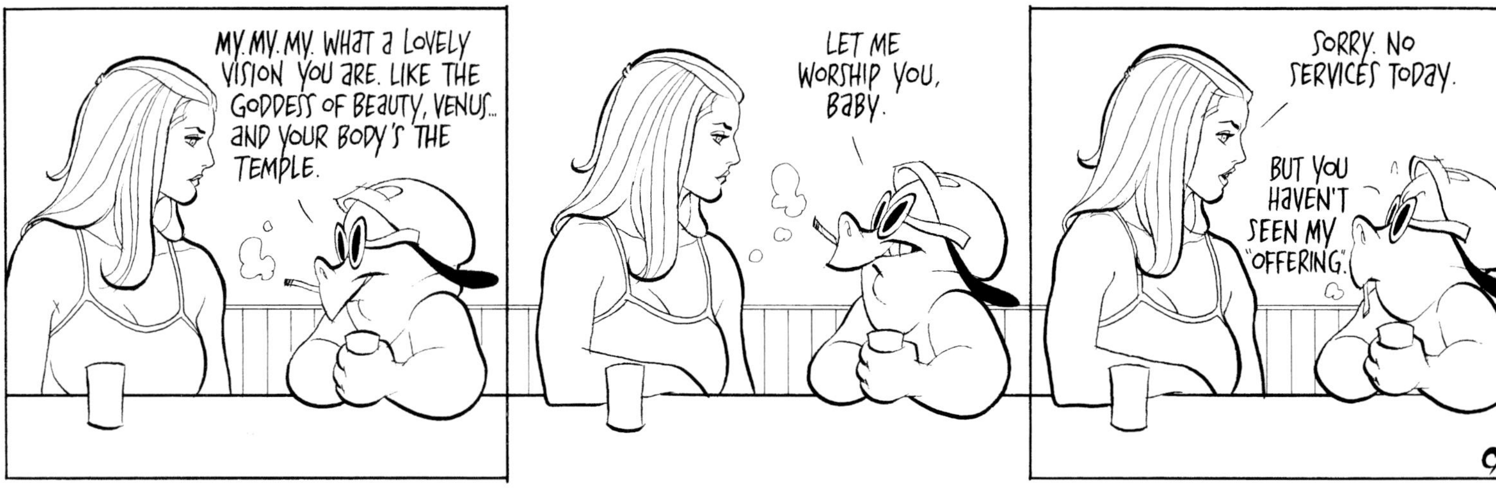
MY. MY. MY. WHAT A LOVELY VISION YOU ARE. LIKE THE GODDESS OF BEAUTY, VENUS... AND YOUR BODY'S THE TEMPLE.
LET ME WORSHIP YOU, BABY.
SORRY. NO SERVICES TODAY.
BUT YOU HAVEN'T SEEN MY "OFFERING."
CHO

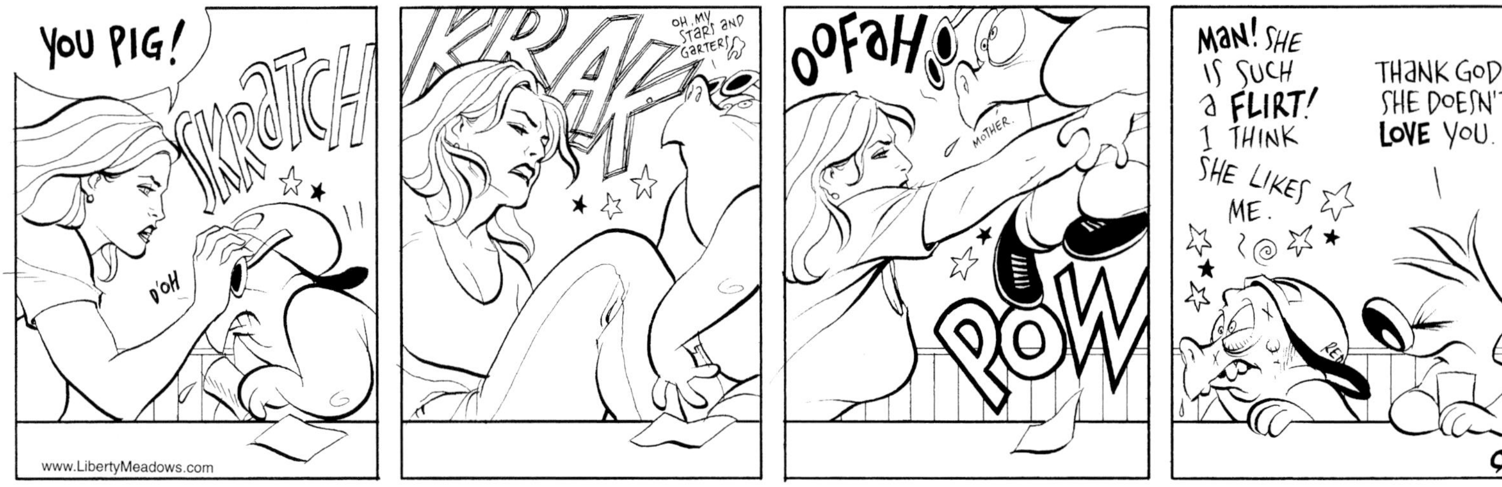
YOU PIG!
SKRATCH
D'OH
www.LibertyMeadows.com
KRAK
OH, MY STARS AND GARTERS!
OOFAH
MOTHER.
POW
MAN! SHE IS SUCH A **FLIRT**! I THINK SHE LIKES ME.
THANK GOD SHE DOESN'T **LOVE** YOU.
CHO

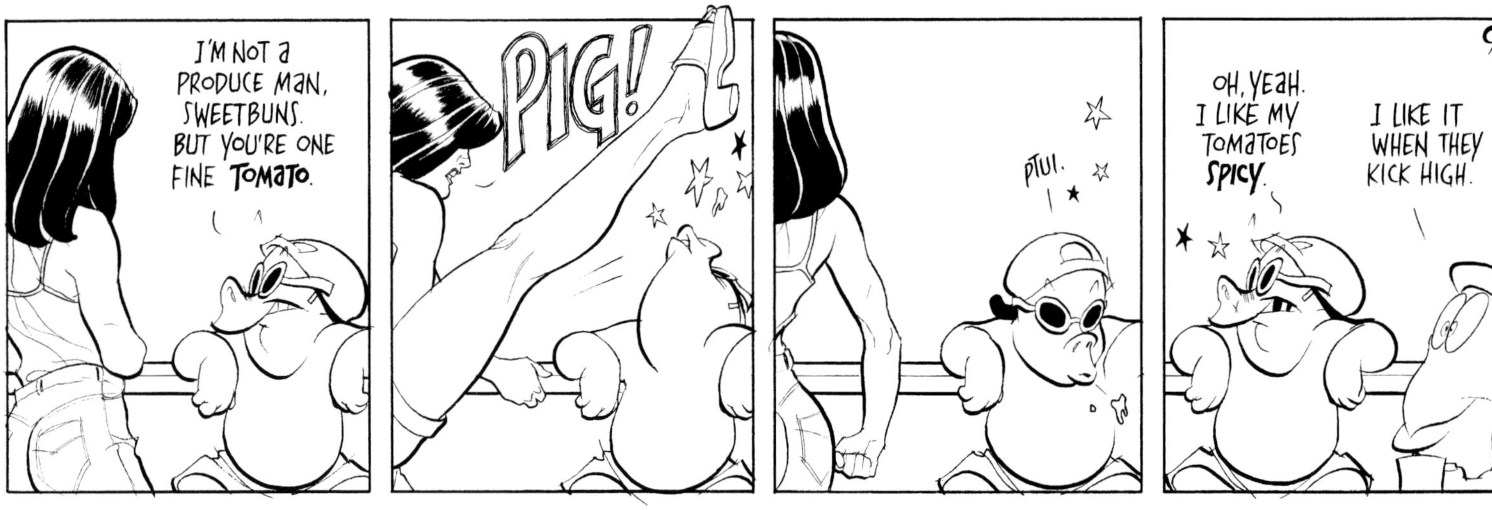
I'M NOT A PRODUCE MAN, SWEETBUNS. BUT YOU'RE ONE FINE **TOMATO**.
PIG!
PTUI.
CHO
OH, YEAH. I LIKE MY TOMATOES **SPICY**.
I LIKE IT WHEN THEY KICK HIGH.

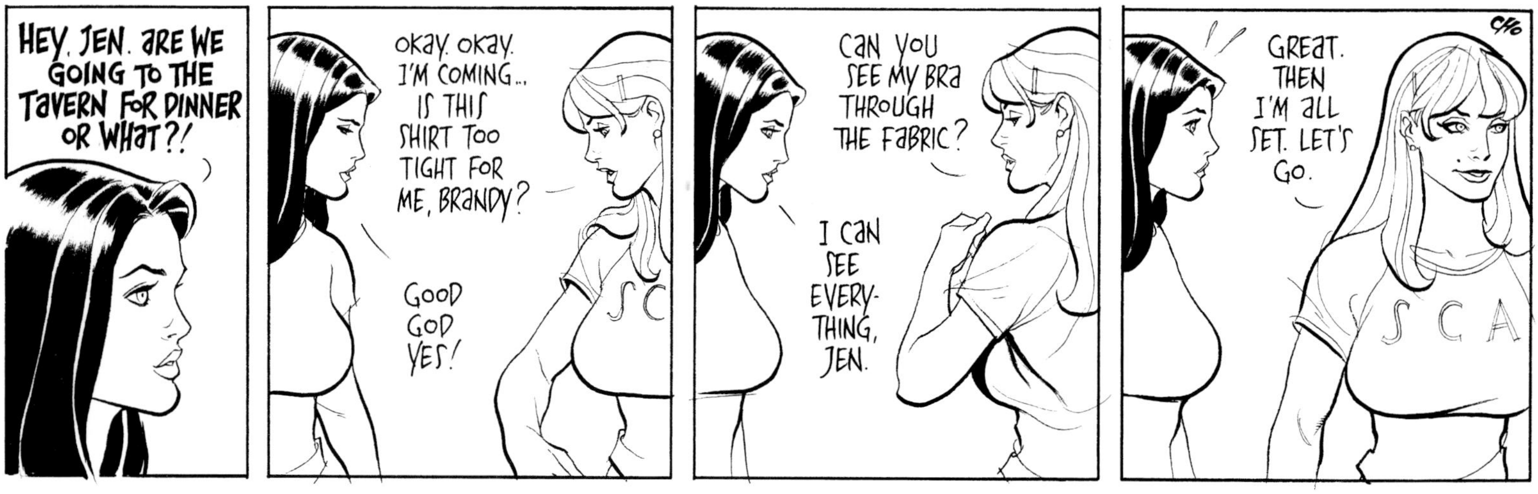
HEY, JEN. ARE WE GOING TO THE TAVERN FOR DINNER OR WHAT?!
OKAY. OKAY. I'M COMING... IS THIS SHIRT TOO TIGHT FOR ME, BRANDY?
GOOD GOD YES!
CAN YOU SEE MY BRA THROUGH THE FABRIC?
I CAN SEE EVERY-THING, JEN.
CHO
GREAT. THEN I'M ALL SET. LET'S GO.

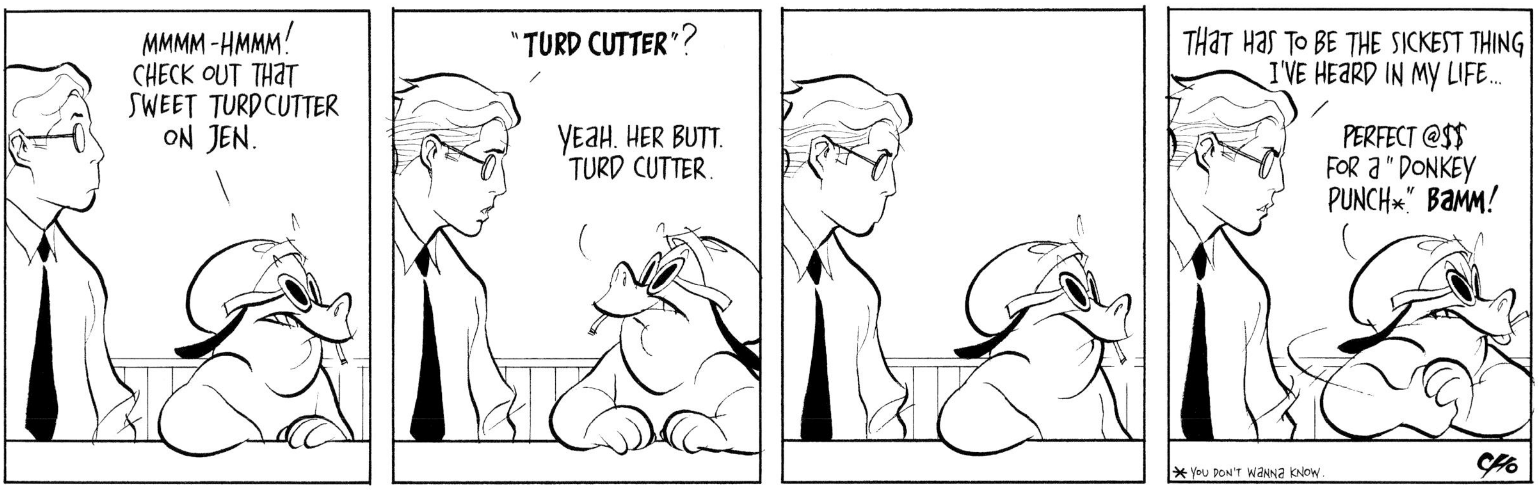
MMMM-HMMM! CHECK OUT THAT SWEET TURDCUTTER ON JEN.
"TURD CUTTER"?
YEAH. HER BUTT. TURD CUTTER.
THAT HAS TO BE THE SICKEST THING I'VE HEARD IN MY LIFE...
PERFECT @$$ FOR A "DONKEY PUNCH*." BAMM!
* YOU DON'T WANNA KNOW.

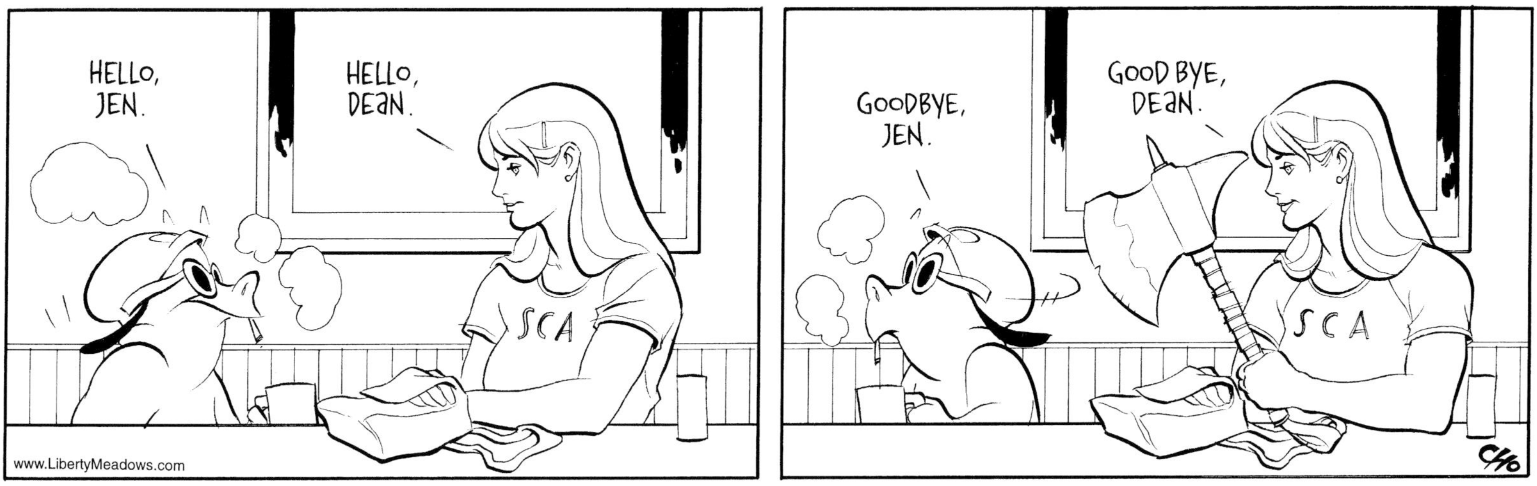
www.LibertyMeadows.com
HELLO, JEN.
HELLO, DEAN.
GOODBYE, JEN.
GOOD BYE, DEAN.

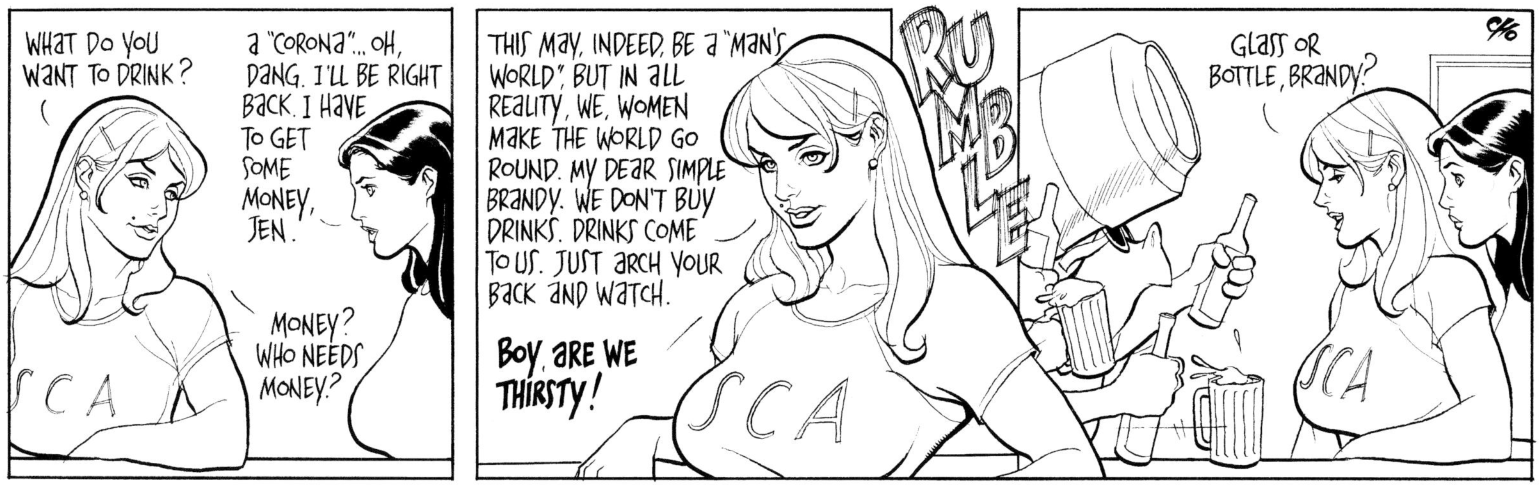
WHAT DO YOU WANT TO DRINK?
A "CORONA"... OH, DANG. I'LL BE RIGHT BACK. I HAVE TO GET SOME MONEY, JEN.
MONEY? WHO NEEDS MONEY?
THIS MAY, INDEED, BE A "MAN'S WORLD," BUT IN ALL REALITY, WE, WOMEN MAKE THE WORLD GO ROUND. MY DEAR SIMPLE BRANDY. WE DON'T BUY DRINKS. DRINKS COME TO US. JUST ARCH YOUR BACK AND WATCH.
BOY, ARE WE THIRSTY!
RUMBLE
GLASS OR BOTTLE, BRANDY?

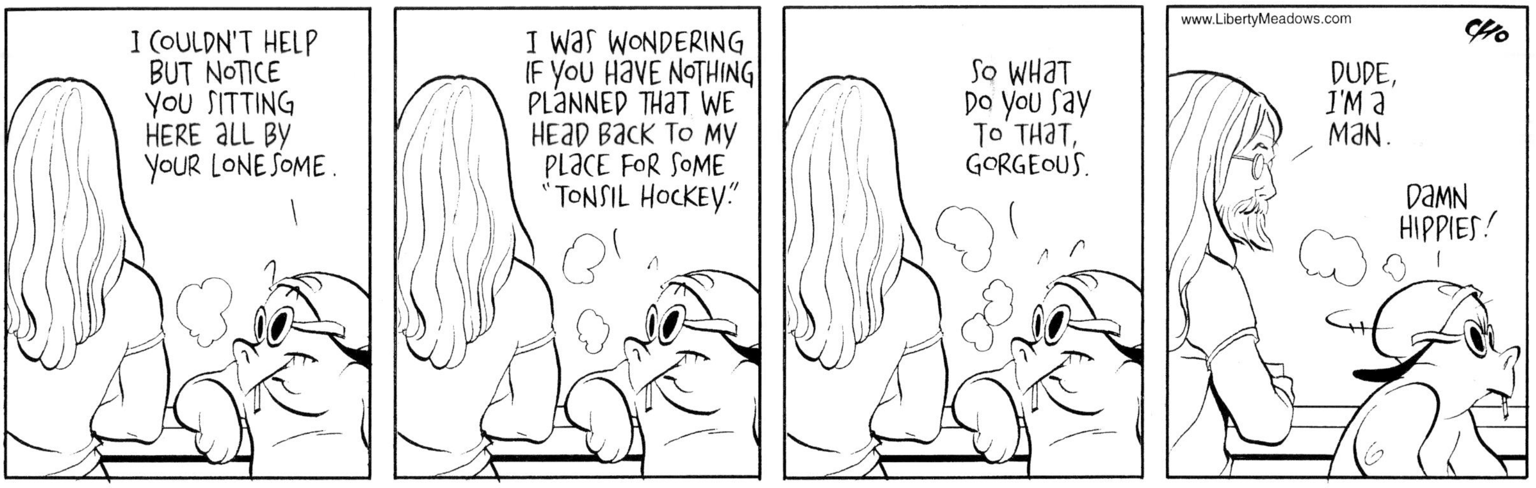
I COULDN'T HELP BUT NOTICE YOU SITTING HERE ALL BY YOUR LONESOME.
I WAS WONDERING IF YOU HAVE NOTHING PLANNED THAT WE HEAD BACK TO MY PLACE FOR SOME "TONSIL HOCKEY."
SO WHAT DO YOU SAY TO THAT, GORGEOUS.
www.LibertyMeadows.com
DUDE, I'M A MAN.
DAMN HIPPIES!

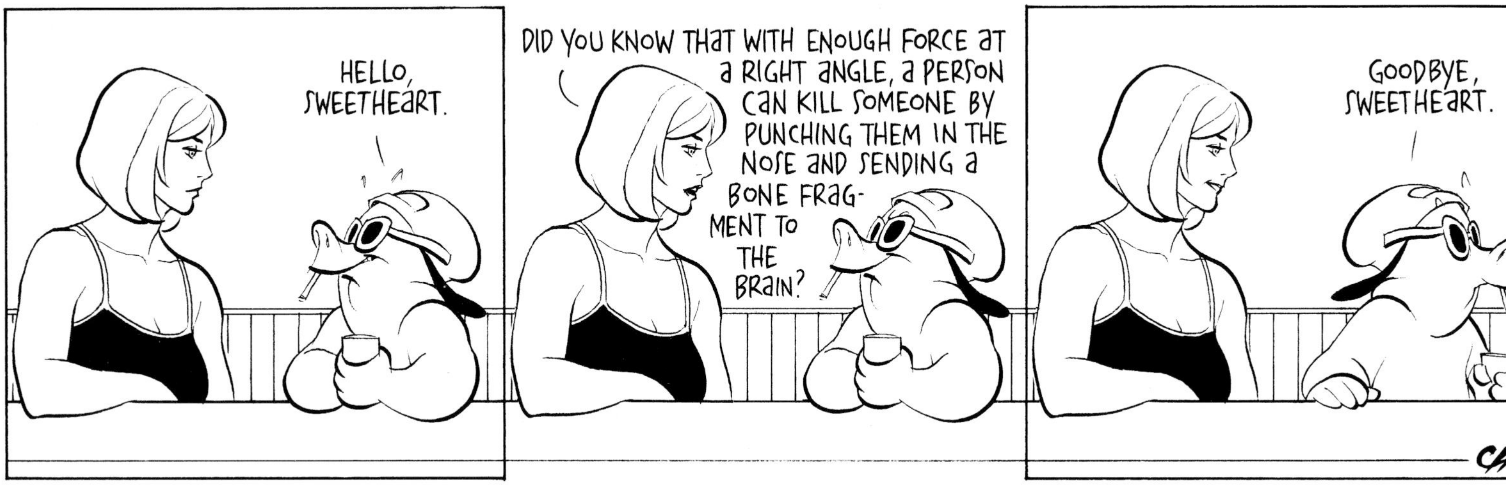
HELLO, SWEETHEART.
DID YOU KNOW THAT WITH ENOUGH FORCE AT A RIGHT ANGLE, A PERSON CAN KILL SOMEONE BY PUNCHING THEM IN THE NOSE AND SENDING A BONE FRAG-MENT TO THE BRAIN?
GOODBYE, SWEETHEART.
CHO

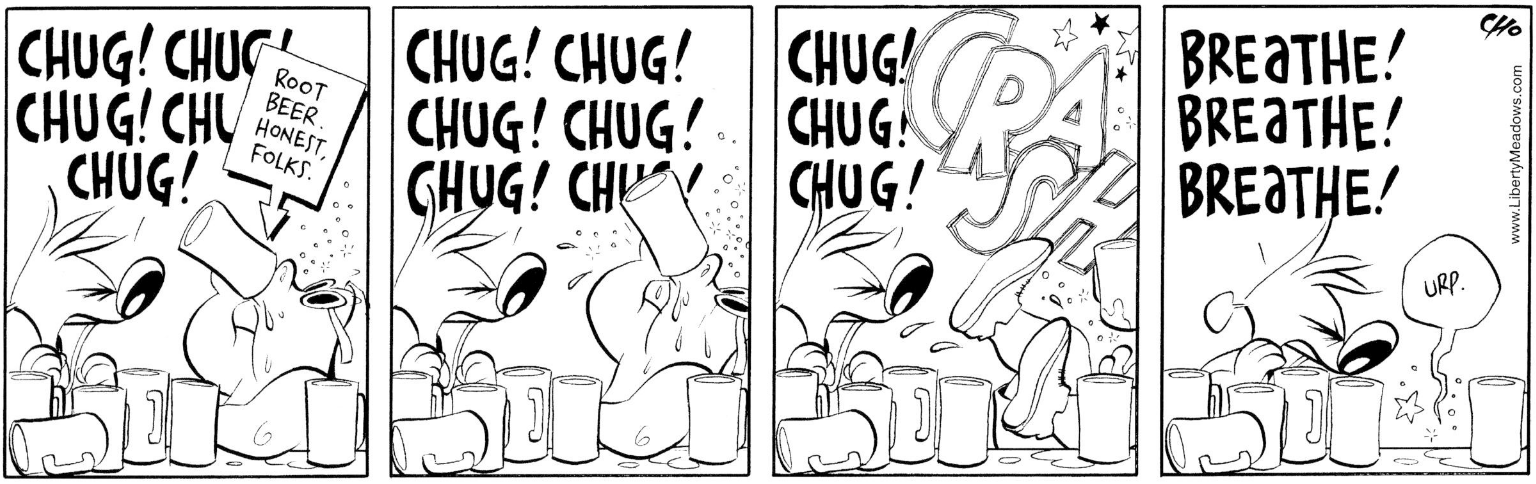
CHUG! CHUG! CHUG! CHU CHUG!
ROOT BEER. HONEST, FOLKS.
CHUG! CHUG! CHUG! CHUG! CHUG! CH
CHUG! CHUG! CHUG!
CRASH!
CHO
BREATHE! BREATHE! BREATHE!
URP.
www.LibertyMeadows.com

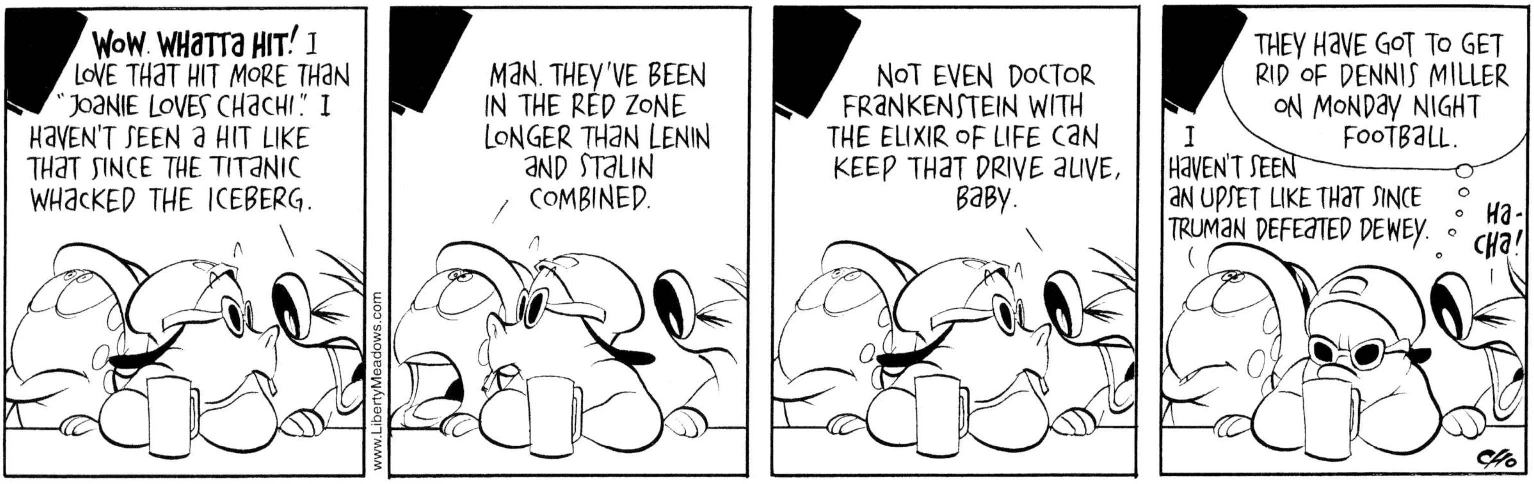
WOW. WHATTA HIT! I LOVE THAT HIT MORE THAN "JOANIE LOVES CHACHI." I HAVEN'T SEEN A HIT LIKE THAT SINCE THE TITANIC WHACKED THE ICEBERG.
www.LibertyMeadows.com
MAN. THEY'VE BEEN IN THE RED ZONE LONGER THAN LENIN AND STALIN COMBINED.
NOT EVEN DOCTOR FRANKENSTEIN WITH THE ELIXIR OF LIFE CAN KEEP THAT DRIVE ALIVE, BABY.
THEY HAVE GOT TO GET RID OF DENNIS MILLER ON MONDAY NIGHT FOOTBALL.
I HAVEN'T SEEN AN UPSET LIKE THAT SINCE TRUMAN DEFEATED DEWEY.
HA-CHA!
CHO

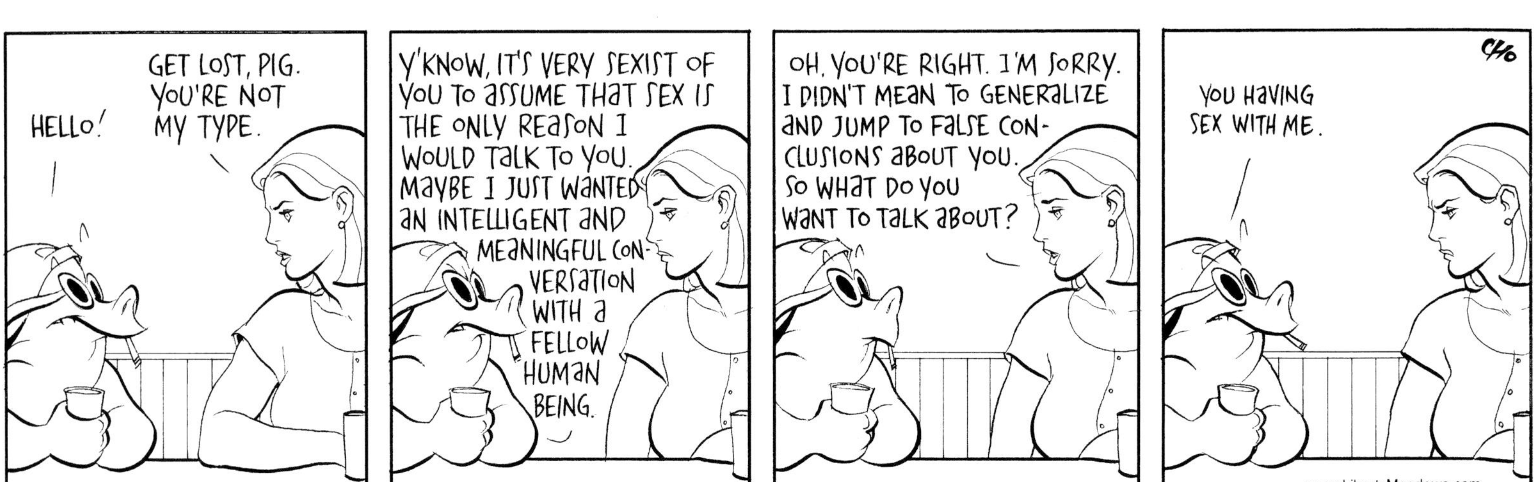
HELLO!
GET LOST, PIG. YOU'RE NOT MY TYPE.
Y'KNOW, IT'S VERY SEXIST OF YOU TO ASSUME THAT SEX IS THE ONLY REASON I WOULD TALK TO YOU. MAYBE I JUST WANTED AN INTELLIGENT AND MEANINGFUL CON-VERSATION WITH A FELLOW HUMAN BEING.
OH, YOU'RE RIGHT. I'M SORRY. I DIDN'T MEAN TO GENERALIZE AND JUMP TO FALSE CON-CLUSIONS ABOUT YOU. SO WHAT DO YOU WANT TO TALK ABOUT?
CHO
YOU HAVING SEX WITH ME.
www.LibertyMeadows.com

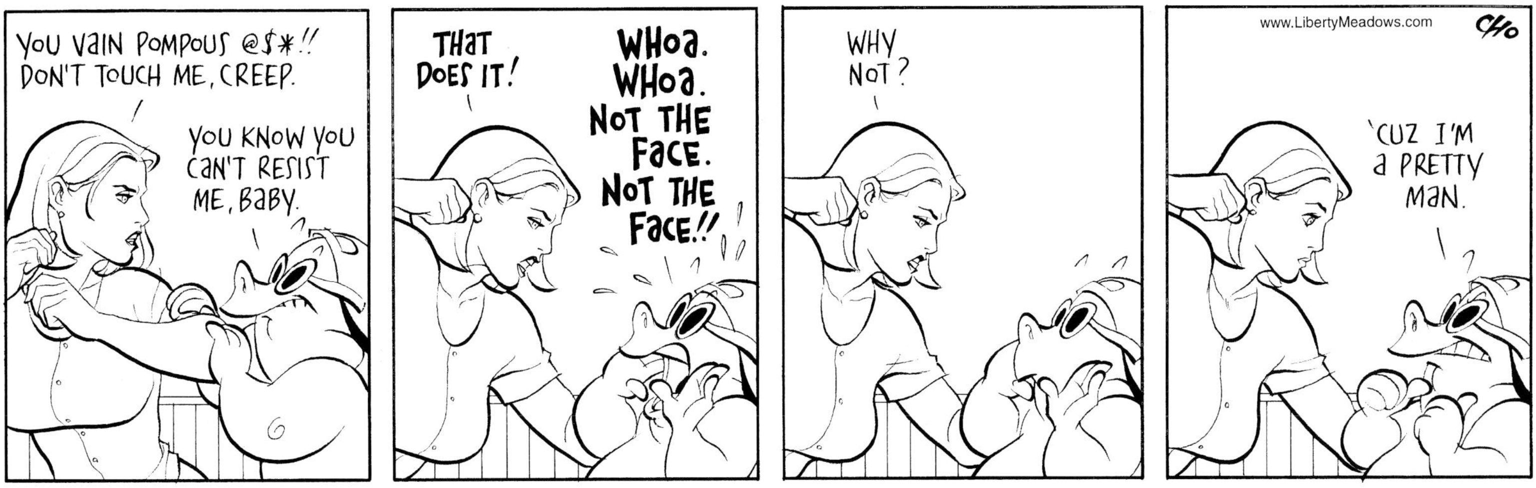
YOU VAIN POMPOUS @$*!! DON'T TOUCH ME, CREEP.
YOU KNOW YOU CAN'T RESIST ME, BABY.
THAT DOES IT!
WHOA. WHOA. NOT THE FACE. NOT THE FACE!!
WHY NOT?
www.LibertyMeadows.com
CHO
'CUZ I'M A PRETTY MAN.

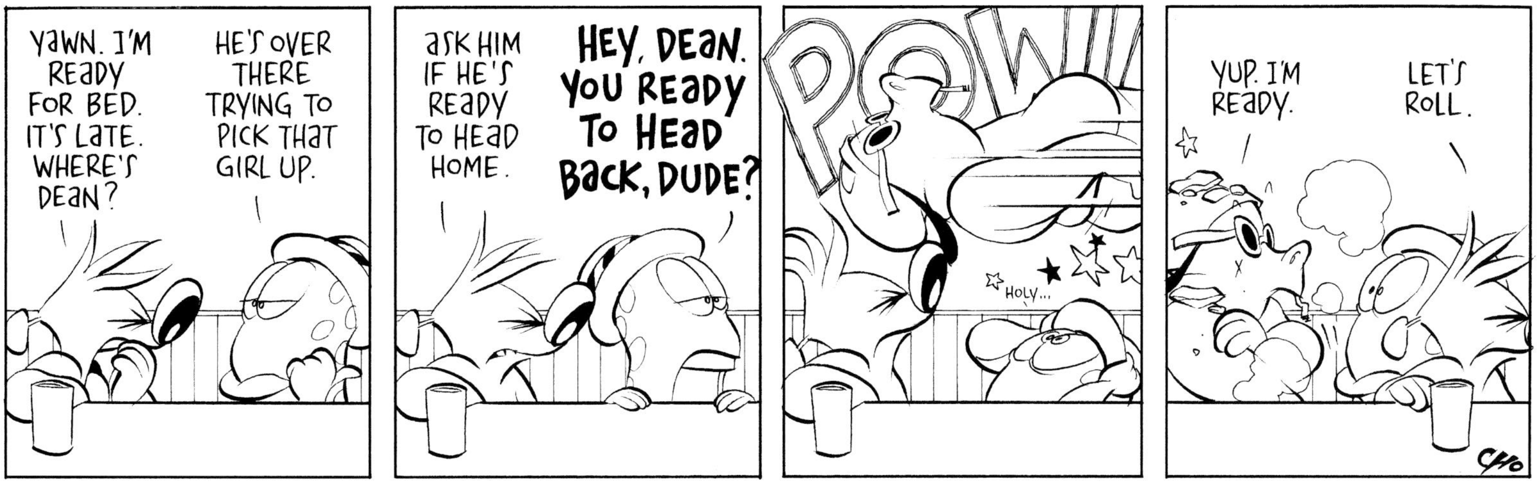
YAWN. I'M READY FOR BED. IT'S LATE. WHERE'S DEAN?
HE'S OVER THERE TRYING TO PICK THAT GIRL UP.
ASK HIM IF HE'S READY TO HEAD HOME.
HEY, DEAN. YOU READY TO HEAD BACK, DUDE?
POW!!!
HOLY...
YUP. I'M READY.
LET'S ROLL.
CHO

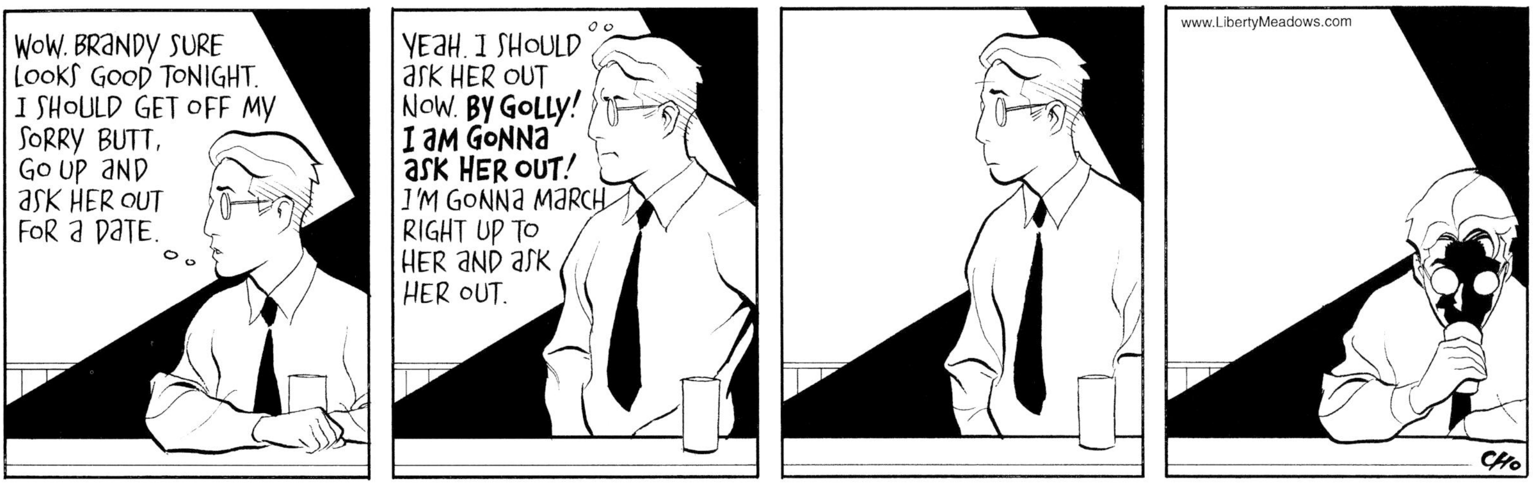
WOW. BRANDY SURE LOOKS GOOD TONIGHT. I SHOULD GET OFF MY SORRY BUTT, GO UP AND ASK HER OUT FOR A DATE.
YEAH. I SHOULD ASK HER OUT NOW. BY GOLLY! I AM GONNA ASK HER OUT! I'M GONNA MARCH RIGHT UP TO HER AND ASK HER OUT.
www.LibertyMeadows.com
CHO

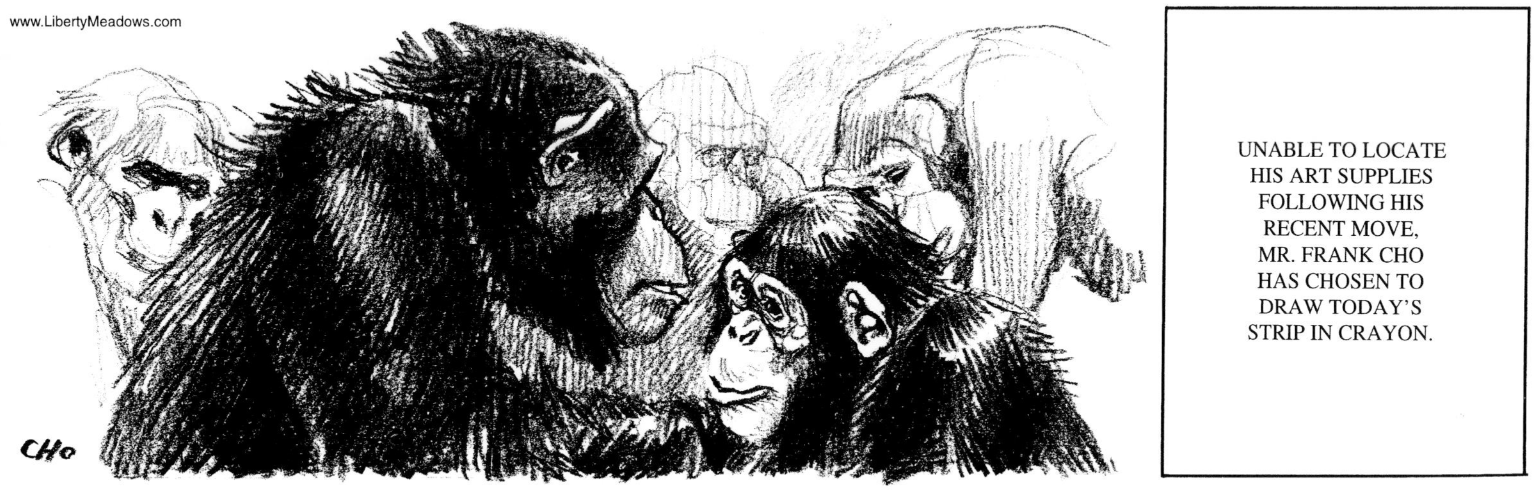
www.LibertyMeadows.com
CHO
UNABLE TO LOCATE HIS ART SUPPLIES FOLLOWING HIS RECENT MOVE, MR. FRANK CHO HAS CHOSEN TO DRAW TODAY'S STRIP IN CRAYON.

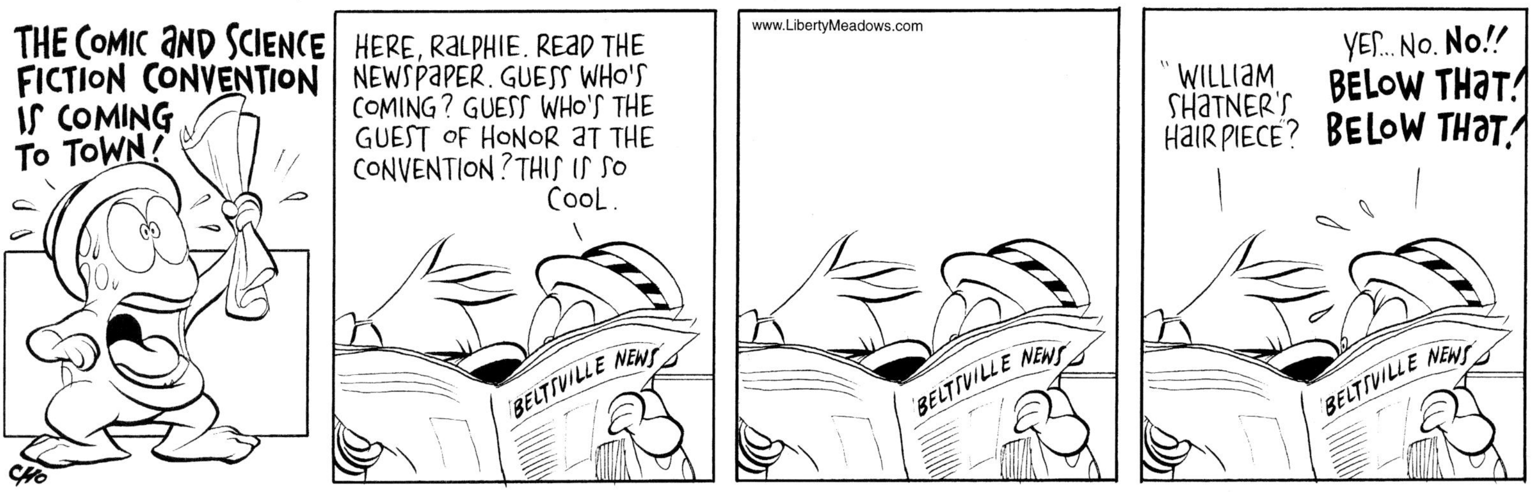
THE COMIC AND SCIENCE FICTION CONVENTION IS COMING TO TOWN!
HERE, RALPHIE. READ THE NEWSPAPER. GUESS WHO'S COMING? GUESS WHO'S THE GUEST OF HONOR AT THE CONVENTION? THIS IS SO COOL.
BELTSVILLE NEWS
www.LibertyMeadows.com
"WILLIAM SHATNER'S HAIRPIECE?
YES... NO. NO!! BELOW THAT! BELOW THAT!
CHO

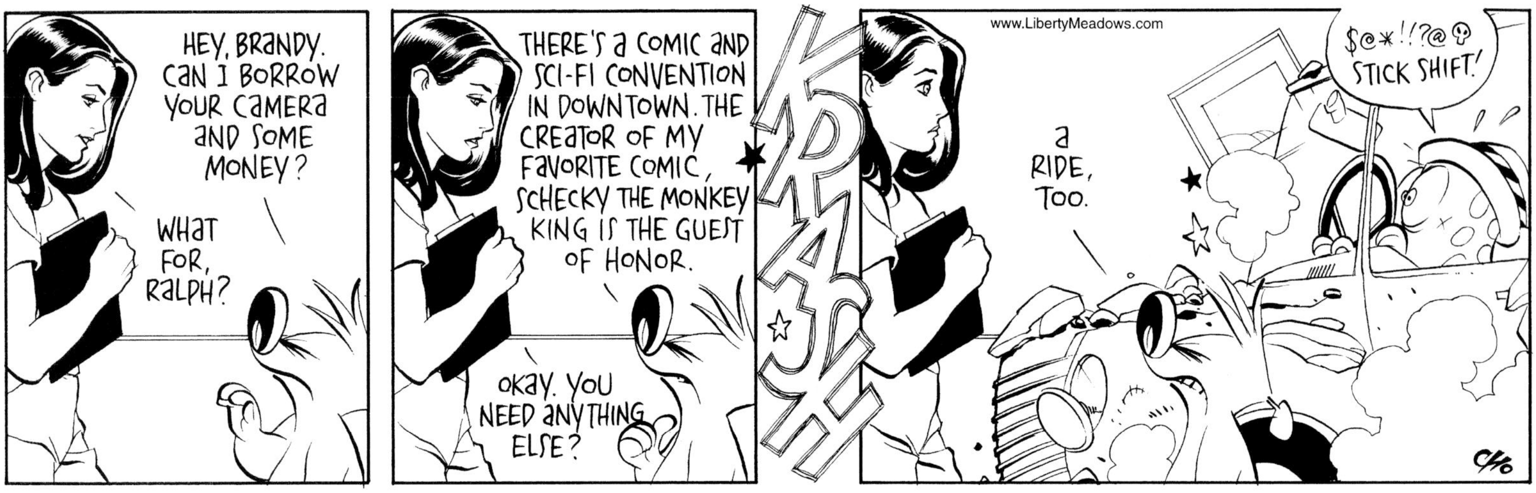
HEY, BRANDY. CAN I BORROW YOUR CAMERA AND SOME MONEY?
WHAT FOR, RALPH?
THERE'S A COMIC AND SCI-FI CONVENTION IN DOWNTOWN. THE CREATOR OF MY FAVORITE COMIC, SCHECKY THE MONKEY KING IS THE GUEST OF HONOR.
OKAY. YOU NEED ANYTHING ELSE?
KRASH
www.LibertyMeadows.com
A RIDE, TOO.
$@*!!?@ STICK SHIFT!
CHO

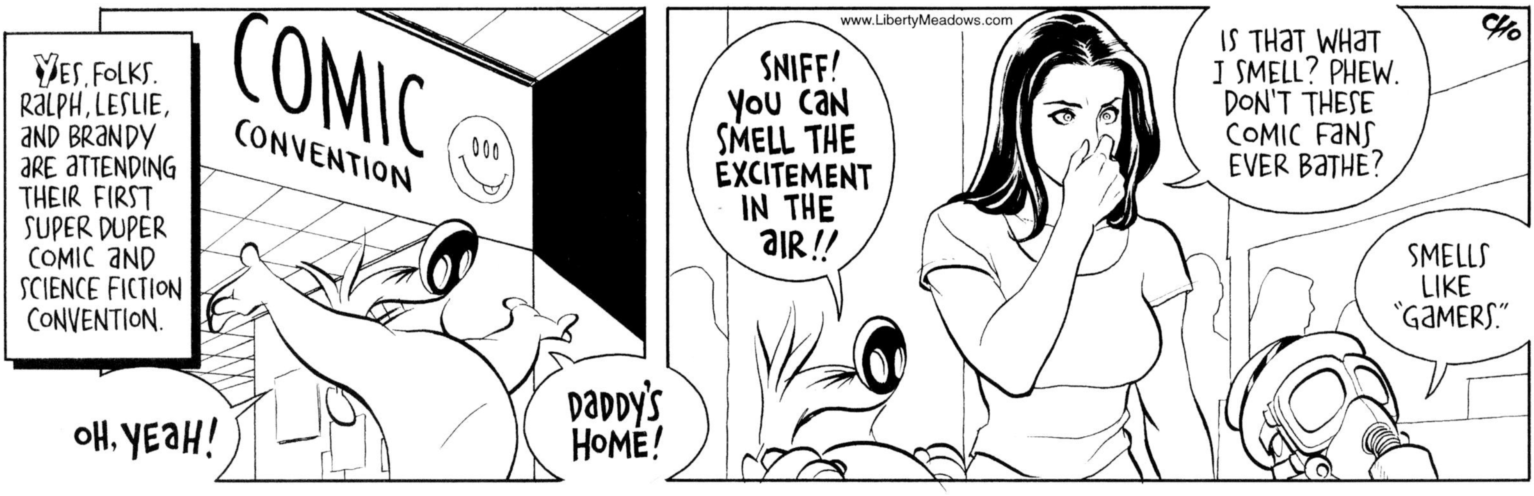
YES, FOLKS. RALPH, LESLIE, AND BRANDY ARE ATTENDING THEIR FIRST SUPER DUPER COMIC AND SCIENCE FICTION CONVENTION.
COMIC CONVENTION
OH, YEAH!
DADDY'S HOME!
www.LibertyMeadows.com
SNIFF! YOU CAN SMELL THE EXCITEMENT IN THE AIR!!
IS THAT WHAT I SMELL? PHEW. DON'T THESE COMIC FANS EVER BATHE?
SMELLS LIKE "GAMERS."
CHO

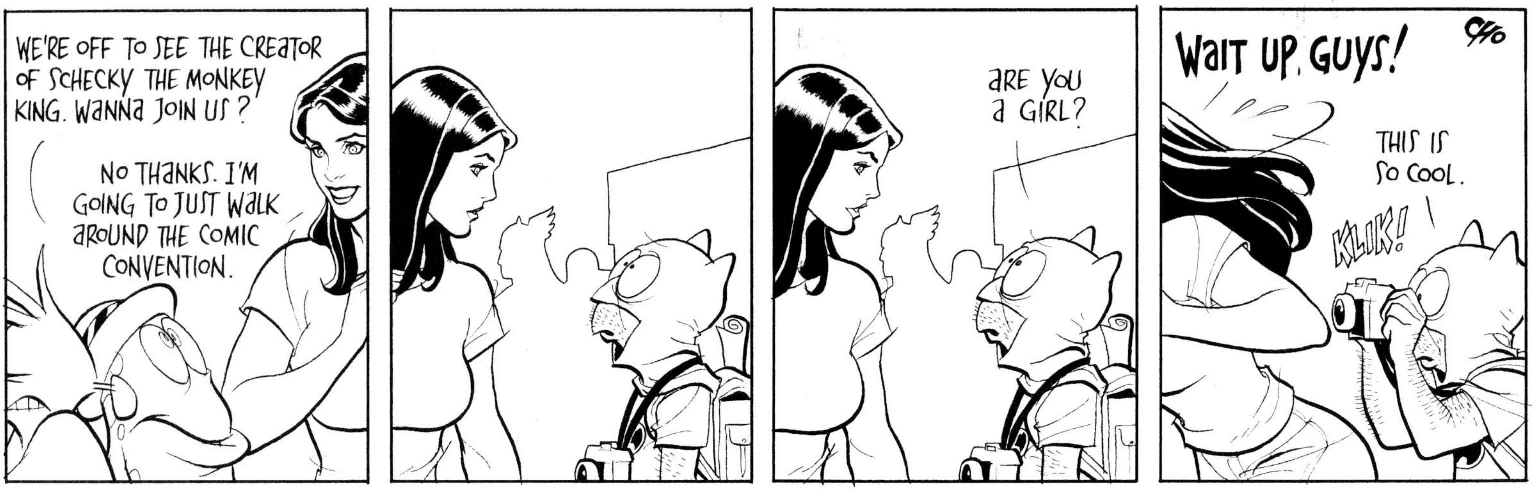
WE'RE OFF TO SEE THE CREATOR OF SCHECKY THE MONKEY KING. WANNA JOIN US?
NO THANKS. I'M GOING TO JUST WALK AROUND THE COMIC CONVENTION.
ARE YOU A GIRL?
WAIT UP, GUYS!
THIS IS SO COOL.
KLIK!
CHO

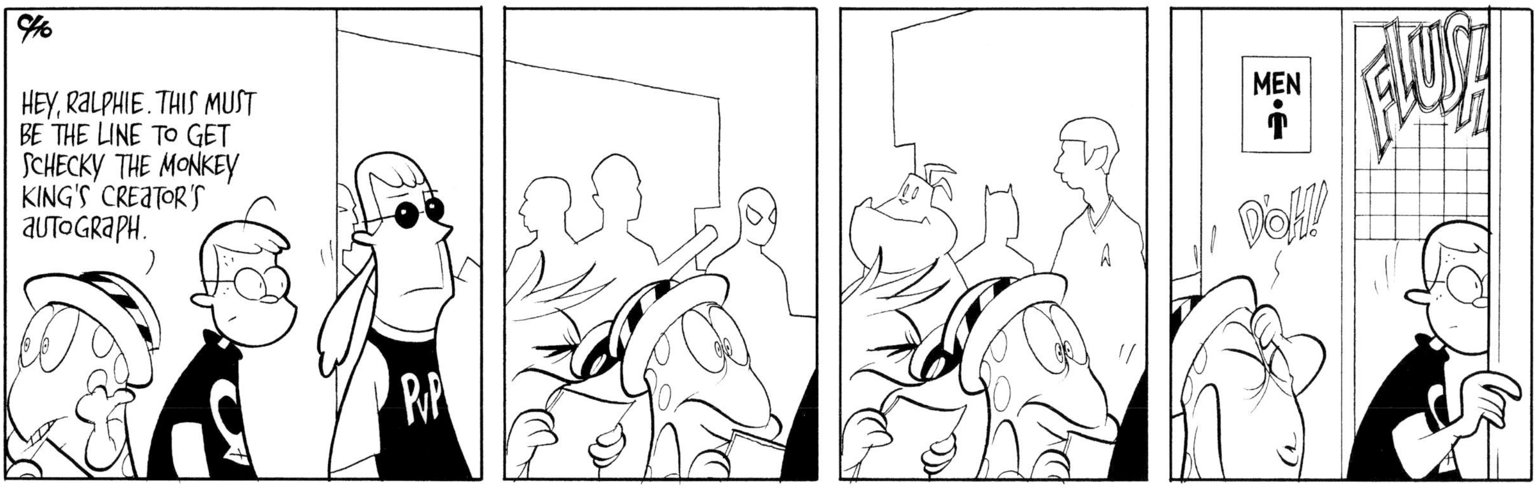
CHO
HEY, RALPHIE. THIS MUST BE THE LINE TO GET SCHECKY THE MONKEY KING'S CREATOR'S AUTOGRAPH.
PvP
MEN
FLUSH
D'OH!

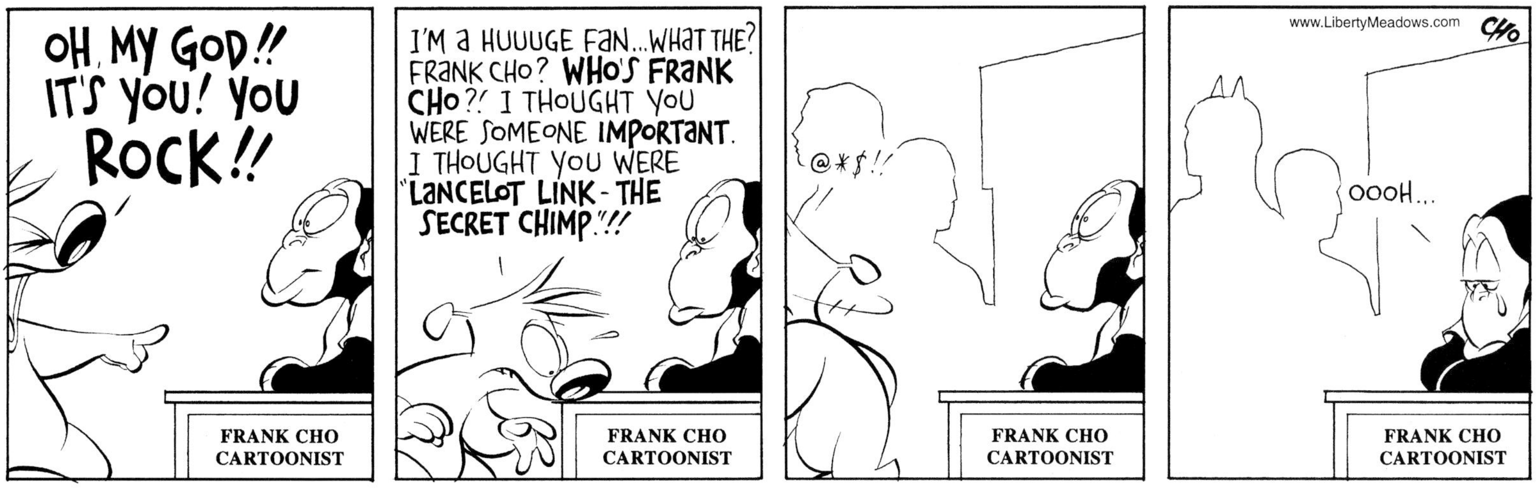
OH, MY GOD!! IT'S YOU! YOU ROCK!!
FRANK CHO
CARTOONIST
I'M A HUUUGE FAN... WHAT THE? FRANK CHO? WHO'S FRANK CHO?! I THOUGHT YOU WERE SOMEONE IMPORTANT. I THOUGHT YOU WERE "LANCELOT LINK - THE SECRET CHIMP"!!!
FRANK CHO
CARTOONIST
@*$!!
FRANK CHO
CARTOONIST
www.LibertyMeadows.com
CHO
OOOH...
FRANK CHO
CARTOONIST

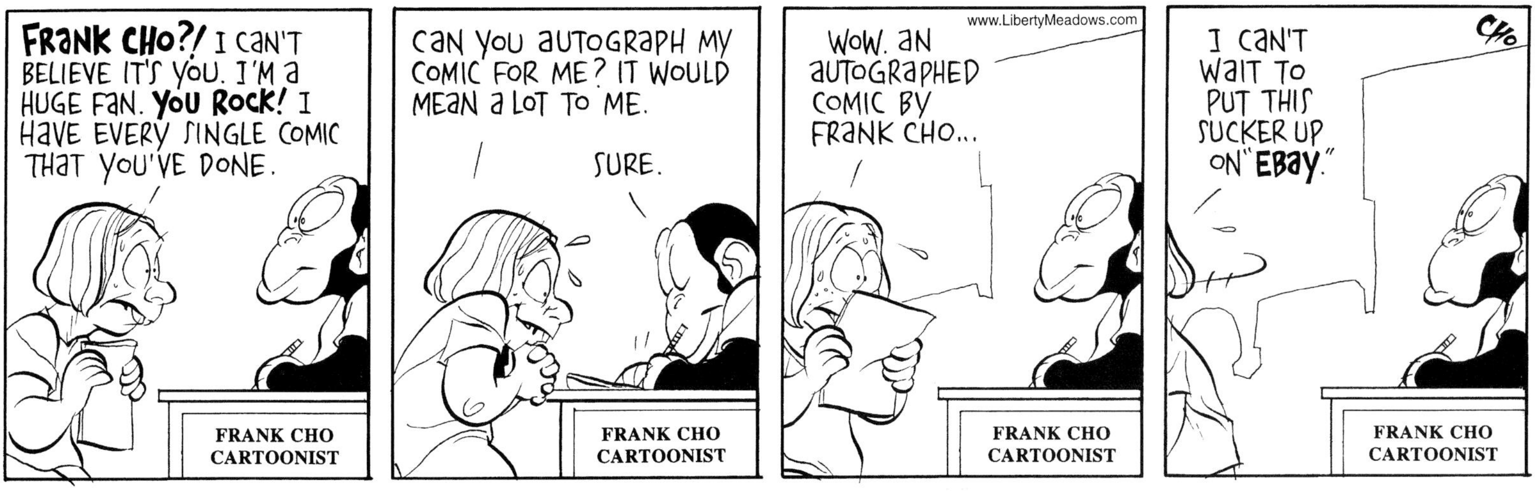
FRANK CHO?! I CAN'T BELIEVE IT'S YOU. I'M A HUGE FAN. YOU ROCK! I HAVE EVERY SINGLE COMIC THAT YOU'VE DONE.
FRANK CHO
CARTOONIST
CAN YOU AUTOGRAPH MY COMIC FOR ME? IT WOULD MEAN A LOT TO ME.
SURE.
FRANK CHO
CARTOONIST
www.LibertyMeadows.com
WOW. AN AUTOGRAPHED COMIC BY FRANK CHO...
FRANK CHO
CARTOONIST
CHO
I CAN'T WAIT TO PUT THIS SUCKER UP ON "EBAY."
FRANK CHO
CARTOONIST

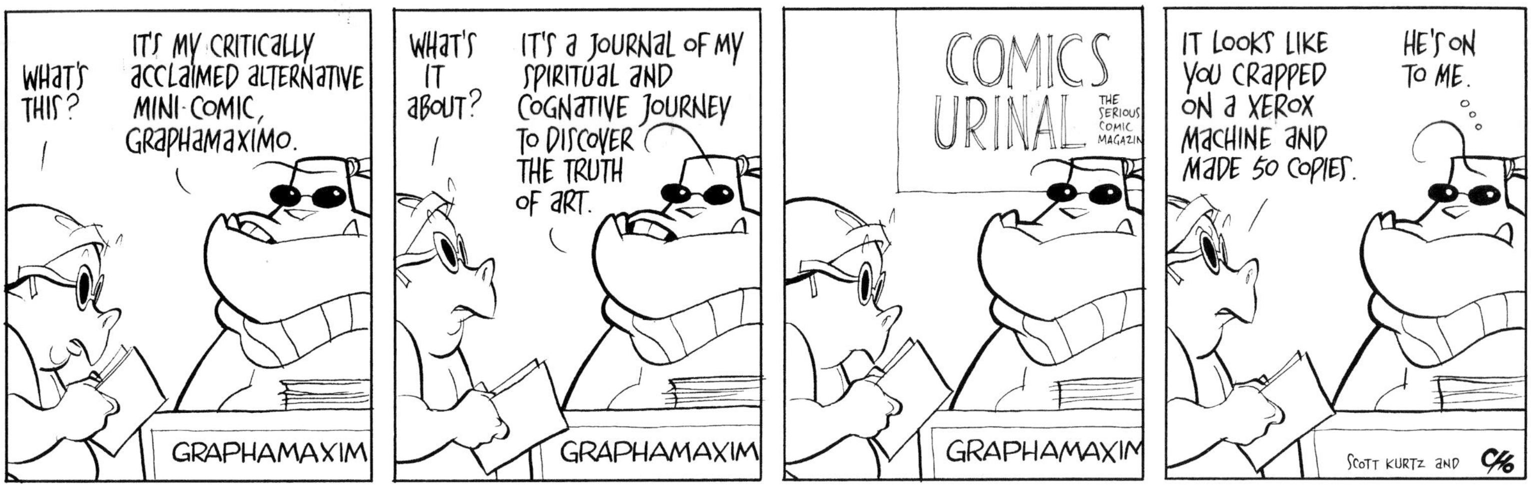
WHAT'S THIS?
IT'S MY CRITICALLY ACCLAIMED ALTERNATIVE MINI-COMIC, GRAPHAMAXIMO.
GRAPHAMAXIM
WHAT'S IT ABOUT?
IT'S A JOURNAL OF MY SPIRITUAL AND COGNATIVE JOURNEY TO DISCOVER THE TRUTH OF ART.
GRAPHAMAXIM
COMICS URINAL
THE SERIOUS COMIC MAGAZIN
GRAPHAMAXIM
IT LOOKS LIKE YOU CRAPPED ON A XEROX MACHINE AND MADE 50 COPIES.
HE'S ON TO ME.
SCOTT KURTZ AND CHO

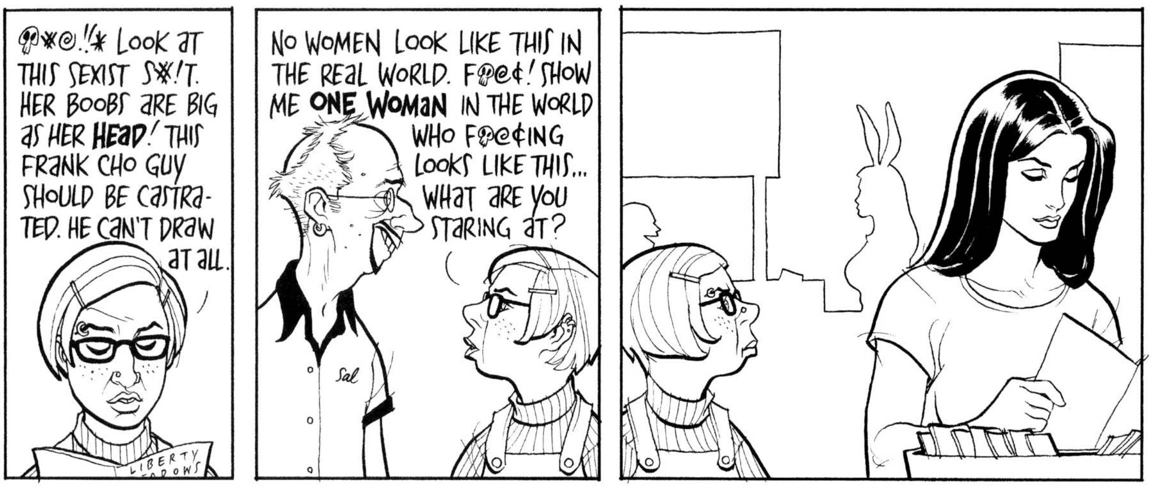
@*@!!✱ LOOK AT THIS SEXIST S*!T. HER BOOBS ARE BIG AS HER HEAD! THIS FRANK CHO GUY SHOULD BE CASTRATED. HE CAN'T DRAW AT ALL.
NO WOMEN LOOK LIKE THIS IN THE REAL WORLD. F@¢! SHOW ME ONE WOMAN IN THE WORLD WHO F@¢ING LOOKS LIKE THIS... WHAT ARE YOU STARING AT?
SAL
OKAY. SHOW ME TWO WOMEN!
WHOA. SPIDER SENSE TINGLING... PANTS SHRINKING...

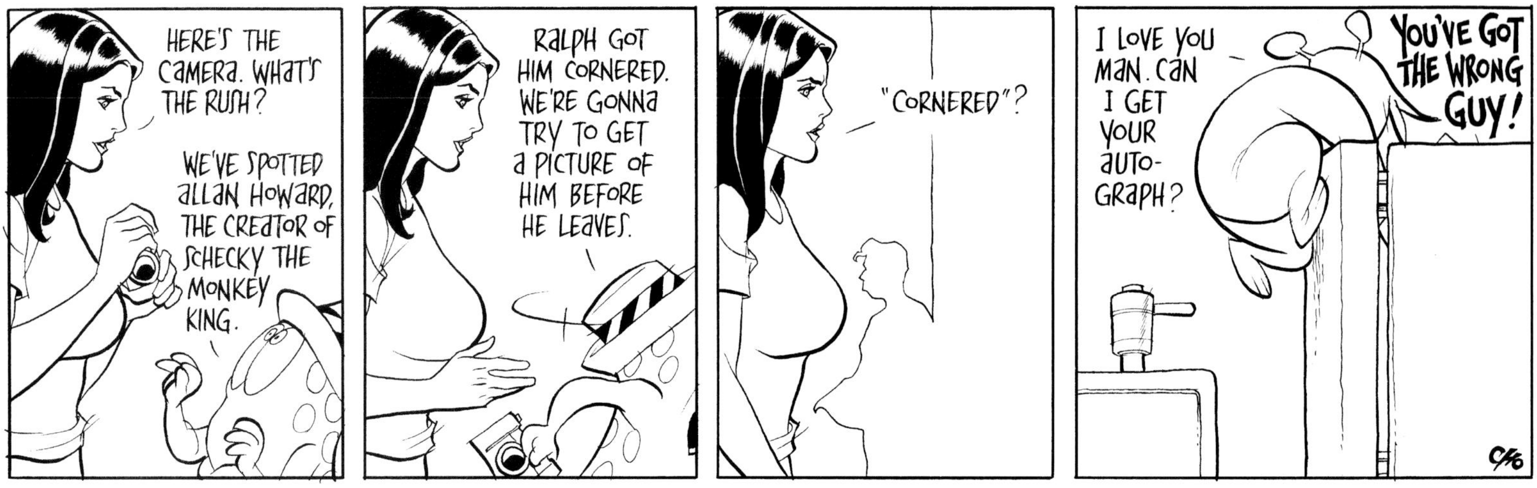
HERE'S THE CAMERA. WHAT'S THE RUSH?
WE'VE SPOTTED ALLAN HOWARD, THE CREATOR OF SCHECKY THE MONKEY KING.
RALPH GOT HIM CORNERED. WE'RE GONNA TRY TO GET A PICTURE OF HIM BEFORE HE LEAVES.
"CORNERED"?
I LOVE YOU MAN. CAN I GET YOUR AUTOGRAPH?
YOU'VE GOT THE WRONG GUY!

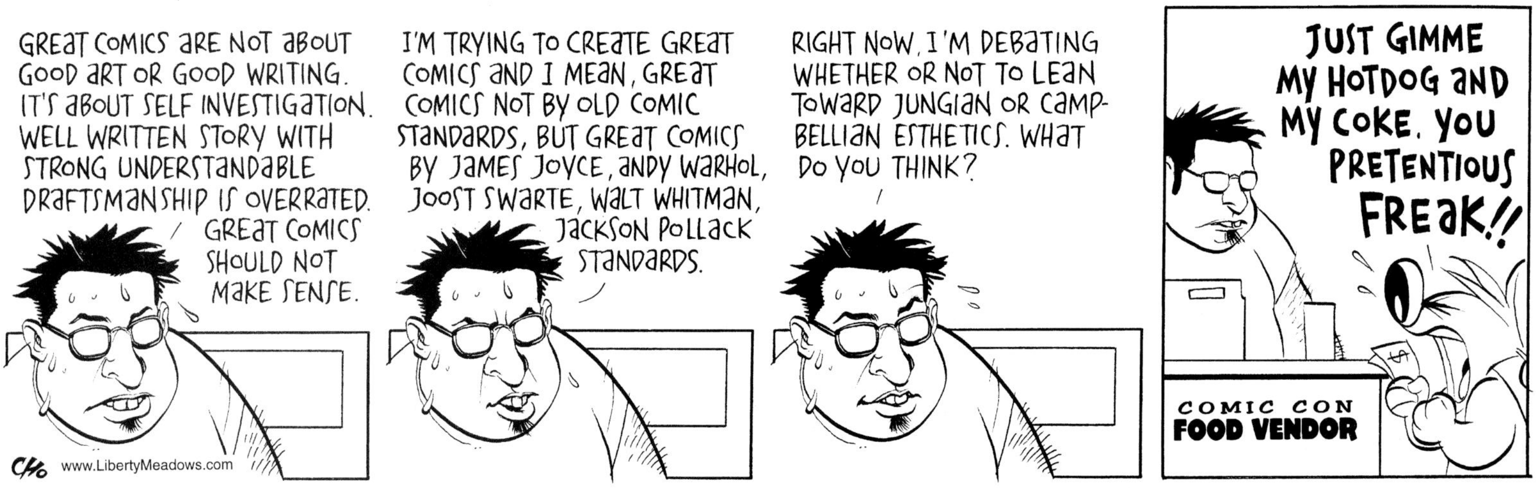
GREAT COMICS ARE NOT ABOUT GOOD ART OR GOOD WRITING. IT'S ABOUT SELF INVESTIGATION. WELL WRITTEN STORY WITH STRONG UNDERSTANDABLE DRAFTSMANSHIP IS OVERRATED. GREAT COMICS SHOULD NOT MAKE SENSE.
www.LibertyMeadows.com
I'M TRYING TO CREATE GREAT COMICS AND I MEAN, GREAT COMICS NOT BY OLD COMIC STANDARDS, BUT GREAT COMICS BY JAMES JOYCE, ANDY WARHOL, JOOST SWARTE, WALT WHITMAN, JACKSON POLLACK STANDARDS.
RIGHT NOW, I'M DEBATING WHETHER OR NOT TO LEAN TOWARD JUNGIAN OR CAMPBELLIAN ESTHETICS. WHAT DO YOU THINK?
JUST GIMME MY HOTDOG AND MY COKE, YOU PRETENTIOUS FREAK!!
COMIC CON FOOD VENDOR

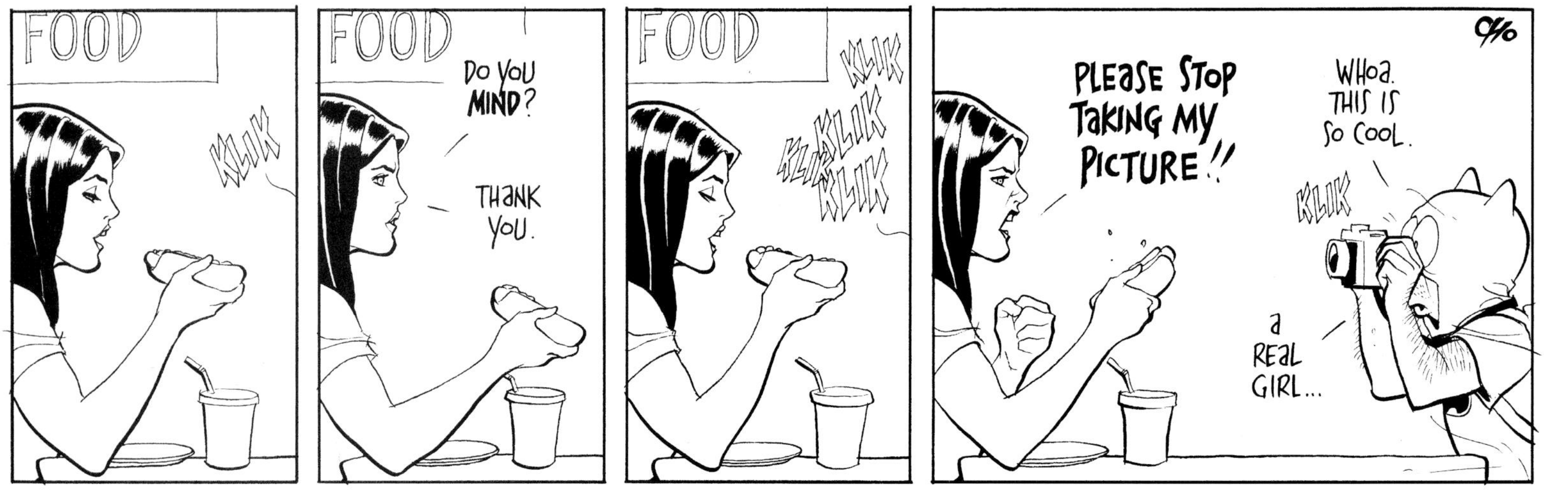
FOOD
KLIK
FOOD
DO YOU MIND?
THANK YOU.
FOOD
KLIK KLIK KLIK KLIK
PLEASE STOP TAKING MY PICTURE!!
WHOA. THIS IS SO COOL.
KLIK
A REAL GIRL...

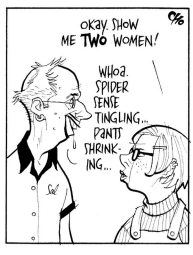

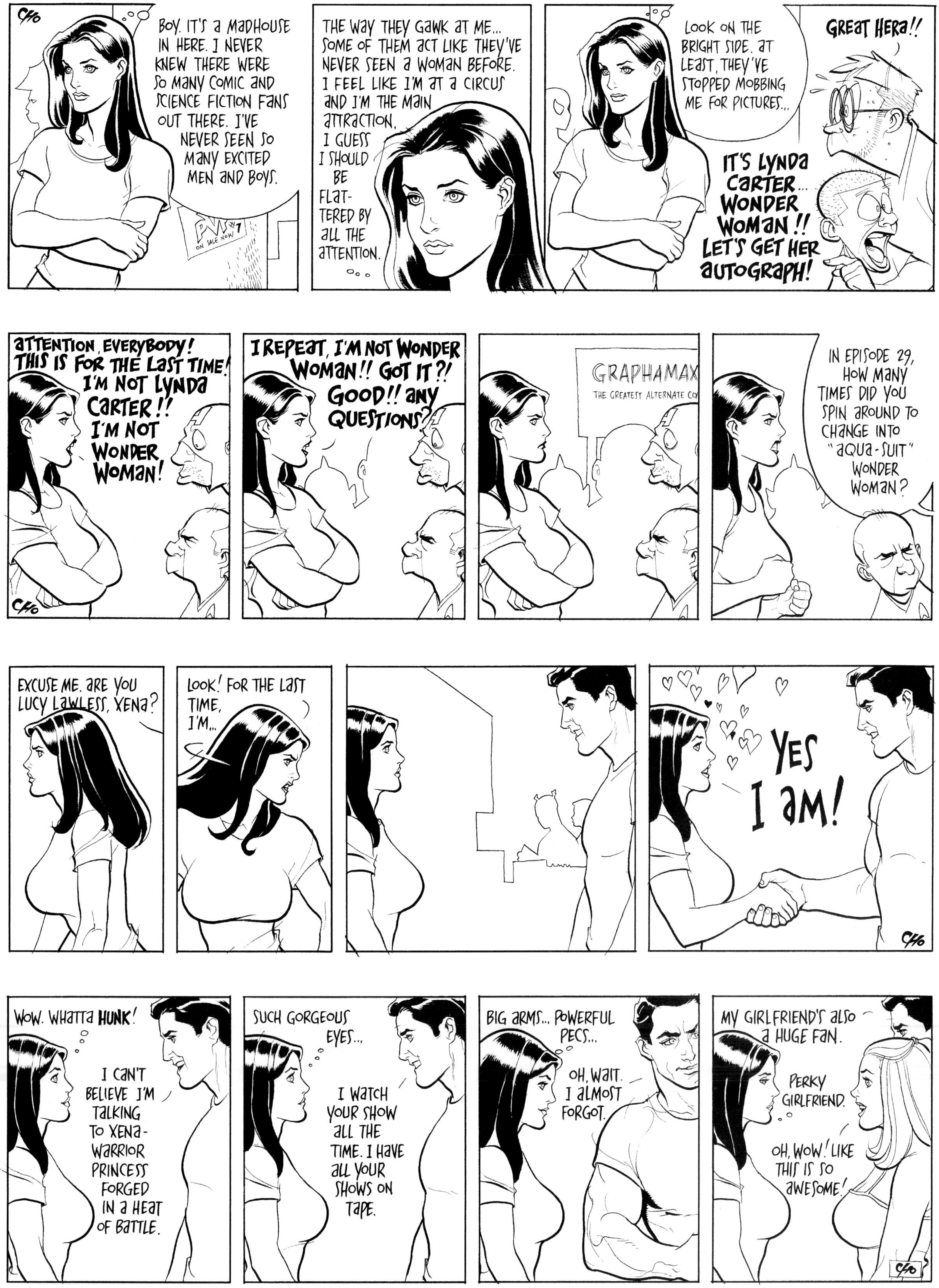
BOY. IT'S A MADHOUSE IN HERE. I NEVER KNEW THERE WERE SO MANY COMIC AND SCIENCE FICTION FANS OUT THERE. I'VE NEVER SEEN SO MANY EXCITED MEN AND BOYS.
THE WAY THEY GAWK AT ME... SOME OF THEM ACT LIKE THEY'VE NEVER SEEN A WOMAN BEFORE. I FEEL LIKE I'M AT A CIRCUS AND I'M THE MAIN ATTRACTION. I GUESS I SHOULD BE FLAT-TERED BY ALL THE ATTENTION.
LOOK ON THE BRIGHT SIDE. AT LEAST, THEY'VE STOPPED MOBBING ME FOR PICTURES...
GREAT HERA!!
IT'S LYNDA CARTER... WONDER WOMAN!! LET'S GET HER AUTOGRAPH!
ATTENTION, EVERYBODY! THIS IS FOR THE LAST TIME! I'M NOT LYNDA CARTER!! I'M NOT WONDER WOMAN!
I REPEAT, I'M NOT WONDER WOMAN!! GOT IT?! GOOD!! ANY QUESTIONS?
GRAPHAMAX
THE GREATEST ALTERNATE CO
IN EPISODE 29, HOW MANY TIMES DID YOU SPIN AROUND TO CHANGE INTO "AQUA-SUIT" WONDER WOMAN?
EXCUSE ME. ARE YOU LUCY LAWLESS, XENA?
LOOK! FOR THE LAST TIME, I'M...
YES I AM!
WOW. WHATTA HUNK!
I CAN'T BELIEVE I'M TALKING TO XENA-WARRIOR PRINCESS FORGED IN A HEAT OF BATTLE.
SUCH GORGEOUS EYES...
I WATCH YOUR SHOW ALL THE TIME. I HAVE ALL YOUR SHOWS ON TAPE.
BIG ARMS... POWERFUL PECS...
OH, WAIT. I ALMOST FORGOT.
MY GIRLFRIEND'S ALSO A HUGE FAN.
PERKY GIRLFRIEND.
OH, WOW! LIKE THIS IS SO AWESOME!

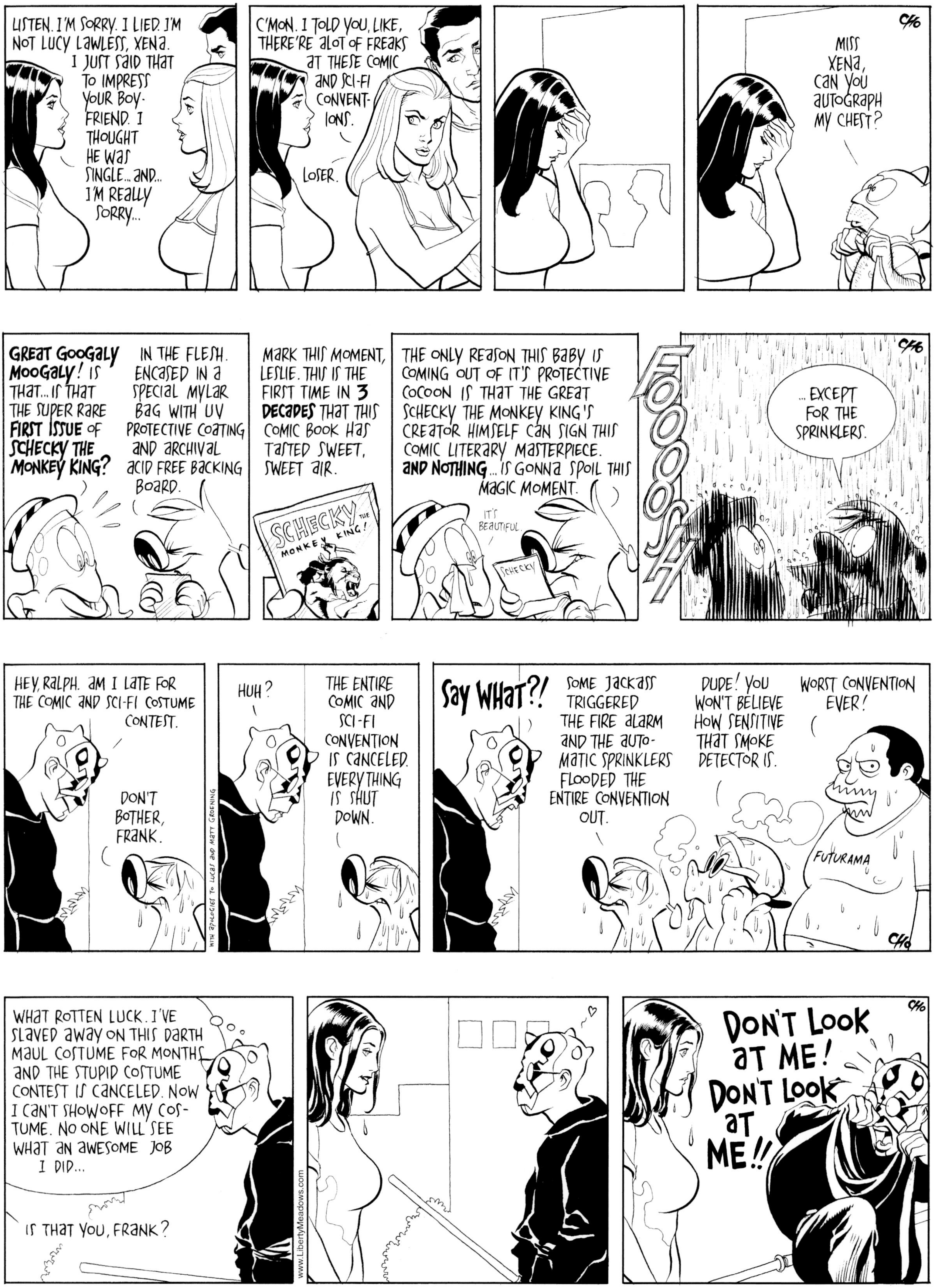
LISTEN. I'M SORRY. I LIED. I'M NOT LUCY LAWLESS, XENA.
I JUST SAID THAT TO IMPRESS YOUR BOY-FRIEND. I THOUGHT HE WAS SINGLE... AND... I'M REALLY SORRY...
C'MON. I TOLD YOU, LIKE, THERE'RE ALOT OF FREAKS AT THESE COMIC AND SCI-FI CONVENT-IONS.
LOSER.
CHO
MISS XENA, CAN YOU AUTOGRAPH MY CHEST?
GREAT GOOGALY MOOGALY! IS THAT... IS THAT THE SUPER RARE FIRST ISSUE OF SCHECKY THE MONKEY KING?
IN THE FLESH. ENCASED IN A SPECIAL MYLAR BAG WITH UV PROTECTIVE COATING AND ARCHIVAL ACID FREE BACKING BOARD.
MARK THIS MOMENT, LESLIE. THIS IS THE FIRST TIME IN 3 DECADES THAT THIS COMIC BOOK HAS TASTED SWEET, SWEET AIR.
SCHECKY THE MONKEY KING!
THE ONLY REASON THIS BABY IS COMING OUT OF IT'S PROTECTIVE COCOON IS THAT THE GREAT SCHECKY THE MONKEY KING'S CREATOR HIMSELF CAN SIGN THIS COMIC LITERARY MASTERPIECE. AND NOTHING... IS GONNA SPOIL THIS MAGIC MOMENT.
IT'S BEAUTIFUL.
SCHECKY
CHO
FOOOOSH
...EXCEPT FOR THE SPRINKLERS.
HEY, RALPH. AM I LATE FOR THE COMIC AND SCI-FI COSTUME CONTEST.
DON'T BOTHER, FRANK.
HUH?
THE ENTIRE COMIC AND SCI-FI CONVENTION IS CANCELED. EVERYTHING IS SHUT DOWN.
WITH APOLOGIES TO LUCAS AND MATT GROENING
SAY WHAT?!
SOME JACKASS TRIGGERED THE FIRE ALARM AND THE AUTO-MATIC SPRINKLERS FLOODED THE ENTIRE CONVENTION OUT.
DUDE! YOU WON'T BELIEVE HOW SENSITIVE THAT SMOKE DETECTOR IS.
WORST CONVENTION EVER!
FUTURAMA
CHO
WHAT ROTTEN LUCK. I'VE SLAVED AWAY ON THIS DARTH MAUL COSTUME FOR MONTHS AND THE STUPID COSTUME CONTEST IS CANCELED. NOW I CAN'T SHOWOFF MY COS-TUME. NO ONE WILL SEE WHAT AN AWESOME JOB I DID...
IS THAT YOU, FRANK?
www.LibertyMeadows.com
CHO
DON'T LOOK AT ME! DON'T LOOK AT ME!!

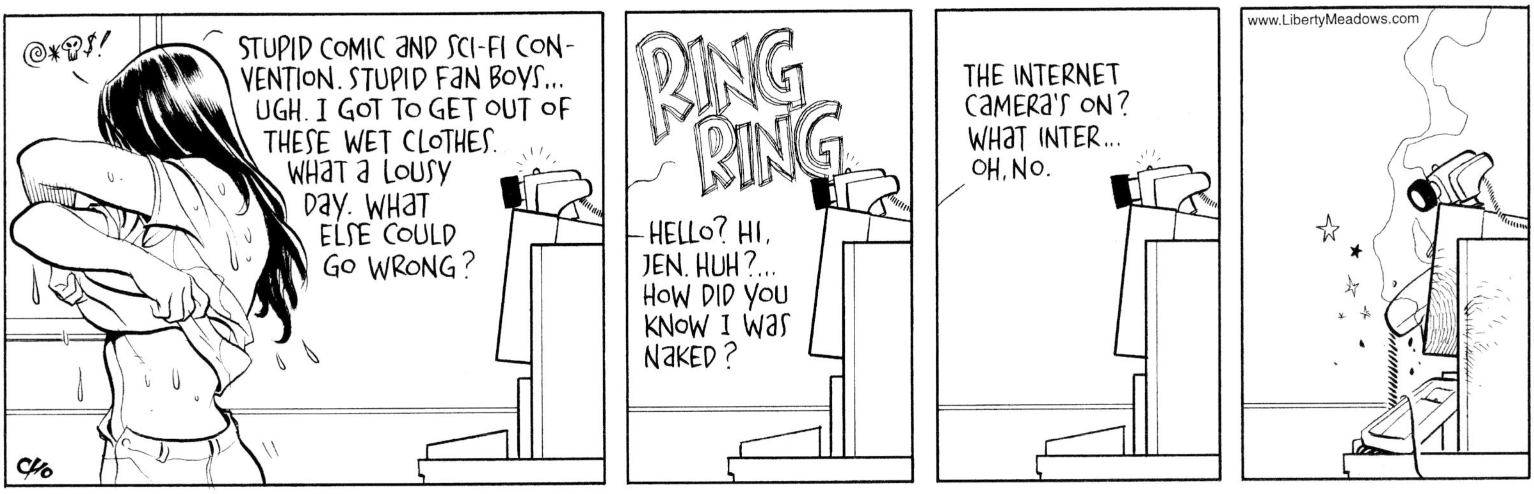
STUPID COMIC AND SCI-FI CONVENTION. STUPID FAN BOYS... UGH. I GOT TO GET OUT OF THESE WET CLOTHES. WHAT A LOUSY DAY. WHAT ELSE COULD GO WRONG?
RING RING
HELLO? HI, JEN. HUH?... HOW DID YOU KNOW I WAS NAKED?
THE INTERNET CAMERA'S ON? WHAT INTER... OH, NO.
www.LibertyMeadows.com
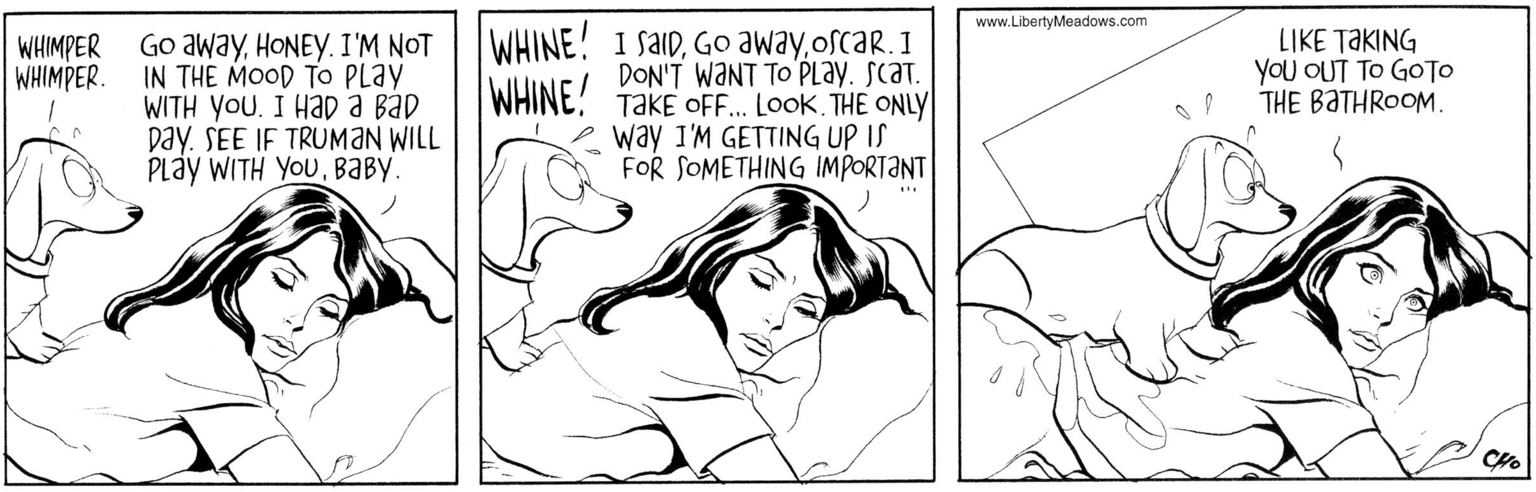
WHIMPER WHIMPER.
GO AWAY, HONEY. I'M NOT IN THE MOOD TO PLAY WITH YOU. I HAD A BAD DAY. SEE IF TRUMAN WILL PLAY WITH YOU, BABY.
WHINE! WHINE!
I SAID, GO AWAY, OSCAR. I DON'T WANT TO PLAY. SCAT. TAKE OFF... LOOK. THE ONLY WAY I'M GETTING UP IS FOR SOMETHING IMPORTANT...
www.LibertyMeadows.com
LIKE TAKING YOU OUT TO GO TO THE BATHROOM.
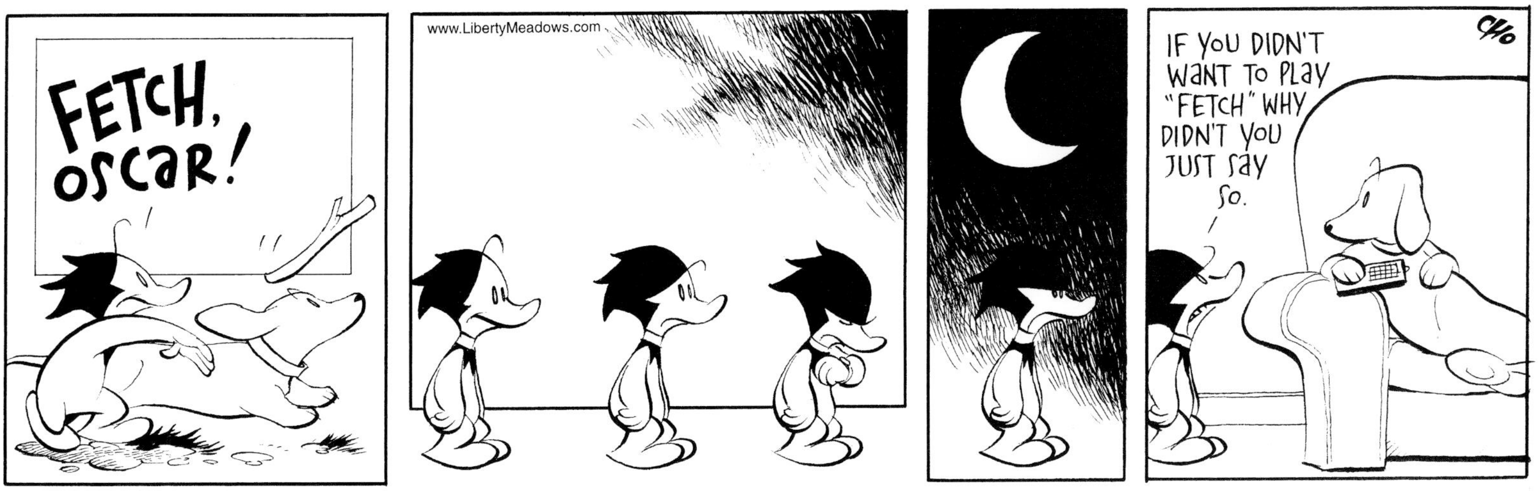
FETCH, OSCAR!
www.LibertyMeadows.com
IF YOU DIDN'T WANT TO PLAY "FETCH" WHY DIDN'T YOU JUST SAY SO.
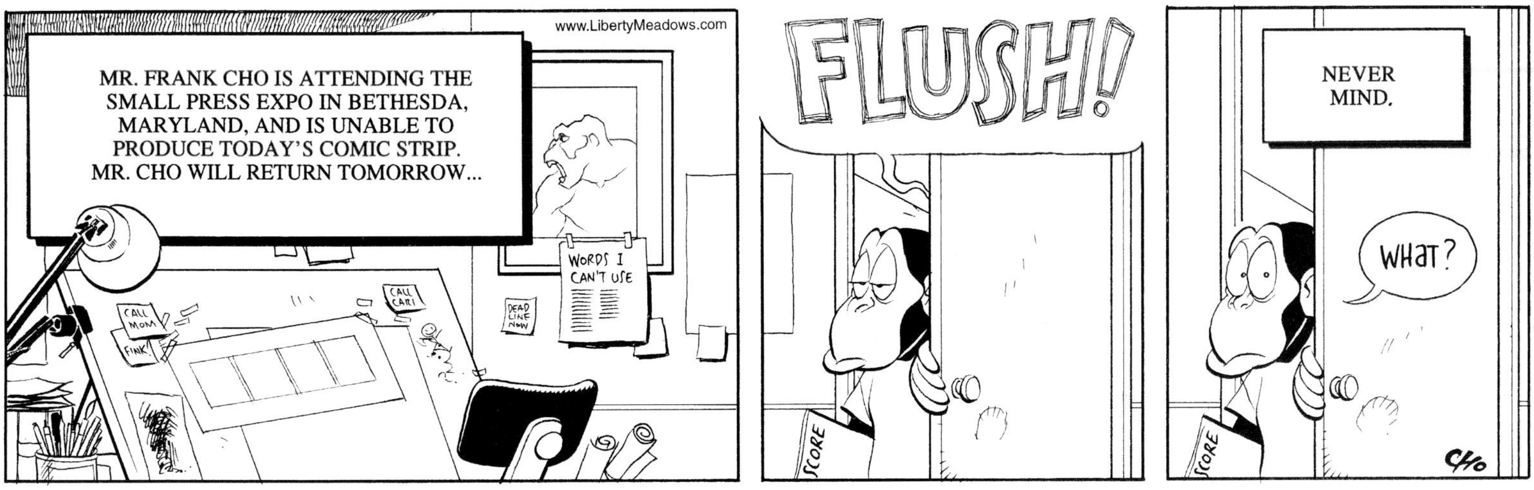
www.LibertyMeadows.com
MR. FRANK CHO IS ATTENDING THE SMALL PRESS EXPO IN BETHESDA, MARYLAND, AND IS UNABLE TO PRODUCE TODAY'S COMIC STRIP. MR. CHO WILL RETURN TOMORROW...
WORDS I CAN'T USE
DEAD LINE NOW
CALL MOM
FLUSH!
SCORE
NEVER MIND.
WHAT?

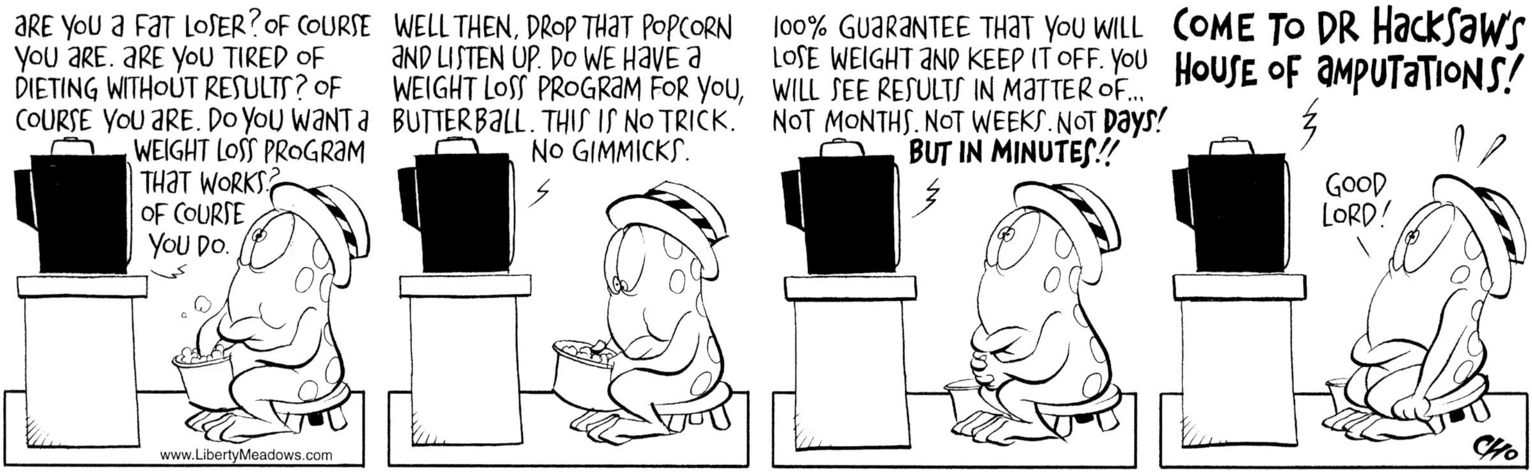
ARE YOU A FAT LOSER? OF COURSE YOU ARE. ARE YOU TIRED OF DIETING WITHOUT RESULTS? OF COURSE YOU ARE. DO YOU WANT A WEIGHT LOSS PROGRAM THAT WORKS? OF COURSE YOU DO.
www.LibertyMeadows.com
WELL THEN, DROP THAT POPCORN AND LISTEN UP. DO WE HAVE A WEIGHT LOSS PROGRAM FOR YOU, BUTTERBALL. THIS IS NO TRICK. NO GIMMICKS.
100% GUARANTEE THAT YOU WILL LOSE WEIGHT AND KEEP IT OFF. YOU WILL SEE RESULTS IN MATTER OF... NOT MONTHS. NOT WEEKS. NOT DAYS! BUT IN MINUTES!!
COME TO DR HACKSAW'S HOUSE OF AMPUTATIONS!
GOOD LORD!
CHO

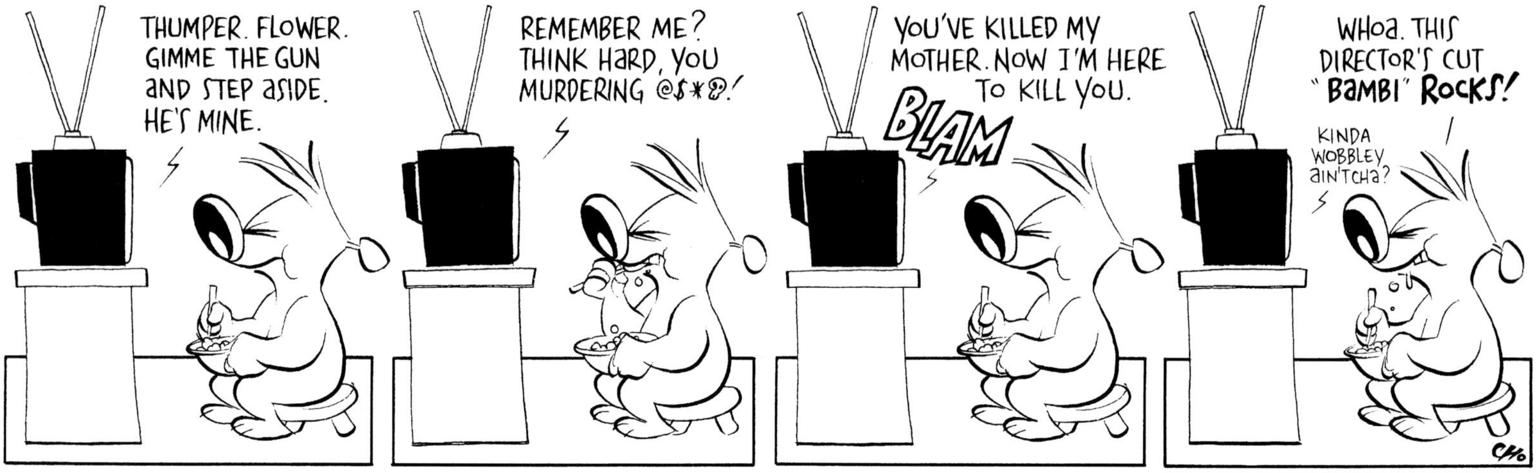
THUMPER. FLOWER. GIMME THE GUN AND STEP ASIDE. HE'S MINE.
REMEMBER ME? THINK HARD, YOU MURDERING @$*&!
YOU'VE KILLED MY MOTHER. NOW I'M HERE TO KILL YOU.
BLAM
WHOA. THIS DIRECTOR'S CUT "BAMBI" ROCKS!
KINDA WOBBLEY AIN'TCHA?
CHO

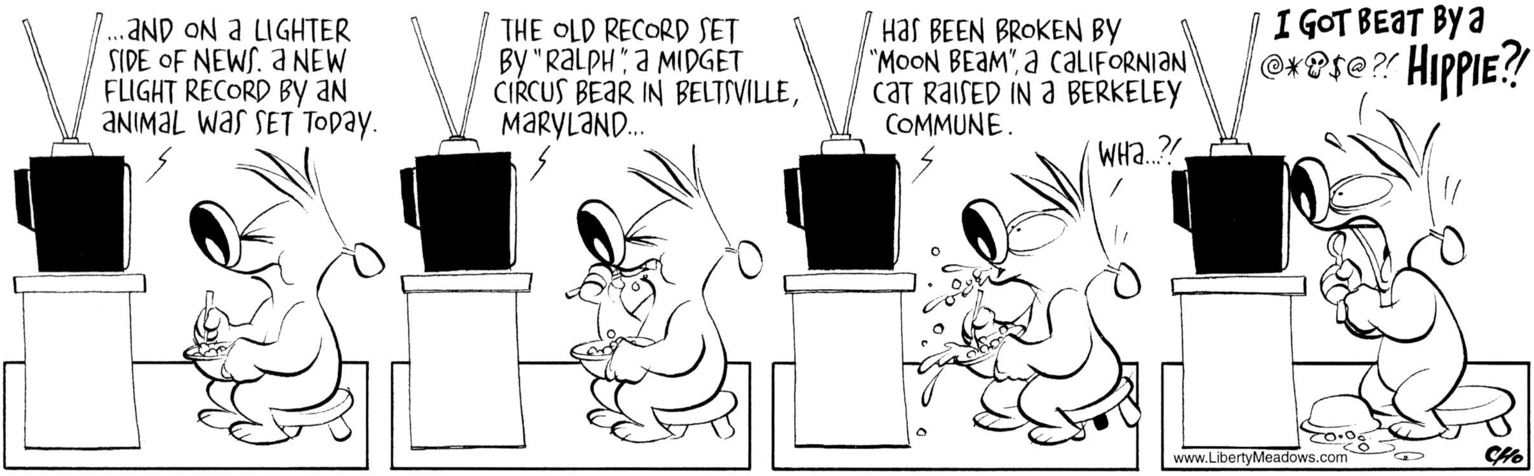
...AND ON A LIGHTER SIDE OF NEWS. A NEW FLIGHT RECORD BY AN ANIMAL WAS SET TODAY.
THE OLD RECORD SET BY "RALPH", A MIDGET CIRCUS BEAR IN BELTSVILLE, MARYLAND...
HAS BEEN BROKEN BY "MOON BEAM", A CALIFORNIAN CAT RAISED IN A BERKELEY COMMUNE.
WHA...?!
I GOT BEAT BY A @*&$@?! HIPPIE?!
www.LibertyMeadows.com
CHO

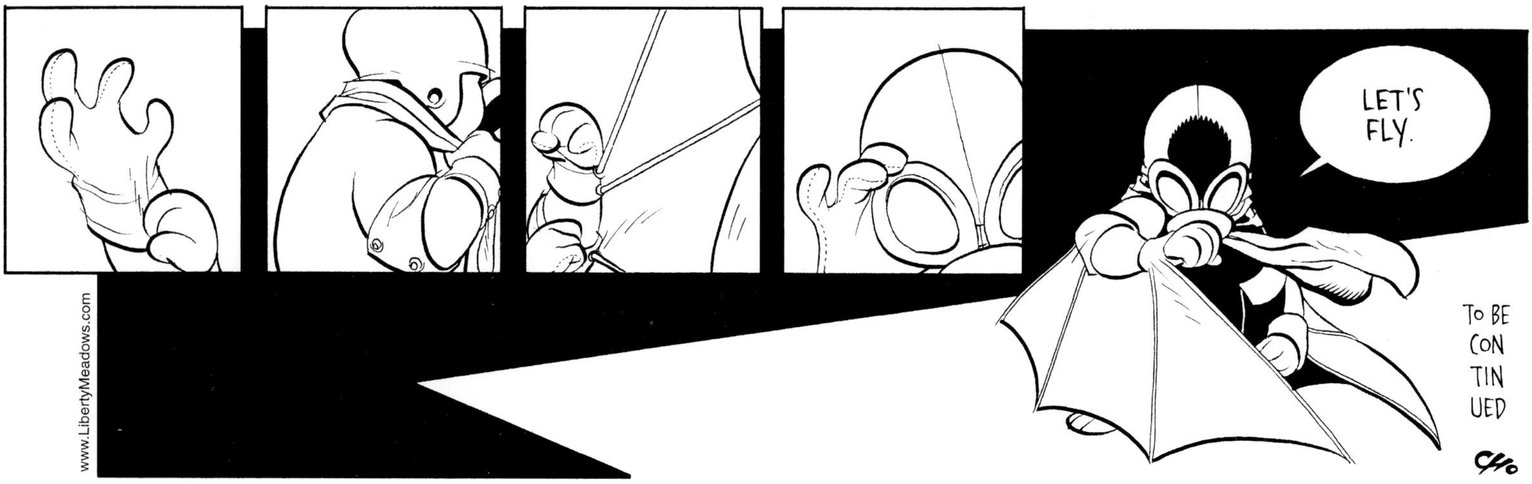
www.LibertyMeadows.com
LET'S FLY.
TO BE CONTINUED
CHO

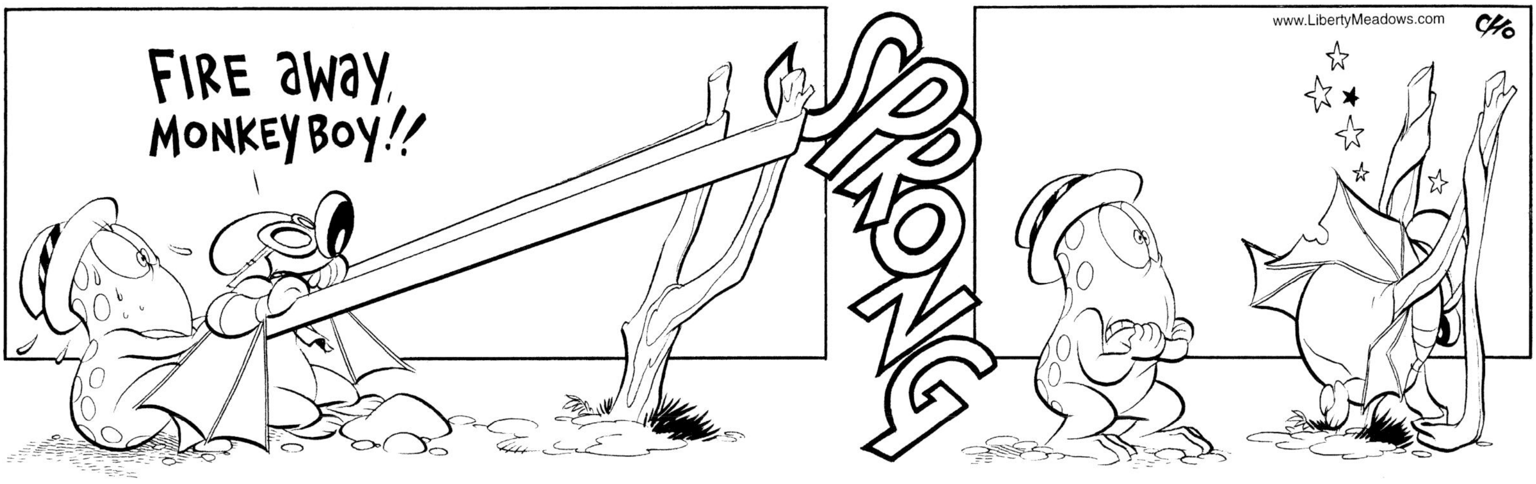
FIRE away, MONKEY BOY!!
SPRONG
www.LibertyMeadows.com
CHO

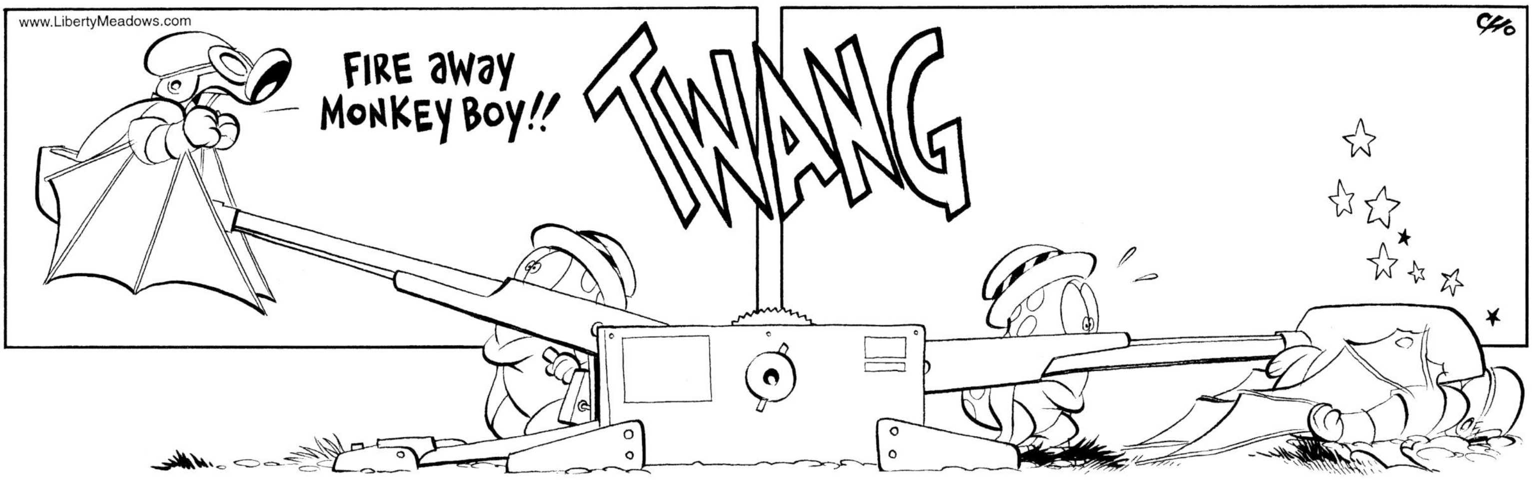
www.LibertyMeadows.com
FIRE away MONKEY BOY!!
TWANG
CHO

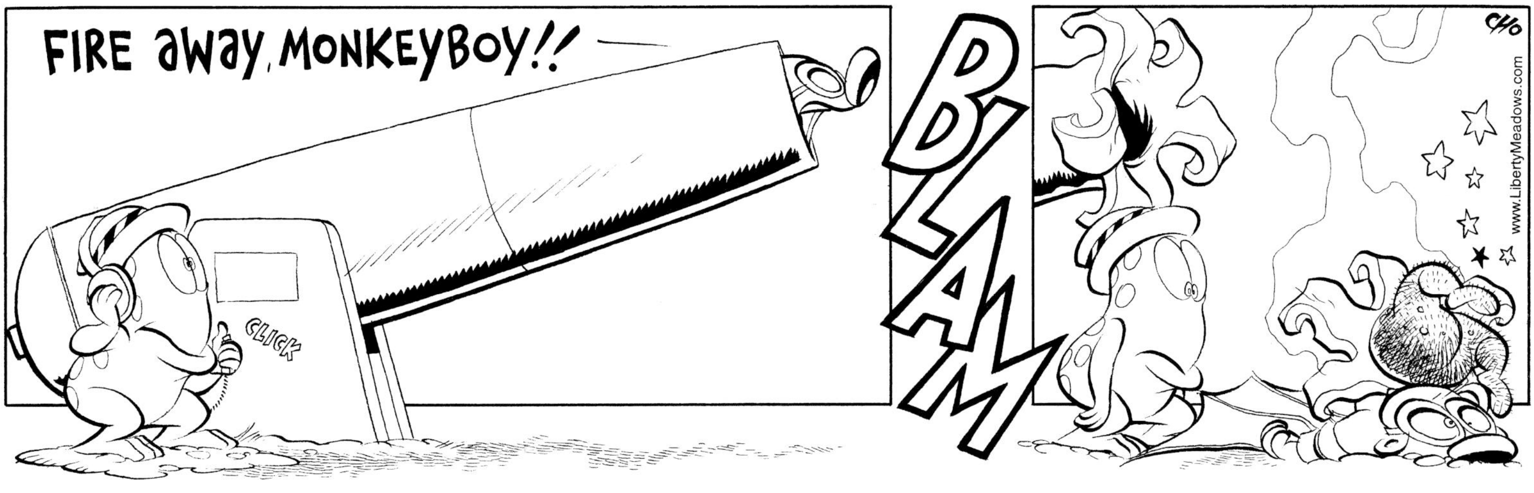
FIRE away, MONKEYBOY!!
CLICK
BLAM
CHO
www.LibertyMeadows.com

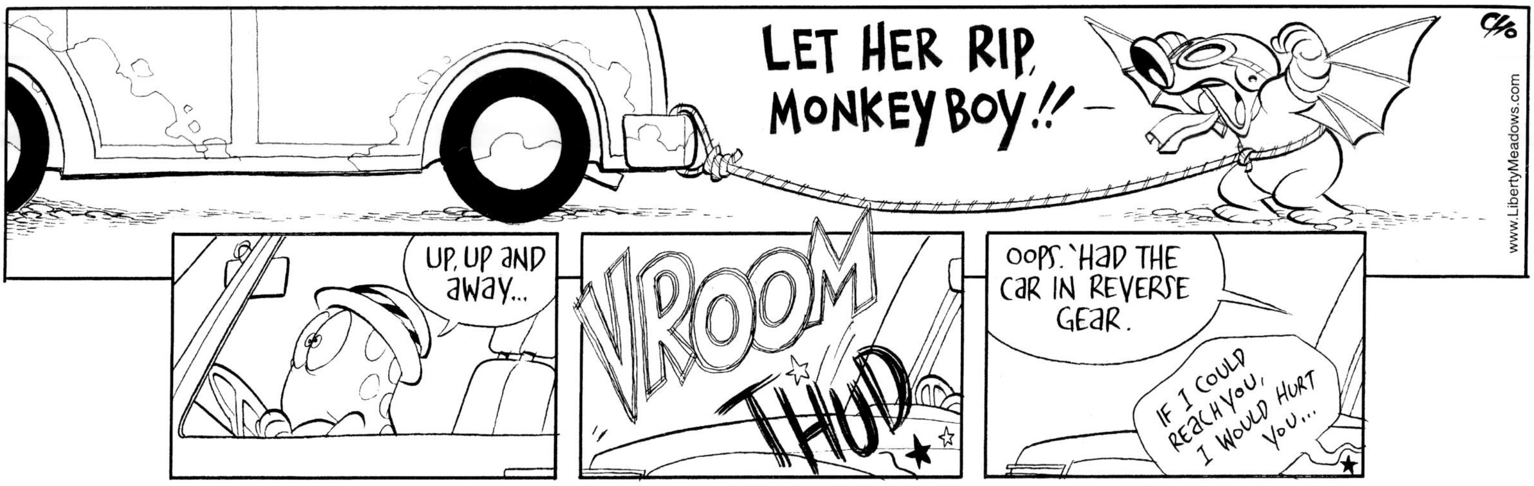
LET HER RIP, MONKEY BOY!!
CHO
www.LibertyMeadows.com
UP, UP AND away...
VROOM
THUD
OOPS. `HAD THE CAR IN REVERSE GEAR.
IF I COULD REACH YOU, I WOULD HURT YOU...

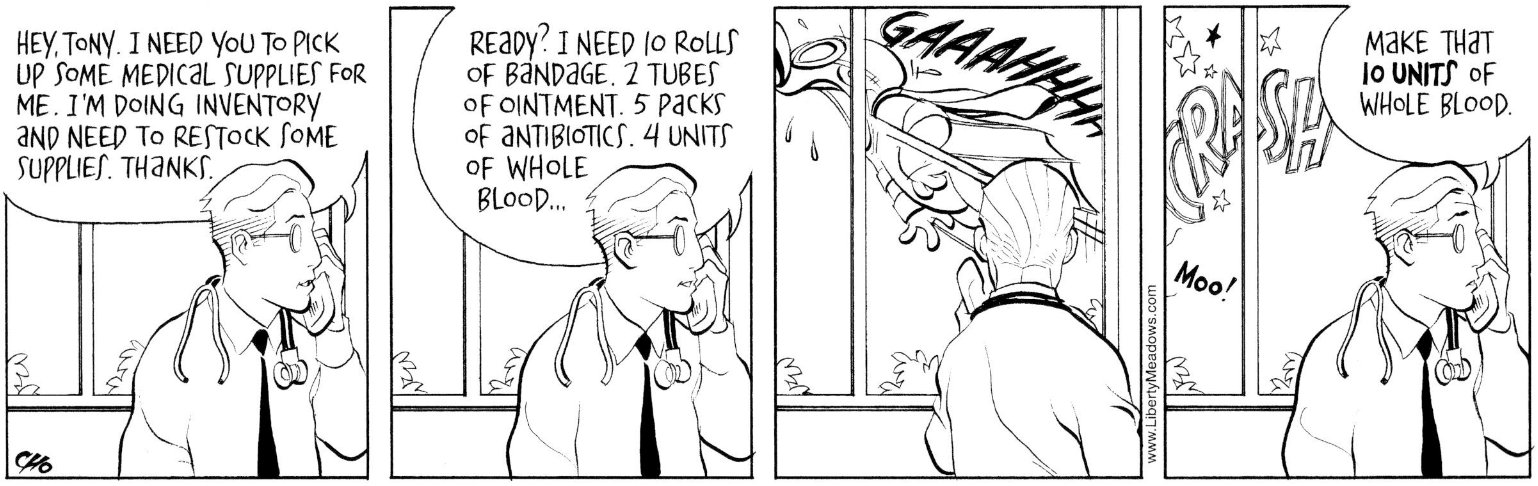
HEY, TONY. I NEED YOU TO PICK UP SOME MEDICAL SUPPLIES FOR ME. I'M DOING INVENTORY AND NEED TO RESTOCK SOME SUPPLIES. THANKS.
READY? I NEED 10 ROLLS OF BANDAGE. 2 TUBES OF OINTMENT. 5 PACKS OF ANTIBIOTICS. 4 UNITS OF WHOLE BLOOD...
GAAAHHH
CRASH
MOO!
www.LibertyMeadows.com
MAKE THAT **10 UNITS** OF WHOLE BLOOD.

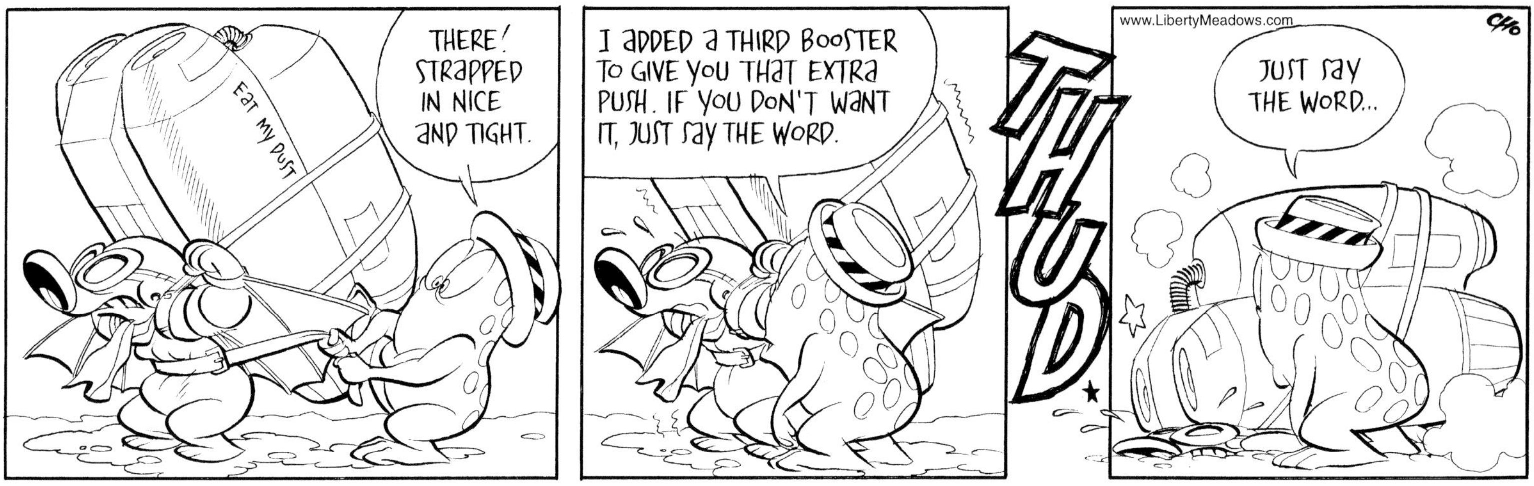
EAT MY DUST
THERE! STRAPPED IN NICE AND TIGHT.
I ADDED A THIRD BOOSTER TO GIVE YOU THAT EXTRA PUSH. IF YOU DON'T WANT IT, JUST SAY THE WORD.
THUD
www.LibertyMeadows.com
JUST SAY THE WORD...

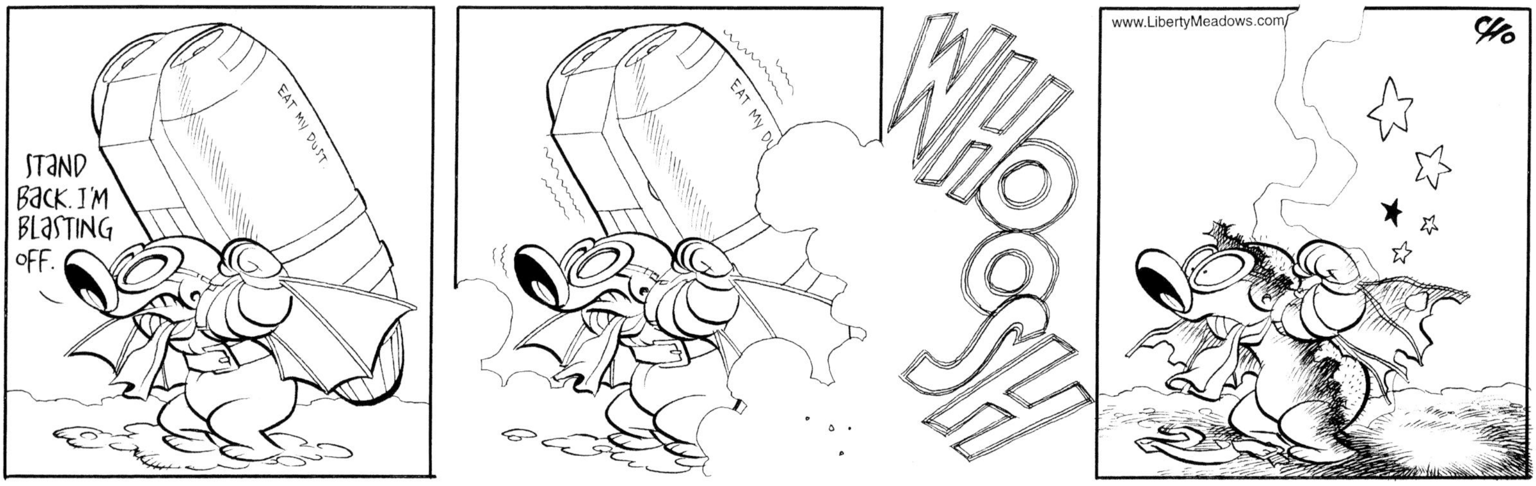
EAT MY DUST
STAND BACK. I'M BLASTING OFF.
WHOOSH
www.LibertyMeadows.com

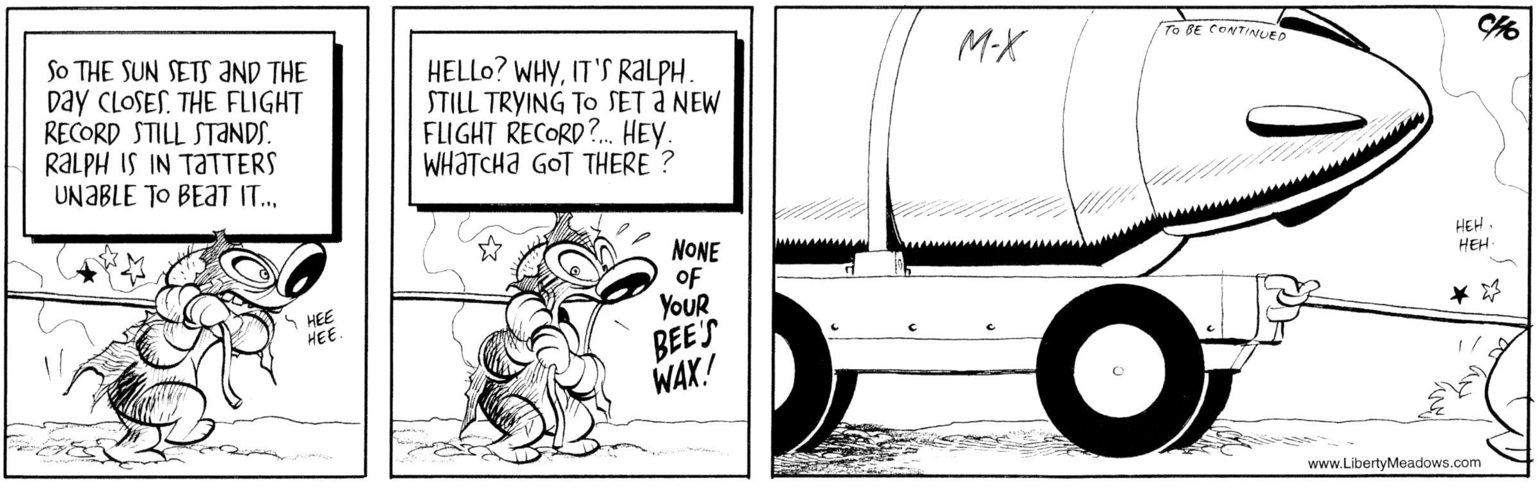
SO THE SUN SETS AND THE DAY CLOSES. THE FLIGHT RECORD STILL STANDS. RALPH IS IN TATTERS UNABLE TO BEAT IT...
HEE HEE.
HELLO? WHY, IT'S RALPH. STILL TRYING TO SET A NEW FLIGHT RECORD?... HEY. WHATCHA GOT THERE?
NONE OF YOUR BEE'S WAX!
M-X
TO BE CONTINUED
HEH. HEH.
www.LibertyMeadows.com

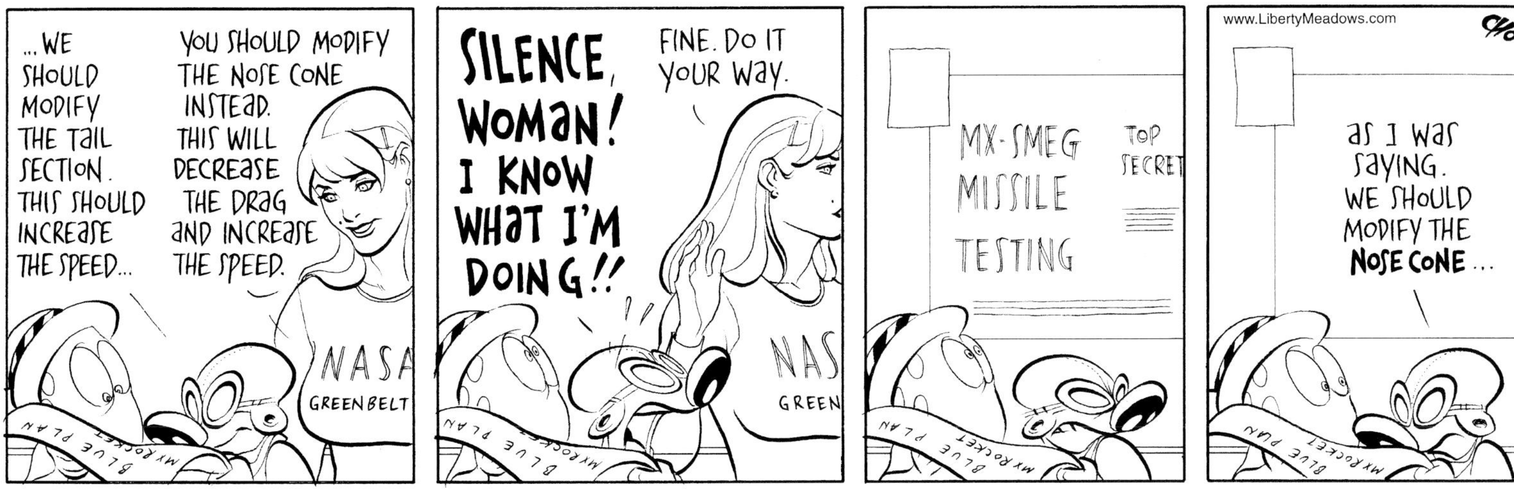
...WE SHOULD MODIFY THE TAIL SECTION. THIS SHOULD INCREASE THE SPEED...
YOU SHOULD MODIFY THE NOSE CONE INSTEAD. THIS WILL DECREASE THE DRAG AND INCREASE THE SPEED.
NASA GREENBELT
BLUE PLAN
MX ROCKET PLAN
SILENCE, WOMAN! I KNOW WHAT I'M DOING!!
FINE. DO IT YOUR WAY.
MX-SMEG MISSILE TESTING
TOP SECRET
www.LibertyMeadows.com
AS I WAS SAYING. WE SHOULD MODIFY THE NOSE CONE...

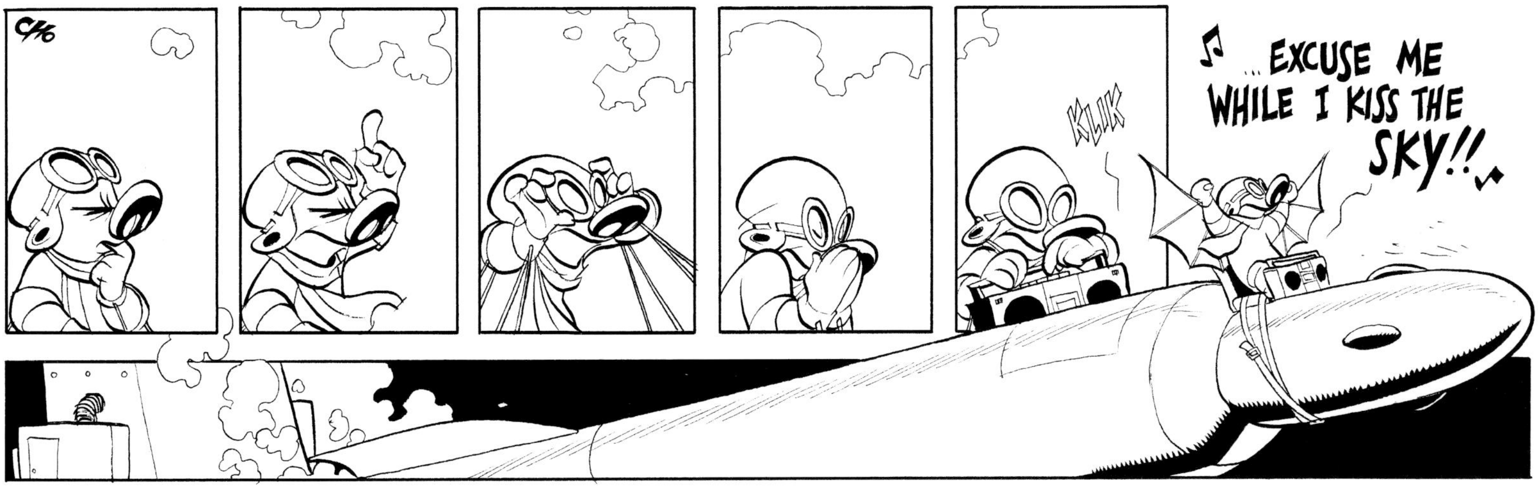
KLIK
...EXCUSE ME WHILE I KISS THE SKY!!

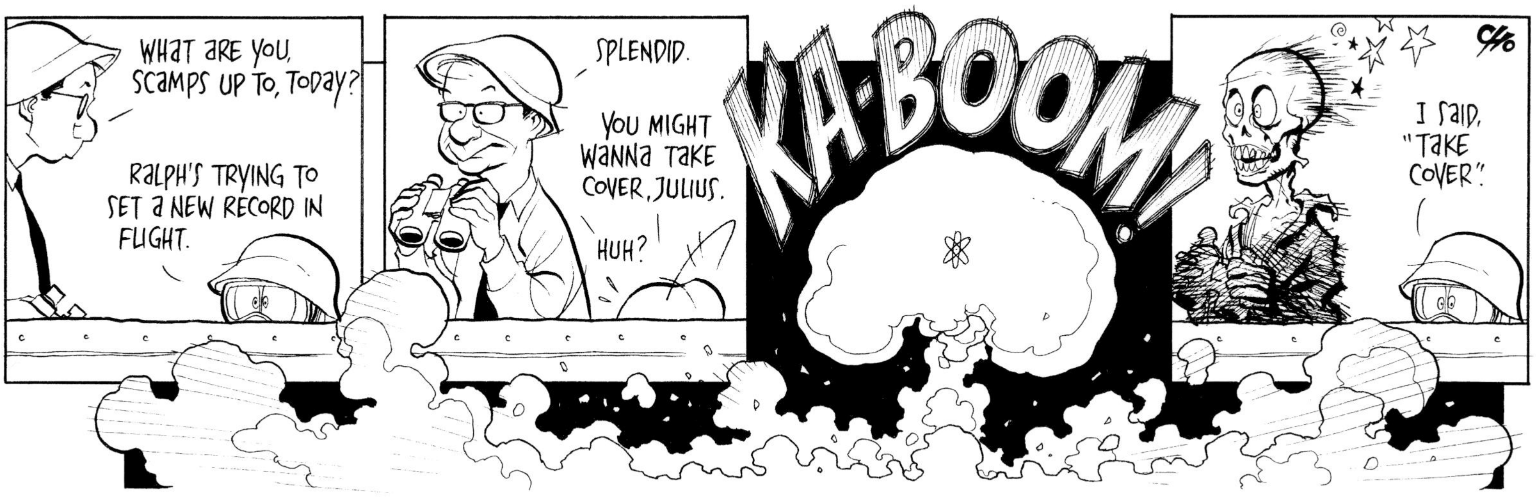
WHAT ARE YOU, SCAMPS UP TO, TODAY?
RALPH'S TRYING TO SET A NEW RECORD IN FLIGHT.
SPLENDID.
YOU MIGHT WANNA TAKE COVER, JULIUS.
HUH?
KA-BOOM!
I SAID, "TAKE COVER".

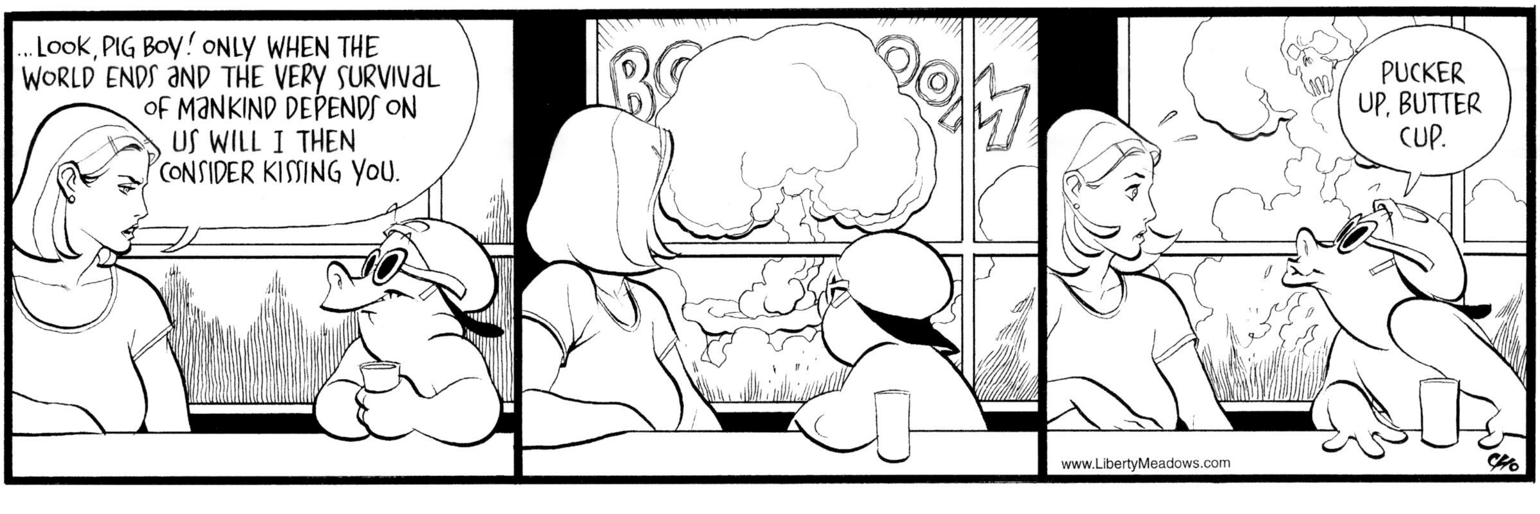
...LOOK, PIG BOY! ONLY WHEN THE WORLD ENDS AND THE VERY SURVIVAL OF MANKIND DEPENDS ON US WILL I THEN CONSIDER KISSING YOU.
PUCKER UP, BUTTER CUP.
www.LibertyMeadows.com

RALPH, YOU JUST BROKE THE WORLD RECORD.
AND SET A NEW MILESTONE IN FLIGHT.
WHAT ARE YOU GOING TO DO NOW?
www.LibertyMeadows.com
I... I.. NEED A BEDPAN.

www.LibertyMeadows.com
THAT'S IT, FRANK. JUST KNOCK ON THE DOOR AND ASK HER OUT.
JUST KNOCK ON THE DOOR AND ASK HER OUT. JUST KNOCK ON THE DOOR...
AW. WHO AM I KIDDING? BRANDY WILL NEVER GO OUT WITH ME.
CHO

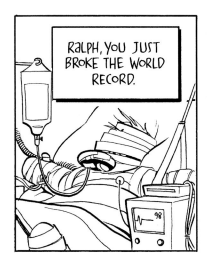

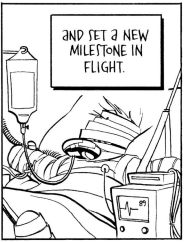

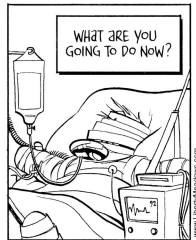

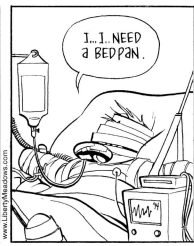

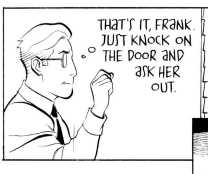

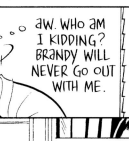

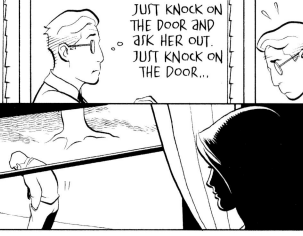

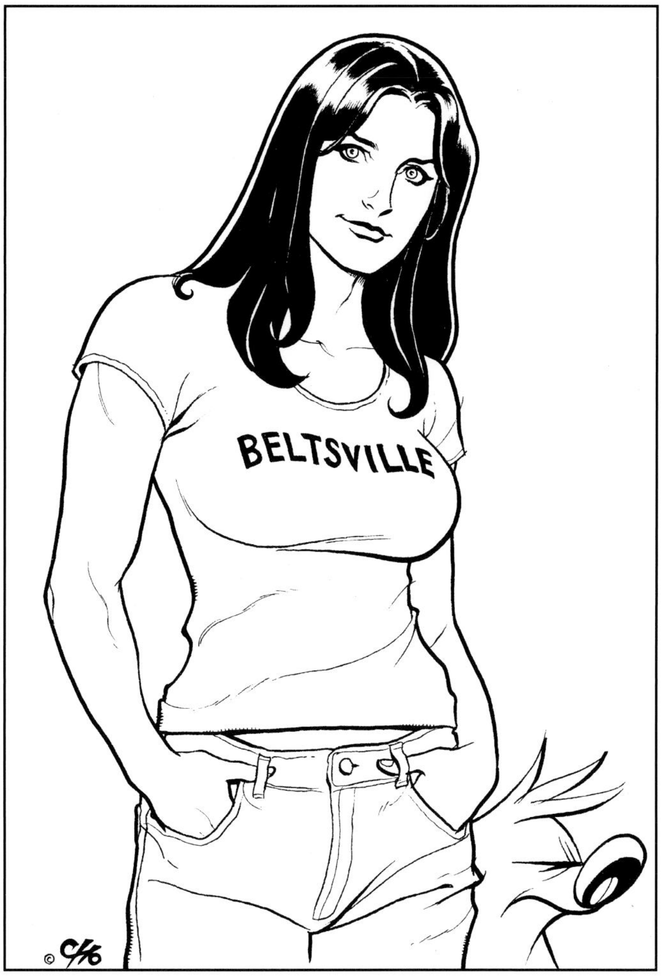
BELTSVILLE

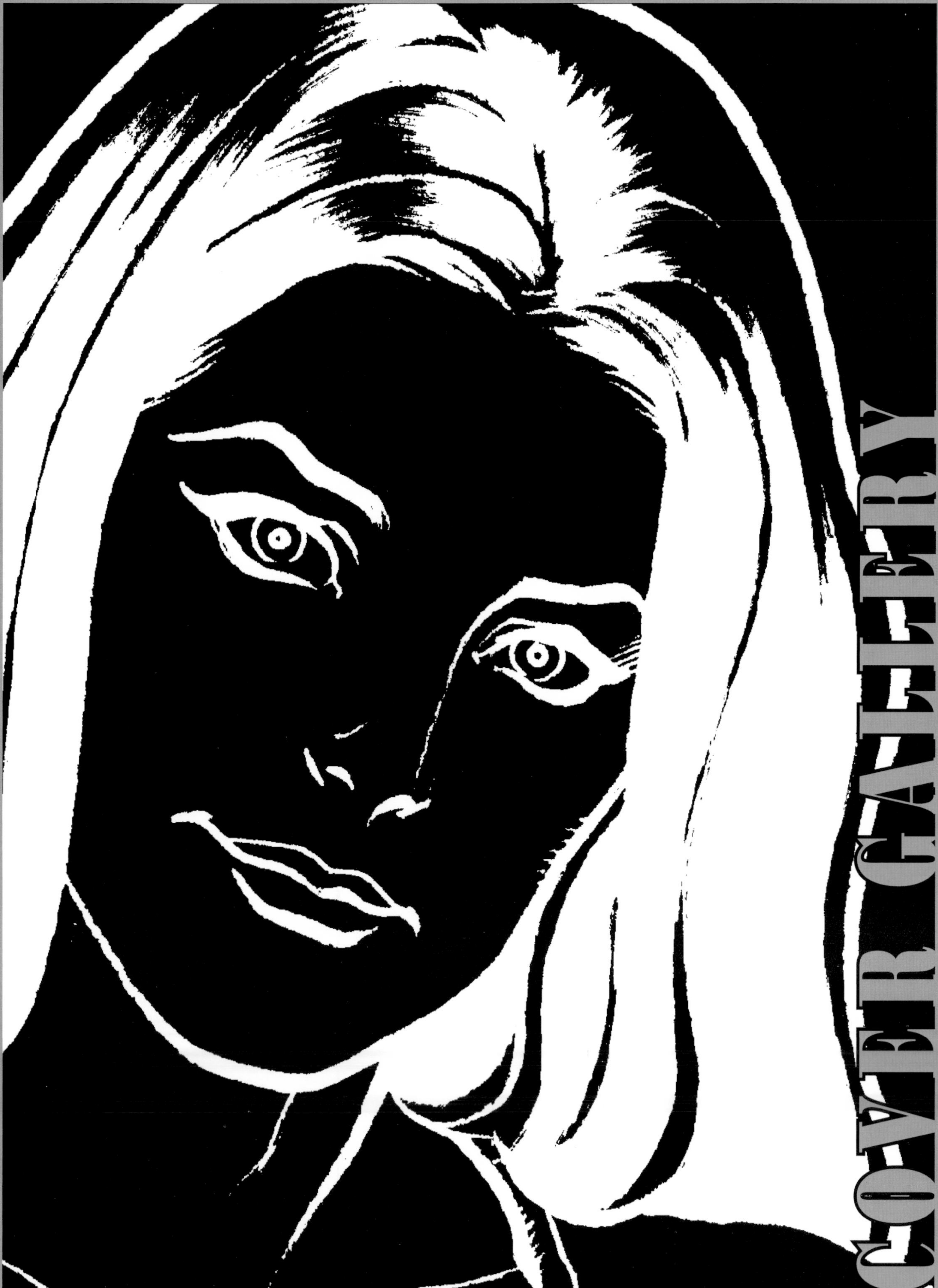
COVER GALLERY

ISSUE 19

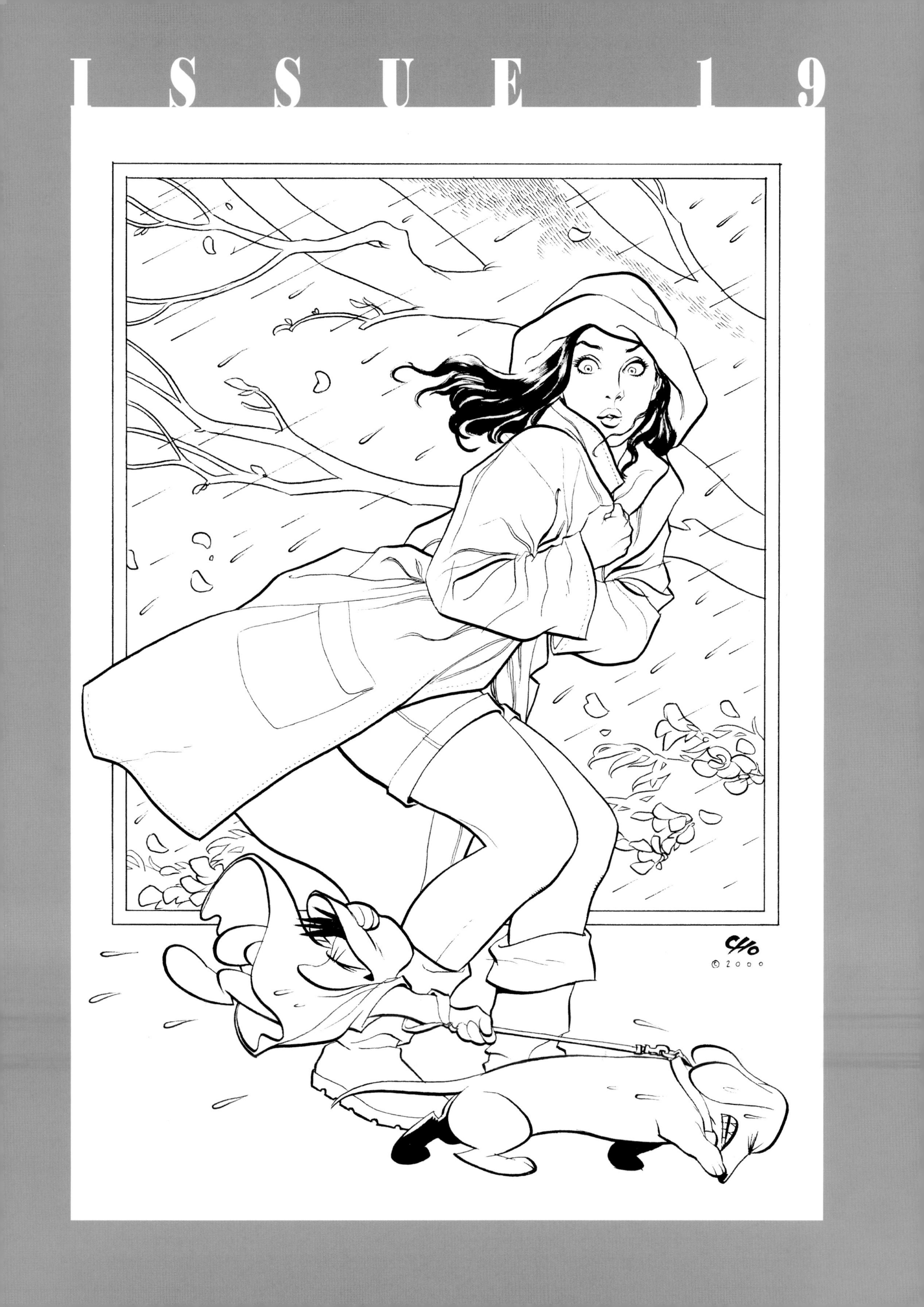
CHO
©2000

ISSUE 20

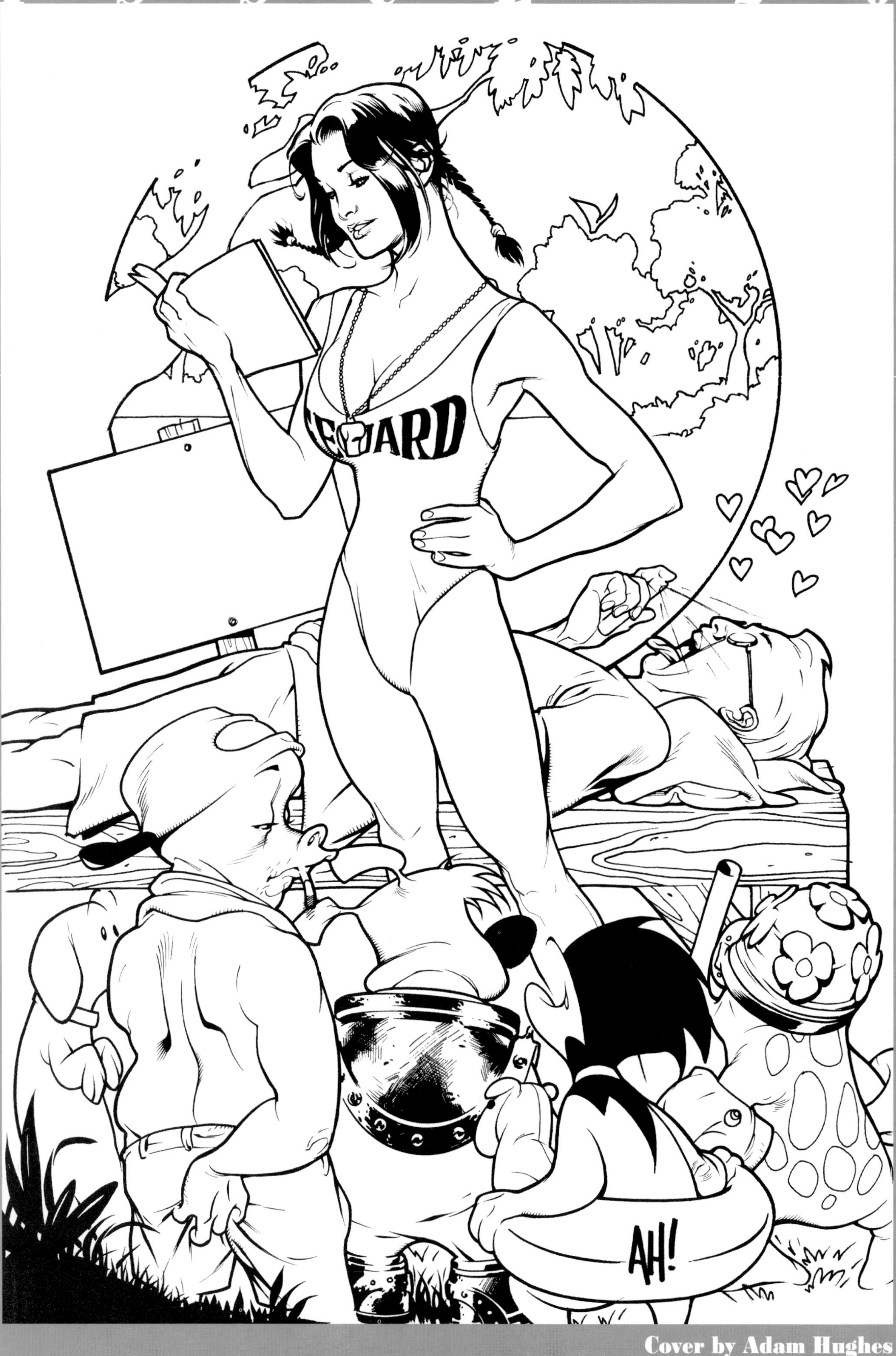

LIFEGUARD
AH!

Cover by Adam Hughes

ISSUE 21

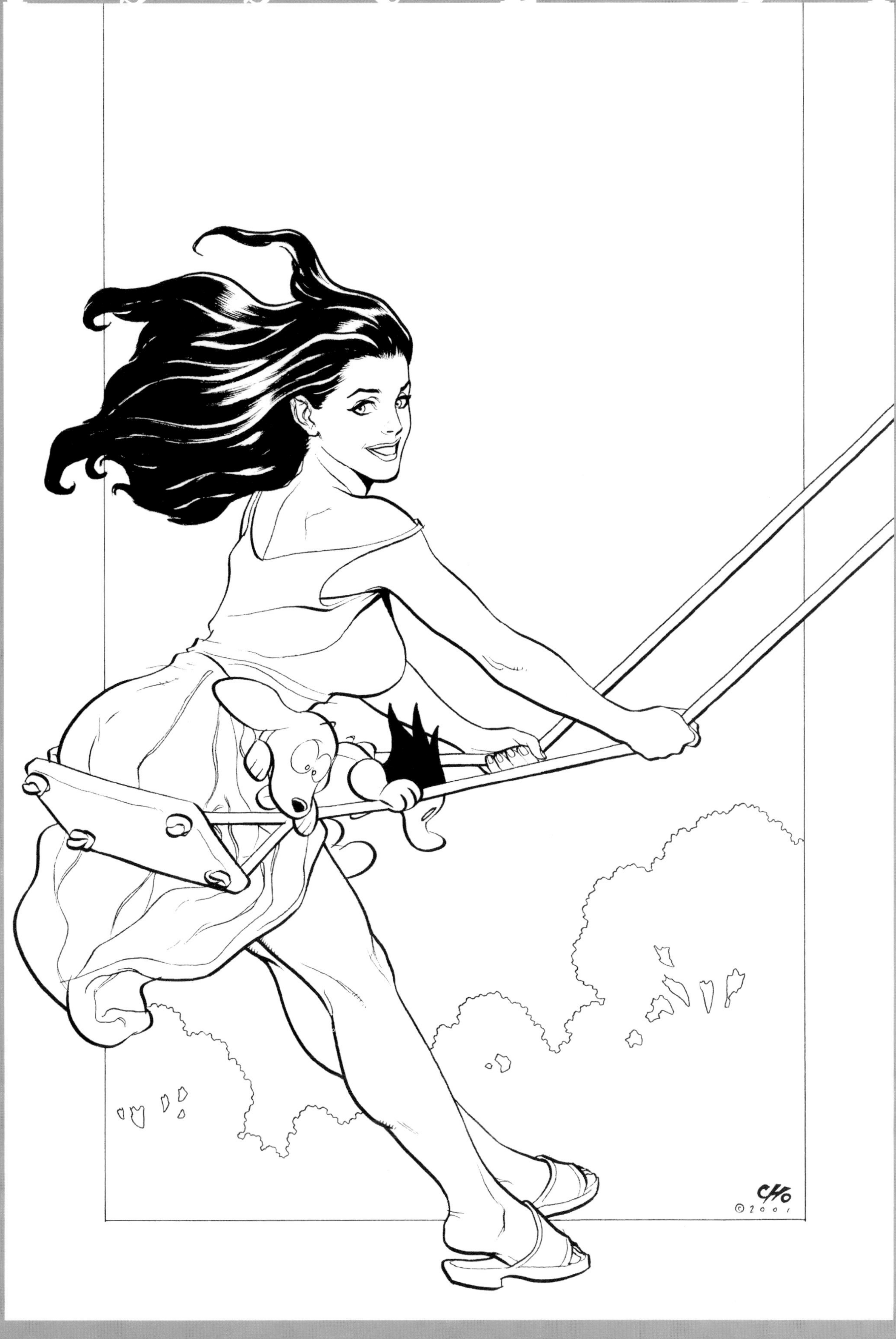
CHO
©2001

ISSUE 22

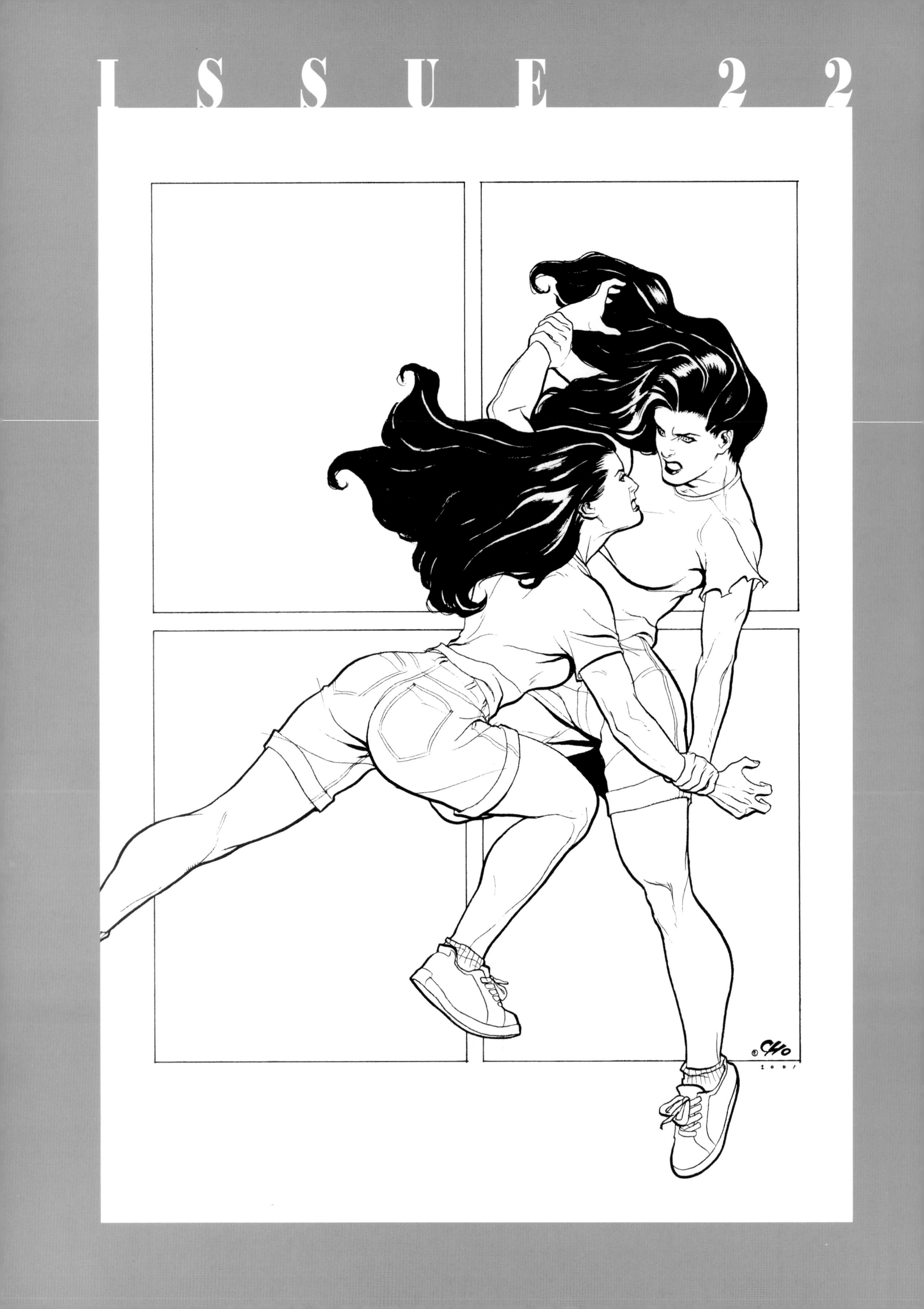
©CHO 2001

ISSUE 23

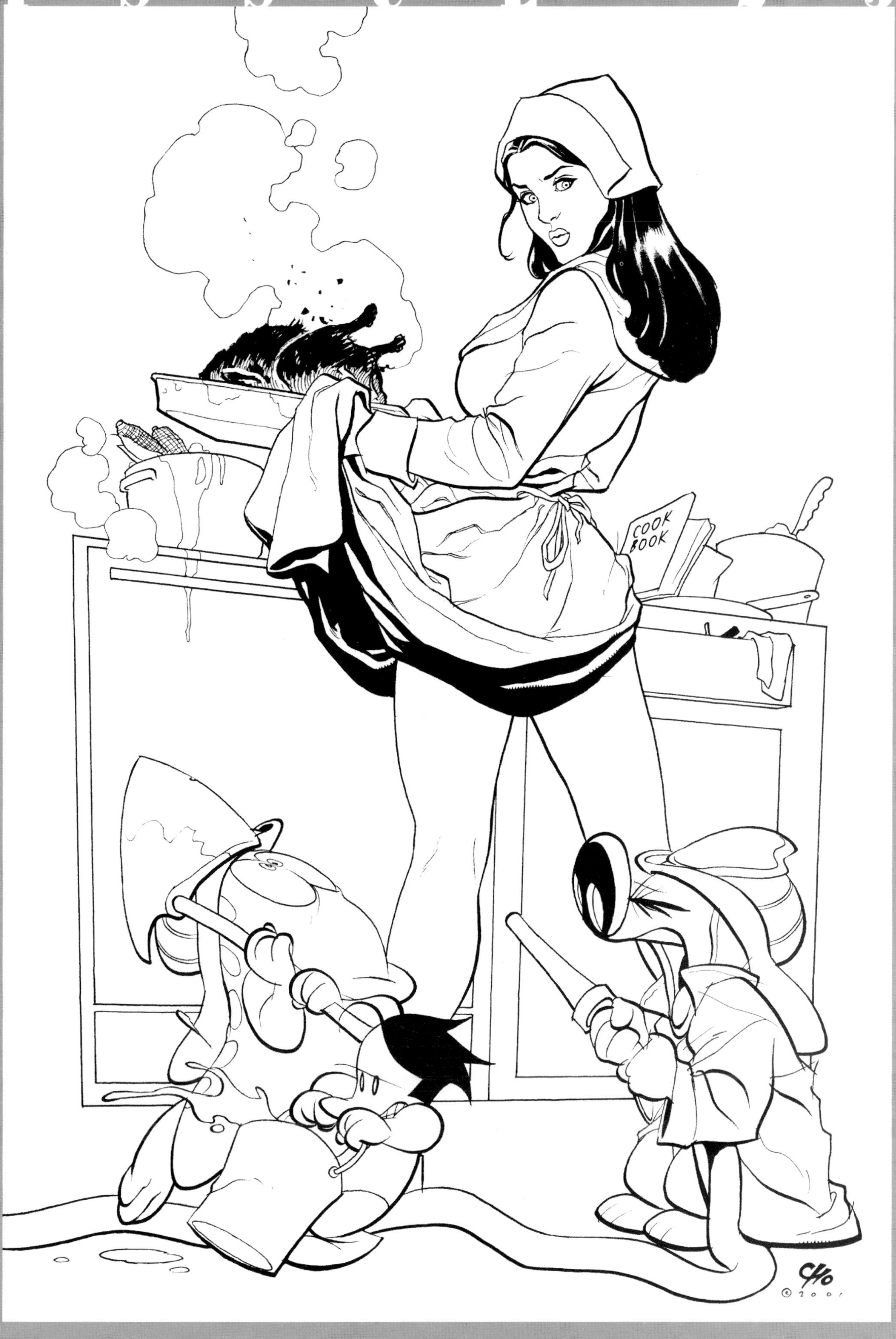
COOK BOOK
CHO
©2001

ISSUE 24

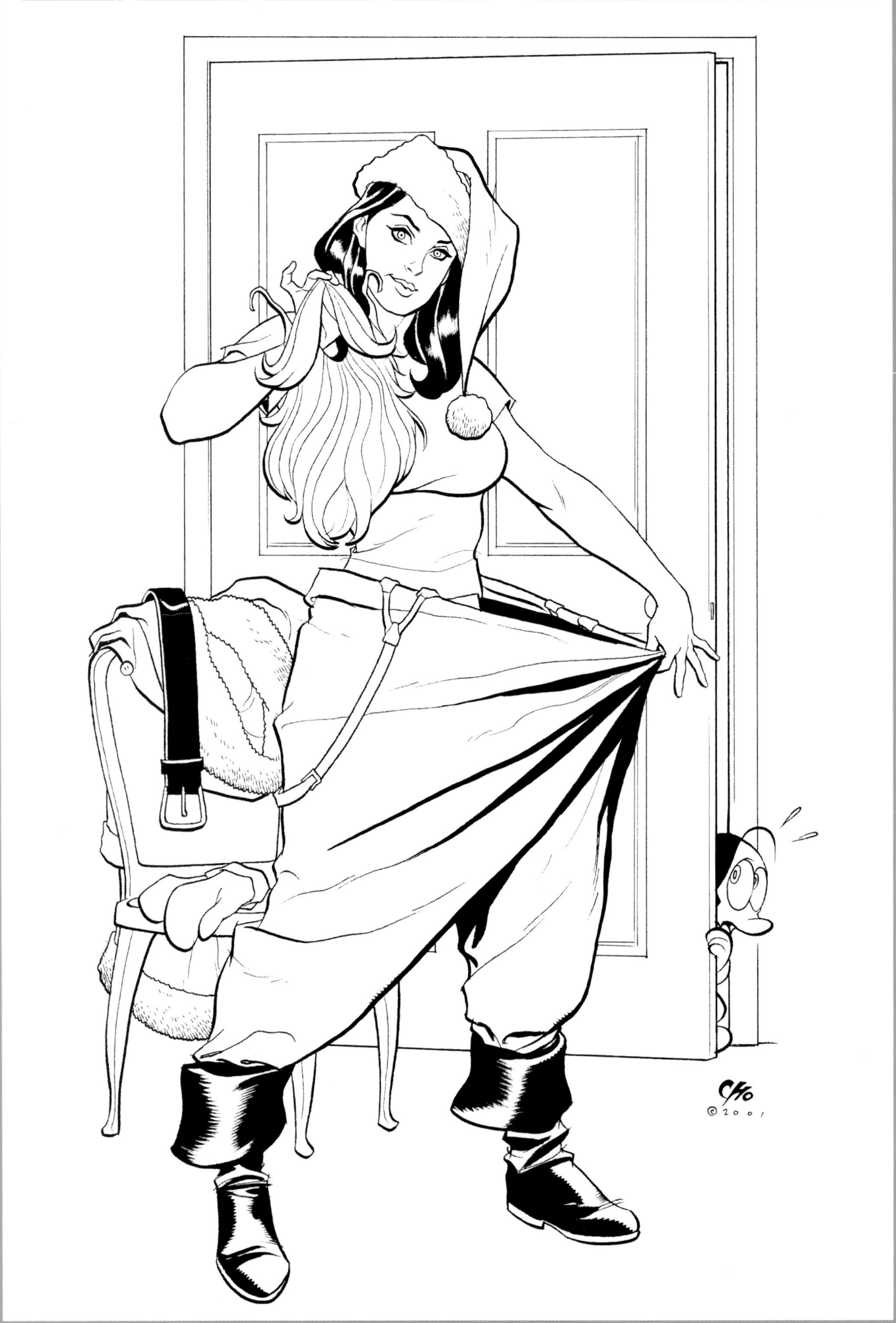
CHO
©2001

ISSUE 25

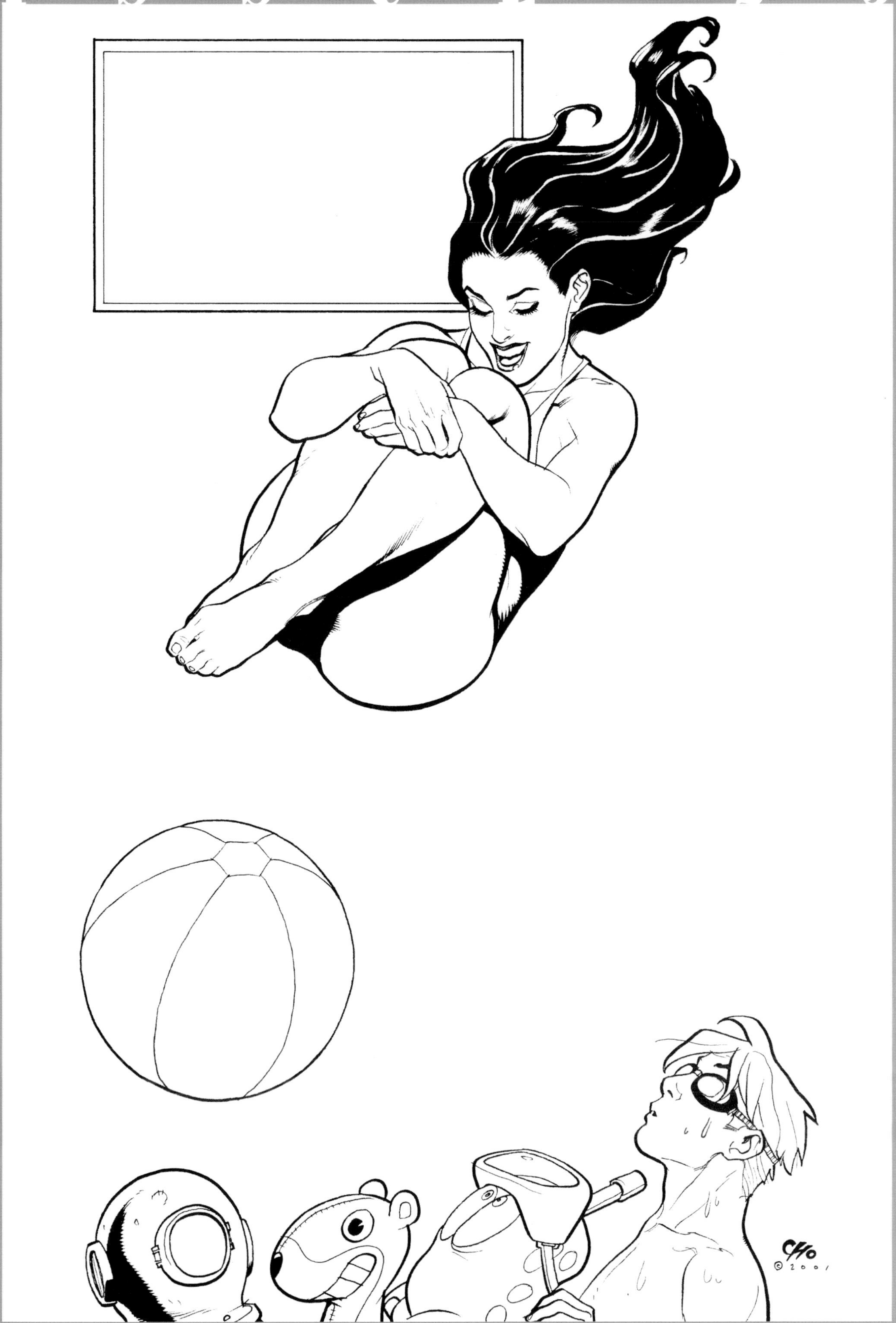
CHO
©2001

ISSUE 26

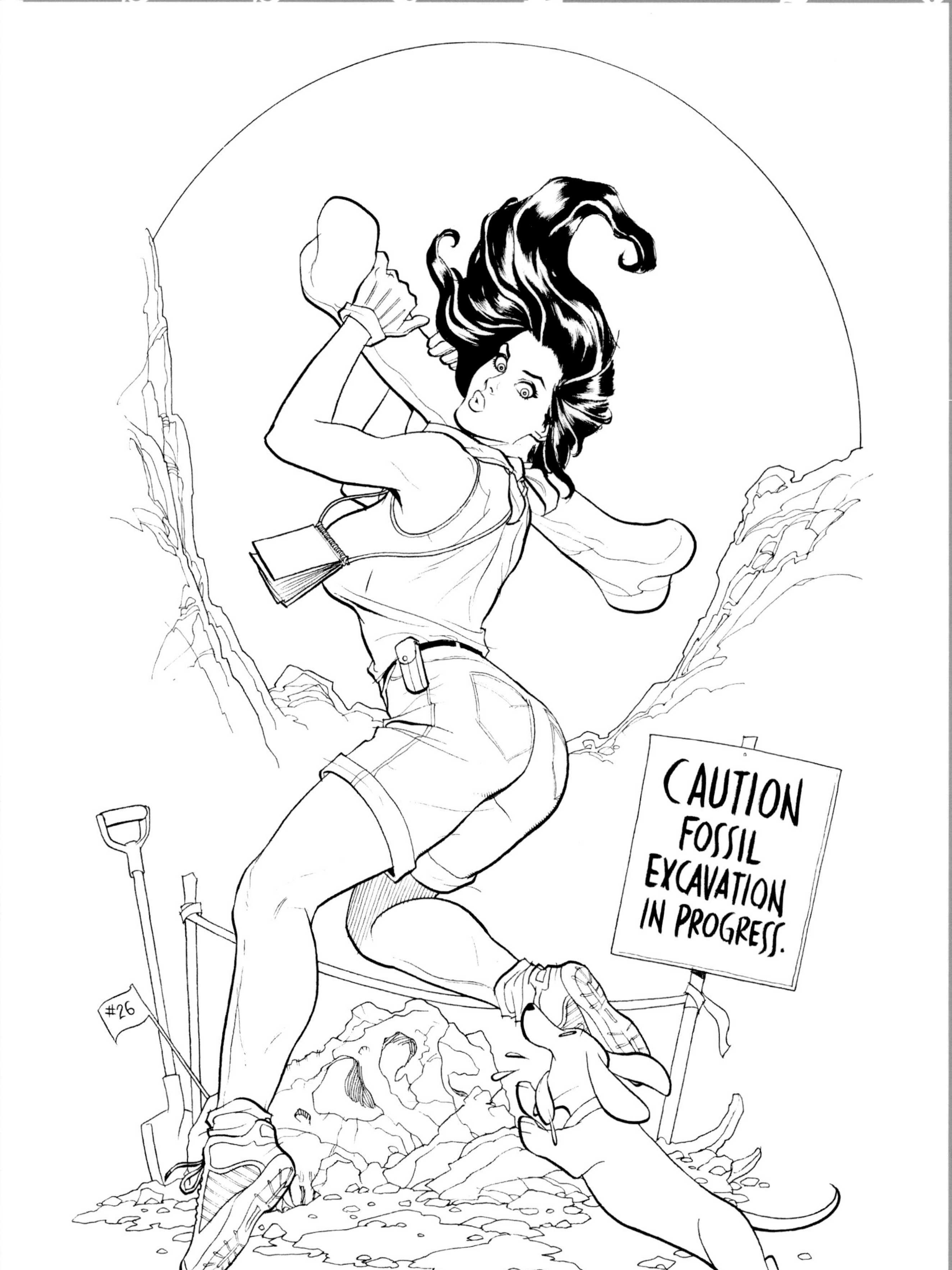
CAUTION
FOSSIL
EXCAVATION
IN PROGRESS.
#26
CHO
©2002

ISSUE 27

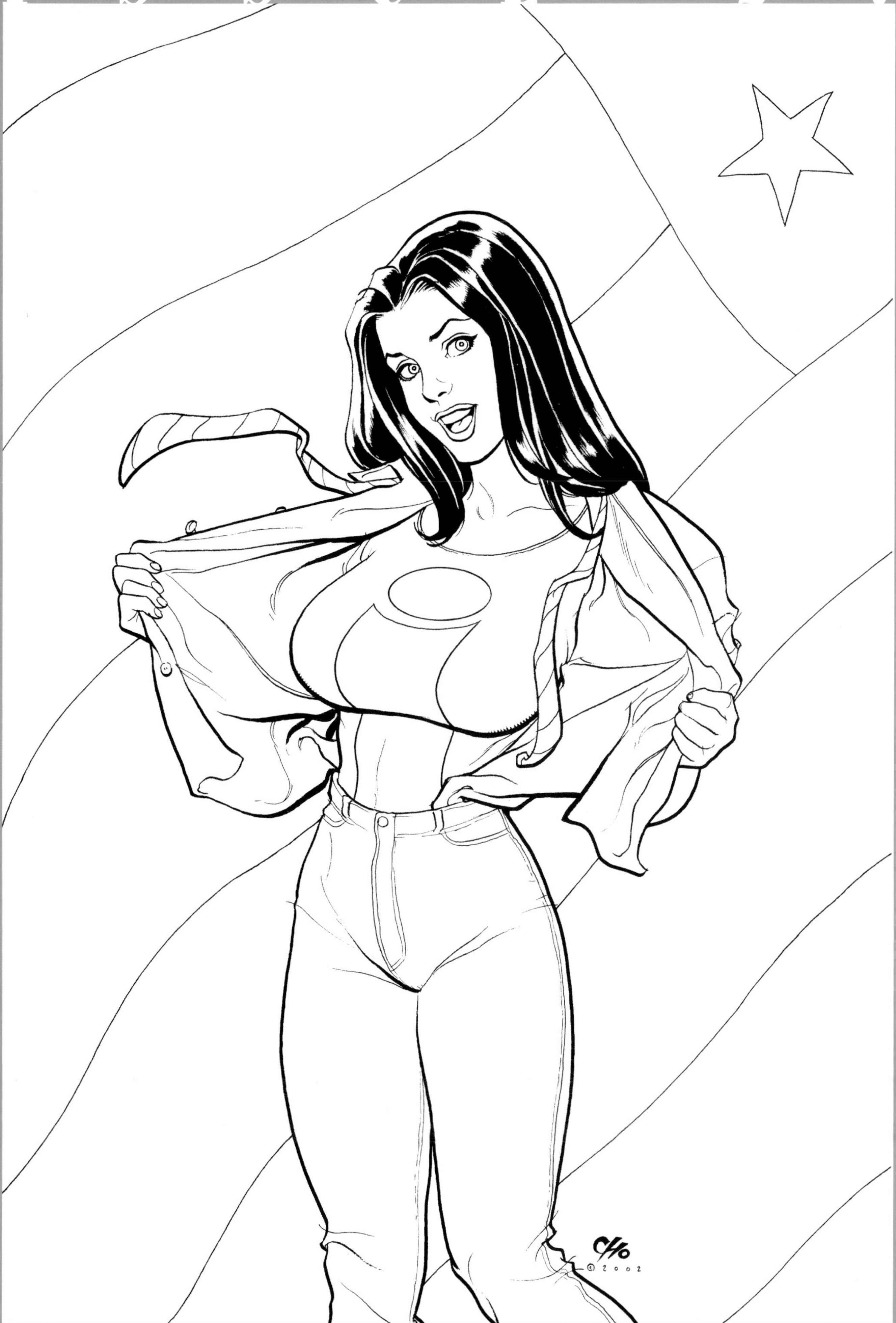
CHO
© 2002

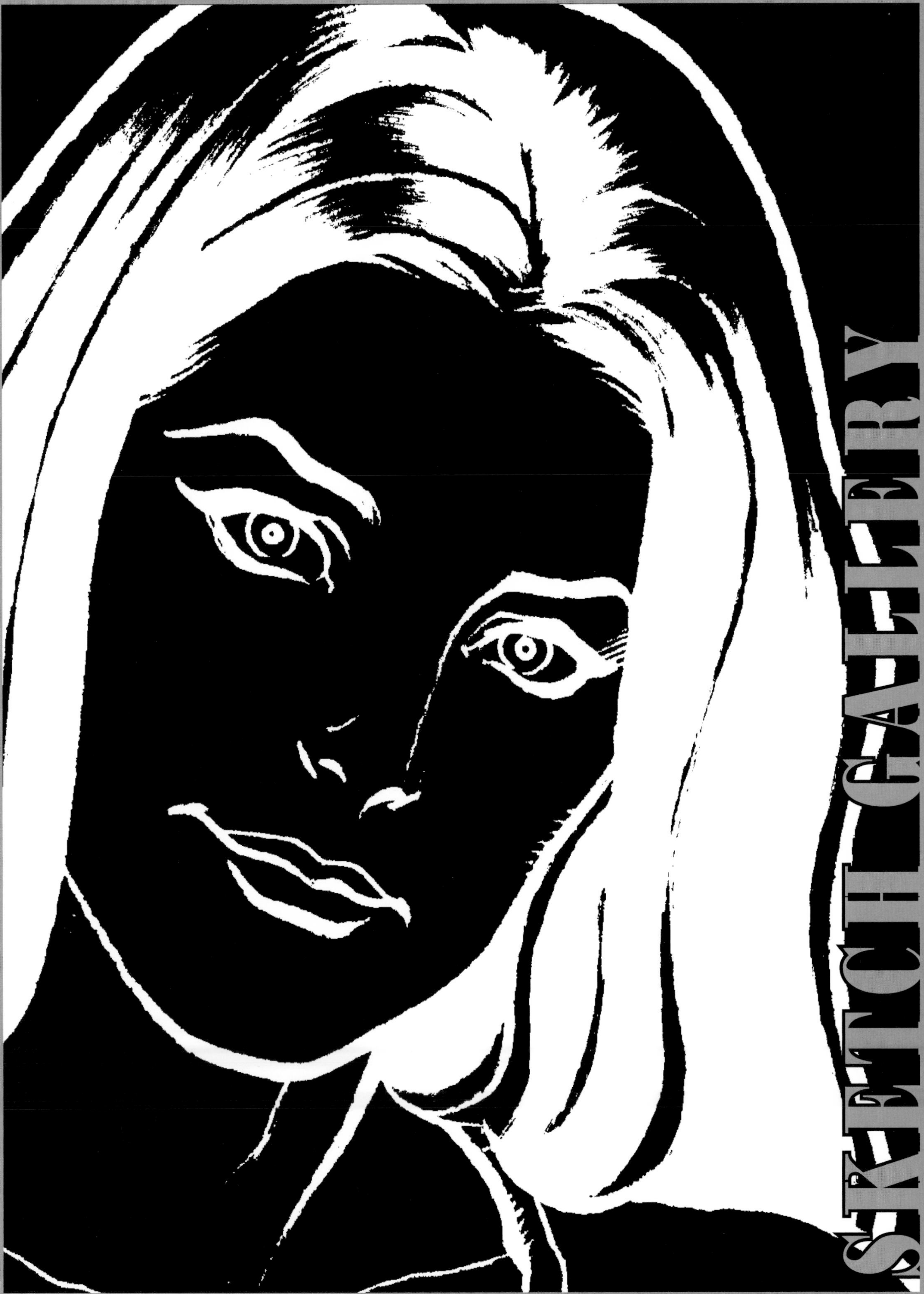
SKETCH GALLERY

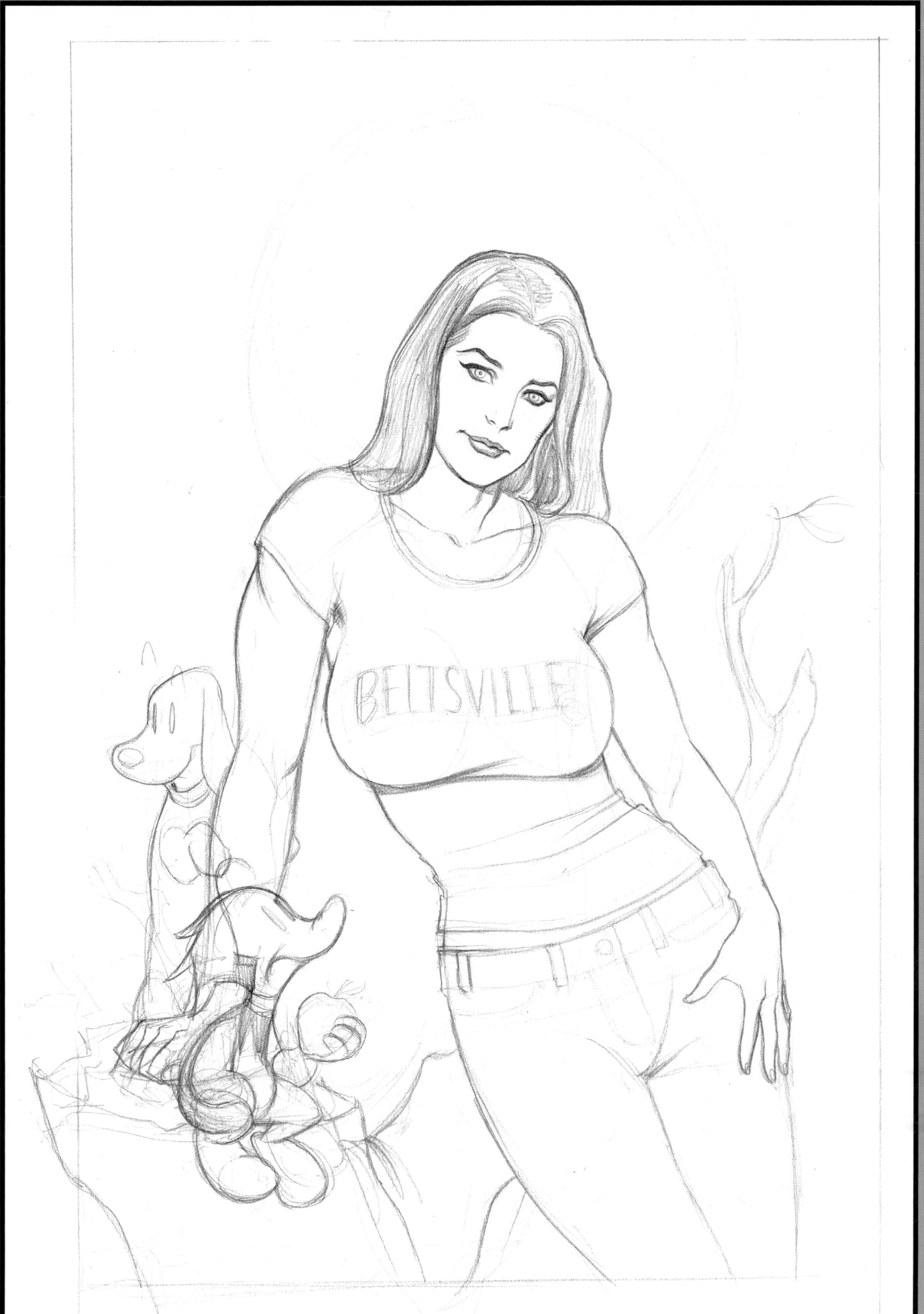
BELTSVILLE

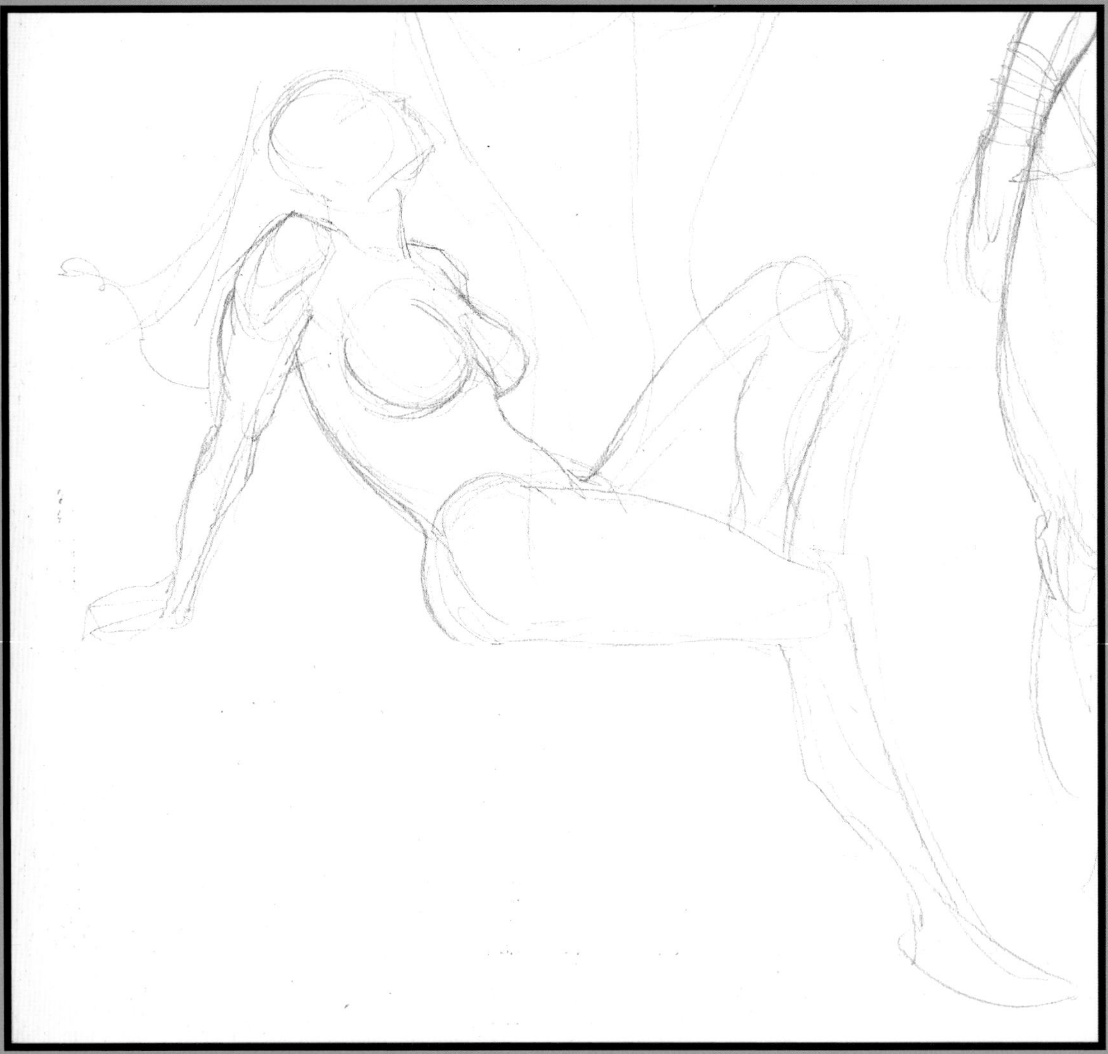

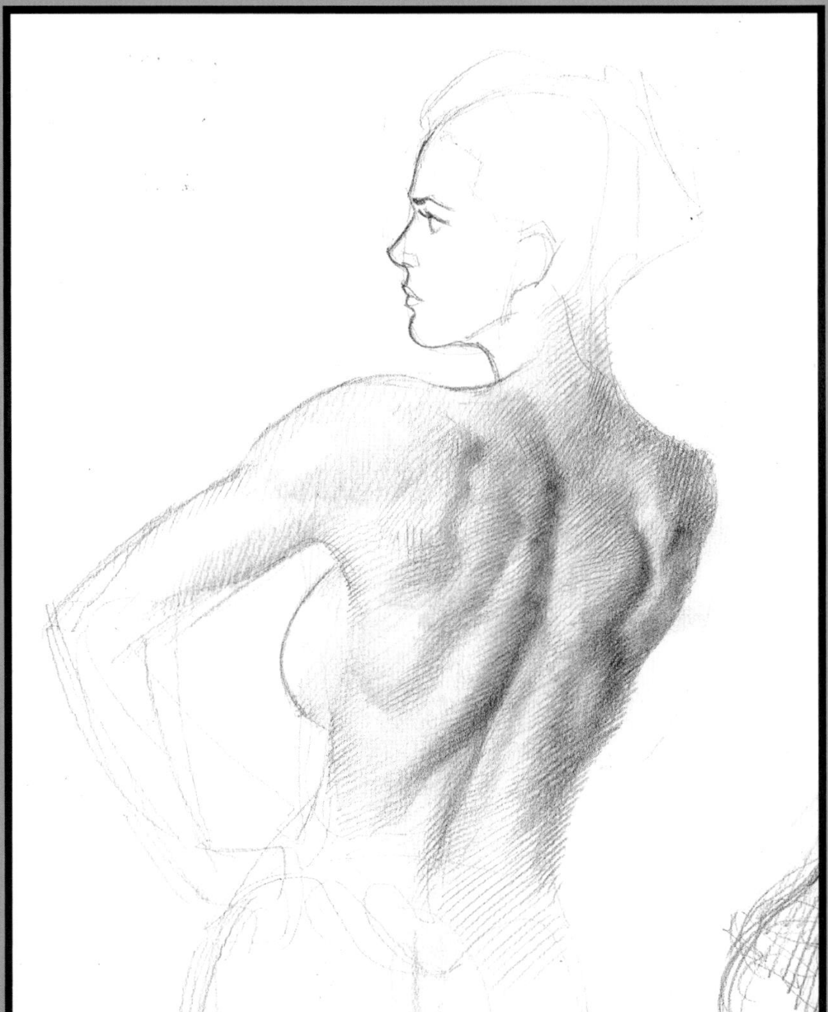

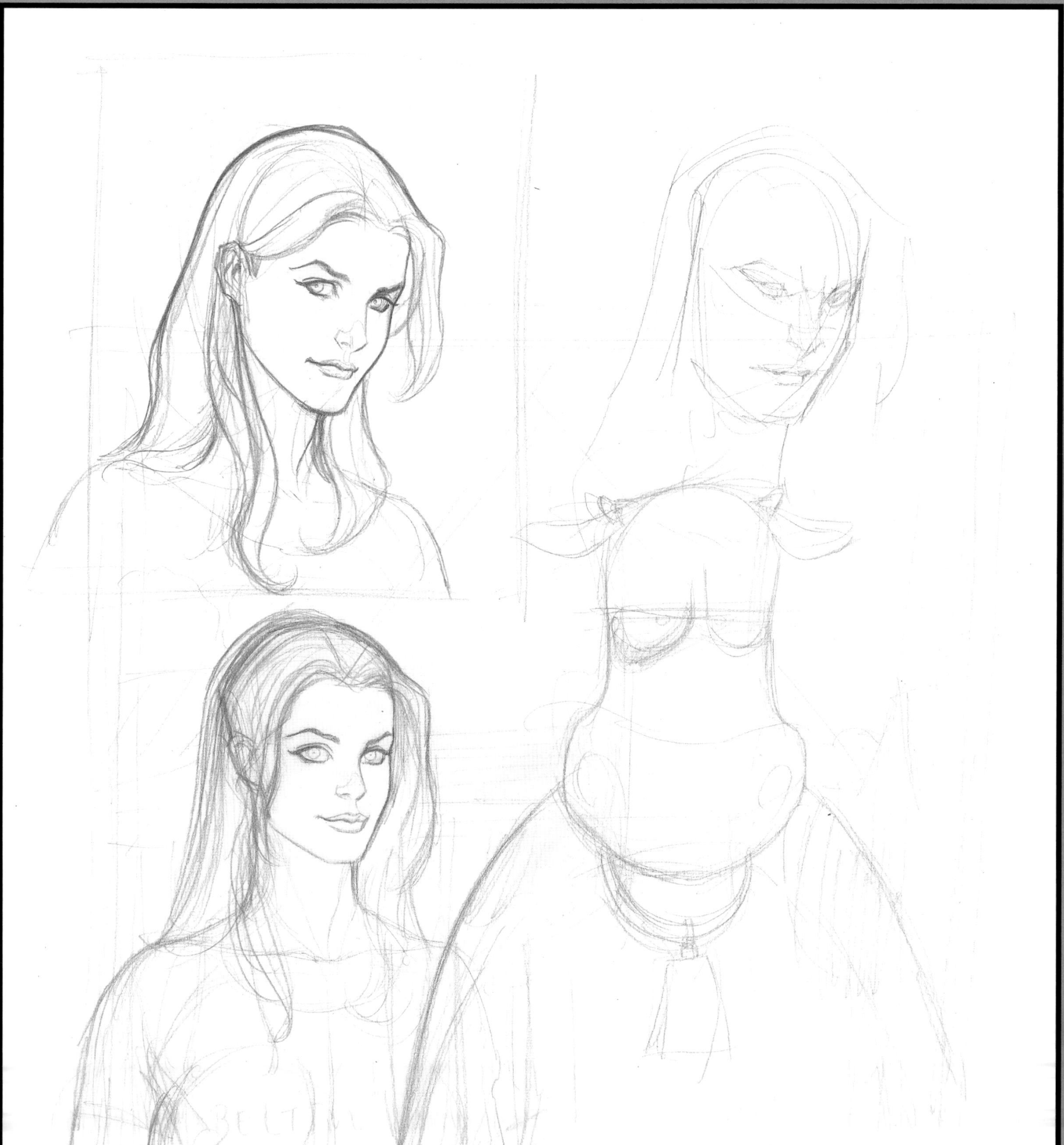

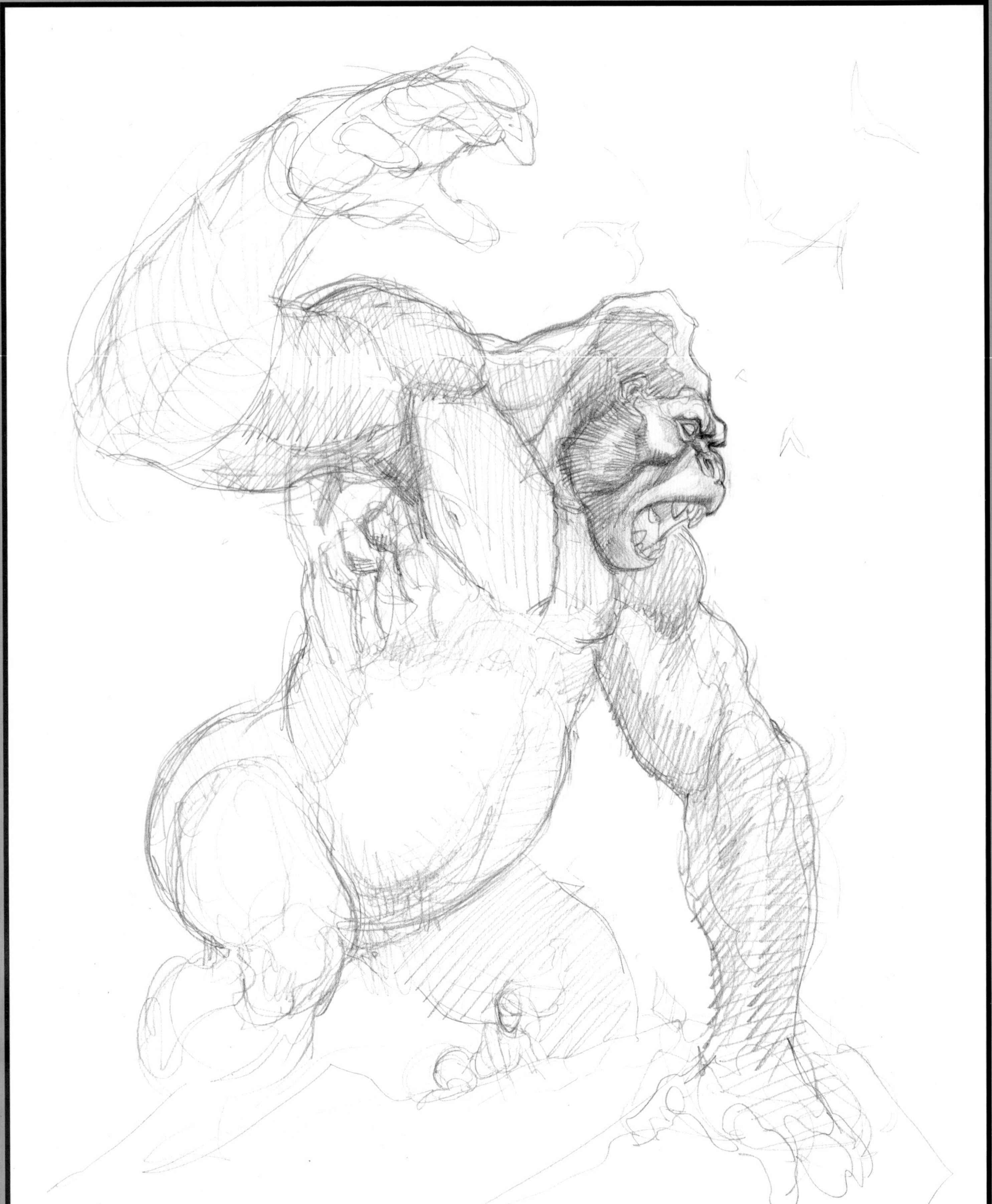

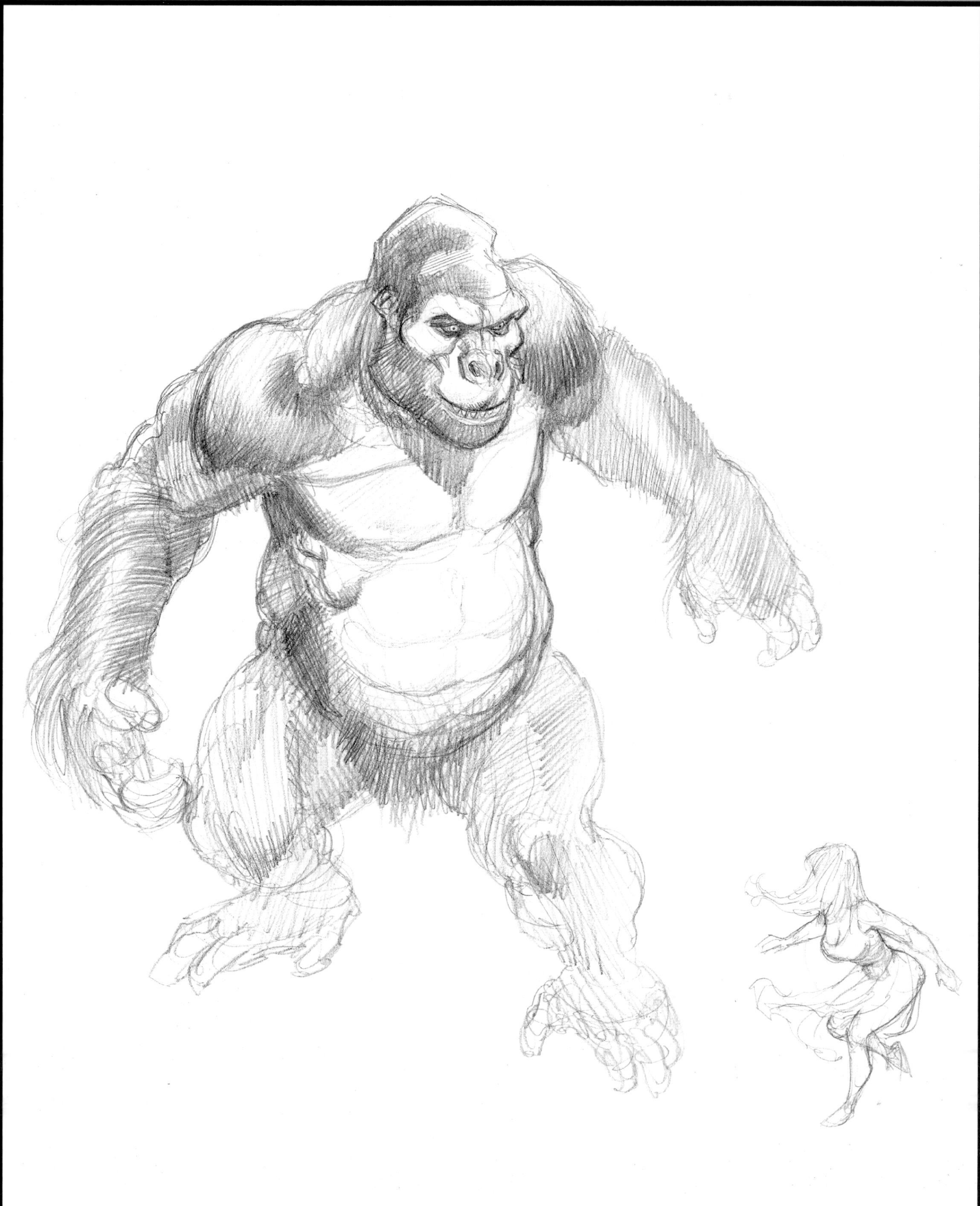

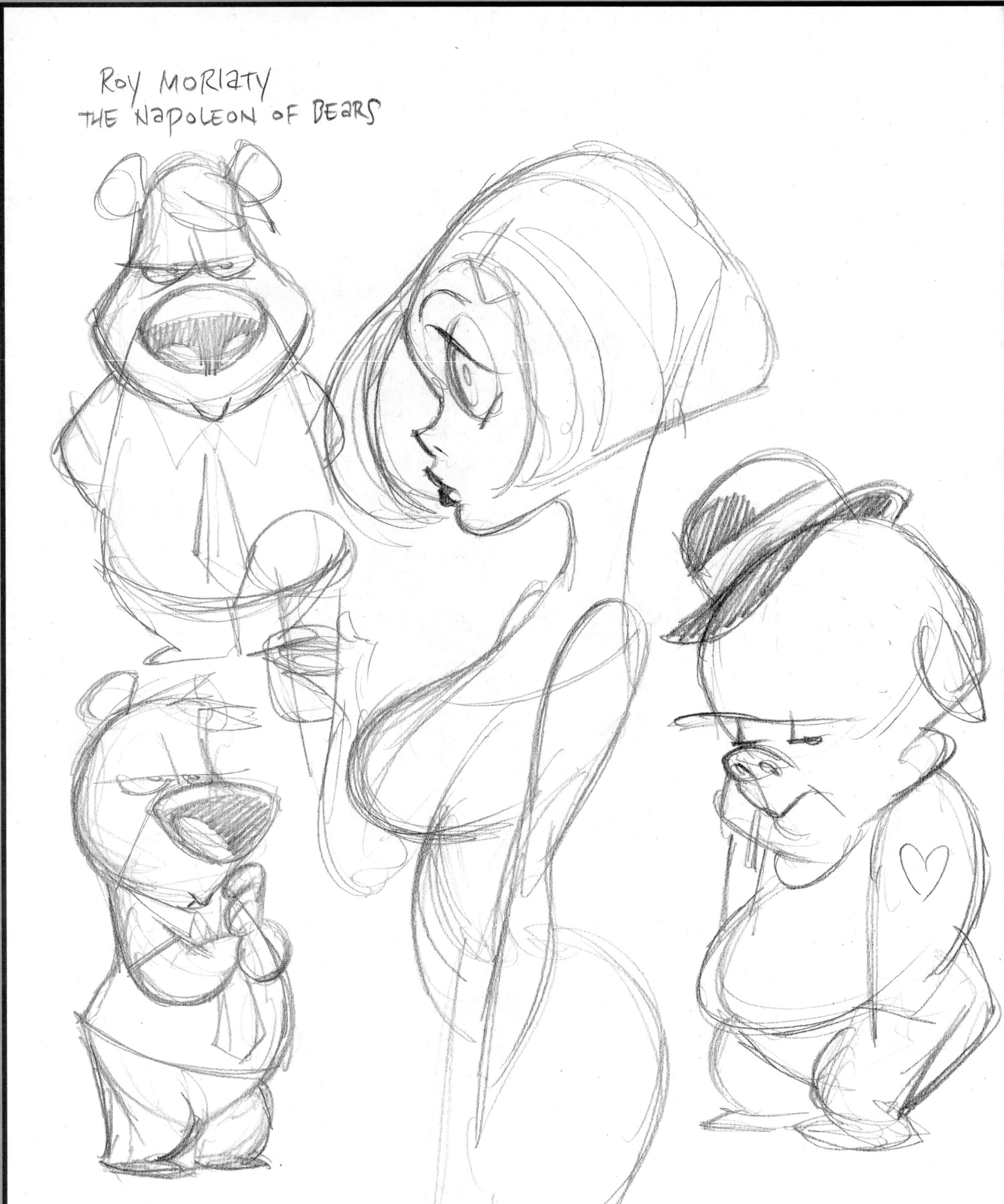
Roy Moriaty
The Napoleon of Bears

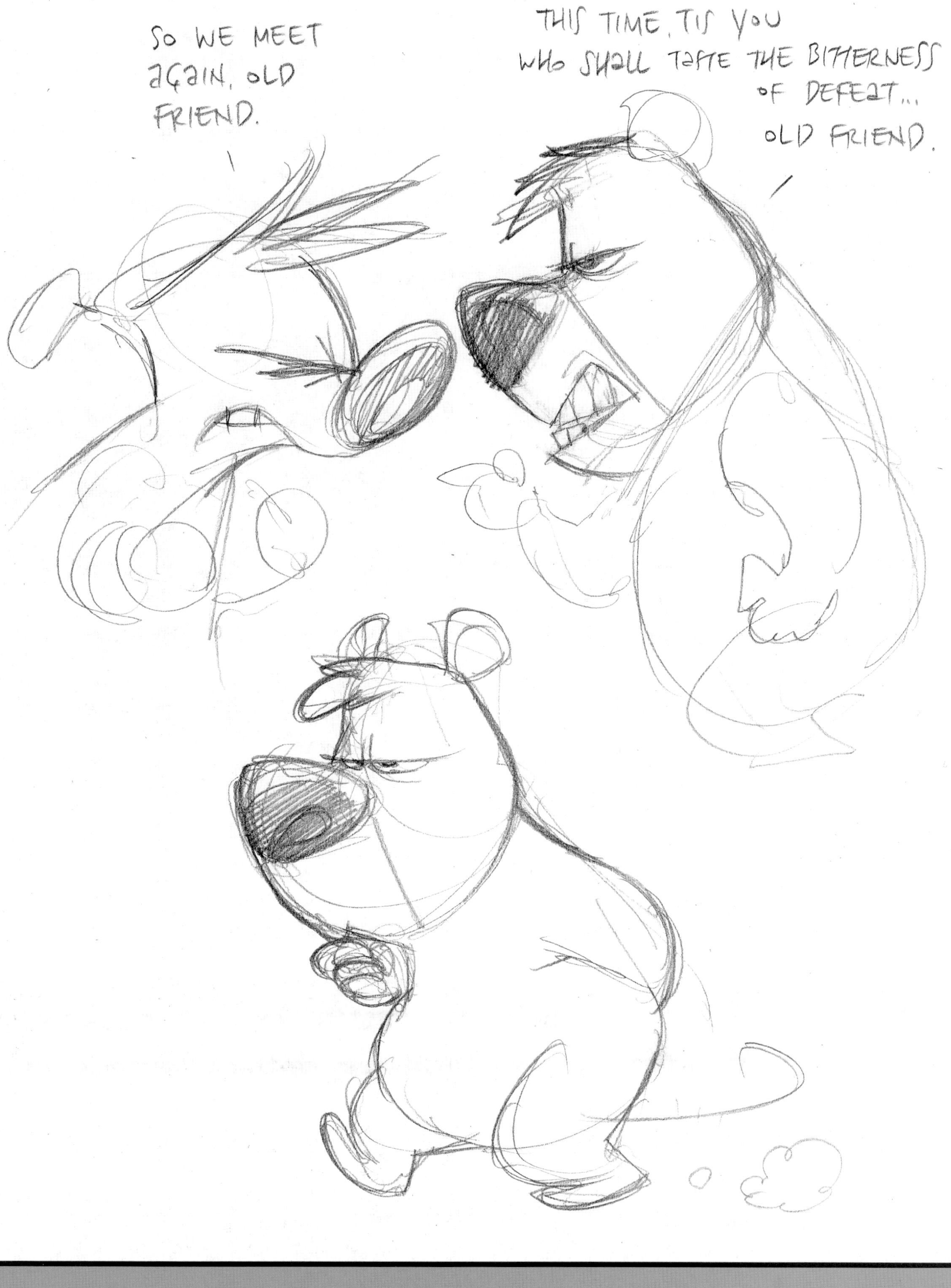
SO WE MEET AGAIN, OLD FRIEND.
THIS TIME, TIS YOU WHO SHALL TASTE THE BITTERNESS OF DEFEAT... OLD FRIEND.

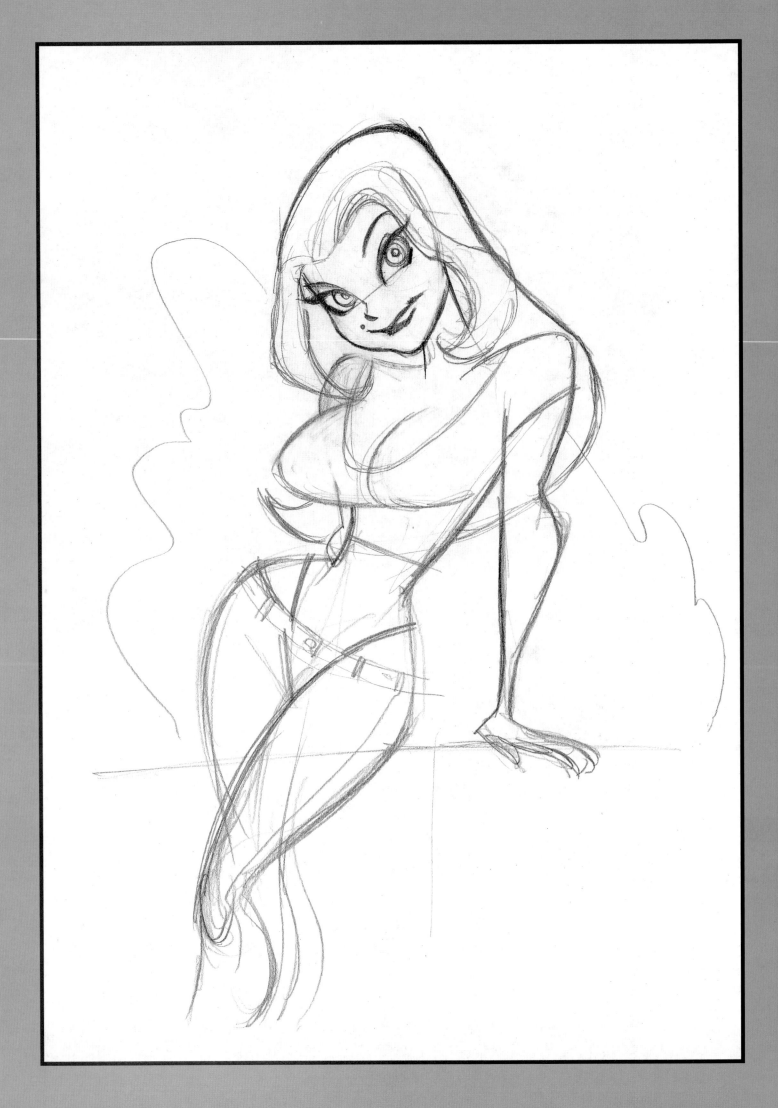

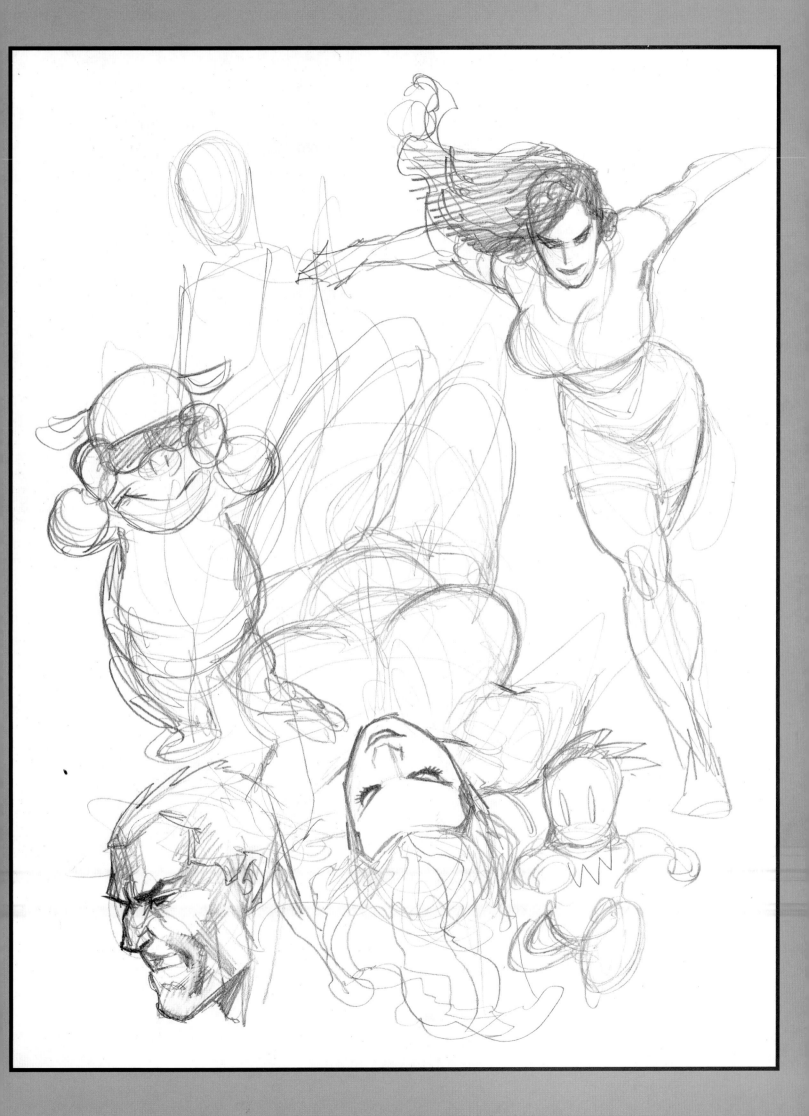

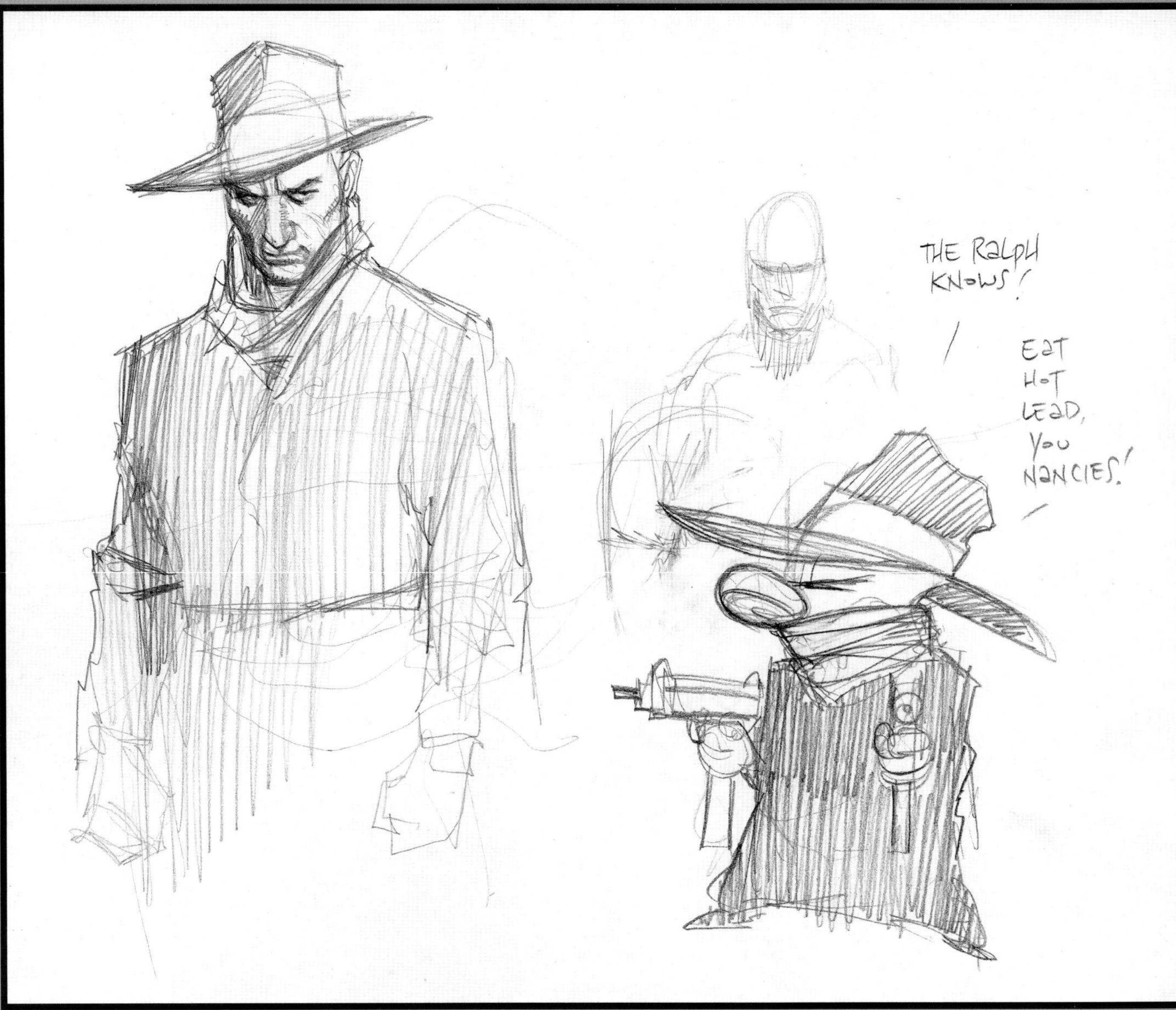
THE RALPH KNOWS!
EAT HOT LEAD, YOU NANCIES!

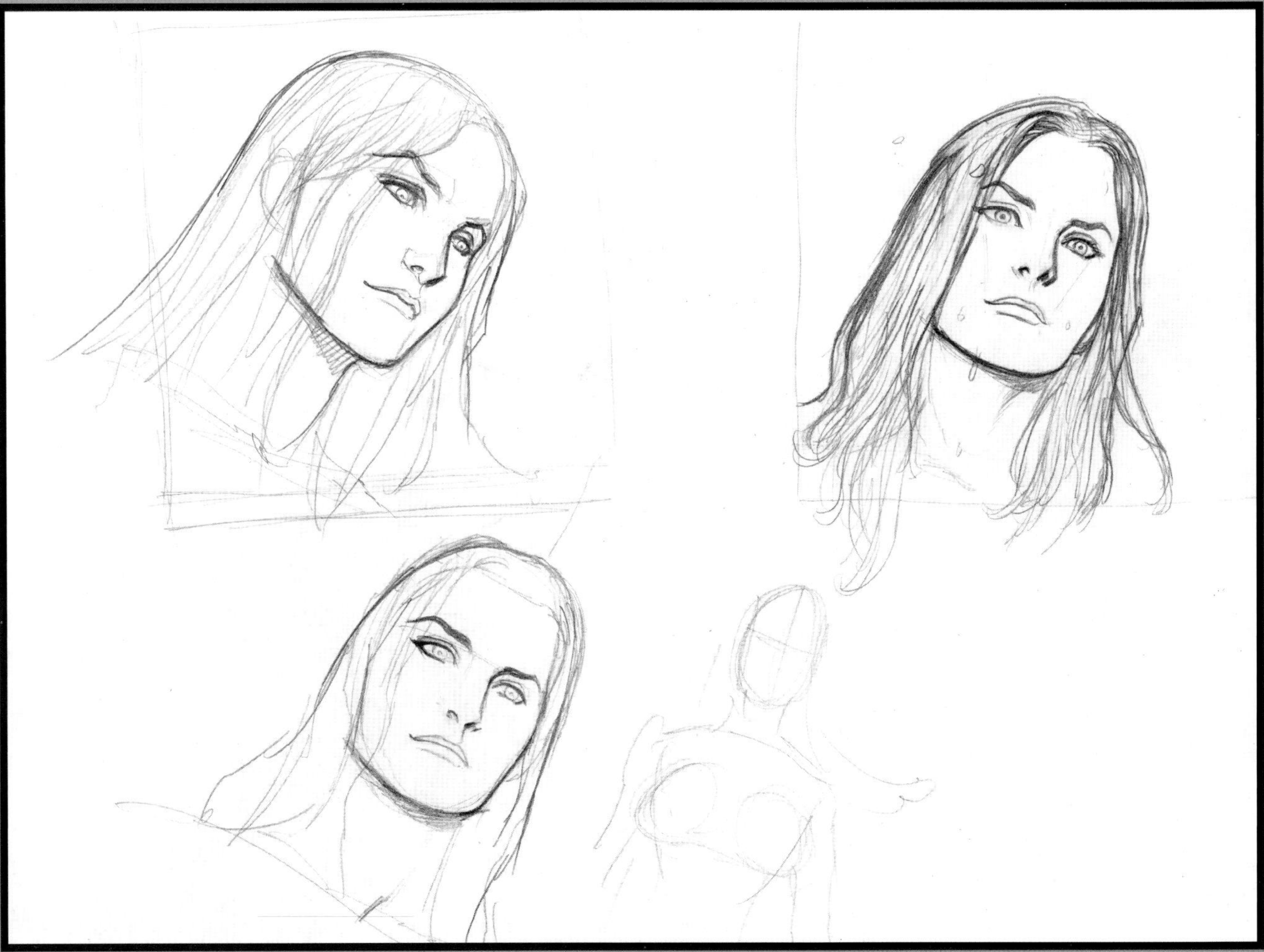

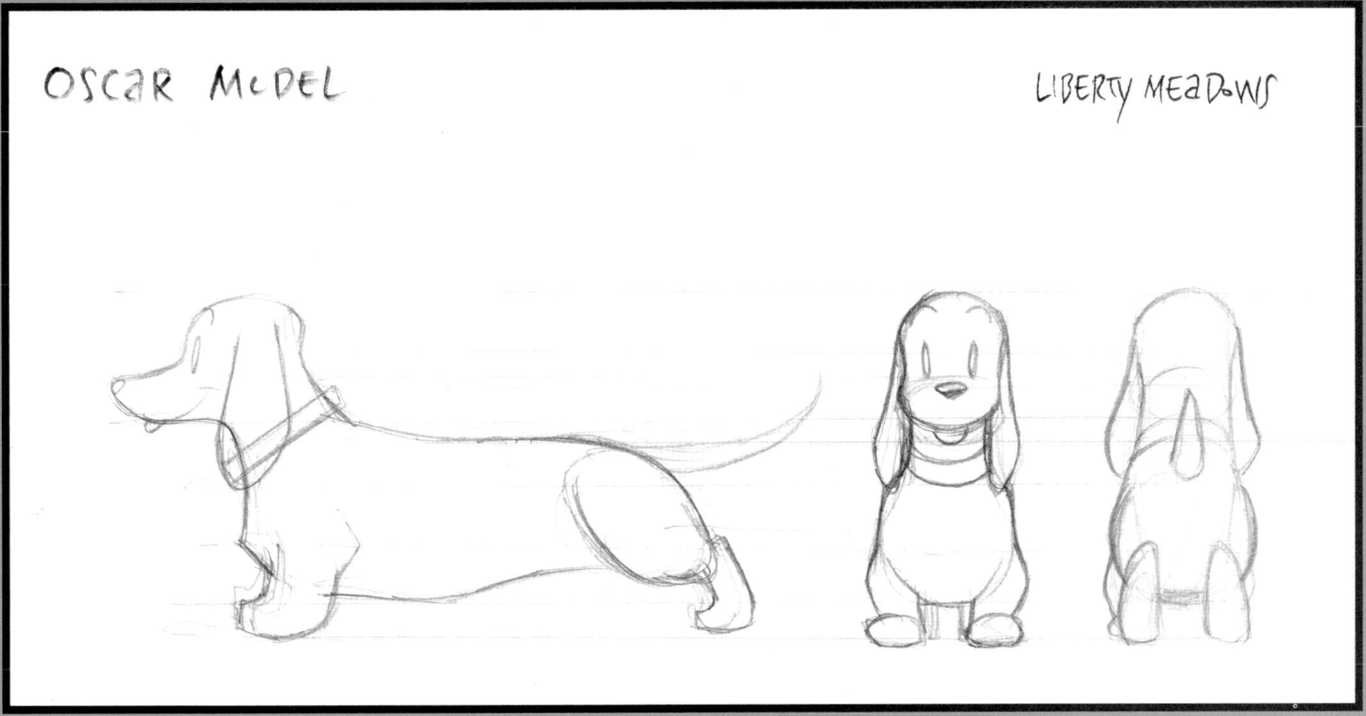
OSCAR MODEL
LIBERTY MEADOWS

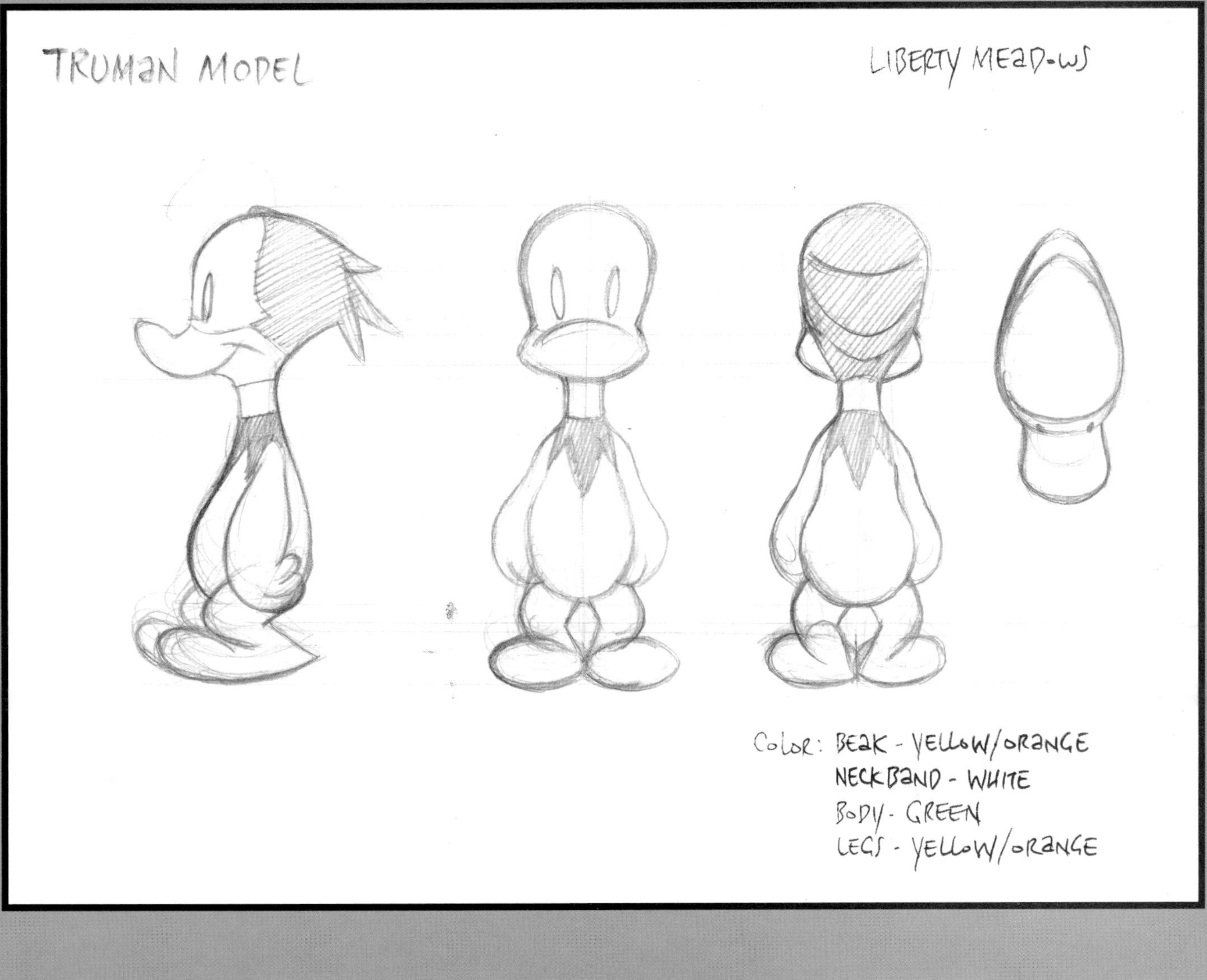
TRUMAN MODEL
LIBERTY MEADOWS
COLOR: BEAK - YELLOW/ORANGE
NECKBAND - WHITE
BODY - GREEN
LEGS - YELLOW/ORANGE

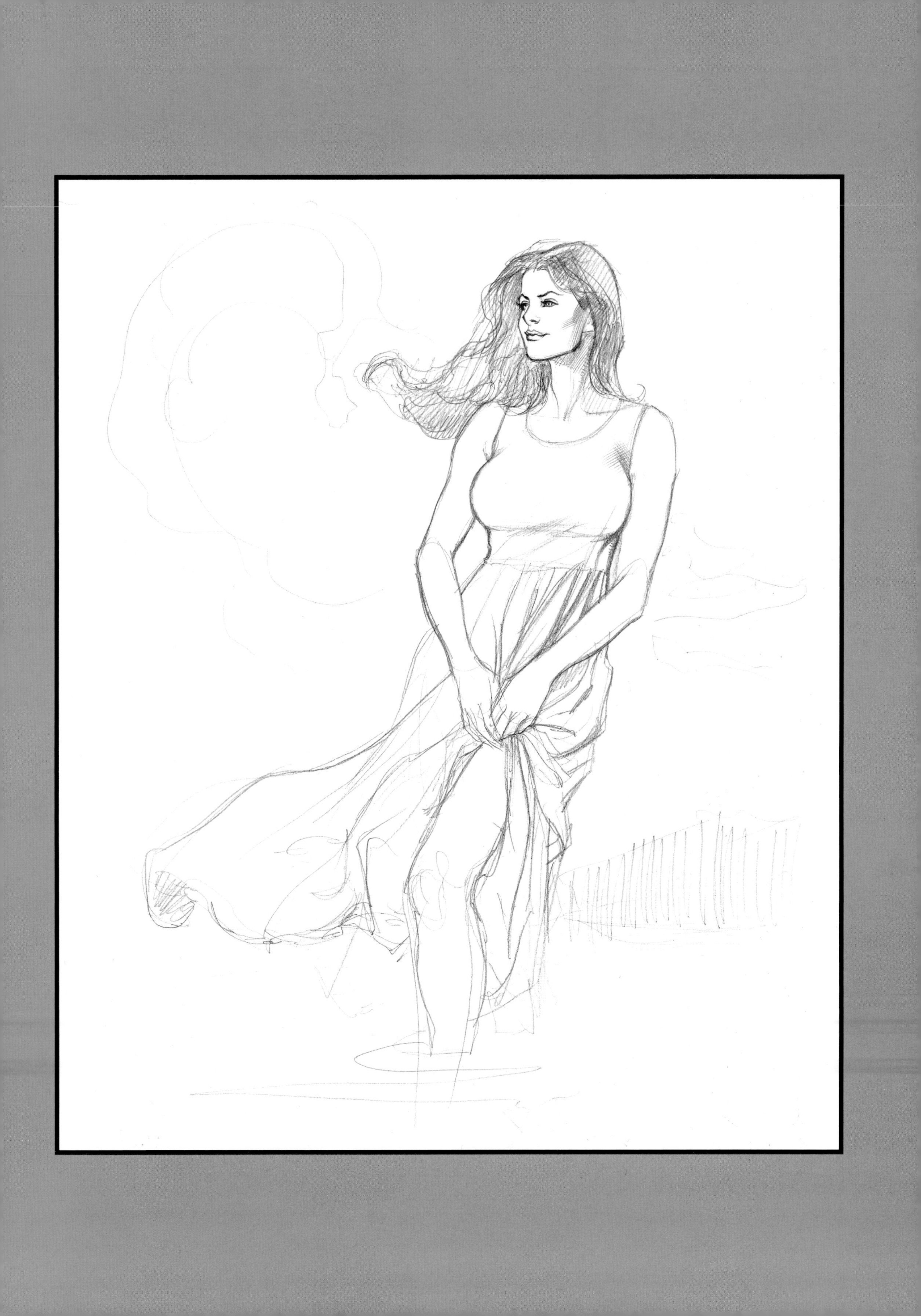

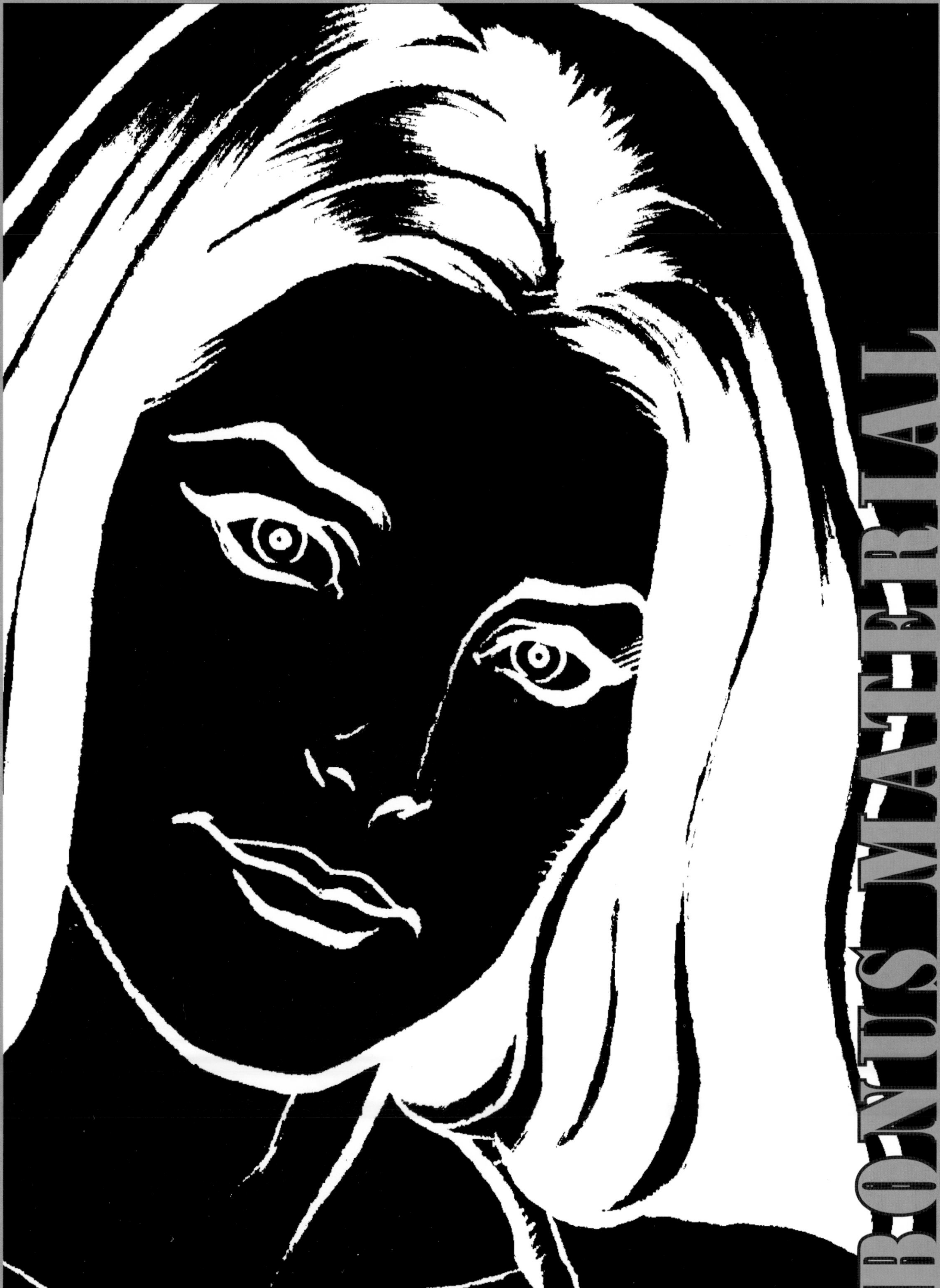
BONUS MATERIAL

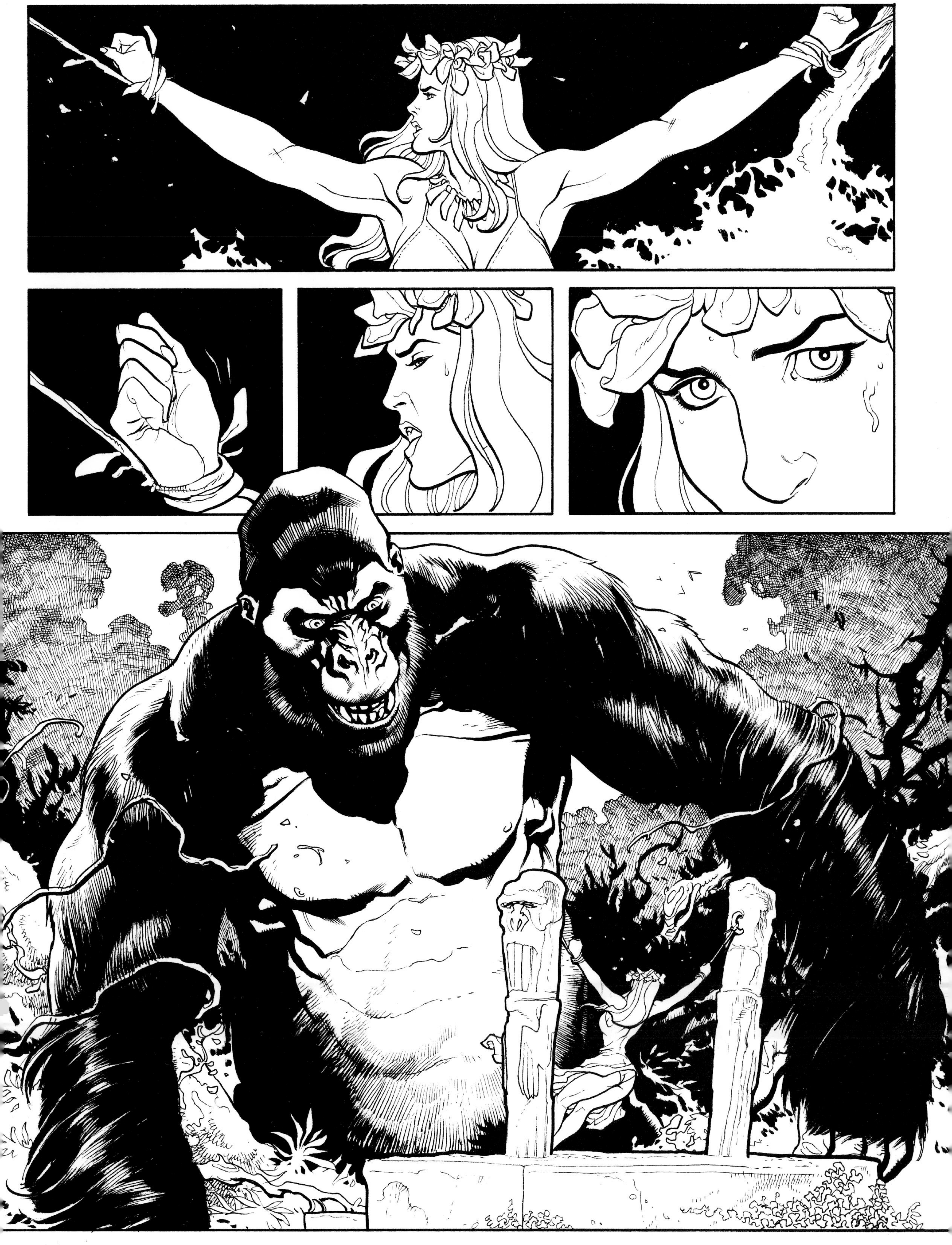

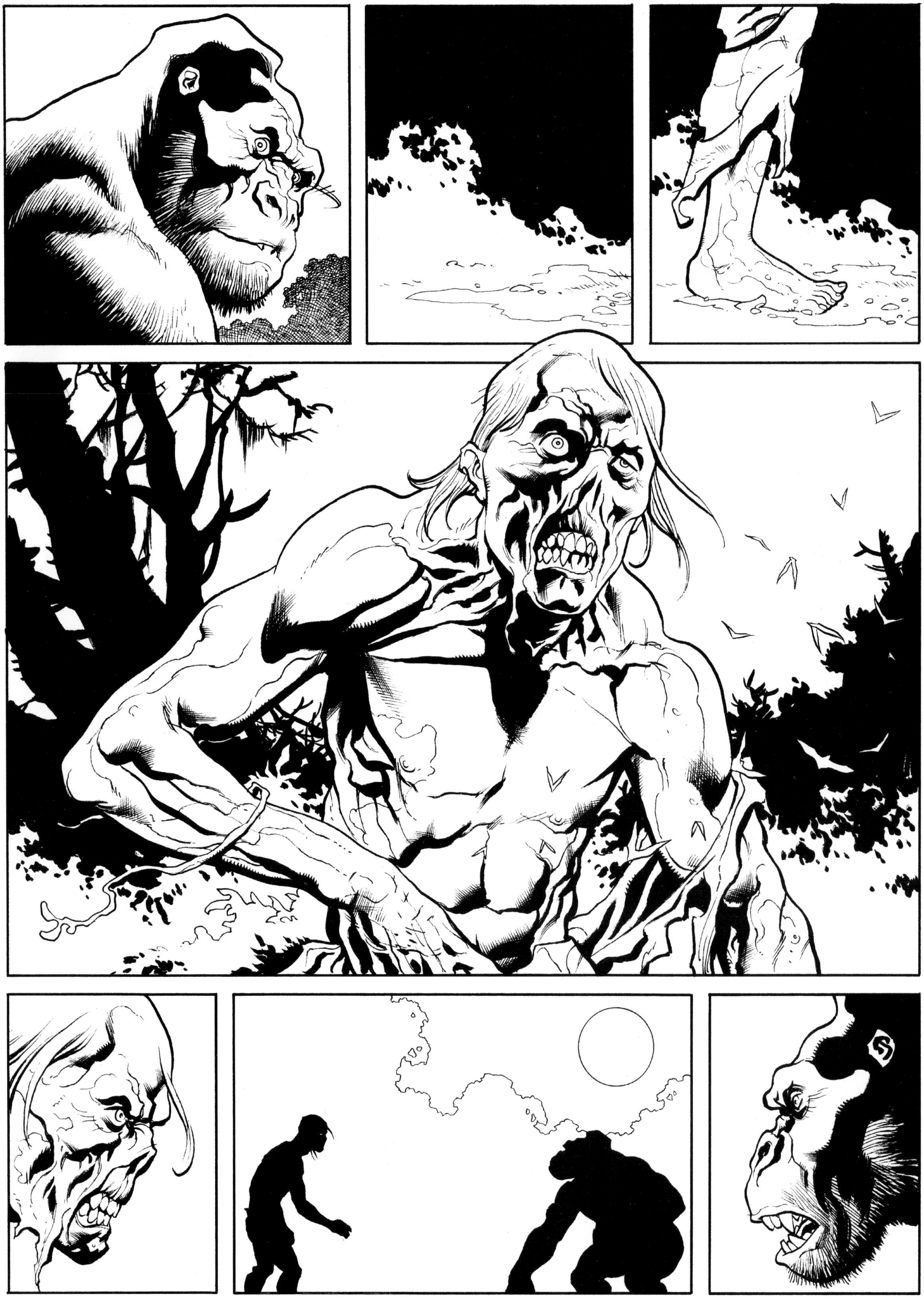

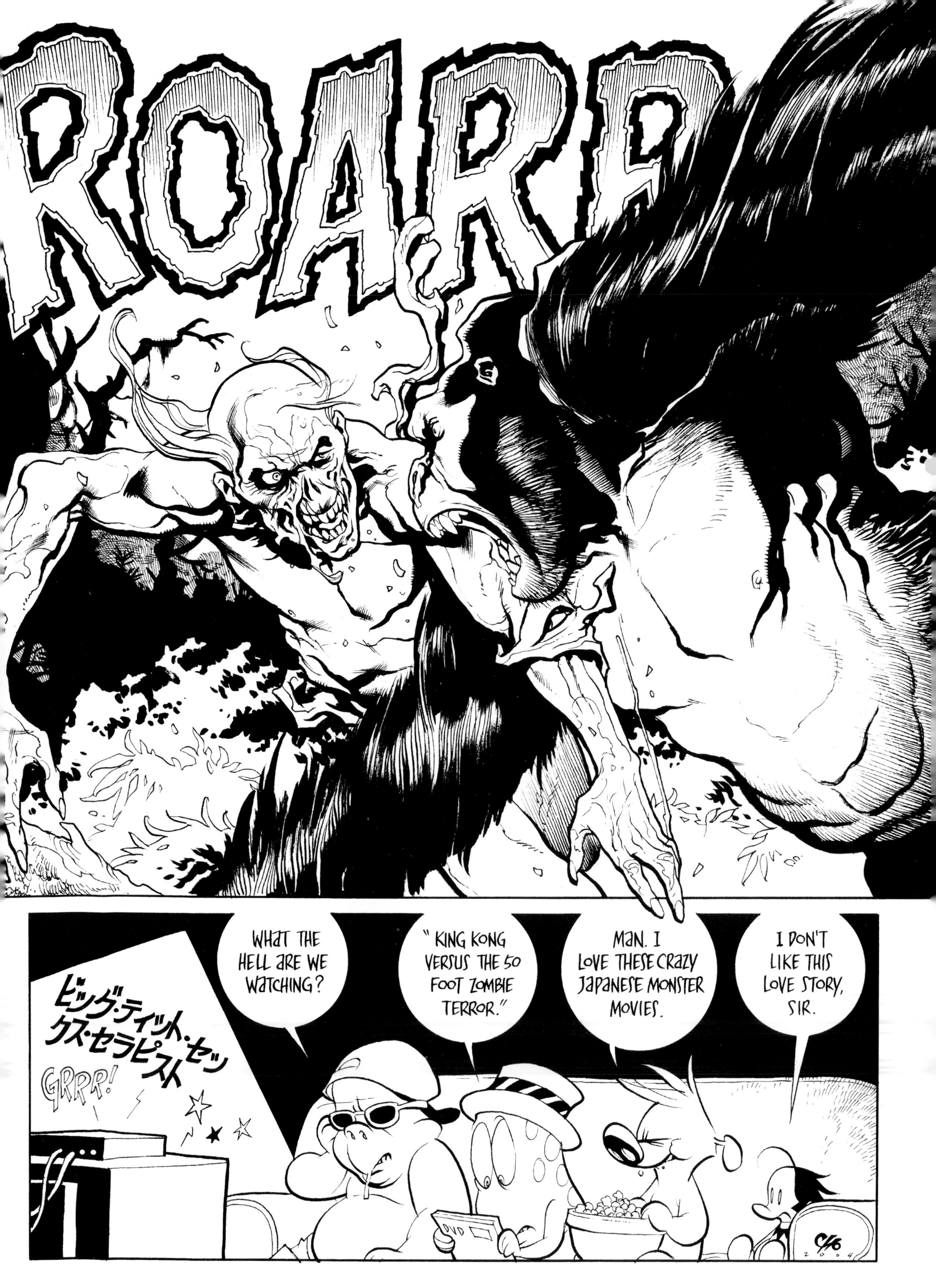
ROARR
ビッグ・ティット・セッ
クス・セラピスト
GRRR!
WHAT THE HELL ARE WE WATCHING?
"KING KONG VERSUS THE 50 FOOT ZOMBIE TERROR."
MAN. I LOVE THESE CRAZY JAPANESE MONSTER MOVIES.
I DON'T LIKE THIS LOVE STORY, SIR.
DVD